The Soviet System in Theory and Practice:
Western and Soviet Views

The Soviet System
in Theory
and Practice

WESTERN AND SOVIET VIEWS

Second, revised edition

Edited by Harry G. Shaffer
The University of Kansas

FREDERICK UNGAR PUBLISHING CO.
New York

Library of Congress Cataloging in Publication Data
Main entry under title:

The Soviet system in theory and practice.

Includes bibliographical references.
1. Soviet Union—Politics and government—1971-
—Addresses, essays, lectures. 2. Soviet Union—Economic
conditions—1918-   —Addresses, essays, lectures.
3. Soviet Union—Social conditions—Social conditions—
1917-   —Addresses, essays, lectures. 4. Communism—
Soviet Union—Addresses, essays, lectures. 5. Communism
—Addresses, essays, lectures. I. Shaffer, Harry G.

DK266.S575   1983   947.084   83-9094

ISBN 0-8044-1828-4

ISBN 0-8044-6857-5 (pbk.)

To my children Bernie, Ron, Lennie, and Tanya,
in the hope that they will learn
to approach all problems with open minds,
always ready to expose themselves to a wide variety of views
before forming their own opinions
on any controversial subject.

Contents

I

Communist Ideology and Morality: The Marxist-Leninist Background

V

B
Elections à la USSR   281

C
The Dissidents   295

VI

VII

Preface to the New Edition

Over eighteen years have passed since the publication of the first edition of *The Soviet System in Theory and Practice*. Much has changed since research for that edition was started two decades ago. In the economic sphere, the Soviet Union has truly become a superpower, with a total industrial output larger than that of the entire world a generation earlier.

In the international sphere, Soviet-U.S. detente has come to an end, at least for the time being, and the armament race has escalated to unprecedented heights. China has remained the Soviet Union's ideological and political adversary but has established more rapport with the United States than previously thought possible. Some Communist countries such as North Korea and Albania have taken an independent course, and the Soviet Union has lost much of its control over Communist parties in the West and especially over the two largest West European Communist parties in Italy and France. In the less developed countries in the world, Soviet influence has met with mixed success. They have lost much of whatever weight they carried in some places, as in Egypt, but have gained tenuous influence elsewhere, as in Angola and Tanzania.

In spite of all changes that have taken place, the Soviet Union's economic and political system has remained fundamentally unchanged. The social ownership of the means of production has been retained, and the system of economic planning and administration, although somewhat altered, is still guided by a central plan that has the force of law. While the head of the party is no longer the dictator Stalin was and does not have even the power Khrushchev once held, the party—and within it the Central Committee, and within that, the Politburo—has retained political dominance.

Taking into account the changes that have taken place, and offering up-to-date views and analyses even of those features of Soviet society and Soviet life that have not changed all that much, only a very few selections dealing with historic events and ideology have been retained from the first edition. Three other selections by Alec Nove, Urie Bronfenbrenner and myself that were originally also included in the first edition have been completely rewritten and brought up to date. All of the other sixty-five selections are new.

Finally, as in the first edition, if the reader finds that some selections, East and West, are more scholarly and others more propagandistic, this is quite intentional. To learn to distinguish between facts and fancy, to question all one reads in this controversial area, is one of the most fascinating challenges facing the student who wishes to understand the Soviet system in theory and practice.

I wish to express my gratitude to all the authors, publishers and editors, and to the Copyright Agency of the USSR for granting permissions to reprint; to Urie Bronfenbrenner and Alec Nove, who allowed me to update and partially rewrite two excellent articles and who took the time to go over them; to my assistant, Ruth Heurtz, who helped in the collection of material from which selections could then be chosen for inclusion; and to the many departmental secretaries who so faithfully and uncomplainingly typed various parts of this manuscript (several parts more than once). Among them I especially note Luanne Best, Ruth Bjorgaard, Marilyn Dechir, Jan Hall, Cheryl Stevens, Susan Wallace, and Jean Yonke. Last, but most certainly not least, I want to thank my friend and colleague, Frank Durgin, from the University of Southern Maine, who took incredibly much time from his own work and family obligations to go over my manuscript word by word, sentence by sentence, and chapter by chapter. He found numerous imperfections, from spelling errors and deficiencies in grammar and sentence structure to statements that needed additional clarification or documentation, and on several occasions he also helped me choose between selections competing for inclusion. It goes without saying that I alone bear full responsibility for any remaining inadequacies; but the book could never have been what it is without his invaluable aid and assistance.

July, 1983   H.G.S.

As this book was being readied for the press, Yuri V. Andropov died, on February 9, 1984. Except for some minor alterations in the tightening of labor discipline and the enhanced delegation of economic decision-making at the micro-level, Andropov did not deviate from the recent policies of the preceding regime during his fifteen months in power. Within three days after his death, the Party's Politburo selected as his successor for the position of Secretary-General Konstantin U. Chernenko, seventy-two years of age, a member of the old guard and a close associate of Brezhnev. He was also later designated President of the USSR. No major alterations in Soviet domestic or foreign policies are anticipated under Chernenko.

January, 1984

Introduction

I was showing some photographs I had taken in Russia to a class of fifth and sixth graders in an American school. Most of the children came from middle class faculty and professional families. Among my pictures were a number of shots of roads lined with young trees.

A child's hand went up: "Why do they have trees along the road?"

A bit puzzled, I turned the question back to the class: "Why do you suppose they have trees?"

Another child's hand rose for eager answer: "So that people won't be able to see what's going on beyond the road."

A girl had a different idea: "It's to make work for the prisoners."

I asked why some of our roads have trees planted along the side.

"For shade," the children said. "To keep the dust down."

Where did the children get the idea that the Russians have different reasons than we have for planting trees?*

URIE BRONFENBRENNER
American social psychologist, Cornell University

THE UNION OF SOVIET SOCIALIST REPUBLICS is a gigantic land that covers one-half of Europe and one-third of Asia; in all, one-sixth of the continental surface of the earth. East-west, the country stretches over a distance of 6,000 miles; when the fishermen on the Bering Strait ready their boats at five in the morning, it is midnight on Lake Baikal in Siberia, while the citizens of Moscow are just sitting down to their dinner at 7 P.M. the evening before. Every third tree on earth grows in this vast land, which leads the world in reserves of many of the raw materials that are essential for today's industrial societies. More than one hundred peoples and nationalities inhabit the territory of the USSR. Over 265 million strong, her population is exceeded only by that of China and India; it increases by about 4 every minute and 6000 every day. Over 90 percent of all Soviet citizens alive today are expected to be living in the twenty-first century.

A generation ago the Soviet people broke the backbone of Hitler's armies at the gates of Leningrad and on the banks of the Volga, at a cost of more than twenty million lives and incalculable material damage. They thereby played an invaluable part in preventing the would-be master race from enslaving the world (just as their forefathers had turned back and destroyed another would-be conqueror's "grand army" and paved the way for the subsequent liberation of Europe more than one-and-a-half centuries ago). Still largely an agricultural country at the outbreak of World War II, the USSR produces today over one-fifth of the world's industrial output. Second only to the United States in industrial and military might, she has been challenging the United States to an economic race, predicting that in the not-too-distant future she will be taking the lead, not only in production but also in the standard of living of her people.

But the Soviet challenge is not merely economic in nature. With its social ownership of the means of production, its political philosophy of "democratic centralism," and its proclaimed goal of a classless society in which each member works according to his ability and receives according to his needs, the Soviet system challenges the political, the social, and the philosophical structure of Western capitalist and semicapitalist democracies. "Never before," says a special issue of *Time*, devoted almost entirely to the USSR,[1] "has it been so important for Americans to be knowledgeable about the Soviet Union, to understand what it has become."

What is this Soviet system whose adherents can be counted in the hundreds of millions, from the jungles of Southeast Asia, from the deserts of Africa and the mountain plateaus of Latin America, to the very hearts of London, Paris, and New York? What is the system—Socialist, Communist, Marxist-Leninist, or whatever it may be called—under which the Soviet people have lived and labored in peace and in war since 1917, and under which they have transformed a semifeudal, semiliterate, and predominantly peasant Russia into the industrial and military colossus of the Union of Soviet Socialist Republics? How does this system—its institutions, its moral foundation, the hopes it holds for the people living under it—resemble those of Western societies and how does it differ from them? What exactly are its accomplishments? What are its major shortcomings? Is it really likely to supersede the economic and political systems of the West, as Marxists have been predicting for over a century?

To find answers to some of the questions above and to evaluate the challenge of the Soviet system, we must understand it as it was intended to be by its ideological creators and as it has evolved during its sixty-five years of existence. To gain such understanding, the Western

---

[1] June 23, 1980, p. 21.

Soviet area specialist studies Soviet source material and the views of
Soviet scholars as well as Western interpretations. The purpose of this
book of readings is to enable students to use such an approach in their
study of the Soviet system, even though they may not be familiar with
the Russian language, nor have the time or the opportunity to dig their
way through countless books, pamphlets, monographs, government publications, magazines, and journals in search of appropriate material on
both sides. To this end, Western anti-Marxist or at least non-Marxist
views in each chapter are confronted by representative selections translated from the writings of Soviet experts on the respective topics. In most
of the chapters, views of Western Marxists are presented also; one contribution (Chapter IV, Selection 14) is by an Indian Marxist, and two
(Chapter IV, Selection 1 and Chapter V, Selection 6) by Western socialists
who classify themselves as non-Marxists. Although necessarily not all-
inclusive, the seven chapters cover a sufficiently wide range of topics to
enable the reader to gain some understanding of the most important philosophical, historical, and political, economic, and social aspects of the
Soviet system. The selections in each chapter were chosen with an eye
to their current applicability and with emphasis on broad, general issues
rather than technical, specialized detail.

As is to be expected, Western non-Marxist scholars vary more
widely in their interpretations of the Soviet system than do Western Marxist scholars. Especially in the case of the more controversial aspects of
the Soviet system (such as, for instance, "Freedom and Democracy")
several Western views, often disagreeing with one another on some major
points, have been included in this book.

Soviet views are more uniform than either Western or Western
Marxist views. But the Soviet Union is no longer the monolithic structure
it used to be in the days of Stalin. Issues varying from the "heredity
versus environment" controversy in genetics to the advisability of de-
centralizing economic decision-making, and from the desirability of reducing specialization for children in secondary schools to the merits of
restricting art to "socialist realism" are debated widely and openly today.
Yet on basic ideological and major policy issues Soviet scholars still profess strong agreement. The selections under Soviet views are therefore
generally representative of officially expressed positions. The views of
dissidents or émigrés, where included (for example, Chapter V, Selection
18), are not listed as Soviet views.

From the selections included in this book, the reader may gain the
impression that apart from somewhat more frequent criticism of certain
aspects of the Soviet system, the views of Western Marxists are very
similar to those of their Soviet peers. It should, therefore, be pointed out
first that I have refrained from including any selections by right-wing anti-
Soviet Socialists or by Trotskyists. Many of the former would refuse to
be classified as "Marxists" altogether (and indeed many of their views

are effectively represented by the "liberal" wing of Western opinion), while the Trotskyists, whatever the merits of their theories, are too few in number and too small in influence among Western Marxists or in the world at large to be represented in a book of readings designed to contrast widely prevalent Western and Soviet views. But because of its interesting analysis and interpretation, and also to give the reader at least one such example, a rather critical, although not truly anti-Soviet, Western Marxist view has been included in the chapter "Soviet Life in General: Some Introductory Observations" (Chapter III, Selection 4).

At this point it may be wise to remind the reader that all Soviet material is presented in English translation and that any translation involves choices that may distort the meaning of the original. The Russian word *bit*, for instance, can be translated as "strike," or "beat"; *goret* as "burn" or "shine"; *krupnyi* as "large" or "important"; *lyubit* as "like" or "love." From these few examples it is evident that even the translator who attempts to be objective may impart connotations that were not intended by the original author. Most of the translations in this volume were originally published by Soviet agencies in Moscow, some by the Soviet Embassies in the United States, England and Canada, two by an American publisher specializing in the translation of foreign-language publications (The International Arts and Sciences Press). Since translators are likely to disagree with one another on how to most faithfully reproduce the meaning of the original text, and since, moreover, in most instances the Russian original was not available anyhow, I have refrained from passing judgment on the precision of the translations of selections included under "Soviet Views."

As final touches were put on the manuscript, a change in the Soviet leadership took place. Leonid I. Brezhnev, for eighteen years Secretary-General of the Party's Central Committee and the last five years also the country's president (official title: Chairman of the Presidium of the Supreme Soviet) died on November 10, 1982, of a heart attack. Yuri V. Andropov, member of the party's top leadership body, the Politburo, and from 1967 to May, 1982, head of the KGB (secret police), became the new party leader. Sometime later he was also appointed to the largely ceremonial position of president.

In spite of the change in leadership, Western analysts anticipate no radical shifts in Soviet economic and political policies, domestic or foreign, in the foreseeable future.

The Soviet System in Theory and Practice
Western and Soviet Views

I

Communist Ideology and Morality: The Marxist-Leninist Background

"Marx's teaching is all-powerful because it is true."

VLADIMIR ILYICH LENIN

"The Soviet system and communist ideology have withstood all kinds of enemy attacks, all tests and trials. We hold firmly to our revolutionary Marxist-Leninist positions. Here we have stood, here we stand, and here we shall stand, since these are the only correct positions."

NIKITA S. KHRUSHCHEV
Former First Secretary, CC CPSU* and Chairman, USSR Council of Ministers

"We shall forever remain unfalteringly faithful to the Leninist principles and precepts that have become firmly enshrined in the life of our Party and state."

YURI V. ANDROPOV
Secretary-General, CC CPSU

EVER SINCE the dawn of history, there have been thinkers who, dissastisfied with the imperfections of the system under which they lived, advocated the establishment of some new order—an order which they perceived as a fairer, happier, better-functioning society, more conducive to the good life than the one under which they had been born and raised. Many of their proposals may have been oversimplified and unrealistic. Yet from the days of Plato or Sir Thomas More to the days of Edward Bellamy and H. G. Wells, farsighted dreamers, through their descriptions of what they considered a more perfect world, have had their impact upon modern economic and political movements. Universal free education; equality before the law, irrespective of race, religion, or coun-

* Central Committee, Communist Party of the Soviet Union.

1

try of origin; a more equitable distribution of wealth and income; the protection of minorities against the tyranny of majorities; the priority of human rights over property rights—these are but a few of the concepts that bear definite traces of utopian ideas, proposed centuries before they became part of the economic policy, the political philosophy, or the legal reality of one or another twentieth-century society.

Many of the essential features of what the Soviets like to refer to as "the moral code of the builders of communism" are also traceable to philosophical and moral precepts developed by utopians long ago. The common ownership of the means of production, the "end of the exploitation of man by man," the perfectibility of man's character, a world united under one government and eventually functioning without a government—all these concepts antedate the birth of Karl Marx (1818–1883), the social philosopher and bearded revolutionist acclaimed by Communists the world over as the founder of the classical Communist movement. And yet, to the Communist mind, Marx is the ideological father, not merely in the sense in which John Locke and Adam Smith are frequently referred to as the fathers of Western political and economic thought, but perhaps more in the sense in which Christianity looks upon Christ.

To the Communist mind, Marx has always been more, much more, than a moral philosopher. And, indeed, Marx was not primarily a moral philosopher who dealt with the "ought to be." Instead, he tried to lay bare the dynamics of social development, tried to discover the laws of nature as they apply to human society in the real world. These, he held, were independent of man's will and would lead mankind towards an ever higher form of human society. In the Communist view, Marx accomplished what he set out to do: he worked out the only valid explanation of all important historical events, and he illuminated the path to the future, to a world of abundance, justice, and freedom for all, a world which will "inevitably" be inherited by the Communist workingman. "By revealing the laws governing the operation and development of the forces of nature and society, genuine science can always foresee the new," proclaims an official Soviet manual on Marxism-Leninism. "The Marxist science of the laws of social development enables us not only to chart a correct path through the labyrinth of social contradictions," it continues confidently, "but to predict the course events will take, the direction of historical progress and the next stages of social advance." And it concludes optimistically, "Marxists have no fear of the future. They represent the class to which the future belongs. . . ."[1] Communists today may disagree with one another as to just exactly what Marx meant, but they are fully agreed that Marx was right. If errors have been made, they were not Marx's errors; they could only be errors of interpretation, "left-wing," "right-wing," "personality-cult-inspired," or "revisionist" deviations from the "true" path.

[1] *Fundamentals of Marxism-Leninism: Manual*, 2nd rev. ed. Foreign Languages Publishing House, Moscow, 1963, p. 17.

In the United States, a 1978 Gallup poll showed that 41 percent of Americans did not know who Karl Marx was. In the Soviet Union, in contrast, as far back as twenty years ago, an advertisement of some of Marx's works had this to say about the essence of Marxist philosophy: "Everyone in the Soviet Union, from a housewife to a high-order scientist, is trained in it. If one does not understand Marxism, one is in the dark about the ideas which represent the Soviet ideology which motivates the Soviet people."[2] Indeed, for the serious student who wants to obtain a *thorough* understanding of Marxian theories, there is no substitute for the study of Marx's original works. But for a brief and clear summary and evaluation of Marxian philosophy, as seen through the eyes of a Western, non-Marxist scholar, it would be difficult to find a better selection than the first one, taken from the 5th edition of Robert L. Heilbroner's well-known book, *The Worldly Philosophers*.

Under the leadership of Vladimir Ilyich Ulianov (1870–1924), better known as Lenin, the first Marxian-type "Dictatorship of the Proletariat" was established in Russia in 1917, but much of Marxian ideology had to be revised, reinterpreted, added to, or subtracted from in the light of the momentous development. How could the revolution take place and succeed in a relatively backward country that had not gone through all the "inevitable" stages of development? What was the role of the peasant in a predominantly peasant society before, during, and after the revolution? What was the function of the Communist party? These and many other questions had to be answered. The answers officially accepted by Soviet and Chinese Communists alike (although they disagree as to the meaning of many of them) can be found in the voluminous pre- and post-revolutionary writings of Lenin.

It is the *Marxist-Leninist* ideology, then, which Communists everywhere acclaim as the "correct" line to which they have been adhering. To its practical application they ascribe the successes of Communist construction in the Soviet Union and in all other countries which have embarked on the Marxist-Leninist path; upon its ability to forecast correctly the future course of events they base their predictions of the advent of a Communist world.

Once again, a detailed study of at least the major writings of Lenin would be essential for a *thorough* understanding of Lenin's contribution to Marxian ideology. Harry G. Shaffer's one-paragraph summary and the excerpts taken from Gerhart Niemeyer's study, presented as Selections 2 and 3 below, can do no more than introduce the reader, in summary form, to Lenin's contributions as seen through the eyes of two Western analysts.

In the fourth selection under "Western Views," Harry G. Shaffer compares communism with fascism, primarily using Fascist Italy and

[2] *All about USSR: A Catalog of Books about the USSR in English, Imported from the Soviet Union,* Catalog Number 26, Cross World Books and Periodicals Inc., Chicago, 1963, p. 17.

Nazi Germany as illustrations. Taking to task those who allege that one
type of dictatorship is just like any other, the author concludes that we
can no longer "afford the erroneous assumption that fascism and communism . . . are but two strands of poison ivy bearing different designations but demanding equal treatment and eradication."

Next, in the two selections under "Western Marxist Views," two
of the foremost American Marxists, Paul M. Sweezy and Leo Huberman,
assisted by Sybil H. May, present the case for Marxian Socialism. To
them the advent of socialism, and eventually of communism, is both morally right and scientifically proven to be not only workable but inevitable.
In greatest confidence, therefore, Sweezy can say that he is "very glad
to leave it to the future to decide" whether Marxists are right or not,
while Huberman and May proclaim: "Socialism is not an impossible
dream. It is the next step in the process of social evolution . . ."

In his writings, Marx dealt primarily with capitalism and with the
development of his main thesis, the inevitability of its downfall. Lenin
elaborated on Marx's few and scattered remarks as to what the societies
of the future—the "Dictatorship of the Proletariat" and the "final stage"
of Communism—would be like. Selection 7 consists of a few quotes from
Lenin's writings to familiarize the reader, albeit to a very limited degree,
with Lenin's train of thought in regard to Communist society during the
transitional and the final stages.

The final selection in this chapter, Selection 8, represents the current Soviet view of the essence of socialism (the Marxist-Leninist type)
and communism. An appendix of important excerpts from Marx and Engels's *The Communist Manifesto* can be found at the end of this chapter.

WESTERN VIEWS

---

1. THE INEXORABLE WORLD
OF KARL MARX*

Robert L. Heilbroner
New School for Social Research

The philosophy is often called dialectical materialism; *dialectical* because
it incorporates Hegel's[1] idea of inherent change, and *materialism* because

---

* Excerpts reprinted from Robert L. Heilbroner, *The Worldly Philosophers*, New York:
  Simon and Schuster, 5th ed., 1980, pp. 141–145 and 151–167, by permission of the author
  and the publisher.
[1] George Wilhelm Friedrich Hegel (1770–1831), German philosopher. [Editor's note.]

it grounds itself not in the world of ideas, but on the terrain of social and physical environment.

"The materialist conception of history," wrote Engels many years later in a famous tract entitled "Anti-Dühring" (it was aimed against a German professor named Eugen Dühring), "starts from the principle that production, and with production the exchange of its products, is the basis of every social order; that in every society that has appeared in history the distribution of the products, and with it the division of society into classes or estates, is determined by what is produced and how it is produced, and how the product is exchanged. According to this conception, the ultimate causes of all social changes and political revolutions are to be sought, not in the minds of men, in their increasing insight into eternal truth and justice, but in changes in the mode of production and exchange; they are to be sought not in the *philosophy* but in the *economies* of the epoch concerned."

The reasoning is not difficult to follow. Every society, says Marx, is built on an economic base—the hard reality of human beings who must organize their activities to clothe and feed and house themselves. That organization can differ vastly from society to society and from era to era. It can be pastoral or built around hunting or grouped into handicraft units or structured into a complex industrial whole. But whatever the form in which men solve their basic economic problem, society will require a whole "superstructure" of noneconomic activity and thought—it will need to be bound together by laws, supervised by a government, inspired by religion and philosophy.

But the superstructure of thought cannot be selected at random. It must mirror the foundation on which it is raised. No hunting community would evolve or could use the legal framework of an industrial society, and similarly no industrial community could use the conception of law, order, and government of a primitive village. Note that the doctrine of materialism does not toss away the catalytic function and creativity of ideas. It only maintains that thoughts and ideas are the *product* of environment, even though they aim to change that environment.

Materialism by itself would reduce ideas to mere passive accompaniments of economic activity. That was never Marx's contention. For the new theory was dialectical as well as materialist: it envisaged change, constant and inherent change; and in that never-ending flux the ideas emanating from one period would help to shape another. "Men make their own history," wrote Marx, commenting on the *coup d'état* of Louis Napoleon in 1852, "but they do not make it just as they please; they do not make it under circumstances chosen by themselves, but under circumstances directly found, given, and transmitted from the past."

But the dialectical—the changeful—aspect of this theory of history did not depend merely on the interplay of ideas and social structures. There was another and far more powerful agent at work. The economic world itself was changing; the bedrock on which the structure of ideas was built was itself in movement.

For example, the isolated markets of the Middle Ages began to lock fingers under the impetus of exploration and political unification, and a new commercial world was born. The old hand mill was replaced by the steam mill under the impetus of invention, and a new form of social organization called the factory came into being. In both cases the determining framework of economic life itself changed its form, and as it did, it forced a new social adaptation from the community in which it was embedded. "The hand-mill gives you society with the feudal lord," Marx wrote, "the steam-mill, society with the industrial capitalist."

And once such a change had taken place, it carried with it a whole train of consequences. The market and the factory were incompatible with the feudal way of life—even though they were born amidst it. They demanded a new cultural and social context to go with them. And they helped in that difficult birthing process by creating their own new social classes: the market nurtured a new merchant class, and the factory gave birth to an industrial proletariat.

But the process of social change was not merely a matter of new inventions pressing on old institutions: it was a matter of new classes displacing old ones. For society, said Marx, is organized into class structures, aggregates of men who stand in some common relationship—favorable or otherwise—to the existing form of production. And economic change threatens all of that. As the organizational and technical forces of production change—as factories destroy handicraft industry, for example—the social relations of production change too; those on top may find the ground cut from under them, while those who were on the bottom may be carried higher. We have seen just such an upset of the relative position of social classes in Ricardo's[2] day in England, when the capitalists, riding the wave of the Industrial Revolution, were threatening to usurp the time-honored prerogatives of the landed gentry.

Hence conflict develops. The classes whose position is jeopardized fight the classes whose position is enhanced: the feudal lord fights the rising merchant, and the guild master opposes the young capitalist.

But the process of history pays no attention to likes and dislikes. Gradually conditions change, and gradually, but surely, the classes of society are rearranged. Amid turmoil and anguish the division of wealth is altered. And thus history is a pageant of ceaseless struggle between classes to partition social wealth. For as long as the technics of society change, no existing division of wealth is immune from attack.

What did this theory augur for the society of Marx and Engels' day? It pointed to revolution—inevitable revolution. For capitalism, according to this analysis, must also contain "forces" and "relations" of

_____

[2] David Ricardo (1772–1823), English economist, follower of Adam Smith, advocate of laissez-faire. [Editor's note.]

production—a technological and organizational foundation, and an architecture of law and political rights and ideology. And if its technical base was evolving, then necessarily its superstructure must be subject to increasing strain.

That is exactly what Marx and Engels saw in 1848. The economic base of capitalism—its anchor in reality—was industrial production. Its superstructure was the system of private property, under which a portion of society's output went to those who owned its great technical apparatus. The conflict lay in the fact that the base and superstructure were incompatible.

Why? Because the base of industrial production—the actual making of goods—was an ever more organized, integrated, *interdependent* process, whereas the superstructure of private property was the most *individualistic* of social systems. Hence the superstructure and the base clashed: factories necessitated social planning, and private property abhorred it; *capitalism* had become so complex that it needed direction, but *capitalists* insisted on a ruinous freedom.

The result was twofold. First, capitalism would sooner or later destroy itself. The planless nature of production would lead to a constant disorganization of economic activity—to crises and slumps and the social chaos of depression. The system was simply too complex; it was constantly getting out of joint, losing step, and overproducing one good while underproducing another.

Secondly, capitalism must unknowingly breed its own successor. Within its great factories it would not only create the technical base for socialism—rationally planned production—but it would create as well a trained and disciplined *class* who would be the agent of socialism—the embittered proletariat. By its own inner dynamic, capitalism would produce its own downfall, and in the process, nourish its own enemy.

It was a profoundly important insight into history, not only for what it betokened for the future, but for the whole new perspective it opened upon the past. We have to come to be familiar with the "economic interpretation" of history, and we can accept with equanimity a re-evaluation of the past with respect to the struggle, say, of the nascent seventeenth-century commercial classes and the aristocratic world of land and lineage. But for Marx and Engels, this was no mere exercise in historical reinterpretation. The dialectic led to the future, and that future, as revealed by *The Communist Manifesto*,[3] pointed to revolution as the destination toward which capitalism was moving. In somber words the *Manifesto* proclaimed: "The development of modern industry . . . cuts

---

[3] *The Communist Manifesto,* written by Marx in collaboration with Engels, was published in 1848. Originally intended as a statement of objectives of the newly formed Communist League, it turned out to be much more than that: it became an attempt to prove the inevitability of the downfall of capitalism and a call to revolution, a program for the future. [Editor's note.]

from under its feet the very foundation on which the bourgeoisie produces and appropriates products. What the bourgeoisie therefore produces, above all, are its own gravediggers. Its fall and the victory of the proletariat are equally inevitable.''. . .

"The history of capitalism," we read in the Program of the Communist International adopted in 1928—a kind of latter-day restatement of *The Communist Manifesto*—"has entirely confirmed the theories of Marx and Engels concerning the laws of development of capitalist society . . . that must inevitably lead to the downfall of the whole capitalist system." What were those laws? What was Marx's prognosis for the system that he knew?

The answer lies in that enormous work *Das Kapital (Capital)*. With Marx's agonizing meticulousness, it is remarkable that the work was ever finished—in a sense it never was. It was eighteen years in process; in 1851 it was to be done "in five weeks"; in 1859 "in six weeks"; in 1865 it was "done"—a huge bundle of virtually illegible manuscripts which took two years to edit into Volume I. When Marx died in 1883, three volumes remained: Engels put out Volume II in 1885 and the third in 1894. The final (fourth) volume did not emerge until 1910.

There are twenty-five hundred pages to read for anyone intrepid enough to make the effort. And what pages! Some deal with the tiniest of technical matters and labor them to a point of mathematical exhaustion; others swirl with passion and anger. This is an economist who has read *every* economist, a German pedant with a passion for footnotes, and an emotional critic who can write that "capital is dead labour, that vampire-like, only lives by sucking living labour" and who tells us that capital came into the world "dripping from head to foot, from every pore, with blood and dirt."

And yet one must not jump to the conclusion that this is merely an irascible text inveighing against the sins of the wicked money-barons. It is shot through with remarks that betray the total involvement of the man with his theoretical adversary, but the great merit of the book, curiously enough, is its utter detachment from all considerations of morality. The book describes with fury, but it analyzes with cold logic. For what Marx has set for his goal is to discover the intrinsic tendencies of the capitalist system, its inner laws of motion, and in so doing, he has eschewed the easy but less convincing means of merely expatiating on its manifest shortcomings. Instead he erects the most rigorous, the purest capitalism imaginable and within this rarefied abstract system, with an imaginary capitalism in which all the obvious defects of real life are removed, he seeks his quarry. For if he can prove that the best of all possible capitalisms is nonetheless headed for disaster, it is certainly easy to demonstrate that real capitalism will follow the same path, only quicker.

And so he sets the stage. We enter a world of perfect capitalism: no monopolies, no unions, no special advantages for anyone. It is a world in which every commodity sells at exactly its proper price. And that proper price is its *value*—a tricky word. For the value of a commodity, says Marx (and Smith[4] and Ricardo before him), is the amount of labor it has within itself. If it takes twice as much labor to make hats as shoes, then hats will sell for twice the price of shoes. The labor, of course, need not be direct manual labor; it may be overhead labor that is spread over many commodities, or it may be the labor that once went into making a machine and that the machine now slowly passes on to the products it shapes. But no matter what its form, everything is eventually reducible to labor, and all commodities, in this perfect system, will be priced according to the amount of labor, direct or indirect, that they contain.

In this world stand the two great protagonists of the capitalist drama: worker and capitalist—the landlord has by now been relegated to a minor position in society. . . . The worker is . . . a free bargaining agent who enters the market to dispose of the one commodity he commands—labor-power—and if he gets a rise in wages he will not be so foolish as to squander it in a self-defeating proliferation of his numbers.[5]

The capitalist faces him in the arena. His greed and lust for wealth are caustically described in those chapters that leave the abstract world for a look into 1860 England. But it is worth noting that he is not money-hungry from mere motives of rapacity; he is an owner-entrepreneur engaged in an endless race against his fellow owner-entrepreneurs; he *must* strive for accumulation, for in the competitive environment in which he operates, one accumulates or one gets accumulated.

The stage is set and the characters take their places. But now the first difficulty appears. How, asks Marx, can profit exist in such a situation? If everything sells for its exact value, then who gets an unearned increment? No one dares to raise his price above the competitive one, and even if one seller managed to gouge a buyer, that buyer would only have less to spend elsewhere in the economy—one man's profit would thus be another man's loss. How can there be profit in the *whole system* if everything exchanges for its honest worth?

It seems like a paradox. Profits are easy to explain if we assume that there are monopolies that need not obey the leveling influences of competition or if we admit that capitalists may pay labor less than it is worth. But Marx will have none of that—this is to be ideal capitalism, which will dig its own grave.

He finds the answer to the dilemma in one commodity that is different from all others. The commodity is labor-power. For the laborer, like the capitalist, sells his product for exactly what it is worth—for its

---

[4] Adam Smith (1723–1790). Scottish economist, father of modern economics. His *Wealth of Nations* is usually accredited as the economic treatise upon which rests the philosophy of a "free enterprise" system. [Editor's note.]

[5] This is a reference to Malthus's theory of population (Thomas Robert Malthus, 1766–1834). Malthus contended that population would always tend to outrun food supply, and that increased incomes would only induce workers to have more children. [Editor's note.]

value. And its value, like the value of everything else that is sold, is the amount of labor that goes into it—in this case, the amount of labor that it takes to "make" labor-power. In other words, a laborer's salable energies are worth the amount of socially necessary labor it takes to keep that laborer alive. Smith and Ricardo would have agreed entirely: the true value of a workman is the money he needs in order to exist. It is his subsistence wage.

So far, so good. But here comes the key to profit. The laborer who contracts to work can ask only for a wage that is his due. What that wage will be depends, as we have seen, on the amount of labor-time it takes to keep a man alive. If it takes six hours of society's labor to maintain a workingman, then (if labor is priced at one dollar an hour), he is "worth" six dollars a day. No more.

But the laborer who gets a job does not contract to work only six hours a day. That would be just long enough to support himself. On the contrary, he agrees to work a full eight-hour, or in Marx's time a ten- or eleven-hour, day. Hence he will produce a full ten or eleven hours' worth of value and he will get paid for only six. His wage will cover his subsistence, which is his true "value," but in return he will make available to the capitalist the value he produces in a full working day. And this is how profit enters the system.

Marx called this layer of unpaid work "surplus value." The words do not imply moral indignation. The worker is entitled only to the *value* of his labor-power. He gets it in full. But meanwhile the capitalist gets the full value of his workers' whole working day, and this is longer than the hours for which he paid. Hence when the capitalist sells his products, he can afford to sell them at *their* true value and still realize a profit. For there is more labor-time embodied in his products than the labor-time for which he was forced to pay.

How can this state of affairs come about? It happens because the capitalists monopolize one thing—access to the means of production themselves. Under the legal arrangements of private property, capitalists "own" jobs, insofar as they own the machines and equipment without which men and women cannot work. If someone isn't willing to work the number of hours that a capitalist asks, he or she doesn't get a job. Like everyone else in the system, a worker has no right and no power to ask for more than his own worth as a commodity. The system is perfectly "equitable," and yet all workers are cheated, for they are forced to work a longer time than their own self-sustenance demands.

Does this sound strange? Remember that Marx is describing a time when the working day was long—sometimes unendurably long—and when wages were, by and large, little more than it took to keep body and soul together. The idea of surplus value may be hard to grasp in a world where the sweatshop is very largely a thing of the past, but it was not merely a theoretical construct at the time that Marx was writing. One example may suffice: at a Manchester factory in 1862 the average work week for a period of a month and a half was 84 hours! For the previous 18 months it had been 78½ hours.

But all this is still only the setting for the drama. We have the protagonists, we have their motives, we have the clue to the plot in the discovery of "surplus value." And now the play is set in motion.

All capitalists have profits. But they are all in competition. Hence they try to accumulate and so to expand their scales of output, at the expense of their competitors. But expansion is not so easy. It requires more laborers, and to get them the capitalists must bid against one another for the working force. Wages tend to rise. Conversely, surplus value tends to fall. . . .

To Smith and Ricardo the solution to the dilemma lay in the propensity of the working force to increase its numbers with every boost in pay. But Marx . . . rules out this possibility. Marx doesn't argue about it; he simply brands the Malthusian doctrine "a libel on the human race"—after all, the proletariat, which is to be the ruling class of the future, cannot be so shortsighted as to dissipate its gains through mere unbridled physical appetite. But he rescues his capitalists just the same. For he says that they will meet the threat of rising wages by introducing *laborsaving machinery* into their plants. This will throw part of the working force back onto the street, and there, as an Industrial Reserve Army, it will serve the same function as Smith's and Ricardo's population growth: it will compete wages back down to their former "value"—the subsistence level.

Now comes the crucial twist. It seems as though the capitalist has saved the day, for he has prevented wages from rising by creating unemployment through machinery. But not so fast. By the very process through which he hopes to free himself from one horn of the dilemma, he impales himself on the other.

For as he substitutes machines for men, he is simultaneously substituting nonprofitable means of production for profitable ones. Remember that in Marx's model of an ideal capitalist world, no one makes a profit by merely sharp bargaining. Whatever a machine will be worth to a capitalist, you can be sure that he paid full value for it. If a machine will yield ten thousand dollars' worth of value over its whole life, our capitalist was presumably charged the full ten thousand dollars in the first place. It is only from his living labor that he can realize a profit, only from the unpaid-for hours of surplus working time. Hence, when he reduces the number or proportion of workers, he is killing the goose that lays the golden egg.

And yet, unhappy fellow, he has to. There is nothing Mephistophelean about his actions. He is only obeying his impulse to accumulate and trying to stay abreast of his competitors. As his wages rise, he *must* introduce laborsaving machinery to cut his costs and rescue his profits—

if he does not, his neighbor will. But since he must substitute machinery for labor, he must also narrow the base out of which he gleans his profits. It is a kind of Greek drama where men go willynilly to their fate, and in which they all unwittingly cooperate to bring about their own destruction.

For now the die is cast. As his profits shrink, each capitalist will redouble his efforts to put new laborsaving, cost-cutting machinery in his factory. It is only by getting a step ahead of the parade that he can hope to make a profit. But since everyone is doing precisely the same thing, the ratio of living labor (and hence surplus value) to total output shrinks still further. The rate of profit falls and falls. And now doom lies ahead. Profits are cut to the point at which production is no longer profitable at all. Consumption dwindles as machines displace men and the number of employed fails to keep pace with output. Bankruptcies ensue. There is a scramble to dump goods on the market, and in the process smaller firms go under. A capitalist crisis is at hand.

Not forever. As workers are thrown out of work, they are forced to accept subvalue wages. As machinery is dumped, the stronger capitalists can acquire machines for less than their true value. After a time, surplus value reappears. The forward march is taken up again. But it leads to the same catastrophic conclusion: competition for workers; higher wages; labor-displacing machinery; a smaller base for surplus value; still more frenzied competition; collapse. And each collapse is worse than the preceding one. In the periods of crisis, the bigger firms absorb the smaller ones, and when the industrial monsters eventually go down, the wreckage is far greater than when the little enterprises buckle.

And then, one day, the drama ends. Marx's picture of it has all the eloquence of a description of a Damnation: "Along with the constantly diminishing number of the magnates of capital, who usurp and monopolize all advantages of this process of transformation, grows the mass of misery, oppression, slavery, degradation, exploitation; but with this too grows the revolt of the working-class, a class always increasing in numbers, and disciplined, united, organized by the very mechanism of the process of capitalist production itself. . . . Centralization of the means of production and socialization of labour at last reach a point where they become incompatible with their capitalist integument. This integument bursts asunder. The knell of capitalist private property sounds. The expropriators are expropriated."

And so the drama ends in the inevitable supersession that Marx had envisioned in the dialectic. The system—the *pure* system—breaks down as it works upon itself to squeeze out its own source of energy, surplus value. The breakdown is hastened by the constant instability that arises from the essentially planless nature of the economy. Although there are forces at work that act to prolong its end, its final death struggle is inescapable. . . . There was no escape from the inner logic: the system would not only destroy itself but, in so doing, would give birth to its successor. . . .

As to what that successor might look like, Marx had little to say. It would be "classless," of course—by which Marx meant that the basis for an economic division of society based on property would be removed once society owned all the means of production of goods. Just how society would "own" its factories; what was meant by "society"; whether there would or could be bitter antagonisms between the managers and the managed, between the political chieftains and the rank and file—none of this did Marx discuss. During a transitional period of "socialism" there would be a "dictatorship of the proletariat"; after that, "pure" communism itself.

Marx, it must be kept in mind, was not the architect of actual socialism. That formidable task would fall to Lenin. *Das Kapital* is the Doomsday Book of capitalism, and in all of Marx there is almost nothing that looks beyond the Day of Judgment to see what the future might be like.

What are we to make of his apocalyptic argument?

There is an easy way of disposing of the whole thing. Remember that the system is built on value—labor value—and that the key to its demise lies in that special phenomenon called surplus value. But the real world consists not of "values" but of real tangible prices. Marx must show that the world of dollars and cents mirrors, in some approximate fashion, the abstract world that he has created. But in making the transition from a value-world to a price-world, he lands in the most terrible tangle of mathematics. In fact he makes a mistake.

It is not an irreparable mistake, and by going through an even worse tangle of mathematics one can make the Marxist equations come out "right"—one can, that is, explain a correspondence between the prices that really obtain in life and the underlying values in terms of labor-time. But the critics who pointed out the error were hardly interested in setting the scheme aright, and their judgment that Marx was "wrong" was taken as final. When the equations were finally justified, no one paid much attention. For regardless of its mathematical purity, there are problems galore in the Marxian model. Can we really use the concept of surplus value in a world of monopolies? Has Marx really disposed of the difficulties of using "labor" as the measuring rod of value?

Questions such as these continue to agitate the world of scholars and have tempted many economists to toss the whole scheme to one side as awkward and inflexible. But to do so overlooks two extraordinary properties of Marx's analysis.

First, it was more than just another "model" of economics. Marx literally invented a new task for social inquiry—*the critique of economics itself*. A great part of *Capital* is devoted to showing that earlier economists had failed to understand the real challenge of the study they undertook. Take, for example, the problem of value that had exercised Smith and Ricardo. Both of them had sought, with varying degrees of success, to show how prices reflected—or failed to reflect—the amounts of labor-time embodied in different commodities.

But this was not the really perplexing question, Marx pointed out. The perplexing question was how one could speak of "labor" as a common denominator of value when the actual labors of men and women were so different. Ricardo spoke of the hours of labor it took to catch a salmon and to kill a deer as establishing their exchange ratios—that is, their prices. But no deer was ever killed with a fishing rod and no salmon caught by a hunter in the woods. How then could one use "labor" as a common denominator to determine exchange ratios?

The answer, said Marx, is that capitalist society creates a special kind of labor—abstract labor, labor that is detached from the special personal attributes of a precapitalist world, labor that can be bought and sold like so much wheat or coal. Hence the real insight of a "labor theory of value" is not the determination of prices, as Smith and Ricardo thought, *but the identification of a kind of social system in which laborpower becomes a commodity*. That society is capitalism, where historical forces (such as the enclosure movement) have created a propertyless class of workers who have no alternative but to sell their labor-power—their sheer ability to work—as a commodity.

Thus Marx invented a kind of "socio-analysis" that put economics itself into a wholly new light. And beyond that signal contribution, Marx's model of capitalism, despite its clumsiness, seemed to come alive, to unfold in an extraordinary manner. Given its basic assumptions—the *mise-en-scène* of its characters, their motives and their milieu—the situation it presented *changed*, and changed in a way that was foreseeable and precise. We have seen what these changes are: how profits fell, how capitalists sought new machinery, how each boom ended in a crash, how small businesses were absorbed in each debacle by the larger firms. Marx called these trends the "laws of motion" of a capitalist system—the path that capitalism would tread over future time. And the astonishing fact is that so many of these predictions have come true.

For profits *do* tend to fall in a capitalist economy. The insight was not original with Marx, nor do profits fall only for the reason he gave. But as Adam Smith or Ricardo or Mill pointed out—and as any businessman will vouchsafe—the pressures of competition and rising wages do indeed cut profits. Impregnable monopolies aside (and these are few), profits are both the hallmark of capitalism and its Achilles' heel, for no business can *permanently* maintain its prices much above its costs. There is only one way in which profits can be perpetrated: a business—or an entire economy—must grow.

But the need for growth implies the second prediction of the Marxist model: the ceaseless quest for new techniques. It was no accident that industrial capitalism dates from the Industrial Revolution, for as Marx made clear, technological progress is not merely an accompaniment of capitalism but a vital ingredient. Business *must* innovate, invent, and experiment if it is to survive; the business that rests content on its past achievements is not long for this enterprising world. Recently one large chemical company announced that 60 percent of its income came from products that were unknown ten years ago; and although this is an exceptionally inventive industry, the relationship between industrial inventiveness and profitability generally holds.

The model showed three more tendencies for capitalism which have also come to pass. We hardly need document the existence of business cycles over the past hundred years or the emergence of giant business enterprise. But we might remark on the daring of Marx's predictions. Cycles were not recognized as inherent features of capitalism by any other economist of Marx's time, although future events have certainly vindicated his prediction of cyclical boom and crash. And in the world of business, when *Capital* appeared, bigness was the exception rather than the rule, and small enterprise still ruled the roost. To claim that huge firms would come to dominate the business scene was as startling a prediction in 1867 as would be a statement today that fifty years hence America will be a land in which small-scale proprietorships will have displaced giant corporations.

Last, Marx believed that the small independent artisan or self-employed worker would be unable to resist the pressures of mass production, and that an ever larger fraction of the work force would have to sell its labor-power on the market—that is, to become a "proletarian." Has that come true? Well, in the first quarter of the nineteenth century about three-quarters of all Americans worked for themselves, on the farm or in small shops. Today only about 10 percent of the labor force is self-employed. We may not think of an office worker or a bus driver or a bank teller as a proletarian, but in Marx's terms these are all workers who must offer their labor power to capitalists, unlike the farmer or the shoe cobbler, who own their own means of production.

All in all, the model displayed extraordinary predictive capacity. And note this: all these changes, vast and portentous as they were, could not have been unearthed purely by examining the world as it appeared to Marx's eyes. For these are historical changes, slow in their unfolding and stretched out over time; as real, but as unnoticeable, as the growth of a tree. It was only by reducing the economic system to a microcosm and then by observing that microcosm in its speeded-up life span that this drift of the future could be apprehended.

It was not, of course, exact. Marx thought that profits would not only fall *within* the business cycle, which they do, but that they would display a long downward secular trend; this does not appear to have taken place. But for all its shortcomings—and it is far from infallible, as we shall see—the Marxist model of how capitalism worked was extraordinarily prophetic.

But everything that Marx had predicted so far was, after all, fairly innocuous. There remained the final prediction of the model; for as the reader will remember, in the end Marx's "pure capitalism" *collapsed*.

Let it be said at the outset that this prediction as well cannot be lightly brushed aside. In Russia and Eastern Europe, capitalism has disappeared; in Scandinavia and Britain it has been partially abandoned; in Germany and Italy it drifted into fascism and emerged from its bath of fire in less than perfect health. And while wars, brute political power, exigencies of fate, and the determined efforts of revolutionaries have all contributed their share, the grim truth is that these changes occurred largely for the very reason Marx foresaw: capitalism broke down.

Why did it break down? Partly because it developed the instability Marx said it would. A succession of business crises, compounded by a plague of wars, destroyed the faith of the lower and middle classes in the system. But that is not the entire answer—we Americans have also had our wars and depressions, and capitalism here is very much alive. Something else spelled the difference between survival and destruction: European capitalism failed not so much for economic as for *social* reasons— and Marx predicted this too!

For Marx recognized that the economic difficulties of the system were not insuperable. Although antimonopoly legislation or anti-business-cycle policies were unknown in Marx's day, such activities were not inconceivable: there was nothing inevitable in the *physical* sense about Marx's vision. The Marxist prediction of decay was founded on a conception of capitalism in which it was *socially* impossible for a government to set the system's wrongs aright; intellectually, ideologically, even emotionally impossible. The cure for capitalism's failings would require that a government would have to rise above the interests of one class alone— and that was to assume that men could free themselves from the shackles of their immediate economic self-interest. Marx's analysis made that doubtful.

And it is just this lack of social flexibility, this bondage to shortsighted interest, that weakened European capitalism—at least until after World War II. For one who has read the works of Marx it is frightening to look back at the grim determination with which so many nations steadfastly hewed to the very course that he insisted would lead to their undoing. It was as if their governments were unconsciously vindicating Marx's prophecy by obstinately doing exactly what he said they would. When in Russia under the Tsars all democratic trade-unionism was ruthlessly stamped out, when in England and Germany monopolies and cartels were officially encouraged, the Marxist dialectic looked balefully prescient indeed. Until very recently, when one considered that in France or

Italy or Greece capitalist governments could not collect taxes they levied on their own business communities, when one inspected the enormous gulf between rich and poor and saw evidence of the total indifference of the former for the latter, one had the uneasy feeling that the psychological stereotypes that Marx cast in his historical drama were all too truly drawn from life.

And it is these very facts that give us the clue as to why capitalism survived in the United States during the years when it languished, or nearly perished, abroad. We had our share of reactionaries and revolutionaries. The economic history of the United States contains more than enough exploitation and ugliness. But capitalism here evolved in a land untouched by the dead hand of aristocratic lineage and age-old class attitudes. To some degree this resulted in a harsher social climate in America than in Europe, for here we clung to the credo of "rugged individualism" long after the individual had been hopelessly overwhelmed by the environment of massive industrialism, whereas in Europe a traditional *noblesse oblige* existed side by side with its unconcealed class divisions. Yet out of the American milieu came a certain pragmatism in dealing with power, private as well as public; and a general subscription to the ideals of democracy which steered the body politic safely past the rocks on which it foundered in so many nations abroad.

It is in these capabilities for change that the answer to Marxian analysis lies. Indeed, the more we examine the history of capitalism, especially in recent decades, the more we learn both to respect the penetration of Marx's thought and to recognize its limitations. For the *problems* that he diagnosed within capitalism are still very much with us, including above all a tendency to economic instability and to the concentration of wealth and power. Yet in different nations these similar problems have been dealt with in strikingly diverse ways. Norway, for example, which is certainly a capitalist nation by Marx's criteria (its means of production are largely privately owned and the market mechanism presumably creates surplus value), has offset the "laws of motion" of capitalism by an extraordinary program of income redistribution that makes Norway one of the most egalitarian nations in the world. Japan, certainly capitalist in structure and outlook, guarantees the *lifetime* employment of all workers in its great corporations, after a probationary period. France has an elaborate system of national planning. England, the very object lesson of a brutal and exploitative capitalism for Marx and Engels, has led the world in the establishment of national health plans, in "cradle-to-grave" social security, low-cost housing, and the like,[6] Sweden, at least as harsh and repressive as England at the time that Marx

---

[6] Under Mrs. Thatcher's Conservative Party government, England retreated somewhat from the British Labor Party's liberal policies; by the early 1980s, West Germany probably provides a better example for Heilbroner's argument than England. [Editor's note.]

wrote, is now perhaps the most democratic nation in the world, with regard to both its political and its economic policy.

Thus it has become clear that capitalism is an economic structure capable of considerable adaptation. This is not to say that capitalism has overcome all its problems. But, given the examples of the Scandinavian countries (not to mention New Zealand or Austria as other instances), it is no longer possible to see in the Marxist scenario the "inevitable" line of evolution of capitalist society. This is not to say, of course, that every capitalist nation will adapt and evolve as the Scandinavian nations have done. In the case of the United States, for example, the flexibility and pragmatism that made capitalism here so much more successful than capitalism abroad during the late nineteenth and early twentieth centuries seem in recent years to have given way to a lesser degree of social responsiveness than we find abroad. It is surely a commentary of great importance that we no longer look to the United States as the model of what a capitalist nation could be with regard to the quality of life that it affords its people, but as the example of a capitalism that has somehow fallen behind in the march and must now strive to catch up.

But the very fact that the United States once was in the vanguard, and that the nations that now lead it were once in the rearguard, is evidence enough that the future is not foreordained. To much of the Communist world, "capitalism" still means a nation built on the stereotypes of English capitalism of the 1850's, with its narrow-minded manufacturers and its reactionary governments, but the achievements (and failures) of the twentieth century show us that capitalism today is as capable of producing a decent or an indecent society as is contemporary socialism.

Yet, shorn of its overtones of inevitable doom, the Marxist analysis cannot be disregarded. It remains the gravest, most penetrating examination the capitalist system has ever undergone. It is not an examination conducted along moral lines with head wagging and tongue clucking over the iniquities of the profit motive—this is the stuff of the Marxist revolutionary but not of the Marxist economist. For all its passion, it is a dispassionate appraisal, and it is for this reason that its somber findings must be soberly considered.

Finally, we must remember that Marx was not just a great economist. In his graveside oration, Engels said that Marx had not only discovered the "special law of motion" of capitalism, but had discovered the "law of development of human history." This is certainly too much to claim, but Engels was not wrong in emphasizing the extraordinary importance of Marx's vision of the historic process as an arena in which social classes struggled for supremacy. Marx taught us not just to look at, but to look *through*, history, just as Freud taught us to look through the façade of personality to the psychic processes within us, or as Plato taught us to look through the screen of unexamined ideas to the veiled questions of philosophy.

That is why Marx's name, like those of Freud and Plato, remains contemporary. Marx is certainly not infallible, for all the idol worship to which he has been subjected. He is better thought of as *unavoidable*—a great explorer whose footprints have been indelibly imprinted on the continent of social thought that he discovered. All who wish to explore that continent further, whether or not they agree with Marx's findings, must pay their respects to the person who first claimed it for mankind.

2. LENIN'S CONTRIBUTION TO MARXIST THEORY: A VERY BRIEF SUMMARY*

Harry G. Shaffer
The University of Kansas

V. I. Lenin (born Vladimir Ilyich Ulianov, and sometimes wrongly called *Nikolai* Lenin, 1870–1924), head of Russia's Bolshevik (Communist) Party, leader of the October (1917) Revolution[1] that brought the bolsheviks to power, and premier of the "first socialist state"—the Soviet Union—from 1918 until his death in 1924, further developed Marx's ideas. He elaborated on the "final stage of capitalism" by investigating the nature of what he called "finance capitalism," "monopoly capitalism," and "imperialism"; he substituted "all toilers" (including especially the peasantry) for the "proletariat" as the ones destined to take over the reins of government from the bourgeoisie; he predicted socialist revolutions not necessarily in the most advanced capitalist countries but in the "weakest links in the capitalist chain"; he converted the structural concept of the Communist Party from that of "Communists [who] do not form a separate party opposed to other working class parties" to that of an organization of professional revolutionaries "who will devote to the revolution not only their spare evenings but the whole of their lives;" and he formulated the concept of "democratic centralism" whereby, during the intermediate phase of socialism, freedom of discussion would be combined with unity of action, and wide political participation of the masses with strict obedience to the leadership.[2]

* Reprinted from Harry G. Shaffer, *The Communist World,* New York: Appleton Century Crofts, 1967, pp. 8–9.
[1] October 25 on the pre-Revolution Russian calendar; November 7 according to the Western calendar which, soon after the Revolution, was adopted by the Soviets.
[2] "Democratic Centralism" means essentially that proposals are subject to discussion and to constructive criticism; but plans, once adopted, must be carried out. This can, in a way, be compared with standard procedure by, let us say, large American automobile manufacturers: wide exchange of ideas in regard to next year's models is encouraged; but once a decision has been reached, and the expensive retooling job has started, the plan must be carried out, at penalty of great losses to the corporation. Note that this explanation of the meaning of "democratic centralism" differs somewhat from the one given by Gerhart Niemeyer below.

3. THE COMMUNIST IDEOLOGY:
LENIN'S CONTRIBUTION*

Gerhart Niemeyer
University of Notre Dame

LENIN'S VIEWS ON CAPITALISM

"Monopoly Capitalism"

Lenin, in his revised description of the present society, derived key ideas from two books: *Imperialism* by J. A. Hobson (1902), which discussed the division of the world among the leading European nations, and *Finanzkapital* by Rudolf Hilferding (1910), which showed how huge banking enterprises controlled vast economic processes. These two ideas Lenin combined into the following picture of the present capitalist society.

The salient feature of modern capitalism is the rule of monopoly. Competition (which Marx said was the basic law of capitalist development) has given way to the concentration of enormous wealth in a few hands.

> . . . This transformation of competition into monopoly is one of the most important—if not the most important—phenomena of modern capitalist economy. . . .[1]

Marx asserted that power in capitalist society belonged to the factory owner who could buy the worker's labor power and employ it to produce surplus value. Lenin says that power now is in the hands of the financier. . . .

> The concentration of production; the monopoly arising therefrom; the merging or coalescence of banking with industry: this is the history of finance capital and what gives the term "finance capital" its content.[2]

Monopoly, in the form of finance capital, governs the present society in all its aspects. . . .

The "Need for Foreign Markets"

The driving power of capitalism, as Lenin describes it, is no longer the need of one capitalist to compete with the other, but the need of the banker-monopolist to export excess capital, obtain more foreign markets, and get them under his exclusive control. . . .

This tendency, according to Lenin, explains not only the political

---

* Excerpts reprinted from *Facts on Communism*, Vol. I, Washington, D.C.: Committee on Un-American Activities, House Document No. 336, 1960.
[1] V. I. Lenin, "Imperialism, The Highest Stage of Capitalism" (January-July 1916), *Selected Works* (New York: International Publishers, 1943), vol. V, p. 15.
[2] *Ibid.*, p. 42.

system under which modern (capitalistic) nations live, but also the international political developments on a world scale:

> Monopolist capitalist combines—cartels, syndicates, trusts—divide among themselves, first of all, the whole internal market of a country. . . .[3]
> [Then] a struggle began which . . . is fittingly called "the struggle for the division of the world."[4]

Division and Redivision of the World

Now, this division of the world is not merely a division of economic spheres of influence, but of political control. This is where imperialism enters.

> . . . Imperialism . . . means the partition of the world, and the exploitation of other countries . . . which means high monopoly profits for a handful of very rich countries. . . .[5]

In such a "parasitic" state, even parts of the working class are corrupted and stop being revolutionary. . . .

The New Image of Capitalism

Now Lenin has just about exchanged all the parts of the Marxist structure for new ones and still retained the structure! The "exploiters" are, in addition to factory owners, the rich countries; the "exploited" are, in addition to industrial workers, the colonies. The "chain of bondage" is no longer the sale of labor-power on the commodity market, but the political control of territory, and the economic control of markets. . . .

Thus, without giving up Marx's idea of the irreconcilable class struggle and Marx's condemnation of the present (capitalist) society, Lenin managed to explain . . . that capitalism has not yet collapsed because the advanced capitalistic societies found a new field of expansion which yielded them new wealth, that the lot of the people under capitalism has improved at the expense of the colonial populations, and that the upper part of the working class has allowed itself to become "corrupted" into preferring this shared wealth to the cause of the revolution. The latter observation served Lenin also as a means to read his opponents, the social-democratic parties, out of the "proletarian movement." . . .

LENIN'S VIEWS ABOUT THE DYNAMICS OF CAPITALISM

Among Marx's basic concepts was also that of the inevitably catastrophic development of capitalism. Lenin did not abandon this concept, either, but gave it a new content that seemed compatible with the all but cata-

---

[3] *Ibid.*, p. 61.
[4] *Ibid.*, p. 64.
[5] *Ibid.*, p. 95.

strophic course which capitalism had taken since Marx wrote. Monopoly capitalism, Lenin said, is the "highest stage" of capitalism.

> . . . Monopoly is the transition from capitalism to a higher system.
> . . . Imperialism is the monopoly stage of capitalism.[6]

In other words, the "higher system," socialism, is at hand. But will it grow organically out of capitalism? Will it emerge peacefully? No, answers Lenin, it will come as the result of "inner contradictions" in the capitalist system in combination with a violent struggle between the ruling powers of that system and the "gravediggers" the system has produced within itself. . . .

"Inherent Contradictions of Imperialism"

There are two kind of "contradictions" which, according to Lenin, contribute to the downfall of the system: the "contradictions" between the leading industrial powers, and that between the rich countries and the emerging power of the formerly colonial areas. . . .

> We ask is there *under capitalism* any means of remedying the disparity between the development of productive forces and the accumulation of capital on the one side, and the division of colonies and "spheres of influence" by finance capital on the other side—other than by resorting to war?[7]
> . . . imperialist wars are absolutely inevitable under *such* an economic system, *as long as* private property in the means of production exists.[8]

Thus, Lenin has now combined "war" with "exploitation" as the evil for which he indicts capitalism.

In the Marxist concept of history, the reader will remember, it appeared inevitable that capitalist society be supplanted by socialist society. Lenin here adds . . . [that] the downfall of capitalism . . . will be hastened by the revolutionary action of all the colonial peoples. . . .

Weaknesses of Lenin's Concept

Lenin's picture of the world as an imperialist, predatory, oppressive system torn by conflict and wars, is, in its way, as impressive at first glance as is Marx's picture of spiralling capitalistic production of wealth and misery. Both have enough support in observable facts to appear plausible. But Lenin's explanation, no less than that of Marx, has been refuted by actual developments. . . . In other words, Lenin's *Imperialism* is—just

[6] *Ibid.,* p. 81.
[7] *Ibid.,* pp. 89, 90.
[8] Lenin, Preface to the French and German editions of "Imperialism, The Highest Stage of Capitalism" (July 6, 1920), *Selected Works* (New York: International Publishers, 1943), vol. V, p. 8.

as little as that of Marx's *Capital*—a true picture of democratic industrial society and its development. . . .

LENIN'S VIEWS OF COMMUNIST REVOLUTION

What Marx left to his followers was the myth of the Socialist Revolution: a great convulsive crisis, a political explosion of the oppressed class of proletarians, which would at one fell swoop end the rule of the bourgeoisie and thus all class societies. . . .

Lenin, while still making full use of the myth of the revolution, saw in practice not one single threshold event that would separate two ages from each other, but rather a protracted struggle extending over an entire epoch, a struggle in which no single event or explosion could accomplish the passage from one age to the other. . . . The period of the struggle extends, in Lenin's views, from the time at which Communist forces organize, through both the bourgeois and socialist revolutions, into an indefinite duration of proletarian dictatorship. . . . Since to Lenin the revolution means not so much a liberating explosion occurring at the point of highest development of capitalism, but rather a protracted class struggle, he made a number of statements which seemed to favor more backward countries as the most suitable theater in which to carry forth this struggle. At any rate, Communist doctrine, evolving from Lenin's concepts, now calls for a concentration of the revolutionary blow on the "weakest link" of the entire "chain" of "imperialism."

Quite logically, then, Lenin expected the revolution in Russia to be decided not solely by the social forces of the proletariat, but rather by the proletariat combined with the peasantry, both led by the party. . . .

Here Lenin has shifted the "proletarian" revolution from advanced capitalist countries to backward countries, he has substituted for the proletariat first the combination of proletariat and peasantry and then "all toilers."

THE COMMUNIST PARTY

Marx, in the Communist Manifesto, had declared that "the Communists do not form a separate party opposed to other working class parties. They have no interests separate and apart from those of the proletariat as a whole." . . .

Lenin insisted on a new type or organization. Although this organization is still called a "party," it is not a genuine political party in the sense of considering itself a part of a whole, nor in the sense of functioning mainly for the purpose of organizing voters in a competitive system of politics. Rather, it was from the beginning envisaged as a combat organization, a kind of ideological-military army. . . .

Lenin set up the Communist Party as an "organization of professional revolutionaries." Such an organization is required, according to Lenin, because the class struggle is above all a "political struggle." . . . The party therefore must be—

> . . . A small, compact core, consisting of reliable, experienced and hardened workers, with responsible agents in the principal districts and connected by all the rules of strict secrecy with the organisations of revolutionaries. . . .[9]

It must consist of people—

> . . . who will devote to the revolution not only their spare evenings, but the whole of their lives. . . .[10]

"Democratic Centralism"

It follows from the entire concept of the party, its purpose as a combat organization, its foundation of "true" theory, its position as the vanguard of history's movement, that there can be no question of democracy within the party. Lenin, as has already been shown, conceived the party as built "from above" rather than "from below." He coined the term "democratic centralism" to denote the combination of two features already foreshadowed in the relation between the party and the masses; strict guidance from a small center and broad "participation" of large numbers of people in the activities flowing from this guidance. . . .[11]

The Party as the Priesthood of "Truth"

The logic of all these ideas points to one final conclusion about the party, a conclusion which has not so much been explicitly stated as a theory, but has been implied as a principle in action: *The party alone is the possessor of truth.* We must recall that truth, for a Communist, is the unfolding movement of social forces, according to the "laws" of history. . . .

The party, in the eyes of Communists, is thus not a mere political expedient but a kind of priesthood administering the truth of history. It is, for Communists, not just an organization but also a spiritual home. At any rate, there can be no other spiritual home for someone committed to the doctrines of the class struggle, the socialist revolution, and the laws of history, as Lenin teaches them. . . .

[9] Lenin, "What Is To Be Done?" (1901–1902), *Selected Works* (New York: International Publishers, 1943), vol. II, p. 133.

[10] Lenin, "The Urgent Tasks of Our Movement" (December 1900), *Selected Works* (New York: International Publishers, 1943), vol. II, p. 14.

[11] Note that this explanation of the meaning of "democratic centralism" differs somewhat from the one in footnote 2, p. 19, of the preceding selection. [Editor's note.]

4. COMMUNISM AND FASCISM: TWO PEAS IN A POD?*

Harry G. Shaffer
The University of Kansas

Born and raised in a nation which has reached unparalleled economic affluence under a democratic free-enterprise system, the majority of Americans have come to regard their political and economic system not only as the very best but as the only acceptable way of life for free people anywhere. Even moderate changes are incorporated but slowly into the "American Way of Life." The extreme political left (communism) and the extreme political right (fascism and nazism), more often than not, are adjudged but poorly disguised tyrannies, alike in all respects except the names of the tyrants. Men like Hitler, Mussolini, Stalin, Brezhnev, Mao Zedong, and Castro tend to be treated as if they were identical in their philosophies and actions—all agents of the devil bent on enslaving suffering mankind for essentially similar purposes and by essentially similar means. Such dictators as Francisco Franco (Spain), Chiang Kai-Chek (pre-Communist China, then Formosa), Fulgencio Batista (Cuba), Shah Mohammed Reza Pahlavi (Iran), and the present leaders of El Salvador, Pakistan, and South Korea, however, have (for reasons of political expediency) at one time or another received the lukewarm if not enthusiastic support of the American government, and the American public has been conditioned to accept them as defenders of Western democracy. Recently, this has been true also of some Central and South American countries.

As of now, well over one-third of the world's population is already within the Communist fold, and many other, smaller nations—both East and West—are ruled over by Fascist-type dictators. Under these circumstances, can we afford the erroneous assumption that fascism and communism—the two major radical challenges to twentieth-century capitalist democracies of the liberal and of the more conservative type alike—are but two strands of poison ivy bearing different designations but demanding equal treatment and eradication?

While great centralization of economic and political power, the one-party system, and the use of force have been manifestations of Fascist and Communist societies alike, the difference between fascism and communism is not merely one of semantics. A thorough comprehension of differences would entail a detailed analysis of several societies, past and present. Hitler's Germany, Mussolini's Italy, Peron's Argentina, Fran-

---

* An early version of this article was published in *Queen's Quarterly*. Vol. LXIX, No. 1, Spring, 1962, pp. 146–156 and reprinted in the first edition of this book (pp. 28–38). It has been largely rewritten.

co's Spain, and Trujillo's Dominican Republic differed widely from one another in many aspects of their ideological, political, economic and social structure, and so do the many right-wing military dictatorships in Latin America and elsewhere today. On the left, as this book goes to press, Andropov's USSR, Deng Xiaoping's China, Kim Il Sung's North Korea, Castro's Cuba, Kadar's Hungary, Hoxha's Albania, LeDuan and Pham Van Dong's Vietnam, and post-Tito Yugoslavia (under the leadership of collective bodies heading the nation and the Communist Party) are hardly deemed homogenous anymore, even by superficial observers (to wit, innumerable disputes among these countries on matters of doctrine and of policy). However, the many very real and fundamental differences between the extreme political right and the extreme political left should be understood by all who live in the Western world, in countries where the course of public and foreign policy is, at least to some extent, still determined by the people.

An outgrowth of mercantilist ideology of the sixteenth, seventeenth, and eighteenth centuries, fascism was launched without any philosophy whatsoever, beyond the vague concept that the leader always knows what's best. In its early history, Mussolini himself denied that fascism had a philosophy, or that it needed one. In 1921, realizing that "if fascism does not wish to die, or worse still to commit suicide, it must provide itself with a doctrine . . . ," he asked that one be written within two months. Obligingly, Giovanni Gentile, fascism's foremost "philosopher," wrote his *Origini e Dottrina del Fascismo*. "The doctrine of Fascism," he expounded, "is not a philosophy in the usual sense of the word . . . nor even a detailed and ultimate political doctrine. It has never desired to tie itself down, as far as the future is concerned. It has often announced reforms when the announcement seemed politically feasible, but, nevertheless, it has not felt itself obligated to the actual execution of such reforms. The decisions of the Duce alone are those which must always be . . . carried out."

Once fascism had gained a foothold in the Western world, it began to develop an ideology that bore clear traces of earlier philosophies. It embodied Machiavelli's and Hobbes's contentions that man is evil and brutish, that he cannot be trusted with liberty and that he must be ruled by force lest confusion and disorder persist. It embraced Nietzsche's views of human weakness and inadequacy (of which democracy, Christianity, equality, and pacifism are prevalent manifestations), to be overcome only by finding the superman capable of ruling. It perverted William James's pragmatism, interpreting it to mean that whatever works is, by definition, right. Adding German nationalism, founded largely upon John Fichte's early ninteenth-century writings, Alfred Rosenberg translated it all into the National Socialist "Weltanschauung" of the Aryan master race whose supremacy is threatened by oriental communism, by Christianity (whose founder was a Jew), and by the decadence of a system of democracy which rewards mediocrity and permits it to rule.

Fascism, its viewpoint somewhat reminiscent of that of the Tories during the American revolutionary period, denies the ability of people to govern themselves as free men and women in a democratic society. Mario Palmieri, Italian social scientist, refers to democracy as "a bastard form of political and social organization. The mass of men," Palmieri proclaims, "is created to be governed and not to govern; is created to be led and not to lead; and is created finally to be slaves and not masters, slaves of their animal instincts, their physiological needs, their emotions and their passions." Mussolini explains that "Fascism asserts the irremediable, fruitful and beneficial inequality of men which can never be leveled permanently by a mere mechanical process such as universal suffrage." And Hitler sums it up and draws the logical conclusion: "There must be no majority decision, but merely a body of responsible persons, and the word 'council' will revert to its ancient meaning. Every man shall have councillors at his side, but the decision shall be made by but one man."

The state, the all-powerful state which stands above the law, is the keystone of Fascist doctrine. "The state is not only the present," Mussolini shouted from his balcony, "it is also the past and above all it is the future. Transcending the brief spell of the life of individuals, the state stands for the immanent conscience of the nation." By superimposing the leadership principle upon the theory of the omnipotence of the state, a system is created which, in Hitler's words, is based upon the maxim: "Authority of every leader towards below and responsibility towards above." The role of the *individual* in such a society was perhaps most clearly stated by one of fascism's best known theoreticians, Alfredo Rocco: "For Fascism, society is the end, individuals the means, and its whole existence consists in using individuals as instruments for its ends."

In the economic sphere, private enterprise, though regulated by the government, is not only permitted but even encouraged, and the profit motive is accepted as a guiding incentive for production, second only to the desire to serve one's country. Article VIII of the Italian Labor Charter of 1926 reads: "The corporate (fascist) state holds that private enterprise in the sphere of production is the most effective and useful instrument in the interest of the nation." Hitler also promised that "Germany will jealously guard the principle of private enterprise in business"; but as Mussolini had before him, he emphasized that "when private interests clash with the interest of the nation, the good of the community must come before the profits of the individual." Hence, both in Hitler's Germany and in Mussolini's Italy, business enterprises, although subordinated to the overall goal and the dictates of the state, remained mostly in private hands and were operated by their owners for the purpose of making a profit within the framework of the rules and regulations imposed on them.

In this respect, certainly, the changes brought about by the advent of fascism were far less sweeping than those resulting from the passage of state power into the hands of the Bolsheviks in the Soviet Union.

Even in times of peace, Germany's and Italy's Fascist economies were oriented towards war. This was only partly due to their inherent spirit of nationalism, to their ambitions to build "a German Reich that would last for a thousand years" and to "re-establish what once was the glory of the Roman Empire." It was only partly due to their belief that "might is right" and that, in Hitler's words, "Nothing will ever grant us life or land for our nation, except the power of a victorious sword." It went much further than that. These modern "supermen"—even more than Sparta's ruling classes during the days of antiquity or Europe's knights during the age of feudalism—looked upon war as desirable for its own sake. "Fascism," Mussolini wrote in an article for the Italian Encyclopedia, ". . . believes neither in the possibility nor in the utility of perpetual peace. It therefore refutes the doctrine of Pacifism . . . *War alone keys up all human energies to their highest tension and puts the stamp of nobility upon those people who have the courage to face it.*"

In disagreement with the teachings of fascism, Socialists and Communists of all shades and leanings believe in the perfectibility of all mankind. People are basically good and capable of being master of their own destiny. Only the economic, social, and political environment (with the stress on "economic") has prevented them from realizing the utmost limits of their capabilities both as productive and as social beings.

Utopian thinkers and writers usually assumed that a change in environment would be adequate to reform immediately what we generally refer to as "human nature." Karl Marx, father of "scientific socialism," was much more realistic. Fully aware that no revolutionary transformation of the economic, political, and social order could possibly usher in the stage of perfect freedom (which he prophesied would be the final destiny of mankind), Marx predicted the advent of an intermediate stage in society's development from capitalist democracy to pure communism. This intermediate stage has been referred to by many designations, such as "socialism" (as contrasted with "communism"), the "Period of Transition," and perhaps most frequently, "the Dictatorship of the Proletariat" (Article 1 of the new Soviet Constitution calls theirs now "a socialist state of the whole people). It is this stage—not "communism"—which the Soviet Union professes to be in at this moment. (This Marx-Lenin type of socialism is basically quite different from moderate, evolutionary, or Fabian types of socialism which combine partial socialization of the means of production with Western-type political democracy. England under the British Labour Party would be an example of such a moderately Socialist democracy.)

Had Marx based his ideology on subjective value judgments, he could never have been recognized as a social scientist. Contrary, however, to a viewpoint rather widely held in the West, his main argument was not that capitalism was inherently bad, and that socialism and communism were better. On the contrary, in 1848 Marx acknowledged in glorious words the accomplishments of bourgeois society which "during its rule of scarce one hundred years [now more than two hundred and thirty years] has created more massive and colossal productive forces than have all preceding generations together." Yet, Marx attempted to prove that the capitalist, free enterprise system was just one of the stepping stones on mankind's arduous climb towards pure communism. Using dialectic materialism and an economic interpretation of history as his basic philosophies, he developed in some two-and-a-half thousand pages of *Das Kapital* his major theories: the labor theory of value, the subsistence theory of wages, the surplus value concept, the law of decreasing profits, the law of capitalist accumulation, the theory of the self-perpetuating concentration and centralization of capital, the theory of the increasing misery of the proletariat, a simplified version of the undercon-sumption-overproduction theory of depressions, and the doctrine of the class struggle. Utilizing these analytical tools with which his name is associated, Marx described capitalism as a system of production in which economic forces would lead eventually to its inevitable downfall. At the time of the breakdown of the old order, the working class would take over the reins of government. Society, not yet ready for pure communism, would now be transformed politically into a dictatorship of the working class.

In marked distinction to Fascist ideology, no Communist ever proclaimed that a dictatorship would be the final goal of mankind. From Marx and Engels to present-day Communist writers, this dictatorship is to be but preparatory for the time when, in Marx's words, quoted also by Lenin, "mankind will inscribe on its banners: From each according to his ability, to each according to his needs." A pure Communist society, then, is mankind's promised land; a society without any government, police force, army, or jails; a society in which perfect freedom reigns; a society in which production will have been developed "to the nth degree"; a society in which people will have been transformed into "social beings" who voluntarily and without special personal reward contribute to the best of their ability and take from the common stores whatever they need. It is this hope of an ideal order in which, quoting Lenin, "the *necessity* of observing the simple fundamental rules of everyday social life in common will have become a *habit*"—it is this promise of a perfect world which communism holds out to the hundreds of millions of its followers. To them, life under a "temporary" dictatorship (which presumably represents them and their interests) does not seem too high a price to pay, especially since most of them have known little freedom in their native lands, and most of their forefathers lived and labored under one or another type of tyranny since time immemorial.

During the intermediate stage, all the means of production are gradually taken over by the government and supposedly operated in the interest of the people. The entire economy is, in a sense, transformed into one gigantic corporation in which every citizen is an equal stockholder and in which the government acts as the board of directors. Though gradually declining in importance as, step by step, the vestiges of capitalist teachings are replaced by Communist indoctrination, monetary incentives are still utilized as essential economic stimuli. While Article 14 of the Constitution of the Soviet Union clearly states that "socially useful work and its results determine a person's status in society," it calls for a combination of "material and moral incentives" and spells out clearly that labor is evaluated and rewarded "in accordance with the principle of socialism: 'From each according to his ability, to each according to his work.'" In Marx's concept of the intermediate stage and in actual practice in the Soviet Union today, the more productive worker has a higher income than his less qualified or less industrious comrade. With his higher income he can purchase more of the consumer goods available but he cannot invest his savings in a business enterprise, for in Socialist-Communist morality it is a crime (once capitalism has been abolished) to derive a profit from the labor of another human being.

How about democracy under the "Dictatorship of the Proletariat"? Democracy is redefined in theory and still more in practice. "Democracy for the vast majority of the people," explained Lenin, "and suppression by force, i.e., exclusion from democracy of the exploiters and oppressors of the people—this is the modification of Democracy during the *transition* from Capitalism to Communism." Democracy for those, then, who at least do not actively oppose the new order, but suppression of "counter-revolutionary enemies of the people" is the admitted redefinition of democracy during the intermediate stage. In Marxist-Leninist ideology, the state has always been "and by its very nature always must be" an agency of oppression used by the ruling class to oppress all other classes. This was so when feudal lords ruled over their land and when absolute monarchs held absolute power. This is so, communism proclaims, when the bourgeoisie rules via universal suffrage which allows the masses, in Marx's words, "once every few years, to decide which particular representatives of the oppressing class should be in parliament to represent and to oppress them." This is also so during the Dictatorship of the Proletariat, when political power has been merely transferred from the bourgeoisie to the proletariat. Only when there are no more classes could the state itslf "wither away" and make room for a perfect, all-inclusive, unlimited democracy.

The extent to which Soviet policy conforms to Marxian ideology is a question of major interest to students of the Soviet economy. The Soviet leadership asserts that theirs is the only correct interpretation and application of Marxist-Leninist teachings. On the other hand, many social scientists in the Western world, including many of laissez-faire, Keynesian, and even some of Socialist leanings, contend that Marx would turn over in his grave were he to know what had been done to his philosophy in the Soviet Union.

It is admittedly difficult to ascertain the extent to which Soviet history and practice have corresponded with, or deviated from, Marxian theory. Marx had predicted that the Dictatorship of the Proletariat would supersede an advanced phase of capitalism, but Russia never went through a stage of industrial capitalism at all. Early endeavors to eliminate money and to introduce a semi-Communist society from the start ("thrust upon us" as a result of the world war, the Revolution, and the Civil War that followed, Lenin said) were quite contrary to Marx's concept of the intermediate stage and failed utterly. The era of the N.E.P. (New Economic Policy) ushered in in 1921 was a period of restoration of order which entailed a substantial degree of de-socialization and amounted, in effect, to a partial return to capitalism—one step backward, so to speak, so that two steps forward could be taken more rapidly in the future. This short-lived readjustment period came to an end seven years later with the introduction of the first Five-Year Plan, which saw the Soviet economy move, with renewed vigor, towards more complete nationalization. Yet even today, the elimination of capitalist incentives and motivation has been but partially accomplished and private enterprise on a limited scale is still permitted. Nonagricultural private entrepreneurship is limited to small productive units and, as the law prevents a private "businessman" from employing anyone, so small a fraction of one percent of total non-farm output is produced by handicraftsmen in business for themselves that it is not even listed in Soviet national income accounts nor deemed of any significance by Western analysts. In the agricultural sector, on the other hand, a kind of free enterprise exists in the form of subsidiary plots. Peasants on state and collective farms (and also other Soviet citizens who wish to spend some of their spare time farming) may devote part of their labor time to their own small private plots, averaging somewhat over an acre in size. These private subsidiary plots (highly productive in output per acre of land but not very efficient per hour of labor bestowed on them) account for about three percent of the total agricultural land area but upward of twenty-five percent of the total agricultural output of the Soviet Union.[1] In violation of Socialist principles, interest is still paid on bank deposits. By means of titles ("Hero of Labor"), honors, and recognition, an attempt is being made to substitute gradually "unselfish, Socialist competition" for monetary incentives, but wage differentials (factory manager

---

[1] Output figures per acre of land on the private plots are somewhat misleading. As a rule, the peasants graze private farm animals on the collective or state farm's land, use without charge some of their collective or state farm's agricultural equipment, grow on their plots high cash-value crops, such as fresh vegetables and fruits, and are allowed to sell them on certain markets at prices dictated by demand and supply.

versus unskilled worker, general versus private in the Red Army) are still substantial and are likely to remain so for some time to come.

Elections in the Soviet Union are not quite so undemocratic as usually visualized in America. Any recognized, organized association such as a labor union, a unit of the army, navy, or air force, a collective or state farm—as well as the local unit of the Communist party, of course—has the right to nominate any man or woman for office, regardless of whether he or she is a member of the Communist party. All nominating organizations, then, send their representatives to a convention for the purpose of selecting the one slate of officers submitted to the electorate for a "yea" or "nay" vote—somewhat comparable to the procedure followed by nominating committees in some of our own democratically run private clubs. Yet it is difficult for us to conceive that such a procedure could be preferable, from the point of view of political freedom, to our system of national elections.

Most important, probably, is the question as to whether there are any indications that the state has started to "wither away." It is true that since Stalin's death, certain changes seem to point to some reduction of centralized control and authority. For instance, machine-tractor stations (once a powerful weapon of centralized control over collective farms) have been abolished, more authority has been given to local management, and force as a means of exacting compliance with rules and regulations has greatly diminished. Yet at best, all this is insufficient evidence that the state has begun to "wither away," and there are even indications of some recentralization since Khrushchev's demise in the mid-1960s. Marxian theory, including the promise of the final stage, is propounded from first-grade classrooms to union halls and mass meetings. Still, the danger that a prolongation of central control will perpetuate the dictatorship unquestionably exist, even if we were to grant the sincerity of the leaders' proclamations. Progress towards economic abundance including free medical services, free education, rent-free housing, free water and heating, free public transportation, etc., has been slower than anticipated in the 1961 Party Program. If it all were to materialize, it would certainly be a great step forward in the direction of a classless society in which goods would be distributed according to needs. But whether it would bring in its wake a significant simultaneous decrease in the centralized political and economic powers of the state, only the future could tell.

Western non-Marxist social scientists show relatively little interest in a detailed theoretical analysis or in constructing a model of the final stage, as they usually consider it utopian, at least in the foreseeable future. Moreover, Western fear of communism is not fear of the promised final stage, but rather of a dictatorship (whether of the proletarian or the one-man type) which repeatedly has shown its readiness to support left-wing revolutionary movements and governments around the globe.

In a tense Western world, moving uneasily along the brink of a nuclear holocaust, the threat posed by such Fascist or semi-Fascist organizations as the American Nazi Party, the KKK, the States Rights Party, or the Minutemen (who in the name of "fighting communism" and often in the name of "preserving American democracy" would destroy all freedom) should not be underestimated. Yet, for many reasons, communism presents a much greater challenge to the survival of Western capitalist society as we know it than fascism.

First of all, while fascism constitutes a potential internal threat to all Western nations, fascist-type right-wing and military dictatorships today have under their control only militarily and economically weak nations. Communism, on the other hand, embraces hundreds of millions of followers in vast areas of the world's potentially most productive regions, and Communist parties rule such superpowers as the USSR and mainland China.

Secondly, with the major Fascist powers defeated in World War II, Fascist expansionist ambitions have, for all practical purposes, come to an end, at least for the time being, while communism is committed to engulf the entire world. Lest it change its views and aims and give up its promise of the final stage, the ideological confrontation and the struggle for the hearts and minds of the people in the Third World will undoubtedly have to continue. Moreover, while Fascist expansionism was always aimed at establishing the Fascist country's hegemony over other nations, communism invites the underprivileged and downtrodden to take over in their own land and reorganize society along Socialist lines without the previous ruling classes—an approach obviously more appealing to the masses in the Third World. (A major East-West military confrontation, on the other hand, must surely be ruled out by followers of Marx, not only because of the unacceptable level of destruction of a nuclear war, but also because it would be totally unnecessary since, Marxist theory holds, the downfall of capitalism is inevitable anyhow.)

Third, since Fascism does not abolish the private ownership of the means of production, it involves mainly a *political change*, and a reemergence of, or a changeover to, a capitalist democracy is quite possible. (After all, the era of mercantilism, when monarchs held absolute power, was a Fascist-type system that gave way all over Western Europe to free-enterprise-type social orders.) Communism, on the other hand, entails such a *complete change* in the economic, social, and political orders of things that a return to a relatively decentralized free enterprise system, guided by the objective forces of the market, seems highly improbable, difficult to accomplish (how does one resell a publicly owned steel industry to private owners, especially in a country in which there are no capitalists?), and unlikely to meet the approval even of citizens dissatisfied with some aspects of socialist rule. (For example, when in 1968 the Czechoslovak leadership attempted to combine economic socialism with a maximum of Western-style political freedom, the great majority of the citizenry apparently approved of it and opposed the Soviet-led Warsaw Pact intervention that followed. But surveys conducted by American university professors on the scene showed that over 85 percent of Czechoslovaks wanted to retain their fundamentally socialist system and had no intention of advocating a "return to capitalism.") Indeed, Marx meant it when he said, "With us it is not a matter of reforming private property, but of abolishing it; not of hushing up the class antagonism, but of abolishing the classes; not of ameliorating the existing society, but of establishing a new one."

Fourth, the Communist policy of expropriation and nationalization of productive facilities has a strong appeal to the masses in the "hungry countries," and any attempt to return private property to the previous owners is unlikely to be interpreted as a "return to liberty" by the many who have little to gain by it.

Fifth, idealists in the "Free World" are much more likely to be impressed by the high moral principles propagated by Communists than by the base appeals of Fascists. Both ideologies demand the unswerving loyalty of their followers. Yet there is a great difference between the oath of blind allegiance Germans had to swear (not to their cause or ideal, not even to their fatherland, but to the person of the Führer) and the Communist demand for adherence to the party line for the proposed goal of "ending the exploitation of man by man." Compare the Fascist dictatorship based on the right of the strong few to rule over the weaker many, a dictatorship which is the end in itself: compare it with Communist totalitarianism which seeks its justification in being a temporary necessity as a means to a moral end. Compare the Fascist view of the world as one consisting of enemies, of inferiors, of lands to be conquered and dominated by the master race: compare it with the Communist view of a world as one consisting of masses of peasants and workers to be awakened to their social responsibilities so that they may throw off the yoke of "wage slavery." Compare the Nazi-adopted "Deutschland, Deutschland über alles" (Germany, Germany above everything), and the Italian "crédere, obbedire, combattere" (believe, obey, fight): compare these with the closing words of the Communist International: "The International Party, shall be the Human Race." Compare the admitted, pronounced, and executed policies of Nazi Germany in the area of race and nationality relationships with Article 34 of the Soviet Constitution: "Citizens of the USSR are equal before the law, without distinction of origin, social or property status, race or nationality, sex, education, language, attitude to religion, type and nature of occupation, domicile, or other status. The equal rights of citizens of the USSR are guaranteed in all fields of economic, political, social and cultural life." Compare Mussolini's view that "all the history of man's civilization, from the caves to civilized or so-called civilized man, is a progressive limitation of liberty": compare this with Marx's economic interpretation of history and its utopian society of perfect freedom at the end of the rainbow. Indeed, fascism offers its adherents only one basic "moral" argument, if such it may be called: "I am better than you are, therefore, I should have the right to rule over you." The Communist, on the other hand, is left with the feeling that he devotes his all to the improvement of the lot of suffering mankind. And the argument that words and deeds do not always jibe is easily countered by the contention that they can fail to jibe only if good people refrain from joining the movement.

Finally, Marx (like laissez-faire economists such as Adam Smith, David Ricardo, Jeremy Bentham, and Alfred Marshall, but unlike Fascist writers and philosophers) presents a scientific approach towards the solution of mankind's problems and this appeals to intellectuals, irrespective of their agreement, disagreement, or partial agreement with his conclusions. Marx's *Das Kapital* is as thorough and comprehensive a study of economic forces prevalent in capitalist society as can be found anywhere. One may question his assumptions, one may take him to task for his overemphasis on supply and underemphasis on demand, one may criticize the oversimplification of his competitive model, one may disagree with some of his interpretations of historic, economic, political, and social data collected during three decades of almost incessant study and research. Yet one cannot help but admire his scientific approach, his attempt to establish scientific truths by logical and by inductive and deductive reasoning, his endeavor to utilize scientific inquiries to discover economic laws and to make valid predictions. Nowhere in Fascist literature (with its appeal to emotions, feelings, and myth, referred to by Bertland Russell as the "revolt against reason") can a comparable work be found. It is not surprising then that so many strongly anti-Marxist social scientists throughout the world have incorporated into their own philosophies one or another of Marx's analytical tools (e.g., the economic interpretation of history), scientific findings (e.g., the recurrence of business cycles) and political predictions (e.g., the growth of monopoly), thus demonstrating the truth embodied in the German proverb: "Der Weise lernt vom Feinde mehr, als der Narr vom Freunde Heer." (The wise man learns more from the enemy than the fool from an army of friends.)

The purported ends of Communists and Fascists, then, are totally different from each other. Even the "Dictatorship of the Proletariat" is superficially similar to Fascism only in some aspects of its political structure, but essentially different in its philosophic approach to the solution of mankind's problems, in the economic structure and social fabric of its society, in its declared goal and at least in some of the ways in which it hopes to achieve it. Last, but by no means least, it differs in its material, moral, psychological, and intellectual appeal to individuals and nations the world over, and in the hopes it holds out to impoverished masses everywhere. To appreciate these fundamental differences between the extreme political right and the extreme political left is imperative, not

merely for the sake of satisfying intellectual curiosity but in the interest
of a realistic approach to foreign and domestic problems.

WESTERN MARXIST VIEWS

---

5. MARXIAN SOCIALISM*

Paul M. Sweezy
Editor, *Monthly Review*

WHAT IS MARXISM?

. . . Marxism is a body of ideas about the nature of the universe, of man,
of society, and of history. It bears the name of Karl Marx, a German who
was born in 1818 and died in 1883, and who lived the latter half of his life
in London. Marx was a man of prodigious learning and enormously powerful intellect, one of the greatest thinkers not only of the nineteenth
century but of all recorded history.

Marx combined in his system of ideas the realistic philosophy of
the English and French Enlightenment, the comprehensive and dynamic
point of view of the German idealist and particularly of Hegel, and the
hardheaded analysis of the capitalist economy which we owe to the great
British classical economists. The result was a brilliant new synthesis
which is both highly original and at the same time stands squarely in the
mainstream of modern intellectual development from the Renaissance
onward. Here, in desperate brevity, are what I understand to be the central elements of the Marxian view of society and history.

The universe is real and existed for eons before there was human
life, or for that matter life of any kind, on our planet. Life here on the
earth is a natural by-product of the earth's cooling, and humanity is the
result of a long process of evolution. In the earliest stages of society,
human labor was still so unproductive that it yielded no surplus over and
above the requirements of life and reproduction. As long as this was true,
men lived in a state of primitive communism—cooperating, sharing, fighting, but not yet exploiting each other.

Later, techniques improved so much that a man could produce a
surplus over and above what he needed for himself, and from this dates
the beginning of economic exploitation and social classes. When one tribe
fought and defeated another, it was now worthwhile to take captive the

* Excerpts reprinted from Paul M. Sweezy, *Marxian Socialism*, Monthly Review Pamphlet
 Series No. 13, 1956, by permission of the author and the *Monthly Review*.

vanquished and force them to work for the victors. Some men became rulers living off the surplus produced by others; while the actual producers lost their independence and spent their lives toiling for their masters. It was in this way that exploitation of man by man and the division of society into classes originated.

But the form of exploitation has not remained unchanged—indeed, nothing remains unchanged, everything is in a constant state of flux. The exploiters seek to expand the surplus at their disposal, and with this end in view they invent and introduce new and better techniques of production; the exploited seek to improve their condition and therefore carry on a never-ending struggle to enlarge their share of the product. As a result the forms of exploitation change, and with them the whole structure of society. At first it was slavery, in which the laborer is the property of his master. Next came serfdom, in which the laborer has attained a certain degree of freedom but is still tied to the soil. And finally there is wage labor, in which the laborer is legally entirely free but must work for the profit of others because he lacks means of production of his own.

A society based on private ownership of the means of production and wage labor is called capitalism. It came into the world first in England and certain parts of Western Europe, not all at once, but gradually and painfully between the sixteenth and nineteenth centuries. It brought with it social and political upheavals, new ways of thinking, and a deep awareness of the vast creative potentials of human labor and industry. Historically speaking, capitalism was a long leap forward. In the words of the *Communist Manifesto*: "It has been the first to show what man's activity can bring about. It has accomplished wonders far surpassing Egyptian pyramids. Roman aqueducts, and Gothic cathedrals: it has conducted expeditions that put in the shade all former migrations and crusades."

But capitalism contains within itself what Marx called contradictions which prevent it from fully realizing the potentials which it was the first to uncover. The capitalist class, comprising those who own the instruments of production and set them in motion, is and must be concerned with making profits, not with the general welfare. Capitalists subordinate other aims to the maximization of profit. In pursuit of this objective, they pay workers as little as they can get away with and steadily introduce labor-saving machinery. The consequence, of course, is to hold down the consuming power of the working class. At the same time, the capitalists restrict their own consumption in the interests of accumulating more and more capital. But accumulating more and more capital means adding to society's productive capacity. We, therefore, have the paradox that capitalism steps on the brake as far as consumption is concerned and on the accelerator as far as production is concerned. This is its basic contradiction, and it cannot be eliminated except through changing the system from one of production for profit to one of production for use.

On the basis of this analysis. Marx believed that it was to the interest of the workers to organize themselves politically in order eventually to gain power and replace capitalism by a system based upon common ownership of the means of production and economic planning, a system to which he and his followers came in time to give the name of socialism. Moreover, Marx had no doubt that the workers would in fact follow this course, and that their growing numbers, importance, and discipline under capitalism would sooner or later ensure their victory. As to *how* the transition would be effected, Marx at first thought that it would have to be everywhere by means of a violent revolution. But as political democracy spread, especially in the English-speaking countries, he modified this view and in the last decades of his life believed that a peaceful and legal transition was quite possible in some countries and under some conditions. "We know," he said in a speech at Amsterdam in 1872, "that special regard must be paid to the institutions, customs, and traditions of various lands; and we do not deny that there are certain countries, such as the United States and England, in which the workers may hope to achieve their ends by peaceful means."

WHAT IS SOCIALISM?

So much then for Marxism. Naturally, my account is oversimplified and very incomplete, but I hope it may serve to give you some idea of the scope and quality of Marx's thought—so different from the impressions which demagogic opponents have always sought to convey. Let us now ask: What is socialism?

Socialism, according to Marx, is the form of society which will succeed capitalism, just as capitalism is the form of society which succeeded feudalism.

The fundamental change would consist in the abolition of private ownership of the means of production. Please note that neither Marx nor (so far as I know) any other modern socialist of importance ever advocated or expected that private ownership of consumer goods would or should be abolished. On the contrary, he favored the multiplication of consumer goods in the hands of the lower-income groups, hence a great extension of private ownership in this sphere.

As to the form of ownership of the means of production which would characterize socialism. Marxists have never been dogmatic. Ownership must be by public bodies, but that does not necessarily mean only the central government: local governments, special public authorities of one sort or another, and cooperatives can also own means of production under socialism. And there can even be a certain amount of private ownership, provided it is confined to industries in which production takes place on a small scale.

A corollary of public ownership of the means of production is economic planning. The capitalist economy is governed by the market, that is to say, by private producers responding to price movements with a view to maximizing their own profits. It is through this mechanism that supply and demand are adjusted to each other and productive resources are allocated to various industries and branches of production. But public bodies have no compelling reason to maximize their profits (though, admittedly, under certain circumstances they may be *directed* to make as much profit as they can). In general, therefore, they must have some other principle to guide their economic conduct, and this can only be the following of a plan which coordinates the activities of all the public bodies.

Now socialists claim that it is precisely the freedom from the necessity to make profits and the coordination of all economic activities by a general plan which allows socialism to overcome the contradictions of capitalism and to develop its resources and technology for the greatest good of the people as a whole. Under such a system, crises and unemployment could only result from bad planning; and while bad planning is certainly not impossible, especially in the early stages of socialist society, there is no reason why planners should not learn to correct their mistakes and to reduce the resulting maladjustments and disproportions to smaller and smaller dimensions.

What about the non-economic aspects of socialism? Here Marx had a well-developed theory. He expected socialism to come first in the more advanced industrialized countries and to build on the political foundations which they had already achieved. Since in such countries the workers were in a majority, he believed that the taking of political power by the working class would mean full democracy and liberty for most of the people, though he also expected that there would be a period of greater or lesser duration when the rights and freedoms of the former exploiters would be subject to certain restrictions. As to the longer-run future, he reasoned that the full development of society's economic potential under socialism would gradually raise the well-being and education of everyone so that eventually all classes and class distinctions would be done away with. When that happened—but not before—the state as a repressive apparatus for dealing with class and other forms of social conflict would "wither away." The final goal of Marx and his followers can therefore be said to be the same as that of the philosophical anarchists. It would be a state of society in which, to quote Marx's words, "the free development of each is the condition for the free development of all" and in which distribution takes place according to the principle "from each according to his ability, to each according to his need."

Others before Marx had had a similar vision of a good society to come—a society of abundance and brotherhood in place of the society of scarcity and alienation which the human race had always been condemned to live in. What particularly distinguished Marx from his predecessors is that he purported to prove that this society of the future, which he called socialism, is not only a dream and a hope but is in fact the next stage of historical evolution. It would not come automatically, to be sure—not as the result of the blind decrees of fate. It would come rather as the result of the conscious, organized activity of working people, the vast majority of mankind. Given this perspective, the task of the humanitarian could only be to devote his energies to educating and organizing the working class to fulfill its historic mission. That, in a word, is what Marxists have been trying to do for nearly a hundred years now.

WAS MARX RIGHT?

Marx's prophetic forecast of the end of capitalism and the opening of a new era in human history was given to the world in the *Communist Manifesto* in 1848. More than a century has passed since. Do the facts of this intervening period permit us to say whether Marx was right or wrong?

In the broadest sense, I do not see how it can be denied that Marx has been brilliantly vindicated. A mighty socialist movement based on the working class grew up during his lifetime. The crises of capitalism, far from abating, grew in intensity and violence, culminating in the holocausts of two world wars. Beginning with the Russian Revolution of 1917, more and more of the earth's population has withdrawn from the orbit of capitalism and has undertaken to reconstruct its economy and society on the basis of public ownership and planning. Today, something like a third of the human race has definitively abandoned private enterprise and, under Communist leadership, is building up a network of planned economies.

But it is not only in Communist-led countries that this is happening, though elsewhere the pace is slower. Since World War II, Great Britain has moved a considerable distance along the road to a socialized economy, and one of the two big political parties is a socialist party. Even more recently, India, next to Communist China the most populous country in the world, has adopted a Five Year Plan which the sober London *Times* calls "India's Socialist Plan."

The fact is that over most of the world's surface the trend is now visibly away from private enterprise and toward public ownership of the means of production, away from market-dominated economies and toward economic planning. Only in the United States and a few countries closely allied to the United States does the trend seem to be in the other direction. Here, it is true, the socialist movement is at a low ebb, and private enterprise is very much in the saddle.

Should we perhaps conclude that Marx was right for the rest of the world but wrong for the United States? Are we the great exception? Or are we merely lagging somewhat behind in a movement which eventually will be as universal as Marx predicted it would? These are crucial questions, especially for us Americans. . . .

There is one respect, and it is an important one, in which Marx was certainly wrong. As I noted earlier, he expected socialism to come first in the most advanced industrial countries. It did not. For reasons having to do with the late 19th- and early 20th-century development of relations between the advanced countries and the colonial and semi-colonial backward countries, the revolutionary movement grew more rapidly and had more opportunities in the backward than in the advanced regions. When the capitalist system was wracked by the destruction and disasters of the two world wars, it broke at its weakest points not at its strongest. Socialism came first to the Tsarist Empire, and spread from there to Eastern Europe and China.

This has, of course, meant that the early stages of the development of socialism have been very different from what Marx foresaw.

The new order could not build directly on the achievements of the old. It had no developed industrial base, no educated and trained labor force, no political democracy. It had to start from scratch and work under conditions of utmost difficulty.

Many people, including Marxists, expected socialism to proceed at once, or at any rate within a short time, to achieve its great goals: an economy of abundance, increasing democracy and freedom for the workers, a richer life for all. It could have happened that way if Britain, Germany, and the United States had been the first great socialist countries. But it could not possibly happen that way in backward Russia standing alone for a whole generation. The industrial base had to be built, and that meant belt-tightening. The Russians had no traditions of democracy and civil liberty, and under the difficult conditions of the '20s and '30s it was natural that a new police state should arise on the foundations of the old Tsarist police state. Moreover, like all police states this one committed excesses and horrors which had little if anything to do with the central tasks of construction the regime had set itself.

Under these circumstances, socialism in practice had little attraction for the people of the advanced countries. The standard of living of those living under it remained abysmally low, and political conduct, both among leaders and between leaders and people, often seemed closer to oriental despotism than to enlightened socialism. It was widely assumed in the West either that the Soviet Union was not socialist at all, or that socialism had been tried and failed.

In the underdeveloped countries, however, the USSR made a very different impression. They saw rapid economic advance, a vast process of popular education, some improvement in living standards—and never having experienced democracy themselves, they hardly noticed its absence in Russia. Communism was imposed on Eastern Europe by the Red Army chasing Hitler back to Berlin, but in China it was the product of a great popular revolution. And it is now expanding its influence throughout the underdeveloped regions of the world. . . .

We come finally to the question of liberty. Here the advanced capitalist countries started with an advantage over the Soviet Union no less enormous than in the field of economics. . . . And yet there is no doubt that the last few years, which happen to be the years since Stalin's death, have witnessed a considerable change in the Soviet world, and the pace of this change has been sharply stepped up. . . .

Suppose socialism shows what Marxists have always maintained, that it is possible to have economic collectivism *and* freedom? Suppose the socialist world overtakes and surpasses the capitalist world not only in production and per capita income, not only in education and science, but also in freedom and respect for the dignity of the individual? What then?

You may think these questions fantastic now. Perhaps. But let me make a suggestion. Let me propose that you file them away in the back of your mind and then bring them out, say once every year, and check the answers you are able to give on the basis of the latest facts available to you. I have no doubt what the answers will be, sooner or later. If I am right, it will be facts and not my arguments that will convince you. And I am very glad to leave it to the future to decide.

6. THE ABC OF SOCIALISM*

Leo Huberman†
Former Co-Editor, *Monthly Review*

Sybil H. May
Former Assistant to the Editors, *Monthly Review*

The only thing most Americans know about socialism is that they don't like it. They have been led to believe that socialism is something to be either ridiculed as impractical, or feared as an instrument of the devil.

This is a disturbing situation. It is a mistake to dismiss or condemn so important a subject on the basis of the extremely superficial and biased accounts of it which are now so widespread in the United States. Socialism is a world-wide movement. The millions who hate it in this country are matched by millions in other countries who rejoice in it. No idea has ever caught the imagination of so many people in so short a time. . . .

Marx saw the capitalist system as part of the history of human development. It was neither permanent nor unchangeable. On the contrary, capitalism was an essentially transitory social system which, like every other form of human society, arose out of the system before, de-

* Excerpts reprinted from Leo Huberman and Sybil H. May, *The ABC of Socialism*, 1953, pp. 3, 40–43, and 62–63, by permission of the authors and the *Monthly Review*. The pamphlet, No. 7 in the Monthly Review Pamphlet Series, is a condensation of Leo Huberman, *The Truth About Socialism*, and is edited by Sybil H. May.
† Deceased

veloped, would decay and be followed by still another system. For Marx, no human society was static—all were in a constant state of flux and change. His job, as he saw it, was to find out what produced the changes in capitalist society—to discover capitalism's "law of motion." He began by trying to explain it and ended not by apologizing for it, as other economists did, but rather by outlining a guide to action for the forces which would create a better society in the future.

Socialists believe that Marx's picture of capitalist society is sound, that it is closer to reality than the picture drawn by non-Marxist economists. On that point Professor Leontief of Harvard University, though he is himself not a Marxist, had this to say to the members of the American Economic Association: "If . . . one wants to learn what profits and wages and capitalist enterprises actually are, he can obtain in the three volumes of *Capital* more realistic and more relevant first-hand information than he could possibly hope to find in ten successive issues of the U.S. Census [or] a dozen textbooks on contemporary economic institutions. . . ."

In the same article, Professor Leontief paid tribute to the many predictions made by Marx which have since been fulfilled: "The record is indeed impressive: increasing concentration of wealth, rapid elimination of small and medium-sized enterprises, progressive limitation of competition, incessant technological progress accompanied by the ever-growing importance of fixed capital, and, last but not least, the undiminishing amplitude of recurrent business cycles—an unsurpassed series of prognostications fulfilled, against which modern economic theory with all its refinements has little to show indeed."

It is interesting to note that about the same time that this Harvard professor felt it necessary to suggest to his fellow economics teachers that they could learn much from Karl Marx, another distinguished scholar was offering similar advice to his colleagues in the field of history. In an article in the *American Historical Review* of October 1935, the late Charles Beard, one of America's most eminent historians, wrote: "It may be appropriate to remind those who may be inclined to treat Marx as a mere revolutionary or hot partisan that he was more than that. He was a doctor of philosophy from a German university, possessing the hallmark of the scholar. He was a student of Greek and Latin learning. He read, besides German, his native tongue, Greek, Latin, French, English, Italian, and Russian. He was widely read in contemporary history and economic thought. Hence, however much one may dislike Marx's personal views, one cannot deny to him wide and deep knowledge—and a fearless and sacrificial life. He not only interpreted history, as everyone does who writes any history, but he helped to make history. Possibly he may have known something."

The working class movement in almost every country of the world, striving to achieve social and economic justice, feels that he may have known something.

The colonial peoples of Asia and Africa, basing their struggles for liberation and independence on his teachings, think that he may have known something.

The countries of eastern Europe, attempting to replace anarchic production for profit with planned production for use, believe that he may have known something.

The privileged few in every capitalist country of the world trying desperately to remain secure on their tottering seats of power, tremble with the fear that he may have known something.

The people in a country one-sixth of the earth's surface, having successfully overthrown capitalism and demonstrated that socialism can end class division and enable man consciously to direct his economy for the welfare of all, are certain that he did know something.

We come now to an analysis of socialism. Let us be clear at the outset that believers in socialism do not argue that the change from private to public ownership of the means of production will solve all man's problems—it will not make angels out of devils, nor will it bring heaven on earth. The claim is made, however, that socialism will remedy the major evils of capitalism, abolish exploitation, poverty, insecurity, and war, and make for greater welfare and happiness of man.

Socialism does not mean piecemeal patchwork reform of capitalism. It means revolutionary change—the reconstruction of society along entirely different lines.

Instead of individual effort for individual profit, there will be collective effort for collective benefit.

Cloth will be made, not to make money, but to provide people with clothes—and so with all other goods.

The power of man over man will be diminished; the power of man over nature will be increased.

The capacity to produce abundance, instead of being strangled by consideration of profit-making, will be utilized to the utmost to provide plenty for all.

The overhanging fear of depression and unemployment, of destitution and insecurity, will vanish with the knowledge that planned production for use insures jobs for all, all the time—economic security from the cradle to the grave.

When success is no longer measured by the size of your pile but by the extent of your cooperation with your fellow man, then the rule of gold will be replaced by the golden rule.

Imperialist wars, which result from the profit-makers' hunt for foreign markets where they can sell "excess" goods and invest "excess" capital will come to an end—since there will no longer be "excess" goods or capital, and no profit-makers.

With the means of production no longer in private hands, society will no longer be divided into classes of employers and workers. One man will not be in a position to exploit another—A will not be able to profit from B's labor.

In short, the essence of socialism is that the country will no longer be owned by a few and mismanaged by them for their own benefit, it will be owned by the people and managed by the people for the benefit of the people.

So far we have dealt only with one part of that "essence" of socialism, the part about the country being "owned by the people"—another way of saying public ownership of the means of production. We come now to the second part of that definition—"managed by the people for the benefit of the people." How will that be accomplished?

The answer to that question is *centralized planning*. Just as public ownership of the means of production is an essential feature of socialism, so, too, is centralized planning.

Now obviously centralized planning for a whole nation is a tough job. It's so tough that many people in capitalist countries—particularly those who own the means of production and therefore think capitalism is the best of all possible worlds—are certain that it can't be done. The National Association of Manufacturers, for example, is emphatic on that point—it has repeated it again and again. Here is one of its plainest, most direct sentences on the subject from its "Platform for American Industry" some years ago: "No small group of men can possess the wisdom, foresight and discernment required to plan, direct, and stimulate successfully the activities of all the people."

Now this charge, if true, is extremely serious in any consideration of socialism. For socialist economy *must* be a planned economy, and if planning is impossible, then socialism is impossible.[1]

Is centralized planning possible? In 1928 something happened which took the question of planning out of the realm of guesswork and brought it down to earth. In 1928, the Union of Soviet Socialist Republics set up its First Five-Year Plan. When that was completed, they started their Second Five-Year Plan, and after that, their Third Five-Year Plan (and so it will go, for ever and ever, so long as Russia is socialized—because as we have seen, a socialist state *has* to have a plan).

Now we need no longer guess whether or not it is possible for a nation to have centralized planning. Now we know. The Soviet Union has tried it. It works. It is possible. . . .

Socialism will not bring perfection. It will not create a paradise. It will not solve all the problems that face mankind.

It is only in artificially created, visionary systems of society, like those of the Utopian Socialists, that sinners become saints, heaven is

---

[1] Market socialists such as Oskar Lange (formerly US and Poland; deceased), Ota Sik (formerly Czechoslovakia), and most Yugoslav economists and planners would probably disagree with a strict interpretation of this statement. [Editor's note.]

brought to earth, and a solution is found for every problem. Marxist socialists have no such illusions. They know that socialism will solve only those problems which can be solved at this particular stage in the development of man. More than that they do not claim. But that much, they feel, will result in a vast improvement in our way of life.

The conscious planned development of the commonly owned productive forces will enable socialist society to attain a far higher level of production than was possible under capitalism. Socialism eliminates capitalist inefficiency and waste—particularly the waste of idle men, machinery, and money in needless depressions; it abolishes the even costlier waste of men and materials in capitalist wars, through the establishment of international peace; it accelerates the speed of technical progress; socialist science, unhampered by capitalist consideration of profit-making as the first and most important goal, makes tremendous strides forward. The standard of living for all is raised as increased production increases the quantity of goods available.

The entire change in the mode of life brings a change in the people who live that life. At first, man will carry with him into socialist society much the same outlook on life and work that he had in capitalist society. Steeped in the competitive atmosphere of capitalism he will not readily accustom himself to the cooperative spirit of socialism; soaked in the capitalist ideology of selfishness he will not quickly switch to the socialist principle of service to his fellow man. This unreadiness to change will even be true of many who have everything to gain from the change from capitalism to socialism; it will, of course, be particularly true of those former ruling class capitalists who lose their wealth and power in the transition from private to public ownership of the means of production.

But as the new socialist system of planned production for use takes root, changes take place in the attitude and development of the people. The capitalist taint in their mental and spiritual outlook fades away and they are reoriented in the spirit of socialism. The new generation, born and bred in the new society, becomes as used to the socialist way of life as the old generation formerly was to the capitalist.

The propagandists for capitalism would have us believe that socialism means the end of freedom. The truth is the exact opposite. Socialism is the beginning of freedom. Socialism is freedom from the evils which most sorely afflict mankind—freedom from wage slavery, poverty, social inequality, insecurity, race discrimination, war.

Socialism is an international movement. Its program in every country of the world is the same—to substitute for the barbaric competitive system, the civilized cooperative commonwealth; to establish the society of the brotherhood of man in which the welfare of each is realized in the welfare of all.

Socialism is not an impossible dream. It is the next step in the process of social evolution. Its time is now.

SOVIET VIEWS

7. LENIN ON COMMUNIST SOCIETY*

From capitalism mankind can pass directly only to socialism, i.e., to the social ownership of the means of production and the distribution of products according to the amount of work performed by each individual. Our Party looks farther ahead: socialism must inevitably pass gradually into communism.

We must take all the culture capitalism left us and build socialism from it. We must take all the science and technology, all the knowledge and the arts. Without that we cannot build the life of communist society.

In the last analysis, productivity of labour is the most important, the principal thing for the victory of the new social system. . . .

The economic basis for the complete withering away of the state is such a high stage of development of communism that the antithesis between mental and physical labour disappears; and, consequently, there disappears one of the principal sources of modern social inequality—a source, moreover, which cannot on any account be removed immediately by the mere conversion of the means of production into public property, by the mere expropriation of the capitalists.

Socialism will shorten the working day, will raise the masses to a new life, will create such conditions for the majority of the population as will enable everybody without exception to perform "state functions", and this will lead to the complete withering away of every form of state in general.

And as soon as equality is achieved for all members of society in relation to ownership of the means of production, that is, equality of labour and equality of wages, humanity will inevitably be confronted with the question of advancing farther, from formal equality to actual equality, i.e., to the operation of the rule, "from each according to his ability, to each according to his needs".

In striving for socialism we are convinced that it will develop into communism and, hence, that the need . . . for the subordination of one man to another, and of one section of the population to another, will vanish altogether since people will become accustomed to observing the elementary conditions of social life without violence and without subordination.

---

* Quotations from the writings of V. I. Lenin. Selected, rearranged, and reprinted from *Soviet Union*, No. 158, 1963, p. 14, by permission of the publisher and the Copyright Agency of the USSR.

The communist organisation of social labour, the first step towards which is socialism, rests, and will do so more and more as time goes on, on the free and conscious discipline of the toilers themselves who have thrown off the yoke both of the landlords and capitalists.

We shall work to eradicate the accursed rule: "every man for himself and god for us all", to eradicate the habit of regarding work only as a duty, and of regarding as legitimate only such work as is paid for at certain rates. We shall work to inculcate in people's minds, to convert into a habit, to introduce in the daily life of the masses, the rule: "all for each and each for all"; the rule: "from each according to his ability, to each according to his needs"; gradually but steadily to introduce communist discipline and communist labour.

The state cannot wither away completely until society implements the rule: "from each according to his ability, to each according to his needs", i.e., when people become so accustomed to observing the basic rules of social life and when their labour is so productive that they will voluntarily work according to their ability.

8. THE ESSENCE OF SOCIALISM
AND OF COMMUNISM*
Novosti Press Agency

Human society, like nature, develops according to its own laws, laws that do not depend on the desire and wishes of the individual. To ignore these laws is tantamount to trying to turn back the wheel of history. Only by accepting this fact can a person obtain a historical perspective and begin to understand the logic of social life. . . .

To discover these laws, however, it is necessary to elucidate the role of material production in the life of society. No society can exist without the production of material wealth indispensable for the life of society. This was accepted by sociologists long before Marx and Engels. The latter, however, established the objective dependence of the system of all social relations on the mode of production of material wealth—a great discovery in social science. . . .

Production relations determine the social nature of each mode of production. Production relations (above all ownership relations) form the basis of any given form of social organisation i.e. the socioeconomic formation. A slave and a slaveowner, a serf and a landlord, a hired worker and a capitalist, differ in their social position because the former work

---

* Excerpts reprinted from *What Is Communism?* (no author given), Moscow: Novosti Press Agency, Publishing House, 1976, pp. 6–9, 44–45, 66–67, 70–75, 80–81, and 108–109, by permission of the publisher and the Copyright Agency of the USSR.

for the latter. The reason for this is quite obvious—the latter are the owners, the proprietors.

Why did slavery replace the ancient communal society only to give way, in turn, to feudalism? Why did capitalism replace feudalism? Because the new form of society was founded on a higher level of mode of production than the preceding stage. Those interested in the historical perspective must make an unbiased analysis of the demands that the contemporary mode of production makes on the social structure.

Anyone in an industrially developed country is familiar with the immense scale of modern production. The huge factories and mines, transport and communications require the collective, joint labor of thousands of workers. But under capitalism the social nature of production conflicts with the private nature of the distribution of what is produced. The main conclusion that follows is that production, which is social in character, cannot function normally or develop fully without breakdowns, recessions or stagnation, unless it is publicly owned, unless it is developed not in the selfish interests of the capitalists but according to a plan and in the interests of the whole of society.

Socialist nationalisation of the main wealth of society is a logical and inevitable solution of this contradiction, and it can only come about through the struggle of the working people for the revolutionary transformation of social relations.

This is the way which was first taken by the peoples of Russia and later on by other countries. This is the way to communist society—the socio-economic formation based on the most humane principles.

WHAT IS THE ESSENCE OF THE SOCIALIST SYSTEM?

The profile of a socialist society (the level of economic and cultural development, the standard of living, political forms, and so on) depends on the concrete historical conditions and traditions of the given country. In a socialist type of society, however, there are some common features which do not depend on the country where it has developed.

Socialist ownership of the means of production makes all people economically equal. And this is the main thing, for in the long run actual equality in all spheres depends on the people's economic position. Without economic power, a person cannot make others work for him, cannot exploit them. For the same reason, he cannot dominate political life, infringe upon other people's rights and make society do his bidding. Under socialism, economic equality means that man's worth is determined by his personality and not his wealth.

Under socialism, social ownership puts an end to the conflicting nature of vital interests of people belonging to different classes, and this is the basis for eliminating dividing lines between classes, for the growing homogeneity of society. . . .

WHAT IS THE ESSENCE OF COMMUNIST SOCIETY?

With the abolition of private property, the antagonism between classes disappears since no one is able to exploit others. The former exploiters also have to learn to earn a living like everyone else. In a socialist society friendly relations develop between the workers, farmers and intellectuals; the social homogeneity of society is continuously furthered. The working classes and social groups together govern their country in the common interest on the basis of broad democracy.

The socialist state's main function becomes the development of the economy and the advancement of science and culture, and seeing that the living standard of the people keeps rising since the state is responsible for public wealth. Therefore the vital interests of the state, social groups and individual citizens no longer clash, they coincide. . . .

When the differences between classes and social groups completely disappear and society becomes socially homogeneous, and when the political functions of the state (as we understand them now) become redundant, the state itself becomes unnecessary.

The very character of the functions which today we designate as state functions will change. Of course, there will continue to be bodies to direct the national economy and plan scientific research. But they will not be state bodies, since their activities will not be determined by political considerations, but exclusively by economic or scientific considerations as the case might be.

As for such classical state institutions as the court, police, security bodies, they will disappear, becoming once and for all a thing of the past.

Communist society is a complex organism based on a high level of social consciousness of all its members. The development of the functions of public control and public regulation assumes ever greater significance. But this control is no longer the control of one social group or of a special apparatus over the behaviour of others. It is, if you like, self-control. That is the basis of self-government. . . .

Visualise for a moment a different level of economic development. Imagine that consumer goods are produced in an incomparably wider variety, of high quality and in abundant quantities. There would be no talk about standardisation of tastes, or of cutting down, or let alone doing away with, the consumer's freedom of choice. The very fact that all goods will be free will ensure the consumer a wider choice which at present is restricted by one's purse. In the future society each member will have the equivalent of a blank check. . . .

Sceptics dismiss this as fantasy. No society, they argue, can allow its members to acquire as much as they want. People have such wants that no amount of wealth could satisfy. But there would not be any motive for people to amass things of value. One must bear in mind that people will have a different psychology. In the capitalist world a person's position in society and his welfare are determined by his possessions. People become obsessed by possessions, making the individual a slave to them. But when there is an abundance of goods and they are freely available, people will have no need to stockpile them. There will be no need to think of leaving an inheritance for the children, as they will have everything they need. Man will cease to be dominated by things. There will be no economic need to possess what a person does not require. The new outlook acquired will be one of the most important guarantees that the needs of all members of a communist society will be fully satisfied.

The last economic fetters will be cast off when these needs are met free of charge. Then people—of course, sensible people, socially conscious and morally sound people, in other words, members of a communist society—will be the first to be genuinely free with regard to their choice of consumer goods and in satisfying their individual tastes.

WHEN WILL THE TRANSITION BE MADE TO THE COMMUNIST PRINCIPLE OF DISTRIBUTION?

It would be wrong to think that one day people will be paying for things and the next day everything will be free. If that were so, there would be a dividing line between socialism and communism. And there is no such clear-cut division. Socialism is the first stage of communism. . . .

WILL THERE BE MORALITY IN A COMMUNIST SOCIETY?

Can any human society exist without a moral code? We are convinced that it cannot. Communism is no exception. . . .

What, specifically, does communist morality require of people? What pattern of behaviour does it regard as moral?

One of the fundamental requirements of communist morality is conscientious labour for the benefit of society. This is regarded as the main measure of a person's sense of duty to society. People in a communist society will also be intolerant of any injustice and have full respect for human dignity. Their main traits will be honesty, truthfulness, sincerity, simplicity and modesty, mutual respect in the family, a dedicated approach to bringing up children, and consideration for the old and sick. . . . Consideration for others and readiness to help at any moment—that is what is appreciated most in the behavior of people in socialist society. . . .

Communist morality is not limited to urging people to be just to each other. It implies the concrete obligation to destroy the very roots of injustice and build a just society. Accordingly, apart from the moral principles that the human race has developed over the ages, the moral code of Communists includes entirely new rules and principles that have been developed in the course of creating and developing the new society:

devotion to the communist cause, love of the socialist motherland and service to the people, proper respect for all socially useful labour, concern for safeguarding and increasing the public wealth, collectivism and fraternal solidarity with the world's working people and friendship with all peoples. *National hostility or racial intolerance in any form are abhorred and considered unworthy of man.*

There can only be a proper moral basis for relations between people when they are genuinely equal, are in the same position with respect to property, and have equal opportunities to satisfy their reasonable requirements. Hence, communist morality upholds collective public ownership and collective labour for the benefit of society as a whole, and not for private interests. That is why it condemns avarice, self-seeking and parasitism. Private ownership which allows one person or a group of people to exploit many divides people, breeds egoism, individualism and antagonism. That is why communist morality is against private ownership.[1]

WILL COMMUNISM ELIMINATE ALL WORRIES, ALL CARES, ALL CONFLICTS?

Communism does not mean a carefree, unshadowed life. It does not mean heaven on earth, or a cloister of quiet and calm. In communist society people will know what it is to tax their capacities to the utmost, they will experience the joy of a difficult job well done, the excitement of scientific research and the bitterness of mistakes. The people of the communist tomorrow will be transforming nature, pitting themselves against its mighty forces, discovering the secrets of the earth and the boundless universe. They will tackle complicated scientific and technical problems, seek to perfect the institutions of self-government and cope with many other tasks that will confront them then. Life will be full; it will have its difficulties and anxieties; there will be losses and sacrifices, doubts and disappointments. There will be risks and danger, heroic deeds and creative inspiration, the joy of victory and the dismay of defeat.

But under communism there will be no class, religious, national or racial antagonisms, there will be no grounds for social and economic conflicts that divide people. Greed and self-seeking will be vices of the past. That does not mean that people will not have any conflicts or that they will never differ in their tastes and views. There cannot be progress without a difference of views, without discussion and debate. Communist society is hardly likely to agree to just mark time. Again, not all people

[1] This refers to the ownership of the means of production. Marxists distinguish carefully between "private" ownership of the means of production and "personal" ownership of consumer goods. It is the former that are to be nationalized, not the latter. Obviously, no one proposes to nationalize an individual's eyeglasses, toothbrushes, or even clothing or furniture. [Editor's note.]

attain the same level of social consciousness; there will be mistakes and misconceptions.

Nor will conflicts of a psychological nature disappear. Even in an atmosphere of confidence, frankness and goodwill such as will prevail under communism, it will still be possible for misunderstandings to arise between people. Some people will like each other, others won't. Different temperaments will clash. There are likely to be conflicts between reason and emotion. . . . There can be differences between parents and children, and between husband and wife. Rivalry in love, and jealousy will probably still exist. There will still be suffering caused by parting, desertion, or unrequited love. The only thing is that in all these situations a spirit of humanity will prevail and personal conflicts will be resolved in a manner worthy of intelligent, morally sound people.

The role of comrades, friends and the collective in educating their fellows and helping them overcome individual inadequacies will be enhanced. Friends will endeavour to ensure that a wrong turn does not lead to actions that could harm someone or those surrounding him, that it does not develop into something that runs counter to the accepted standards of social behaviour.

In every way the pattern of life will be much healthier and more reasonable than it is today, and people will gradually cast off many harmful habits.

WILL CRIME REMAIN?

There will be no or very little crime. A communist society makes it possible, for the first time in history, to wipe out crime. This is not wishful thinking, but something that can really come about.

What is the basis for this conviction? Primarily because crime is not something that the human race is saddled with for ever. Man is not born a criminal—a violator of the peace, a trickster, a robber or a murderer. It is the environment that makes him one. Greed, cupidity, robberies and crimes of violence occur only because of social conditions, because of the injustice and evils stemming from exploitation, oppression, and the injust distribution of wealth.

People could argue—that may well be the case, but does not crime still exist in a socialist society?

Yes, so far it does. The replacement of one social system by another does not mean the automatic uprooting of this social evil that has existed through the ages. . . .

Socialism creates the conditions affording each person an opportunity of developing high moral qualities and a high level of social consciousness. . . . So, although crime still exists in the USSR and there are still violations of the law and the standards set by society, we are confident that this is something that is becoming part of the past.

The incidence of crime keeps falling, and especially so with regard to the gravest crimes. . . .

WILL COMMUNISM LAST FOR EVER?

Communism is not the end, but the beginning of the real history of society. Preceding civilisations have given man immense material and cultural wealth but, even so, they were all just a preface to real history, for society's development was an unconscious spontaneous process. Each man was aware of his own doings, determined his own goals and acted consciously, but society as a whole developed without a definite aim, was unaware of where it was heading and of the laws of its own development. Consequently, the uncomprehended motive forces of social development were blind, often destructive forces.

Mankind's transition to communism is the beginning of the conscious, purposeful, planned guidance of social processes. . . .

Communists set themselves the task of building a society of genuine social justice, of complete equality for all. As to its further development, we can only make guesses. . . . History will have to supply the final answers.

APPENDIX

"Proclaimed by the founders of Marxism, the immortal slogan 'Working men of all countries, unite!' has become the call for the international struggle of working people against all forms of enslavement, social as well as national."

YURI V. ANDROPOV
Secretary-General, Central Committee, Communist Party of the Soviet Union.

The then newly organized League of Communists (consisting predominantly of German émigré workers) held its first two meetings in London in 1847. Marx and Engels attended the second meeting and were commissioned to prepare a new program for the League. The League itself lasted only another five years, but its program, *The Communist Manifesto,* has remained the fundamental, basic document of Communist parties throughout the world. Reproduced below are major parts of Sections I and II; Section III, entitled "Socialist and Communist Literature" deals predominantly with various types of socialism such as feudal socialism, petty bourgeois socialism and utopian socialism. Primarily to distinguish the new movement from these other types of socialism, which Marx and Engels opposed, the authors used the word "Communist" rather than "Socialist" in the *Manifesto*. From Section III, only the last part is reproduced here. It deals with the relationship of Communists to other parties and ends in the famous words that have become the motto of Communists everywhere: "Working men of all countries, unite!"

The Communist Manifesto

Karl Marx and Friedrich Engels

A specter is haunting Europe—the specter of Communism. All the powers of old Europe have entered into a holy alliance to exorcise this specter: Pope and Tsar, Metternich and Guizot, French Radicals and German police-spies.

Where is the party in opposition that has not been decried as communistic by its opponents in power? Where is the Opposition that has not hurled back the branding reproach of Communism, against the more advanced opposition parties, as well as against its reactionary adversaries?

Two things result from this fact:

I. Communism is already acknowledged by all European powers to be itself a power.

II. It is high time that Communists should openly, in the face of the whole world, publish their views, their aims, their tendencies, and meet this nursery tale of the specter of Communism with a manifesto of the party itself.

To this end, Communists of various nationalities have assembled in London, and sketched the following manifesto, to be published in the English, French, German, Italian, Flemish and Danish languages:

I: BOURGEOIS AND PROLETARIANS[1]

The history of all hitherto existing society is the history of class struggles.

Freeman and slave, patrician and plebeian, lord and serf, guild-master and journeyman, in a word, oppressor and oppressed, stood in constant opposition to one another, carried on an uninterrupted, now hidden, now open fight, a fight that each time ended, either in a revolutionary reconstitution of society at large, or in the common ruin of the contending classes.

In the earlier epochs of history, we find almost everywhere a complicated arrangement of society into various orders, a manifold gradation of social rank. In ancient Rome we have patricians, knights, plebeians, slaves; in the Middle Ages, feudal lords, vassals, guild-masters, journeymen, apprentices, serfs; in almost all of their classes, again, subordinate gradations.

The modern bourgeois society that has sprouted from the ruins of feudal society has not done away with class antagonisms. It has but established new classes, new conditions of oppression, new forms of struggle in place of the old ones.

Our epoch, the epoch of the bourgeoisie, possesses, however, this distinctive feature: it has simplified the class antagonisms. Society as a whole is more and more splitting up into two great hostile camps, into two great classes directly facing each other—bourgeoisie and proletariat. . . .

Modern industry has established the world market, for which the discovery of America paved the way. This market has given an immense development of commerce, to navigation, to communication by land. This

---

[1] By bourgeoisie is meant the class of modern capitalists, owners of the means of social production and employers of wage labor. By proletariat, the class of modern wage laborers who, having no means of production of their own, are reduced to selling their labor power in order to live. [This footnote was prepared by Friedrich Engels for an 1888 edition of the *Manifesto*—Editor's note.]

development has, in its turn, reacted on the extension of industry; and in proportion as industry, commerce, navigation, railways extended, in the same proportion the bourgeoisie developed, increased its capital, and pushed into the background every class handed down from the Middle Ages. . . .

[T]he modern bourgeoisie is itself the product of a long course of development, of a series of revolutions in the modes of production and of exchange.

Each step in the development of the bourgeoisie was accompanied by a corresponding political advance of that class. An oppressed class under the sway of the feudal nobility, an armed and self-governing association in the medieval commune; here independent urban republic (as in Italy and Germany), there taxable "third estate" of the monarchy (as in France); afterwards, in the period of manufacture proper, serving either the semi-feudal or the absolute monarchy as a counterpoise against the nobility, and, in fact, corner stone of the great monarchies in general, the bourgeoisie has at last, since the establishment of Modern Industry and of the world market, conquered for itself, in the modern representative state, exclusive political sway. The executive of the modern state is but a committee for managing the common affairs of the whole bourgeoisie.

The bourgeoisie, historically, has played a most revolutionary part.

The bourgeoisie, wherever it has got the upper hand, has put an end to all feudal, patriarchal, idyllic relations. It has pitilessly torn asunder the motley feudal ties that bound man to his "natural superiors," and has left no other nexus between man and man than naked self-interest, than callous "cash payment." It has drowned the most heavenly ecstasies of religious fervor, of chivalrous enthusiasm, of philistine sentimentalism, in the icy water of egotistical calculation. It has resolved personal worth into exchange value, and in place of the numberless indefeasible chartered freedoms, has set up that single, unconscionable freedom—Free Trade. In one word, for exploitation, veiled by religious and political illusions, it has substituted naked, shameless, direct, brutal exploitation. [Yet] . . . The bourgeoisie . . . has been the first to show what man's activity can bring about. It has accomplished wonders far surpassing Egyptian pyramids, Roman aqueducts, and Gothic cathedrals; it has conducted expeditions that put in the shade all former Exoduses of nations and crusades. . . .

The bourgeoisie, during its rule of scarce one hundred years,[2] has created more massive and more colossal productive forces than have all preceding generations together. Subjection of nature's forces to man, machinery, application of chemistry to industry and agriculture, steam navigation, railways, electric telegraphs, clearing of whole continents for cul-

---

[2] As this book goes to press in 1983, it would be 135 years (since *The Communist Manifesto* was first published in 1848). [Editor's note.]

tivation, canalization of rivers, whole populations conjured out of the ground—what earlier century had even a presentiment that such productive forces slumbered in the lap of social labor?

We see then: the means of production and of exchange, on whose foundation the bourgeoisie built itself up, were generated in feudal society. At a certain stage in the development of these means of production and exchange, the conditions under which feudal society produced and exchanged, the feudal organization of agriculture and manufacturing industry, in one word, the feudal relations of property became no longer compatible with the already developed productive forces; they became so many fetters. They had to be burst asunder; they were burst asunder.

Into their place stepped free competition, accompanied by a social and political constitution adapted to it, and by the economical and political sway and the bourgeois class.

A similar movement is going on before our own eyes. Modern bourgeois society with its relations of production, of exchange and of property, a society that has conjured up such gigantic means of production and of exchange, is like the sorcerer who is no longer able to control the powers of the nether world whom he has called up by his spells. For many a decade past the history of industry and commerce is but the history of the revolt of modern productive forces against modern conditions of production, against the property relations that are the conditions for the existence of the bourgeoisie and of its rule. It is enough to mention the commercial crises that by their periodical return put the existence of the entire bourgeois society on its trial, each time more threateningly. In these crises a great part not only of the existing products, but also of the previously created productive forces, are periodically destroyed. In these crises there breaks out an epidemic that, in all earlier epochs, would have seemed an absurdity—the epidemic of over-production. Society suddenly finds itself put back into a state of momentary barbarism; it appears as if a famine, a universal war of devastation, had cut off the supply of every means of subsistence; industry and commerce seem to be destroyed, And why? Because there is too much civilization, too much means of subsistence, too much industry, too much commerce. The productive forces at the disposal of society no longer tend to further the development of the conditions of bourgeois property; on the contrary, they have become too powerful for these conditions, by which they are fettered, and so soon as they overcome these fetters, they bring disorder into the whole of bourgeois society, endanger the existence of bourgeois property. The conditions of bourgeois society are too narrow to comprise the wealth created by them. And how does the bourgeoisie get over these crises? On the one hand by enforced destruction of a mass of productive forces; on the other, by the conquest of new markets, and by the more thorough exploitation of the old ones. That is to say, by paving the way for more extensive and more destructive crises, and by diminishing the means whereby crises are prevented.

The weapons with which the bourgeoisie felled feudalism to the ground are now turned against the bourgeoisie itself.

But not only has the bourgeoisie forged the weapons that bring death to itself; it has also called into existence the men who are to wield those weapons—the modern working class—the proletarians.

In proportion as the bourgeoisie, i.e., capital, is developed, in the same proportion is the proletariat, the modern working class, developed— a class of laborers, who live only so long as they find work, and who find work only so long as their labor increases capital. These laborers, who must sell themselves piecemeal, are a commodity, like every other article of commerce, and are consequently exposed to all the vicissitudes of competition, to all the fluctuations of the market. . . .

No sooner is the exploitation of the laborer by the manufacturer so far at an end that he receives his wages in cash than he is set upon by the other portions of the bourgeoisie, the landlord, the shopkeeper, the pawnbroker, etc.

The lower strata of the middle class—the small tradespeople, shop-keepers, and retired tradesmen generally, the handicraftsmen and peas-ants—all these sink gradually into the proletariat, partly because their diminutive capital does not suffice for the scale on which modern industry is carried on, and is swamped in the competition with the large capitalists, partly because their specialized skill is rendered worthless by new meth-ods of production. Thus the proletariat is recruited from all classes of the population.

The proletariat goes through various stages of development. With its birth begins its struggles with the bourgeoisie. At first the contest is carried on by individual laborers, then by the work people of a factory, then by the operatives of one trade, in one locality, against the individual bourgeois who directly exploits them. They direct their attacks not against the bourgeois conditions of production, but against the instruments of production themselves: they destroy imported wares that compete with their labor, they smash to pieces machinery, they set factories ablaze, they seek to restore by force the vanished status of the workman of the Middle Ages.

At this age the laborers still form an incoherent mass scattered over the whole country, and broken up by their mutual competition. If anywhere they unite to form more compact bodies, this is not yet the consequence of their own active union, but of the union of the bourgeoisie, which class, in order to attain its own political ends, is compelled to set the whole proletariat in motion, and is moreover yet, for a time, able to do so. At this stage, therefore, the proletarians do not fight their enemies, but the enemies of their enemies, the remnants of absolute monarchy, the landowners, the non-industrial bourgeois, the petty bourgeoisie. Thus the whole historical movement is concentrated in the hands of the bourgeoisie; every victory so obtained is a victory for the bourgeoisie.

But with the development of industry the proletariat not only increases in number; it becomes concentrated in greater masses, its strength grows, and it feels that strength more. The various interests and conditions of life within the ranks of the proletariat are more and more equalized, in proportion as machinery obliterates all distinctions of labor, and nearly everywhere reduces wages to the same low level. The growing competition among the bourgeois, and the resulting commercial crises, make the wages of the workers ever more fluctuating. The unceasing improvement of machinery, ever more rapidly developing, makes their livelihood more and more precarious; the collisions between individual workmen and individual bourgeois take more and more the character of collisions between two classes. Thereupon the workers begin to form combinations (trades unions) against the bourgeois; they club together in order to keep up the rate of wages; they found permanent associations in order to make provisions beforehand for these occasional revolts. Here and there the contest breaks out into riots.

Now and then the workers are victorious, but only for a time. The real fruit of their battle lies, not in the immediate result, but in the ever-expanding union of the workers. This union is helped on by the improved means of communication that are created by modern industry, and that place the workers of different localities in contact with one another. It was just this contact that was needed to centralize the numerous local struggles, all of the same character, into one national struggle between classes. But every class struggle is a political struggle. And that union, to attain which the burghers of the Middle Ages, with their miserable highways, required centuries, the modern proletarians, thanks to railways, achieve in a few years.

This organization of the proletarians into a class, and consequently into a political party, is continually being upset again by the competition between the workers themselves. But it ever rises up again, stronger, firmer, mightier. It compels legislative recognition of particular interests of the workers, by taking advantage of the divisions among the bourgeoisie itself. Thus the ten-hours' bill in England was carried.

Altogether, collisions between the classes of the old society further in many ways the course of development of the proletariat. The bourgeoisie finds itself involved in a constant battle, at first with the aristocracy; later on, with those portions of the bourgeoisie itself, whose interests have become antagonistic to the progress of industry; at all times with the bourgeoisie of foreign countries. In all these battles it sees itself compelled to appeal to the proletariat, to ask for its help, and thus to drag it into the political arena. The bourgeoisie itself, therefore supplies the proletariat with its own elements of political and general education;

in other words, it furnishes the proletariat with weapons for fighting the bourgeoisie.

Further, as we have already seen, entire sections of the ruling classes are, by the advance of industry, precipitated into the proletariat, or are at least threatened in their conditions of existence. These also supply the proletariat with fresh elements of enlightenment and progress.

Finally, in times when the class struggle nears the decisive hour, the process of dissolution going on within the ruling class, in fact within the whole range of old society, assumes such a violent, glaring character that a small section of the ruling class cuts itself adrift and joins the revolutionary class, the class that holds the future in its hands. Just as, therefore, at an earlier period, a section of the nobility went over to the bourgeoisie, so now a portion of the bourgeoisie goes over to the proletariat, and, in particular, a portion of the bourgeois ideologists, who have raised themselves to the level of comprehending theoretically the historical movement as a whole.

Of all the classes that stand face to face with the bourgeoisie today, the proletariat alone is a really revolutionary class. The other classes decay and finally disappear in the face of modern industry; the proletariat is its special and essential product.

The lower middle class, the small manufacturer, the shopkeeper, the artisan, the peasant, all these fight against the bourgeoisie, to save from extinction their existence as fractions of the middle class. They are therefore not revolutionary, but conservative. Nay, more, they are reactionary, for they try to roll back the wheel of history. If by chance they are revolutionary, they are so only in view of their impending transfer into the proletariat; they thus defend not their present, but their future interests; they desert their own standpoint to place themselves at that of the proletariat. . . .

In the conditions of the proletariat, those of old society at large are already virtually swamped. The proletarian is without property; his relation to his wife and children has no longer anything in common with the bourgeois family relations; modern industrial labor, modern subjection to capital, the same in England as in France, in America as in Germany, has stripped him of every trace of national character. Law, morality, religion, are to him so many bourgeois prejudices, behind which lurk in ambush just as many bourgeois interests.

All the preceding classes that got the upper hand, sought to fortify their already acquired status by subjecting society at large to their conditions of appropriation. The proletarians cannot become masters of the productive forces of society, except by abolishing their own previous mode of appropriation, and thereby also every other previous mode of appropriation. They have nothing of their own to secure and to fortify; their mission is to destroy all previous securities for, and insurances of, individual property.

All previous historical movements were movements of minorities, or in the interest of minorities. The proletarian movement is the self-conscious, independent movement of the immense majority, in the interest of the immense majority. The proletariat, the lowest stratum of our present society, cannot stir, cannot raise itself up, without the whole superincumbent stratum of official society being sprung into the air.

Though not in substance, yet in form, the struggle of the proletariat with the bourgeoisie is at first a national struggle. The proletariat of each country must, of course, first of all settle matters with its own bourgeoisie. . . .

The essential condition for the existence and for the sway of the bourgeois class is the formation and augmentation of capital; the condition for capital is wage labor. Wage labor rests exclusively on competition between the laborers. The advance of industry, whose involuntary promoter is the bourgeoisie, replaces the isolation of the laborers, due to competition, by their revolutionary combination, due to association. The development of modern industry, therefore, cuts from under its feet the very foundation on which the bourgeoisie produces and appropriates products. What the bourgeoisie therefore produces, above all, are its own grave-diggers. Its fall and the victory of the proletariat are equally inevitable.

II: PROLETARIANS AND COMMUNISTS

In what relation do the Communists stand to the proletarians as a whole?

The Communists do not form a separate party opposed to other working class parties.[3]

They have no interests separate and apart from those of the proletariat as a whole.

They do not set up any sectarian principles of their own, by which to shape and mold the proletarian movement.

The Communists are distinguished from other working-class parties by this only: 1. In the national struggles of the proletarians of the different countries, they point out and bring to the front the common interests of the entire proletariat, independently of all nationality. 2. In the various stages of development which the struggle of the working class against the bourgeoisie has to pass through, they always and everywhere represent the interests of the movement as a whole.

The Communists, therefore, are on the one hand, practically, the most advanced and resolute section of the working-class parties of every country, that section which pushes forward all others; on the other hand, theoretically, they have over the great mass of the proletariat the advan-

[3] Note that this concept was changed by Lenin. Nowadays, Communists generally do form separate parties. Even in the GDR, the Socialist Unity Party of Germany (Sozialistische Einheitspartei Deutschland) is essentially a Communist party. [Editor's note.]

tage of clearly understanding the line of march, the conditions, and the ultimate general results of the proletarian movement.

The immediate aim of the Communists is the same as that of all the other proletarian parties: formation of the proletariat into a class, overthrow of the bourgeois supremacy, conquest of political power by the proletariat.

The theoretical conclusions of the Communists are in no way based on ideas or principles that have been invented, or discovered, by this or that would-be universal reformer.

They merely express, in general terms, actual relations springing from an existing class struggle, from a historical movement going on under our very eyes. The abolition of existing property relations is not at all a distinctive feature of Communism.

All property relations in the past have continually been subject to historical change consequent upon the change in historical conditions.

The French Revolution, for example, abolished feudal property in favor of bourgeois property.

The distinguishing feature of Communism is not the abolition of property generally but the abolition of bourgeois property. But modern bourgeois private property is the final and most complete expression of the system of producing and appropriating products that is based on class antagonisms, on the exploitation of the many by the few.

In this sense, the theory of the Communists may be summed up in the single sentence: Abolition of private property.[4] . . .

Let us now take wage labor.

The average price of wage labor is the minimum wage, i.e., that quantum of the means of subsistence which is absolutely requisite to keep the laborer in bare existence as a laborer. What, therefore, the wage laborer appropriates by means of his labor merely suffices to prolong and reproduce a bare existence. We by no means intend to abolish this personal appropriation of the products of labor, an appropriation that is made for the maintenance and reproduction of human life, and that leaves no surplus wherewith to command the labor of others. All that we want to do away with is the miserable character of this appropriation, under which the laborer lives merely to increase capital, and is allowed to live only in so far as the interest of the ruling class requires it.

In bourgeois society, living labor is but a means to increase accumulated labor.[5] In Communist society, accumulated labor is but a means to widen, to enrich, to promote the existence of the laborer. . . .

And the abolition of this state of things is called by the bourgeois abolition of individuality and freedom! And rightly so. The abolition of

---

[4] By private property, as distinguished from personal property, Marx refers to the private ownership of the means of production and not to the individual ownership of durable consumer goods (See also footnote, p. 52). [Editor's note.]

[5] Accumulated labor, in this context, refers to labor embodied in machinery. [Editor's note.]

bourgeois individuality, bourgeois independence, and bourgeois freedom is undoubtedly aimed at.

By freedom is meant, under the present bourgeois conditions of production, free trade, free selling and buying.

But if selling and buying disappears, free selling and buying disappears also. This talk about free selling and buying, and all the other "brave words" of our bourgeois about freedom in general, have a meaning, if any, only in contrast with restricted selling and buying, with the fettered traders of the Middle Ages, but have no meaning when opposed to the Communist abolition of buying and selling, of the bourgeois conditions of production, and of the bourgeoisie itself.

You are horrified at our intending to do away with private property. But in your existing society, private property is already done away with for nine-tenths of the population; its existence for the few is solely due to its nonexistence in the hands of those nine-tenths. You reproach us, therefore, with intending to do away with a form of property, the necessary condition for whose existence is the non-existence of any property for the immense majority of society.

In one word, you reproach us with intending to do away with your property. Precisely so; that is just what we intend.

From the moment when labor can no longer be converted into capital, money, or rent, into a social power capable of being monopolized, i.e., from the moment when individual property can no longer be transformed into bourgeois property, into capital, from that moment, you say, individuality vanishes.

You must, therefore, confess that by "individual" you mean no other person than the bourgeois, than the middle-class owner of property. This person must, indeed, be swept out of the way, and made impossible.

Communism deprives no man of the power to appropriate the products of society; all that it does is to deprive him of the power to subjugate the labor of others by means of such appropriation.

It has been objected that upon the abolition of private property all work will cease, and universal laziness will overtake us.

According to this, bourgeois society ought long ago to have gone to the dogs through sheer idleness; for those members who work acquire nothing, and those who acquire anything do not work. . . .

But don't wrangle with us so long as you apply, to our intended abolition of bourgeois property, the standard of your bourgeois notions of freedom, culture, law, etc. Your very ideas are but the outgrowth of the conditions of your bourgeois production and bourgeois property, just as your jurisprudence is but the will of your class made into a law for all, a will whose essential character and direction are determined by the economic conditions of existence of your class.

The selfish misconception that induces you to transform into eternal laws of nature and of reason, the social form springing from your present mode of production and form of property—historical relations that rise and disappear in the progress of production—this misconception you share with every ruling class that has preceded you. What you see clearly in the case of ancient property, what you admit in the case of feudal property, you are of course forbidden to admit in the case of your own bourgeois form of property.

Abolition of the family! Even the most radical flare up at this infamous proposal of the Communists. . . .

Do you charge us with wanting to stop the exploitation of children by their parents? To this crime we plead guilty.

But, you will say, we destroy the most hallowed of relations, when we replace home education by social.

And your education! Is not that also social, and determined by the social conditions under which you educate, by the intervention direct or indirect, of society, by means of schools, etc.? The Communists have not invented the intervention of society in education; they do but seek to alter the character of that intervention, and to rescue education from the influence of the ruling class.

The bourgeois claptrap about the family and education, about the hallowed correlation of parent and child, becomes all the more disgusting the more, by the action of modern industry, all family ties among the proletarians are torn asunder, and their children transformed into simple articles of commerce and instruments of labor.[6] . . .

The Communists are further reproached with desiring to abolish countries and nationality.

The working men have no country. We cannot take from them what they have not got. Since the proletariat must first of all acquire political supremacy, must rise to be the leading class of the nation, must constitute itself *the* nation, it is, so far, itself national, though not in the bourgeois sense of the word.

National differences and antagonisms between peoples are daily more and more vanishing, owing to the development of the bourgeoisie, to freedom of commerce, to the world market, to uniformity in the mode of production and in the conditions of life corresponding thereto.

The supremacy of the proletariat will cause them to vanish still faster. United action of the leading civilized countries at least is one of the first conditions for the emancipation of the proletariat.

In proportion as the exploitation of one individual by another is put an end to, the exploitation of one nation by another will also be put an end to. In proportion as the antagonism between classes within the nation vanishes, the hostility of one nation to another will come to an end.

The charges against Communism made from a religious, a philo-

---

[6] At the time Marx wrote, economic necessity forced many, and in some places most, workers' families to send their children to the mines and factories at an early age where they labored for long hours and low pay under highly hazardous and unhealthy conditions. [Editor's note.]

sophical and, generally, from an ideological standpoint are not deserving of serious examination.

Does it require deep intuition to comprehend that man's ideas, views, and conceptions, in one word, man's consciousness, changes with every change in the conditions of his material existence, in his social relations and in his social life?

What else does the history of ideas prove than that intellectual production changes its character in proportion as material production is changed? The ruling ideas of each age have ever been the ideas of its ruling class.

When people speak of ideas that revolutionize society, they do but express the fact, that within the old society the elements of a new one have been created, and that the dissolution of the old ideas keeps even pace with the dissolution of the old conditions of existence.

When the ancient world was in its last throes, the ancient religions were overcome by Christianity. . . .

"Undoubtedly," it will be said, "religious, moral, philosophical and juridical ideas have been modified in the course of historical development. But religion, morality, philosophy, political science, and law constantly survived this change."

"There are, besides, eternal truths, such as Freedom, Justice, etc., that are common to all states of society. But Communism abolishes eternal truths, it abolishes all religion, and all morality, instead of constituting them on a new basis; it therefore acts in contradiction to all past historical experience."

What does this accusation reduce itself to? The history of all past society has consisted in the development of class antagonisms, antagonisms that assumed different forms at different epochs.

But whatever form they may have taken, one fact is common to all past ages, viz., the exploitation of one part of society by the other. No wonder, then, that the social consciousness of past ages, despite all the multiplicity and variety it displays, moves within certain common forms, or general ideas, which cannot completely vanish except with the total disappearance of class antagonisms.

The Communist revolution is the most radical rupture with traditional property relations; no wonder that its development involves the most radical rupture with traditional ideas.

But let us have done with the bourgeois objections to Communism.

We have seen above that the first step in the revolution by the working class is to raise the proletariat to the position of ruling class, to win the battle of democracy.

The proletariat will use its political supremacy to wrest, by degrees, all capital from the bourgeoisie, to centralize all instruments of production in the hands of the state, i.e., of the proletariat organized as the ruling class; and to increase the total of productive forces as rapidly as possible.

Of course, in the beginning, this cannot be effected except by means of despotic inroads on the rights of property, and on the conditions of bourgeois production; by means of measures, therefore, which are unavoidable as a means of entirely revolutionizing the mode of production.

These measures will, of course, be different in different countries.

Nevertheless, in the most advanced countries, the following will be pretty generally applicable:

1. Abolition of property in land and application of all rents of land to public purposes.
2. A heavy progressive or graduated income tax.
3. Abolition of all right of inheritance.
4. Confiscation of the property of all emigrants and rebels.
5. Centralization of credit in the hands of the state, by means of a national bank with state capital and an exclusive monopoly.
6. Centralization of the means of communication and transport in the hands of the state.
7. Extension of factories and instruments of production owned by the state; the bringing into cultivation of waste lands, and the improvement of the soil generally in accordance with a common plan.
8. Equal obligation of all to work. Establishment of industrial armies, especially for agriculture.
9. Combination of agriculture with manufacturing industries; gradual abolition of the distinction between town and country, by a more equable distribution of the population over the country.
10. Free education for all children in public schools. Abolition of children's factory labor in its present form. Combination of education with industrial production, etc.

When, in the course of development, class distinctions have disappeared, and all production has been concentrated in the hands of a vast association of the whole nation, the public power will lose its political character. Political power, properly so called, is merely the organized power of one class for oppressing another. If the proletariat during its contest with the bourgeoisie is compelled, by the force of circumstances, to organize itself as a class; if, by means of a revolution, it makes itself the ruling class, and, as such, sweeps away by force the old conditions of production, then it will, along with these conditions, have swept away the conditions for the existence of class antagonisms and of classes generally, and will thereby have abolished its own supremacy as a class.

In place of the old bourgeois society, with its classes and class antagonisms, we shall have an association in which the free development of each is the condition for the free development of all. . . .

III (Part): Position of the Communists in Relation to the Various Existing Opposition Parties

Section II has made clear the relations of the Communists to the existing working class parties, such as the Chartists in England and the Agrarian Reformers in America.

The Communists fight for the attainment of the immediate aims, for the enforcement of the momentary interests of the working class; but in the movement of the present, they also represent and take care of the future of that movement. In France the Communists ally themselves with the Social-Democrats, against the conservative and radical bourgeoisie, reserving, however, the right to take up a critical position in regard to phrases and illusions traditionally handed down from the great Revolution.

In Switzerland they support the Radicals, without losing sight of the fact that this party consists of antagonistic elements, partly of Democratic Socialists, in the French sense, partly of radical bourgeois.

In Poland they support the party that insists on an agrarian revolution as the prime condition for national emancipation, that party which fomented the insurrection of Cracow in 1846.

In Germany they fight with the bourgeoisie whenever it acts in a revolutionary way, against the absolute monarchy, the feudal squirearchy, and the petty bourgeoisie.

But they never cease, for a single instant, to instill into the working class the clearest possible recognition of the hostile antagonism between bourgeoisie and proletariat, in order that the German workers may straightway use, as so many weapons against the bourgeoisie, the social and political conditions that the bourgeoisie must necessarily introduce along with its supremacy, and in order that, after the fall of the reactionary classes in Germany, the fight against the bourgeoisie itself may immediately begin. . . .

The Communists disdain to conceal their views and aims. They openly declare that their ends can be attained only by the forcible overthrow of all existing social conditions. Let the ruling classes tremble at a Communist revolution. The proletarians have nothing to lose but their chains. They have a world to win.[7]

Working men of all countries, unite!

---

[7] While this is obviously a call to revolution, Marx did say that a revolution may not be necessary in all cases. In an often-quoted speech he gave in 1872 at the Hague Convention of the First International (an organization to which belonged socialist and Communist parties and labor unions in various countries) Marx said, "But we do not assert that the way to reach this goal is the same everywhere. We know that the institutions, the manners and the customs of the various countries must be considered, and we do not deny that there are countries like England and America . . . where the worker may attain his objective by peaceful means." [Editor's note.]

II

Stalin: Great Leader or Cruel Despot?

"There was an interesting difference between Lenin and Stalin: Lenin forgave his enemies, Stalin killed his friends."

NIKITA S. KHRUSHCHEV

"Stalinism is the only true Marxism-Leninism."

LOZARI NREGI
Albanian Delegate to an International Conference of World War II Partisans in Rome

"In abusing Stalin, Khrushchev is in fact wildly denouncing the Soviet system and state. His language in this connection is by no means weaker but is actually stronger than that of such renegades as Kautsky, Trotsky, Tito, and Djilas."

EDITORIAL DEPARTMENTS OF COMMUNIST CHINA'S *PEOPLE'S DAILY* AND *RED FLAG*, 1963

SPACE LIMITATION does not allow for an extensive analysis of Russia's prerevolutionary and the Soviet Union's postrevolutionary history. But to place Soviet life into its proper perspective, to round out the picture of Soviet economic and political institutions as they evolved over the past three-score years, and to provide the reader with an albeit limited blackground, this brief chapter on the Stalin era has been included here.

For almost three decades—from the death of Lenin in 1924 to his own death in 1953—Joseph Stalin (1879–1953) ruled the Soviet Union with an iron hand, often as tyrannically as any oriental potentate had ever ruled over his subjects. Eliminating his former comrades-in-arms one by one, Stalin first turned against the Trotskyist radicals who favored the immediate support of world-wide revolutions, as opposed to his plan to perfect "socialism in one country," the USSR, and then to proceed from there. Having defeated the left-wing opposition and driven Trotsky[1] into

---

[1] Leon Trotsky, 1877–1940, Chief organizer of the revolutionary Red Army, and, from 1918 to 1925, People's Commissar for Military and Naval Affairs.

exile in 1928 (where he was assassinated eleven years later, presumably on Stalin's orders), Stalin then turned against the "right-wing opportunists and bourgeois nationalists." Opposed to radical collectivization and industrialization at the expense of current consumption, these "right-wing deviationists" favored a more gradual introduction of changes, at a speed that would not call forth the bitter antagonism of the peasants. The leaders of these moderate forces, men like Bukharin,[2] had almost all been active revolutionists during the days of the establishment of the Soviet Union, had fought on Lenin's side against the White Russians and the foreign armies, and had given their full support to Stalin in his fight against the Trotskyites. Now their turn had come. During the purges of the 1930's, one after another faced charges of treason and eventually the firing squad.[3]

In the meantime Stalin proceeded to pursue his goal of rapidly industrializing the Soviet Union. Opposition was ruthlessly shattered; peasants who refused to cooperate with the collectivization program or the enforced delivery of grain to the state at almost confiscatory prices were shipped to Siberia by the hundreds of thousands; and improvements in living standards were postponed,[4] since all available resources not absolutely required to meet minimum consumption needs were utilized to build up the military and industrial might of the USSR. The sacrifices exacted from the population at large and from the peasantry in particular were appalling, but some of the objectives were undoubtedly achieved. Even today, some thirty years after Stalin's death, it is not easy to form a judgment as to whether, within the framework of the type of planned economy that was being built, more permissive policies would have led to equally rapid industrialization. If not, could a less-well-prepared USSR have withstood the brutal onslaughts of the Nazi war machinery and turned the tide in World War II against the would-be master race bent on enslaving the world?

Under the given conditions, then, was Stalin an historical, objective necessity? Although by no means in complete disagreement, Alec Nove and Leopold Labedz cross swords on this issue under "Western Views" below.

Throughout the days of his regime, in classrooms and assembly halls, in newspapers, books, and radio broadcasts, on the stage and on the screen, Stalin was hailed as the benevolent father and magnanimous mentor, the protector of the socialist motherland, the "greatest genius of mankind." Whatever he personally may have contributed or failed to contribute to the war effort, it was under his leadership that the Nazi

---

[2] Nikolai Ivanovich Bukharin, 1888–1938.

[3] Some but by no means all of those purged have since been cleared posthumously of all charges.

[4] In fact, living standards dropped sharply during the early 1930's, and some Western economists would argue that the 1928 levels were not reached again until as late as 1955.

invaders were driven from Soviet soil and the red flag carried deep into the heart of Europe. By the end of World War II, Stalin was acclaimed by one and all in the USSR as the "wise leader and military commander," the "organizer of victory." The first selection under "Soviet Views" gives a few examples of the glorification of Stalin during his lifetime.[5]

Soon after the end of World War II, Stalin once again turned against his former friends and comrades. If his "excesses" had ever been in any way "justifiable" in prewar days to eliminate political opponents and speed the process of industrialization, their recurrence at a time at which a unified nation had come to accept its new social order as the best way of life and him as its revered leader could be ascribed only to paranoic suspicion. Doubtful of the loyalty of even his closest associates, Stalin returned to the terror tactics of the 1930s. Thousands of faithful party members and ardent supporters of Soviet communism were arrested on the slightest suspicion, tried before mock courts, and summarily executed for crimes to which all of them "confessed." Did other party leaders, men like Khrushchev, know about all of this? Here is Khrushchev's answer:

> The question arises whether the leading cadres of the Party knew about, for example, the arrests of people in that period. Yes, they did. But did they know that absolutely innocent people were arrested? No, they did not. They believed Stalin and could not dream that repressions could be used against honest people devoted to our cause.[6]

Stalin died in 1953, and a nation mourned the leader who had guided its destiny for an entire generation. His body was placed next to that of Lenin in the Soviet Union's most hallowed shrine, the Mausoleum in Red Square, and millions filed by in the days and months and years that followed. "At Stalin's funeral many, including myself, were in tears," Khrushchev admitted frankly. "These were sincere tears, for although we knew about some of Stalin's shortcomings, we believed in him."[7]

At the Twentieth Party Congress, in 1956, came the now famous secret session in which Khrushchev denounced Stalin. Here is Nathaniel Weyl's description of the proceedings, taken from his introduction to the English translation of Khrushchev's speech:

> We know something of the atmosphere in which Khrushchev's speech was delivered. Sixteen hundred delegates to the Party Congress met behind locked doors. Not even foreign Communist fraternal delegates were permitted inside. The address lasted until four in the morning. Khrushchev reportedly broke

[5] The phrases in quotes were titles bestowed upon Stalin by Khrushchev. See *Soviet World Outlook: A Handbook of Communist Statements,* Department of State Publication 6836, released July, 1959, p. 43.

[6] From a speech by Nikita S. Khrushchev, delivered on March 8, 1963. Translated in *Current Soviet Documents,* April 5, 1963, p. 13.

[7] *Ibid.,* p. 15.

down in tears four times; some thirty delegates fainted or had sei-
zures.

    This was not a cold, Machiavellian performance, but an in-
tensely emotional and disturbing ritual in which men who had lived
in fear, under terror, in a miasma of lies spoke out to an audience
which was also partly guilty. . . .

    . . . When they learned what sort of man Stalin had actually
been, when they were told about crimes which they had perhaps
previously heard rumors of, but had tried to deny even in the privacy of their own thoughts, clearly they could not dissociate themselves emotionally or morally as if they had been mere bystanders
and not participants and accomplices.[8]

The second selection under "Soviet Views" consists of excerpts
from Khrushchev's condemnation of Stalin. It should be noted, however,
that Stalin was taken to task only for having brought about the execution
of *loyal* comrades on trumped-up charges. Stalin's purges of left- and
right-wing deviationists were still officially approved by the Party. Here
is the way a 1960 Soviet edition of the *History of the Communist Party
of the Soviet Union* reported Stalin's actions against his political opponents:

    . . . As an outstanding theoretician and organizer, he led
the fight against the Trotskyists, Right-wing opportunists, and
bourgeois nationalists, against the intrigues of the capitalist encirclement. He rendered great services not only in ensuring the
victory of Socialism in the U.S.S.R., but also in developing the
world Communist and liberation movement. This naturally earned
him great prestige and popularity. However . . .[9]

The denunciation of Stalin was undertaken for the declared purpose
of assuring that "phenomena of this kind would never again arise in the
Party and country."[10] If ever Stalinist methods and practices were to be
discontinued, if ever Stalinist attitudes and approaches were to be
changed, the Stalin myth had to be unmasked for, in the words of an
eminent American author, editor, and social critic,

    . . . Stalin was not just a tyrant who brought a reign of terror
and suppression to the Russian people. He exerted a profound
influence on the form and direction of the Communist Party, on
approaches to major problems, on the thought patterns of the people. And before the effects could be extirpated, the cause had to
be clearly defined.[11]

Once Stalin had been exposed, the Soviet Union and all the Eastern

---

[8] Nathaniel Weyl's Introduction to *The Anatomy of Terror*, Public Affairs Press, 1956, p.
14.
[9] *History of the Communist Party of the Soviet Union*, Foreign Languages Publishing House,
1960, pp. 670–71.
[10] *Ibid.*, p. 670.
[11] Norman Cousins, "Listening to Ivan Denisovich," *Saturday Review*, February 9, 1963,
p. 18.

European bloc countries, except Albania, proceeded to erase one by one the vestiges of the Stalin cult. His pictures were taken down; his statues were removed from their pedestals; the names of streets, places, towns, collective farms, and cooperative and state enterprises were changed. Even the hallowed name of Stalingrad, where the Nazi armies met their first major defeat, was changed to Volgograd. In the meantime, the accusations against Stalin mounted in vigor and bitterness. For years thereafter, in issue after issue of the leading Soviet newspapers and historical journals there appeared obituaries on the anniversaries of the birth of former leading Communists, eulogizing their contributions to the cause, and ending in words such as these: "His [V. P. Zatonsky's] devotion to the ideals of Marxism-Leninism, his unusual courage and heroism, his close ties with the people, his internationalism, the purity of his actions and thoughts—all this was unjustly deleted from history, along with his name, in the period of the Stalin cult."[12] Sometimes the phrasing was simpler but no less revealing: "Yuri Mikhailovich perished in 1941, a victim of the repressions of the cult of the individual."[13]

By the time the Twenty-Second Party Congress met in 1961, the Party was ready to take the final step: Stalin's body was removed from the Lenin Mausoleum and his remains were reduced to ashes. Most of the Communist world approved, but the Chinese Communists (and their Albanian comrades) didn't. The latter did not sanctify Stalin, who for years had refused to support their struggle against the Chiang Kai-shek regime. They did not pronounce him faultless. They admitted that he had erred, and they did not even deny that "innocent people . . . were wrongly convicted." But, balancing his accomplishments against his shortcomings, they proclaimed that he was "primarily correct" and that his faults had been "secondary." The last selection of this chapter is an exposition of the point of view promulgated loudly, clearly and incessantly by the Chinese Communists in the late 1950s and throughout the 1960s. There are no indications that the Chinese have altered their views on Stalin since then. There has been no official denunciation of Stalin, no extensive or severe criticism. But since President Nixon's historic trip to China in February, 1972, that ushered in a new era in Chinese-American relations, the Chinese have basically remained silent on this politically loaded issue.

The Soviets, on the other hand, appear to have come closer to the Chinese position in recent years. While still critical of Stalin for having committed "errors" and "excesses," one can once again find reports praising him for his role as the Soviet leader before, during, and after the "Great Patriotic War." He is certainly no longer the nonperson he was during the post-1961 Khrushchev era.

[12] *Voprosii istorii KPSS,* No. 9, September, 1963. Translated in *The Current Digest of the Soviet Press,* October 9, 1963, p. 23.
[13] *Izvestia,* August 27, 1963. Translated in *The Current Digest of the Soviet Press,* September 18, 1963, p. 41.

WESTERN VIEWS

1. WAS STALIN A "HISTORICAL NECESSITY"?

A. WAS STALIN REALLY NECESSARY?*

Alec Nove
University of Glasgow

Stalin has suffered a dramatic post-mortem demotion, and a monument to his victims is to be erected in Moscow. The present Soviet leadership is thus disassociating itself publicly from many of the highly disagreeable features of Stalin's rule, while claiming for the Party and the Soviet system the credit for making Russia a great economic and military power. Is this a logically consistent standpoint? How far was Stalin, or Stalinism, an integral, unavoidable, "necessary" part of the achievements of the period? How much of the evil associated with the Stalin system is attributable to the peculiar character of the late dictator, and how much was the consequence of the policies adopted by the large majority of the Bolshevik party, or of the effort of a small and dedicated minority to impose very rapid industrialisation on a peasant country?

To ask these questions is of interest from several standpoints. Firstly, in trying to answer them we might be able to see a little more clearly the meaning of such misused terms as "determinism," causality, or the role of personality in history. Secondly, an examination of the circumstances which brought Stalin to power and led to—or provided an opportunity for—crimes on a massive scale is surely of very practical interest, since it might help in understanding how to avoid a repetition of these circumstances, particularly in those underdeveloped countries which are being tempted by their very real difficulties to take the totalitarian road.

To some people, the word "necessary" smacks of "historicism," of a belief in inevitability, or suggests that the author wishes to find some historic justification, a whitewash to be applied to Stalin and his system. This is far from being my intention. "Necessity" is used here with no moral strings attached. If I say that to travel to Oxford it is necessary to go to Paddington station, this implies no approval, moral or otherwise,

* Reprinted from *Encounter*, April, 1962, pp. 86–92, by permission of the author and the publisher.

of the service provided by the Western Region of British Railways, still less of the project of making the journey to Oxford. It is simply that *if* I wish to do A, it involves doing B.

It is true that there may be alternatives. One might, for instance, do not B but C, or D. Thus I could go to Oxford by car, or by bus. However, it could be that these physically possible methods are not in fact open to me: I may not own a car, and shortage of time precludes taking the bus. Thus a judgment on the "necessity" or otherwise of an action in pursuit of a given purpose requires some consideration of what could have been done instead.

The range of choice is not, in practice, limited only by what is *physically* possible. There are also actions which are excluded by religious or ideological principle. For example, it is not in fact open to a rabbi to eat a ham sandwich or an orthodox Hindu to eat cow-meat. Thus if an "alternative" happens to involve such acts, it is not *for them* an alternative at all. This is because, were they to act otherwise, they would cease to be what they in fact are. A rabbi does not eat pork; were he to do so, he would not be a rabbi. The fact that he is a rabbi would also affect his outlook, his "freedom" to choose between alternative modes of conduct, where religious law is less strict: for instance, there is nothing in the Talmud or in Deuteronomy about smoking on the Sabbath, but rabbis would tend to be the kind of people who, faced with this "new" problem, would give the answer "no."

Thus, to come nearer our subject, there may have been a number of solutions to the problems posed by Russia of the 'twenties which the Communists could not have chosen because they were Communists, and in considering the practical alternatives before them we have to bear this in mind. In doing so, we are by no means driven to any generalisations about the "inevitability" of the Russian revolution or of the Bolshevik seizure of power, and *a fortiori* we need not assume that non-Bolsheviks could not have found some other ways of coping with the problems of the period. (Indeed, though the problems would still have been acute, they might in important respects have been different.) Before his assassination in 1911, the last intelligent Tsarist prime minister, Stolypin, expressed the belief that his land reform measures would create in about twenty years a prosperous peasantry which would provide a stable foundation for society and the throne. No one will know if he would have been right, if he had not been murdered, if the Tsar had been wise, if Rasputin had not existed, if the war had not broken out. . . . But of what use is it to indulge in such speculations? A 19th-century Russian blank-verse play provides, if somewhat inaccurately, a relevant comment:

> *If, if, if grandma had a beard,*
> *She would be grandpa. . . .*

In assessing the choices open to the Bolsheviks in, say, 1926, the events before that date must be taken as given. The real question, surely, is to consider the practical alternatives which Stalin and his colleagues had before them.

In doing so, we should certainly not assume that what happened was inevitable. "Necessity" and "inevitable" are quite distinct concepts, though some critics seem to confuse them. Two simple and probably uncontroversial propositions will illustrate this: it was necessary for 18th-century Poland to make drastic changes in its constitution if she were to survive as an independent state; and for China around 1890 a strong, modernising government was urgently necessary if many disasters were to be avoided. Yet the "necessary" steps were not taken and the disasters occurred. Unless we believe that whatever was not avoided was for that reason unavoidable, we would wish to examine the actions which men took, their choices between *available* alternatives, and see whether viable alternatives in fact existed.

At this point, many historians tend to brush aside impatiently any talk of what might have been; they are concerned, they would claim, with chronicling and explaining what was. Curiously, this line is often taken both by those who believe in strict historical determinism, *i.e.*, that what happened *had* to happen, and by those who consider history to be merely a chronological series of events, *i.e.*, that by implication *anything* could have happened. Both these apparently opposite extremes agree in not examining the actual possibilities as they were seen by the statesmen of the period. Yet how can one speak meaningfully of the reasons for, or causes of, any political act unless one implicitly or explicitly considers what could have been done instead? In other words, we must be concerned with freedom of choice, or its converse, necessity, whether we like it or not, unless we hold either that freedom of choice is infinite or that it is non-existent.

There are several more things to be said on the subject of "necessity." One of these concerns what might be called consequences of consequences, or indirect effects. For example, it is difficult to marry a wife without simultaneously acquiring a mother-in-law. Or, moving nearer to our subject, a sergeant is an unavoidable element in an army, and the needs of discipline involve giving him power over his men which he is likely to abuse. Bullying N.C.O.'s are likely to be found if an army exists, and so, given the necessity for an army, they become an inevitable consequence of its existence, just as the mother-in-law is an unavoidable appendage of a "necessary" wife. Thus, getting still nearer to the point, a situation which requires many bureaucrats, or which gives exceptional power to many policemen, may bring into action certain forces, certain behavioural tendencies, which are typical of bureaucrats or policemen and which, though not needed or desired as such, cannot in the circumstances be avoided.

The saying that "you cannot make omelettes without breaking

eggs" (or its Russian equivalent: "if you chop trees, the chips fly") has been used so often as an excuse for excesses and crimes, that we sometimes forget that you really *cannot* make omelettes without breaking eggs. . . .

Now on to Stalin, or rather to Stalinism, since the idea of "necessity" does not of course mean that the leader had to be a Georgian with a long moustache, but rather a tough dictator ruling a totalitarian state of the Stalinist type. What were the practical alternatives before the Bolsheviks in the late 'twenties, which contributed to the creation of the Stalinist régime, or, if one prefers a different formulation, gave the opportunity to ambitious men to achieve so high a degree of absolutism?

The key problem before the Bolsheviks concerned the linked questions of industrialisation and political power. They felt they had to industrialise for several reasons, some of which they shared with non-Bolshevik predecessors. Thus the Tsarist minister, Count Witte, as well as Stalin, believed that to achieve national strength and maintain independence, Russia needed a modern industry, especially heavy industry. The national-defence argument, re-labelled "defence of the revolution," was greatly strengthened by the belief that the Russian revolution was in constant danger from a hostile capitalist environment, militarily and technically far stronger than the USSR. Then there was the belief that the building of socialism or communism involved industrialisation, and, more immediately, that a "proletarian dictatorship" was insecure so long as it ruled in an overwhelmingly petty-bourgeois, peasant, environment. There had to be a large increase in the number and importance of the proletariat, while the rise of a rich "kulak" class in the villages was regarded as a dangerous (or potentially dangerous) resurgence of capitalism. It was clear, by 1927, that it was useless to wait for "world revolution" to solve these problems. These propositions were common to the protagonists of the various platforms of the middle 'twenties. Thus even the "moderate" Bukharin wrote: "If there were a fall in the relative weight of the working class in its political and its social and class power, . . . this would subvert the basis of the proletarian dictatorship, the basis of our government."[1] He too spoke in principle of the "struggle against the kulak, against the capitalist road," and warned of the "kulak danger."[2] He too, even in the context of an attack on Zinoviev and the "left" opposition, argued the need for "changing the production relations of our country."[3]

Until about 1927, a rapid rise in industrial production resulted from the reactivation of pre-revolutionary productive capacity, which fell into disuse and disrepair in the civil war period. However, it now became

[1] "The Results of the United Plenum of the Central and Control Commissions of the Party" (1927).
[2] Speech on "The Results of the 14th Party Congress" (5th January, 1926).
[3] Speech to the XXIII special conference of the Leningrad provincial party organisation (1926).

urgent to find material and financial means to expand the industrial base. This at once brought the peasant problem to the fore. The revolution had distributed land to 25 million families, most of whom were able or willing to provide only small marketable surpluses. Supplies of food to the towns and for export fell, peasant consumption rose. Yet the off-farm surplus must grow rapidly to sustain industrialisation, especially where large-scale loans from abroad could scarcely be expected. As the "left" opposition vigorously pointed out, the peasant, the bulk of the population, had somehow to be made to contribute produce and money, to provide the bulk of "primitive Socialist accumulation."

The arguments around these problems were inextricably entangled in the political factional struggles of the 'twenties.[4] The moderate wing, led by Bukharin, believed that it was possible to advance slowly towards industrialisation "at the pace of a tortoise,"[5] a pace severely limited by what the peasant was willing to do voluntarily. This was sometimes described as "riding towards socialism on a peasant nag." The logic of this policy demanded priority for developing consumers' goods industries, to make more cloth to encourage the peasants to sell more food. At first, Stalin sided with the moderates.

The case against the Bukharin line was of several different kinds. Firstly, free trade with the peasants could only provide adequate surpluses if the better-off peasants (*i.e.,* those known as *kulaks*) were allowed to expand, since they were the most efficient producers and provided a large part of the marketable produce. Yet all the Bolshevik leaders (including, despite momentary aberrations, Bukharin himself) found this ideologically and politically unacceptable. A strong group of independent, rich peasants was Stolypin's dream as a basis for Tsardom. It was the Bolshevik's nightmare, as totally inconsistent in the long run with their rule or with a socialist transformation of "petty-bourgeois" Russia. But this made the Bukharin approach of doubtful internal consistency. This was understood at the time by intelligent non-party men. Thus the famous economist Kondratiev, later to perish in the purges, declared in 1927: "If you want a higher rate of accumulation . . . then the stronger elements of the village must be allowed to exploit (the weaker)," in other words that the "kulaks" must expand their holdings and employ landless labourers.[6] The "peasant nag" could not pull the cart; or it, and the peasant, would pull in the wrong direction.

A second reason concerned the pace of the tortoise. The Bolsheviks were in a hurry. They saw themselves threatened by "imperialist interventionists." Even though some war scares were manufactured for

---

[4] See A. Erlich: *The Soviet Industrialisation Debate* (Harvard, 1960) for a most valuable account of the interaction between the debates and the economic realities of the period. The account given here is necessarily oversimplified.
[5] Paper read at a plenum of the Agricultural Economics Research Institute, Moscow, 1927.
[6] Bukharin's words, speech of 5th January, 1926.

factional reasons, the Party as a whole believed that war against them would come before very long. This argued not merely for speed, but also for priority to *heavy* and not light industry, since it provided a basis for an arms industry. Still another reason was a less tangible but still very real one: the necessity of maintaining political *élan*, of not appearing to accept for an indefinite period a policy of gradualism based on the peasant, which would have demoralised the Party and so gravely weakened the régime. It was widely felt, in and out of Russia, that by 1927 the régime had reached a *cul-de-sac*. I have in front of me a contemporary Menshevik pamphlet published abroad, by P. A. Garvi,[7] which describes its dilemma quite clearly, and indeed the political and economic problem was extremely pressing: to justify its existence, to justify the Party dictatorship in the name of the proletariat, a rapid move forward was urgent; but such a move forward would hardly be consistent with the "alliance with the peasants" which was the foundation of the policy of the moderates in the 'twenties. Stalin at this point swung over towards the left, and his policy of all-out industrialisation and collectivisation was a means of breaking out of the *cul-de-sac,* of mobilising the Party to smash peasant resistance, to make possible the acquisition of farm surpluses without having to pay the price which any free peasants or free peasant associations would have demanded. He may well have felt he had little choice. It is worth quoting from the reminiscences of another Menshevik, who in the late 'twenties was working in the Soviet planning organs: "The financial base of the first five-year plan, *until Stalin found it in levying tribute on the peasants, in primitive accumulation by the methods of Tamerlane,* was extremely precarious. . . . (It seemed likely that) everything would go to the devil. . . . No wonder that no one, literally no one, of the well-informed economists, believed or could believe in the fulfillment (of the plan)."[8]

It does not matter in the present context whether Stalin made this shift through personal conviction of its necessity, or because this seemed to him to be a clever power-manœuvre. The cleverness in any case largely consisted in knowing that he would thus strengthen his position by becoming the spokesman of the view which was widely popular among Party activists. The "leftists," destroyed organisationally by Stalin in earlier years, had a considerable following. Stalin's left-turn brought many of them to his support—though this did not save them from being shot in due course on Stalin's orders. It is probably the case that he had at this time genuine majority support within the Party for his policy, though many had reservations about certain excesses, of which more will be said. But if this be so, the policy as such cannot be attributed to Stalin personally, and therefore the consequences which flowed from its adoption must be a matter of more than personal responsibility.

[7] *Zakat bolshevisma* (Twilight of Bolshevism) (Riga, 1928).
[8] N. Valentinov, in *Sotsialisticheskii Vestnik* (New York), April, 1961. (Emphasis mine.)

Let us examine some of these consequences. Collectivisation could not be voluntary. Rapid industrialisation, especially with priority for heavy industry, meant a reduction in living standards, despite contrary promises in the first five-year plans. This meant a sharp increase in the degree of coercion, in the powers of the police, in the unpopularity of the régime. The aims of the bulk of the people were bound to be in conflict with the aims of the Party. It should be added that this conflict is probably bound to arise in some form wherever *the state* is responsible for financing rapid industrialisation; the sacrifices are then imposed by political authority, and the masses of "small" people do not and cannot provide voluntarily the necessary savings, since in the nature of things their present abstinence cannot be linked with a future return which they as individuals can identify. However, this possibly unavoidable unpopularity was greatly increased in the USSR by the sheer pace of the advance and by the attack on peasant property, and, as we shall see, both these factors reacted adversely on production of consumers' goods and so led to still further hardships and even greater unpopularity. The strains and priorities involved in a rapid move forward required a high degree of economic centralisation, to prevent resources from being diverted to satisfy needs which were urgent but of a non-priority character. In this situation, the Party was the one body capable of carrying out enormous changes and resisting social and economic pressures in a hostile environment; this was bound to affect its structure. For a number of years it had already been in process of transformation from a political into a power machine. The problems involved in the "revolution from above" intensified the process of turning it into an obedient instrument for changing, suppressing, controlling.

This, in turn, required hierarchical subordination, in suppression of discussion; therefore there had to be an unquestioned commander-in-chief. Below him, toughness in executing unpopular orders became the highest qualification for Party office. The emergence of Stalin, and of Stalin-type bullying officials of the sergeant-major species, was accompanied by the decline in the importance of the cosmopolitan journalist-intellectual type of party leader who had played so prominent a role earlier.

The rise of Stalin to supreme authority was surely connected with the belief among many Party members that he was the kind of man who could cope with this kind of situation. Of course, it could well be that Stalin tended to adopt policies which caused him and his type to be regarded as indispensable, and he promoted men to office in the Party because they were loyal to him. Personal ambition, a desire for power, were important factors in shaping events. But this is so obvious, so clearly visible on the surface, that the underlying problems, policy choices and logical consequences of policies need to be stressed.

Let us recapitulate: the Communists needed dictatorial power if they were to continue to rule; if they were to take effective steps towards industrialisation these steps were bound to give rise to problems which would require further tightening of political and economic control. While we cannot say, without much further research, whether a Bukharinite or other moderate policy was impossible, once the decision to move fast was taken this had very radical consequences; the need for a tough, coercive government correspondingly increased. Given the nature of the Party apparatus, the mental and political development of the Russian masses, the logic of police rule, these policies were bound to lead to a conflict with the peasantry and to excesses of various kinds. Thus, given the premises, certain elements of what may be called Stalinism followed, were objective "necessities." In this sense, and to this extent, Stalin was, so to speak, operating within the logical consequences of Leninism.

It is an essential part of Lenin's views that the Party was to seize power and use it to change Russian society; this is what distinguished him from the Mensheviks who believed that conditions for socialism should ripen within society. Lenin also suppressed opposition parties and required stern discipline from his own followers. (It is impossible to ban free speech outside the Party without purging the Party of those who express "wrong" views within it.) Indeed Lenin promoted Stalin because he knew he was tough, would "prepare peppery dishes," though he had last-minute regrets about it. While it would be going too far to describe Stalin as a true Leninist, if only because Lenin was neither personally brutal nor an oriental despot, Stalin undoubtedly carried through some of the logical consequences of Lenin's policies and ideas. This remains true even though Lenin thought that the peasant problem could be solved by voluntary inspiration, and would probably have recoiled at the conditions of forced collectivisation.

Is it necessary to stress that this does not make these actions right, or good? Yes, it is, because so many critics assume that to explain is to justify. So it must be said several times that no moral conclusions follow, that even the most vicious acts by politicians and others generally have causes which must be analysed. We are here only concerned to disentangle the special contribution of Stalin, the extent to which Stalinism was, so to speak, situation-determined. This is relevant, indeed, to one's picture of Stalin's personal responsibility, but in no way absolves him of such responsibility. If in order to do A it proves necessary to do B, we can, after all, refuse to do B, abandon or modify the aim of attaining A, or resign, or, in extreme circumstances—like Stalin's old comrade Ordzhonikidze—commit suicide.

But Stalin's personal responsibility goes far beyond his being the voice and leader of a party majority in a given historical situation. For one cannot possibly argue that all the immense evils of the Stalin era flowed inescapably from the policy decisions of 1928–29. In assessing

Stalin's personal role in bringing these evils about, it is useful to approach the facts from two angles. There was, first, the category of evils which sprang from policy choices which Stalin made and which he need not have made; in other words we are here concerned with consequences (perhaps necessary) of unnecessary decisions. The other category consists of evil actions which can reasonably be attributed to Stalin and which are his direct responsibility.

Of course, these categories shade into one another, as do murder and manslaughter. In the first case, the evils were in a sense situation-determined, but Stalin had a large hand in determining the situation. In the second, his guilt is as clear as a politician's guilt can be.

The most obvious examples of the first category are: the brutality of collectivisation and the madly excessive pace of industrial development. In each case, we are dealing with *"excessive excesses,"* since we have already noted that collectivisation without coercion was impossible, and rapid industrialisation was bound to cause stresses and strains.

Take collectivisation first. Some over-zealous officials were presumably bound to overdo things, especially since the typical Party man was a townsman with no understanding or sympathy for peasants and their problems. But these officials received orders to impose rapid collectivisation, to deport *kulaks,* to seize all livestock, and Stalin was surely the source of these orders. The deportation of the *kulaks* (which in reality meant anyone who voiced opposition to collectivisation) removed at one blow the most efficient farmers. There had been no serious preparation of the measures, no clear orders about how a collective farm should be run. Chinese experience, at least before the communes, suggests that milder ways of proceeding are possible. In any event, the attempt to collectivise all private livestock ended in disaster and a retreat. It is worth reproducing the figures from the official handbook of agricultural statistics:

LIVESTOCK POPULATION (Million of Head)

	1928	1934
Horses	32.1	15.4
Cattle	60.1	33.5
Pigs	22.0	11.5
Sheep	97.3	32.9

Yet already by 1934 private livestock holdings were again permitted, and in 1938 over three-quarters of all cows, over two-thirds of all pigs, nearly two-thirds of all sheep, were in private hands. This is evidence of a disastrous error.

Its consequences were profound. Peasant hostility and bitterness were greatly intensified. For many years there were in fact no net investments in agriculture, since the new tractors merely went to replace some of the slaughtered horses. Acute food shortage made itself felt—though the state's control over produce ensured that most of those who died in the resulting famine were peasants and not townsmen. But once all this happened, the case for coercion was greatly strengthened, the need for police measures became more urgent than ever, the power of the censorship was increased, freedom of speech had still further to be curtailed, as part of the necessities of remaining in power and continuing the industrial revolution in an environment grown more hostile as a result of such policies. So Stalin's policy decisions led to events which contributed greatly to the further growth of totalitarianism and the police state.

The same is true of the attempt to do the impossible on the industrial front in the years of the first five-year plan. Much of the effort was simply wasted, as when food was taken from hungry peasants and exported to pay for machines which rusted in the open or were wrecked by untrained workmen. At the same time, the closing of many private workshops deprived the people of consumers' goods which the state, intent on building steelworks and machine-shops, was quite unable to provide. Again, living standards suffered, the hatred of many citizens for the régime increased, the N.K.V.D. had to be expanded and the logic of police rule followed. But Stalin had a big role in the initial decisions to jump too far too fast.[9] (It is interesting to note that Mao, who should have learnt the lessons of history, repeated many of these mistakes in China's "great leap forward" of 1958–59, which suggests that *there are certain errors which Communists repeatedly commit,* possibly due to the suppression, in "anti-rightist" campaigns, of the voices of moderation and common sense.)

One of the consequences of these acute hardships was isolation from foreign countries. Economists often speak of the "demonstration effect," *i.e.,* of the effect of the knowledge of higher living standards abroad on the citizens of poor and under-developed countries. This knowledge may act as a spur to effort—but it also generates resistance to sacrifice. Stalin and his régime systematically "shielded" Soviet citizens from knowledge of the outside world, by censorship, by cutting off personal contacts, by misinformation. The need to do so, in their eyes, was greatly increased by the extent of the drop in living standards in the early 'thirties.

But we must now come to Stalin's more direct contribution to the brutality and terrorism of the Stalin era.

There was, firstly, his needless cruelty which showed itself already in the methods used to impose collectivisation. The great purges were

---

[9] N. Jasny, in his *Soviet Industrialisation, 1938–52* (Chicago, 1961), has much to say about the chaotic planning of the early 'thirties.

surely not "objectively necessary." To explain them one has to take into account Stalin's thirst for supreme power, his intense pathological suspiciousness, *i.e.*, matters pertaining to Stalin's personal position and character. These led him to massacre the majority of the "Stalinist" central committee elected in 1934, who had supported or at the very least tolerated Stalin's policies up to that date. The facts suggest that they believed that relaxation was possible and desirable; many of them seem to have died for the crime of saying so. Nor was there any "police logic" for the scale and drastic nature of the purges. Indeed, the police chiefs figured prominently among the victims. True, there was a kind of "snowballing" of arrests, which might have got out of control in 1938, but this was due largely to the effect of the terror on the police, who had to show zeal or go under. Nor can any "necessity" explain the post-war repressions, the death of Voznesensky, the so-called "Leningrad affair," the shooting of the Jewish intellectuals, the "doctors' plot." Stalin played so prominently a personal role in establishing a reign of terror in the Party and the country that he must bear direct responsibility even where executions were the result of false information supplied to him by his subordinates for reasons of their own.

The atmosphere of terror had, of course, far-reaching consequences in every sphere of Soviet life. It became particularly grotesque and purposeless in the last years of Stalin, when the social and economic developments, plus victory in war, provided the Soviet régime with a much firmer base among the people, so that a considerable part of the discontent was the result, rather than the cause, of repressive measures. Many obviously overdue reforms had to await his death. As did Tsar Nicholas I, a century earlier, Stalin was able to delay "necessary" changes.

Many other examples can be given of the personal role of Stalin. On the economic front, the miserable state of the peasants in 1953 was due largely to Stalin's obstinate refusal to face the facts and listen to serious advice. He contributed greatly to wasteful and grandiose schemes to "transform nature," and to a wasteful and grandiose style of architecture. In the military field, history will, I think, support Khrushchev's accusation that Stalin's inability to see the signs of a German attack, his unwillingness to allow preparations, his massacre of the best Soviet officers, all made a personal contribution to the Russian disasters of 1941. Stalin personally insisted on his own deification, the rewriting of history, the creation of myths. Some myths were based on lies which he himself publicly uttered. For instance, in 1935 he announced: "We have had no poor for two or three years now"—and this when bread had reached the highest price, in relation to wages, that it had ever attained in Soviet history. Or equally ridiculous was his claim, in 1947, that Moscow "had completely abolished slums." In this personal way he made impossible all serious discussion either of living standards or the housing problem, just as his wildly false assertions about "Bukharin and Trotsky, agents of Hitler and the Mikado," made the writing of Soviet history impossible in Russia. One could argue that the myth about "voluntary collectivisation" was an objectively necessary lie, in the sense of transcending Stalin's personality; indeed, this lie figures in the Party programme adopted by the 22nd Congress last November [1961]. But Stalin's lies went very much beyond this, and beyond the distortions and myths which can be ascribed to other politicians in other countries.

Throughout Russia, officials at all levels modelled themselves on Stalin, and each succeeded in imposing more unnecessary misery on more subordinates, stultifying initiative, penalising intelligence, discouraging originality. The price of all this is still being paid.

The urgent need to prepare for war has often been advanced as an excuse for Stalin's industrial "tempos" and for the terror. This can hardly be accepted. In the worst years of social coercion and over-ambitious plans, *i.e.*, 1929–33, Hitler was only just climbing to power, and Comintern policy showed that he was not then regarded as the main enemy. It is possible that Stalin was liquidating all potential opponents in the Purges of 1936–38 as a precaution in case war broke out, though this seems doubtful for a variety of reasons. But it is quite false to use the result of the war as ex-post-factum justification of Stalinism. Perhaps, with less harsh policies, the greater degree of loyalty in 1941 would have offset a smaller industrial base? In any event the Purges not only led to the slaughter of the best military officers but also halted the growth of heavy industry.

The attentive reader will have noticed that this analysis has some features in common with Khrushchev's. Before 1934, Stalin had been carrying out policies which commanded the assent of a majority of the Party and which, like collectivisation, had been accepted as necessary and irreversible by the bulk of Party members, whatever their reservations about particular mistakes and acts of brutality. However, after that date he took more and more personal, arbitrary measures, massacred much of the Party, behaved like an oriental despot. It is true that he was also arbitrary before 1934, and that he took some wise decisions after that date; but there is a case for placing a qualitative change around then.

But this is by no means the end of the matter. It is not only a question of making some obvious remarks concerning Khrushchev's own role during the terror. Of much more general significance is the fact that the events prior to 1934, including the building-up of Stalin into an all-powerful and infallible dictator (by men many of whom he afterwards massacred), cannot be disassociated from what followed; at the very least they provided Stalin with his opportunity. This is where the historian must avoid the twin and opposite pitfalls of regarding what happened as inevitable, and regarding it as a chapter of "personalised" accidents. At each stage there are choices to be made, though the range of possible choices is generally much narrower than people suppose. In 1928 any practicable Bolshevik programme would have been harsh and unpopular. It might not have been *so* harsh and unpopular but for choices which need not necessarily have been made. If before 1934, *i.e.,* in the very period of maximum social coercion, Stalin truly represented the will of the Party, and Khrushchev argues that he did, some totalitarian consequences logically follow. One of these, as already suggested, is the semi-militarised party led by a *Fuehrer,* a dictator, because without an unquestioned leader the consequences of the policies adopted could not be faced.

But, even if it is true that the triumph of a dictator may be explained by objective circumstances which certainly existed in the Soviet situation, the acts of a dictator once he has "arrived" involve a.considerable (though of course not infinite) degree of personal choice. Those who gave him the opportunity to act in an arbitrary and cruel way, who adopted policies which involved arbitrariness and coercion on a big scale, cannot ascribe subsequent events to the wickedness of one man or his immediate associates and claim that their hands are clean, even indeed if they were shot themselves on Stalin's orders. The whole-hog Stalin, in other words, was not "necessary," but the possibility of a Stalin was a necessary consequence of the effort of a minority group to keep power and to carry out a vast social-economic revolution in a very short time. And *some* elements of Stalinism were, in those circumstances, scarcely avoidable.

The serious problem for us is to see how far certain elements of Stalinism, in the sense of purposefully-applied social coercion, imposed by a party in the name of an ideology, are likely or liable to accompany rapid economic development even in non-Communist countries.

For it is surely true that many of the problems tackled by Stalin so brutally are present elsewhere, though events in the USSR were, of course, deeply affected by peculiar features of Russia and of Bolshevism. The West should indeed emphasize the high cost in human and material terms of a Stalin, and show that the rise of such a man to supreme power in the Soviet Union was, to use the familiar Soviet-Marxist jargon phrase, "not accidental." Indeed, some Western historians who normally write "personalist" and empiricist history will begin to see the virtues of an approach they normally deride as "historicist"; they will analyse Soviet history to establish patterns, regularities, "necessities" which lead to Stalin. By contrast, an embarrassed Khrushchev will be—is being— forced to give an un-Marxist emphasis to personal and accidental factors.

But, of course, we must not confine our search for "necessities" in history only to instances which happen to serve a propagandist purpose. This would be a typically Soviet approach to historiography, only in reverse. It is particularly important to think very seriously about the interrelationship of coercion and industrialisation, about the nature of the obstacles and vicious circles which drive men to think in totalitarian terms. Unless we realise how complex are the problems which development brings, how irrelevant are many of our ideas to the practical possibilities open to statesmen in these countries, we may unconsciously drive them towards the road which led to Stalin. They cannot be satisfied with "the pace of a tortoise."

B. WAS STALIN REALLY NECESSARY?: A COMMENT*
Leopold Labedz
Associate Editor, *Survey*

Alec Nove's article, "Was Stalin Really Necessary?" is very stimulating. Although his answer to the basic question posed is not quite clear, one can agree with most of what he says. Still, my own inclination is to say "Quite, quite unnecessary!" and so I should like to make a few comments on the way Nove handled the three central issues:

1. What is the meaning of historical necessity?
2. Was the forcible collectivisation necessary?
3. Was the Great Purge linked with the 1929–31 economic up-heaval or was it only a consequence of Stalin's "excesses"?

1. Nove argues that historical necessity is not historically immanent (why exactly is it historical?) but is to be understood as the existence of objective and subjective factors limiting the range of possible choice. The subjective factors are concerned with the Aristotelian essences of those taking decisions. "A rabbi does not eat pork; were he to do so, he would not be a rabbi." Similarly: "there may have been a number of solutions to the problems posed by Russia of the 'twenties which the Communists could not have chosen because they were Communists." That may be true, but if historical necessity is so defined then each régime carries within it its own "inevitability." The Indian Congress Party, for instance, cannot do certain things without ceasing to be an Indian Congress Party, and Soviet Russia's "historical necessities" are thus irrelevant to it by definition. Is this the conclusion Mr. Nove wanted to draw? He rightly rejects Marxist "historical inevitability," but then in his reasoning the belief in it is surely a subjective factor without which the Soviet Communists would not be Communists. It thus follows that, however mistaken and however "voluntaristic" their acts, they are in Nove's scheme in a sense all "necessary" by definition. This is, of course, part of a genuine paradox; but it largely rests on how the words "possible" and "necessary" are defined. Is this begging the whole question? If "really necessary" is not the same as "historically necessary," why is it not?

2. The answer to the second question is given in the affirmative:

* Reprinted from Leopold Labedz, "Nove on Stalin," *Encounter,* August, 1962, pp. 93–94, by permission of the author and the publisher.

Yes, Nove argues, forcible collectivisation was necessary. This is not the answer implied by Gomulka, and Khrushchev himself admitted at the 22nd Congress the possibility of a different road to socialism in countries "where peasants are deeply attached to private property." The Polish Communists have quickly reproduced this passage offering a doctrinal legitimation of their present practice. If this is so, doesn't it cast doubt on the "necessity" of Stalin's forcible collectivisation? Peasants every-where are attached to their property; so were they in Russia. It is inter-esting to compare Nove's conclusions on the subject with those given in the official Polish Communist theoretical journal *Nowe Drogi* (No. 12, 1961):

> Apart from objective factors there are also subjective fac-tors. There are no situations in which the Party or the individuals do not have possibility of choice, in which definite problems can-not be solved by different methods, less costly, and avoiding many unnecessary sufferings and negative effects.

Would Nove reject this in favour of the Khrushchevian justification of Stalin's "necessities" (*minus* his "excesses")? Is there not enough evidence that the whole monstrous character of Soviet collectivisation was connected more with *political* than with economic necessities?

3. According to Nove, forcible collectivisation stemmed from ob-jective necessities and only its excesses (which Stalin also condemned) resulted from subjective factors and indirect effects. This apparently is not the case with the great purges of 1936–38. In his view, "the great purges cannot possibly by derived from any 'objective necessity' arising from past policies. They can be derived from Stalin's thirst for supreme power, his intense pathological suspiciousness."

This is an astonishing argument. It is enough to look at the record (for example, in the chapter on the subject in Leonard Schapiro's history of *The Communist Party of the Soviet Union*) to see that historical evi-dence points to a precisely opposite conclusion. The Great Purge was more than intimately linked with the past policies of forcible collectiv-isation. Nobody, of course, would deny Stalin's "thirst for power," but this was also an operative factor in the previous instances. "Given the nature of the system," Stalin had at each stage been taking decisions which largely conditioned his subsequent actions (and "Stalin would not be Stalin, if he had done otherwise").

Collectivisation may be regarded either as an end in itself, or as a means to secure industrial growth. In the former case, the problems be-setting Soviet agriculture today cast doubt on the economic rationality of collectivisation; in the latter case, in the perspective of 1931, Stalin may well have felt that the drastic method of squeezing agriculture in order to build industry quickly may be the only one, but three decades later this does not seem so certain and there is no reason to fall into the trap of *post hoc ergo propter hoc* type of reasoning. In any case the economic perspective is not the only one. What may seem economically necessary may not be "really necessary" if the human price to be paid is too high. It is only too easy to confuse retrospectively doctrinal necessity with economic necessity and then make it into a "historical necessity".

The exclusively economic perspective probably accounts for Nove's conclusion on the great purges. "Objective necessity" in this context means for him more or less plausible economic reasons; and these, he seems to suggest, may have justified drastic steps in 1931 but not after 1934 when the economic situation improved. But in political perspective there were apparently reasons more compelling than the economic one for Stalin to act as he did.

For an economist there may be a temptation to qualify economic reasons as "objective necessity", but not political reasons. This reflects a certain economic determinism. It is an oversimplification to regard Stalinism as just a function of the necessities of industrialisation in "backward Russia". Stalin had risen to power before his "second revolution" and not as a result of it. There is no historical reason to confer an economic justification on his would-be imitators in the underdeveloped countries, however harsh may be the conditions of the industrial "take-off" in them.

C. WAS STALIN REALLY NECESSARY?: A REJOINDER*

Alec Nove
University of Glasgow

It is always a pleasure to cross swords with my old friend Leopold Labedz, who never fails to be a stimulating opponent. He takes me to task for my judgment of the necessity or otherwise of Stalin. I do not deny the validity of some of his comments, but on occasion he seems to misunderstand what I was trying to say. My article was concerned, first, to discuss the personal role of Stalin, *i.e.,* the extent to which his terror régime was situation-determined; secondly, I was concerned to identify the extent to which the situation itself, including the horrors of forced collectivisation, flowed from the existence of a Communist dictatorship which was trying to industrialise a predominantly peasant country quickly. I do not pretend that these are the only questions which should be asked in a survey of the political and economic history of the Soviet Union. Nor indeed are they the kind of questions which permit of a definitive answer. They are, nonetheless, matters which are interesting to discuss.

I do not quite understand the point of Labedz's criticism of my discussion of necessity. He both accepts and rejects the proposition that the choices of politicians are limited by their own ideological attitudes

* Reprinted from Alec Nove, "Was Stalin Necessary?", *Encounter*, November 1962, pp. 93–94, by permission of the author and the editor.

and beliefs. Surely, if one is trying to identify the role of an individual, it is significant to identify the ideological limitations on his choice which would apply not only to him but also to the overwhelming majority of his party comrades. For example, no leader of the British Labour Party is in a position to de-nationalise an existing nationalised industry, and this is surely an elementary political fact. A Conservative is less limited in this respect, though no doubt he would be precluded by his beliefs from advocating certain solutions which would be acceptable to the Labour Party. All this is obvious, and I do not see why the same kind of logic cannot be applied to the choices available to the Bolsheviks. Labedz complains that "if historical necessity is so defined, then each régime carries with it its own inevitability." The word "inevitability" is his, not mine. It does carry with it its own limitations on the range of practicable choices. He points out that, if my logic were valid, the Indian Congress Party must be seen as having a different field of choices from that which was or would be available to the Communists. A minute's reflection would cause him to see that this is not only the case, but self-evidently the case. Why is this a criticism?

Labedz also asserts that I expressed the view that "forcible collectivisation was necessary." In doing so he again shows a misunderstanding of the subject of my article, which was Stalin and not collectivisation as such. I carefully made the point that non-Communists would have found some totally different solution; I also quite specifically left open the question of the possible viability of alternative policies. What I tried to do was to stress the considerations which led to the decision to impose collectivisation, looking for the impersonal logic of events, noting that the bulk of the Communist Party, including former oppositionists, rallied round the Party in its campaign against the peasants. All this is relevant to the assessment of Stalin's personal role. I also noted that voluntary collectivisation was a nonstarter in the circumstances, and that in those same circumstances forced collectivisation would be associated with excesses. The actual methods used, not without a great deal of personal encouragement from Stalin, led to excesses and brutalities on a vast scale. What happened then is not part of any model for underdeveloped countries to follow. It is rather a terrible warning, and I never suggested otherwise.

Labedz roundly asserts that I deny any connection between collectivisation and the great purge. Perhaps he would re-read my article, where I devote much space to establishing the connection between the harshness and brutalities of collectivisation and the increasing intensity of police repression. But the events which followed Kirov's death, and especially the great massacres of 1936–38, were no *necessary* consequence of the events before 1934. Labedz seems to overlook the distinction between a causal connection and a necessary connection, though admittedly the distinction is never absolute, but is rather one of degree.

Of course the events of 1929–34 were part of the essential background of the purges. But was it a logical consequence of collectivisation for Stalin to massacre the majority of the members of his own faction, the very men who carried collectivisation through? Is there not some evidence for the proposition that this massacre followed an attempt by his colleagues to restrain Stalin's growing arbitrariness and blood-letting? True, the earlier events created an atmosphere in which a mass purge became possible. However, as recent Chinese experience suggests, disastrous "leaps forward" can sometimes be followed by a sinking of differences in an effort to put matters right, rather than by mass shootings.

Labedz would seem to ascribe to me the belief that I accept only economic and social logic, and not a political logic of events. This is surely not the case. The desire of the Communist leadership to maintain itself in power was an essential element in the choices which they made, including the decision to collectivise. The relative importance of this aspect of the decision is a matter on which legitimate disagreement is possible, but I nowhere denied that this was a significant factor. Did the events of 1936–38 follow from political necessity? If they did, and I failed to allow for this, I am guilty of error. However, despite carefully reading Schapiro's book, I still believe that what I called the "whole-hog Stalinist terror" was primarily aimed at securing the absolute dictatorship of Joseph Stalin, over the Party and everyone else. (Schapiro's chapter on the purges is entitled: "Stalin's Victory Over the Party"!) I say this while entirely accepting the proposition that political logic led to toughness and to numerous restrictions on human freedom. It is true that the power manœuvring of Stalin did indeed have its own logic and its own "irregularities." However, since my paper was concerned with identifying Stalin's personal role, I naturally treated actions in furtherance of Stalin's career as attributable to Stalin rather than to the impersonal logic of events. I am surprised that Labedz should be so insistent on historical inevitability and the inexorable march of History, etc., etc. On other occasions he and those who think like him seem to take a somewhat different view of the role of personality.

D. WAS STALIN REALLY NECESSARY?: A REPLY TO THE REJOINDER*

Leopold Labedz

Associate Editor, *Survey*

Having formulated the problem "of the necessity or otherwise of Stalin", Alec Nove is still reluctant to give an explicit answer to his own question,

---

* Hitherto unpublished manuscript. Originally prepared for the Dallin-Brzezinski seminar at the Russian Institute of Columbia University, it has been slightly revised by the author, especially for publication here. Included herein by permission of the author.

despite my promptings. Instead, he tries to turn the tables by reversing
the charge and accusing me of being "insistent on historical inevitability
and the inexorable march of History". I admire his polemical skill, but
one should not exaggerate: not only have I not expressed in my letter
anything remotely connected with such argument, it was most emphatically directed against it.

Nove dissociated himself in his article from historicism; nevertheless, he did betray a certain tendency towards determinism. Apart from
the general Khrushchevian character of his analysis (which he admits),
implying the "necessity" of Stalin before 1934, there was a somewhat
selective impatience with historical "might-have-beens" ("If, if, if
grandma had a beard, she would be grandpa") and also the familiar,
though qualified, stress that "we sometimes forget that you really *cannot*
make omelettes without breaking eggs".

We also sometimes forget that those who accept the "necessary
evil" in history, eventually tend to stress more and more the "necessity"
and less and less the "evil". It is all too easy to dismiss historical "might-
have-beens" in the name of "realism"; but those who reject historical
determinism cannot dismiss them in principle. If it is admitted that we
have our choices in facing the problems of today, the same surely must
apply to the problems of yesterday. Hence, unless we believe in historical
inevitability, we have to accept the idea of historical "might-have-beens".
Nove's arguments reflect less a consistent method of analysis than an
attitude of mind.

It is ironical that he should insist so much on the necessity of
collectivization now that Khrushchev himself told an American journalist
that "We are paying now for Stalin's mistakes in agriculture" (*New York
Times,* April 26, 1962). Replying to the Chinese attacks, the Yugoslav
Communists emphatically rejected the necessity of collectivization, saying that it "would provoke an open conflict between the state and the
peasants" (*Komunist,* November 7, 1963). Indeed, this has been the case
in all the countries of the Soviet bloc where it was imposed upon the
countryside. A public opinion poll recently conducted among the Polish
farmers amply confirms it: only 2.2 percent among them are ready to
accept the collective farm as a solution of the agricultural problems (*The
Polish Sociological Bulletin,* No. 1, 1963).

The "necessity" of Stalinist collectivization cannot be seriously
argued on economic grounds, and even less so on social grounds. It is
only "necessary" for political reasons and then it is *post hoc* dressed up
as a "historical necessity". The subsequent "ideological superstructure"
is buttressed by the doctrinal myth of historical inevitability. Nove does
not believe in it, but he falls into some methodological fallacies usually
connected with it.

His definition of "necessity" may not in his view be historicist, but in effect it reintroduces inevitability through the back door. If subjective ideological belief makes for him an action "necessary" (not characteristic, or appropriate, or likely, but necessary), then in case of Bolsheviks it is also *ipso facto* inevitable, because of their belief in historical inevitability. We are all aware of the Popperian "self-fulfilling prophecy" but that should make it easier to avoid the pitfalls of "historical necessity". Indeed, Nove's reasoning simply confuses the probability of action and its necessity. It is pointless to argue at one and the same time, as Nove did in his article, that forcible collectivization was necessary for the Communists and then to declare that after all there is always a choice: one can even "like Stalin's old comrade Ordzhonikidze—commit suicide". The chief architect of the forcible collectivization would have been somewhat perplexed by this combination of the logic of historical determinism with the existentialist free choice. He was never reluctant in breaking eggs, but his actions were supported, as Djilas reports, by a belief in their "historical inevitability" and because of this, within the framework of Nove's own formulation, his range of choice was limited and *his* suicide did not enter into it.

The confusion stems from postulating "essences" of the actors on the historical scene in analysing their political actions. It is perfectly obvious that their ideological beliefs make some actions more likely than others; still, they can change their ideological beliefs, and within a given ideological framework there is also a margin of choice. Not only non-Communists would have found a different solution to the problem of industrialization, many Communists would have done it too. Nove refers to Erlich's book on the Soviet industrialization debate, but he seems to have completely missed its main point, which contradicts his own. Erlich points out that none of the various proposals discussed in the Soviet economic debates between 1924 and 1928 was eventually implemented and that the participants in these debates, all of them Communists, perished in the great purge.

> All of them—Left, Right, or Center—operated under the assumption that in the sphere of economic policy there are resistances of material which call not for a smashing knock-out blow but for some kind of coexistence of heterogeneous socio-economic setups for a long time to come.

However, when Stalin eliminated the Left and then the Right opposition, the time for economic arguments was over, and they were replaced by what Erlich calls "the meat-axe technique." Butchers may well be economically more necessary than economists, but one must not jump to conclusions about their historical necessity. Economic goals can be reached in a variety of ways and 'great leaps forward' are not always successful. Yet certain types of omelettes cannot be made without breaking eggheads—and economists, of all people, should remember this. Erlich's conclusion shows that, unlike Nove, he is well aware of it:

> The rapid-fire industrialization and sweeping collectivization were not merely devices of economic policy, but means of extending the direct control of the totalitarian state over the largest possible number within the shortest time.

In the light of this conclusion by another economist, the inconsistency of Nove's analysis is all the more striking. His treatment of the great purge stands in contrast to his attitude towards collectivization. The latter was, but the former was not "objectively necessary". Thus the logic of 'necessity' is applied to the economic but not to the political sphere. One can reject it in both cases, as I do; or rationalize them in both cases, as Stalin did; but one cannot apply it in one case, but not the other, without committing a methodological fallacy.

SOVIET VIEWS

---

2. PAGES FROM THE PAST: IN PRAISE OF STALIN*

The Sun . . .
The heart of every Soviet citizen is warmed by his love of Stalin. In all languages of the world, humanity glorifies his name, the name of the promoter of popular happiness, of the head of working humanity.

PRAVDA, DECEMBER *10, 1949.*

The Father . . .
He is friend of the sun
He will disarm all his foes.
Your name is on our lips,
Your heart is in our hearts,
Your will in our deeds.
Stalin, the father, has sixteen daughters—
Sixteen loving Republics.

PRAVDA, DECEMBER *11, 1949.*

* Reprinted from *Problems of Communism,* March–April, 1963, p. 87, by permission of the United States Information Agency.

The Ubiquitous . . .
Stalin! Always we hear in our souls his dear name. And here, in the Kremlin, his presence touches us at every step. We walk on stones which he may have trod only recently. Let us fall on our knees and kiss those holy footprints.

> FROM *ZEMLIA RUSSKAIA* [RUSSIAN LAND],
> BOOK PUBLISHED BY KOMSOMOL, *1946.*

Author of Creation . . .
O Great Stalin, O Leader of the Peoples,
Thou who didst give birth to man,
Thou who didst make fertile the earth,
Thou who dost rejuvenate the centuries,
Thou who givest blossom to the spring . . .

> PRAVDA, AUGUST *28, 1936.*

Omnipotent Sire . . .
I love a young woman with a renewed love and I shall perpetuate myself in my children—all thanks to Thee, great educator Stalin. . . . And when the woman I love presents me with a child, the first word it shall utter will be: Stalin.

> PRAVDA, FEBRUARY *1, 1935,* QUOTING A
> WRITER BY NAME OF AVIDIENKO.

That naughty Yossif . . .
. . . I feel no more than in my twenties since Stalin taught me to under-stand the meaning of life and art. . . .

> IZVESTIA, DECEMBER *2, 1936,* QUOTING A
> VENERABLE SOVIET ACTRESS.

He drives . . .
Stalin is the driver of the locomotive of history.

> PRAVDA, DECEMBER *26, 1939.*

He personally . . .
. . . foresees and determines the plan for the development of our country for long historical periods. . . .

> PRAVDA, DECEMBER *21, 1949.*

. . . examined all the main questions of Soviet technical history. . . .

> RADIO MOSCOW, DECEMBER *28, 1949.*

. . . attended to gas conversion in Moscow.

> MOSCOW BOLSHEVIK, APRIL *9, 1949.*

. . . [was responsible] for planting eucalyptus trees on the coast of the Black Sea, cultivating melons in the Moscow region and extending the cultivation of branched wheat. . . .

PRAVDA, DECEMBER *21, 1949.*

. . . bestows daily attention on the development of public health. . . .

MEDICAL WORKER, NOVEMBER *5, 1952.*

. . . inspires Soviet male and female physical culturists to achieve new successes in sport for the glory of the great socialist Homeland.

PRAVDA, MAY *26, 1952.*

He is . . .
. . . the greatest Marxist, the great Leninist, the brilliant continuer of the great cause of Marx-Engels-Lenin. . . .

SOVIET STATE AND LAW,
NO. *4, 1950,* p. *79.*

. . . the greatest scholar of our epoch. . . .

PRAVDA, NOVEMBER *25, 1946.*

. . . the creator of the Soviet Armed Forces, the great military leader of modern times . . . the creator of the progressive Soviet military science. . . .

N. BULGANIN IN PRAVDA,
DECEMBER *21, 1949.*

. . . the greatest man on our planet.

K. VOROSHILOV, IN *STALIN AND THE ARMED FORCES OF THE USSR,*
MOSCOW, *1951,* p. *81.*

. . . the best that humanity possesses. For Stalin is hope; he is expectation; he is the beacon that guides all progressive mankind. Stalin is our banner! Stalin is our will! Stalin is our victory!

NIKITA SERGEYEVICH KHRUSHCHEV, AS
QUOTED IN PRAVDA, JANUARY *31, 1937.*

3. AN ANATOMY OF TERROR*

Nikita S. Khrushchev

Former First Secretary, Central Committee of the Communist Party of the Soviet Union,
and Former Chairman of the U.S.S.R. Council of Ministers

The objective of the present report is not a thorough evaluation of Stalin's life and activity. Concerning Stalin's merits, an entirely sufficient number of books, pamphlets and studies had already been written in his lifetime. The role of Stalin in the preparation and execution of the Socialist Revolution, in the Civil War, and in the fight for the construction of Socialism in our country is universally known. Everyone knows this well. At the present we are concerned with a question which has immense importance for the Party now and for the future—(we are concerned) with how the cult of the person of Stalin has been gradually growing, the cult which became at a certain specific stage the source of a whole series of exceedingly serious and grave perversions of Party principles, of Party democracy, of revolutionary legality. . . .

In December 1922 in a letter to the Party Congress Vladimir Ilyich [Lenin] wrote: "After taking over the position of Secretary General, Comrade Stalin accumulated in his hands immeasurable power and I am not certain whether he will be always able to use this power with the required care." . . .

Vladimir Ilyich said: "Stalin is excessively rude, and this defect, which can be freely tolerated in our midst and in contacts among us Communists, becomes a defect which cannot be tolerated in one holding the position of the Secretary General. Because of this, I propose that the comrades consider the method by which Stalin would be removed from this position and by which another man would be selected for it, a man, who above all, would differ from Stalin in only one quality, namely, greater tolerance, greater loyalty, greater kindness and more considerate attitude toward the comrades, a less capricious temper, etc." . . .

As later events have proven, Lenin's anxiety was justified: in the first period after Lenin's death Stalin still paid attention to his [i.e., Lenin's] advice, but later he began to disregard the serious admonitions of Vladimir Ilyich.

When we analyze the practice of Stalin in regard to the direction of the Party and of the country, when we pause to consider everything which Stalin perpetrated, we must be convinced that Lenin's fears were

* From Khrushchev's 1956 address to the Twentieth Party Congress of the Communist Party of the Soviet Union. Excerpts reprinted from *The Anatomy of Terror*, 1956, by permission of the Public Affairs Press.

justified. The negative characteristics of Stalin, which, in Lenin's time, were only incipient, transformed themselves during the last years into a grave abuse of power by Stalin, which caused untold harm to our Party.

We have to consider seriously and analyze correctly this matter in order that we may preclude any possibility of a repetition in any form whatever of what took place during the life of Stalin, who absolutely did not tolerate collegiality in leadership and in work, and who practiced brutal violence, not only toward everything which opposed him, but also toward that which seemed to his capricious and despotic character, contrary to his concepts.

Stalin acted not through persuasion, explanation, and patient cooperation with people, but by imposing his concepts and demanding absolute submission to his opinion. Whoever opposed this concept or tried to prove his viewpoint, and the correctness of his position—was doomed to removal from the leading collective and to subsequent moral and physical annihilation. This was especially true during the period following the XVIIth Party Congress, when many prominent Party leaders and rank-and-file Party workers, honest and dedicated to the cause of Communism fell victim to Stalin's despotism. . . .

Stalin originated the concept "enemy of the people." This term automatically rendered it unnecessary that the ideological errors of a man or men engaged in a controversy be proven; this term made possible the usage of the most cruel repression, violating all norms of revolutionary legality, against anyone who in any way disagreed with Stalin, against those who were only suspected of hostile intent, against those who had bad reputations. . . .

Stalin . . . used extreme methods and mass repressions at a time when the revolution was already victorious, when the Soviet state was strengthened, when the exploiting classes were already liquidated and Socialist relations were rooted solidly in all phases of [the] national economy, when our Party was politically consolidated and had strengthened itself both numerically and ideologically. It is clear that here Stalin showed in a whole series of cases his intolerance, his brutality and his abuse of power. Instead of proving his political correctness and mobilizing the masses, he often chose the path of repression and physical annihilation, not only against actual enemies, but also against the Party and the Soviet government. Here we see no wisdom but only a demonstration of the brutal force which had once so alarmed V. I. Lenin.

Lately, especially after the unmasking of the Beriya gang, the Central Committee looked into a series of matters fabricated by this gang. This revealed a very ugly picture of brutal willfulness connected with the incorrect behavior of Stalin. As facts prove, Stalin, using his unlimited power, allowed himself many abuses, acting in the name of the Central Committee, not asking for the opinion of the Committee members nor even of the members of the Central Committee's Political Bureau; often he did not inform them about his personal decisions concerning very important Party and government matters. . . .

Stalin's willfulness vis-à-vis the Party and its Central Committee became fully evident after the XVIIth Party Congress which took place in 1934.

Having at its disposal numerous data showing brutal willfulness toward Party cadres, the Central Committee had created a Party Commission under the control of the Central Committee Presidium; it was charged with investigating what made possible the mass repressions against the majority of the Central Committee members and candidates elected at the XVIIth Congress of the All-Union Communist Party (Bolsheviks).

The Commission has become acquainted with a large quantity of materials in the NKVD archives and with other documents and has established many facts pertaining to the fabrication of cases against Communists, to false accusations, to glaring abuses of Socialist legality—which resulted in the death of innocent people. It became apparent that many Party, Soviet and economic activists, who were branded in 1937–1938 as "enemies," were actually never enemies, spies, wreckers, etc., but were always honest Communists; they were only so stigmatized and often, no longer able to bear barbaric tortures, they charged themselves (at the order of the investigative judges—falsifiers) with all kinds of grave and unlikely crimes. The Commission has presented to the Central Committee Presidium lengthy and documented materials pertaining to mass repressions against the delegates to the XVIIth Party Congress and against members of the Central Committee elected at that Congress. These materials have been studied by the Presidium of the Central Committee.

It was determined that of the 139 members and candidates of the Party's Central Committee who were elected at the XVIIth Congress, 98 persons, i.e., 70 percent, were arrested and shot (mostly in 1937–1938).

The same fate met not only the Central Committee members but also the majority of the delegates to the XVIIth Party Congress. Of 1966 delegates with either voting or advisory rights, 1108 persons were arrested on charges of anti-revolutionary crimes, i.e., decidedly more than a majority. This very fact shows how absurd, wild and contrary to common sense were the charges of counter-revolutionary crimes made out, as we now see, against a majority of participants at the XVIIth Party Congress. . . .

Stalin deviated from the clear and plain precepts of Lenin. Stalin put the Party and the NKVD up to the use of mass terror. . . . This terror was actually directed not at the remnants of the defeated exploiting classes but against the honest workers of the Party and of the Soviet State; against them were made lying, slanderous and absurd accusations concerning "two-facedness," "espionage," "sabotage," preparation of fictitious "plots," etc. . . .

Now when the cases of some of these so-called "spies" and "sab-oteurs" were examined it was found that all their cases were fabricated. Confessions of guilt of many arrested and charged with enemy activity were gained with the help of cruel and inhuman tortures.

At the same time Stalin, as we have been informed by members of the Political Bureau of that time, did not show them the statements of many accused political activists when they retracted their confessions before the military tribunal and asked for an objective examination of their cases. There were many such declarations, and Stalin doubtless knew of them.

The Central Committee considers it absolutely necessary to inform the Congress of many such fabricated "cases" against the members of the Party's Central Committee elected at the XVIIth Party Congress. . . .[1]

Only because our Party has at its disposal such great moral-political strength was it possible for it to survive the difficult events in 1937–1938 and to educate new cadres. There is, however, no doubt that our march forward toward Socialism and toward the preparation of the country's defense would have been much more successful were it not for the tre-mendous loss in the cadres suffered as a result of the baseless and false mass repressions in 1937–1938. . . .

Facts prove that many abuses were made on Stalin's orders without reckoning with any norms of Party and Soviet legality. Stalin was a very distrustful man, sickly suspicious; we knew this from our work with him. He could look at a man and say: "Why are your eyes so shifty today," or "Why are you turning so much today and avoiding to look me directly in the eyes?" The sickly suspicion created in him a general distrust even toward eminent Party workers whom he had known for years. Every-where and in everything he saw "enemies," "two-facers" and "spies."

Possessing unlimited power he indulged in great willfulness and choked a person morally and physically. A situation was created where one could not express one's own will.

When Stalin said that one or another should be arrested, it was necessary to accept on faith that he was an "enemy of the people." Mean-while, Beriya's gang, which ran the organs of the state security, outdid itself in proving the guilt of the arrested and the truth of materials which it falsified. And what proofs were offered? The confessions of the ar-rested, and the investigative judges accepted these "confessions." And how is it possible that a person confesses to crimes which he has not committed? Only in one way—because of application of physical methods of pressuring him, tortures, bringing him to a state of unconsciousness, deprivation of his judgement, taking away of his human dignity. In this manner were "confessions" acquired. . . .

---

[1] Now follow some specific examples of such allegedly fabricated cases. [Editor's note.].

The power accumulated in the hands of one person, Stalin, led to serious consequences during the Great Patriotic War. . . .[2]

All the more shameful was the fact that after our great victory over the enemy which cost us so much, Stalin began to downgrade many of the commanders who contributed so much to the victory over the enemy, because Stalin excluded every possibility that services rendered at the front should be credited to anyone but himself. . . .

Not Stalin, but the Party as a whole, the Soviet Government, our heroic army, its talented leaders and brave soldiers, the whole Soviet nation—these are the ones who assured the victory in the Great Patriotic War. . . .

The magnificent and heroic deeds of hundreds of millions of people of the East and of the West during the fight against the threat of Fascist subjugation which loomed before us will live centuries and millennia in the memory of thankful humanity. . . .

Comrades, let us reach for some other facts. The Soviet Union is justly considered as a model of a multi-national State because we have in practice assured the equality and friendship of all nations which live in our great Fatherland.

All the more monstrous are the acts whose initiator was Stalin and which are rude violations of the basic Leninist principles of the nationality policy of the Soviet State. We refer to the mass deportations from their native places of whole nations, together with all Communists and Komsomols without any exception; this deportation action was not dictated by any military considerations.

Thus, already at the end of 1943, when there occurred a permanent break-through at the fronts of the Great Patriotic War benefiting the Soviet Union, a decision was taken and executed concerning the deportation of all the Karachai from the lands on which they lived. In the same period, at the end of December 1943, the same lot befell the whole population of the Autonomous Kalmyk Republic. In March 1944 all the Chechen and Ingush peoples were deported. . . . The Ukrainians avoided meeting this fate only because there were too many of them and there was no place to which to deport them. Otherwise, he would have deported them also.

Not only no Marxist-Leninist but also no man of common sense can grasp how it is possible to make whole nations responsible for inimical activity, including women, children, old people, Communists and Komsomols, to use mass repression against them, and to expose them to misery and suffering for the hostile acts of individual persons or groups of persons.

[2] Now follows a long list of accusations charging Stalin with incompetent leadership and with many errors in the conduct of the war. Special stress was put on the "grievous consequences" resulting from the unjustified annihilation of military commanders and political leaders. [Editor's note.]

After the conclusion of the Patriotic War the Soviet nation stressed with pride the magnificent victories gained through great sacrifices and tremendous efforts. The country experienced a period of political enthusiasm. The Party came out of the war even more united; in the fire of the war Party cadres were tempered and hardened. Under such conditions nobody could have even thought of the possibility of some plot in the Party.

And it was precisely at this time that the so-called "Leningrad Affair" was born. As we have now proven, this case was fabricated. Those who innocently lost their lives included Comrades Voznesensky, Kusnetsov, Rodionov, Popkov, and others. . . .

Stalin became even more capricious, irritable and brutal; in particular his suspicion grew. His persecution mania reached unbelievable dimensions. Many workers were becoming enemies before his very eyes. After the war Stalin separated himself from the collective even more. Everything was decided by him alone without any consideration for anyone or anything.

This unbelievable suspicion was cleverly taken advantage of by the abject provocateur and vile enemy, Beriya, who had murdered thousands of Communists and loyal Soviet people. . . .

The willfulness of Stalin showed itself not only in decisions concerning the internal life of the country but also in the international relations of the Soviet Union.

The July Plenum of the Central Committee studied in detail the reasons for the development of conflict with Yugoslavia. It was a shameful role which Stalin played here. The "Yugoslav Affair" contained no problems which could not have been solved through Party discussions among comrades. There was no significant basis for the development of this "Affair"; it was completely possible to have prevented the rupture of relations with that country. This does not mean, however, that the Yugoslav leaders did not make mistakes or did not have shortcomings. But these mistakes and shortcomings were magnified in a monstrous manner by Stalin, which resulted in a break of relations with a friendly country. . . .

Let us also recall the "Affair of the Doctor-Plotters." Actually there was no "affair" outside of the declaration of the woman doctor Timashuk, who was probably influenced or ordered by someone (after all, she was an unofficial collaborator of the organs of State security) to write Stalin a letter in which she declared that doctors were applying supposedly improper methods of medical treatment.

Such a letter was sufficient for Stalin to reach an immediate conclusion that there are doctor-plotters in the Soviet Union. He issued orders to arrest a group of eminent Soviet medical specialists. He personally issued advice on the conduct of the investigation and the method of interrogation of the arrested persons. He said that the academician Vinogradov should be put in chains, another one should be beaten. Present at this Congress as a delegate is the Former Minister of State Security, Comrade Ignatiev. Stalin told him curtly, "If you do not obtain confessions from the doctors we will shorten you by a head."

Stalin personally called the investigative judge, gave him instructions, advised him on which investigative methods should be used; these methods were simple—beat, beat, and once again beat.

Shortly after the doctors were arrested we members of the Political Bureau received protocols with the doctors' confessions of guilt. After distributing these protocols Stalin told us, "You are blind like young kittens; what will happen without me? The country will perish because you do not know how to recognize enemies."

The case was so presented that no one could verify the facts on which the investigation was based. There was no possibility of trying to verify facts by contacting those who had made the confessions of guilt.

We felt, however, that the case of the arrested doctors was questionable. We knew some of these people personally because they had once treated us. When we examined this "case" after Stalin's death, we found it to be fabricated from beginning to end.

This ignominious "case" was set up by Stalin; he did not, however, have the time in which to bring it to an end (as he conceived that end), and for this reason the doctors are still alive. Now all have been rehabilitated; they are working in the same places they were working before; they treat top individuals, not excluding members of the Government; they have our full confidence; and they execute their duties honestly, as they did before.

In organizing the various dirty and shameful cases, a very base role was played by the rabid enemy of our Party, an agent of a foreign intelligence service—Beriya, who had stolen into Stalin's confidence. . . .[3]

Beriya was unmasked by the Party's Central Committee shortly after Stalin's death. As a result of the particularly detailed legal proceedings it was established that Beriya had committed monstrous crimes and Beriya was shot.

The question arises why Beriya, who had liquidated tens of thousands of Party and Soviet workers, was not unmasked during Stalin's life? He was not unmasked earlier because he had utilized very skillfully Stalin's weaknesses; feeding him with suspicions, he assisted Stalin in everything and acted with his support. . . .

Comrades! The cult of the individual has caused the employment of faulty principles in Party work and in economic activity; it brought about rude violation of internal Party and Soviet democracy, sterile ad-

[3] Now follows an account of some of the crimes allegedly committed by Beriya. (Beriya, by the way, is often spelled "Beria" in English transliteration.) [Editor's note.]

ministration, deviations of all sorts, covering up of shortcomings and varnishing of reality. Our nation gave birth to many flatterers and specialists in false optimism and deceit.

We should also not forget that due to the numerous arrests of Party, Soviet and economic leaders, many workers began to work uncertainly, showed over-cautiousness, feared all which was new, feared their own shadows and began to show less initiative in their work. . . .

Comrades!

If we sharply criticize today the cult of the individual which was so widespread during Stalin's life and if we speak about the many negative phenomena generated by this cult which is so alien to the spirit of Marxism-Leninism, various persons may ask: How could it be? Stalin headed the Party and the country for 30 years and many victories were gained during his lifetime. Can we deny this? In my opinion, the question can be asked in this manner only by those who are blinded and hopelessly hypnotized by the cult of the individual, only by those who do not understand the essence of the revolution and of the Soviet State, only by those who do not understand, in a Leninist manner, the role of the Party and of the nation in the development of the Soviet society.

The Socialist revolution was attained by the working class and by the poor peasants with the partial support of middleclass peasants. It was attained by the people under the leadership of the Bolshevik Party. Lenin's great service consisted of the fact that he created a militant Party of the working class, . . . became its experienced leader, and led the working masses to power, to the creation of the first Socialist State.

You remember well the wise words of Lenin that the Soviet State is strong because of the awareness of the masses that history is created by the millions and tens of millions of people.

Our historical victories were attained thanks to the organizational work of the Party, to the many provincial organizations, and to the self-sacrificing work of our great nation. These victories are the result of the great drive and activity of the nation and of the Party as a whole; they are not at all the fruit of the leadership of Stalin, as the situation was pictured during the period of the cult of the individual.

If we are to consider this matter as Marxists and as Leninists, then we have to state unequivocally that the leadership practice which came into being during the last years of Stalin's life became a serious obstacle in the path of Soviet social development. . . .

Some comrades may ask us: Where were the members of the Political Bureau of the Central Committee? Why did they not assert themselves against the cult of the individual in time? And why is this being done only now?

First of all we have to consider the fact that the members of the Political Bureau viewed these matters in a different way at different times. Initially, many of them backed Stalin actively because Stalin was one of the strongest Marxists and his logic, his strength and his will greatly influenced the cadres and Party work.

It is known that Stalin, after Lenin's death, especially during the first years, actively fought for Leninism against the enemies of Leninist theory and against those who deviated. Beginning with Leninist theory, the Party, with its Central Committee at the head, started on a great scale the work of Socialist industrialization of the country, agricultural collectivization and the cultural revolution. At that time Stalin gained great popularity, sympathy and support. The Party had to fight those who attempted to lead the country away from the correct Leninist path; it had to fight Trotskyites, Zinovievites and rightists, and the bourgeois nationalists. This fight was indispensable. Later, however, Stalin, abusing his power more and more, began to fight eminent Party and government leaders and to use terroristic methods against honest Soviet people. . . .

In the situation which then prevailed I have talked often with Nikolai Aleksandrovich Bulganin; once when we two were traveling in a car, he said, "It has happened sometimes that a man goes to Stalin on his invitation as a friend. And when he sits with Stalin, he does not know where he will be sent next, home or to jail."

It is clear that such conditions put every member of the Political Bureau in a very difficult situation. And when we also consider the fact that in the last years the Central Committee Plenary sessions were not convened and that the sessions of the Political Bureau occurred only occasionally, from time to time, then we will understand how difficult it was for any member of the Political Bureau to take a stand against one or another injust or improper procedure, against serious errors and shortcomings in the practices of leadership.

Comrades: We must abolish the cult of the individual decisively, once and for all; we must draw the proper conclusions concerning both ideological-theoretical and practical work.

It is necessary for this purpose:

First, in a Bolshevik manner to condemn and to eradicate the cult of the individual . . . and to fight inexorably all attempts at bringing back this practice in one form or another.

To return to and actually practice in all our ideological work the most important theses of Marxist-Lennist science about the people as the creator of history and as the creator of all material and spiritual good of humanity, about the decisive role of the Marxist Party in the revolutionary fight for the transformation of society, about the victory of Communism.

In this connection we will be forced to do much work in order to examine critically from the Marxist-Leninist viewpoint and to correct the widely spread erroneous views connected with the cult of the individual in the sphere of history, philosophy, economy and of other sciences, as well as in the literature and fine arts. It is especially necessary that in the immediate future we compile a serious textbook of the history of our Party which will be edited in accordance with scientific Marxist objectivism, a textbook of the history of Soviet society, a book pertaining to the events of the Civil War and the Great Patriotic War.

Secondly, to continue systematically and consistently the work done by the Party's Central Committee during the last years, a work characterized by minute observation in all Party organizations, from the bottom to the top, of the Leninist principles of Party leadership, characterized, above all, by the main principle of collective leadership, characterized by the observation of the norms of Party life described in the Statutes of our Party, and finally, characterized by the wide practice of criticism and self-criticism.

Thirdly, to restore completely the Leninist principles of Soviet Socialist democracy, expressed in the Constitution of the Soviet Union, to fight willfulness of individuals abusing their power. The evil caused by acts violating revolutionary Socialist legality which have accumulated during a long time as a result of the negative influence of the cult of the individual has to be completely corrected.

Comrades!

The XXth Congress of the Communist Party of the Soviet Union has manifested with a new strength the unshakable unity of our Party, its cohesiveness around the Central Committee, its resolute will to accomplish the great task of building Communism. And the fact that we present in all their ramifications the basic problems of overcoming the cult of the individual which is alien to Marxism-Leninism, as well as the problem of liquidating its burdensome consequences, is an evidence of the great moral and political strength of our Party.

We are absolutely certain that our Party, armed with the historical resolutions of the XXth Congress, will lead the Soviet People along the Leninist path to new successes, to new victories. . . .

CHINESE COMMUNIST VIEWS

---

4. ON THE QUESTION OF STALIN*
Editorial Departments of the "People's Daily" ("Renmin Ribao") and the "Red Flag" ("Hongqi")

The question of Stalin is one of worldwide importance which has had repercussions among all classes in every country and which is still a sub-

* Excerpts reprinted from *Peking Review*, Sept. 20, 1963, pp. 8–15.

ject of much discussion today, with different classes and their political parties and groups taking different views. It is likely that no final verdict can be reached on this question in the present century, but there is virtual agreement among the majority of the international working class and of the revolutionary people, who disapprove of the complete negation of Stalin and more and more cherish his memory. . . .

The great Soviet Union was the first state of the dictatorship of the proletariat. In the beginning, the foremost leader of the party and the government in this state was Lenin. . . . After Lenin's death, Stalin became not only the leader of the party and government of the Soviet Union but the acknowledged leader of the international communist movement as well.

It is only 46 years since the first socialist state was inaugurated by the October Revolution [66 years, as this book goes to press in 1983]. For nearly 30 of these years Stalin was the foremost leader of this state. Whether in the history of the dictatorship of the proletariat or in that of the international communist movement, Stalin's activities occupy an extremely important place. The Chinese Communist Party has consistently maintained that the question of how to evaluate Stalin and what attitude to take toward him is not just one of appraising Stalin himself; more important, it is a question of how to sum up the historical experience of the dictatorship of the proletariat and of the international communist movement since Lenin's death.

Comrade Khrushchev completely negated Stalin at the 20th Congress of the CPSU. He failed to consult the fraternal parties in advance on this question of principle, which involves the whole international communist movement, and afterwards tried to impose a fait accompli on them. . . . But no one can deny the international significance of the historical experience of the first state of the dictatorship of the proletariat, or the historical fact that Stalin was the leader of the international communist movement; consequently, no one can deny that the appraisal of Stalin is an important question of principle involving the whole international communist movement. . . .

The CCP[1] has invariably insisted on an overall, objective, and scientific analysis of Stalin's merit by the method of historical materialism and the presentation of history as it actually occurred, and has opposed subjective, crude, and complete negation of Stalin by the method of historical idealism and the willful distortion and alteration of history.

The CCP has consistently held that Stalin did commit errors, which had their ideological as well as social and historical roots. It is necessary to criticize the errors Stalin actually committed, not those groundlessly attributed to him, and to do so from a correct stand with correct methods, but we have consistently opposed improper criticism of Stalin. . . .

[1] China's Communist Party. [Editor's note.]

Stalin fought Tsarism and propagated Marxism during Lenin's lifetime; after he became a member of the Central Committee of the Bolshevik Party headed by Lenin he took part in the struggle to pave the way for the 1917 revolution; after the October Revolution he fought to defend the fruits of the proletarian revolution.

Stalin led the CPSU and the Soviet people, after Lenin's death, in resolutely fighting both internal and external foes, and in safeguarding and consolidating the first socialist state in the world.

Stalin led the CPSU and the Soviet people in upholding the line of socialist industrialization and agricultural collectivization and in achieving great successes in socialist transformation and socialist construction.

Stalin led the CPSU, the Soviet people, and the Soviet Army in an arduous and bitter struggle to the great victory of the antifascist war.

Stalin defended and developed Marxism-Leninism in the fight against various kinds of opportunism, against the enemies of Leninism, the Trotskiyites,[2] Zinovievites, Bukharinites and other bourgeois agents.

Stalin made an indelible contribution to the international communist movement in a number of theoretical writings which are immortal Marxist-Leninist works.

Stalin led the Soviet party and government in pursuing a foreign policy which on the whole was in keeping with proletarian internationalism and in greatly assisting the revolutionary struggles of all peoples, including the Chinese people. Stalin stood in the forefront of the tide of history guiding the struggle, and was an irreconcilable enemy of the imperialists and all reactionaries.

Stalin's activities were intimately bound up with the struggles of the great CPSU and the great Soviet people and inseparable from the revolutionary struggles of the people of the whole world.

Stalin's life was that of a great Marxist-Leninist, a great proletarian revolutionary.

It is true that while he performed meritorious deeds for the Soviet people and the international communist movement, Stalin, a great Marxist-Leninist and proletarian revolutionary, also made certain mistakes. Some were errors of principle and some were errors made in the course of practical work; some could have been avoided and some were scarcely avoidable at a time when the dictatorship of the proletariat had no precedent to go by. In his way of thinking Stalin departed from dialectical materialism and fell into metaphysics and subjectivism on certain questions, and consequently he was sometimes divorced from reality and from the masses. . . . In the work led by Stalin of suppressing the counterrevolution, many counterrevolutionaries deserving punishment were duly punished, but at the same time there were innocent people who were wrongly convicted, and in 1937 and 1938 there occurred the error of en-

---

[2] The name is usually spelled "Trotsky," but in this translation from the Chinese it is spelled "Trotskiy" throughout the text. [Editor's note.]

larging the scope of the suppression of counterrevolutionaries. In the matter of party and government organization, he did not fully apply proletarian democratic centralism and, to some extent, violated it. In handling relations with fraternal parties and countries he made some mistakes. He also gave some bad counsel in the international communist movement. These mistakes caused some losses to the Soviet Union and the international communist movement.

Stalin's merits and mistakes are matters of historical, objective reality. A comparison of the two shows that his merits outweighed his faults. He was primarily correct, and his faults were secondary. In summing up Stalin's thinking and his work in their totality, surely every honest communist with a respect for history will first observe what was primary in Stalin. Therefore, when Stalin's errors are being correctly appraised, criticized, and overcome, it is necessary to safeguard what was primary in Stalin's life, to safeguard Marxism-Leninism which he defended and developed.

It would be beneficial if the errors of Stalin, which were only secondary, are taken as historical lessons so that the communists of the Soviet Union and other countries might take warning and avoid repeating those errors or commit fewer errors. . . .

Khrushchev has abused Stalin as a "murderer," a "criminal," and "bandit," a "gambler," a "despot of the type of Ivan the Terrible," "the greatest dictator in Russian history," a "fool," an "idiot," and the like. When we are compelled to cite all this filthy, vulgar, and malicious language, we are afraid it may soil our pen and paper.

Khrushchev has maligned Stalin as "the greatest dictator in Russian history." Does this not mean that the Soviet people lived for 30 long years under the "tyranny" of "the greatest dictator in Russian history" and not under the socialist system? The great Soviet people and the revolutionary people of the whole world completely disagree with this slander! . . .

If his memory is not too short, Khrushchev ought to remember that at a mass rally held in Moscow in January 1937 he himself rightly condemned those who had attacked Stalin, saying, "In lifting their hand against Comrade Stalin, they lifted it against all of us, against the working class and the working people! In lifting their hand against Comrade Stalin, they lifted it against the teachings of Marx, Engels, and Lenin!" Khrushchev himself repeatedly extolled Stalin as an "intimate friend and comrade-in-arms of the great Lenin," as "the greatest genius, teacher, and leader of mankind," and "the great, ever-victorious marshal," as "the sincere friend of the people" and as his "own father."

If one compares the remarks made by Khrushchev when Stalin was alive with those made after his death, one will not fail to see that Khrushchev has made a 180-degree turn in his evaluation of Stalin. . . .

The opportunists in the history of the international communist movement were unable to negate Marx, Engels, or Lenin by vilification, nor is Khrushchev able to negate Stalin by vilification. As Lenin pointed out, a privileged position cannot insure the success of vilification. Khrushchev was able to utilize his privileged position to remove the body of Stalin from the Lenin Mausoleum, but try as he may, he can never succeed in removing the great image of Stalin from the minds of the Soviet people and of the people throughout the world. Khrushchev can utilize his privileged position to revise Marxism-Leninism one way or another, but try as he may, he can never succeed in overthrowing Marxism-Leninism which Stalin defended and which is defended by Marxist-Leninists throughout the world. . . .

Long live the great revolutionary teachings of Marx, Engels, Lenin, and Stalin!

III

Soviet Life Today: Some Introductory Observations

"In this confrontation of two worlds—the socialist and the capitalist—socialism has the advantage of stable economic growth, steadily rising living and cultural standards, the soundness of Marxist-Leninist ideas, social justice, humanism, genuine democracy and our socialist way of life whose motto is: All in the name of Man, all for the benefit of Man."

> NIKOLAI A. TIKHONOV
> Chairman, USSR Council of Ministers

"With every passing year, the Soviet citizen will ever more fully avail himself of the fruits of his successes and ever more clearly feel the advantages of the socialist way of life."

> LEONID I. BREZHNEV
> Late Secretary-General, CC CPSU and Chairman, Presidium of the Supreme Soviet

"Communists should know that in all events, the future belongs to them."

> VLADIMIR ILYICH LENIN

TO MILLIONS of pro-Soviet Communists the world over, the Union of Soviet Socialist Republics represents the ray of light in an otherwise rather dark world, the beacon of hope, the fulfillment of a dream, the promise of a marvelous future for all mankind. Here is a symbol to be looked up to, an example to be followed. It is the first land in which the scourge of unemployment, "wage slavery," and "the exploitation of man by man" has been abolished forever, the first land in which the means of production belong to all the people and are operated in their interests by their elected government. It is a land of promise, a land with continuously rising living standards, in which no one can get rich at someone else's expense. It is a land on the verge of achieving the ultimate in human accomplishments.

111

But there are millions of others to whom the Soviet Union presents a quite different image. They see it as a gigantic slave labor camp, ruled over by tyrannical masters bent on enslaving all of mankind. They see it as a nation ever ready to stir up revolutions in the "Free World," to pit brother against brother and countryman against countryman in an effort to divide and conquer. They see the Communist leaders as men willing to take advantage of any opportunity to further their goal, unhesitatingly willing to lie, to cheat, to kill in order to advance their cause.

What is the Soviet Union *really* like? Is it heaven on earth? Is it a living hell? Or is it, perhaps, somewhere in between, a country with considerable accomplishments to its credit, and with severe shortcomings on the debit side of the ledger? It is hoped that this book will shed a little light upon these questions, that it will give the readers some insight into Soviet life today, as they become better acquainted with Western and Soviet views on a variety of topics concerning present-day Soviet society. This chapter is intended as a preliminary survey. Many points, merely touched upon here, will be examined at greater length in chapters to come.

In the first selection under "Western Views," Alexander Dallin points to "bias and blunders" in American studies of the USSR. On one end of the spectrum he sees a "general reluctance to acknowledge *any* positive accomplishments in the Soviet period," at the other end, pro-Soviet distortions "rooted in wishful thinking." Warning about "persistent failures in our efforts to understand and explain Soviet reality," he admonishes that "clearly the time has come to reexamine underlying assumptions." Next, in a somewhat similar vein, Alec Nove, Chairman of the Department of International Studies at the University of Glasgow, writes that "Russians and Americans have some pretty fantastic views about one another." In an article in which he tries to separate Soviet realities from myths about the USSR, he cautions the reader to beware of extreme views. "It is not that the USSR is just, free, or affluent. It is none of these things," he says; but on the other hand, he warns, "the 'totalitarian slave state' caricature simply does not correspond to reality" either.

Urie Bronfenbrenner, in the third selection, portrays in great detail what he calls the "mirror image" in Soviet-American relations, trying to show both on the basis of his research and his personal observations that "the Russians' distorted picture of us is curiously similar to our view of them."

In this chapter, two Western Marxist views are presented. The first is a rather critical Marxist article by the editorial board of *Canadian Dimension*. Tracing the development of Soviet socialism back to its ideological origins in the middle of the nineteenth century, the authors charge that "a change in the formal property relations towards state ownership . . . and the replacement of the market system by central planning—as fundamental and far-reaching as these are—do not constitute a socialist revolution." They see great progress in many areas ("remarkable" in-dustrialization, rising living standards, elimination of inflation and un-employment, health, education and recreational facilities, "among the best in the world," etc.) But on the other hand, they are taking the Soviet Union to task for continuing political repression and, in the economic sphere, for fostering "bourgeois values, bourgeois criteria of success, bourgeois tastes and kinds of behavior all within the bosom of socialist property relations." They conclude that the Soviet Union today is "a society half-way between capitalism and socialism" but that in spite of its shortcomings, there is not sufficient evidence to write it off as a country on the capitalist path.

In the second Western Marxist view, Howard L. Parsons, Profes-sor and Chairman of the Department of Philosophy at the University of Bridgeport, takes a more positive position on Soviet achievements. Fo-cusing his attention on the development of the "new person" in the Soviet Union, he "passes over the complexities of a 60-year history and the problems yet to be solved," problems of which "the Soviet people, the CPSU, and the leaders are well aware." While concentrating on the re-lationship between the individual and society, he nevertheless tries to give the reader a feel for life in the USSR as a whole, touching on many aspects thereof, such as living standards, crime, and the desire for peace. Painting a favorable picture, he concludes that "in this 60-year-old col-lective movement toward equality of opportunity and fulfillment, in this affirmation of human life for all, the Soviet people have begun to create simultaneously a new person, a new society, and a new world."

The final selection in this chapter represents the official Soviet position. Taken from a 1977 resolution of the Soviet Communist Party's Central Committee, it is an albeit rather glorified summary-account of Soviet achievements over the six decades since the October Revolution and description of the fabric of life under socialism. It contains no ref-erences to lingering problems, no expression of awareness of flaws or shortcomings, and no admissions of remaining gaps to be closed such as the reader will encounter in subsequent Soviet views on more specific issues—for instance on economic performance or living standards. Point-ing to a current, deepening "general crisis of capitalism," it concludes that "socialist organization of economic, political and intellectual life has demonstrated that only socialism opens the way to solving the most im-portant and outstanding problems of our time that affect all mankind."

WESTERN VIEWS

1. BIAS AND BLUNDERS IN AMERICAN STUDIES ON THE USSR*

Alexander Dallin
Stanford University

Western Sovietologists have often been scornful of the layman's ignorance and misunderstanding of Soviet affairs—and not without reason. The resting place of American views of Russia and communism is littered with the carcasses of incomprehension and misperception which, were they not so sad, would be funny. It has been a pathetic and perdurable obsession, even since the dispatch in November 1917 that Lenin had died in Switzerland two years earlier and that the impostor who was taking over Petrograd was some unknown named Zederblum;[1] and the rhapsodic exclamations of those who "had seen the future" in Lenin's Russia and found that "it works." Until the Second World War countless Americans "still envisaged the Russian social structure in terms of bomb-and-whisker Bolshevik stereotypes: sexual promiscuity; . . . the encouragement of abortion; the abandonment of babies; . . . and the encouragement of defiance among the younger generation."[2] And during the war, a former U.S. ambassador to Moscow assured his audience that Stalin's word was "as safe as the Bible."[3]

American attitudes and views, it has been correctly remarked, have often revealed more about the United States than about the USSR. Even those who had every opportunity to be informed, such as newspapermen and government officials, predicted time and again that the Soviet regime was about to collapse, go capitalist, be overthrown, or launch a major attack on the West. One public figure predicted in 1956: "Within the next twenty years, Soviet Communism will collapse under the weight of its economic fallacies, its political follies, and the pressure of a restive, discontented population. . . . The Soviet empire will fall apart as one satellite

---

* Excerpted and somewhat rearranged from *Slavic Review*, Vol. 32, Number 3, Sept., 1973, pp. 560–576. Reprinted in this form by permission of the author and the publisher.
[1] *The North American Review*, cited in Peter G. Filene, *Americans and the Soviet Experiment, 1917–1933* (Cambridge, Mass., 1967), pp. 33–34.
[2] Thomas A. Bailey, *America Faces Russia* (Ithaca, 1950), p. 292. In a Senate speech on April 28, 1920, Senator Henry L. Myers denounced the Bolshevik barbarians for "nationalizing" all women, destroying "the home, the fireside, the family, the cornerstones of civilization," and undertaking to demolish "what God created and ordained." As Filene puts it, "The Bolsheviks became convenient monsters to be dressed with one's favorite prejudices or fears" (*Americans and the Soviet Experiment*, p. 46).
[3] *Daily Worker* (New York), Feb. 25, 1942.

after another attains its own liberation. The Communist hierarchy will destroy itself by internal struggles for power and will be displaced by a military dictatorship, which, in turn, will give way to representative government."[4] And each such forecast could be matched by another, foreseeing on the contrary the relentless forward march of conquering Red hordes.

Understandably there has been confusion and uncertainty, even in official quarters. Former vice-president of the United States, Hubert H. Humphrey, once confessed: "I knew so little about Russian history that I was very poorly equipped intellectually or by experience or by aptitude to deal with the top man of the Soviet Union. . . . And so few of our people in public life have any knowledge at all of these areas of the world, so few of us. We deal so superficially, it's really almost frightening how superficial we are. And is it any wonder that we have such misleading headlines?"[5]

To the policy-maker the Communist world was a baffling conundrum long before Vietnam appeared on his mental map. On July 8, 1918, Woodrow Wilson wrote Colonel House: "I have been sweating blood over the question what is right and feasible to do in Russia. It goes to pieces like quicksilver under my touch. . . ."[6] And in 1961, when in a briefing on John F. Kennedy's boat, off Hyannis Port, the discussion shifted to "Communist China," the president called forward, "Jackie, we need the Bloody Marys now!"[7]

But how much better have we "professionals" done? I need not dwell on the remarkable growth of Soviet studies in the United States— not only in numbers but also in quality and sophistication. Yet it is precisely because the best work has been of such high quality that we must, I submit, be more seriously and systematically concerned with the persistent failures in our efforts to understand and explain Soviet reality— past, present, and future. . . .

I am not here concerned with errors of specific fact, be it Soviet harvest statistics or the organization of the Central Committee Secretariat. These errors are natural and under the circumstances unavoidable. It is more bothersome that serious blunders occurred in the middle range of analysis—that is, in what should be the most promising and fruitful dimension of our research. Thus it used to be axiomatic that the Soviet system required an omnipotent dictator. Well, where is he today? And what lessons have we drawn from his absence? Ten years ago [1963] a panel of highly qualified experts agreed that the Soviet Union could not, in the foreseeable future, both catch up with the United States in strategic

---

[4] David Sarnoff, *Looking Ahead* (New York, 1968), p. 267.
[5] Address at the Annual Dinner of the American Council of Learned Societies, Washington, D.C., Jan. 20, 1966; in ACLS *Newsletter*, January-February 1966, p. 10.
[6] Charles Seymour, ed., *The Intimate Papers of Colonel House*, 4 vols. (Boston, 1926–28), 3:398.
[7] Arthur M. Schlesinger, Jr., *A Thousand Days* (New York, 1965), p. 423.

weapons and also increase the standard of living of its population. It has done so. Ten to fifteen years ago most specialists on the USSR held that Moscow would not sign and abide by any international treaty limiting its production, testing, or deployment of nuclear weapons. But it has done so. Virtually none of us would have envisaged, five years ago, that the Soviet authorities could permit tens of thousands of their Jewish citizens to emigrate, whatever the conditions and difficulties. . . . When the Politburo ousts Khrushchev (and the Central Committee approves), manifestly the axiom which says that the power of the Number One man in the Soviet system cannot be successfully challenged needs to be overhauled. When it is argued that the Soviet system must rely on massive coercion because popular loyalty or socialization will never suffice to dispense with purges and mass terror, and then the regime does dispense with them, clearly the time has come to reexamine some underlying assumptions. . . .

Who cannot recall some of the countries which—we were told— Moscow was taking over or was about to seize? Greece, Finland, Ghana, Guinea, Egypt, the Congo, Indonesia, Iraq, and all the rest. Was there ever a corresponding acknowledgment that these countries were in fact not under Soviet control or no longer actively threatened (if they ever had been)? One need hardly dwell on the possible implications of such a tendency, which (if anyone took us at all seriously) could easily set off patterns of self-fulfilling prophecies. . . .

All too often we find a general reluctance to acknowledge *any* positive accomplishments in the Soviet period, as if the image of the system must be primitively homogeneous in all respects.

Two or three recent examples may illustrate this point. In the last few years we have witnessed new Soviet attempts to tighten political controls over arts and letters; but some of our colleagues who (properly) bemoan this trend never got themselves to recognize that these controls had earlier been loosened at all. And a good many of those who (very justly) condemned the Soviet occupation of Czechoslovakia in 1968 had never acknowledged that the country had slipped from its erstwhile satellite status in the first place. I also detect a novel nostalgia for Nikita Khrushchev on the part of some colleagues who evinced no particular affection for him while he was in office. . . .

Some of the past distortions have been rooted in wishful thinking. Even during the post-Stalin period we may all have had lapses of overoptimism. As late as 1968 many competent students (along with Alexander Dubček)[8] believed that Moscow would be constrained to tolerate systemic

[8] Head of Czechoslovakia's Communist Party and government in 1968 who attempted to combine economic socialism with Western-type political democracy and freedom. In August of 1968, Warsaw Pact nations under Soviet leadership marched into Czechoslovakia and ended the "Prague spring." The following year, Dubček was deposed as First Party Secretary, lost his place on the Party Central Committee. Subsequently he was appointed Czechoslovakia's ambassador to Turkey (1969–70); as this book goes to press, he is an inspector in a forestry enterprise in Bratislava. [Editor's note.]

diversity and dissent within its sphere. Some of the more extravagant arguments about "convergence" and the periodic assertions (not by Maoists but by "capitalist" observers) that the Soviet Union is "reverting to capitalism" have been little better than silly. . . .

And yet, it seems to me, the most damaging patterns of misinterpretation have continued to be located at the opposite end of the spectrum. As some of my examples should have illustrated, the single most characteristic bias has been the denial of actual or latent diversity, variety, change, or choice. This has been only too congruent with the psychological requisites of the "image of the enemy." . . .

Military planners are said to be bound to operate on the basis of "worst-case analysis." Given any situation in which two or more possible explanations or projections may fit the case, it is their predisposition to assume "worst things first." Unwittingly we have often been inclined to follow the same kind of prescription in our own work. . . .

We need not, I submit, engage in orgies of self-flagellation over our failure to predict discrete events. Not only observers at a distance (with the scant information at their disposal, for example, about elite attitudes and leadership conflicts in the Soviet Union) but even insiders are unable to predict specific occurrences. The classic example is Nikita Khrushchev's own failure to anticipate his ouster in October 1964. He, of all people, surely should have had access to the relevant intelligence. . . .

There is little we can do about the errors of analysis which are due to the nature of the Soviet system and the inherent limitations of the state of the art. Other blunders, however, have been due primarily to ourselves and to the biases which we unwittingly absorb from our political environment. If this is so, then a greater awareness of such shortcomings and a greater openness to alternative interpretations should be the first conditions for avoiding such failures in the future.

2. THE USSR: MYTHS AND REALITIES*

Alec Nove
University of Glasgow

Once in the course of a discussion I was asked whether, in my view, the Russians misunderstood America more or less than the Americans mis-

* An earlier version of this article was published in the *Lawrence Daily Journal World*, January 21, 1963. It was updated and in part rewritten, especially for inclusion here, by Harry G. Shaffer. Professor Nove then checked the revised version, made corrections and alterations, and put final touches on it. The sections from the original version are reprinted by permission of the publisher. (The *Lawrence Daily Journal World* is the daily paper of Lawrence, Kansas, the home of the University of Kansas. During the fall semester, 1962/63, Professor Nove held a Distinguished Rose Morgan Visiting Professorship at the University of Kansas.)

understood Russia. After some reflection—the answer is by no means obvious—I expressed the opinion that possibly the American view is the more unbalanced. By the American view I certainly do not mean that of American experts on the Soviet Union. It is with the nonspecialists that I am concerned, the politically conscious man-in-the-street, or even intellectuals who specialise in other subjects. Here one encounters views that seem to be wildly off the mark, even more so than some peculiar views about the United States which are held in Russia.

The reader may well be surprised by such a judgment and will rightly wish to know the reasoning behind it. Is it not a fact, he might ask, that a Soviet citizen is presented by his authorities with a highly slanted and propagandist view of the world in general, and of the United States in particular? Is he not almost wholly cut off from access to outside sources of information? Is not the American who wishes to study Soviet reality able to do so from the several different points of view, which are freely accessible to him? All this is true, and yet. . . .

The first point to make is that the Soviet citizen has long ago learnt to take the official propaganda with a pinch of salt, and particularly when it is describing the "miserable life" which the masses are supposed to lead in Western countries. In my own conversations in the Soviet Union, I formed the impression that many citizens overcompensate for the propaganda and possibly believe that conditions of life in the West are better than in fact they are.

The Russians have always had an inferiority complex about their general level of culture and technique. They regard themselves as inferior in table manners, women's fashions, automobile design and even science. There is a general predisposition to believe that everything in the West is likely to be better than anything Russian. The loud official propaganda to the contrary is partly to be explained by the need felt to combat this tendency. One of the effects of official efforts to conceal the truth is to heighten the curiosity which the majority of Soviet citizens feel about what is really going on in the West.

It is worth mentioning in passing that the failures of official propaganda in this matter are just one small example of the limitations of indoctrination. A good deal of the misunderstanding of what goes on in Russia is caused by the misuse of such terms as totalitarianism, brainwashing and slavery. I still remember, some years back, after watching the brilliantly made movie, *The Manchurian Candidate*, I wondered what proportion of the audience had been brainwashed into believing its underlying assumptions about brainwashing. For years I have been wondering whether the repeated presentation of fiendishly clever Russian indoctrinators does not have the effect of unnecessarily making the enemy seem "ten feet tall." In fact, Soviet attempts at indoctrination are usually conducted with great lack of imagination, and are appallingly dull. On occasion this fact is referred to in the Soviet press. I recall a cartoon in

Krokodil concerning the notorious inadequacy of antireligious propaganda. The drawing shows a priest talking to a woman cleaner in his church. The following is the conversation:

> CLEANER: I hear that an intelligent lecturer on atheism is being sent to our district.
> PRIEST: Do not worry, my dear. Miracles do not happen.

Another point to make is that the Soviet educated classes have a considerable knowledge of, and a very great interest in, Western literature. It used to be said that they believed that England is still the country described by Dickens, since under Stalin only pro-Communist living writers were translated, with comparatively few exceptions. This is no longer the case. Many modern American and British writers are known and admired. It is true that selection of material for translation remains slanted. For example, Graham Greene is known to the Soviet public mainly by *The Quiet American* and *Our Man in Havana*. Nonetheless, the improvement since Stalin's death, some thirty years ago, is unquestionable. Though human contact with Westerners is still far from free, there is much more of it, and a growing number of Soviet citizens, no doubt carefully screened, actually travel abroad as tourists. They tell their friends, when they return, what they have seen. With mass arrests a thing of the past, people do talk much more freely than was possible before. Also, many people listen to foreign broadcasts; there is no difficulty in buying a radio set with short wave reception.

Needless to say, it is not being argued that the Soviet citizen has an accurate picture of life in the West, still less that his government wishes him to have one. But the American citizen's picture of the USSR may be even less accurate.

What are the most commonly held erroneous views found in the United States? The first and most pervasive is a persistent refusal to accept that Stalin is dead. Some excellent Western writers have given a most vivid and basically truthful picture of the Stalin terror, and in most people's minds that picture has not been replaced by any other. Those who study the Soviet Union do know, of course, that the era of Stalin terror has long been over, that the concentration camps were largely emptied under Khrushchev, more than twenty-five years ago, and that no one appears to have been shot for a political offense since 1954, with the only exception of Colonel Oleg Penkovsky, convicted of spying for the British, who faced a firing squad on March 16, 1963, and of V. Kolinin, who confessed to spying for the CIA and was sentenced to death in December, 1981.

But much of the public does not seem to know. One can judge this by the kind of propagandist material which is thought to have a popular appeal in this country. One still encounters American films that seem to be based on the idea that mass arrests of terrified slaves are an everyday occurrence in the Soviet Union. I doubt if such films could be shown in London, as they would probably be laughed off the screen. Here they appeal, as do certain extreme Right statements, to a ready-made belief that Brezhnev was Stalin (Joseph Alsop once even called Krushchev a Hitler), and therefore evil incarnate—and Andropov will probably be even worse. At the level of "mass culture," i.e., in pulp magazines, this attitude towards the Russians takes the form of picturing degenerate monsters in Soviet army uniforms whipping half-clad maidens, to cite an example that was on sale when I visited the U.S. a while back. How can one explain such vicious rubbish to a well-meaning visitor from the East?

By contrast, there is very little interest indeed in Soviet literature in the United States. Admittedly, a good deal of it is rather dull, but this is far from explaining the fact that for the vast majority of literate Americans the only books written in Russia for the past thirty-five years are *Dr. Zhivago* and books by such émigré dissidents as Solzhenitsyn.

It is lack of interest, of any real curiosity, rather than lack of information, which may be at the root of misunderstandings. Sensible interpretations of the USSR do get published, of course, in large paperback editions; one excellent example is Hedrick Smith's *The Russians,* a model of balanced high-level journalism at its best. But they do little to alter the commonly held view. Perhaps this rests on a psychological need to see the enemy as a devil, to disregard evidence which modifies the picture of a slave state ruled by professional criminals. I sometimes feel that this attitude has a basically honorable explanation. Decent people are apt to be worried about a situation in which bombers and ICBMs are apparently poised ready for the slaughter of many millions of fellow human beings, and it is certainly easier to reconcile oneself with this if one is dealing with devils.

The "totalitarian slave state" caricature simply does not correspond to reality. Russian people laugh, love, go to football games, quarrel, cheat, complain, travel in overcrowded subways and behave like normal human beings most of the time. Even the higher authorities have some human feelings, of which vodka is obviously one. In practice it is physically impossible for Moscow to order everyone's lives, even though from time to time it has tried to do so. Perhaps Stalin got nearer to paralyzing spontaneous human activity than anyone did before him. However, most fortunately, he died thirty years ago.

A few American liberals, conscious of the false view of Russia held by so many of their countrymen, swing to the other extreme and maintain that the Soviet Union is or has become free. This is going too far altogether. The Communist monopoly of power is a fact, arbitrary and unjust actions by party officials do occur, freedoms of speech and assembly are still curtailed, the arts are still subject to strict party supervision, and "elections" to representative bodies are still votes for the single candidates running for each position. There are ways of ensuring Communist control over political and social life without actually shooting anyone. While people are not hungry, the food is often of poor quality, with certain items unavailable for months at a time, and shortages have recently grown worse. Much building is certainly going on, but the housing problem, although greatly improved in recent years, remains acute. While the Russian church is active and is not directly persecuted, the situation of a regular churchgoer is not a comfortable one. He is free to go, but this will certainly not help his career. I have heard of students dismissed from a teacher's training college for attending church on the grounds that they may pass on beliefs to schoolchildren. And the toleration extended to the Orthodox and Baptist churches does not cover some of the smaller Christian sects. Jews, too, have much to complain about.

It is not that the USSR is just, free, or affluent. It is none of these things. The point is that it is evolving and that we must, under no circumstances, regard Soviet society as being frozen into some kind of unchangeable totalitarian mold. While in the most recent years we have seen some regrettable increases in repressive measures against dissidents, it is remarkable how many things that were forbidden or unavailable twenty years ago have become part of normal life. There are open controversies in such diverse fields as literature, economics, music. Even back during the Khrushchev days, the communist leadership's attempt to prevent showings of abstract art elicited protest letters signed by large numbers of Soviet intellectuals, which were referred to in the press, an event inconceivable ten years earlier. Or to take examples of a more material kind: we recall (perfectly true) scores of Russian soldiers stealing watches when they reached central Europe in 1945. They were worth their weight in gold in the soldiers' imagination, because such things were simply unavailable to the ordinary man in Russia. Yet today, watches and also cameras have become plentiful, as any visitor to the USSR can see. Most homes have television sets, radios, and refrigerators, although the quality is sometimes mediocre. So, alongside many shortages, inconveniences, and oppressive regulations, there is progress. There is also much lack of discipline, petty corruption, pilfering, and drunkenness. Controls are often ineffective.

Lastly, it is worth stressing one point that seems to me significant. We rightly deplore the fact that the Communist governments of such countries as Czechoslovakia or East Germany have been put there by the Russians. Their policies reflect the Moscow line rather than the needs of their own countries (although the same can hardly be said anymore about Yugoslavia, or even Romania). In fact this is a serious source of weakness of Communist parties in much of Eastern Europe. Nationalist sentiments are against them. This is very obvious today in Poland. But clearly, we cannot see Russia itself in the same light. If Prague obeys Moscow, Moscow obeys whom, or what? The Soviet Community Party, while of course not democratically expressing the views of the citizens, does express in many ways the deep nationalist sentiments which penetrate Russian society and the Communist leadership itself. Despite all ideology, national interest is a powerful force. The Communist leadership has many unlovely features. But even the unlovely features are very Russian—just as there is, close beneath the surface among some Soviet intellectuals, another and much more attractive Russian tradition, inherited from the humanistic ideas so well expressed in nineteenth-century literature.

Both Russians and Americans have some pretty fantastic views about one another. I know of no instrument that can measure degrees of fantasy, so the views expressed above can neither be qualified nor proved right. But in a sense the errors that the Russians make are the more excusable. The American government does not, unlike its Russian counterpart, make efforts to prevent its people from learning about the other side.

3. THE MIRROR IMAGE IN SOVIET-AMERICAN RELATIONS: A SOCIAL PSYCHOLOGIST'S REPORT*

Urie Bronfenbrenner
Cornell University

I should explain by way of introduction that I have visited the Soviet Union several times over the past twenty years. The primary purpose of my trips has been to become acquainted with scientific developments in my field, which is social psychology. But in addition to visiting laboratories at universities and institutes, I wanted also to become acquainted with *living* social psychology—the Soviet people themselves.

Having knowledge of the language, I was able to go about alone, without a guide. Accordingly, after spending the first two or three days of my visit in a particular city at scientific centers, I would devote the remaining days to walking about the town and striking up conversations with people in public conveyances, parks, stores, restaurants, or just on the street. Since foreigners are a curiosity (a bit less in recent years than in the past, but still a curiosity, nevertheless), and since I was obviously a foreigner (though, I quickly learned, not obviously an American), people were eager to talk. But I also went out of my way to strike up conversations with people who weren't taking the initiative—with fellow passengers, with strollers in the park, with children and old people. Or I

* An earlier version of this article was published in *The Journal of Social Issues,* Vol. XVII, No. 3, 1961. It was updated and in part rewritten, especially for inclusion here, by Harry G. Shaffer. Professor Bronfenbrenner then checked the revised version, made corrections, and alterations, and put final touches on it. The sections from the original version are reprinted by permission of the publisher.

would enter a restaurant deciding in advance to sit at the third table on the left with whomever should turn out to be there. (In Soviet restaurants it is not uncommon to share a table with strangers.)

These conversations convinced me that the great majority of Russians feel a genuine pride in the accomplishments of their system and a conviction that Communism is the way of the future, not only for themselves but for the rest of the world as well. For several reasons my Soviet journey was a deeply disturbing experience. But what frightened me was not so much the facts of Soviet reality as the discrepancy between the real and the perceived. At first I was troubled only by the strange irrationality of the Soviet view of the world—especially their gross distortion of American society and American foreign policy as I knew them to be. But on the very first trip in the summer of 1960, there gradually came an even more disquieting awareness—an awareness which I resisted and still resist. Slowly and painfully, it forced itself upon me that *the Russians' distorted picture of us was curiously similar to our view of them—a mirror image.* But of course our image was real. Or could it be that our views too were distorted and irrational—a mirror image in a twisted glass?

Over the years, I have become increasingly convinced of the existence of just such a mirror image. During the brief years of detente, it seemed to fade somewhat into the background; but since the deterioration of U.S.-Soviet relations in the wake of the Afghanistan intervention and the subsequent Olympics boycott and Polish crisis, it seems to have experienced a rebirth, indeed to have come back with a vengeance, this time in color on a 26-inch screen, and backed by a hundredfold escalation of ever more frightful weapons of destruction on both sides. And under the new administration that took over in Washington in 1981, an awesome assymetry appears to have developed: we seem to see an even more distorted picture of "the enemy" in our mirror than they see in theirs.

It was—and is—a frightening prospect. For if such reciprocal distortion exists, it is a psychological phenomenon without parallel in the gravity of its consequences. For this reason, the possibility deserves serious consideration.

Let us then briefly examine the common features in the American and Soviet view of each other's societies. For the Russian's image I drew mainly not on official government pronouncements but on what was said to me by Soviet citizens in the course of our conversations. Five major themes stand out.

1. *They* are the aggressors

The American view: Russia is the warmonger bent on imposing its system on the rest of the world. Witness Cuba, Czechoslovakia, Angola, Ethiopia, and now Afghanistan. The Russians have hundreds of missiles aimed at Western Europe, but denounce as unwarranted aggression our proposal to rectify the balance by placing Pershing II and cruise missiles in Western Europe. Thus the Soviet Union makes meaningful disarmament impossible by insisting on agreements that would assure the military superiority of the communist countries over the West.

The Soviet view: America is the warmonger bent on imposing its power on the rest of the world and on the Soviet Union itself. Witness American intervention in 1918, Western encirclement after World War II with American troops, bases and nuclear devices on or close to every border of the USSR (e.g. in West Germany, Turkey, South Korea), intervention in Korea, Vietnam, El Salvador. After years of work to reach a SALT agreement, America has refused to ratify it, has now started a new arms race of hitherto unheard of proportions and, using an alleged and unfounded "threat" by the Soviet Union to Western Europe and the Persian Gulf area as a pretext, is now talking about using nuclear weapons in a "limited" nuclear war.

2. *Their* government exploits and deludes the people

The American view: Convinced Communists, who form but a small proportion of Russia's population, control the government and exploit the society and its resources in their own interest. To justify their power and expansionist policies they have to perpetuate a war atmosphere and a fear of Western aggression. Russian elections are a travesty since only one party appears on the ballot. The Russian people are kept from knowing the truth through a controlled radio and press and conformity is insured through stringent economic and political sanctions against dissident individuals or groups.

The Soviet view: A capitalistic industrial-militaristic clique controls the American government, the nation's economic resources, and its media of communication. This group exploits the society and its resources. It is in their economic and political interest to escalate their military power and to engage in militaristic expansion. The American people are kept from knowing the truth through a monopoly-controlled radio and press and through economic and political sanctions against anti-establishment elements.

3. The mass of *their* people are not really sympathetic to the regime

The American view: In spite of the propaganda, the Soviet people are not really behind their government. Their praise of the government and the party is largely perfunctory, a necessary concession for getting along. They do not trust their own sources of information and have learned to read between the lines. Most of them would prefer to live under our system of government if they only could.

The Soviet view: Unlike their government, the bulk of the American people want peace. Thus, the majority disapproved of American aggression in Vietnam and they disapprove now of American corporate investments in South Africa, support of the military junta in El Salvador, and of vastly increased military expenditures at the expense of social programs and education. But of course they can do nothing since their welfare is completely under the control of the ruling financier-militaristic clique. ("You Americans are such a nice people; it is a pity you have such a terrible government.")

4. *They* cannot be trusted

The American view: The Soviets do not keep promises, and they do not mean what they say. While they claim to believe in the right of all countries to determine their own destinies, their agents are stirring up trouble all over the Third World, while their Cuban cronies are sending troops to Africa to support rebellions against legitimate governments there. Their talk of peace is but a propaganda maneuver. Everything they do is to be viewed with suspicion, since it is all part of a single coordinated scheme to further aggressive Communist aims.

    The Soviet view: The Americans do not keep promises and they do not mean what they say. Their phony charges of "Soviet aggression" and their refusal to ratify the SALT agreement are ample evidence that they have no real intention of disarming. Everything the Americans do is to be viewed with suspicion (e.g., they preach nonintervention but support antisocialist forces in Poland and ferment terrorism in African and Latin American countries that have overthrown colonial and capitalist-supported regimes that used to exploit the people.

5. *Their* policy verges on madness

The American view: Soviet insistence on their right to support "national liberation movements," their encouragement of terrorist activities as evidenced by their support of Quaddafi, the huge build-up of their armed forces, the large number of SS-20 missiles targeted on every West European capital are prima-facie evidence of what they *really* mean by "peaceful coexistence." It is only due to the restraint of the Western alliance and of the United States in particular that Soviet provocations have not precipitated World War III.

    The Soviet view: The American position on such crucial problems as disarmament, Cambodia, Afghanistan and China shows what they really stand for. In Cambodia, they support the Pol-Pot regime in the UN, which they themselves labeled the most genocidal regime in history; in Afghanistan, they are supplying weapons to a small minority of counter-revolutionary religious fanatics bent on overthrowing the country's legal government; and they are giving their support and even offering weapons to China so as to reinforce the regime's anti-Soviet posture. They have now started to increase rapidly their nuclear arsenal, including the dreadful neutron bomb, a truly capitalist weapon that destroys "only" life but leaves property untouched. Were it not for Soviet prudence and restraint, the support of Fascist regimes in El Salvador or the encouragement of antisocialist counterrevolutionaries in Poland, could easily have precipitated World War III.

It is easy to recognize the gross distortions in the Soviet views summarized above. But is our own outlook completely realistic? Are we correct, for example, in thinking that the mass of the Soviet people would really prefer our way of life and reject their own? Certainly the tone and tenor of my conversations with Soviet citizens hardly support this belief.

But, you may ask, why is it that other western observers do not report the loyalty and commitment which I encountered?

I asked this very question of newspaper men and embassy officials in Moscow. Their answers were revealing. Thus, one reporter replied somewhat dryly, "Sure, I know, but when a Communist acts like a Communist, it isn't news. If I want to be sure that it will be printed back home, I have to write about what's wrong with the system, not its successes." Others voiced an opinion expressed most clearly by representatives at our embassy. When I reported to them the gist of my Soviet conversations, they were grateful but skeptical: "Professor, you underestimate the effect of the police state. When these people talk to a stranger, especially an American, they *have* to say the right thing."

The argument is persuasive, and comforting to hear. But perhaps these very features should arouse our critical judgment. Indeed, it is instructive to view this argument against the background of its predecessor voiced by the newspaperman. To put it bluntly, what he was saying was that he could be sure of getting published only the material that *the American people wanted to hear*. But notice that the second argument also fulfills this objective, and it does so in a much more satisfactory and sophisticated way. The realization that "Soviet citizens *have* to say the right thing" enables the Western observer not only to discount most of what he hears, but even to interpret it as evidence in direct support of the West's accepted picture of the Soviet Union.

It should be clear that I am in no sense here suggesting that Western reporters and embassy officials deliberately misrepresent what they know to be the facts. Rather I am but calling attention to the operation, in a specific and critical context, of a phenomenon well known to psychologists—the tendency to assimilate new perceptions to old, and unconsciously to distort what one sees in such a way as to minimize a clash with previous expectations. A number of leading social psychologists, notably Heider (1958), Festinger (1957), and Osgood (1960), have emphasized that this "strain toward consistency" is especially powerful in the sphere of social relations—that is, in our perceptions of the motives, attitudes, and actions of other persons or groups. Specifically, we strive to keep our views of other human beings compatible with each other. In the face of complex social reality, such consistency is typically accomplished by obliterating distinctions and organizing the world in terms of artificially-simplified frames of reference. One of the simplest of these, and hence one of the most inviting, is the dichotomy of good and bad. Hence we often perceive others, be they individuals, groups, or even whole societies, as simply "good" or "bad." Once this fateful decision is made, the rest is easy, for the "good" person or group can have only desirable social characteristics and the "bad" can have only reprehensible traits. And once such evaluative stability of social perception is established, it is extremely difficult to alter. Contradictory stimuli arouse only anxiety and resistance. When confronted with a desirable characteristic of something already known to be "bad," the observer will either just not "see" it, or will reorganize his perception of it so that it can be perceived as "bad." Finally, this tendency to regress to simple categories of perception is especially strong under conditions of emotional stress and external threat. Witness our readiness in times of war to exalt the virtues of our own side and to see the enemy as thoroughly evil.

Yet another social psychological phenomenon has direct relevance for the present discussion. I refer to a process demonstrated most dramatically and comprehensively in the experiments of Solomon Asch (1956), and known thereby as the "Asch phenomenon." In these experiments, the subject finds himself in a group of six or eight of his peers all of whom are asked to make comparative judgments of certain stimuli presented to them, for example, identifying the longer of two lines. At first the task seems simple enough; the subject hears others make their judgments and then makes his own. In the beginning he is usually in agreement, but then gradually he notices that more and more often his judgments differ from those of the rest of the group. Actually, the experiment is rigged. All the other group members have been instructed to give false responses on a predetermined schedule. In any event, the effect on our subject is dramatic. At first he is puzzled, then upset. Soon he begins to have serious doubts about his own judgment, and in an appreciable number of cases, he begins to "see" the stimuli as they are described by his fellows.

What I am suggesting, of course, is that the Asch phenomenon operates even more forcefully outside the laboratory where the game of social perception is being played for keeps. *Specifically, I am proposing that the mechanisms here described contribute substantially to producing and maintaining serious distortions in the reciprocal images of the Soviet Union and the United States.*

My suggestion springs from more than abstract theoretical inference. I call attention to the possible operation of the Asch phenomenon in the Soviet-American context for a very concrete reason: I had the distressing experience of being its victim. While in the Soviet Union I deliberately sought to minimize association with other Westerners and to spend as much time as I could with Soviet citizens. This was not easy to do. It was no pleasant experience to hear one's own country severely criticized and to be constantly out-debated in the bargain. I looked forward to the next chance meeting with a fellow Westerner so that I could get much-needed moral support and enjoy an evening's invective at the expense of Intourist and the "worker's paradise." But though I occasionally yielded to temptation, for the most part I kept true to my resolve and spent many hours in a completely Soviet environment. It was difficult, but interesting. I liked many of the people I met. Some of them apparently liked me. Though mistaken, they were obviously sincere. They wanted me to agree with them. The days went on, and strange things began to happen. I remember picking up a Soviet newspaper which featured an account of American activities in the Near East. "Oh, what are they doing now!" I asked myself, and stopped short; for I had thought in terms of "they," and it was my own country. Or I would become aware that I had been nodding to the points being made by my Soviet companion where before I had always taken issue. In short, when all around me saw the world in one way, I too found myself wanting to believe and belong.

And once I crossed the Soviet border on my way home, the process began to reverse itself. The more I talked with fellow Westerners, especially fellow Americans, the more I began to doubt the validity of my original impressions. "What would you expect them to say to an American?" my friends would ask. "How do you know that the person talking to you was not a trained agitator?" "Did you ever catch sight of them following you?" I never did. Perhaps I was naive. But, then, recently I reread a letter written to a friend during the last week of my stay. "I feel it is important," it begins, "to try to write to you in detail while I am still in it, for just as I could never have conceived of what I am now experiencing, so I suspect, it will seem unreal and intangible once I am back in the West." The rest of the letter, and others like it, contain the record of the experiences reported in this account.

In sum, I take my stand on the view that there *is* a mirror image in Soviet and American perceptions of each other and that this image represents serious distortions by *both* parties of realities on either side. . . .

WESTERN MARXIST VIEWS*

---

4. SIXTY YEARS OF RUSSIAN COMMUNISM†
Editorial Board
Canadian Dimension

"A spectre haunts Europe—the spectre of Communism"—the opening words of the Communist Manifesto written by Marx and Engels in 1848.

---

* Note that the first is a rather critical, and the next a rather approbatory, Western Marxist view.

† Reprinted from "60 Years of Russian Communism," *Canadian Dimension*, Vol. 12, No. 7, 1978, pp. 14–21, by permission of the publisher.

The founders of the communist movement were right. The Capitalist world was then undergoing a profound economic and political crisis. Industrial capitalism had successfully uprooted millions of peasants, artisans and shopkeepers but it was less successful in finding them work. Businessmen themselves feared that the first stage of industrial capitalism might also be its last.

There was a real crisis, but it did not result in a communist revolution. Looking back we can see that what Marx and Engels were observing was not the end of capitalism but its "teething" period. As it emerged in the ensuing decade with the railway and steamship boom, the gold discoveries and the spread of the factory system throughout Europe, Marx and Engels gradually resigned themselves to the fact that they would not live to see the revolution.

Towards the end of the century competitive capitalism began to give way to monopoly capitalism; England was forced to share its dominant position with the other industrial powers especially Germany and the U.S.A.; and capitalism spread to the remotest corners of the globe, creating one-crop economics in Latin America, Asia and Africa, each becoming entirely dependent upon the developed industrial world for its outlets.

The new era of expansion created a crisis for Marxism and led some, like the German Edward Bernstein, to revise the revolutionary imperative of Marx and replace it with "evolutionary socialism". Others were making different revisions. Lenin began writing about imperialism. Under its strains, he said, the revolution would break out not in the centres of world capitalism but in the peripheral regions, what he termed "capitalism's weakest links". In these areas, liberal democratic forces would be too immature to carry through the bourgeois revolution and the proletariat would push it through and from there to socialism.

This is what happened—beginning in Russia in 1905, in Mexico 1910, China 1911 and Russia again 1917—the Bolshevik revolution where one-sixth of the earth's surface was removed from world capitalism.

The strategy of the Bolsheviks was predicated on the confidently-held belief that the torch kindled in Russia would ignite the socialist revolution in western Europe. With the support of the European proletariat, Russia would be enabled to complete its socialist revolution and build a socialist society. The task—Lenin had said again and again, and there was universal agreement on this—was too heavy for backward Russia to carry out alone. Left to itself, it would either be crushed or become brutalized in the economically and culturally primitive Russian environment.

The Red Army, organized and led by Leon Trotsky, turned back the intervention of the western powers, but the Bolsheviks waited in vain for the revolution in Europe. In the autumn of 1923, when the German proletariat for the third or fourth time since 1918 suffered a crushing defeat, leaders in Moscow finally resigned themselves to the fact that the European revolution was still a long way off. In light of this, they accepted

Stalin's formula of "socialism in one country"—itself a revision of the first order.

Many socialists in the west have come to look upon the experience of the Soviet Union as a great set back for world socialism. "If that is what socialism is like, who wants it"? Certainly socialism in the USSR has been a brutalizing experience and a deadly one for many of its participants. To deny that or explain it away by casual references to "errors" or "the cult of personality" is to fly in the face of historical evidence—not only the evidence of a Solzenytsin, but also of a Nikita Khrushchev. But to leave it at that is to ignore other equally important historical facts.

It would be unfair to suppose that Stalin deliberately and consciously sought isolation. Again and again approaches were made to the western world. Again and again they were rejected. Canada, under the leadership of MacKenzie King was one of the most hostile of western nations. Only under the stress of war[1] and even then at the last possible moment, did western nations overcome their bitter antagonisms. And once the war was over the iron curtain descended again.

Socialist revolutions, of course, cannot count on the support or even the neutrality of the ruling class of capitalist countries. But they have every reason to count on the support of the working class in these countries. We in the west bear a heavy responsibility for the predicament of the Soviet Union—and the similar predicament of China, Vietnam, Cuba, etc. Our failure to promote socialism in the west is at least partly to blame for their failure to advance more easily and less painfully.

The Bolshevik revolution began in an atmosphere of idealism bordering on Utopia. Marxism—the Marxism of Marx, Engels, Lenin, Luxemburg, Trotsky and Gramsci—stood on the shoulders of western bourgeois liberal democracy. The Socialist revolution was never intended to abandon democratic ideals, but to fulfill them in a manner that capitalism was incapable of doing. Many of the first legislative acts and declarations of the Soviet regime were inspired by this tradition. But the workers who were called upon to build the first socialist order had been for generations the victims of economic misery, only recently emerged from serfdom. They had been subjected to political repression more extreme than in any other great country. The socialist order in Russia could draw neither upon the wealth created by past capitalist accumulation, as Marx had presupposed, nor upon the political experience fostered by bourgeois democracy as also presupposed by Marx. Instead it inherited the hidden force of the Russian past—autocracy, bureaucracy and political and cultural conformity. The revolution wasn't destroyed. It was harnessed to the backward environment of Russia and so it gave birth to backward socialism.

To begin with the Bolshevik party was the expression of a smart and concentrated proletariat, without a wide class base in relation to the

---

[1] Reference to World War II. [Editor's note.]

country as a whole. The country was reduced to an ungovernable economic chaos by the World War and the Civil War. Large numbers of the urban proletariat, the base of the Bolsheviks, were killed off or dispersed. In the circumstances, Lenin had no alternative but to launch a strategic retreat, the New Economic Policy, which re-established private ownership in some sectors of the economy and a return to the market system. Within'a few years the economy had recovered to its pre-revolutionary level of economic activity. Now the question was posed, where to go from here.

This was the liveliest political and cultural period in the history of the revolution, with much social experimentation and fairly open debate. But it also marked the beginning of the rise of a bureaucratic party and state apparatus that gradually concentrated economic and political control in its hands. Indeed this was the subject of a vigorous debate launched by Trotsky in 1923 who argued that the bureaucratization of the party machinery had developed to unheard of proportions. There were 20,000 party officials, most of whom were appointed rather than being elected by the party's 400,000 members. Party members, he said, should exercise the right to criticism "without fear and without favour." He chastized the party machine for intimidating and "terrorizing" those who put forward opposing points of view. But not even Trotsky and his followers were advocating a workers' democracy at this point. Like their opponents they were against allowing rival socialist parties to operate freely. But was it possible that the party could be an island of freedom in a society governed by dictatorial rule?

The state of affairs which gave rise to this debate had deeper roots than Stalin's ambition for personal power. Revolutionary consciousness had barely penetrated the Russian population. Severe shortages and economic hardships resulted in widespread apathy and pockets of hostility among the masses of people. In this context the revolution was held together by the massive political machine built up in the earliest days. Stalin was the political expression of this rising bureaucracy.

This was no "dictatorship of the proletariat". It wasn't even a "dictatorship for the proletariat", for there was barely a proletariat to dictate on behalf of. It was at this stage, a dictatorship of a party bureaucracy to build a proletariat. The major question was how this was to be accomplished.

One faction called for a continuation of the New Economic Policy, a gradual industrialization that would be achieved by encouraging the growth of prosperous private farmers that would, through market incentives produce an agricultural surplus to feed the cities and gain much needed foreign exchange.

The corollary was an industrialization policy that would produce farm implements and the consumer goods needed to entice the peasants. The architect of this strategy was Nicolai Bukharin.

The opposing faction, led by Trotsky and Preobrazhensky argued that this strategy would endanger the revolution by making it dependent upon the grasping Russian muzhik[2] who would hold the country to ransom to win a greater advantage for themselves. They advocated a strategy of encouraging the formation of collective farms, of rapid industrialization and the institution of central economic planning.

With Stalin's support, the Bukharanites held the day. Whether through faulty implementation, as some now contest, or because of the inherent weakness of the strategy, the Russian economy soon faltered. The cities were faced with famine as the poor peasants consumed most of their produce and the more prosperous ones stored their surpluses to force up prices. Forced requisitions exacerbated the problem and set in motion a vicious cycle which the leadership could see no way out of except by a crash program of collectivization combined with accelerated industrialization. Thus the first Five-Year Plan launched in 1929. Not a single Bolshevik group or faction thought of an industrialization so intensive and rapid or of a collectivization so total and rapid as that which Stalin initiated. He was possessed by the idea that he could achieve a miraculous transformation of Russia by a single tour de force.

The isolation of the Russian revolution compelled it to rely on its own resources. As the isolation became permanent, the Bolsheviks were driven farther back into the Russian past. Joseph Stalin was a throw-back to Peter the Great as he determined to drive the revolution forward at all costs through forced collectivation and torrid industrialization. Like Ivan the Terrible, he protected himself from potential treachery by eliminating every possible rival, terrorizing and liquidating not only the survivors of the ancien regime but also every one of the original Bolsheviks who together with Lenin and himself had led the revolution. (As one writer has said, Stalin "had more Communists on his conscience than had hitherto been exterminated by the entire world bourgeoisie"). Just as medieval Russia had been suffocated by ecclesiastical orthodoxy, so Soviet Russia became suffocated by party orthodoxy that claimed a monopoly over all philosophy, literature and art.

> In leaving us, Comrade Lenin ordained us to hold high and keep pure the great title of member of the party. We vow to thee, Comrade Lenin, that we shall honourably fulfill this thy commandment.

These were the opening words of Stalin's oath to Lenin read at the second congress of the Soviets, a remarkable reflection of the way Lenin's crisp and analytical rationalistic style was transformed by Stalin whose revolutionary invocations sound like something borrowed from an Orthodox Prayer Book.

[2] In Czarist Russia, a peasant. [Editor's note.]

Marx described the first stage of industrialization as "primitive capital accumulation": "capital comes (into the world) dripping from head to foot, from every pore, with blood and dirt". He recalls "the bloody discipline by which the free peasants of England were made into wage-earners . . . the disgraceful action of the state which employed the police to accelerate the accumulation of capital by increasing the degree of exploitation of labour". Stalin introduced the same practices in the forced collectivization of the conservative, superstitious Russian Muzhik, in the military-style discipline of early Soviet factories, in the grossly unequal wages and the vicious piece-work system brought in to stimulate production, in the elimination of trade unions as defensive organizations for workers, in the horrendous labour camps set up for political dissidents. In primitive Russia socialism also came into the world "dripping from head to foot, from every pore, with blood and dirt".

But come into the world it did. The impact of the second revolution launched by Stalin in 1929 was far more sweeping and radical for Russia's 160 million people than the first. Within a few decades, backward Russia became one of the world's greatest industrial powers. Tens of millions of illiterate people were made to learn to read and write. The nationalities of Central Asia were dragged out of their nomadic past and involved in the circuit of modern life. And Soviet Russia was instrumental in saving the world from Nazi Germany.

How are we to assess the Russian Revolution today, sixty years later? Whatever else one might say, it was surely one of the greatest turning-points in history, comparable with the French Revolution and perhaps surpassing it in significance. A beacon of hope to some, the work of Satan to others, its influence remains powerful throughout the world. It has clearly played an instrumental role in assisting numerous peoples—the Cubans, Chinese, Koreans, Vietnamese, Angolans and others—in breaking away from the grip of western imperialism. Whether in the process it has launched its own "social imperialism" as the Chinese now insist, we regard as dubious. We view this accusation as more akin to the dangerous and tragically incorrect theory of "social fascism" that the communist parties themselves hurled at the social democrats in the early thirties. The consequence of that horrendous error led to the rise of Hitler and World War Two. We can only hope that the theory of "social imperialism" and the disunity of the socialist world that it reflects, will not bring about the same tragic result.

But did the Bolshevik Revolution inaugurate a "new civilization" as its proponents then and now insist? If by "new civilization" is meant a society whose means of production are owned by the state and whose economy is centrally and comprehensively planned according to priorities set by the state—then the answer must be "yes". These fundamental changes were achieved, not on the morning after the revolution, for the chaos and destruction created by World War One, the Civil War and the western intervention forced a necessary strategic retreat. Only with the drive towards collectivization of agriculture and the first five-year plan did the state sector triumph over the private sector. Shortly thereafter Stalin declared that the USSR had achieved socialism. Socialist property relations were now in place. The advance towards communism was guaranteed as succeeding Five-Year plans would provide the material base for increased production and more consumer goods for all. . . .

It was forty years ago when Stalin made his declaration that socialism and a class-less society had been achieved. In that short period Russia has undergone a remarkable industrialization. The living standard of Soviet citizens has gradually improved, though it is still well below North American levels. For a people deprived of basic security so often and for so long, this is a highly significant accomplishment. Whatever the other shortcomings of the Soviet economy, Russian workers do not have to worry about employment or uncontrollable inflation. Their health, education and recreation facilities are among the best in the world. Correct legal procedures are scrupulously followed unlike the days of lawlessness under Stalin. Political offenders don't stand a chance of winning in court, but they are able to insist upon their rights and defend themselves publicly. The emergence of open political discontent and the struggle for civil liberties during the past decade reflects an important evolution within Soviet society.

But has Soviet Russia actually advanced towards the Marxist vision of a communist society—towards the dissapearance of class division—towards the withering away of the state as an instrument of repression—towards overcoming the crippling forms of the division of labour— the authoritarian and hierarchical organization of work—towards abolishing the distinction between manual and mental labour and between country and city—towards a system of distribution according to needs?

We are not so naive to believe that this vision can ever be perfectly realized or that it can be achieved overnight. As Marx himself said, the society that follows the overthrow of capitalism is "in every respect, economically, morally, and intellectually, still stamped with the birthmarks of the old society from whose womb it emerges". Capitalism and communism will be separated not by years or even decades but by a whole historical epoch. The capitalist revolution culminated in the 17th century but capitalist man did not emerge full blown for two hundred years. We cannot expect that the transition from capitalist man to communist man will take any less time.

It would be entirely wrong, therefore, to dismiss Soviet socialism because the Russian muzhik of 1917 has not been transformed into communist man some 60 years later.

Yet there are grounds for seriously questioning whether the USSR is still advancing along the socialist path towards communism. . . .

Sixty years of Soviet history has many lessons to teach. The one we have chosen to stress is that a change in the formal property relations towards state ownership, as fundamental and far-reaching as this is—and the replacement of the market system by central planning, as fundamental and far-reaching as this is—do not in themselves constitute a socialist revolution.

State planners rather than corporations determine what will be produced and how. The profit motive in a formalistic sense has been abolished. Yet material self-interest still dominates, and it is increasingly individualized self-interest rather than the collective needs of society. Soviet citizens, with notable exceptions are individually motivated, like the citizens of capitalist societies to promote their own private interest. The Soviet economy is firmly grounded on the principle of using differential rewards to secure the kinds and amounts of work needed to propel it forward. . . .

The Soviet State has fostered bourgeois values, bourgeois criteria of success, bourgeois tastes and kinds of behaviour all within the bosom of socialist property relations. The Soviets have produced an unhappy, some would say grotesque hybrid—socialist property relations and a capitalistic mode of operation. A strange new synthesis.

The result must be a growing material inequality. . . .

Reliance on private gain fostered a system of petty sabotage as workers and managers distorted the targets set by the planners when this would bring them greater material rewards. As centralized administrative planning entered a period of crisis during the 1950's and 1960's the Soviet Union and the countries of Eastern Europe were led to introduce reforms which gave greater autonomy to enterprise managers and placed emphasis on producing the planned output at minimum cost—by tying bonuses more closely to profits. And Soviet managers were sent to business schools in the United States to learn the latest techniques in capitalist management. These reforms have had little effect and today Soviet leaders are looking to technological advances imported from the west as a way out of the economic difficulties. . . .

We do not conclude from all of this that Soviet Russia has stepped off the socialist path and that it is speedily and irreversibly moving towards a collectivist capitalism. Some have come to this conclusion but we are not persuaded that there is sufficient evidence to warrant a write-off. We see it rather as a society half-way between capitalism and socialism, having elements of both. . . .

The Soviet Union no longer stands as the one Communist State. There are now several and together they rule over more than half the world's population.[3] Nor is the Communist Party of the USSR still the indisputable leader of the Communist world. It resembles more a Com-

---

[3] More than one-third might be closer. [Editor's note.]

munist Commonwealth, although Moscow is still resisting the idea of this kind of pluralism.

Capitalism in the west has experienced more than one trauma in the past half century—but it has proved to be a more flexible system than Marx and Engels thought possible. It learned from the Great Depression and World War II that it must and could incorporate a greatly expanded role for the state. The crisis of the '70's propels it towards even more state involvement—towards some version of state capitalism.[4] The Communist Parties of the west have responded to changing circumstances by altering their strategies which involve abandoning many of the original precepts designed by Lenin and redesigned by Stalin. To their credit, several Communist parties have not only declared their independence from the USSR but have publicly criticized the way political dissent is smothered there and political dissenters are mistreated. . . .[5] Russia has the material and military base today, yet it appears to have lost its socialist dynamic. When bureacratic solutions replace political ones, it is only a matter of time before a new ruling class emerges, now based on its control over that same bureaucracy. The socialist revolution cannot rest during the period of rapid accumulation. If it does not go forward through struggles against the state and party bureaucracies, a new system of exploitation will be born.

A few years before he died the widely respected writer Isaac Deutscher[6] delivered a speech which he titled, "On Socialist Man". This excerpt provides a fitting conclusion to our statement.

> "It was once said of the Jesuits that, having failed to raise earth to heaven, they dragged heaven down to earth. Similarly, Stalin and Stalinism, failing to raise a poverty-stricken and miserable Russia to Socialism, have dragged down socialism to the level of Russian misery. It may be argued that they had to do it. Even if that were so, we have to do something else: We have to raise socialism back to its own height. . . . We must restore the image of socialist man to all its spiritual splendour. We must restore it in our own minds first and then, fortified in our conviction and rearmed politically, we must carry socialist consciousness and the socialist idea back to the working class."

---

[4] In England and the United States this trend was reversed, at least for the time being, when Margaret Thatcher was elected British prime minister in 1979, and Ronald Reagan President of the United States in 1980. [Editor's note.]

[5] The large Communist parties of France and Italy have done this, but not the Communist Party of the United States. [Editor's note.]

[6] Isaac Deutscher (1907–1967), while a Marxist, was a determined opponent of Stalinism for more than forty years. He was expelled from the British Communist party in 1932, and for most of his life thereafter was not affiliated with any political party, group, or sect. [Editor's note.]

5. LIFE IN THE SOVIET UNION: SIXTY YEARS OF PROGRESS TOWARD HUMAN FULFILLMENT*

Howard L. Parsons
University of Bridgeport

In ancient class societies humanistic prophets and seers dreamed of a time to come when human personality and society would be fulfilled—when individual persons would be compassionate, cooperative, intelligent, esthetic, and fully realized in all their human powers, and when just and prosperous social arrangements would encourage and enable persons to be so. The Jewish prophets proclaimed peace among all nations. Plato in *The Republic* wrote of "the education of our heroes," and the author of The Revelation to John wrote that he "saw a new heaven and a new earth" as a voice from heaven declared that God "shall wipe away all tears" and "death shall be no more" (21:1, 4). But these dreams proved fruitless so long as societies remained class societies dominated by small groups ruling over slaves, serfs, or wage laborers. In October of 1917 in Russia the first successful socialist revolution smashed class rule there once and for all; and for the first time in history the people of a society organized themselves and their resources to set out on the grand experiment of creating "heroes" and "a new earth"—a society of abundance, equality, and human fulfillment, and a world of peace.

Have the people of the Soviet Union succeeded in their struggle to create "a new person"? I believe so. Not completely, of course; for such creation is never fully finished. But they are far enough along the way so that we can see a distinctive kind of personality emerging in large numbers and clearly differentiated from the kinds living in class societies past and present.

I want to examine briefly four ingredients in their success; collectivism, equality, the affirmation of human life, and the full development of human potentialities. In this examination I have necessarily passed over the complexities of a 60-year history and the problems yet to be solved. That there are such problems the Soviet people, the CPSU, and the leaders are well aware.

Collectivism. The collective philosophy, attitude, and practice is the primary distinguishing feature of Soviet socialist society. Socialism means that individual personality is profoundly social both as fact and

* Reprinted from Howard L. Parsons, "The New Person in the Soviet Union: Sixty Years of Progress Toward Human Filfillment," in Marilyn Bechtel, David Laibman, and Jessica Smith (editors) *Six Decades That Changed the World*, New York: NWR Publications, Inc., 1978, pp. 229–38 by permission of the author and the publisher.

value, as actuality and possibility. Dating from Neolithic society or earlier, the *theory* of personality as social found expression in many of civilization's ancient philosophies and religions. In modern times the great
utopians articulated it, and Marx defined the human being as "the total
unity of his primary interpersonal relations." But only in socialist societies have people really applied this theory to social conditions to create
and discover its truth in living human practice.

From the earliest age in the Soviet Union, "mine is ours; ours is
mine" is the rule. Blocks are built so that children *must* engage the help
of others in order to move them. Children are nurtured not only by their
parents; relatives, teachers, older children, and strangers in general look
after them (so that strictly speaking the "stranger" is usually the unknown
friend). Urie Bronfenbrenner, in his *Two Worlds of Childhood: U.S. and
U.S.S.R.,* reports the following incident:

> Our youngest son—then four—was walking briskly a pace
> or two ahead of us when from the opposite direction there came
> a company of teenage boys. The first one no sooner spied Stevie
> than he opened his arms wide and, calling *"Ai Malysh!"* [Hey,
> little one!], scooped him up, hugged him, kissed him resoundingly,
> and passed him on to the rest of the company, who did likewise,
> and then began a merry children's dance, as they caressed him
> with words and gestures.

In addition to his or her nurtured and responsible role in the close-
knit Soviet family, every schoolchild participates in a series of collectives
to which he is responsible: his row of double-seated desks, his classroom,
and his school organization as a whole (*druzhina*). Each classroom functions as a unit of the Octobrists (ages 7 to 9) and the Pioneers (ages 10
to 15). The Komsomol (Young Communist League), consisting of more
than half of those eligible from age 16 to 28, includes both high school
youth and graduates. To participate in such collectives is for the child
and youth to be and to become quite a different person from one who
lives in the individualistic society of capitalism. It is to grow up into a
truly *socialized* person.

Every adult, moreover, continues to participate in collectives, with
their corresponding rights and duties. Work, expected and required of all
able-bodied Soviet citizens, is the principal way in which the Soviet adult
person contributes to and receives from others. From his membership in
a collective at his place of work, every adult derives housing rights, travel
rights, recreational opportunities, insurance, educational advantages,
nursery school privileges for children, and other benefits. Besides the one
or more families to which the Soviet adult belongs, he participates in many
other collective activities—political groups, recreational and library
clubs, artistic societies, etc.

Unlike the worker in capitalist society, the Soviet worker does not
work principally to "make money" and thereby to survive and help his

family to survive. He works principally to express his own life, to co-operate with others, to provide his share of wealth for the collective good, and to receive in turn as he has worked. This reciprocity is possible because the classless Soviet society had long since wiped away the antagonism of worker and worker, of worker and owner, and of citizen and government which characterizes capitalist society. The workers' sense that this factory, this farm, belongs to *them* induces a feeling of willing engagement and a sense of meaningful activity in life: the worker feels that his work counts, that it makes a difference, that it is his own contribution to the collective good, material and moral, to which he belongs. The alienation endemic to workers under capitalism is gone.

The fraternal spirit that imbues the family and working unit extends throughout the nation and into international relations. The Soviet Union is a multinational state uniting a rich diversity of ethnic, racial, cultural, and linguistic traditions. This in itself is a signal achievement in a century in which the disease of racism has reached a peak in fascist states like Nazi Germany. . . . The Soviet fraternal attitude reaches beyond the borders of the Soviet Union to embrace the peoples of many other nations throughout the world.

Because bourgeois analysts presuppose an inherent antagonism between individual personality and society, the relation of these two in the Soviet Union is usually a puzzle to them. The "priority of social interests" for them means a suppression of individual interests and personality. But in Soviet theory and practice the individual personality is not something *apart* from society. The personality is *defined* by social relations, beginning with the family and work unit and reaching out to the whole of society and its relations with the nonhuman ecological order. This dynamic interdependence wherein individuals strengthen and create one another, society, and nature is both an ultimate fact and a supreme value. It calls for a whole code of ethics that in its form and application is really new in human history. We can say that to the extent that people are socialized in this sense, they become truly moral; for to be moral is in the original and fundamental sense to help as many people as possible, including oneself, to live and to live well.

Soviet society demands of each individual person the development, exertion, and contribution of his abilities to the social fund of goods, services, and gifts of character. This places a large burden on each personality, calling him or her to do his share for the good of the whole. From the outside this looks like a heavy weight for individual conscience to bear. The stated objectives of education, for example, the rules for the various youth organizations, and the code of the builders of communism are very demanding. But from an early age children receive from people generally repeated encouragement for doing their duties and self-discipline in responding to the demands of the collective becomes second nature. . . .

Soviet society generates in its children and adults a great deal of security, both economic and psychological, as well as a great outward and inward sense of peace. When I first arrived in the Soviet Union in 1964 I experienced a very strong impression of people sure of themselves and their station on this earth, a people busy, serious, and happy, a people certain they had a firm hold on their life and their future, a people who knew they could do and would do what they set out to do, a people whose deep sense of security with themselves gave them the strength to reach out to other people and nations for the collective security in the world that their government had striven for so patiently for so many decades. During my subsequent half dozen visits to the Soviet Union this impression of security has recurred with the same vividness.

In the past half-century crime has declined by 71.5 per cent while the population has increased by 117 million. A society that has reduced this rate to one of the lowest levels in the modern world, has no organized crime, no profit-making crime (as in the sale of arms, drugs, bets), and no profiteering by individuals and the media by the depiction of crime (via TV, radio, newspaper, journal, fiction, science, cinema, comics, etc.), and has eradicated the social crimes of racism and illiteracy, must surely be creating "the new person" in large numbers.

Soviet people, as compared with people in western capitalist countries, seem to me to be less egocentric and more sociocentric, to have a keener sense of their moral obligations to others, society, and nature, to be more solicitous about children, the disadvantaged, and the elderly, to be less obsessed with the acquisition and accumulation of material goods, to be more peaceful in handling the conflicts in their interpersonal lives, and to be less interested in money. Many whom I have met, especially young people, seem remarkably indifferent to money. Why? In capitalist society money is the all-powerful god, since survival itself depends on the individual's getting it by hook or crook, by job or rob. Under Soviet socialism the state guarantees a job, subsidized food and housing prices, socialized medical care, state-supported education, and an ample pension. Why worry about survival in such a society? So as a rule Soviet people don't.

The Soviet people *do* worry about one thing: the threat to human survival posed by the arms race and weapons of mass destruction. They worry because they have lost more by war than any other people. They have struggled mightily to build it back again, they are well on the way to winning a world of "the new person" both for themselves and all others, and they are loath to lose it all in the most stupid crime and irrevocable folly.

Soviet society presupposes a "general will" or common interest which unites all individual persons and in which, as Rousseau put it, "each necessarily submits to the conditions which he imposes on others—an admirable union of interest and justice." In the more concrete formulation of Marxism-Leninism, what binds people together is their working class interest in survival and development. That generic human interest, which always expresses itself in social form, gives rise to particular and individual interests that become interlocked with other particular interests. While there is no pre-established harmony of particular interests in Soviet society, the prevailing disposition is to presume that such harmony is more or less possible and to drive toward it. This drive is a collective drive. Both goal and method are collective.

Unlike our own, this society is unified and inspired by a single pervasive philosophy—communism, taught implicitly and explicitly. Every secondary school student in his or her last year must study a full course of economics, philosophy, and scientific communism and must pass an examination in dialectical and historical materialism. As one Soviet philosopher, Professor Yuri Konstantinovich Melvil, said "In the Soviet Union philosophy is essential to education; each person must understand *what* he does and *why* he does it." . . .

Under Marxist-Leninist theory, each person in principle holds an equal right in the collective power and value of society. That society is in fact defined by the linkage of all individual wills regulating each other. Correspondingly, each person submits himself to the rule of the whole body politic. All rights pertaining to the individual are derived from and are conditioned by the right of the society to exist and develop. The rights of the individual person to the free exercise of religion, and freedom of speech, press, and assembly—which in the Constitution of the United States are beyond the power of the Congress to abridge—are not absolute under Soviet socialism. The right to life for all citizens as it is guaranteed by the Soviet state is the ultimate right, preceding and undergirding all other rights. In their very bones the Soviet people know this from their life-and-death struggle to survive. War and war-mongering are intolerable. No person has the right to advocate the reversion of a socialist state to a capitalist one, or to preach racism. No one has the right to propose or practice the destruction of the people's sovereignty, self-determination, peace, and social ownership of the means of production. The Soviet people accept this definition of rights. They accept the new Constitution's prescription of social duty for all citizens.

Equality. The sense of equality among the Soviet people is widespread. One can observe this in the homes, factories, offices, shops, streets, buses, and trains, where people speak to each other and defend their rights as equals. The sense of rank and status so common in countries like England and France is absent in the Soviet Union. A young research worker in psychology once told me that from time to time he would see Khrushchev in his neighborhood, where the former Premier then lived after his retirement. I expressed some surprise at the casual way in which he reported this fact, and his reply was that no one in the neighborhood took special note of him. He was one of the Soviet masses—no better, no worse. When American journalists, hypocritically expressing sympathy for Krushchev, complained that Soviet society should pay more respect to their retired leaders, they not only failed to understand the thought and values of the Soviet people; they betrayed their own class snootiness. . . .

Much has been made of how Soviet "bureaucracy" crushes individuality and equality. Of course every government or institution of any size requires bureaus with routinized procedures of administration (*i.e.*, a bureaucracy); and every bureaucracy is infected with some inefficiency, rigidity, looseness, personal whim and arbitrariness, "influence," and unfairness. I have not found the bureaucracies in the Soviet Union worse in these respects than those in capitalist countries. And there one finds resistance to and criticism of inefficient bureaucracy. The criticism is of bureaucracy and not of socialism, and it is made from a sense of loyalty to Soviet society and socialism. The Soviet people view bureaucracy as "our" problem, and scientists interpret it as a stage in the evolution of the management of social affairs that will be superseded as automation takes over such management.

Economic equality in a society where wage differentials remain is enhanced by the "public consumption funds," which constitute that portion taken from the national income to be "distributed among members of society as gratuitous material benefits and services and as money allowances of various kinds." Through such funds, which comprise more than one-third of the aggregate revenue of the average industrial worker family, people obtain free medical help, free education and advanced training, diverse benefits, pensions, scholarships, paid leaves, and free or subsidized accommodation at sanatoriums and holiday homes for adults and at kindergartens and nursery schools for children. Also, two-thirds of the cost of maintaining dwellings, libraries, clubs, etc. comes from such funds. The proportion of these consumer benefits for those in lower income brackets is three times as high as for those in upper income brackets. In this way the inequities of income are reduced.

The principle of equality means that access to resources and assumption of obligations apply indifferently to *all* people. . . .

The Affirmation of Human Life. In opposition to the anxiety, pessimism, obsession with death, and escapism of much of bourgeois society, Soviet society is optimistic and life-affirming. For it, all significance for us is created by us *in this life* here and now—and by others in human history, workers past and future, who are linked to us by common struggle, labor, thought, love, art, and play. Human beings and their development—within the congenial environment of society and nature—are taken as final values.

Soviet socialism is inspired by daring ideals, and this daring is grounded in a hard-headed realism to match that and make it creative, effecting powerful changes in the material and social world. Theory and practice confirm the facts that (1) human begins have the possibilities for healthy, constructive development in creative interaction with others and nonhuman nature, and (2) that these possibilities *can* and *will* be realized in the course of human history.

The Soviet conviction in progress is grounded in their own 60-year historical experience as well as in their observation of and solidarity with struggles of workers and peasants in many countries. To win the civil war and the war of intervention (losing 13,000,000 people); to combat famine; to construct, from a poorly developed capitalist base, the foundation for a modern society in industry, agriculture, and other spheres of applied science and technology; to beat back the forces of fascism in the Great Patriotic War; to reconstruct the country which had lost over 20,000,000 people and one-third its industrial base—all that was almost superhuman. No people have had to struggle against so much and for so much in such a short time. Only an indomitable love of life—of their own persons, their families, their soil, their communities, their Socialist Motherland—would impel them to do so. While bourgeois nations elicited patriotic heroism from their soldiers and citizens in the war against fascism, the heroism of the Soviet people in that war reached a scale without parallel in human history.

Not only in their collective exertion to build a better material world do the Soviet people express their love of life. They express it also in their sports and recreation, in their appetite for travel and new experiences, and perhaps most of all in their hearty personal relations with one another and with people of other countries. Scientists, taxi drivers, elevator operators, hotel floor supervisors—they all love to converse, to find out about strangers and their families, to tell them about their families. They are the kind who make good neighbors—ready to give a hand in trouble, lending a sympathetic ear, tender and protective toward children. (A babe-in-arms in an elevator or shop is likely to create a minor sensation, as women of all ages cluster and buzz around to have a look, and, most of all, to hold it and play with it.) As much as any people, perhaps more, they love a good party, where food and drink, stories and jokes, talk and toasts, singing and dancing, bring people together in a union of feeling that complements and celebrates the union of common endeavor.

The Soviet love of people is carried out in acts that objectively help people to live and to fulfill themselves. I have already referred to the large network of collective institutions at home that do this. In foreign relations, we observe comparable objective activity in material and moral aid to national liberation movements and in the 60-year-old political movement for peaceful coexistence, disarmament, and detente. I recently thanked a prominent Soviet sociologist for organizing an international symposium on philosophy and social progress and for the expenditure of time and money on it. He spontaneously replied: "What is money compared to the cause of peace and the saving of mankind?"

The love of life and the longing for peace among the Soviet people reflects a new level of material and moral development in human history. Normally all peoples love life and long for peace. But when social and individual existence rise to the point where the great mass of people in a nation experience day by day in their family living, in their work, and in their national life as a whole the joy of collective work and fulfillment, that love and longing rise to a qualitatively new level. "The new person" exists in such large numbers in the Soviet Union that, taken together, they compose a powerful new social force among the 150 nations on our planet. That is a force that demands peace as a necessary condition for the life of all people, and that demands human life and its fulfillment as the final reason and value of why we are here.

The Full Development of Human Potentialities. Socialist society proceeds by concentrating on constructing an economy that will satisfy all survival needs—the needs for food, water, clothing, shelter, sanitation, medical care, safety, etc.—and at the same time assembling institutions that will provide resources and opportunities for people to fulfill distinctively human needs. These latter are the needs for interpersonal relations enjoyed for their own sake (friendship, love), for rest and relaxation, for esthetic creation and experience, for cognition, for play, for dreaming and meditation, for sensuous enjoyment, for selfless surrender, for gaiety. As work becomes more efficient through improved tools and machines, these needs with their corresponding values can be cultivated.

Thus we can see in Soviet history for the past 60 years a whole social organism developing, a whole ecological system, with first the ground being cleared of a rotten social system of poverty and oppression, then a physical basis laid down for modern technology, then a more and more easy and comfortable physical life for people, and gradually and simultaneously the release of human energies from social production into the domain of personal fulfillment.

Take two of the most elementary things, food and literacy. Food for *everyone*! That achievement is the Soviet people's own answer to their deep, desperate cry of "Peace, bread, and land!" 60 years ago. That achievement is unprecedented in human history. When I tell my American students this, they don't seem impressed, and the main reason, I think, is that they have never been hungry and don't vividly foresee they might be. But the hungry masses of the world have been impressed, and almost one-third of them have followed the lead of the Soviet Union into socialism—in their own ways, of course, as Lenin anticipated.

The first step to developed culture, after the care and the feeding of the body, is literacy. The Soviet people, between the two world wars, "accomplished more to raise the literacy of an entire nation than had ever before been achieved in all recorded history" (Carroll Atkinson and Eugene T. Maleska, *The Story of Education*, p. 179). Literacy opens the door to endless corridors of developed culture, the enrichment of consciousness, community with others, and scientific practice, the mark of developed humanity. That is the way of our true human fulfillment—of our true human history, as Marx called it.

Fulfillment includes not only the satisfaction of all our generic human needs. It is also the fulfillment of these needs in the aggregate and in unison, so as to realize what we call the unique human personality or character. That is the meaning of the communist principle "From each according to his abilities, to each according to his needs."

What happens to talents in the Soviet Union? Have a look. The arts—music, painting, sculpture, theater, dance, literature, architecture; the sciences, theoretical and applied; engineering; philosophy; athletics; military sciences; chess; space exploration; circuses; puppet theater; etc.—virtually all fields testify to the development of talent in such numbers and depth that makes it outstanding. What is notable in the Soviet Union is the scale on which talent is identified and educated. Soviet society is a planned society; hence the development of talent is planned.

In this 60-year-old collective movement toward equality of opportunity and fulfillment, in this affirmation of human life for all, the Soviet people have begun to create simultaneously a new person, a new society, and a new world. . . .

SOVIET VIEWS

6. 1917–1977: SIX DECADES OF PROGRESS*
Central Committee, CPSU

Six decades ago, Russia's heroic proletariat, led by the Bolshevik Party with Lenin at the head, launched a resolute assault on the bourgeois-landowner system and overthrew it. For the first time in history the struggle of the working people against exploitation and social and national oppression ended in complete victory.

The triumph of the October Revolution—the major event of the 20th century—radically changed the course of development of mankind. The Great October Socialist Revolution was a natural outcome of social development and class struggle in a society ruled by monopoly capital. The victorious Revolution gave birth to the world's first socialist

* Reprinted from *1917–1977 On the 60th Anniversary of the Great October Socialist Revolution* (Resolution of the CPSU Central Committee of January 31, 1977), Moscow: Novosti Press Agency Publishing House, 1977, pp. 3–23, by permission of the publisher and the Copyright Agency of the USSR.

state. . . . The Great October Revolution opened up a new era, an era of mankind's transition from capitalism to socialism, an era of struggle, as Lenin put it, "to liberate nations from imperialism, to put an end to wars among nations, to overthrow capital and to achieve socialism."

The October Revolution demonstrated in a profound and comprehensive manner the working class's great liberating role which is of world significance.

The victory of the October Revolution marked a historical turning point in the destinies of the peoples of our country.

The proletariat of multinational Russia was destined to play the difficult but at the same time honoured role of pioneer in the building of a new society. The working class, expressing the vital interests of the absolute majority of the people, and acting in alliance with the working peasantry, secured victory for the Revolution and took over power. The broadest sections of the working people, and all progressive workers in the field of science and culture, accepted the Revolution and followed the working class. . . .

The establishment and strengthening of Soviet power as a form of dictatorship of the proletariat ensured freedom and democracy for the great majority of working people, a kind of democracy which did not and could not exist in any capitalist country. . . . The conditions in which the building of a new society in our country began were marked by a low level of development of the productive forces and low cultural standards inherited from tsarist Russia, the predominance of small-commodity agricultural production, and the dire consequences of the First World War, the Civil War and foreign intervention. And the Soviet people had to accomplish that task in an extremely difficult situation, being encircled by hostile capitalist countries.

Within a historically brief period, socialist industrialization, collectivization of agriculture, a cultural revolution and a just and correct solution of the nationalities question transformed our homeland into a great socialist power.

Nazi Germany's treacherous attack interrupted the Soviet people's peaceful labour. In that long war, the grimmest of all our country had ever known, the Soviet people performed a feat which was unparalleled in history. They were able not only to defend their own freedom and independence, but also to contribute decisively to saving European and world civilization from destruction by the fascist barbarians.

After the Great Patriotic War had ended, in which they performed unprecedented feats, the Soviet people carried out heroic exploits in peaceful labour, rebuilding the cities, villages and industrial enterprises ravaged by the war.

The achievements of the homeland of the October Revolution over a period of six decades convincingly show that socialism has attained unprecedented rates of progress in all areas of life of society.

The country's economy had changed radically. Despite the fact that out of the 60 years of the Soviet state's existence the country had to spend nearly 20 years on fighting wars imposed on our people and on subsequent economic rehabilitation, its national income in 1976 was 65 times greater than before the Revolution. Today as many products are manufactured in two and a half days as were made in all of 1913.

Our country accounted for only slightly over four per cent of world industrial production before the Revolution; today its share is 20 per cent. The Soviet Union produces more pig iron, steel, oil, iron, manganese and chrome ores, coal and coke, cement, tractors (in aggregate engine capacity), diesel and electric locomotives, cotton, flax, mineral fertilizer, and many other goods, than any other country.

Social plagues such as hunger, poverty, unemployment, and social and national oppression, inherent in capitalism, have been eradicated once and for all in our country. The real incomes of industrial and construction workers are ten times higher than in 1913, and of farmers, 14 times. A colossal programme for the construction of housing and of cultural and communal services has been carried out. Most old cities have been rebuilt and many new ones have sprung up; the appearance of the countryside has changed. Today more new housing is turned over for tenancy in the country every two years than all of Russia's cities had before the Revolution. All Soviet citizens get free medical assistance and are guaranteed just social maintenance.

A social task of immense historical significance, that of ensuring women's genuine equality, has been accomplished in our country. Soviet women play an important role in all spheres of social life. The Soviet people deeply respect women as mothers, women as workers, women who are actively participating in the building of communism.

Socialism has provided unlimited access to knowledge and the riches of culture for working people. Nearly three-quarters of all adults were illiterate in pre-revolutionary Russia. Today over three-quarters of all working people in the country have a higher or a 10-year or 8-year secondary education. More than 93 million people are studying at all educational levels. The transition to universal 10-year secondary education has been completed in the main. Soviet literature and art are flourishing and are making a notable contribution to world culture.

Socialism has opened up limitless possibilities for the development of science and has made science serve the people. The country has nearly 1.3 million scientists, or 108 times more than in 1913. Soviet science has achieved major successes in the study of the processes of social development and it has reached the foremost frontiers in several fields of mathematics, mechanics, quantum electronics, solid-state physics, nuclear energy, chemistry, biology, space research, Earth sciences, and many other fields of knowledge.

The most important result of the Soviet people's dedicated work is a society of advanced socialism which has been built in our country. On the basis of a dynamic development of economy, the social mould of Soviet society has been changing and acquiring new features. Class distinctions are withering away, while the society's social composition is becoming more homogeneous. The alliance of the working class, the collective-farm peasantry and the people's intelligentsia, with the working class playing the leading role, has become a firm and unbreakable foundation for a new historical community that has been born in the country— the Soviet people.

The fraternal friendship and unity of all nations and nationalities that make up the great and strong Union of Soviet Socialist Republics are firm and solid. The formation of the USSR and its successful development are the triumph of the Leninist nationalities policy conducted by the CPSU, a striking evidence that this policy is truly internationalist, and a great gain of socialism. . . . Real equality of all nations and nationalities in all spheres of the society's activities has been ensured; a culture that is national in form and socialist in content has flourished, and a true fraternity of working men irrespective of their nationality, a fraternity cemented by common interests and goals, and by the Marxist-Leninist ideology, has been established. . . .

The Soviet man has been moulded and has matured in the course of creative revolutionary endeavours, in the struggle for freedom, and in the day-by-day work of building socialism. By his great labour feats and creative accomplishments, by his supreme staunchness and courage during the severe trials of the Great Patriotic War, and by his unselfish concern for the destinies of his class brothers throughout the world, the Soviet man has proved his profound devotion to the ideals of communism and his ardent patriotism and internationalism. He has combined ideological conviction and great energy, a constant striving for the summits of knowledge and culture, and the spirit of collectivism and comradely assistance. The Soviet man has a deep affection for his socialist homeland. His work for the cause of communism has become part and parcel of his life and he draws inspiration from it.

The present stage of development of Soviet society is characterized by the further strengthening and development of socialist statehood and by consistent improvement of socialist democracy.

Socialist democracy expresses and protects the people's interests and serves the cause of communism. It embraces all aspects of the life of society—economic, political and intellectual, and creates conditions for the all-round development of the individual. The Soviet people are the true and the sole master of the country. All major questions of the country's political, economic, social and cultural life are discussed, and decisions are made, with the broadest and direct participation of workers, farmers and intellectuals. The democratic nature of our society is most vividly seen in the many-sided activities of the Soviets of Working People's Deputies—the most representative organs of people's power. An important part in the life of Soviet society is played by trade unions which enjoy extensive rights and possibilities in solving social and economic problems. An active part is played by the Leninist Komsomol, an organizer of Soviet youth and a reliable assistant and reserve of the Party.

The entire heroic history of the Soviet people, their victories on the battlefield and on the work front, and their outstanding achievements cannot be separated from the work of the Communist Party, the leading and guiding force of our society.

The present period is characterized by a greater role of the Party in guiding society and by an intensification of its theoretical, political and organizational work. Of great importance in this respect is the fruitful and constructive work of the Central Committee of the CPSU and its Politburo headed by L. I. Brezhnev, General Secretary of the CPSU Central Committee, an outstanding political leader and statesman of our time, a faithful Marxist-Leninist and a tireless fighter for the cause of communism. . . .

Today, when the general crisis of capitalism has considerably deepened and its irreconcilable contradictions have become aggravated, the struggle against exploitation, against monopoly domination, and for democracy and socialism is steadily growing in scope. The proletariat is in the vanguard of this struggle. The strike movement, directed against exploitation, unemployment, the soaring cost of living, against the attempts to shift the burden of the economic crisis onto the shoulders of the working people, has reached its highest level in recent decades. Resistance to the reactionary policies of big business is growing. The fascist dictatorships in Portugal and Greece have collapsed. The Franco regime in Spain has disintegrated.

The colonial system of imperialism has disintegrated under the powerful pressure of the national liberation movement. . . .

The Soviet Union and other socialist countries are giving every support to the developing countries in their struggle to realize their legitimate aspirations, to free themselves completely from imperialist exploitation, to win the right to manage their own affairs. . . .

While firmly repulsing all the machinations of the enemies of peace and socialism, the Soviet Union and other fraternal socialist countries are at the same time working to further promote changes in the international situation that are favourable to peace and social progress, to make detente a continuous, an ever more effective, universal and an irreversible process embracing all continents, to bring about the transition to stable and fruitful peaceful cooperation among countries, and to achieve practical results in the field of disarmament—in the first place, nuclear disarmament. . . .

The October Revolution is a social and political event whose greatness stands out still more clearly and boldly as mankind advances along the road of social progress.

The epoch-making significance of the victory of the October Revolution and of the experience of real socialism is that they have provided an example of the most fair organization of society in the interests of the working people.

Socialism is a society of real humanism. Its chief value is the working man. Everything for the benefit of man, for the sake of man—this is the basic meaning of the new socialist way of life.

Socialism is a society of emancipated labour, of genuine democracy, of real freedom of the individual and of the most advanced science and culture. It abolishes all forms of oppression, guarantees the right to work, education, leisure and recreation, and full employment, and creates real possibilities for an all-round development of creative energy of every member of society.

Socialism is a society of social optimism. It gives the working man firm confidence in the morrow, in a happy future for his children, and in material security in old age.

Socialism brings the peoples new, equal relations, mutually advantageous cooperation and peace. It opens before the peoples of the developing countries, suffering from the consequences of colonialism and neocolonialism, the prospect of doing away with their economic backwardness within a historically short period, the prospect of social emancipation and all-round progress.

Socialist organization of economic, political and intellectual life has demonstrated that only socialism opens the way to solving the most important and outstanding problems of our time that affect all mankind. Socialism alone is capable of ridding mankind forever from the threat of an all-out, devastating war involving the use of weapons of mass annihilation, and of preserving and improving the natural environment.

The brightest hopes of working people of all countries are associated with socialism. In this lies the force of example of the October Revolution, and of the achievements of the Soviet Union and all the countries of the socialist community. . . . .

IV

The Soviet System of Government

"All power in the USSR belongs to the people."
CONSTITUTION OF THE USSR, ART. 2

"Led by the Leninist Party, the Soviet people are confidently advancing along the road of communist construction."
NIKOLAI A. TIKHONOV
Chairman, USSR Council of Ministers

"The legitimate object of government is to do for a
community of people whatever they need to have
done, but cannot do at all, or cannot do well, in their
separate individual capacities."
ABRAHAM LINCOLN

IN MUCH OF the Western world, and these days especially in the United
States, the Soviet system of government is seen as the polar opposite
of that prevalent in the U.S., Canada, Western Europe, Australia and
New Zealand. The conventional view holds that "theirs" is a dictatorship,
"totalitarian, undemocratic, and repressive," with little hope for meaningful change, as long as the Communists remain in power. "Ours" in
the "Free World," on the other hand, is a democracy, "pluralistic, representative, and open," with the government "the servant of the people
and not their master." But there are others in the West, among them
students of comparative social systems who, although non-Marxists themselves, hold such views to be gross exaggerations of differences between
East and West. To them, our system does not appear so perfect, nor the
Soviet system so evil as the conventional wisdom would have it. As regards the Soviet system, they do not deny the powerful role of the party
in a one-party governmental structure, the single list of candidates in
national elections, nor the existence of certain restrictions on free speech.
Advocacy of racial discrimination or of war, for instance, is prohibited

151

under Soviet law, and advocating a return to capitalism would be greatly discouraged, to put it mildly. Yet many such non-Marxist critics of the "conventional" position maintain nevertheless that the great majority of Soviet citizens stand behind the regime. Here is how one critic explains it:[1]

> Some may argue that political legitimacy has not been achieved in the Soviet Union, that the people there are cowed into silence, that they fear their government and grudgingly obey it rather than suffer suppression by the omnipresent KGB. This is a misreading of the nature of contemporary Soviet society. It may be depressing, or paradoxical, or simply incredible, but contemporary Soviet society is built upon a solid foundation of regime support. Coercion by the secret police cannot explain the wide acceptance of the regime's platitudes and promises by the Soviet man-in-the-street. For this one must turn to the regime's tight control and regulation of school curricula, supervision of the entire output of the mass media, isolation of the entire Soviet society from most outside (foreign) influences, and effective penetration of group activities to force individual conformity to regime-sponsored group norms. Of course, everyone knows that there are dissidents in Russia, that there is a *samizdat* (the underground, carbon-copy "press"), that writers have been tried and condemned for their "anti-Soviet" prose, that there is a Solzhenitsyn, that there was a Pasternak. We do not wish to disparage the importance of this phenomenon. Quite the contrary, we wish to stress the courage of the individuals involved, for they must fight not only the secret police, but also the orthodox indignation, or mere indifference of the vast majority of their fellow citizens. The small minority of dissidents, who have escaped the web of indoctrination, are isolated and rendered ineffective by the vast net of regime legitimacy which surrounds them in the "working masses."

Western pro-Soviet Marxists, however, go beyond such a position and argue that the USSR's social system is actually freer and more truly democratic than any to be found in the West.

This chapter concerns itself with the structure of the Soviet Union's political fabric. Part A deals with the role and the functions of the Communist Party of the Soviet Union (CPSU) which, East and West agree, represents the real center of power in the USSR. Part B scrutinizes the Soviet governmental apparatus proper, with special attention focused on the Supreme Soviet, the country's highest legislative body. Part C devotes itself to a brief analysis of the new, 1977, Soviet Constitution, the "fundamental law of the land." An extensive treatment of freedom, democracy and related issues as applicable to the USSR is relegated to the next chapter.

---

[1] Jerome M. Gilson, *British and Soviet Politics: Legitimacy and Convergence*, Baltimore: Johns Hopkins University Press, 1972, p. xi.

A
The Party

"The CPSU exists for the people and serves the people. The Communist Party determines the general perspectives of the development of society, the course of domestic and foreign policy, and directs the constructive work of the Soviet people."

NOVOSTI PRESS AGENCY

"As an orchestra conductor sees to it that all the instruments sound harmonious and in proportion, so in social and political life does the party direct the efforts of all people towards the achievement of a single goal."

NIKITA A. KHRUSHCHEV,
Former First Secretary, CC CPSU and Chairman,
USSR Council of Ministers

"To strengthen the unity of the Party and the people, to firmly follow the great Leninist behests—this is the pledge for all our future victories."

YURI V. ANDROPOV
Secretary-General, CC CPSU

Article 6 of the Constitution of the USSR states: "The leading and guiding force of Soviet society and the nucleus of its political system, of all state organizations and public organizations, is the Communist Party of the Soviet Union."

And so it is. Not a legislative, executive, or judicial branch of the Soviet government per se, but the Communist Party of the Soviet Union, the CPSU (and within the party, the Central Committee, the Politburo it elects from among its members, and the party head—the Secretary-General of the CPSU Central Committee) represents the real center of power and decision-making in the USSR. If a disagreement had ever arisen between Leonid Brezhnev, who headed the party from 1964 until his death in 1982, and Alexei Kosygin, who as chairman of the USSR Council of Ministers was the head of the government, there is little doubt that the head of the party would have prevailed. Similarly, today Yuri Andropov would surely have his way over Nikolai Tikhonov, who replaced Kosygin in October of 1980.

Less than 7 percent of the Soviet population—some 17.5 million

Soviet citizens in 1981—are members of the CPSU. But one would be sadly mistaken to assume that this apparently small percentage indicates lack of party support among the Soviet people. To understand why party membership is so restricted one has to understand the purpose, functions, and structure of the CPSU and, for that matter, of other *ruling* Communist parties as well.

There is a world of difference between such Western political parties as the American Democratic or Republican party on the one hand and the Communist Party of the Soviet Union on the other. The basic difference is that in the United States the citizen chooses his or her party; in the Soviet Union, the party chooses its members. In the United States, one becomes a Democrat or a Republican simply by saying that one is a Democrat or a Republican and voting in the primaries. The party has no right or power to tell members what to do or not to do or how to conduct themselves . . . it cannot penalize them, it cannot expel them. In 1980, if a Democrat joined "Democrats for Reagan," or a Republican "Republicans for Carter," or if either campaigned for Anderson or for any other minority-party candidate, there was really nothing the party could do about it. But the Communist Party of the Soviet Union is not that kind of party.

The CPSU is a selective, leadership party. Virtually all prospective members nowadays start preparing for possible party membership in their earliest childhood. Preschoolers join the Octobrists; once in school, they join the Young Pioneers, a sort of politically oriented and trained boy/girl scout organization. In their late teens they are eligible for membership in the *komsomol,* the party's youth auxiliary. Then, in their twenties, they may apply for membership in the party. Their application must be endorsed by three individuals who have been members of the CPSU for at least five years. If accepted, they then become candidate members of the party. During the probationary period, the aspiring members are tested for political, professional and moral qualities, and not all applicants make it. If any of those who are accepted as members subsequently prove themselves unworthy, they can be expelled from the party. Between 1975 and 1980, one-and-a-half million of the "finest members of the working class" were admitted to party membership; but 91,000 of the candidate members failed to make the grade and 300,000 members were expelled "for deeds incompatible with the name of Communist."[1]

Party membership is helpful, although not absolutely essential, for professional advancement. Even in the Supreme Soviet, the highest legislative governmental body in the USSR, a substantial minority are not party members; and at all levels of government, about half of elected and appointed officials are "non-Party Bolsheviks" (more recently also often

[1] L. I. Brezhnev, *Report of the Central Committee of the CPSU to the XXVI Congress of the Communist Party of the Soviet Union*, Moscow: Novosti Press Agency Publishing House, 1981, p. 69.

referred to as "non-Party people") which means that they basically sub-scribe to Marxist-Leninist ideology but have either not chosen to become party members or have not been accepted. Many Soviet citizens choose not to join the party because party membership does not have only ad-vantages; it also entails obligations and duties. There are frequent and time-consuming meetings, committees to serve on, special assignments to be carried out. Moreover, party members agree to dedicate themselves fully to the party and to place the interest of the cause, as interpreted by the party leadership, over and above their own personal interests. If, for instance, an industrial worker in Tashkent decides to move to Kharkov and find a job there, he is basically free to do so; but if he is a party member and the party tells him that he is needed in Tashkent, he must either remain there or take the consequence, which would usually mean forfeiture of his Party membership.

The party membership forms the base; it elects the delegates to the party Congress, the next echelon in the Soviet Union's power struc-ture; the party Congress, in turn, elects the Central Committee, currently approximately 360 strong, which, together with some less exalted party committees, is responsible for nominations and appointments to the so-called *nomenklatura*, the list of approximately 250,000 most important economic and political positions in the Soviet Union (such as newspaper editors, high trade union officials, directors of major enterprises, heads of research institutes, members of the Council of Ministers, etc.). Finally, the Central Committee elects from among its members the Politburo, that small group of individuals (at present, 13 full and nine nonvoting candidate members) which essentially determines and controls the domestic and foreign policies of the USSR. And on top of the power hierarchy is the secretary-general of the CPSU Central Committee, no longer the one-man ruler Stalin once was, but still the single most powerful individual in the country.

No one, East or West, really questions the leadership role of the CPSU. But how much power does it, its Central Committee, its Politburo, or its secretary-general really have? What is its role and what are its functions in the Soviet Union's governmental structure? How internally democratic is the party structure? How representative is the party of the true interests and aspirations of the Soviet people? What are the rights, what are the duties, and what are the moral convictions of its rank-and-file membership? The four Western and three Soviet selections in Part A of this chapter address themselves to these and related issues.

In the first selection, Mary McAuley, a self-styled Socialist but non-Marxist, investigates the political changes from the days when Stalin, as a virtually omnipotent potentate, ruled with an iron hand not so much through but over the party and the nation to more recent days when no single individual holds such power and when "even Khrushchev, at his zenith . . . could not prevent his own ouster." John N. Hazard, next, focuses on the internal power structure in the party and addresses himself specifically to questions of the extent of democracy and discipline within the rank and file, as seen through the eyes of a critical Western analyst. Robert G. Wesson, third, discusses the functions and purposes of the party and comments on special privileges, but also on limitations of power of the party elite. M. Lewin, in the final Western contribution, describes the main instruments and methods by which the party carries out its functions and perpetuates itself in power. Although critical overall, all four Western analysts would probably agree with the conclusion reached by one of their colleagues that the "Soviet leadership does seem to have presided over the evolution of a viable political model."[2]

In the fifth selection, the first under "Soviet Views," the Novosti Press Agency presents the official Soviet position on the achievements of the party, its role in Soviet society, its composition and leadership, and the "democratic principles" by which it operates. The sixth and seventh selections respectively deal with the "moral code of the builders of communism," as spelled out in the Party Programme, and the duties and rights of party members as decreed in the 1966 revision of the Communist party rules and reaffirmed by party Congresses since.

WESTERN VIEWS

---

1. POLITICAL CHANGE SINCE STALIN*
Mary McAuley
University of Essex

(I)

With the industrialization and collectivization campaigns at the end of the twenties, the leading party organs took direct control of an economic transformation of society. Central planning of the distribution of resources, control of the means of coercion and communication—all were concentrated in the hands of one authority. In other words, we have the emergence of an extremely powerful central authority.

As the thirties progess, the form of this central authority changes. One man—Stalin—emerges as the unquestioned leader. Enveloped in a cult, he stands above a number of huge hierarchical institutions, centered

---

[2] Roy D. Laird, *The Soviet Paradigm*, New York: The Free Press, 1970, p. xix.
* Reprinted from Mary McAuley, "Political Change Since Stalin," *Critique* No. 2, Spring, 1974, pp. 23–36, by permission of the author and the Editorial Board of *Critique*.

in Moscow, and subordinate finally to him alone. These institutions, the most important of which were the secret police, the party apparatus, the military and the big industrial ministries, overlapped with one another in the sense that personnel from the first two worked in all different types of organizations, but at the same time vied with each other for their share of resources, for the extension and maintenance of their authority. Thus, although centralized and overlapping, the big institutions developed into separate empires and it was Stalin, at the top, who held them together. All, in terms of personnel, suffered badly in the purges. And as an institution the party lost its position as the dominant authority in society. It was relegated to being merely one of the organizations responsible for executing policy. . . . Policies were made by Stalin, in conjunction with one or two leading individuals, to be passed down and obeyed blindly. Policies originated at the top, there was no public discussion, no discussion of alternatives. . . .

The industrialization campaign, which began in the late twenties, entailed drastic social change: with the shift of resources into industry, we have the creation of an industrial labour force out of peasant or previously unemployed labour; in the course of twenty years, the rural population shrinks to half the total population; a new Soviet intelligentsia is trained. In other words, the political changes that occurred or the kind of political edifice that characterized the Stalin period was constructed against the background of an industrial revolution. If one couches the discussion in such general terms as these, it appears that we have two separate phenomena—the industrial transformation of a society and the shift from party-rule to an extraordinary one-man dictatorship—which do not necessarily relate one to another.

(II)

By the late twenties the Bolshevik leadership had accepted that resources for investment were not going to come from outside and were not going to come from voluntary saving. Some sections of society, at least, were going to have to forgo present consumption; this would involve decisions from above and means of enforcing them. Furthermore, given that they wished to change the pattern of production, the structure of the economy, they had to find means to achieve this. Any such change involves the reallocation or movement of labour. How were they to bring about the desired redistribution? The options open to them (and indeed to anyone desiring to affect change) were material incentives, coercion or the direction of labour, and moral incentives. If moral incentives are not working, then one is left with a choice between coercion and material incentives or a combination of the two. From the beginning of the 30s, the Soviet leadership used all three. It was also necessary to devise a system for directing and managing the economy. The leadership had accepted that

all the individual producing units, if left alone were not going to produce
the kind of increase in GNP or social wealth that they wished for. Some
kind of aggregate decision-making was necessary and a method of executing decisions that would ensure they were carried out. Given the unpopularity of the decisions, some kind of hierarchical system of directives
or incentives, or a combination of both seemed the obvious 'rational'
solution.

       Thus, the means that the Soviet leadership adopted in initiating the
industrialization campaign ran counter to some of the original aims of the
revolution, and posed problems for others. . . . Central planning and control of resources and a hierarchical system of administration dealt a final
blow to social control from below, and increased the number of officials
administering the system. But the point to be made here is that the way
in which the leadership used these 'new' or 'necessary' means was extreme. . . . What was happening to society affected the party in a number
of different ways. A few of them are worth mentioning. Firstly, within
the party, one had the emergence of sectional interests and competition
for resources between those responsible for different sectors; secondly,
there was the increasing use of the party as an administrative machine
by the leadership (a return in some ways to civil war methods) whereby
one's duties as a party member were simply to obey orders swiftly without
questioning; and thirdly, at the same time, at least among some sections,
a growing unease at the unexpected drop in consumption, the obsession
with investment, and the plight of the peasants. As it turned out, Stalin
solved the problem by decimating the party, ending its role as a decision-
maker, and reducing it to merely part of the administrative mechanism,
with authority to act at lower levels as a coordinator of activity and watch-
dog. . . .

       From 1936–37 until his death, the Soviet Union had in Stalin one
'wise' leader who stood above all the competing, specialized factions; he
could discover the correct policies, those which served the social interest
as defined by him. This solution to the decision-making problem had certain consequences. Firstly, since only the leader was responsible for defining what were socially desirable goals and deciding what was the best
way to achieve them, subordinates concentrated entirely on their specific
tasks and ignored any wider questions. Their world was limited to their
little empire; their position depended upon its importance and its success
in fulfilling tasks set from above. This encouraged thinking in sectional
terms. Secondly, since the leader alone was responsible for initiating policy, to propose a change was unwise in that it implied a criticism of the
present policy produced by Stalin; it was in one's interest to suggest that
all was well. As a consequence the dictator would and did tend to produce
the same package deal, unless faced by a drastic situation which could
no longer be hidden from him. Furthermore, it was physically impossible

for one man to follow or take an interest in all aspects of policy. Again
he would tend only to intervene in an emergency, or in a purely arbitrary
fashion. He would tend to rely on on-going policies. Under such a system
existing institutions strengthen their position and existing priorities
harden. Thus, for example, we find the temporary aims of the first five-
year plan—notably the relation between investment and consumption and
the stress on heavy industry—becoming untouchable principles; we find
the aim of securing grain reserves for the state (which was only one of
the original aims behind collectivization) becoming the be-all and end-all
of agricultural policy. We find an acceptance of income differentials and
a privileged position for those in administrative or other elite positions.

In summary, the Stalinist system posited certain relatively simple
goals (the growth of the major branches of heavy industry and military
might), and used methods to achieve these which were pretty effective,
i.e. there was one policy maker who stated that this was in the social
interest, and no questions were asked; it employed a hierarchical system
of directives plus coercion and fear, plus an incentive system geared to
increase production of these goods (the less important branches mopped
up what was left). The communist party's task was to see that the priorities
were observed and to coordinate activity at lower levels. . . .

(III)

Against this background, I now want to look at the political changes that
have occurred since Stalin's death. The following seem to me the most
important: the ending of terror, the replacement of a one-man dictatorship
by collective leadership or shifting coalitions, the introduction of new
policies accompanied by the existence of public discussion, albeit limited,
of policy alternatives, and the reemergence of the party as the dominant
political authority. That these are related one to another can be seen if
we look at them in some detail. To do this we have to begin by looking
at the actions of the top leadership, following Stalin's death. The kind of
political situation which existed was one in which the actions of individuals at the top could have far-reaching consequences, it was one in which
initiative was going to come from inside the leadership. In the post-Stalin
environment, control was so tight and any experience of organizing from
below so slight that it is hard to see changes being effected from below.
The initiative lay with the new leaders and the question they were faced
with was "what shall we replace Stalin with?" It took perhaps ten years
for the question to be answered, for a new status-quo to emerge, one in
which lines of authority are fairly well-established and the main direction
of policy clearly discernible. But it is an uneasy situation and one which
has presented the leadership with far more problems than, I think, they
ever expected.

Whether one is talking of the Stalin or the contemporary period, it remains true that the leadership, controlling as it does the allocation of resources in a centrally-planned economy, the means of communication and coercion, and exempt from any elective system, is a much more powerful institution vis-a-vis the rest of society than its counterparts in the west. This is important because it affects the way political change takes place. On the one hand, scope for political initiative lies to a much greater extent within the hands of a relatively small group and it is freer to act than its western counterpart; on the other, the rigid system which enables it to retain its position limits its scope of action. . . . In referring to the abolition of terror, I mean the end to arbitrary arrest and sentencing as it existed under Stalin. Then any action or lack of it could lead to arrest, which was unpredictable. Since the mid-fifties the individual or official has had a pretty good idea of the kind of behaviour that merits the attention of the secret police. If he is brought in for questioning, it will be for something he is aware of. . . .

The effect of the ending of terror had important consequences at the top—on the way the leadership is formed and remains in office, and on the formation of policy. With the liquidation of Beria[1], the way lay open for policy disagreements within the leadership and the need to form internal coalitions to try to get policy through. . . .

Under Stalin it was he who found the 'correct' policy—that which was best and which, therefore, would be accepted by all right-minded people. After his death, no one individual had the stature to be able to claim that his policy was the correct one; furthermore conflicting proposals were being put forward. In this situation it was desirable to produce evidence for the correctness of one's proposals and evidence, naturally, consisted in the support verbal and otherwise of as many influential people as possible and a sprinkling of the 'masses'. By influential is meant those who occupied leading positions within their own hierarchies—ministers, party officials, academics, specialists. This is not to suggest that suddenly there was a free-for-all in the discussion of policy proposals; on the contrary, some policies—notably those relating to the curbing of the secret police—were taken without wider discussion, and the securing of alliances within the Politburo was still undoubtedly the major preoccupation of individual members. However, what is true is that a new element had been introduced. An individual who could claim and produce support for his proposals was, *ceteris paribus*, in a stronger position than his colleague who had none.

---

[1] Lavrenti Pavlovich Beria, member of the Politburo, commissar for internal affairs and head of the secret police under Stalin, was arrested on July 10, 1953, four months after Stalin's death, and charged with "criminal anti-Party and anti-State activities." In December, 1953, it was announced that he had been convicted of high treason and executed. [Editor's note.]

Since 1957 three factors—careful attention to colleagues' views, promotion of supporters to key positions, and the gaining of support from influential organizations or spokesmen—have been important in deciding both specific policy issues and the question of the leadership. Since 1957 the top leader, be it Khrushchev or Brezhnev, has had to take all three into account. He may be able on a particular issue, to win by relying on one, but he cannot rely on it permanently nor afford to make a practice of it. Even Khrushchev, at his zenith, failed to get certain policies through and, finally, could not prevent his own ouster. Despite the greater sharing of top offices that has characterized the post-Khrushchev leadership, and the care taken to prevent any one individual building up a dominant group of his own supporters within the Politburo, the factors that govern political leadership have not changed in any important respects since 1957. Hence to contrast the present 'collective leadership'[2] with Khrushchev's 'one-man rule' is misleading. The political style may have changed and some of the policies but, as an institution, the Politburo's position vis-a-vis other institutions has not changed, and the individuals within it rely on the same factors to retain their places. What held the Brezhnev-Kosygin administration together (and what holds the Andropov-Tikhonov administration together now) is the extent of agreement between the leading individuals on policy or, perhaps, the unwillingness of any of them to propose major policy changes that would split the leadership. . . .

(IV)

The remaining important change to be considered is the re-emergence of the party as the dominant political authority. Whereas under Stalin the party, secret police, military and ministers jostled uneasily together, today the party stands pre-eminent. It is within the top echelons of the party that decisions affecting the leadership are taken; the party apparatus controls appointments and acts as the main executive branch; its network of party groups flung across society provides the base of the organization. But although the form the party takes, its organizational structure and its dominant position may be reminiscent of a pre-Stalin period, it is the product of a different environment. Hence it is misleading to talk of the re-emergence of the party if this is taken to imply the rebirth of the same institution.

Today's party dominates because it has either absorbed other institutions, or because they have been abolished, or because of a combination of the two. The political leadership brought the secret police and military under its control, decimated the police as an institution, called

---

[2] Brezhnev-Kosygin until October, 1980, Brezhnev-Tikhonov afterwards, and Andropov-Tikhonov since Brezhnev's death. [Editor's note.]

itself a party leadership and then, under Khrushchev, elevated the status of the apparatus. The abolition of the big, industrial ministries[3] further enhanced the latter's position. But what do the new party structures consist of? To what extent do they resemble the old? If one looks at the Central Committee which began to re-emerge, at least as a consultative body, one finds that there are representatives from the apparatus, the ministries, secret police and military, from the trade unions and republics, and a sprinkling of other institutions. Thus in the Central Committee are brought together, under the party umbrella, a cross section of high-ranking officials. The disparate institutions have, in this sense been merged together to form a new authority, which only in name resembles the old.

At the same time the old apparatus itself has been changing. Since the mid-fifties the leadership has followed a policy of recruiting professional specialists into the apparatus and demanding specialization within it. As might be expected this has not been an altogether smooth process—there have been frictions between the different types of apparatchik and some confusion over what is expected of an official. But I think it true to say that the leadership views the apparatus and more particularly the future of the apparatus as being one of professional-technical people with expertise in particular areas.

Given both the new political structures at the top and the changing apparatus, the reintroduction of the ministries does not affect the situation. They assume the place of a new branch of the civil service, subordinate to politicians of the Politburo or secretariat. The lobbies or groupings that one would expect to find would be sectional ones (secretariat official responsible for chemicals plus minister for chemicals versus the steel lobby) rather than party officials versus ministerial officials.

In theory, the party, containing as it does representatives of the different groups or classes (and I say groups because of attention paid to this in recruitment) unites them all, and serves the social interest. . . . The trouble is that the more initiative or criticism is allowed, the more the disagreements become apparent. In the attempt to include in the party all sections of society, the leadership produces a party which reflects the social chequerboard of competing units and conflicting views. (This is not meant to suggest that party composition reflects social composition. Of course it does not—with its heavy relative weighting in favour of the intelligentsia. The trend towards increasing the proportions of workers in the party does not seem to be significant in any way—given that decision-

---

[3] Under Khrushchev, the economy's administration by branches of industry, headed by industrial ministries, was replaced by regional administration, with the country subdivided into 105 economic areas, each under the jurisdiction of a regional economic council (*sovnarkhoz*). After Khrushchev's ouster, the *sovnarkhozy* were abolished and the industrial ministries again took up their traditional roles, somewhat modified by "economic reforms" which gave somewhat greater decision-making power at the micro-level to the industrial enterprises themselves and, more recently, to enterprise associations which stand between the ministries and the enterprises. [Editor's note.]

making within the party is reserved for the intelligentsia.) If one did have
genuine party democracy, the party would disintegrate into fragments.
Hence the leadership must continue with hierarchical control within the
party and tight limits on discussion both to safeguard its own position and
to hold the party together as an institution since it is not clear that anything
else holds it together.

2. THE COMMUNIST PARTY: THE HARD CORE OF THE SOVIET SYSTEM OF GOVERNMENT*

John N. Hazard
Columbia University

A description of the Soviet system of government must begin differently
from an account of North American or West European democracy. The
latter would focus upon the operation of instruments through which the
public expresses its will. Western political scientists are now centering
their attention upon pressure groups, upon parliaments and their committees, upon law which enables the individual to speak his mind without
fear of retaliation. Soviet parliamentary institutions and pressure groups
work differently, for these serve as focal points from which the influence
of leaders is radiated throughout the populace. Only informally do strata
with specific interests exert influence upon policy formulation. The key
to the functioning of the Soviet system is the leadership group. The 1977
Soviet Constitution (Art. 6) reaffirms this fact. Study must begin, therefore, with the Communist Party.

While the Communist party is called a "political party" in textbooks from the U.S.S.R. and from elsewhere abroad, it is so different
from Western political parties that some Westerners have suggested that
another term be invented for it. A look at the characteristics of the Communist party as a political organization will both indicate its distinguishing
elements and help to suggest the features of Western political parties that
are essential to preservation of intra-party democracy and of a political
party's function in a democratic system of government.

The key terms in any characterization of the Communist party are
"centralized structure" and "discipline." Armies, too, are structured centrally and require discipline of the troops. . . . Yet the Communist party
would not attract members if it were structured completely on army

* Excerpts reprinted from John N. Hazard, *The Soviet System of Government,* 5th Edition,
Chicago: University of Chicago Press, 1980, pp. 15–28 and, 38, by permission of the author
and the University of Chicago Press, © 1957, 1960, 1964, 1968, 1980 by the University of
Chicago.

lines. . . . Ever since the American and French revolutions, too many people, even in Russia, have dreamed of democracy and of mass determination of policy to be attracted to a political party without a show of these.

Thus the leaders of the Communist party have found it necessary to provide a mechanism through which the rank-and-file members appear to have the opportunity to choose their own leaders and to influence policy. Having created this mechanism in a form susceptible of democratic use, they have felt it necessary to devise a subtle system of counterweights to prevent an overturn of their leadership and an adoption of policies contrary to their desires. The Communist leaders have devised a name for this system of mass participation subject to counterweight control. They have called it "democratic centralism."

THE FORMALITIES OF COMMUNIST PARTY STRUCTURE

How is the system operated? The democratic feature comprises two elements, the first of which is the choice of officers. Party members at the level that would be called a platoon in an army are given the formal right to elect every year their "secretary of the primary party organization." The party members in the primary organization, who may be as few as three or as many as three hundred, also are given the formal opportunity to choose delegates at intervals to attend periodic conferences of delegates from primary party organizations within a geographical area corresponding to a county or a large city. These conferences meet seldom, being required by the Communist party rules to convene only at two-year intervals. When the delegates meet they choose from their number a smaller group, called a "committee," to meet every three months. This committee proceeds to select its executive bureau, including several secretaries, who must be confirmed in office by the provincial committee. One of the secretaries is designated "first secretary," and, in practice, it is he who runs the bureau and the affairs of the committee in general.

The large conference of delegates from the party organizations within the various counties and large cities also elects a delegate to attend periodically, at intervals of two or three years, a superior meeting called a "provincial conference," or, in the small republics not divided into provinces, a "republic congress. . . .

When the provincial party conference meets, its delegates take steps similar to those taken in the various county conferences. They choose their own "committee," which, in turn, selects an executive bureau including several secretaries. The provincial committee meets only every four months, but its executive bureau is on call at all times. The provincial party conference in each of the four larger republics also selects a group of delegates to proceed, at five-year intervals, to the capital of the republic within which the province or very large city is situated. Again the same procedure is followed in the choice of an executive body: the republic congress chooses a committee, called in this instance a "central committee," and the central committee then chooses an executive bureau including several secretaries. The delegates to the republic party congress also name a group of delegates to proceed to the quinquennial all-Union congress in Moscow.

To this pattern of ever higher party bodies leading up through the republics to Moscow, an exception is provided by the largest republic, that comprising the Great Russian ethnic element of the population. In this large republic, called the Russian Soviet Federated Socialist Republic, stretching from Leningrad across Siberia to Vladivostok, there is no republic party congress. The various provincial party conferences send their delegations directly to the all-Union meeting in Moscow. . . .

The All-Union meeting in Moscow, composed of delegates from republic party congresses and from the various provincial conferences of the Russian Republic, is called "The All-Union Communist Party Congress." It is of very large size. It has always been large, and since 1961 has been increased threefold with a change in ratio of delegates to party members. At the twenty-fifth congress of 1976, 4,998 delegates represented the 15,694,187 full and candidate members.[1] Being large, its importance seems to outsiders as more symbolic than real, for no floor debates or divided votes occur. Still, the congress has utility. For the leadership, it periodically legitimates its role by providing public evidence of rank and file support. For the delegates, it provides an opportunity to see and meet leaders; to gain orientation in political, economic and social problems by listening to reports; to share experience with peers during corridor and hotel conversations; and, perhaps most importantly, to sense the exhilaration of being recognized as an important cog in a machine proclaimed from the congress tribune as infallible and invincible. This experience can contribute to morale when the delegate returns home to find often frustrating tasks requiring party guidance for solution.

The All-Union Communist Party Congress chooses by vote its own "committee" to conduct the policy-making function between congresses. It is called the Central Committee of the Communist Party. As named in 1976 at the twenty-fifth congress, it numbered 288 members and 139 alternates, the latter having no vote but enjoying the right to attend meetings. Vacancies among the voting members are filled from the alternate panel. The congress also names a "central auditing committee" to monitor finances.

The Central Committee chooses its steering committee from its own members, in accordance with party tradition dating from pre-revolutionary Russia. As *Political Buro* its task was then, and remains today, direction of highest policy. . . . Its membership consisted of 13 members

[1] As of early 1983, party membership was close to 18 million. [Editor's note.]

and 9 candidates in late 1979. It is the key policy making institution of the party.

Ostensibly to provide rotation in positions on the executive bodies at each level within the party, the 1961 rules introduced a requirement of rotation in office and in 1966 the principle of rotation was reaffirmed. . . .

What has been a considerable staff or "apparatus" serves the Central Committee as a secretariat, headed by a "General Secretary" and including a varying number of "secretaries"—in 1978, ten. Although this staff has been reduced under resolution of the twentieth party congress after Stalin's death, it seems still to number about one thousand. It is divided into sections, each headed by a secretary or some member of the Central Committee. Several of the secretaries are also members of the Political Buro, and they wield much more power than might be supposed from the example of secretarial positions elsewhere. . . .

CONTROLS WITHIN THE PARTY

The creation of a hierarchy of party agencies is an attempt to meet the desire of the rank and file to share in the selection of its leaders. Share they do, yet there are controls so that this selection cannot result in the overturn of the leaders. . . .

One measure of control is inherent in the nature of this very hierarchy. Because there are no direct elections of top Communist party officials, a wave of mass discontent over party leadership would have to exist for several years and sweep almost the whole country to be reflected in the top echelons. The rank and file can influence only the choice of their committee and of their delegate to the next higher party conference. By their committee they are insulated even from selection of the party secretary, who in practice controls the destiny of a primary party organization. Top party officials are chosen by the small Central Committee of the party, and this in turn can be reconstituted only once in five years by The All-Union Party Congress. . . .

A second measure of control lies in the nominating and electing procedure within the party. Nominations are prepared by the first secretary at the level of the primary party organization and by the executive bureau at higher levels. These individuals can, and usually do, assure their own election by placing only their own names on the ballot. . . .

SELECTION OF PARTY MEMBERS

A third measure of control, in addition to the intraparty measures of the multi-stepped system of elections and the self-nominating procedure adopted for these, lies in a careful selection of candidates from among those who express their desire for party membership. Not every applicant is admitted to membership. In 1978 the total party membership constituted only about 9 per cent of the adult population of the U.S.S.R.

The small number of members in the Communist party is the result of a selection system devised to eliminate from consideration all but those most devoted to the cause of the party—those who can be expected to be willing and able to accept party discipline. The selection process is placed within the authority of primary party organizations, which are established at places of employment such as factories, government offices, collective or state farms, divisions of railways, large department stores, universities, and army units. The Communist party leaders have indicated their feeling that those who know a person at work know a great deal about him because the good and the bad in a man or a woman appear more clearly at work than in social activities. Application for candidate membership must be filed, therefore, with the primary party organization at the applicant's place of work, and he is judged by those who in party thinking know him best.

An application must be accompanied by recommendations from three persons who have been members of the Communist party for at least five years. These are not lightly given, because those who recommend and vouch for a candidate are subject to penalties, including loss of their own Communist party membership, if he proves to be a serious misfit within the party. . . .

When an application has passed the scrutiny of the primary party organization to which it is delivered, it is reviewed by the district committee of the county or big-city Communist party conference to which the primary party organization concerned sends a delegate. If this superior, and presumably more reliable, body approves the recommendation of admission made by the primary party organization, the applicant has passed the first barrier. He is not yet a member of the party, for he must prove his worth during a period of trial.

During a candidate's period of trial, which is currently established at one year, he is subjected to rigid tests in the form of duties such as propagandizing with party doctrine groups among whom he circulates. If he shows himself to be well disciplined and effective, he is admitted to full membership by the primary party organization in which he has been a candidate, but only after repeating all the steps required for his original admission to candidacy. If, after one year, discussion within the primary party organization concludes that a candidate has not proved himself worthy of membership, and if the county or city party committee agrees, he is dropped from candidacy and returns to the ranks of non-party people from which he came. . . .

In its formalized selection of members the Communist party reveals one of the primary distinctions between itself and the mass political parties familiar to the student of politics in the United States and in many other countries. In the West, parties other than the Communist party generally provide no such process for the selection of members. In most parties there is required no more than a declaration of membership, and there is no obligation to perform duties or to accept any form of discipline. Even representatives of these parties within the various parliaments or congresses of the West generally consider themselves free to oppose their leaders if they think that a decision has been unwise.

LIMITATIONS ON EXPRESSION OF OPINION

The extent to which opinion may be expressed on matters of policy has come to be a measure of a democratic system of government, and the designers of the Communist party have found it necessary to provide a semblance of honor of this measure both to hold the loyalty of party members and to attract outsiders into the ranks. Again, however, there seems to have been a problem of providing a means for popular expression of opinion and at the same time of devising a counterweight. The party leaders seem to want to be sure that expressions of opinion will never result in the adoption of a policy before the highest officers of the Communist party have had an opportunity to consider its prospective influence upon the course of events.

In defining democratic centralism, the rules drawn up by the Communist party leaders and adopted formally by The All-Union Communist Party Congress establish the outlines of the control mechanism. Every party member is given the formal right to express his opinion within the group to which he belongs, whether it be his primary party organization or a higher-level conference to which he is a delegate. This right is widely advertised by the Communist party press as indicative of the democratic character of the Communist party.

Having given the formal right of free speech to party members within their organizations, the draftsmen of the party rules provided a counterweight. The rules declare that members shall not be permitted to form a voting bloc, known in party parlance as a "faction," within the organization to which they belong. This restriction means that while a member is permitted to rise in his place and speak his mind at a party meeting, he may not have consulted with friends in advance to solicit their support of his views so that his speech will not be the solitary one on the subject he espouses. Nor may he have bargained with others to vote for his project in exchange for his subsequent vote in favor of some project dear to their hearts. . . .

There is yet another formal counterweight to the democratic right of free speech guaranteed to individual members within the party. It lies in the obligation established by the rules that when a decision has been taken, it is binding upon all those who shared in it, even if they voted against it on the floor. They are not permitted to argue for its reversal until it has been tried to the satisfaction of the leaders. The decision is binding upon them until opened again for discussion.

DISCIPLINE FOR PARTY MEMBERS

Discipline within the Communist party is enforced in two principal ways, by persuasion and by punishment of violators. Persuasion plays a part greater than is often appreciated outside the U.S.S.R., for though the Communist party is a relatively small core of persons guiding the destinies of the entire country and thus attracts people who enjoy the perquisites of power, there are here, as among any group of leaders, not only those who enjoy a sense of power but also those who have a sense of mission. It is upon those individuals who seek admission to, and continue within, the party because they have a sense of mission that persuasion especially acts as a means of enforcing discipline. These have joined voluntarily, and they remain voluntary. To be sure, if they resigned they would be considered "quitters" and would lose favor both with those whom they left behind in the party and also with millions more who have not desired or could not gain membership but who accept party values. But while such social opprobrium is to be reckoned with before resigning, there is a still stronger force for those who feel a sense of mission—the force created by a consuming interest, without which life would not be worth living.

To those who have entered the Communist party with a sense of mission, the party leaders who seek to win them to a point of view have only to explain policy in terms of improving conditions within the U.S.S.R. and even, eventually, throughout the world—the declared mission of the party. If the explanation is well phrased and convincing, it will be seized upon and incorporated as a design for living without serious question. For such persons, persuasion is a mighty instrument of control, and the training of Communist party secretaries, on whom the primary burden of persuasion rests, includes a very extensive portion of the art of effective public speaking.

Punishment awaits those party members who feel less or no sense of mission and are not persuaded by argument to accept the orders of their superiors within the party. It takes several forms. There are the moderate forms of admonition, reprimand, and censure, which are entered on the registration card. There is also the harsher form of reduction to candidate status for one year. The most severe form consists of expulsion from the party: for the disillusioned party member who has compelling personal reasons for remaining within the party while disliking official policy, the threat of expulsion is a strong incentive to conform. . . .

Members of the Central Committee of the party, and of the executive committees at each lower level within the party hierarchy, are protected against disciplinary action by the primary party organization to which they belong. Under the rules, penalties may be exacted of such persons only if approved at a full meeting of the Central Committee or of the executive committee concerned, and then only when a two-thirds majority consents. The leadership has thus assured itself of no surprise from below.

While expulsion and eclipse of political opponents in the Soviet manner is shocking to Westerners accustomed to parliamentary procedures created to assure respect for dissident views, the analyst who fails to draw comparisons with Stalin's procedures will miss what is happening in the Soviet Union. There is a growing sense of moderation, still far short of what is expected in a stable government in the West, but one which has reached a point of qualitative difference in the politics of the Communist party. It is the intellectuals who are forcing the change, and it is their influence within the party to which moderates look to prevent a slipping back into old techniques.

3. THE PARTY AND ITS LEADERSHIP ELITE: MORE CONTINUITY THAN CHANGE*

Robert G. Wesson
Hoover Institution

It is easy to define the Communist Party of the Soviet Union as an organization composed of recognized members and candidate members, who officially totaled 16,203,446 in November 1977. However, this definition is hardly satisfactory. The membership never acts as a body, and the ordinary members have slight influence or initiative; very little is known of them beyond a few unreliable statistics. For most political purposes, the party consists of the apparatus, the professional party people, a self-selected and fairly clearly set-off group consisting of about 1.5 percent of the membership, that directs and guides the entirety and through it Soviet society. If these members form the elite, the essential nucleus is what Lenin called the "Old Guard" of the party, the oligarchy currently composed of about twenty-five men at the summit of power—the Politburo plus the Secretaries of the Central Committee. In his time Lenin was equated with the party in the minds of many; and in Stalin's day, the dictator with his coterie was almost equivalent to the party.

On the other hand, there is no real reason to draw a line at formal

* From Robert G. Wesson, *Lenin's Legacy: The Story of the CPSU*, Stanford, Calif.: Hoover Institution Press, 1978, pp. xv–xvi and 255–69. Reprinted by permission of the publishers, Hoover Institution Press. Copyright © 1978 by the Board of Trustees of the Leland Stanford Junior University.

membership in the CPSU. The Komsomol, the youth auxiliary of the party, is a kindred organization through which young people normally pass on the way to party careers. Members, especially leaders, of trade unions, and activists in local councils or soviets and many other organizations, are· *ipso facto* affiliated with the party. In a sense, all Soviet citizens are party-bound in that they are expected to respect and serve the party, the sovereign institution of their lives. In Lenin's words, which are frequently cited in the contemporary Soviet press. "The Party is the intelligence, honor, and conscience of our era." It is the focus of the Soviet world, around which nearly everything revolves.

The Communist Party of the Soviet Union also has branch parties, such as the Ukrainian, Tadzhik, and Lithuanian parties, that are integrated into its structure. Nearly a hundred offspring are informally joined to it. All non-Soviet Communist parties are directly related to Lenin's party; most of them were formed by Comintern or Soviet agents and shaped in accordance with Lenin's conditions and in imitation of his example. Some of these, the parties of Mongolia, North Korea, Poland, East Germany, Czechoslovakia, Hungary, Romania, and Bulgaria, were lifted to power by Soviet forces; with the partial exception of the Romanian party, they remain relatively faithful to the wishes and policies of the CPSU. Parties that came to power largely or entirely on their own, those of Yugoslavia, Albania, China, and Indochina, are independent or hostile, but they continue to revere the founder, Lenin. The Cuban party, too, was a child of the Leninist family before Castro adopted it as a vehicle of his rule. The many nonruling parties are mostly loyal to the Soviet Fatherland of the Workers; many of them amount to branches of the Soviet party.[1]

The influence of Lenin's party is much broader still. Many parties that avoid overt identification with the Soviet-led Communist movement, and a large fraction of intellectuals, especially of Third World countries, are Communist, or leftist, oriented. The Marxism of most of the world is not Social Democratic but Leninist in inspiration.

Whatever we may think of Lenin's party, it has proved itself effective. Against competitive philosophies, it gained power and held it when few thought this possible. It made a new, and in many ways pathbreaking, government, won the civil war, and transformed its great realm socially and economically according to preconceived ideas to an extent never before attempted by any state. The party could acquire the status it did only because it genuinely fulfilled important functions and did not operate solely for its members and direct beneficiaries. . . .

"The Communist Party incorporates the collective intelligence, will, and wisdom of the Soviet people. The destiny and aspirations of the

---

[1] Mostly, perhaps, but it no longer holds true for the large nonruling Communist parties of Europe. [Editor's note.]

Soviet people are fused forever with their beloved party, and their great deeds in the making of the communist society.''[2] Whether or not the Soviet peoples are married forever to their beloved party, it is clear that the organization founded by Lenin has become an extraordinarily powerful and effective instrument for the guidance and governance of an immense domain. As it has taken shape under Lenin and Stalin and matured to the settled times of Brezhnev, the party has become perhaps the most complex social structure in history, with interlocking lines of responsibility and control along and between many layers of authority, all designed, expertly and cunningly, to mobilize the will of many under the leadership of few, just as Lenin proposed in *What Is to Be Done?*

The party that began as a collection of a few odd radicals united by their dedication to activism and their willingness to accept the chieftainship of Lenin, has become a well-trained, harmonious, skilled group of administrators.

Party control of the government and of all other major organizations was doubly and triply assured, through control at each level of administration by means of the local party committee, through the power of the leadership to make all appointments of any significance, and through the organization of the party members within any organization (the "party fraction") into a group that was responsible to party authorities and charged with directing the policies of the organization—from a sports club to a ministerial office to the Academy of Sciences or a military unit. . . .

This means that the Communist party has become to a degree that is novel in history an organized and purposefully directed political elite or ruling class. It forms a self-conscious in-group, offering power and privileges and demanding in return total loyalty—the loyalty and dedication that are necessary to make the system work. Its cohesion is, and has always had to be, strong enough to prevent any sector of the party from linking its discontents with the discontents of the nonparty masses; it has always been treasonous to appeal to workers or peasants (or the party membership) for support against any party policy, no matter how misguided. The party elite has thus become the modern equivalent of a feudal nobility, enjoying a monopoly of power far beyond that of any historic nobility.

The party tries to recruit people who distinguish themselves in any approved way, from scientists to athletes. It wants in its ranks those who are in any manner leaders of society, so that it can bring them under party discipline and guidance and make them sharers in the rulership. But it cannot be doubted that entry into the party, which is governed by the party group and the secretaries, is easier for the offspring of party members, although data to support (or refute) this theory have not been pub-

[2] I. Yudin and Yu Malov, "The Intelligence, Honor and Conscience of Our Era," *Partinaia zhizn* 13 (July 1976).

lished. In the tightly knit elite group, the children of the faithful old hands are certain to have the inside track, partly because no one wants to offend longtime comrades, and partly because they are known and reliable. . . .

Probably the chief objective of the leadership is stability, the maintenance of a condition that is approximately the best that can be devised for its beneficiaries. A major preoccupation, more important than economic growth, is the avoidance of a new purge, and the best guarantee of the safety of each is the immunity of all. The Soviet elite is like a club that may be exclusive in admissions but that seldom pushes members out. It is a cruel thing to punish a longtime colleague even though he may be losing his powers of concentration, especially inasmuch as, in Soviet society, he has nowhere else to go; and everyone in authority has an interest in the principle that positions are for keeps. For the superiors, it is like turning a faithful old servant out into the cold; for equals, the loss of one is a threat to all. . . .

The higher ranks of the party are increasingly clublike and positions are more stable. Some people stay at one post for decades. For example, B. P. Beshchev became Deputy Minister of Railroads in 1944 and Minister in 1948; he was still in that post in 1977.[3] Andrei Gromyko became Deputy Foreign Minister in 1946, at the age of thirty-seven, when the system was more fluid. He became Foreign Minister in 1957, and still held that position in 1977, having far outlasted all his colleagues of major powers. Such fixity of tenure is regarded as a positive achievement, favoring expertise.

Fixity in positions is synonymous with aging, and the Leninist youth movement has become a gerontocracy. Lenin was the oldest major figure in his party, at age forty-seven, when the revolution was made. The average age of Bolshevik delegates to the Congress of Soviets in November 1917 (those who answered questionnaires) was twenty-nine. . . . In 1939 the Soviet elite was among the youngest to rule a modern state; by 1959 it was among the oldest.

Recent congresses have ceased reporting in detail on the age composition either of the congress or of the party. . . . The members of the Politburo in 1966 averaged 57.5 years of age, in 1971 they averaged 61 years, and in 1976 the average age was 66 years. Brezhnev, who was 70 at the end of 1976, was the youngest of the four top figures at that time, including Podgorny (73), Kosygin (72)[4] and Suslov (74).

The Soviet leader is thus surrounded by a group of elder statesmen who must feel themselves approximately his equals and whom he can get rid of only with great difficulty, if at all. They are generally more interested in checking the power of the leader than in giving him unrestricted powers. At the same time, it is harder for him to build up the unconditionally

---

[3] Now deceased. [Editor's note.]

[4] Tikhonov was 75 when he took Kosygin's place in October, 1980, and Andropov was 68 when he became head of the party in 1982. [Editor's note.]

dedicated following he must have to operate arbitrarily in the Soviet system. The office of General Secretary confers not so much power as the means of building power. But however much power the General Secretary may build, it is certain to be far less than Stalin enjoyed. He is no longer very free to reward by promotions, since positions only gradually become vacant. He cannot demote freely without the concurrence of his colleagues, who are in principle opposed to demotion. Furthermore, the ruthless, ignorant men whom Stalin raised to do his bidding are no longer available, or they are no longer welcome. Everyone in the upper levels of the hierarchy has been there a long time and has acquired a higher education, which gives self-confidence if not breadth of vision. . . . "Trust in cadres" comes naturally when all have been through the same schools and have climbed the career ladders together, but it means a restricted leader; without the power of purge, there is no real dictator. . . .

The Secretary-General appears to be powerful in doing what the party wants. He never fights the machine or his fellow oligarchs. Unlike the American president, the General Secretary can at any given time make only minor changes in his government, and he has to clear policy with a cabinet he cannot change. Consequently, he can become gradually more influential through the cumulative effect of his influence over appointments, but he can embark on no bold initiatives in either foreign or domestic policies. To push anything very hard might well draw down his limited stock of power. . . .

There seem to be loose lobbies in the system, such as the military, the police, the advocates of heavy industry, the party apparat, and the ministerial bureaucrats, but the only pressures seem to be those of self-interest. The alliances fluctuate, and groups are more capable of defending their positions than of pushing any positive programs. If there are contrary tendencies toward the slackening or tightening of controls, none of them push hard or far; confrontation is avoided, and so far as it exists, it is kept quiet. The compromises that are reached involve policies less than persons, and an individual may be entrusted with the execution of a policy that is contrary to his own. Groups are held together by mutual advantage; political progress depends upon the members of the collective helping one another, and a shift to another group makes a person seem disloyal. The principle is loyalty to the party. Again stability is more important than change, harmony is preferred to movement.

Fixity of personnel is almost equivalent to fixity of policy; to embark on new programs usually requires putting new people in charge. Since there is no great drive to change, in any case, the settled party rulership has become remarkably conservative. Even formal change comes very hard. Khrushchev proposed in January 1959 that the 1936 "Stalinist" constitution be replaced. Three years later, in April 1962, a drafting commission was formed, and it was reconstituted under the chairmanship of Brezhnev after Khrushchev's fall. Nothing was revealed of the debates or proposals, but the new constitution was promised for the fiftieth anniversary of the revolution in 1967, as well as several times since then. It was finally unveiled in June 1977 in connection with Brezhnev's assumption of the presidency, and the changes it made were almost entirely declarative or cosmetic. In 1935 Stalin decided on a new constitution to reflect his achievements, and it was produced in a few months. In another minor way, the party finds itself paralyzed in replacing the symbols of the Stalin era. The words of the national anthem hailing Stalin were dropped in 1956; twenty-one years later, the commission produced verses almost unchanged except for dropping the name of Stalin.

Similarly, basic dogmas live on. The old priority of heavy industry has become increasingly irrelevant in the age of plastics and computers, but it has been retained ever since Stalin put it in place in his First Five Year Plan. Agriculture is also locked into the system of huge centralized and politically directed collective and state farms and the cultural scene is also frozen, with only marginal relaxation of censorship and of the required adherence to the canons of socialist realism, and there are no positive new directions. . . .

Since change is unwelcome, the system rests its legitimacy increasingly on tradition, the momentum of the going concern, and the inability or unwillingness of most people—especially those in positions of influence—to demand change. The Soviet citizen, knowing only the present political system, educated to it and submerged in it, can hardly conceive of anything very different. Even its critics and opponents are generally convinced that whatever its faults, the Soviet regime represents socialism, or public ownership of the means of production; hence it is basically of a superior order and cannot be opposed. People grumble but accept the rulership. The bureaucrats who run the economy, the press, the Writers' Union, and the scientific institutes apparently like things the way they are. The workers do not mind if the intellectuals are kept under pressure in the name of socialism, and the party democratically makes some concessions, mostly but not entirely concessions of form, to the less educated. . . .

The party has thus settled into place as the monolithic edifice of power, but its ability to work its will has decreased as its will has withered, and its authority is crumbling around the edges. Police repression is arbitrary, but like the official ideology, it lacks real conviction, hesitates a little in the face of public opinion at home and abroad, and is only partially effective. An opposition movement has grown up that is small but well publicized and determined. For a tiny sector of the intelligentsia, repugnance for the established order has become a matter of principle. Like the tsarist state, the Soviet order must seemingly live with intellectual dissidence, and it risks embittering without crushing. The non-conformists are of many shades, from neo-Stalinists and neo-Leninists to Russians and other nationalists, advocates of civil rights, and a few liberal democrats. Physically they are impotent, and they are far better known (as are Andrei Sakharov and Alexander Solzhenitsyn) in the West than in their homeland. . . .

In a dynamic world in which to stand still is to regress, the party seems fixed in its patterns of power and belief. It is aging at a time when renovation is indispensible, and it is losing morale when high morale is required to avoid putrefaction. The question is whether the system can break out of its mold without destroying itself.

At best, this would be a formidable task. . . .

The crux of the problem may be as follows: those who might possibly be able to effect change, the oligarchs at the summit (it is by no means certain that they could in fact really reform the system) have a very strong personal interest in maintaining the structure as is, which may well be the only way it can be maintained. . . . On the other hand, those outside who are in a better position to perceive a need for change and who might gain, or at least would not lose, by it, are kept as powerless as the party can manage. . . .

4. THE CPSU'S MONOPOLY OF POLITICAL POWER*

M. Lewin
University of Birmingham

The distinctive feature of the Soviet political system is that it is a one-party system. The ruling party has an undisputed monopoly of power. In Western countries, and particularly in the United States, one-party systems came to be seen, especially during the Cold War, as the embodiment of all that is evil in politics. The origins of the one-party system were traced to Lenin's *What Is To Be Done?*, and some saw the whole thing as a kind of conspiracy by Lenin. Once the Cold War subsided, however, it became clear that the one-party system was not just the product of one mind, one movement or one country but was a genuine creation of history. One-party systems have appeared in all kinds of countries, with all kinds of attributes and all kinds of labels. We can nowadays study a whole range of one-party systems. Some are important instruments of economic and social development, some are rather instruments of destruction, some are both at different periods of their development. Some exhibit liberal or democratic tendencies; others degenerate into oppressive machines ma-

* Reprinted from M. Lewin, "The Communist Party, Yesterday and Today," in R. W. Davies, ed., *The Soviet Union*, London: George Allen & Unwin Publishers Ltd., 1978, pp. 73–79, by permission of the publisher.

nipulated by despots. Matters are much more complicated than might have been supposed, especially as we can also observe some democratic processes degenerating. To understand the Soviet Communist Party, we evidently need to examine it as one specific case in a variety of one-party systems.

Perhaps the central feature of the Soviet Party, like other Communist Parties, is that it has an official ideology which it imposes on society. This ideology, 'Marxism-Leninism', claims monopoly of ideological life and enforces it as far as it can. Purporting to possess the capacity to formulate a scientific theory of history, society and even philosophy (though some of these claims are, in practice, somewhat diluted today), the Party considers itself to be the 'guide' for the whole of Soviet society. 'Guide' could, of course, mean different things in different circumstances. The Soviet Party is not merely concerned with formulating ideology, but also with the making of policy; indeed it frequently not merely supervises the implementation of policies but even implements them itself directly. It is thus both a governmental party, and a *party-government*: its top leadership is in fact responsible for central government, and its intermediate agencies guide the local government. In addition, the scope of Party policy making is enormous. National economic planning, education, culture and arts—the whole range of social phenomena—are all officially claimed to fall into the Party's purview. Such a party, if it actually does what it claims—and this is so far still the case— can be seen as an agency of comprehensive social planning, shaping, or trying to shape, social forces according to its conceptions and objectives.

What are the main instruments and methods by which the Party carries out this vast range of functions?

First, the enforcement of a monopoly ideology was, and up to a point still is, a powerful instrument for securing a high degree of uniformity of views in society. At the same time it provides a common language between the masses and their rulers and a common frame of reference for the rulers and the different influential groups or elites.

Second, all the leading personnel throughout the USSR—people in positions of responsibility in government, science, trade unions and so on—are trained by the Party or under its supervision and selected for their posts by the Party authorities.

Third, the whole nation is being educated and heavily propagandised under the control of or by the Party. The monopoly on power and ideology is supplemented by the monopoly on means of communication and information. . . .

Fourth, cultural activities, especially art and literature, have to follow prescribed paths and are supervised by powerful censors.

Fifth, the Party is organised so as to enable it to control the governmental machinery and, either through it or, when necessary, directly, the whole of social life. The central leadership, the Politburo, is elected

by and formally responsible to the Central Committee, which includes all
the leading officials of the Party, the government and the most important
other organisations. The Politburo has at its disposal the Secretariat of
the Central Committee which is organised like a miniature government,
with departments responsible for supervising the main branches of industry, culture and science, the police and the army, propaganda and
education. Thus Premier Kosygin's[1] ministers are supervised by parallel
departments in the Central Committee although the Premier and his two
deputies are themselves Politburo members. The Central Committee departments also control the Party itself, with its ubiquitous network of
Party branches in every factory, office or school.

Finally, the social composition of the Party membership is regulated so as to ensure that different classes of society are represented in
it in proportions considered appropriate by the central authorities. In
particular, citizens of talent and position either reach leading positions
because they are Party members or are asked to join because they can
be influential among their peers.

All these are impressive political organisational methods which
help the Party to run the country, to raise it to a high position in world
affairs and to create a powerful viable system. . . .

So much for the secrets of the Party's success. But now let us
briefly review some sources of tension and failure. In fact, some of the
factors which made for success are also at the same time creating trouble.
The one-party monopoly, and the very insistence of the leadership on
ideological and political unity, is in itself a major source of trouble. All
rulers probably prefer a situation in which they can afford to disregard
or suppress all kinds of anarchic, irresponsible opponents and feel free
to devise their policies without interruption. But the strong, disciplined
Party machinery shaped by the years of forced industrialisation and world
war is now faced by a new, diversified, complex and quickly changing
society. This complexity of the social body cannot be evaded. The purges
which, forty years ago, a capricious ruler carried out in order to eliminate
political risks for himself stemming from diversity, cannot easily be repeated today.

So, unavoidably, pressure groups are being formed and have to be
accommodated at least to a certain extent. . . . Uniformity of thought
just does not exist in the Soviet Union, and its leaders are aware of it. Careful observation shows the existence of different and competing political
trends of different denominations, which cannot express themselves
freely, but constitute subterranean currents, and penetrate the Party too.
So far the Party retains its monolithic conceptions and is not ready to
permit the emergence of different political groups even within the Party

[1] After sixteen years as chairman of the USSR Council of Ministers, Alexei Kosygin (quite
sick at the time) resigned in October, 1980 and died two months later. He was replaced
by Nikolai Tikhonov. [Editor's Note.]

itself. It is therefore inadequately equipped to deal with political diversity and strife and may one day be forced to learn bitter lessons. The pretence of political uniformity is as detrimental to political development as enforced cultural and artistic uniformity is detrimental to culture and art. In the field of sciences, some of them extremely sensitive to economic and military development, the sheer need for survival as a state often forced the leaders to abandon narrow-minded claims; in order to progress in physics, biology, cybernetics and mathematical economics, the state had to relinquish cherished practices. Some social sciences are still the victim of ideological stifling, but here too the same trend is discernible: a modern society cannot be run adequately without training its leading personnel in a spirit of independence in searching for solutions to political and social problems. Sociology therefore had to be allowed, though efforts are made to keep it from overstepping the limits of a practical, problem-solving technique. But it is only cultural diversity, intellectual and political challenge and a free flow of information which allow both the development of sciences and the training of open-minded elites and leaders. In fact, there is growing pressure on the Party for access to ever more information in different fields, without which the complex process of training leading personnel is constantly hampered.

Though Soviet citizens have many opportunities to exert their talents and initiative in many fields of private, social and professional endeavours, they are still denied freedom of political activity—other than apparatus politics inside the monopolistic party—and greatly hindered in the public exercise of critical and creative thinking in the spheres of political judgement and social and philosophical opinion. Much private discussion however does take place, in itself an indicator of the existence of a sharp problem.

The increasing number of such thinking people may tend to get alienated from their political system and retreat into cynicism or indifference, if they are not persuaded that 'the system is thinking too'. Obviously, many important problems cannot be raised on a national scale unless a debate is asked for by the government—and many problems which cannot be resolved, let alone noticed, without social pressure, tend to accumulate or suppurate. At the same time, leaders who are not elected or openly tested tend to be of the type that is considered suitable by those responsible for their selection but not necessarily acceptable to public opinion. The fact that they cannot be removed by any regular procedure creates either a sense of helplessness about politics, or deep dissatisfaction and even opposition.

In my own view, the Soviet system has entered a stage in which it will bear many pressures for change and is on a threshold of important transformations. Is the straitjacket put by political institutions on society really unbearable and crisis-laden? What will be the eventual direction of political change? Is there a channel for democratic change within the

Soviet political system? Are there Soviet forms of democracy which could emerge within the framework of a one-party system?

Such problems are not easy to answer and they need a lot of thought, further study and also waiting and seeing.[2]

SOVIET VIEWS

---

5. THE COMMUNIST PARTY OF THE SOVIET UNION*
Novosti Press Agency

THE CPSU: STAGES OF HISTORY†

On the night of October 25 (November 7, New Style), 1917, as the result of a victorious armed uprising of revolutionary workers, soldiers and sailors led by the Leninist Party of Bolsheviks, the bourgeois Provisional Government was overthrown and political power in Russia passed into the hands of the Soviets of Workers', Soldiers' and Peasants' deputies. The first Soviet Government, the Council of People's Commissars, headed by Lenin was formed.

The affirmation of Soviet power in Russia was the logical outcome of the work conducted by the Leninist Party and directed toward establishing a democratic republic and setting up a people's government whose task was to carry out socialist transformations of society. . . .

The Soviet people led by the Marxist-Leninist Party are advancing steadfastly toward their great goal—the building of a Communist society where the principle of "from each according to his ability, to each according to his needs" will be implemented. The road traversed by the nation—from the setting up of the first underground Marxist groups and leagues of struggle for the emancipation of the working class to the functioning of a 17-million-strong party which is at the head of the world's first socialist state, the Union of Soviet Socialist Republics—was not an easy one.

[2] For a variety of views on "freedom and democracy" in the USSR per se, see Chapter V, Part A below. [Editor's note.]

* Unless otherwise indicated, this selection has been rearranged and reprinted from "The Communist Party of the Soviet Union," *Soviet News*, Feb. 24, 1981, pp. 64–65, by permission of the publisher and the Copyright Agency of the USSR.

† The subsection "The CPSU: Stages of History" has been reprinted from *The CPSU: Stages of History*, 3rd enlarged edition, Moscow: Novosti Press Agency Publishing House, 1980, pp. 6, 7, and 85, by permission of the publisher and the Copyright Agency of the USSR.

Under the guidance of the Communist Party the Soviet people had beaten back, in a life-and-death struggle, the onslaught of the enemies of the revolution during the years of foreign intervention and the Civil War (1918–20), and, by self-sacrificing efforts, had rehabilitated the devastated economy. In the grim years of invasion by Nazi hordes (1941–45) the Communist Party was the inspiring force in the people's armed struggle against fascism. Today, the Communist Party is taking every necessary measure to considerably increase the well-being and raise the cultural level of the Soviet people, and to promote the cause of peace throughout the world.

The Leninist Communist Party has traversed a glorious road ever since its founding in 1903. From a comparatively small underground organization it has grown into a mighty army of Communists more than 17 million strong, the ruling party of the world's first socialist state. . . .

Under the Party's guidance the Soviet people are confidently marching along the path to communism. . . .

ROLE IN SOVIET SOCIETY

The Communist Party plays the leading role in the Soviet political system. This is fully reflected in the Constitution of the USSR. It is stated there that the CPSU is the leading and guiding force of Soviet society and the nucleus of its political system. This is really nothing out of the ordinary— as long as states continue to exist they are and will be guided by political parties which express the will of the classes that rule them.

The CPSU's leading position in Soviet society is based on its vast experience in political, organisational and ideological work. The Party is the central core of all state and public organisations, and directs their efforts towards a single objective. Only Party leadership enables the state and public organisations to co-ordinate their work and move in the same direction. The Party coordinates their actions, and by doing so gives these actions the greatest impact and meaningfulness in terms of benefitting the people.

It would be very wrong to confuse the CPSU's leading position in Soviet society with the practical day-to-day guidance of the country's affairs. This is exercised by the many elected organs of legislative authority—the Soviets of People's Deputies. The CPSU can neither adopt nor annul laws—this is the prerogative of the Soviets. The leading role of the CPSU consists primarily in the working out of political decisions which are subsequently presented for consideration by state organs.

CONDITIONS OF ADMISSION

People are admitted to the CPSU on their personal merits and following a personal choice. Any Soviet citizen—industrial worker, peasant, intellectual—who has excelled at his job and in public work, can apply for membership.

The admission procedure is not simple. First, a person applies to be a candidate member, following the submission of recommendations from three members of the CPSU who have each been at least five years in the Party and have been acquainted with the applicant either at their place of work or in public activity for at least a year. These communists are responsible to the Party organisations for presenting an objective description of the political, professional and moral qualities of the person they recommend.

The question of admission is resolved at a general meeting of the primary Party organisation, and the decision is then approved by the district or town committee of the CPSU.

A year later the candidate member is admitted to full membership. Again recommendations are necessary, as is a decision by the meeting of the local Party branch, and approval by a higher Party body.

The conditions of admission to the CPSU are the same for representatives of all strata of Soviet society (workers, peasants, intellectuals), for men and women, and for people of all nations, large and small.

CPSU membership does not bring with it any privileges. As far as social rights are concerned, communists and people who do not belong to the Party are equal. This applies to things like remuneration for work, acquiring a flat, etc.

The principal responsibility of a communist—something which Party members also regard as a privilege—is to serve as an example in work, studies and daily life.

As it is always concerned about its qualitative composition, the CPSU drops people from membership who violate the Party Rules and discredit the name of a communist. During the exchange of Party cards in the early 1970s, 347,000 people were denied new membership cards.

The probation period is a very good way of seeing that only the most worthy become Party members; in the five years leading up to 1977, over 100,000 people did not prove their worth, and were not raised from candidate members to full Party members.

COMPOSITION

Even in our period of developed socialism, when the CPSU has become the party of the entire people, it is still by origin the party of the working class.

Party organisations increase their membership primarily by admitting the best representatives of the working class. In the first half of the 1950s, 28.3 per cent of those admitted as candidate members were industrial workers, who made up approximately a third of the Party membership of the time.

But between the 24th (1971) and 25th (1976) Congresses 57.6 per cent of those joining the Party were industrial workers.

In the three years following the 25th Congress, 58.9 per cent of those admitted as candidate members were industrial workers.

At present there are more than seven million industrial workers in the CPSU, accounting for 42.7 per cent of the Party membership.

The Party is striving to strengthen its position primarily among that sector of working people engaged in production. In 1978, 73.2 per cent of those who entered the Party worked in this sphere. In recent years Party membership has become much larger primarily in the industries which determine scientific and technical progress.

Over ten per cent of those accepted as candidate members of the CPSU are peasants, and peasants as a whole account for 13.2 per cent of the Party membership.

Intellectuals play quite a considerable role in the Party. Approximately one in five specialists is a communist. Two-thirds of the country's Doctors of Science and half the Candidates of Science belong to the Party.

CPSU membership is steadily being supplemented with young people—mainly the best members of the Komsomol. In 1978, 73.4 per cent of those accepted as candidate members of the CPSU were Komsomol members.

An important aspect of the development of the CPSU is the increasing involvement of women, whose political activity is growing. In recent years, 32 per cent of those accepted as candidate members of the Party have been women. In 1979, more than a quarter of all members of the CPSU were women.

CONGRESS—THE SUPREME ORGAN

The CPSU Congress is the Party's highest body.

Congresses are held on a broadly democratic basis, with totally free discussion of all questions. Delegates to the Congress from all Party organisations are elected by secret ballot. Each and every communist has the right and the opportunity to address the Party Congress directly. All Congress decisions are binding on all Party organisations, all Party members and all candidate members.

Congress decisions cannot be changed or annulled by anyone or any organ, except the next Party Congress.

Each Party Congress is a stage in the Party's life and development. The Congress evaluates the results of past endeavours, and decides on the most topical and important questions.

The central committee must call Party Congresses at least once every five years. There must be at least six weeks between the announcement and agenda of a Party Congress and its opening date. The basis of representation at the Congress is determined by the central committee.

Extraordinary Congresses may also be convened, either by the central committee on its own initiative or on the demand of Party organisations representing at least a third of all Party members represented at the previous Congress. The extraordinary Congress is considered valid if at least half the Party membership is represented.

There have been two extraordinary Congresses, both called on the initiative of the central committee. The extraordinary 7th Congress was held in the spring of 1918 to decide the question of whether or not to sign the Brest Treaty. The extraordinary 21st Congress was held in January-February 1959. It discussed and approved the control figures of the Seven-Year Plan of the country's economic development.

LEADING BODIES

The CPSU central committee guides all the activity of the Party between Congresses. Its decisions are always based on the general guidelines approved by the Congresses. It is a collegiate body.

The 25th Congress elected 287 full members and 139 alternate members to the central committee (alternate members take part in the plenary meetings of the CPSU central committee with speaking rights but no vote).

The central committee members come from a wide range of nationalities and include Party leaders and statesmen, industrial officials, administrative personnel, leading workers in all areas of the economy, military people, diplomats, scientists and scholars, writers, lawyers, etc. Although elected to the highest Party body, they continue to work in their respective jobs. Central committee members and alternate members travel to Moscow from across the country for the central committee plenary meetings, which are usually held twice a year.

The central committee elects a secretariat from among its members. The secretariat directs the everyday work of the central committee, primarily concentrating on choosing personnel and ensuring that decisions are carried out.

The relative significance of the Congress and the central committee plenary meeting can be seen from the following: the 1976–80 Five-Year Plan was adopted by the 25th Party Congress, but the plans for each single year of that period were adopted by the plenary meetings of the central committee; the guidelines for Soviet foreign policy over the past decade were mapped out by the 24th and 25th Party Congresses, while current problems were considered by the plenary meetings.

Collective leadership

In between plenary meetings the work of the central committee is supervised by the political bureau, which is elected by the plenary meeting.

Between the 24th and 25th Congresses, the political bureau met 215 times (an average of once every eight days).

The political bureau, and the central committee as a whole, abide strictly by the basic principle of the CPSU—collective leadership.

The general secretary of the CPSU central committee is also elected by the plenary meeting of the central committee. It is not necessary to go into details about the great authority that a general secretary exercises and his important role as the Party leader who bears personal responsibility for the work of the central committee and the carrying out of Congress decisions. But this does not change the basic principle of the inner-life of the CPSU—that of collective leadership.

Within the central committee and the political bureau the general secretary, like other members of these collegiate organs, has only one vote, and his opinions and suggestions can only be considered accepted if they are supported by the majority of the members.

DEMOCRATIC PRINCIPLES OF ACTIVITY*

Membership of the CPSU is voluntary. The Party has long-established democratic traditions.

The basic principle and the Party's organisational structure and activity is democratic centralism. Without democracy it is impossible for Party members to express their opinions and without centralism it is impossible to achieve unity of action and to carry out Party decisions.

Democracy within the Party is ensured by the following principles: all leading Party bodies are elective; Party leadership is collective; the leading Party bodies are responsible and accountable to rank-and-file Party members; Party work is made public; all Party members enjoy equal rights and have equal responsibilities.

Centralism means discipline and unity. The decisions and directives of higher Party bodies are binding on the lower Party organisations; the minority must submit to the decision of the majority.

Under the Party Rules every Party member has the right to criticise and to express his opinion on any question.

There are no limits to discussions of problems within the Party, but as soon as a decision has been adopted by the majority, it becomes binding for all members of the Party organisations, including those whose opinion on the matter differed.

The Constitution of the USSR guarantees every person the right to submit suggestions to government bodies and public organisations about how to improve their work, and to criticise their shortcomings. In

---

* The second, third, and fourth paragraph of this subsection, and the first sentence of the fifth paragraph, have been reprinted (and inserted here) from *Yearbook '80 USSR*, Moscow: Novosti Press Agency Publishing House, p. 65, by permission of the publisher and the Copyright Agency of the USSR.

the four years since the 25th Party Congress, 9,400,000 letters have come to the central committee of the CPSU, the central committees of the Communist Parties of the Union Republics, and territorial, regional, city and district Party committees. Almost five and a half million people (5,400,00) made verbal statements to these bodies.

The suggestions and requests contained in the letters, just like the opinions, are reflected in the resolutions of the CPSU central committee and the USSR Council of Ministers, and in speeches by Party and government leaders. Local Party and governmental bodies more and more often submit specific proposals to all-union and Republican ministries and administrations in pursuit of the questions which people have raised.

6. THE MORAL CODE OF
THE BUILDERS OF COMMUNISM*

Programme of the Communist Party of the Soviet Union[1]

The Affirmation of Communist Morality. In the course of transition to communism, the moral principles of society become increasingly important; the sphere of action of the moral factor expands and the importance of the administrative control of human relations diminishes accordingly. The Party will encourage all forms of conscious civic self-discipline leading to the assertion and promotion of the basic rules of the communist way of life.

The Communists reject the class morality of the exploiters; in contrast to the perverse, selfish views and morals of the old world, they promote communist morality, which is the noblest and most just morality, for it expresses the interests and ideals of the whole of working mankind. Communism makes the elementary standards of morality and justice, which were distorted or shamelessly flouted under the rule of the exploiters, inviolable rules for relations both between individuals and between peoples. Communist morality encompasses the fundamental norms of human morality which the masses of the people evolved in the course of millenniums as they fought against vice and social oppression. The revolutionary morality of the working class is of particular importance to the moral advancement of society. As socialist and communist construction progresses, communist morality is enriched with new principles, a new content.

* Reprinted from *Programme of the Communist Party of the Soviet Union,* Moscow: Foreign Languages Publishing House, 1961, pp. 108–9, by permission of the Copyright Agency of the USSR.
[1] The Programme of the CPSU, adopted by the Twenty-Second Party Congress in October, 1961, is still the official Party program in 1981.

The Party holds that *the moral code of the builder of communism* should comprise the following principles:

devotion to the communist cause; love of the socialist motherland and of the other socialist countries;

conscientious labour for the good of society;[2]

concern on the part of everyone for the preservation and growth of public wealth;

a high sense of public duty; intolerance of actions harmful to the public interest;

collectivism and comradely mutual assistance: one for all and all for one;

humane relations and mutual respect between individuals—man is to man a friend, comrade and brother;

honesty and truthfulness, moral purity, modesty, and unpretentiousness in social and private life;

mutual respect in the family, and concern for the upbringing of children;

an uncompromising attitude to injustice, parasitism, dishonesty, careerism and money-grubbing;

friendship and brotherhood among all peoples of the USSR; intolerance of national and racial hatred;

an uncompromising attitude to the enemies of communism, peace and the freedom of nations;

fraternal solidarity with the working people of all countries, and with all peoples.

7. DUTIES AND RIGHTS OF MEMBERS OF THE CPSU

Party Congresses of the CPSU

It is the duty of a Party member:

(a) to work for the creation of the material and technical basis of communism; to be a model of the communist attitude towards labour; to raise labour productivity; to display the initiative in all that is new and progressive; to support and propagate advanced methods; to master technology, to improve skills; to protect and increase socialist

---

[2] The original version contained the additional sentence, "he who does not work, neither shall he eat." The Soviet Constitution of 1936, specifying that work is a matter of duty and honor for every *able-bodied* citizen, also contained that phrase. It was, however, dropped in the new 1977 constitution and was therefore omitted from the text here also. [Editor's note.]

public property, the mainstay of the might and prosperity of the Soviet country;

(b) to put Party decisions firmly and steadfastly into effect; to explain the policy of the Party to the people; to help strengthen and multiply the Party's bonds with the people; to be considerate and attentive to people; to respond promptly to the needs and requirements of the working people;

(c) to take an active part in the political life of the country, in the administration of state affairs, and in economic and cultural development; to set an example in fulfilment of public duty; to assist in developing and strengthening communist social relations;

(d) to master Marxist-Leninist theory, to improve ideological knowledge, and to contribute to the moulding and education of the man of communist society. To combat vigorously all manifestations of bourgeois ideology, remnants of a private-property psychology, religious prejudices, and other survivals of the past; to observe the principles of communist morality, and place public interests above personal;

(e) to be an active proponent of the ideas of socialist internationalism and Soviet patriotism among the working people; to combat survivals of nationalism and chauvinism; to contribute by word and by deed to the consolidation of the friendship of the peoples of the USSR and the fraternal bonds linking the Soviet people with the peoples of the countries of the socialist camp, with the proletarians and other working people in all countries;

(f) to strengthen to the utmost the ideological and organisational unity of the Party; to safeguard the Party against the infiltration of people unworthy of the lofty name of Communist; to be truthful and honest with the Party and the people; to display vigilance, to guard Party and state secrets;

(g) to develop criticism and self-criticism, boldly lay bare shortcomings and strive for their removal; to combat ostentation, conceit, complacency, and parochial tendencies; to rebuff firmly all attempts at suppressing criticism; to resist all actions injurious to the Party and the state, and to give information of them to Party bodies, up to and including the CC CPSU;[1]

(h) to implement undeviatingly the Party's policy with regard to the proper selection of personnel according to their political qualifications and professional qualities;

(i) to observe Party and state discipline, which is equally binding on all Party members. The Party has one discipline, one law, for all Communists, irrespective of their past services or the positions they occupy;

[1] From "The Rules of the Communist Party of the Soviet Union," as adopted by previous party Congresses, in force in 1981. Reprinted from *Soviet Union*, March, 1981, p. 8, by permission of the publisher and the Copyright Agency of the USSR.

(j) to help, in every possible way, to strengthen the defence potential of the USSR; to wage an unflagging struggle for peace and friendship among nations.

A Party member has the right:

(a) to elect and be elected to Party bodies;

(b) to discuss freely questions of the Party's policies and practical activities at Party meetings, conferences and congresses, at the meetings of Party committees and in the Party press; to table motions; to express openly and uphold opinions until the Party organisation concerned adopts a decision;

(c) to criticise any Communist, irrespective of the position he holds, at Party meetings, conferences and congresses, and at the plenary meetings of Party committees. Those who commit the offence of suppressing criticism or victimising anyone for criticism are responsible to and will be penalised by the Party, to the point of expulsion from the CPSU;

(d) to attend in person all Party meetings and all bureau and committee meetings that discuss the member's activities or conduct;

(e) to address any question, statement or proposal to any Party body, up to and including the CC CPSU, and to demand an answer on the substance of his address.

B
State and Government

"The Union of Soviet Socialist Republics is a socialist state of the whole people, expressing the will and interests of the workers, peasants, and intelligentsia, the working people of all the nations and nationalities of the country."

CONSTITUTION OF THE USSR
Art. 1

"Comrade Workers! Remember that you yourselves now administer the State. Your Soviets are henceforth the organs of state power, organs with full powers, organs of decision."

VLADIMIR ILYICH LENIN

The highest legislative body in the Soviet Union, the Supreme Soviet of the USSR, is similar in structure to our Congress. It consists of two chambers, with the deputies of one elected on the basis of population, as are the delegates to the U.S. House of Representatives, and those of the other on a territorial basis, as are U.S. senators. Similar legislative bodies exist at the Republic level, comparable to our state legislatures in structure, and at lower levels of the Soviet state structure. The highest executive body is the Council of Ministers of the USSR, prior to 1946 known by the designation of Council of People's Commissars. Nominally, it is responsible for the enforcement of the laws passed by the Supreme Soviet and for other designated tasks, such as the development of economic policy, general guidance in foreign relations, and directing the general organization of the country's armed forces. In fact, the Council of Ministers is responsible, above all, for carrying out the policies decided by the party's Politburo.

In a sense, the most interesting aspect of the Soviet Union's political structure is the interlocking relationship between the CPSU and the various legislative, executive and administrative units of the Soviet state and government. That the CPSU is the dominating authority, empowered to make all final decisions if it so desires—on this issue, there is no dispute. But does this leave any functions of importance at all for the various levels of state and government, or are these merely showpieces ordered to approve and carry out party policies? This question bears further analysis.

The first selection of Part B of this chapter (Selection 8), taken from the *Europa Yearbook,* consists of a brief description of the Soviet Union's state and governmental structure. In Selection 9, Stephen White presents a critical Western view on the role and functions of the Supreme Soviet. While he agrees with other Western analysts that its authority is very limited since the CPSU holds ultimate power, he finds nevertheless that on close inspection, subjects debated by the deputies in that parliamentary body are "by no means trivial or remote from the daily concerns of those who nominally elect them." Selection 10, representative of the official Soviet position, supplies a more detailed description of the various levels of the country's state and government machinery than did Selection 8 and gives a somewhat different flavor. It conveys the impression that all units have vital functions to perform, from the local Soviets (councils) which "independently decide matters that come within their competence" to the Supreme Soviet, which "is empowered to define fundamentals of legislation" and the USSR Council of Ministers, "the highest executive and administrative body of state authority in the USSR." The final selection in this part of Chapter IV deals with the aims and functions of the Soviet state as seen through Soviet eyes, and addresses itself also briefly to the matter of "socialist legality."

WESTERN VIEWS

---

8. THE STRUCTURE OF
THE SOVIET STATE AND GOVERNMENT:
AN INTRODUCTION*
Europa Yearbook 1981

Under the 1977 Constitution, the Soviet Union is formally a federal state comprising 15 Union (constituent) Republics of equal status. . . . Some Union Republics contain Autonomous Republics and Autonomous Regions. The Russian Soviet Federative Socialist Republic (R.S.F.S.R.) also includes 10 National Areas.

The highest organ of state power is the bicameral legislature, the Supreme Soviet of the USSR, comprising the Soviet (Council) of the Union, with 750 members elected from constituencies, and the Soviet of

* Rearranged and reprinted from *Europa Year Book 1981*, London: Europa Publications Limited, 1981, pp. 1217, 1218 and 1255, by permission of the publisher.

Nationalities, with 750 members (32 from each of the Union Republics; 11 from each of the 20 Autonomous Republics; five from each of the eight Autonomous Regions; one from each of the 10 National Areas). . . . Members are directly elected (from a single list of candidates) by universal adult suffrage and serve five-year terms. At elections in March 1979, official figures state that over 99 per cent of the electorate voted.

The Soviet of the Union represents the common interests of all citizens, irrespective of their nationality. The Soviet of Nationalities represents the specific interests of each nation. These two chambers are vested with equal powers to initiate legislation, have equal terms of office, simultaneous sessions. Approval of both chambers is required for a bill to be passed.

The Supreme Soviet adopts and repeals laws, sees that the Soviet Constitution is observed, takes decision on the most important questions of internal and external policy, forms the leading bodies of the State, controls the work of state bodies and officials.

At a joint session the members elect the Presidium of the Supreme Soviet (39 members) to be the legislature's permanent organ. The Presidium, led by a Chairman, functions as a collective Head of State. The Supreme Soviet also appoints the Council of Ministers, headed by a Chairman, to form the executive and administrative branch of government, responsible to the Supreme Soviet.

The Presidium of the Supreme Soviet is a permanent body elected by a joint meeting of the Soviet of the Union and the Soviet of Nationalities. It consists of a Chairman, a First Vice-Chairman, 15 Vice-Chairmen, a Secretary and 21 members. It is fully accountable to the Supreme Soviet; between sessions it considers and settles all the main questions of state administration and controls the work of subordinate bodies. Meetings are convened by the Chairman about every two months.

Each of the 15 Union Republics has a constitution and state structure on the same pattern as the central government, with a unicameral Supreme Soviet and a Council of Ministers to deal with internal affairs.

Political power is held by the highly centralized Communist Party of the Soviet Union (CPSU), described in the constitution as "the leading and guiding force of Soviet society". The CPSU is the only legal party, has an absolute monopoly of power in all political affairs and controls government at all levels. . . .

9. THE USSR SUPREME SOVIET: HOW MUCH AUTHORITY AND POWER?*

Stephen White
University of Glasgow

The USSR Supreme Soviet has not generally been accorded praise by Western scholars. Although nominally the Soviet Union's national legislature, the "highest body of state authority of the USSR," according to the 1977 Constitution (Art. 108), the Supreme Soviet, for the more than forty years of its existence, has been a much less influential body than its formal position might suggest. It meets relatively infrequently: at least twice a year as specified by the Constitution (Art. 112), but usually for only two or three days on each of these occasions, making it among the world's assemblies least frequently in session. Its deputies are chosen by a selection process dominated by the Communist Party of the Soviet Union, to which about three-quarters of all candidates normally belong. There is no choice of party or even of candidates at the polls; the single agreed slate goes forward as the "bloc of Communist and non-party candidates," and since the Second World War it has never received less than 99 percent support. A process of recall exists by which deputies can be replaced if an error appears to have been made in their selection (Art. 107). Usually, however, there is no need, since the deputies greet with unanimous enthusiasm each and every proposal submitted to them by the Soviet government, the Council of Ministers. It is perhaps not surprising that such an assembly normally has not been taken seriously by scholars or by the mass public in the Western liberal democracies.

For example, the late Merle Fainsod, in a classic account of the mid-1960s, wrote that in comparison with the fairly active involvement of local Soviets in community affairs "the role of the Supreme Soviet appears more strictly ornamental." Its commissions worked within sharply circumscribed limits and discharged a largely perfunctory role; its proceedings on the whole conveyed the impression of a "well-rehearsed theatrical spectacle from which almost all elements of conflict have been eliminated." The slight budgetary modifications and criticisms of government ministers that took place, he wrote, gave "every impression of being part of a prepared script." All important decisions came ready-made from the party leadership; the task of the Supreme Soviet was "not to question but to execute, to clothe the Party thesis in the garb

* Reprinted from Stephen White, "The USSR Supreme Soviet: A Developmental Perspective," *Legislative Studies Quarterly,* V, 2, May, 1980, pp. 247–48, 254, 257–58, 260–61, and 271–72, by permission of the author and the publisher. © Comparative Legislative Research Center of the University of Iowa.

of constitutional legality.''[1] Other writers have described Supreme Soviet sessions as "mere ceremonies of ratification, characterised by set speeches rather than debate, and by unanimous acceptance of legislation introduced by government spokesmen" which do "little more than emphasize the unity of party and non-party citizens and provide an opportunity for re-affirming support for the leadership."[2] To writers of this view, the Supreme Soviet is "not a real legislature but a rubber stamp."[3]

A number of other scholars have taken a more charitable view of the Supreme Soviet's powers, or at least of the potential for its further development. Jerome Gilison, for instance, concedes that the Supreme Soviet's discussions and meetings were indeed "perfunctory" and "stage-managed" for perhaps the first three decades of its existence (1936–1966); since Stalin, however, and more especially since Khrushchev, who was hostile to any enlargement of the role of the Soviets, the Supreme Soviet has made a "modest—but in terms of past history, impressive—comeback as an institution with more than purely symbolic functions."[4]

The responsibilities of the Supreme Soviet deputy, once elected, are not unduly onerous. The sessions, or meetings, are short and relatively infrequent; deputies, who are all part-time, are released from their work to attend meetings and can usually accomplish a good day's shopping while in the capital; and they have relatively few formal duties to perform except for taking part in votes that are in all but exceptional circumstances unanimous. Many of them, indeed, seem not to take the formal proceedings very seriously at all. According to a *New York Times* report of a recent session, for instance:

> Some of the deputies listened attentively. Some read *Pravda*. . . .
> Many, by chatting among themselves, created a buzz when speakers on the rostrum drew a breath, or yielded to their successors.
> A few deputies appeared to be asleep.[5]

There must clearly be some justification, on this basis, for writers such as Merle Fainsod to have taken sessions of the Supreme Soviet to be no more than "rallies of the faithful" at which the proposals of the government are "unanimously hailed and unanimously ratified," their only purpose being to give a spurious constitutional legitimacy to decisions taken elsewhere by the Communist Party leadership.[6]

Yet, considered more closely, the subjects on which Supreme So-

---

[1] Merle Fainsod, *How Russia is Ruled,* Rev. ed. Cambridge, Mass.: Harvard University Press, 1965, p. 384.

[2] M. McAuley, *Politics and the Soviet Union,* Harmondsworth, Eng.: Penguin, 1977, p. 204.

[3] John A. Armstrong, *Ideology, Politics and Government in the Soviet Union,* 3rd ed., New York: Praeger, 1978, pp. 164–65.

[4] Jerome M. Gilison, *British and Soviet Politics: Legitimacy and Convergence,* Baltimore and London: Johns Hopkins University Press, 1972, p. 50.

[5] Quoted in Gilison, *op. cit.,* p. 91.

[6] Fainsod, *op. cit.,* p. 384.

viet deputies have recently engaged in debate have been by no means trivial or remote from the daily concerns of those who nominally elect them. Since August 1966, for instance, the Supreme Soviet has discussed the Soviet health service (June 1968 and December 1969), marriage and family law (June 1968), labour law (July 1970), criminal law (July 1969) and the educational system (July 1973), as well as a number of important economic matters. During 1977 and 1978, a series of discussions considered important constitutional measures concerning citizenship, the electoral system and so forth. The number of participants in discussion on the floor of the Supreme Soviet itself is often limited, but a full discussion takes place beforehand in the relevant standing commissions and most bills are published in the press or at least submitted to the institutions most directly concerned before a final text is adopted. The draft law on marriage and the family, for instance, provoked no fewer than 7,000 proposed amendments in this way, and there were more than 3,000 suggested changes to the draft education law in 1973. Proposals of this kind are considered by the relevant standing commissions and in many cases changes in the draft are reported to take place as a result.

The increasing number and influence of the standing commissions, indeed, particularly since 1966, are perhaps the most compelling evidence that the Supreme Soviet may be said to have extended its authority over the period we have been considering. . . .

The standing commissions have averaged between one and three meetings a year since their foundation, though all of them additionally take part in the joint discussion of the plan and budget that occurs every year during the month before the Supreme Soviet itself considers them. In sum, however, the number of meetings of all commissions taken together has increased very considerably, as has the number of deputies involved in their deliberations. Deputies who are members of other commissions or "representatives of state and public organs and organisations, scientific institutions, specialists and scholars" may also be invited to take part in the work of a commission in a consultative (nonvoting) capacity, thus further extending their representative character. . . .

The crucial question, of course, is whether the Supreme Soviet's more developed committee structure and widening sphere of interests mean it is becoming a more important and influential political actor. . . . The broadening competence of the Supreme Soviet need mean no more than the transfer of a number of more or less technical matters to a subordinate assembly in which they can be given at least the appearance of a public hearing. To scholars of the Fainsod school, there can be no question here of the increasing influence of the Supreme Soviet as such; the party leadership have simply found it convenient to make somewhat more use of the Supreme Soviet than in the past, entrusting more noncontroversial matters to its attention and giving the largely honorific deputies a little more to do while in no way relaxing the party's ultimate control. What has been given to the Supreme Soviet, in this analysis, could just as easily be taken away.

There probably can be no conclusive answer to questions such as these, any more than to questions about where power "really" lies in political systems elsewhere; it may be possible to reformulate the question, however, along the lines suggested by Jerry Hough[1] in writing of the development of "constitutional" or "institutional" restraints in Soviet politics. The kind of restraints mentioned by Hough include limitations on the ability of the leader to execute political opponents, to override expert knowledge and the interests of major social groups, and to restrict individual freedom beyond a certain point. Restraints of this kind may mean no more than a willingness by the political leadership to exercise their considerable powers with discretion. If such restraints persist over a long time, however, Hough argues,[2] they are likely to become conventions that are more or less taken for granted within the political system and are likely to resist challenge. In the case of the Supreme Soviet, we may argue similarly, what may initially have been a tactic or concession— that it should enjoy an enlarged sphere of influence and a more active committee structure—may become, over time, a convention that is more or less "built into" the political system. Then this enlarged sphere of influence may be capable of resisting challenge, in much the same way that conventions of this kind have acquired constitutional force in countries such as Great Britain.

In the absence of detailed evidence on the inner workings of Soviet politics, we cannot reliably determine whether any conventions of this kind have emerged in the relations between (for instance) the Supreme Soviet and the Presidium and Council of Ministers that are nominally responsible to it, or between party and state organs more generally. There are, however, a number of ways in which we can test for the emergence of regular and predictable exercises of authority by the Supreme Soviet itself.[3]

The conclusions of this study may be briefly stated:

1. The USSR Supreme Soviet has not radically extended its authority, gradually displacing the party Central Committee as the major forum for the resolution of societal disputes as some writers in the 1950s thought possible. It has, nonetheless, secured

---

[1] Jerry F. Hough, "The Soviet Experience and the Measurement of Power," *Journal of Politics* 37 (August, 1975): 685–710.

[2] Jerry F. Hough, *How the Soviet Union is Governed: An Extensively Revised and Enlarged Edition by Jerry F. Hough of Merle Fainsod's How Russia is Ruled*, Cambridge, Mass. and London: Harvard University Press, 1979, pp. 554–55.

[3] Space limitation precludes a detailed discussion of the tests proposed by the author. Suffice it here to present the author's conclusions. The reader interested in the more technical details will have to turn to the original article. [Editor's note.]

and retained a position as an institutional actor of by no means negligible importance, more important certainly than many writers in the Fainsod school have normally been willing to allow it.

2. The degree to which the Supreme Soviet is representative of the major social groups of the USSR—women, workers and peasants, young people, and non-party members—has been steadily increasing from convocation to convocation. The Supreme Soviet, however, has become less representative of the nationalities of the USSR, mainly because of the equal representation of all the union republics irrespective of population within the Council of Nationalities.

3. The number of sessions, days of meeting, speeches delivered to the Supreme Soviet and interpellations all increased remarkably up to the fourth convocation in the mid-1950s, but have since shown a tendency to decline. An examination of the agendas of the sessions that have taken place, however, shows that the Supreme Soviet has been increasingly concerned with domestic socioeconomic rather than foreign policy issues, and that it has considered basic legislation in many areas of Soviet life. This does not suggest a body that has become marginal to the Soviet political process.

4. Perhaps more important, the system of standing commissions originally established in 1938 has developed further, particularly since 1966, and now embraces 16 separate commissions in each chamber with a total membership in excess of three-quarters of all deputies. The standing commissions have met more frequently than the Supreme Soviet as a whole and appear to have played an important role in the oversight of government performance (*kontrol*), although their role in amending and initiating legislation is by no means to be neglected.

5. The legislative output of the Supreme Soviet increased considerably between the third and fourth convocations, at the beginning of the 1950s, but has since declined somewhat. Its present legislative output nonetheless remains higher than for any period up to the 1950s.

6. The impact of the Supreme Soviet upon the legislation it does consider is more difficult to establish. Patterns of budgetary spending, however, have shown a tendency to move from defense toward social and economic purposes, and a study of the distribution of the additional expenditure voted by the Supreme Soviet every year shows that the resources made available have been devoted consistently and increasingly toward sociocultural purposes and to a somewhat lesser extent toward expenditure by the union republics through the union republican budgets.

Although the precise connections remain to be specified empirically, this provides at least external evidence of the emergence of some form of "linkage politics" in the USSR, with deputies consistently maximising the resources devoted to the purposes of most immediate benefit to their constituents.
7. The Supreme Soviet appears to have played a minor role in the redistribution of resources between the union republics of the USSR.

SOVIET VIEWS

---

10. NATIONAL AND STATE STRUCTURE*
Novosti Press Agency

The USSR is a country with a population of 265 million—a family of over 100 nations and nationalities.

The USSR is a Socialist state of the whole people. All power in the Soviet Union belongs to the people. The people exercise state power through Soviets of people's deputies—elective bodies, which constitute the political foundation of the USSR.

The Union of Soviet Socialist Republics is an integral, federal, multinational state formed on the principle of Socialist federalism as a result of the free self-determination of nations and the voluntary association of 15 equal Union Republics. The Union Republics are inhabited by people of many nationalities; autonomous republics, autonomous regions, and autonomous areas are included in their territories.

Each **Union Republic** is a sovereign socialist state. It has its own Constitution conforming to the Constitution of the USSR and taking note of specific national, economic or other features of the republic. Each Union Republic has its own highest bodies of state authority—the Supreme Soviet and its Presidium, the Council of Ministers, and its own Supreme Court, its own civil, criminal, labour, family and other laws, its own judicial system and its own anthem, flag, emblem and capital. . . .

Each **Autonomous Republic** is a national-state entity and an integral part of the Union Republic in which it is incorporated. It also has its own

---

* The first three paragraphs of this selection have been taken from *USSR: The State Structure*, Moscow: Novosti Press Agency Publishing House, 1978 (open-up-pamphlet; pages not numbered); the rest from *USSR Yearbook '80*, Moscow. Novosti Press Agency Publishing House, 1980, pp. 55–60. Reprinted by permission of the publisher and of the Copyright Agency of the USSR.

Constitution, its own bodies of authority, its own territory, its own judicial system, its own laws, and its own capital, emblem and flag.

The USSR unites fifteen Union Republics: the Russian Soviet Federative Socialist Republic and the Ukrainian, Byelorussian, Uzbek, Kazakh, Georgian, Azerbaijan, Lithuanian, Moldavian, Latvian, Kirghiz, Tajik, Armenian, Turkmen and Estonian Soviet Socialist Republics.

All nations and nationalities are ensured true equality in social, political, economic and cultural matters. A citizen of any race or nationality enjoys the same rights as all the rest, without any privileges.

There are twenty Autonomous Republics within the Union Republics, of which sixteen are in the Russian Federation.

Each **Autonomous Region** is a national territorial entity which, by virtue of the specific national composition and customs of its population, enjoys administrative autonomy. It has its own bodies of state authority, court and procurator's office: all these bodies, as well as schools, cultural and public organisations and the press base their work on the native language of the regional population.

There are eight **Autonomous Regions** within the Union Republics.

Each **Autonomous Area** is a national territorial entity which is also distinguished by its specific national composition and customs, but which has a comparatively small population. National areas are to be found only in the Russian Federation. There are ten of them.

Administrative-territorial units in the USSR are villages, settlements, districts in big cities, towns, rural districts and regions; and in the Russian Federation—also areas and territories.

THE SOVIETS OF PEOPLE'S DEPUTIES

The Soviets of People's Deputies constitute a single system of elective, representative bodies of state authority. Hence the term—Soviet rule.

The principle of democratic centralism, namely, the electiveness of all bodies of state authority from the lowest to the highest, their accountability to the people and the obligation of lower bodies to observe the decisions of higher ones, is basic to the functioning of the Soviet state. It also means combining central leadership with local initiative and creative activity.

The Soviets are a school of state and public administration for millions of people. The Soviets have a 30-million army of volunteer assistants.

The Soviets embrace both legislative and executive powers. They not only pass laws and take decisions but also ensure their execution and decide all questions of political, economic, social and cultural development on their territory.

A **people's deputy** has the right to address inquiries to all state bodies and public organisations on the territory covered by the Soviet.

All those to whom the deputy addresses inquiries, including ministers, are obliged to receive the deputy without delay and to reply to his or her inquiry within three days.

A deputy is authorised to inspect the work of offices, enterprises, collective and state farms and to demand the speediest solution of questions raised by electors.

All deputies enjoy immunity. They may not be prosecuted, arrested or subjected to administrative penalties imposed by court procedure without the consent of the Soviet to which they have been elected.

Deputies exercise their powers without payment and without discontinuing their regular employment or duties. When it is necessary for a deputy to work on one of the Soviet's commissions, he is released from his regular employment while retaining his average earnings.

In their work the deputies are guided by the interests of the state as a whole; they also take into consideration the requirements of the people of their election districts and do their best to carry out the electors' mandates. The mandates as a rule deal with such matters as the improvement of the work of local enterprises, housing construction, extension of the network of children's institutions, out-patient clinics, hospitals and educational institutions, the repair of roads, and the work of transport facilities.

According to the Constitution it is the duty of a deputy to report on his work in the Soviet to his electors and to the work collectives and public organisations which nominated him.

If a deputy fails to live up to the expectations of his electors and does not perform his duties conscientiously, he or she can be recalled at any time from the Soviet following a decision of the majority of the electors. In this case new elections are held.[1]

The system of Soviets: Each Soviet exercises supreme authority in its respective area and all the Soviets constitute a single system of bodies of state authority. This system comprises the Supreme Soviet of the USSR, the Supreme Soviets of the fifteen Union Republics, the Supreme Soviets of twenty Autonomous Republics and 50,662 local Soviets.

Each Soviet sets up respective bodies of state administration: either Councils of Ministers or executive committees.

The Supreme Soviet of the USSR is the highest body of state authority in the country. It expresses the sovereignty of the whole Soviet people and consists of two Chambers each having equal rights: the Soviet of the Union, representing the common interests of all working people irrespective of nationality, and the Soviet of Nationalities, representing the particular interests of each nationality and national group stemming from the specific features of their economy, history, culture, traditions and customs.

[1] For Western and Soviet views on elections in the USSR, see Chapter V, Part B below. [Editor's note.]

Its present-day composition is as follows: 522 deputies are workers (34.8 per cent), and 244 collective farmers (16.3 per cent) or 766 (51.1 per cent) taken together. Among deputies 1,075 (71.7 per cent) are Party members and candidate-members, thus 425 (28.3 per cent) are non-Party. Four hundred and eighty-seven deputies (32.5 per cent) are women. People under 30 years of age number 317 (21.1 per cent), and YCL members, 207 (13.8 per cent).

Both Chambers are elected on the same day and have equal terms of office—five years—and equal powers of initiating legislation. A law is considered adopted when it has been passed in each Chamber by simple majority.

The Supreme Soviet is empowered to define fundamentals of legislation, to exercise guidance of the country's economy, to draft and endorse state plans for economic and social development and a single state budget, to determine prices and wages policy, to decide on questions of war and peace, to ensure sovereignty, protect state frontiers and the territory of the country, direct the Armed Forces, ensure representation in international relations, deal with foreign trade, and decide many other issues of all-Union importance.

The Presidium of the Supreme Soviet of the USSR is a standing body and the highest body of state authority in the country. It is elected at a joint sitting of both Chambers and consists of a Chairman, a First Vice-Chairman, 15 Vice-Chairmen (one from each Union Republic), a Secretary and 21 members. The Presidium is accountable to the Supreme Soviet for all its activities. Between sessions of the Supreme Soviet and within the limits stipulated in the Constitution it exercises the functions of the highest body of state authority.

Standing Commissions of the Supreme Soviet of the USSR are set up by each of its two Chambers. At the present time each Chamber has 16 identical commissions: the credentials; legislative proposals; planning and budget; foreign affairs; youth affairs; women's living and working conditions; maternity and child care; industry; transport and communications; construction and building materials industry; agriculture; consumer goods and trade; health and social security; education and culture; domestic services and municipal services; nature conservation; and science and technology.

The tasks of these commissions are to draft legislation and exercise control over the implementation of laws and the work of administrative bodies. Some 1,070 deputies, or over two-thirds of all deputies, are members of these commissions.

Heads of ministries and departments regularly report to the commissions. Commission members carry out constant work connected with the preparation of new decisions, the elucidation of the views of deputies who are in constant touch with their constituencies, and the co-ordination of proposals. It is this unseen but continuous work that enables Soviet leaders competently to decide fundamental issues of the development of the USSR.

The Council of Ministers of the USSR, i.e. the government, is the highest executive and administrative body of state authority in the USSR. It is formed by the Supreme Soviet at a joint sitting of both Chambers and consists of a Chairman, Vice-Chairmen, Ministers, Chairmen of State Committees and Chairmen of the Councils of Ministers of the Union Republics. It works on a collegial basis. All its decisions and ordinances are issued solely on the basis of and in pursuance of the laws of the USSR.

The Council of Ministers is responsible and accountable to the Supreme Soviet.

The Supreme Soviets of the Union and Autonomous Republics are the highest bodies of state authority in their respective republics. They have one chamber and are elected for a term of five years. The number of deputies depends on the size of the republic's population, the quotas of representation being defined in the Constitution of each republic. For example, at present the Supreme Soviet of the Russian Federation has 904 deputies, the Ukraine—570, Byelorussia—430, Turkmenia—300, and so on.

The rights vested in the Supreme Soviets include adopting the Constitution, issuing the republic's laws, endorsing plans for economic and social development and the republic's budget, and supervising the work of state bodies and officials.

The Supreme Soviets of the republics form the highest bodies of state authority in the republic—the Presidiums of the Supreme Soviets, the Councils of Ministers and the Supreme Courts.

Local Soviets exercise state authority and independently decide matters that come within their competence in their respective administrative divisions—from a territory to a rural community.

Local Soviets direct state, economic, social and cultural development within their territory, ensure observance of the laws, the protection of citizens' rights and the maintenance of law and order, and endorse plans for economic and social development and the local budget. They are in charge of the land, guide the work of local industry, exercise control over industrial enterprises subordinate to ministries, over clubs, libraries and theatres, organise the work of trading enterprises and educational establishments, ensure adequate health services for the population, and see to the payment of state pensions and benefits. In other words they take care of people's everyday needs.

Local Soviets have the right to discuss matters of nation-wide importance and to submit their proposals to the appropriate bodies. All local Soviets are elected for a term of two and a half years. Soviets of territories and regions usually comprise 100 deputies, those of districts—75 deputies, cities—50, and settlements and villages—25.

Functioning under local Soviets are street and house management committees, parents' committees, women's councils, councils dealing with cultural matters and other public organisations that unite millions of enthusiasts.

At the elections to the present local Soviets nearly 2,200,000 deputies were elected. Of this number 68 per cent are workers and collective farmers. Half of the deputies are women, and 30 per cent of the deputies are people under 30 years of age. Fifty-six per cent are not Party members.

At each election the composition of local Soviets is substantially changed. For example, nearly half the deputies elected had not been deputies during the previous term. This means that new millions of working people are going through the school of state administration.

People's control: Lenin, the founder of the Soviet state, saw the main task of people's control bodies to be enabling broad sections of the people to supervise all state affairs and learn the art of administration.

Teams and posts of people's control are set up at practically all industrial enterprises, offices, collective farms and other organisations. Their members are elected for a term of two years at general meetings of all those employed there. At present over 9,500,000 industrial workers, collective farmers and office employees are members of people's control bodies.

People's controllers check up on the fulfilment of state plans, combat violations of state discipline, parochial tendencies and instances of excessive attention to departmental interests, bad management and squandering, lovers of red-tape and bureaucrats.

The people's control bodies make wide use of the press, radio and television. The extensive participation of the population in people's control, and the wide publicity given to the work of its bodies ensure their high prestige and efficiency. Decisions and recommendations of people's control bodies are binding on the heads of enterprises and organisations at all levels, including members of the government.

11. THE SOVIET SOCIALIST STATE*
Novosti Press Agency

ESSENCE OF THE SOVIET STATE

As was the case with all other states that preceded it, the socialist state, too, emerges as an instrument of political power of one of the social classes. . . . At the same time, it differs in principle from the states that came before it. First—and most important of all—the socialist state is an

* Reprinted from *Fundamentals of Political Knowledge,* Moscow: Novosti Press Agency Publishing House, 1980, pp. 108–115, by permission of the publisher and of the Copyright Agency of the USSR.

instrument of political power of a   ss which not only does not exploit
anyone, but sets out to free from exploitation all working people. Second,
the working class does not seek to perpetuate its rule. It needs the state
only for a definite historical period, as an instrument of building the new
society. After fulfilling its tasks, the state shall wither away and be replaced by communist public self-government. And lastly, the working
class draws into administering the state, first, its ally—the working peasantry, and then, after the exploitative classes have been abolished, the
whole people. . . .

Indeed, the essence of the Soviet state was, at first, the dictatorship
of the proletariat, without which it was impossible to suppress the resistance of the overthrown oppressor classes to the people's revolutionary
will and organize the masses for building a happier life. With the abolition
of the exploitative classes, the need for the dictatorship gradually disappeared, and the Soviet state became a political organization of the whole
people or *a state of the whole people.*

It is easy to see that this is the logical development of the essence
of the socialist state. Of course, the working class—numerically the
strongest, economically the most important, and the most politically
aware—continues to play a leading part in society and exerts a decisive
influence on state affairs. But, acting together with its allies, the collective
farmers and the people's intelligentsia, it does not establish any privileges
for itself, and power in the country belongs to the entire Soviet people.

As the essence of the socialist state develops, it becomes necessary
to bring in line with it the forms and methods of state administration, to
improve the socialist political system. This problem was solved by the
adoption of a new Constitution of the USSR on October 7, 1977.[1]

The state is the backbone of this system; it includes the Communist
Party as a political public organization, the trade unions, the Young Communist League, co-operatives and other public organizations, and work
collectives.

The basic principles of the Soviet political system are: democratic
centralism, socialist legality, and Communist Party leadership. From the
standpoint of the methods of its activity, this system is characterized by
a combination of representative and direct people's government, and the
main direction in which it develops is the further unfolding of socialist
democracy.

AIMS AND FUNCTIONS OF THE STATE OF THE WHOLE PEOPLE

The *supreme goal* of the Soviet state is the building of a classless communist society in which there will be public, communist self-government.

The *main aims* of the people's socialist state are: to lay the material

---

[1] For details on the new Soviet Constitution, see part C of this chapter below.

and technical foundation of communism, to perfect socialist social relations and transform them into communist relations, to mould the citizen
of communist society, to raise the people's living and cultural standards,
to safeguard the country's security, and to further the consolidation of
peace and development of international co-operation. . . . The following
are the main functions of the Soviet state:

Organization of economic activities. As it is in charge of public
property, the state plans and directs the development of all branches of
the economy; ensures growth of labour productivity and efficiency of
production, and the improvement of the quality of work; takes measures
towards the protection and scientific, rational use of the country's natural
resources; exercises control over the amount of labour and the amount
of consumption; keeps account of the people's property; regulates individual labour activities; deals with questions of mechanization and automation of production processes, and so on.

We have enumerated only some of the aspects of the activity carried out by the state in organizing the economy, but they are sufficient
to show the great scope of its work. The same can be said with respect
to *the social and cultural* function of the state. Here the state promotes
the growth of the social homogeneity of society, namely, the elimination
of class differences and the all-round development and drawing together
of all the peoples of the Soviet Union; organizes systems of public education, health protection, social security, trade and public catering, communal services and amenities, and public utilities; takes steps to raise the
people's living standards and improve working conditions, provides for
the training of scientists; and implements measures to protect, augment
and make extensive use of society's cultural wealth for the moral and
aesthetic education of the Soviet people, for raising their cultural level.

Another function of the Soviet state is *to maintain law and order.*
Acting on the basis of socialist legality, it safeguards the interests of society and the rights and freedoms of citizens, sees to it that they fulfil their
civic duties, organizes the system of people's control which combines
state control and public control by working people in enterprises, collective farms and institutions, administers justice and ensures observance
of the country's laws, and settles economic disputes.

The Soviet state also has important functions connected with the
country's external relations. One of them is *defense of the socialist Motherland,* for which the USSR maintains armed forces, supplied with everything necessary to ensure the security and defence capability of the country, and has instituted universal military service. The other is the
implementation of the country's *foreign policy* which is aimed at ensuring
international conditions favourable for building communism in the USSR,
and which stems from the internationalist duty of the Soviet people to
the working people of the world, and from the Soviet Union's responsibility to the world community.

The Soviet state promotes and strengthens friendship, co-operation, and comradely mutual assistance with other socialist countries on the principle of socialist internationalism, and takes an active part in socialist economic integration and the socialist international division of labour. It supports the struggle of peoples for national liberation and social peace, and builds its foreign relations on the principles of peaceful co-existence. . . .

SOCIALIST LEGALITY

Strict and uniform observance of laws by all state bodies, officials, and citizens is one of the principles of the Soviet state. Socialist legality provides for the establishment of strict and just public order in conformity with Soviet law, i.e. the sum total of rules (rules of conduct) expressing the will of the whole people.

Laws of the USSR are enacted by the Supreme Soviet or by a nationwide vote (referendum) held by its decision.

Laws of a union republic are enacted by its Supreme Soviet or by a referendum, and are effective on its territory.

It is the duty of all state bodies to exercise control over the observance of the country's laws, ensure public order and protect citizens' rights and interests. But there are bodies which concern themselves exclusively with these matters. These bodies are the courts and the Procurator's Office.

In the USSR justice is administered only by the courts. The Soviet judicial system follows the state structure of the country and the territorial-administrative division of union republics. District courts elected by citzens form its basis. Judges of these courts are elected for a term of five years, and people's assessors, for a term of two and a half years. Higher courts are elected by corresponding Soviets of People's Deputies for a term of five years. The Supreme Court of the USSR is elected by the Supreme Soviet. It is the highest judicial body in the USSR and supervises the activities of all other courts.

Soviet justice is notable for consistent democratism and legality. The hearing of civil and criminal cases in all courts is collegial; judges and people's assessors are independent and subject only to the law; proceedings in all courts are open to the public—hearings *in camera* are allowed only in special cases provided for by law; defendants are guaranteed the right to legal assistance; no one may be adjudged guilty of a crime and subjected to punishment as a criminal except by the sentence of a court and in conformity with the law.

C
The Constitution

"The great achievements of our society of developed socialism are recorded in the new Constitution of the USSR."

NIKOLAI A. TIKHONOV
Chairman, USSR Council of Ministers

"The Soviet people . . . hereby affirm the principles of the social structure and policy of the USSR, and define the rights and obligations of citizens, and the principles of the organization of the socialist state of the whole people, and its aims, and proclaim these in the Constitution."

CONSTITUTION OF THE USSR
Preamble

"The new Soviet Constitution is justly called the law of life of developed socialist society. . . . We have not created the Constitution as a stage prop. It has to be fulfilled and will be fulfilled in all its parts. It has to become and will become a powerful instrument in the further development and deepening of socialist democracy."

LEONID I. BREZHNEV
Late Secretary-General, CC CPSU and Chairman, Presidium of the Supreme Soviet

On June 4, 1977, after many years of preparation dating back to the Khrushchev era, Soviet newspapers published a draft of a new constitution, the fourth in Soviet history and the first in over forty years. After an extensive, nationwide discussion which resulted in millions of proposals and suggestions submitted for consideration to the framers, an altered, final version of the new "Fundamental Law" was adopted by a special session of the Supreme Soviet of the USSR on October 7, 1977.

In the United States, the U.S. Constitution is proclaimed the highest law in the land, but the meaning of this statement is not always clear. The U.S. Supreme Court has the power to declare unconstitutional state laws as well as acts of Congress, but over time, with new judges on the bench, the Supreme Court has often reversed itself. It has let stand laws once held in violation of the Constitution (child labor laws, for instance), while holding to be unconstitutional what previously had been considered lawful (such as segregation in public schools)—so much so that some political scientists have said that "the Constitution is what the courts say it is." To still get on the books a law declared unconstitutional by the courts, the U.S. Constitution can be amended (which requires ratification by two thirds of the states), and then the courts interpret precisely what the amendment means.

In the Soviet Union, the constitution is also proclaimed the highest law in the land, but the meaning of this statement is even more shrouded in unclarity. In elaborating on the powers of the CPSU, the "leading and guiding force of Soviet society and the nucleus of its political system, of all state organizations and public organizations," Article 6 of the Soviet Constitution states that "all party organizations shall function within the framework of the Constitution of the USSR." But precisely what does this mean? Can anyone challenge the constitutionality of an action of the Communist Party of the Soviet Union? And is the new Soviet Constitution a progressive document that truly reflects the legal needs of a "developed socialist society," as the Soviet Constitution claims it is, or is it merely a document designed to "freeze Soviet political structures" and to "re-affirm the determination to avoid change," as some Western analysts assert? These and related issues are discussed in the contributions to this, the last part of Chapter IV. (The important issues of freedom, democracy, and human rights, while touched upon here, are treated in detail in the next chapter.)

In Selection 12, Robert Sharlet sees the new 1977 Soviet Constitution as an important, comprehensive document, a "Brezhnev Constitution" (as differentiated from the previous 1936 "Stalin Constitution"), aimed at bringing an "authoritative and definitive end to de-Stalinization" by "constitutionalizing both the accomplishments and the limits of de-Stalinization." Next, under "Western Marxist Views," John J. Abt briefly outlines the essence of the four Soviet Constitutions (1918, 1924, 1936 and 1977), each of which, he writes, "marks a new stage in the progress of the first land of socialism." In Selection 14, R. R. Sharma, a self-proclaimed Indian Marxist who heads the Centre for Soviet and East European Studies at Jawaharlal Nehru University, New Delhi, India, discusses in some length the drafting as well as the structure and the contents of the new constitution which he views as "a historically re-markable document." In the final selection of this chapter, an article by Soviet journalist and commentator on Soviet law, Irina Trofimova, praises the new Soviet Constitution as the Fundamental Law and as "a political doument of global significance, summing up the sixty years' experience of the Soviet state."

WESTERN VIEWS

12. DE-STALINIZATION AND SOVIET CONSTITUTIONALISM*

Robert Sharlet
Union College

The 1977 constitution, superseding the "Stalin constitution" of 1936, provides an unusual opportunity to explore in broad outline the question of change and continuity in the Soviet system since Stalin. As the most ambitious constitutional description of the shape and appearance of the Soviet system to date, the new document represents a careful distillation of six decades of Soviet rule and particularly of the developments of the post-Stalin period.[1] Consistent with Soviet political tradition, the new constitution is more important for its comprehensive spirit than for its function as a fundamental legal document; it represents a broad, historical policy statement or, more precisely, a "metapolicy": a policy on policy making and implementation. However, departing from past practice, the constitution of 1977 is intended as a prescriptive and normative declaration, signaling the party's public commitments with regard to nearly all aspects of the Soviet system. In the absence of the Stalinist reliance on terror, and given the post-Stalin leadership's much greater dependence on public consensus requiring the maintenance of the elite's credibility, these constitutional commitments have not been made lightly.

The 1977 constitution is clearly a metapolicy to be taken seriously. The Brezhnev regime attempted to use the document as a means for codifying both the scope and the limits of de-Stalinization. De-Stalinization as post-Stalin reform has generally been taken to mean decentralization and the diffusion of administrative authority as well as the debureaucratization of leadership and the depoliticization of social initiative. Among other things, this broad reform has resulted, in practical terms, in increased operational independence for middle-level political, administrative, and economic elites; solicitation and accommodation of expert advice in policy making; invigoration of secondary organizations

---

* Reprinted from Robert Sharlet, "De-Stalinization and Soviet Constitutionalism," in Stephen F. Cohen, Alexander Rabinowitch, and Robert Sharlet, *The Soviet Union Since Stalin*, Bloomington: Indiana University Press, 1980, pp. 93–94 and 106–7, by permission of the author and the publisher.

[1] As with the previous constitutions, the new document is primarily reflective of the Soviet system. However, by design, the 1977 constitution also has programmatic content to a far greater extent than its predecessors. See Robert Sharlet, "The New Soviet Constitution," *Problems of Communism*, September–October 1977, pp. 5–8.

and the stimulation of mass participation in the implementation of official policy, and a less coercive social policy toward the individual. . . .

Although the Soviet constitution of 1977 bears the discernible imprints of Lenin, Stalin, and Khrushchev, Brezhnev's "signature" is evident throughout the document as well, especially in what appears to be his attempt finally to lay to rest Stalin's ghost as a divisive issue in Soviet leadership politics. Characteristically, his approach to this problem was to seek a pragmatic compromise. By constitutionalizing both the accomplishments and the limits of de-Stalinization, Brezhnev presided over the creation of a centrist post-Stalin constitution that is neither anti-Stalin nor neo-Stalinist.

However, it cannot be denied that the constitution of 1977 is a triumph for conservatism in Soviet politics. Although it may be a centrist document in the letter, a tilt toward the conservative camp is evident in its spirit. Since the constitution was drafted under the aegis of a conservative leadership, it embodies the extremely cautious and tightly controlled conception of change characteristic of the conservative reaction led by Brezhnev against Khrushchev's reformism from 1964 on. Fundamentally, the 1977 constitution is a document of the post-Stalin and post-Khrushchev status quo. Stability is based on a "juridicized" society peopled by citizen-conservators constitutionally charged with a host of duties. These duties range from "socially useful" employment and the protection of public property to the preservation of culture and the conservation of nature.[2]

Presumably one of Brezhnev's major purposes was to bring an authoritative and definitive end to de-Stalinization and what it came to mean politically—the politics of reformism—by codifying its scope and limits in the new constitution, the first since Stalin. It is characteristic of Brezhnev and his conservative colleagues that they chose a legal instrument to carry out this political purpose. Traditionally, law in Soviet society has been considered a stabilizing force and has been philosophically and functionally juxtaposed to the dynamism of politics. In this sense, Soviet history can be viewed as a cycle of political change followed by consolidation through law. Hence, it is not surprising that the reform-to-reaction cycle of post-Stalin politics in the USSR has been defined in the basically conservative form of law. Whether or not this juridical framework will succeed in the long-term containment of the reformist impulse in Soviet society remains, of course, to be seen.

Beyond arresting reformist change, Brezhnev seemed to want to leave behind the constitution of 1977 as a monument to his "administration," fixing in place the modernized, institutionalized, and now presumably stabilized Soviet system, if his eventual legacy remains intact.

---

[2] See the 1977 constitution, Arts. 12, 14, 60, 61, 67, and 68, respectively.

WESTERN MARXIST VIEWS

13. THE FOUR SOVIET CONSTITUTIONS*
John J. Abt
Constitutional lawyer and counsel for the Communist Party, USA

The draft of a new Constitution of the USSR was approved by the Presidium of the Supreme Soviet in May, 1977 and presented to the people for nationwide discussion and proposed amendments before its submission to the Supreme Soviet for final action in October.

Publication of the draft invites comparison with its predecessors of 1918, 1924 and 1936. Each of the four Constitutions marks a new stage in the progress of the first land of socialism.

The earliest was adopted nine months after the Revolution when the young state, ravaged by four years of imperialist war and beleaguered by the armies of fourteen foreign powers and of counterrevolutionary White Guard generals, retained control only of Central Russia, while the Ukraine, the Caucasus, Central Asia, Siberia and other former Russian territories were under enemy occupation. The Constitution for what was then called the Russian Soviet Federal Socialist Republic declared as its goal "the abolition of the exploitation of men by men" and the establishment of a socialist society. It then proceeded to codify the measures already taken toward realization of this noble objective.

It nationalized the land, the banks and foreign trade and provided for "a first step" in nationalizing the means of industrial production and transportation. It guaranteed national self-determination in a land which under the tsars had been a prison of nations, "Leaving to the workers and peasants of every people to decide . . . whether or not they desire to participate, and on what basis, in the Federal Government." It abolished racial and national discrimination, gave equal rights to women, and "sets itself the task of furnishing full and free education" to a population then 75 per cent illiterate.

It established a dictatorship of the proletariat, disenfranchising the propertied classes, giving industrial workers approximately three times the representation of peasants in the central government, and depriving all individuals and groups "of rights which could be utilized by them to the detriment of the Socialist Revolution." It fixed the voting age at 18

* Reprinted from John J. Abt, "The New Soviet Constitution," in Marilyn Bechtel, David Laibman, and Jessica Smith, eds., *Six Decades That Changed the World*, New York: New World Review Publishers, Inc., 1978, pp. 149–52 by permission of the publisher.

and set up a structure of government vesting "all the central and local power" in the Soviets of Workers, Soldiers and Peasant Deputies. These were delegate bodies which, at the local level, were elected by meetings of voters at their work places, such as factories, army units and rural villages. Higher bodies, including the central government, were elected by the delegates to the next lower bodies. All delegates were subject to recall.

By 1922, after four years of devastating civil war and foreign intervention, the Revolution was victorious throughout the country as it exists today, except for the Baltic States which federated in 1939 and the territory acquired following World War II. As the enemy was driven out, Soviet Republics were established in the liberated areas. Initially, they entered into a loose federation with the RSFSR but soon found a closer union necessary. This was decided on at a Congress of the constituent republics in 1922 and formalized in 1924 by adoption of the Constitution of the Union of Soviet Socialist Republics. Its primary innovation was the creation of a federal structure which provided for a strong central government while guaranteeing each constituent republic the fullest local and cultural autonomy and equal participation in the central government. This was secured by providing for the establishment for each of six Union Republics of a government elected by its citizens and a bicameral Central Executive Committee of the Union in which one chamber was elected on the basis of population while the other gave equal representation to each Union Republic, with the proviso that all action required the concurrence of both chambers.

If the 1924 Constitution marked the victory of the Revolution, its successor, adopted 12 years later, marked the victory of socialism. In little more than a decade, the face of the nation had been transformed. Agriculture was all but completely socialized by the system of collective and state farms. All industry was publicly owned, and output increased seven times. Socially owned wealth had risen from 48 per cent to 95.8 per cent of the country's fixed capital. Unemployment had been done away with by 1931, and illiteracy substantially eradicated.

The 1936 Constitution expressed the essence of this transformation by declaring the USSR to be "a socialist state of workers and peasants" in which capitalist exploitation of man by man had been replaced by the socialist principle, "From each according to his ability, to each according to his work."

The enormous progress made in industrializing the country and socializing agriculture made it possible for the state to provide its people, and for the 1936 Constitution to guarantee them, the most basic of all human rights—the right to work, to rest, to security in old age and disability, to free medical care, and to free education at every level.

The 1936 Constitution likewise reflected the victory of socialism by democratizing the electoral system. There being no exploiters to disenfranchise, the vote was given to all citizens at the age of 18, with eligibility for public office at 23, excepting only those legally certified as insane. The disproportion between urban and rural representation in the soviets was eliminated. Direct election by secret ballot at all levels of office was provided for. Territorial election districts, each with the same number of inhabitants, replaced the former work-place districts. The Central Executive Committee was replaced by a bicameral Supreme Soviet of the USSR composed of a Soviet of the Union and a Soviet of Nationalities.

In the 40 years since the 1936 Constitution proclaimed the victory of socialism, the Soviet Union has developed into a mature socialist society. Recovering from the incalculable losses of World War II, it has increased the overall volume of industrial production 29 times until it stands at 85 per cent of the US level and has surpassed the latter in steel, coal, oil and other key indicators. In the same period, socialized agriculture has increased output 3.2 times. Per capita real income doubles every 15 years and is more than five times higher than in 1936. Accompanying the betterment of the material conditions of the people has been a change in their social relations. Soviet society has become increasingly homogeneous as the differences in educational level and mode of life between town and country and between manual and intellectual workers have narrowed. Similarly, the equality of the nations comprising the Soviet Union which the 1936 Constitution guaranteed as a matter of law has now become equality in fact as affirmative action by the central government has raised the economic and cultural level of the formerly underdeveloped republics of Central Asia and elsewhere to a parity with what had been industrially advanced areas of the country.

As a result of these profound changes, the Soviet state is no longer characterized as a dictatorship of the proletariat but has developed into a form described as a state of the whole people.

The change in the international position of the Soviet Union has been no less far-reaching. No longer isolated by capitalist encirclement, it has become a member of a powerful socialist community. At the same time, dozens of new states in Asia and Africa have thrown off the colonial yoke and taken an anti-imperialist course of development with the aid and support of the socialist community of nations. As a result, the world balance of forces has been altered to the point where the prevention of world war has become a realistic possibility.

The new Constitution builds on the foundation laid by its predecessors, taking into account the tremendous advances of the last 40 years in the life of the country and in the international arena. Like them, it is at once a programmatic document which sets forth the principles and goals applicable to the present stage of Soviet society and a codification of the nation's major social advances and political structure.

The draft's preamble characterizes the Soviet Union as a "developed socialist society" having "mature social relations" in which the state, after fulfilling the tasks of the dictatorship of the proletariat, "has become a state of the whole people" where "the law of life is the concern of all for the welfare of each and the concern of each for the welfare of all." Unlike any of its forerunners, the preamble then sets its sights on the transition to communism, the highest stage of socialist society. It states:

> The supreme purpose of the Soviet state is to build a class-less communist society. The principle tasks of the state are: to build the material and technical basis of communism, to perfect socialist social relations, to mould the citizen of communist society, to raise the living standard and cultural level of the working people, to ensure the country's security, to help strengthen peace and to promote international cooperation. . . .

AN INDIAN MARXIST'S VIEWS

14. SOME PARAMETERS OF THE NEW SOVIET CONSTITUTION*

R. R. Sharma†

Chairman, Centre for Soviet and East European Studies,
Jawaharlal Nehru University

The new Soviet Constitution—adopted on 7 October 1977, now declared as the national Constitutional Day—epitomizes what Brezhnev called "the whole sixty years' development", as well as continuity and break with the past. The Constitution of 1936 is clearly transcended, and yet that Constitution looms large in the background as a basic constitutional document with a certain politico-ideological framework within which the present Constitution has been structured. Despite the fact that the new Soviet Constitution is more comprehensive in its scope and content, its ideological genetic affinity with the Constitution of 1936 has to be seen and emphasized. The underlying Marxian political logic in the structural totality of the new Constitution has been distinctly retained from the past with suitable clarifications and additions. From this standpoint, the new Soviet Constitution appears to be a more carefully drafted document, one

* Reprinted from *International Studies*, April–June, 1979, pp. 209–15, by permission of the author and the publisher.

† Dr. Sharma is Chairman of the Centre for Soviet and East European Studies at Jawaharlal Nehru University, New Delhi, India.

which has the merit of projecting a clear and neat perspective of the Soviet State and society, and the socio-economic and political metamorphosis that has occurred during the last sixty cataclysmic years. The Soviet system has greatly matured since 1936. Hence the characterization of the present Constitution as the Constitution of Developed Socialism.

Our intention here is to discuss not only the structural content and scope of the new Soviet Constitution but also the constitution-making process, which in some ways is self-explanatory of the functionality of the Soviet political system itself.

CONSTITUTION IN THE MAKING

Even a cursory glance at the new Constitution clearly shows that it is a more neat and structurally better-framed document than the Constitution of 1936. No other living Constitution has known such detailed discussion, intensive work, and even anxious waiting. In sharp contrast to the Constitution of 1936, the present Constitution was in the making for nearly fifteen long years, The Constitutional Commission to draft the new Soviet Constitution was formally appointed in 1962. Its work appeared to have slowed appreciably after the removal of Khrushchev in 1964. The Constitutional Commission was reorganized and activated in 1966. It was initially headed by Khrushchev, and subsequently by Brezhnev, and was comprised of seventy-five members. Twenty-three new members were added to the Commission in April 1977 to replace those who had retired in the intervening years. The Constitutional Commission included, to quote Brezhnev, "experienced party and Government workers, collective farmers, the intelligentsia, eminent scientists and legal specialists". Debate and discussion even at the drafting stage was extensive and far-reaching. It was "twice considered" by the Plenary meetings of the Central Committee of the Communist Party of the Soviet Union (CPSU), and we are further informed by G. Romanov—a member of the Politburo, and also of the Constitutional Commission—that at the drafting stage "repeated" and wide discussions were held in the Politburo, the Central Committee, and other State institutions, as also with jurists, sociologists, historians, and representatives of mass social organizations.[1]

The draft constitution was exposed to nation-wide "political" discussion soon after the Plenary Session of the Central Committee late in May 1977. According to Brezhnev, the draft constitution was debated by "over eighty per cent" of the adult population resulting in "400,000 proposals for amendments" intended to clarify, improve, and supplement the draft proposals. In the light of these proposals as many as 110 Articles of the draft were amended, and a completely new Article was added. The

[1] This contrasts sharply with the making of the Constitution in 1936. The work of the Constitutional Commission, as also the discussion on the draft, was completed in a little over a year. The Constitution was ratified early in December 1936.

discussion in the Sureme Soviet enhanced the number of amendments and clarifications to a total of 150. Obviously the magnitude and scope of the discussion and "commentary" on the draft stands out in bold relief as a watershed in mass political mobilization and participation in the functionality of the Soviet system. Brezhnev was thus close to reality in claiming that the discussion had in fact transcended the "framework of an analysis of the text itself. It had developed into a frank commentary truly by the whole people, on the key aspects of our life."[2] The entire socio-political procedure of constitution-making has thus a certain bearing on the functionality of the Soviet political system, which, at its present stage of development, clearly seeks to involve "representatives of all strata of population" for further "invigoration of all social life" in the country. This level of participation in "government and people's control bodies", Brezhnev claimed, is bound to "transform" the Soviet State into "self-government" and Socialist democracy. He of course conceded that progress on these lines was "steady and slow", but he believed that the programmatic aspects of the new Constitution "will contribute effectively to the attainment of this important goal". . . .

Various suggestions which emerged in the course of the extensive constitutional debate were intended to emphasize the need to strengthen further the actual functioning of Soviet democracy. Comprehensive constitutional guarantees were sought to ensure meaningful participation of the people in improving the democratic functioning of the system and the elimination of whatever possibility there was of illegal "persecution" of Soviet citizens.[3] A large number of participants in the debate, therefore, suggested that it was important not only to uphold the principle of "Socialist legality" but also to devise an institutionalized mechanism that would ensure a much wider participation of the people than had till then been possible and to strengthen their control function. Further, there was a suggestion that all party organizations should function within the framework of the Soviet Constitution and that the "role of the party and its growth in the future" should be clearly and "precisely stated in two or three places in the Constitution", especially in the chapter on the basic rights and duties of citizens. Perhaps the implication was that even a "leading and guiding force" like the CPSU should not in future be able to transgress its constitutionally specified political role in a manner that would violate the principle of "Socialist legality". Thus public comment centered round the issues of mass political and socio-economic participation and "Socialist legality". . . .

---

[2] The Soviet Press and academic journals vibrated with sharply conflicting views and suggestions on the draft between June and October 1977.

[3] Brezhnev in his speech before the Supreme Soviet on 4 October 1977 pointed out how several letters received from Soviet citizens had reported "disgraceful instances of abuse of State power."

STRUCTURE OF THE NEW CONSTITUTION

The Preamble of the new Soviet Constitution, "preserving the continuity" of ideas from the Constitutions of 1924 and 1936, conceptualizes itself as the "Fundamental Law" of the land and declares that the building of a "classless Communist society" would be the "supreme goal" of the Soviet State. This obviously is a programmatic delcaration, the functional content of which is writ large in other parts of the Constitution as well. Here the present Constitution makes a significant departure from the Constitution of 1936, which did not go beyond the framework of recording in legislative terms what has already been achieved and won in actual fact. . . . The structure of the present Constitution thus transcends the 1936 document in so far as it is not only reflective but also programmatic in its scope and content. It seeks to relate itself to the specifics of the historical imperative of current and future socio-economic development.

Of course, the new Constitution makes a detailed account of nearly all major socio-economic and legislative developments since the Soviet Revolution. The great volume of these crucial changes is catalogued in Sections 1-2 of the new Constitution, which deal with socio-political and economic institutional structures and with the relationship between the State and the individual. The so-called special chapter on the aims and principles of Soviet foreign policy also is included in these sections. Collectively, these two sections comprise seven chapters and sixty-nine Articles. . . . What clearly emerges from these two sections is the implicit recognition that the Soviet State must subserve the socio-economic and ideological props of the Soviet system, i.e. "the extension of Socialist democracy" (Article 9).

The most strategic departure from the Constitution of 1936 is distinctly conceptualized in the "Socialist State of the whole people [Article 1], expressing the will and interests of workers, peasants, and intelligentsia". This epitomizes the evolution of the system from the notion of "dictatorship of the proletariat", which the Constitution of 1936 embodied. The conceptualization of the system as a State of the whole people derives its legitimacy from the Soviet perception of the process of radical transformation of the socio-economic configuration of Soviet society. In 1936 the Soviet State was viewed as "a Socialist State of workers and peasants" in which the peasantry was the socially dominant class required to function in conditions of working-class hegemony.

The productive forces have registered a sharp growth since 1936. The working class has emerged as the largest social group: it now constitutes 62 per cent of the total population. (In 1936 it used to be only 31 per cent of the total population.) The impressive development of the productive forces is conceptualized in the notion of Developed or Mature Socialism. . . . The strength of the economic base and the rapid growth of its vast infrastructure, the tremendous improvement in educational and technical skills, the large reduction in the income differentials, etc. have narrowed the areas of socio-economic diversity and have consequently drawn the main social classes and national groups closer in terms of Socialist social relations. . . . This had its corresponding impact in drawing together various socio-economic groups; their income and educational differentials has been reduced, and nearly 73 per cent of the workers and over 56 per cent of the collective farmers have received the benefit of secondary and specialized education.[4]

To put it briefly, the notion of Developed Socialism thus intrinsically incorporates the concept of State of the whole people. In fact the two are viewed as complementary. They are reinforced by Article 2 of the Constitution, which speaks of the "exercise of State power through Soviets of People's Deputies". The Soviet Constitution of 1936 spoke of "Soviets of Working People's Deputies". The Soviet conception of the system as a "state of the whole people" is not likely to find favour with the orthodox Marxists, but it certainly calls for thoughtful consideration and serious discussion.

The interest of the Soviet leadership in involving the greater mass of people in economic, political, and cultural subsystems is further operationalized in Articles 5–8, which spell out the scope of mass participation and the legislative role of the various mass organizations. . . .

The right to "small-scale" private property (Article 17), initially guaranteed in Article 9 of the Soviet Constitution of 1936, remains with minor changes.[5] Actually, there was a lively debate in the Soviet Press on the demand that it should be abolished. However, in his speech before the Supreme Soviet in October 1977 Brezhnev argued that "small-scale" holdings, mainly agricultural, which "do not involve exploitation", had "a useful role to play in our economy *at the present stage*". He thus gave indication of the possibility of their abolition at some suitable future date. Articles 13–14 of the new Constitution make it clear that property "owned or used cannot be [the] means of deriving unearned income" and that a citizen's "status in society" is to be determined really by "socially useful work". These Articles are thus directed against the phenomenon of social parasitism. Their spirit is made more explicit in Article 60 (in the section on rights and duties), which reads: "Evasion of socially useful work is incompatible with the principles of Socialist society."

---

[4] The new Constitution goes beyond the Constitution of 1936 in envisaging "universal compulsory secondary education, and broad development of vocational, specialized secondary and higher education" as its programmatic objective (Article 56). Productive efforts in this direction will have the effect of further reducing distinction between mental and physical labour, country and town, and even the income structure.

[5] This refers to private ownership of the means of production. Article 17 reads: "In the USSR, the law permits individual labour in handicrafts, farming, the provision of services for the public and other forms of activity based exclusively on the personal work of individual citizens and members of their families. The state makes regulations for such work to ensure that it serves the interests of society." [Editor's note.]

The so-called special chapter on foreign policy (Chapter 4, Articles 28–30) briefly reiterates the objectives of Soviet foreign policy. These notably include peaceful co-existence, support for movements for national liberation, and universal and complete disarmament. Some of the well-known provisions of the Helsinki Conference, such as inviolability of frontiers, respect for human rights and fundamental freedoms, respect for international law, etc., have also been included (Article 29). Article 30 deals with the principle of "Socialist internationalism" and co-operation among Socialist states.

The next part of the Soviet Constitution deals with the strategic problem of relationship between the State and the individual (Articles 33–69). This part attracted wide attention both within and outside the country, and the commentary on these Articles was also suitably reported in the Soviet Press.[6] It distinctly identifies the basic economic, political, and cultural rights, as well as the corresponding duties and obligations of a Soviet citizen. It marks a distinct advance from the provisions of the previous Constitution in that it enlarges the basic structure of rights and duties. It also provides for further Constitutional guarantees with respect to economic and socio-cultural rights. Obviously this has been made possible by the maturity of the economic system, which corresponds to the "developed" stage of Socialism. . . .[7]

In contrast to the Constitution of 1936, there are specific Constitutional provisions and guarantees now with respect to universal employment. These include "the right to choose one's trade or profession, the type of job" (Article 40), the right to economic security (Article 42–43), the right to housing and other utility services (Article 44), and the right to enjoy cultural benefits (Article 46). The economic rights enshrined in the Constitution are so rich and so extensive in scope that they may fairly be regarded as reflective of the immense growth of productive forces in Soviet society. They also testify to the commencement of a new stage in the economic development of Soviet society.

Likewise the ambit of personal, civil, and participatory rights and freedoms in the new Constitution is considerably wider than it was in the Constitution of 1936. However, both constitutions conceptualize a close nexus between rights and social obligations, which are deemed "inseparable" (Article 59). The large body of legislation on criminal procedural law enacted since the end of the 1950s is significantly incorporated in the new Constitution. These laws are intended to ensure the inviolability of the guaranteed civil and personal rights in the light of the specific codification of the "due process" of law, which is sufficiently amplified in Section 7, dealing with justice, arbitration, etc. Notably the so-called

---

[6] The nationwide discussion which reflected a wide spectrum of views was given adequate space in the national press, particularly in *Pravda, Izvestiya, Komsomolskaya Pravda,* etc.

[7] The issues of freedom and democracy in the USSR and of the rights and duties of the Soviet citizens are covered in greater detail in Chapter V below. [Editor's note.]

"extra-legal" and "special courts" referred to in the Constitution of 1936 (Article 102) no longer exist. There is no mention of these courts in the new Constitution. Article 155 proclaims complete judicial independence. Emphasizing the "due process" of law and the independence of the Judiciary in his speech before the Central Committee Plenum in May 1977, Brezhnev asserted that there would be no return to the "illegal repression" of the late 1930s. The inviolability of these rights has been further strengthened by a number of guarantees provided in the criminal codes and "other legislative acts" of the various Union Republics.

Perhaps the most characteristic feature of the new Constitution is the enlargement of a remarkable variety of participatory rights. These are intended to ensure meaningful scope for mass involvement in public life. The specified participatory rights are both individual and institutional (group) in scope and character. Their focus seems to have been sharpened after the wide public debate that followed the publication of the draft constitution early in June 1977. The final basket of participatory rights includes the right to submit proposals to State bodies to improve their policies or functioning, the right to criticize their performance (Article 46), the right to lodge complaints against State officials and others, and also the right to seek "legal compensation" from courts for "damages" caused by "unlawful actions by State organizations" (Article 58). This is sought to be ensured by appropriate Constitutional guarantees, clarified in each Article, for their enforcement and compliance, such as time-bound consideration of proposals, complaints, etc.

Additionally, the structure of participatory rights has been strengthened in Chapters 13, 14, and 19 of the new Constitution, which seek to enhance the functional role of people's deputies of the local Soviets, as also of other local bodies of State authority. The responsibilities of people's deputies in local decision-making to ensure "all-round economic and socio-cultural development of their areas" (Article 147) are sought to be institutionalized by means of the provision for "electors' mandate" (Article 102). The strategic significance of this new Article is, as Brezhnev put it, to fulfil the "diverse" requirements of "group" or "institutional" interests—a clear acknowledgement of the fact that there is a plurality of group interests calling for protection. Likewise economic enterprises have been constitutionally allowed greater initiative and participation in micro planning and decision-making. The scope of workers' participation is also sought to be enhanced in enterprise management (Articles 15 and 16). These, thus, constitute the additional dynamic linkages with the envisaged goals of participatory self-government, greater functional autonomy of the local institutions, and the advancement of scientific-technological revolution.

Finally, the new Constitution retains the structure of federal arrangement of Union-Republic relationships and division of State powers. In fact the Constitutional Commission had received some proposals suggesting "the elimination" of the Union and autonomous Republics and the incorporation of the "concept of an integral *Soviet nation*" in the Constitution. If accepted, this would have basically altered the existing federal scheme, drastically curtailed the sovereignty of the Union Republics, and eliminated the Chamber of Soviet of Nationalities of the Supreme Soviet. The Constitutional Commission rejected the proposals. . . . While preserving the basic federal framework, the functional ethos embodied in the new Constitution seems to favour institutional decentralization. . . .

The new Soviet Constitution is thus a historically remarkable document which lists the cumulative achievements of the Soviet system since 1936. It also seeks to project a programmatic orientation by stipulating an activization of the work of the lower organs of State power and other institutions and an expansion of their rights in the creative guidance of the economy, culture, etc. It codifies the source of power, which is the broad mass of "all people". It seeks to ensure their greater participation in socio-political and economic spheres of public activity. . . .

Basically, the undercurrent theme in the extension of the process of Socialist democracy, or, as Chkhikvadze puts it, the main "merit" of the new Constitution, is that it has "mapped out the main lines for the further improvement of Socialist democracy."[8] Ever since the Twenty-First Congress of the CPSU Soviet leaders have been increasingly occupied with the problem of extending the scope of people's participation in the functionality of the system. Soviet sociologists are reported to have told Professor Gouldner that "a habit of waiting for directions from the top had emerged in the past, from past situations . . . but we are trying to extend democracy in our country and, with this, a greater respect for the individual person".[9] The new Soviet Constitution appears to reflect a committee effort in that direction.

SOVIET VIEWS

15. OUR NEW CONSTITUTION*
Irina Trofimova
Soviet journalist and legal analyst

The Constitution was adopted on October 7 (1977), at the closing meeting of the special session of the U.S.S.R. Supreme Soviet in the Kremlin. As

[8] V. Chkhikvadze, "Soviet Constitution: An Inspiring Example," in *International Affairs* (Moscow), Jan., 1978, p. 28.

[9] A. Gouldner, *The Coming Crisis of Western Sociology* (London, 1971), p. 457.

* Reprinted from *New Times*, No. 42, October, 1977, pp. 4–5, by permission of the Copyright Agency of the USSR.

one of the deputies aptly put it, doing the will of the Soviet people, their representatives have legislatively secured the character of the society of developed socialism which today constitutes the highest achievement of social progress. Codified in this momentous document are the broad and manifold rights and freedoms the Soviet citizen enjoys, as also his lofty duties to society. This is the code whereby the Soviet people will now live and work and by which they will measure their progress.

"Years will pass and decades," Leonid Brezhnev said, "but this day in October will for ever remain in the people's memory as vivid testimony to the genuine triumph of the Leninist principles of democratic government. The farther our society advances along the road to communism, the more obvious will be the vast creative potentialities of socialist democracy—government by the people, government for the people—reflected in the new Constitution."

The Soviet people did not receive their Fundamental Law from "above." They themselves are its architects. More than 140 million people took part in discussing the draft of the Constitution. It was a truly nationwide discussion. The draft was examined thoroughly and competently, and this is yet another distinctive feature of the society of developed socialism in which we live. The Soviet people's competence in dealing with state affairs has grown immeasurably. Ours is a society of educated people. Here is one figure cited at the Supreme Soviet session: 73.2 per cent of the workers have a higher or secondary (complete or incomplete) education. Millions of working people have gone through the school of state administration in the local Soviets. Our people have not only acquired the right to rule the destinies of their country; they have been given the conditions enabling them to perform this mission.

In the course of the discussion of the draft Constitution Soviet people raised questions relating to fundamentally important aspects of the life of society. The additions, clarifications and amendments were directed above all at deepening and improving the wording of the basic laws of the social system of the U.S.S.R., at defining more clearly the role of labour under socialism. . . .

There were about 400,000 suggestions for amendments and the Constitution Commission could not consider and submit them all to the Supreme Soviet session. Some were essentially correct, but were of limited nature, while others were incorrect in principle. It was suggested, for instance, to introduce in the Constitution the concept of an integral Soviet nation, eliminating the Union and Autonomous Republics or drastically curtailing the sovereignty of the Union Republics. . . . The argument was that a new historical community—the Soviet people—has taken shape in our country. But socio-political unity does not at all imply the disappearance of national distinctions. It would be unwise artificially to speed the objective process of the coming together of the nations and nationalities of our country.

The wide range of proposals, including those that could not be accepted for one reason or another testified to the unrestricted character of the discussion. In many ways it was more than just an analysis of the text itself. It was a frank exchange of views on questions of immediate concern to Soviet people.

The discussion of the draft of the Fundamental Law was continued at the Supreme Soviet session. It was not a ceremonial session, although the importance of the question considered gave it an air of solemnity. The deputies advanced many interesting suggestions. Valentina Nikolayeva-Tereshkova, Chairman of the Soviet Women's Committee, and Zoya Pukhova, manager of the Ivanovo Textile Mill, proposed to add to Article 35 a clause providing for the gradual reduction of working time for mothers with small children. Maira Amantayeva, a teacher from Kazakhstan, expressed the wish to see inscribed in the Constitution the provision that spiritual values should be used for the moral and esthetic upbringing of the Soviet people. Deputies Grigory Romanov and Kazimir Lushnevsky proposed that the obligation of the Soviets of People's Deputies and the bodies they set up to report regularly to the population on their work and the decisions they adopt be inscribed in the Constitution.

If one compares the draft with the final text, one will see that the latter was considerably enriched by the suggestions advanced. Behind each line of the Fundamental Law is the collective wisdom of the people.

The Constitution is a political document of global significance summing up the sixty years' experience of the Soviet state and illustrating our achievements. It is the law of life of developed socialist society. Leonid Brezhnev's report to the session analyzed the Constitution and presented an integral picture of mature socialism, its economic and political systems, the social structure and spiritual life of our society, its foreign policy. The Fundamental Law ensures that the tasks, structure, functions and work procedure of state bodies conform to the present stage of development of our state.

There is a vast distance—not in time but in terms of accomplishment—between mature socialism and its beginnings. "It is a society in which powerful productive forces . . . have been created," the Constitution says. Behind this terse line is a whole epoch in our life. Implicit in it is the enthusiasm of the people who built the Magnitogorsk Steel Mill and who lived on meager rations and in unheated barracks; the first outlines of the GOELRO (Electrification of Russia) Plan, and the modest— by present standards—DIP lathes of which the country was then proud. It stands also for our first atomic power stations and giant works and the flight of scientific and technical thought that has paved man's path to the stars. New gauges, new dimensions, new deep-going processes have emerged in every sphere of our society's life.

As the socialist state advances, millions of citizens take an increasingly active part in the work of administrative bodies, in the management of production and distribution, in the people's control system and in judicial bodies, in the elaboration of cultural and social policies. Our statehood is gradually developing into communist social self-government. As Leonid Brezhnev pointed out, this is of course a long process, but it is going steadily forward. The dialectics of social development was taken into account in drawing up the Fundamental Law; it ensures extension of socialist democracy, giving full rein to the tendency towards self-government.

The role of the Communist Party naturally becomes all the greater at the new stage of development, whenever more complex and responsible tasks of communist construction are being tackled. The Constitution secures the Party's role as the leading and guiding force of Soviet society and outlines its sphere of action. Article 6 says that the Communist Party, armed with Marxism-Leninism, determines the general perspectives of the development of society and the course of the home and foreign policy of the USSR, directs the great constructive work of the Soviet people, and imparts a planned, theoretically substantiated character to their struggle for the victory of communism. . . .

The Soviet people heartily approve of the leading role of our Leninist Party, being secured in our Fundamental Law. The Party has won the people's trust by faithfully serving their interests. In the most trying periods of the history of the Soviet state—when we were setting our poverty-ridden, hungry country on its feet and in the years of life-and-death struggles against aggressors—the Communists were always in the van, where the difficulties were the greatest.

Probably only the Soviet people and our friends abroad, those who know Soviet history not only by hearsay but who took part in making it, can fully appreciate what is behind every chapter, every article and every line of the Fundamental Law.

The Constitution has attracted attention in all countries. It is being studied and talked about.

World public opinion particularly notes that the Soviet Union is the first country in history to make defence of peace a constitutional principle. It would not be a bad thing, says American lawyer Charles J. Faulkner, if the countries developing the neutron bomb and advocating its manufacture—the bomb which jeopardizes the most vital human right, the right to life—would follow the Soviet example and adopt a similar law.

With the adoption of the new Constitution, the Communists and all Soviet people see once again, as it were, the grandeur of what their country has achieved and its growing influence on the development of global processes.

V

Freedom and Democracy

"Everyone has the right to life, liberty and security of person."

UN DECLARATION OF HUMAN RIGHTS
Article 3

"We know not only from theory but also from long years of practice that genuine democracy is impossible without socialism and that socialism is impossible without a steady development of democracy."

LEONID I. BREZHNEV
Late Secretary-General, CC CPSU and Chairman, USSR Council of Ministers

"Proletarian government is a dictatorship with respect to the exploiters, but a democracy with respect to the working people."

FUNDAMENTALS OF POLITICAL KNOWLEDGE
Novosti Press Agency

ACCORDING TO Marxist-Leninist theory, the state, by its very nature, must always be an apparatus of coercion, used by the ruling class to keep all other classes subdued. Patricians, feudal lords, and absolute monarchs in turn utilized the agency of the state to oppress all other classes, and the same holds true for the bourgeoisie, which built new societies on the ruins of the old. The overthrow of the capitalist order and the subsequent transfer of power from the bourgeoisie to the proletariat cannot bring in its wake an immediate end to all oppression either, since during the dictatorship of the proletariat the last vestiges of capitalism must be wiped out once and for all, in order to enable society to embark on its transition to communism. However, during this preparatory stage, political power (the power to oppress) is no longer in the hands of the wealthy few. For the first time in history the workers, the vast majority, have taken over the reins of government and are able to enjoy democratic rights and freedoms. The bourgeoisie, the small minority, having lost political power, has now become the oppressed class. For the

225

time being, then, there are still oppressors and oppressed. Only in the final stages of perfect communism, when there are no longer any class distinctions, will *all* people

> gradually become accustomed to the observance of the elementary rules of social life that have been known for centuries and repeated for thousands of years in all school books; they will become accustomed to observing them without compulsion, without subordination, without the special apparatus for compulsion which is called the state.[1]

Perfect freedom and perfect democracy are thus impossible, according to Marxist-Leninist theory, so long as there is any state at all. But on the other hand, as the transitional stage of the dictatorship of the proletariat moves in the direction of communism, as class distinctions begin to disappear and the state itself begins to "wither away," freedom and democracy are supposed to become *more* perfect, *more* complete.

It is undeniable that great changes have taken place in the Soviet Union since the days of Stalin, when footsteps in the hall were sufficient to make people tremble in their own home. But whether these changes are merely superficial or truly fundamental, whether they are temporary or likely to be permanent, and whether or not they show promise of leading to further improvement—these are matters on which observers are by no means in complete agreement. Where does the Soviet Union stand today, as far as freedom and democracy are concerned? What is likely to be her future course? It is hoped this chapter will lead to a better understanding of these issues, or at least of the complexity of problems they present.

In Part A of this chapter, Marxists and non-Marxists debate the meaning of freedom and democracy and present a wide variety of views on the extent to which freedom and democracy actually prevail in the Soviet Union and to which progress has or has not been made in recent years. Part B deals specifically with the controversial problem of Soviet style elections, part C, finally, offers divergent views on the number, role and significance of Soviet "dissidents."

---

[1] V. I. Lenin, *State and Revolution*, New York, International Publishers Co. Inc., 1932, p. 74.

A
How Much Freedom, How Much Democracy in the USSR?

"The Soviet Revolution has given an unprecedented impulse to the development of democracy in breadth and in depth, democracy, that is, for the working people oppressed by capitalism, democracy for the overwhelming majority of the people, socialist democracy."

VLADIMIR ILYICH LENIN

"As regards genuine human rights, historical experience has shown that such rights can be ensured only by the socialist system. The right to work, the right to education, to social security, the right to elect and to be elected to the government and administrative bodies of all levels, the right to criticize and control one's work, the right to participate in the discussion and adoption of decisions, including decisions on matters of national importance—such is our socialist democracy in action. . . . Legal action is taken in conformity with Soviet law in the case of individuals who engage in anti-Soviet propaganda and agitation designed to undermine or weaken the established social and political system in our country, or [in the case of individuals] who systematically spread deliberate falsification vilifying the Soviet state or social system."

PRAVDA EDITORIAL

"Proletarian government is a dictatorship with respect to the exploiters, but a democracy with respect to the working people."

FUNDAMENTALS OF POLITICAL KNOWLEDGE
Novosti Press Agency

How much freedom, how much democracy is there in the USSR today? To a great extent, the answer to the question depends upon exactly what one means by the terms freedom and democracy. Contrary to rather widely held views, these terms are not easily definable. Nowhere in the world is one completely free to do as he pleases. In the United States, people are not free to drive their cars as fast as they wish, to practice medicine without proper accreditation, to be married to two or three spouses simultaneously, to advertise their flourishing marihuana cigarette business by giving free samples to high school boys, or to do any of a million other things prohibited by law. Even the meaning of freedom of speech is limited by court interpretation. "The most stringent protection of free speech would not protect a man in falsely shouting 'fire' in a theater and causing a panic," wrote Justice Oliver Wendell Holmes in a Supreme Court decision which effectively restricted freedom of speech in cases where it would result in a "clear and present danger."[1]

Is the answer, perhaps, that freedom means and ought to mean an individual's right to do as he pleases as long as his actions do not bring harm to others? This may seem acceptable, but who is to determine what is and what is not harmful to one's fellow man or to society? The United States and the Soviet Union are in full agreement that the freedom to purchase and sell human beings on the market is not a freedom that ought to be legally permitted (although no federal law prohibited slavery in the United States during the first eighty-four years of her existence as a "free and independent" nation.) Strangely enough, the United States and the Soviet Union are also in essential agreement on the correctness of at least some of the above mentioned laws against what have come to be called "crimes without victims." These are illegal acts which it would be difficult to prove harmful to individuals other than the ones voluntarily engaged in them (such as smoking marihuana, marrying more than one spouse, etc.). The United States and the Soviet Union are not in agreement, however, as to whether the freedom of an individual to own productive property and to earn a profit from such ownership is harmful to society. What to the U.S. appears to be a constitutional if not an inalienable right, important for the economic well-being of the nation and vital for the maintenance of individual freedom, is, in the eyes of the Soviet Union, nothing but a continuation of the age-old "exploitation of man by man," clothed in modern dress.

As long as their words and deeds are merely offensive or obnoxious but do not represent a "clear and present danger," Americans are relatively free to advocate racial discrimination or war, to make highly derogatory statements and bring charges of incompetence, irresponsibility, or even dishonesty against the country's top leaders, or to join a party, such as the American Nazi Party, which openly proposes the abolition of all democratic institutions. But to the Soviets, such acts constitute not freedom but license, abuses of liberties. Such liberties are carefully weighed against other social values, such as equality, justice, peace, or political stability. And so, Soviet laws do not permit the advocacy of war or racial discrimination, nor do they permit the spreading of "deliberate lies" or the commission of acts deemed harmful to the Soviet state and

---

[1] Schneck v. United States of America, 249 U.S. 47,1919, p. 52.

social system. On the other hand, the Soviet concept of freedom, but not the American, includes "the right to work, to rest and leisure, to free education and free medical services, to material security in old age and in case of illness or disability."[2] "The Soviet worker," wrote Giuseppe Boffa, former chief correspondent of Italy's Communist newspaper *L'Unità* some twenty years ago, "is free in a way an American worker can never be. The Soviet worker is free of a thousand restrictions to which a capitalist worker is subject, not necessarily by law, but by economic pressures, customs and habits. These restrictions under capitalism, which flow from the threat of unemployment, the difficulty of getting an education, the fear of illness—all these are unknown to the Soviet worker. They must be kept in mind even when considering the political limitations on democracy imposed on Soviet workers in past periods".[3]

Article 39 of the new Soviet Constitution states that the "enjoyment by citizens of their rights and freedoms must not be to the detriment of the interests of society or the state, or infringe on the rights of other citizens." Many Westerners interpret this as an undue restriction that effectively nullifies any guarantees of freedom in the USSR (see, for example, Selection 3 below). But Marxists disagree. American constitutional lawyer and counsel for the Communist Party of the United States, John J. Abt, for instance, considers such a qualification of Soviet constitutional guarantees of freedom merely "the Soviet equivalent of the 'clear and present danger' limitation of First Amendment rights in the United States. Under this limitation, the advocacy of ideas may be restrained or punished if found to "threaten the national security or public peace," the only difference being that such limitation in the U.S. is supplied by Supreme Court interpretations, while in the Soviet Union it is explicitly stated in the constitution. As to Soviet restrictions being unnecessarily extensive, Abt argues:

> One may disagree with the extent of Soviet restraints on freedom of expression as excessive and lacking justification in any actual or threatened injury to the fabric of socialist society. But criticism must be tempered by the knowledge that from the moment of its birth, the Soviet Union has been the target of a conspiracy by the capitalist powers to overthrow, dismember or strangle it by every available means including war, quarantine, "containment," "massive retaliation," "positions of strength," subversion, and discriminatory trade practices, and that these policies have by no means been abandoned today.[4]

---

[2] *Programme of the Communist Party of the Soviet Union*, (adopted by the Twenty-Second Congress of the CPSU on October 31, 1961, and still in force today), Moscow: Foreign Languages Publishing House, 1961, p. 17. Selection 9 below elaborates on this paragraph of the 1961 *Programme*.

[3] Giuseppe Boffa, *Inside the Khrushchev Era*, New York: Marzani and Munsell Publishers, 1959, p. 192.

[4] John J. Abt, "The New Soviet Constitution," in *Six Decades That Changed the World*, New York: New World Review Publications, Inc., 1978, p. 154.

Indeed, freedom is a complex issue. In some languages, the word freedom does not exist in the abstract, i.e., one cannot say that a person is free, but rather only that he is free of hunger, free of anxiety over unemployment, free of an obligation. And as to democracy, some see its true measure not in the governmental structure or the number of competing parties but rather, in the final analysis, in how it responds to the needs of the people.

To give the reader a broad overview of the spectrum of views on "freedom and democracy" in the Soviet Union, a wide variety of non-Marxist and Marxist contributions are presented below.

In the first selection, Anatol Rapoport shows how difficult it is even for well-meaning American and Soviet citizens to communicate when they discuss "democracy" in their respective countries. Next, William N. Loucks and William G. Whitney find the Soviet Union less democratic and more restrictive than Western democracies but see indications that "a further loosening of individual choice will occur." James D. Forman, in the third selection, finds restrictions in the Soviet Union so severe that "for anyone accustomed to Western freedoms, the situation in Russia would be intolerable." Still, he acknowledges that "the Soviet Union has come a long way from the serfdom of just over a hundred years ago" and he states unequivocally that the Soviet people as a whole are loyal to their government: they don't want to overthrow it, he says, they merely "want more out of it." In the fourth selection, Stanley Rothman and George W. Breslauer, and in the fifth, D. Richard Little, discuss mass political participation, its role and its significance in the Soviet Union, and they draw comparisons with the United States. Both find popular political involvement important and more widespread in the USSR, but both agree that it still plays but a very minor role in the selection of leaders and the formulation of a national policy (although the former two, but not the latter, also question how much impact mass political participation really exerts in the United States). Finally, Roy Turner, Australian Labor Party Representative in the Upper House of New South Wales, a self-proclaimed "democratic socialist" but not a Marxist, explains and asks his readers to understand that, contrary to Western practice, Soviet constitutional law is based on the theory that individual freedoms and social obligations must be inseparably associated, lest the individual be alienated from society.

The first selection under "Soviet Views," (Selection 7), taken from Lenin's *State and Revolution*, summarizes in concise form the Marxist-Leninist view on democracy under various social systems. There is democracy for "an insignificant minority" under capitalism, democracy for "the vast majority" but not for the "exploiters and oppressors of the people" after the downfall of capitalism on the road to communism, and full and complete democracy "without any exceptions whatever" in the final stage of perfect communism. Next, V. Denisov, former Deputy-

Editor-in-Chief of the Novosti Press Agency, explains the true meaning of freedom and democracy in socialist society—as outlined in the Programme of the CPSU—which, the Marxist-Leninist view holds, must be based on guaranteed economic security.

In 1949, the General Assembly of the United Nations adopted the "Universal Declaration of Human Rights," with 48 countries (including the United States) voting for it and 8 countries (including the Soviet Union) abstaining. It spelled out not only political rights, such as freedom of speech, freedom of peaceful assembly, and freedom of movement (stressed as essential for human rights by the United States), but also such economic rights as the right to work, the right to a standard of living adequate for health and well-being, and the right to periodic holidays with pay (issues emphasized in the Soviet concept of human rights). As a matter of fact, many parts of the Soviet Constitution's Chapter 7 on "The Basic Rights, Freedoms, and Duties of Citizens of the USSR" (Articles 39–69) are very similar in content and wording to articles contained in the UN Universal Declaration of Human Rights. The ninth selection consists of the Soviet Constitution's articles 39–69, with comparable articles from the UN Declaration of Universal Human Rights reprinted next to them, where applicable, for comparison.

The last three contributions to Part A of this chapter, respectively by Soviet journalist I. Alexandrov, Soviet law expert Valentin Patyulin, and an editorial from *Kommunist*, elaborate on various aspects of the Soviet position on freedom and democracy in the USSR, including, for example, freedom of religion, freedom from discrimination, freedom to emigrate, etc., as well as restrictions on liberties, because "under socialism, freedom of the individual and his development do not at all mean unrestrained arbitrary actions on the part of the individual."

WESTERN VIEWS

1. WHAT IS DEMOCRACY?*

Anatol Rapoport
University of Michigan

American newspapers insist that the United States is a democracy and that the Soviet Union is a tyranny. The Soviet jurist Vyshinsky in his

* Reprinted from Anatol Rapoport, *Science and the Goals of Man*, 1950, pp. 46–47, by permission of Harper & Row, Publishers. Copyright, 1950, by Harper & Row, Publishers.

book on Soviet law declares that the Soviet Union is a "million times
more democratic" than the most democratic of the "bourgeois" countries. Who is right? Who is wrong? Instead of asking such a question, let
us see this verbal fight in terms of a communication process. Are the
Americans and the Russians communicating when they call their respective countries "democracies" and their neighbors' countries "tyrannies"?

How does the conviction "United States is a democracy" arise?
To begin with, this conviction is implied in the Constitution, where it is
stated that the power of government of the United States resides in the
elected representatives of the people. The Russians too have a constitution, where it is stated that the power of government resides in the
elected representatives of the people. Democracy is implied in many other
aspects of American life, frequent elections, unrestricted criticism of government officials and of the party in power, free education, frequent examples of "successful" careers, etc., etc. The Russian also has many of
these things to show. Elections are also frequent. Government officials
are not only criticized but often actually "purged," educational opportunities are widespread, and so are "successful" careers (from lathe
worker to factory director, from peasant to party functionary, etc.).

"But," says the American newspaper editor, "this is only sham.
You may have elections, but there is only one list of candidates to choose
from. Your successful careers depend not only on ability but also to a
great extent on conformity to the party line, etc., etc."

"On the contrary," says the Russian journalist, "it is your democracy that is a sham. You have two parties, but they both represent
the capitalists. You disfranchise many of your people because of the color
of their skin. Your successful careers are often the rewards not of public
service but of unscrupulous methods and profiteering at the expense of
other people's misery, etc., etc."

Let us consider this argument about democracy as a discussion in
good faith, not as a camouflage for "I am afraid of you and I hate you."
Why do such arguments fail to effect agreement? Inasmuch as they contain no value judgments, they seem to be built on assertions about things.
The controversy is not about which country is "better" or more "moral"
(such a controversy would be about the speakers, not about the countries),
but about which is the more "democratic." Such an argument is an attempt to reduce a controversy about values into a more objective discussion, presumably about "facts." . . . Here the opponents apparently
agree on basic "values" (democracy is good). They try to be objective.
They try to cite only facts. Still they get nowhere. The discussion invariably degenerates into a certain pattern:

"We have achieved universal literacy."

"Ah, but you are told what to read. Now, *we*, have freedom of
expression."

"Ah, but most of your press is controlled by monopoly interests. *We* have *n*-tupled our production."

"By using forced labor. We still have the world's highest standard of living."

"And lynchings," says the Russian.

2. THE INDIVIDUAL AND
THE SOVIET STATE*
William N. Loucks and William G. Whitney
Wharton School, University of Pennsylvania

THE INDIVIDUAL AND THE STATE

When one examines the Soviet system from the viewpoint of the traditional values of the Western world, considerable doubts about its ultimate merit arise. Western traditions hold the individual to be the end toward which political and economic activity is directed. The individual's freedom and ability to develop personal potentialities to the full is the final criterion by which our institutions, processes, and historical trends are judged. Although activities are limited by law, these limitations are grounded on the necessity to restrict one individual's actions in order to assure others their inherent rights. We have a concept of the common good—the necessity for group or communal action in certain limited spheres—in order that individuals, as such, may enjoy full lives. The great force protecting the individual is pluralism: in a multiparty political system; in relatively free economic enterprise and competition; in independent newspapers, books, and magazines; in religious freedom and tolerance; in varied state and private educational systems and institutions; and in unrestrained activities in the sciences and the arts.

The absence of pluralism in the Soviet system opposes it to Western philosophies and ideals. Sovereignty in the Soviet Union resides in the Communist Party—the single legal party—and not in the government with its ostensibly popularly elected assemblies (soviets). Within the Party, sovereignty centers in a small circle of Party officials, which, while the personages change, remains a self-selected, self-perpetuating, all-dominating power bloc. This is not to say that this self-selected power elite does or can do whatever it personally may prefer; there is an outside limit in the tolerance of the masses. In the Soviet Union this outside limit is kept inactive by the ubiquity of government as an agent of the Party. The government owns and operates practically all industrial enterprises and

* Reprinted from William N. Loucks and William G. Whitney, *Comparative Economic Systems*, Ninth Edition, New York: Harper & Row, Publishers, 1973, pp. 329–331, by permission of the publisher.

a constantly enlarging portion of agricultural units; government or Party appointees edit and government presses publish all newspapers and journals, and government presses publish all books; religion in any traditional sense is experiencing a planned withering away; and education is exclusively a function of government. Only in the arts and sciences does pluralism have some reality, and in the arts this is well confined by Party influence.

The persistence of restrictions on the free flow of artistic and intellectual ideas long after they represent any immediate threat to political stability may indicate an ingrained bureaucratic distrust of creative expression in nonpluralistic societies. Although the methods of repressing dissent have become more subtle, the possibility of loss of privileges, bans on publication, or even involuntary incarceration in "mental" hospitals exerts a chilling effect on intellectual activity. Life for most Russian citizens goes on in a bland, routine way; any society imposes sanctions on rebellious or deviant behavior, but in Russia the detection mechanism is omnipresent and the price of misbehaving greater than in the West. . . .

In the Soviet Union all industrial employees work for the government, either directly in state-owned and operated enterprises or in closely controlled producers' cooperatives. The peasant farmer either works directly for the government on a state farm or, aside from time spent on his private plot, in collective-farm activities. The skill or type of ability the industrial worker achieves and the attainments of the professional worker are related directly to the amount and type of education or training the government makes available. In addition, an enormous number of people are employed by the hierarchy of governmental administrative, planning, and management agencies, and by the Communist Party apparatus.

Finally, our evaluation of the Soviet system must not be concluded without noting the reply of Soviet Marxism to these questions. The contemporary domination of government and Party, they declare, is simply a way station along the path to full communism; it is only in this latter state of human living that complete consumer sovereignty can prevail. Only then will a person be really free, the hard and disagreeable work having been taken over by machinery and some measure of socially useful effort having become an inherent ingredient of individual happiness; only then will class divisions and distinctions have disappeared, and no symbols of class remain; and only then will true pluralism in its full meaning prevail, with its benefits freely available to all. This surely has the ring of the highest idealism. The present Soviet Communist Party leaders admit that entry into such a stage of human society first requires proliferation of society's economic productive power—now sought through powerful government and Party use of planned scientific development and industrial automation. The leaders also contend that the beginnings of ultimate full communism and the attendant absence of restrictive government are now visible in the Soviet Union.

This, of course, raises the question of the goals and motivations of present and future political leaders in the Soviet Union. Is affluence a goal in itself, or is it also a means of increasing the freedom and dignity of the individual? Will the levers of economic and social control be relinquished now that the initial rationale for them—rapid modernization of the economy—has largely been achieved? Will a pent-up mass demand for greater civil liberties emerge the way the demand for consumer-durable goods has recently required the attention of economic planners? Indications are that a further loosening of individual choice will occur, but like all processes of social change it will occur unevenly and with unforeseen side effects and political ramifications.

3. HOW MUCH FREEDOM IN THE USSR?*
James D. Forman
Author of books in comparative politics

With the spread of education so necessary to an advanced industrial society, a tentative intelligentsia has appeared in Russia. Though in no position to seriously threaten the Soviet monolith, these few daring thinkers have at least questioned communist ideas that formerly were never questioned. While the present party bosses would hesitate to use guns against their striking workers, they have been heavy-handed in dealing with dissent, ever since the brief flowering of freer literature under Khrushchev. Consequently, a vast underground literature called *Samizdat*—"self-publishing"—has been handtyped and circulated. It has led to unrest and a tightening of control. In 1968 several writers, among them Aleksandr Ginzburg and Yuri Galanskov, received prison terms of five and seven years for "upsetting" the Soviet community. In 1974 Alexander Solzhenitsyn, winner of the Nobel prize for literature, was expelled from the Soviet Union for his opinions. The visual artist has a bit more leeway than the writer. Portraits, still lifes, and landscapes inherently are nonpolitical. Should the artist paint a robust lumberjack felling a tree, the Ministry of Culture would guarantee sales and throw in an additional annual stipend. On the other hand, if the artist's wood gatherer were a threadbare peasant woman piling twigs into a baby carriage, the state might well take offense and ban the work. Few Soviet artists have sought

* Reprinted from James D. Forman, *Communism: From Marx's Manifesto to 20th Century Reality*, New York-London: New Viewpoints (A Division of Franklin Watts,) 2nd ed., 1979, pp. 25–30, by permission of Franklin Watts, Inc. (Copyright © 1972, 1979 by James D. Forman).

out such confrontations. Though admitting a political limitation on the subject of his art (most modern art is considered "decadent" and therefore forbidden public exhibition), one patriotic artist pointed out rather fatuously that he was not on the other hand commercially enslaved by the necessity of making a living, as is the case with the Western artist.

Though in 1975 the Helsinki accords were signed, calling for the free movement of peoples and ideas, Russia has done nothing to implement the terms, and dissent has fallen to a low ebb. In connection with the sixtieth anniversary of the Soviet Union in 1977, an amnesty for prisoners pointedly failed to include prisoners of a political nature. One may observe, however, that this is an improvement over the past. Stalin would have had the lot of them shot. But it is still far from the tradition of individual freedom and liberty accepted in the West. . . .

For anyone accustomed to Western freedoms, the situation in Russia would be intolerable. Opportunities for choosing one's own employment are limited,[1] and to work purely as an individual is almost impossible. Foreign travel is limited to the highest party members. Religion is officially regarded as an impediment to the attainment of true freedom of conscience—yet it remains a powerful force among large elements of the population. So in practice a priest who limits himself strictly to church matters, mass, confession, baptism, is not interfered with. But when religion enters into everyday life, as with the fundamentalist Pentecostal sect, its members are harassed and humiliated. Yet with all this, the Russian citizen of today can look back on a blacker past and say: We are not starving. No one will come to shoot us in the night. In general, the courts of the Soviet Union deal out fair and folksy justice. A man can be heard, even if now and then the laws are changed to raise the penalty after the crime has been committed, a sort of ex-post-facto treatment that would turn an American judge's hair white.

An example of the difference in attitude between the Western democracies and the Soviet Union, between the emphasis on the individual and his fulfillment as opposed to the fulfillment of the state, often at the individual's expense, occurs in the Russian's so-called Parasite Law. Under this law, anyone who is not gainfully and usefully employed for

[1] In industry, Soviet workers are generally free to change jobs at will [as a matter of fact, some 20 million do each year (Boris Alexeyev, "World's Highest Employment Rate: Some Built-In Problems," *Soviet Panorama*, Feb. 29, 1980, p. 59)], subject only to the requirement prevalent all over Europe that they give two weeks notice (in the USSR, extended in 1981 to four weeks). The only exceptions are university students, who upon graduation are supposed to repay society for their tuition-scholarship and stipend by working for two to three years in their own profession at a place assigned to them (although the law does not provide for any penalties for those who don't abide by this rule, see also p. 353, footnote 4); and secondly, members of the Communist party are supposed to put the interests of the party before their own. If they do not want to do what the leadership tells them, they may lose their party membership. Collective farmers, on the other hand, are supposed to petition the general membership meeting since there are accounts to be settled, shares to be determined, if possible, replacements to be found (the Soviets complain that too many are leaving the farms), etc. [Editor's note.]

the good of society may be uprooted from his home and sent to a specified location where work will be provided. Candidates for this administrative extralegal punishment include pimps and prostitutes and anyone who gets drunk regularly or works irregularly. There are merits in such a proceeding. How quickly the streets of New York City could be cleaned up by regimented vagrants! But there are grave dangers. What does a court define as useful employment? Does it include critical writers? Avant-garde painters? Or does it not?

Nevertheless, the Soviet Union has come a long way from the serfdom of just over a hundred years ago. A counterrevolution today is unthinkable. True, there is some discontent, but not so much because of the limitation of freedoms known in the West that few Russians have ever experienced. Rather, it is an unhappiness at the continued low standard of living, poor and limited housing, the unavailability of the material plenty that is known to exist elsewhere and that might be more available to Soviet citizens if the command economy were directed away from enhancing a powerful state to providing its individual members with the comforts of life. There is little disloyalty. The people don't want to overthrow their government. They simply want more out of it. And at the top there is a very complacent aristocracy, not one established by birth and automatic inheritance, but by party devotion and ability.

Russians today still like to voice the old formulas of Marx and Lenin. They have reason for pride in the emergence of a great nation and cause, too, for disillusionment with their ideology, which has become but a thin crust spread over a very large pie. In theory, they are a classless society, yet a ruling clique has emerged within the institutional embodiment of the party. And what may be spoken of as the dictatorship of the proletariat is, in fact, the dictatorship of a new Soviet bureaucracy.

Whatever happens, a return to Stalinism is as unlikely as is the traditional communist goal of a classless society. A popular Soviet anecdote says: "Communism is just over the horizon, but the horizon is an imaginary line and as you approach it, it recedes." The truth is the Soviet Union is becoming a country, not a cause, and at the November 7, 1977, sixtieth-anniversary parade honoring the birth of the Soviet Union, Defense Minister Marshal Dmitri Ustinov was undoubtedly speaking for the vast majority of Russians when he justified the display of military might by saying, "So that no one will dare disturb our tranquil life." The revolution is over in Russia. Visionary power has died and political ideals are largely relegated to the classroom. Brezhnev has given the country years of stability with old-style totalitarianism gradually giving way to a more tolerant authoritarianism. But Brezhnev [is dead] and his colleagues are aging. The next generation of leaders will in general be better educated and less ideological. They may be experimenters in reform and liberalization, though initially they may, to solidify their positions, have to take a tough, even militant stance. Nevertheless, peace is fundamentally de-

sired, as is world trade and Western technology, and with it all must come
a spilling over of the Western life style. The Soviet Union has long been
a model for communism around the world. It may remain so. But though
its power is unquestioned, its desirability as a model for emerging nations
depends on its ability to keep up with the times.

4. MASS POLITICAL PARTICIPATION*
Stanley Rothman
Smith College
George W. Breslauer
University of California, Berkeley

Since 1957, the Soviet government has tried to draw more of its citizens
into the administrative process as a means of both checking the work of
governmental departments and helping in the performance of certain routine, nontechnical tasks. In addition to the two or three million citizens
who serve as members of the standing commissions of local soviets, other
millions participate in the activities of such local organizations as voluntary militia squads, street committees, house committees, and parents'
committees. Some of these groups have a degree of authority. They scrutinize such things as the operation of schools, clinics, libraries, local transport, environmental quality, sanitary services, and the quality of consumer goods production. Or, like the people's militia and comrades'
courts, they help the authorities make sure that citizens behave properly.

Other groups supplement the work of the public authorities: they
complete minor housing repairs, including the planting of gardens and
repainting, or take over work that was once performed by a department
of local government. For example, volunteer financial bureaus have been
set up to explain the tax laws; other groups acquaint citizens with their
rights under the different pension laws, and still others establish voluntary
fire brigades. The single largest group of unpaid workers is still the volunteer militia, of which there are some seven million. In all, though, from
twenty to thirty million citizens are involved at any given time in these
varied forms of public service.

In addition to these forms of public activity, Soviet citizens are
encouraged to send letters to newspapers and to governmental or Party
agencies when they have complaints about local conditions or local officials. And they do so on a large scale, for tens of thousands of such
letters are received each month. It is almost impossible, however, to judge

the effectiveness of such appeals. The media do follow up many letters with investigations of local conditions, and with periodic exposes about an incompetent or corrupt local official. However, newspaper editors decide which letters to publish or follow up, and they often pass complaints directly to the offending governmental department, thereby keeping the protest "within channels". . . .

Yet many complaints do receive a proper response, either from local authorities themselves (a good number of whom, after all, are honest and competent), or from higher-level officials who have an interest in receiving complaints about local grievances. Ruling over a highly bureaucratized system, they are to some extent cut off from accurate information about local conditions. Indeed, Soviet leaders routinely refer to such extraofficial communications from the masses as "signals." The regime's primary concern is to respond to accumulating grievances before they reach a flash point, and to respond in a way that will not cast doubt on the legitimacy of the system and the current Party program. Accordingly, a local official will be periodically dismissed or denounced, and the masses will be encouraged to assimilate a human, rather than a systemic, explanation of the cause of the grievance.

The simultaneous large-scale involvement of Party and non-Party people in the administration of local-government policy indicates the continued strength of the participatory elements of Soviet ideology. Without much doubt, the increase in participation, which began under Khrushchev, was a genuine effort to move closer to that day when the administration of policy would be a function of the people rather than of the official state apparatus. Under Khrushchev, moreover, there were tentative efforts to encourage the masses to take political initiatives that had not been given prior approval by "trusted" and "reliable" state or party officials. These efforts, however, were ended with Khrushchev's overthrow. On those few occasions when volunteer groups have stepped out of line and seemed to be exerting independent and spontaneous initiative, they have been severely criticized. In most cases, those in charge of volunteers are now reliable Party activists who may even hold official positions in the state apparatus.

Indeed, the participatory element in Soviet theory and practice has a strongly statist tinge to it. . . . While volunteer groups do indeed check on administrative malfeasance and misfeasance, the citizen has little or no direct say over priorities and policy. Full-time officials within the bureaucracy exercise a near-monopoly of significant political initiative. Moreover, the principle of mass involvement in the administration of public affairs is geared principally toward the educational function of exposing citizens to collectivist values, socializing them into those values, and reinforcing this educational process through active involvement in public activity. In this way, a new communist morality is ostensibly inculcated in Soviet citizens.

To assess just how voluntary mass participation of this sort is, or just how enthusiastic, is a difficult exercise. That this involvement has permitted the Soviets to reduce the size of their official governmental apparatus on the local level is unquestionably true. It is also true that . . . it has enabled some retired people, such as pensioners, to find something to do that gives them a sense of dignity. Depending on the type of issue involved, it is also probably the case that many Soviet citizens find such mass involvement to be meaningful and proper. Never having participated in a political system that gave them an opportunity to assist in determining national policy and priorities, they may well attach greater significance to involvement in local, routine, or technical decision-making than would citizens raised in pluralistic systems. Moreover, most of the evidence at our disposal suggests that very few Soviet citizens see through the human explanations offered by the regime when failures occur. Yet, in the absence of public opinion surveys on all these questions, we cannot advance very far beyond guesswork.

It would, of course, be a mistake to overstate the differences between mass political participation in the U.S.S.R. and in Western pluralistic systems. Despite their right to choose leaders through open electoral competition, citizens in the West have relatively little direct influence on the formulation of most policy. In fact, in recent years citizens have realized this and become increasingly cynical about their leaders. Moreover, large numbers of citizens are apathetic and passive, preferring to leave the game of politics to others. To the extent that mobilized citizens directly shape the decisions of their leaders, these tend to be matters of primarily local importance. In fact, recent scholarly emphasis on the elitist character of politics even in liberal-democratic societies has led some Western observers to explicitly discount differences in mass political participation in the Soviet Union and the West. The forms and mechanisms of such participation are different, they argue, but the impact is the same.

Such a position, in our opinion, goes much too far. It ignores the many recent instances of mass mobilization in the West that have had considerable impact on critical national policy outcomes. One can hardly imagine the abolition of compulsory military service in the United States, for example, without such political pressure—nor could one imagine the more recent pardon of draft resisters. In France, a public referendum forced Charles DeGaulle out of office, while public exposure was surely crucial in forcing Richard Nixon's resignation as President of the United States. The fact that masses in the West do not exercise their right to organize pressure groups, publicize their demands, and mobilize others may indicate cynicism and apathy—or it may simply mean that many of these individuals have not felt sufficiently deprived by the system to take action. Indeed, the importance of *opportunities* for *potential* political mobilization in the eyes of the citizenry would probably become most obvious were a political leader or party to try to abrogate these rights.

That the Soviet system differs from liberal-democratic systems with respect to the nature of mass participation is obvious. Which of the two systems is *better* is a separate issue, and one that will depend on one's values. Nonetheless, there are obvious strengths and weaknesses to each. Systems that provide opportunities for autonomous public mobilization tend to be more flexible in anticipating crises before they occur, and in drawing previously neglected groups into the political process. However, they suffer the drawback of not being able to regulate the pace at which public issues are raised, and may suffer crises of instability if public mobilization outpaces the responsive capacities of the political system. Soviet-type systems, in turn, have the advantage of being able to suppress demands when the system becomes overloaded, and to manipulate a relatively passive population. These systems suffer the disadvantage, however, that when the patience of the masses wears thin (as in Poland during the 1970s), it tends to express itself in anomic outbursts of considerable intensity. Such crises may seriously undermine the legitimacy and stability of the system. We should add, though, that there is no evidence currently to suggest that the patience of the Soviet masses is wearing thin. Most Soviet citizens, it would appear, have internalized the norms of the political culture, and can barely conceive of alternatives to it.

Not *all* Soviet citizens, though. A small number of dissidents are both alienated from the system and prepared to demand a fundamental change in the terms of political participation in the U.S.S.R.

5. MASS POLITICAL PARTICIPATION IN THE U.S. AND THE USSR*

D. Richard Little
San Diego State University

FEW CONCEPTS in the contemporary political lexicon have had more diverse meanings attributed to them than "political participation." At one extreme in the definitional continuum is the traditional Western-democratic notion of participation as involving activities which result in effective control over political leaders by citizens acting upon rational and informed judgments about major policy alternatives. At the other extreme is the image of totalitarian participation, according to which cit-

* Excerpted from *Comparative Political Studies*, Vol. 8, No. 4, January, 1976, pp. 437–55 by permission of the publisher, Sage Publications, Beverly Hills, California and London.

izens are manipulated and coerced into hyperactive support of the policies of self-appointed leaders who are totally impervious to public opinion.

Somewhere between these extremes lies a third model which describes participation as real and psychologically satisfying to individual citizens but in fact based upon self-delusion and the myth that such participation has an effect on government. As Jacques Ellul poses it, the reasoning is: "Democracy is good. To have democracy, the citizen must participate; thus, what I am doing is my form of participation; it is real. Not to do it would be to despair of everything. . . ."[1] This is what has been called the "democratic myth of citizen competence," and it provides the primary explanation for the effective functioning of American democracy. . . .

The principal concern of this study is political participation by individual citizens, rather than by professional political elites or interest groups. Our focus, therefore, is on the average citizen in each nation. An analysis of mass political participation involves three major aspects: (1) the types of political activities in which citizens engage; (2) the conditions under which those activities take place; and (3) the significance they have for the political system as a whole. . . .

Voting in the Soviet Union is not legally compulsory, as it has been at one time or another in Austria, Belgium, Holland and Switzerland, but the political pressures on Soviet citizens to vote are sufficient to ensure that over 99% of the people vote in every election, national, regional, and local. . . .

Despite the official pressure on Soviet citizens to enter into the activities of party and government sponsored organizations, the number who actually do is probably lower than in the United States. Approximately 20,000,000 Soviet people are members of public organizations in local communities, although Soviet sources put the number much higher. Whatever the exact number, the involvement of citizens in local organizations concerned with community problems is within a common range in both countries. . . .

Campaign activities draw upon the efforts of millions of Soviet citizens, just as they do Americans. Soviet national election campaigns last about two months, and the campaigning is extremely intensive. The party leadership mobilizes millions of "agitators" and "propagandists," as well as ordinary citizens, to publicize the election, explain the issues and programs which the party considers important, and ensure that the entire population goes to the polls. The weeks preceding the election see the formation of countless study circles, discussion groups, campaign meetings, door-to-door canvassing, rallies, demonstrations and speeches.

The fact that Soviet elections are non-competitive, and therefore that the outcome is known before the election is held, does not diminish

[1] J. Ellul, *The Political Illusion*, New York: Random House, 1967, p. 196.

the importance of the campaign to the Soviet leadership. For beyond the recruitment function which elections perform in Western countries, they also perform, in all political systems, important educational, socializing and mobilizing functions. We have no accurate figures on how many Soviet citizens participate in campaign activities, but it is unlikely that any large body of citizens can escape some minimal involvement in the process. By contrast, less than one American in five even occasionally attends political meetings or rallies. . . .

The inclination of a private citizen to contact a government official depends on a variety of factors, including his psychological make-up, his social status, and his political acumen. Contacting in the American context is directed either toward social and communal outcomes or toward the satisfaction of personalized requests. This type of participation differs from electoral activities in two important ways: it is engaged in alone (that is, in "participatory settings devoid of counterparticipants") and it requires a relatively high degree of individual initiative.

In the Soviet Union, contacting is also a prominent form of political participation. Citizens are encouraged to write letters to newspapers and to government offices to voice complaints or make suggestions on matters of policy, and such organizations are obliged to follow up matters raised in such letters. Contact with officials is also encouraged by the requirement that deputies to Soviets at all levels must spend considerable time meeting with constituents and exploring individual concerns, actions for which they are periodically held accountable.

Although there are informal limits to this process, fragmentary evidence indicates that Soviet citizens make extensive use of this sort of input. . . .

The act of forming an independent citizens' committee to pressure the government on some social problem is no doubt rarely if ever indulged in by Soviet citizens. The political leadership does not countenance overt attempts to do so and unofficial attempts would bear considerable risk. There are, however, a very large number of officially sanctioned citizen groups operating under the jurisdiction of local Soviets and other public organizations, to which millions of Soviet citizens belong. Many of these groups may perform the same functions for the citizen as do independent committees in the American context.

Whether this is so depends on whether the interests being promoted in such groups are genuinely shared by the participants or are governmental interests in support of which a recalcitrant population is being mobilized. In a careful study of the matter, Adams[2] concludes that citizen interests are in fact being widely promoted through this mechanism. She argues that such groups "must honestly be acknowledged as 'self-interest groups' at the local levels of Soviet society. While the citizen in these

[2] J. S. Adams, (1973) "The people as monitors of Soviet bureaucracy." (unpublished)

groups may be pursuing goals of mutual benefit to the state and himself, and while the self-interest group as such remains anathema to some party ideologues, self-interest groups nevertheless exist in the Soviet Union at local levels, and they are multiplying and growing stronger.'' A group formed to protest the Soviet invasion of Czechoslovakia would clearly be beyond the pale, but many groups exist for the purposes of improving housing conditions, the quality of consumer goods, the operation of schools and other public institutions, the ecological quality of the country and similar matters. Many citizens' groups in the United States have similar purposes.

The membership of citizens in political organizations, particularly parties, is difficult to compare across national boundaries, for the term has different meanings in different political systems. This is especially true in comparing the Soviet Union and the United States, for these states represent polar extremes in the definition of membership. The very formal nature of party membership in the Soviet Union, involving a period of candidacy, sponsorship by active members, regular dues, and significant responsibilities, contrasts sharply with the loose relationships most Americans have with political parties. Some 75% of Americans "identify" with a party but only 8% fall in the category of "members," and this figure includes membership in other political organizations and clubs as well. Appropriately, American observers speak of party affiliation rather than party membership.

Where only a single, dominant political party exists, the concept of "identifying" with that party has little meaning, since there is no alternative. Formal membership in the CPSU is held by approximately 10% of the adult population.[3] In addition, millions more Soviet citizens of voting age belong to the Komsomol, which is a party organization open to people 14 to 28 years of age. The Komsomol has some 27 million members, about half of the age group. It is clear that formal, regular involvement in political party activity is more widespread in the Soviet Union than in the United States. . . .

The conclusion which emerges from a consideration of these political activities seems inescapable: the Soviet population participates more extensively in political activities than does the American population. Insofar as substantial popular involvement in these particular activities defines a participant political system, the Soviet Union is a more highly participant one than is the United States. Indeed, the image of the United States as a highly participant system is refuted by statistics: most acts of political participation are performed by only a small segment of the citizenry. . . .

While observers of the Soviet Union have long recognized the high level of political activity engaged in by its citizens, most have denied that

[3] Around 18 million in 1983. [Editor's note.]

this constitutes genuine political participation. Their arguments generally rest on the insistence that the concept of "participation" includes qualitative as well as quantitative characteristics. . . .

Other authors have argued that a basic difference exists between "participation" and "mobilization," and that the Soviet Union is an archetypical example of a system which has mobilized its population to fulfill the objectives of the party elite rather than permitted it to participate in defining and implementing those objectives. The vast complex of organizations and processes in which Soviet citizens are involved is viewed as a network of "transmission belts" for the communication and implementation of the policies of the elite. Related to this idea is the argument that participation is significant only when it affects the "input" side of the governmental process, that is when it has a direct effect on decision-making and policy formulation. It is generally recognized that Soviet citizens are widely involved in the implementation of party policies, but this tends to be defined as "obedient participation" or the political behavior of subjects rather than citizens.

By contrast, American political participation is pictured as voluntary rather than mobilized, derived from civic attitudes essential to democratic participation, directed toward inputs rather than outputs, and reflected in a highly responsive political system. . . .

It is the thesis of this paper that this is not the case, that in fact the conditions under which citizens participate in politics in the two countries are sufficiently similar that the concept "political participation" needs to be redefined in such a way as to apply to both cases. To examine the thesis, the analysis which follows will explore each of the characteristics indicated above as distinguishing Soviet from American participation.

"Mobilization of the masses" is much used by Soviet political writers. What they understand by it is perhaps not too remote from what we mean by "public relations." . . . In the Soviet Union nearly all decisions are made in this way—that is, the members of the public are not led to an understanding of them by the processes of the market and need to have the decision "sold" to them after it is taken. Hence we have "mobilization," which aims at informing people as to what has been decided . . . and at building a positive attitude of acceptance of the decision.

There are both broad and narrow concepts of "mobilization" and this one is decidedly in the latter category, focusing as it does on the generation of public support for particular political decisions. . . .

Since change is endemic in all societies, so also is the process of acculturation by which peoples adapt to evolving values and cultural innovations. Societies differ in terms of the extent to which political elites attempt to accelerate the rate of acculturation and in this sense the Soviet Union falls into the category of states where the political leadership has been committed to compression of time and social distance, where one

of the main functions of politics is the rapid involvement of peripheral
members of society. . . . For that reason, the process of mobilization in
the Soviet Union has been far more visible than in countries where the
pace has been slower. Nevertheless, regardless of the rate, mobilization
takes place in any society over time. And even among societies undergoing rapid mobilization, some have far more pluralistic political structures
than others. . . .

In both the American and Soviet political systems, much of the
impetus for political participation arises not out of the private motives of
concerned citizens, but as a result of mobilization by a variety of institutional and social agencies. There is, of course, a substantial difference
in the manner in which this process takes place in the two countries.
Mobilization in the Soviet Union is overt, intense, and heavily promoted
by governmental and party agencies. In the United States, mobilization
is more subtle and decentralized, and occurs principally through organizational and social influences, which, of course, are also present in the
Soviet political system.

One effect of political mobilization in any society is to constrict,
either overtly or subtly, the individual's free choice of whether to become
involved in politics or not. The intensity of Soviet mobilization has persuaded some observers that voluntarism is virtually nonexistent, and that
Soviet citizens have no choices to make in determining their political
involvement. . . .

In the very limited sense that all Soviet citizens must vote in every
election, and probably are more or less compelled to attend an occasional
rally or political meeting, this is accurate. However, I would argue that
there are numerous options for political involvement open to Soviet citizens, and that, in fact, the choices presented by these options are more
significant to the individual than are similar choices in the American context.

The Soviet citizen must choose, first of all, whether to go beyond
a perfunctory obeisance to the rituals of political life, and thus to take
seriously his prescribed role in committees, meetings, election campaigns
and similar activities. . . .

A more serious choice facing all Soviet citizens is whether to seek
membership in the Communist Party. This bears little resemblance to an
American citizen's decision to "affiliate" with one of the political parties,
for the consequences of the decision to the Soviet citizen are highly significant. Membership in the party can positively affect one's career, his
access to political leaders, his income, his information about the political
system, and his upward social mobility. On the other hand, it also places
a citizen under serious obligations, toward which failure to devote oneself
sufficiently can have serious negative consequences.

Among party members, a further choice exists with even more
serious implications. This involves a decision whether to remain a "rank

and file" member of the party or to become a member of the "aktiv."
The former are defined by Meyer as

> those whose activities as Party members are part-time only, be-
> cause they earn their living by holding jobs in some non-Party
> agency. They are thus performing their Party work in addition to
> their more regular duties. The *aktiv*, in contrast, comprises those
> people whose employer is the Party and who are therefore full-
> time Party officials—professional Communists, as it were.[4]

A very different level of commitment and obligation is associated with
each of these relationships to the party, and the choice is not lightly made.

Individuals who decide as young adults to pursue nonparty careers
may still have to face the question of party membership later on: . . . a
significant number of persons in the upper ranks of the CPSU are co-
opted into the party in mid-career. For the most part, they are individuals
who have had successful careers in industry, agriculture, education or in
other fields. Recognizing that opportunity for further advancement in
managerial positions may be enhanced by party membership, some of
them (by no means a majority) join the party at that point. The decision
to do so, or not, relates directly to the aspirations and ambitions of the
individual, as well as to the party's willingness to accept him to membership. . . .

More generally, the element of choice is an important component
in the political life of Soviet citizens, just as it is in the United States.
The difference is that in the Soviet Union, choices are more serious and
significant to the individual citizen. By comparison, movement in and out
of the political arena in the United States is, for most people, a relatively
casual matter, which involves neither great advantages nor great disad-
vantages.

The extent to which both Soviet and American citizens become
involved in political activities depends partly on subjective attitudinal
factors. . . .

There is no doubt that most Americans feel they should participate
in politics and would be able to do so if they tried. . . . Yet, this sense
of competence

> is certainly not matched by actual political behavior. In the first
> place, only a small proportion of those respondents who say they
> could influence the government report that they have ever at-
> tempted such influence. And even if those who think they could
> influence governmental decisions were to attempt to do so—which
> is unlikely—they would almost certainly not have the success that
> they believe they would have.[5]

If it is true then, as a general proposition, that large numbers of
citizens can be subjectively but not objectively competent, then the com-

---

[4] A. Meyer, *The Soviet Political System*, New York: Random House, 1965, p. 135.
[5] G. A. Almond, and S. Verba, *The Civic Culture*, Boston: Little, Brown, 1968, p. 245.

mon perception of the Soviet Union as dominated by an authoritarian elite does not rule out the possibility that Soviet citizens may nevertheless experience a relatively high degree of subjective competence. In both nations, after all, the idea of mass control over political leaders is a fundamental tenet of the ideology and is symbolically reinforced through the continual process of acculturation and through mass participation in parliamentary institutions. . . .

In the case of the Soviet Union, we have virtually no reliable, quantitative data on Soviet attitudes or judgments regarding their political system. The point of the above argument, however, is that even if there should be widespread dissatisfaction among Soviet citizens with the political system or its policies, this would not necessarily be evidence that the people do not participate actively and voluntarily in the political process. . . .

A further characteristic usually imputed to democratic participation is that it involves inputs rather than outputs. . . .

In practice, the input-output distinction is far too simple to be of much use in analyzing participation. The process of governance presents citizens with a wide range of access points, including the formulation of general policy, the overall administration of that policy, its application to specific cases, evaluation of the policy and its administration, amendments in practice, ad hoc interpretations, and the individual performance of administrators. The citizen may find any one of these phases of governance significant to his personal interests. . . .

The importance to citizens of policy implementation is particularly great in a system, like the Soviet Union, where high-level comprehensive planning is used extensively to implement national objectives. The greater the insistence of political leaders on integrating the myriad activities of a complex social system, the more irrationalities will appear on lower levels, and the more people will find it important to try to affect the implementation of the plan. . . .

Empirical studies of policy-making in the Soviet Union lend support to this position. In reviewing studies of seven policy areas, Juviler and Morton conclude that "implementation is often the heart of the policy-making process. Laws and Party resolutions (the results of decisions) are merely plans of action. They are theoretical solutions until proven in application, and are often unenforceable without administrative and popular support."[6]

There is, therefore, no reason to think of "input participation" as necessarily more significant to the individual citizen than "output participation," even if such a distinction were a useful one to maintain. . . .

This is not to argue that Soviet and American citizens have equal, or even comparable, influence on their respective governmental pro-

[6] P. Juviler, and H. Morton, *Soviet Policy-Making*, New York: Praeger, pp. ix–x.

cesses, but only to suggest that the input-output dichotomy is of little help in identifying the differences in participation in the two nations. The question of influence on government arising from mass political participation remains to be considered, and is the subject of the following section.

In their systemic model, Almond and Verba have distinguished between the citizen and the subject in terms of the participation of each in the governmental process. "The competent citizen," they say "has a role in the formation of general policy. Furthermore, he plays an *influential* role in this decision-making process: he participates by using explicit or implicit threats of some form of deprivation if the official does not comply with his demand." The subject, on the other hand, "does not participate in making rules, nor does his participation involve the use of political influence. His participation comes at the point at which general policy has been made and is being applied."[7]

By those definitions, the great majority of both Soviet and American citizens could be classified as subjects rather than citizens. Most readers would have little hesitancy about assigning the Soviet populace to that category, but a description of the American people as subjects requires discussion. The evidence on the role, attitudes and effectiveness of American citizens in politics is far too voluminous even to summarize here, but the argument can be made by reference to the conclusions of some of these studies.

A conclusion which is by now widely accepted by students of popular participation in America is that large numbers of citizens are uninformed about politics, indifferent to it, and inactive in the political arena, and that most of the rest participate only passively.

The direct communication of policy preferences is, however, only one of the two principal means by which, according to democratic theory, the public controls the government. The other is, of course, through elections. In the United States, candidates for political offices are normally nominated on the basis of contested primary elections and party conventions, and elected by popular vote. In the Soviet Union, elections are noncompetitive, as there is only one candidate for each office and each candidate must have the approval of the Communist Party. A minuscule proportion of the Soviet population normally votes against the party candidate, but this has no effect on the election.

There is no doubt that the American public does affect the selection, from among a very limited number of alternative candidates, of its elected officials through the electoral process, and that the Soviet public does not. But our concern is not with recruitment but with policy formulation, since that is the process by which public needs and desires are met or not met. The power to choose leaders has little significance unless that power can be converted into influence over policy-making.

[7] Almond and Verba, *op. cit.*, pp. 168–69.

To bring about this conversion, voters would have to have clear ideas as to what policies they wished to see enacted by government; they would have to know where each candidate stood on those issues; and they would have to vote for candidates on the basis of their positions on the issues. But the fact is, as studies of voting behavior have repeatedly demonstrated, that none of these characteristics accurately describes voting in America. "It appears," Verba and Nie conclude,[8] "that few citizens know what they want. They do not have clear and consistent positions on the important issues of the day. Attitudes on public issues are lightly held and answers to survey questions on specific issues facing the nation often appear to have a random quality."

Furthermore, they state,[9] "the public has little information on which candidate takes which position during an election. In fact, they may know almost nothing about candidates." Finally, the majority of voters do not cast their votes with policy objectives in mind, so that the common contention that elected officials have received policy mandates from the electorate is rarely true. In fact, "there is evidence that a prime motivation for voting is the gratification of the act itself—not some expected outcome.". . .

On the basis of the arguments in this paper, a modification is needed, one which separates the concept of "participation" from its traditional Western liberal-democratic context. Stripped of its ideological content, the concept appears in a simpler and more useful form. It allows us to begin with the mere association of individuals with others in various types of political activities and to relate those activities to the basic characteristics of the political system. It allows us, in other words, to analyze the relationship of participation to popular influence on policy-making and recruitment because we have not defined those consequences as inherent parts of the idea of participation. And it allows us to relate the ideas of participation to a broader range of experiences, recognizing that churchgoers, football players, ballet dancers, and conscript armies are all participants in their respective activities despite the fact that few have any significant control over the rules of the game or the consequences of their involvement.

Viewed in this way, mass political participation may be defined as the involvement of individual citizens in collective political activities related to the functions performed by the formal institutions of the political system. A participant political system is one in which the involvement is (relatively) widespread and frequent.

In terms of this definition, both the American and Soviet political systems are participant systems, with the Soviet somewhat more so than

---

[8] S. Verba, and N. Nie *Participation in America*, New York: Harper & Row, 1972, p. 104.
[9] *Ibid.*, p. 103.

the American. That is, the Soviet people as a whole are involved more frequently and in greater numbers in collective, politically related activities than are the American people. In both cases, active participation results in relatively little issue-communication to political leaders, although somewhat more in the American than in the Soviet system. In both, there are numerous choices to be made regarding the degree of individual participation in politics, although the choices are personally more significant to the Soviet citizen than to the American. In both systems, the mobilization of political support for the system is a constant and pervasive phenomenon, although in the Soviet Union it is more centralized and overt than in the United States.

The general conclusion of this analysis is that mass political participation can exist in political systems of widely varying characteristics. Thus, it exists in systems in which it has virtually no impact on the recruitment of political leaders or the generation of national policy (such as the U.S.S.R.) as well as in systems in which the popular vote is a crucial element in the selection of leaders (such as the U.S.). The stark differences between the political systems of the two countries lie not so much in their participatory mechanisms as in the characteristics of the systems themselves. Whether popular participation results in a change of leadership or policy depends on the basic distribution and exercise of power within each political system. Participation is thus an important and relatively independent variable in the analysis of whole systems of political life.

6. RIGHTS PLUS OBLIGATIONS UNDER SOVIET LAW*

Roy Turner†

Lawyer, Sydney, Australia, and Labor Party Delegate,
Upper House of New South Wales

An interesting fundamental of legal theory in the Soviet Union is that consideration of the rights and freedoms of man is not divorced from his

---

* Reprinted from Roy Turner, *Law in the USSR*, Moscow: Novosti Press Agency Publishing House, 1981, pp. 29–32, by permission of the author, the publisher and the Copyright Agency of the USSR.
† At the invitation of his Soviet colleagues, Mr. Turner visited the Soviet Union in 1978. He visited and observed many legal institutions in Moscow and Leningrad, talked to leading Soviet lawyers and legal experts as well as other public officials and private citizens, and wrote his book after returning to Sydney. Mr. Turner represents the Australian Labor Party which, he explained in a letter to this editor, is a democratic and socialist, but not a Marxist, party.

obligations. Separation of rights and freedoms from obligations may be a growing characteristic . . . . in some sections in the West; such separation is absent from the social, political and legal conditions of socialist society in the USSR.

Reading the 174 articles of the Constitution, the rights of the citizens are spelt out but so also are their obligations. These obligations are of prime importance. Perhaps in this way the document is unique. The preamble and the Constitution must be read as a whole document so as to appreciate that although the USSR is a federal state with 15 states or Union Republics, and, to this extent, similar in construction governmentally to Australia, the USA and Canada, the philosophy is quite different.

> "It is a society in which the law of life is concern of all for the good of each and concern of each for the good of all. It is a society of true democracy, the political system of which ensures effective management of all public affairs, ever more active participation of the working people in running the state, and the combining of citizens' real rights and freedoms with their obligations and responsibility to society."

This reference to the obligations of the citizens as well as their rights is the tandem that people living in another economic and social system tend to overlook. We, in our system, do not put to the forefront the obligations of our citizens. . . .

My study of existing Soviet constitutional law shows that it not only provides a concept of rights coupled with obligations, but is based on the theory that to divorce rights from obligations is to alienate the individual from society and, even more so, from the socialist state based on the people as a whole. This alienation causes a separation of man from his living environment.

The cult of the autonomous individual means that ultimately people do not belong to anything. They are unable to identify themselves with anything outside themselves. This is the basic cause of the overwhelming loneliness and retreat into the frustration of individualism that curses societies of the modern world. It is a basic factor in the individualist "one-out" or "look after Number One" tendencies that are strong characteristics of capitalist society.

Legal scholars of socialist law I spoke with in the USSR say that the democratic status and equality of the individual under socialism, irrespective of origin, social or property status, nationality, sex, education, attitude to religion, occupation, residence and other circumstances show how the rights and freedoms of the individual are guaranteed in fact by the economic and political system of socialism.

These basic concepts of the freedom of the individual associated inseparably with social obligations . . . cause most of the confusion and criticism in the West when examining law in the USSR.

SOVIET VIEWS

7. "DEMOCRACY" UNDER CAPITALISM, SOCIALISM AND IN THE FINAL STAGE OF PERFECT COMMUNISM*

V. I. Lenin

The transition from capitalist society—which is developing towards Communism—to a communist society is impossible without a "political transition period," and the state in this period can only be the revolutionary dictatorship of the proletariat.[1]

What, then, is the relation of this dictatorship to democracy?

The *Communist Manifesto* simply places side by side the two concepts: "to raise the proletariat to the position of the ruling class" and "to win the battle of democracy." On the basis of all that has been said above, it is possible to determine more precisely how democracy changes in the transition from capitalism to Communism.

In capitalist society, . . . democracy is always hemmed in by the narrow limits set by capitalist exploitation, and consequently always remains, in reality, a democracy for the minority, only for the propertied classes, only for the rich. Freedom in capitalist society always remains about the same as it was in the ancient Greek republics: freedom for the slave-owners. . . .

Democracy for an insignificant minority, democracy for the rich—that is the democracy of capitalist society. If we look more closely into the machinery of capitalist democracy, we shall see everywhere, in the "petty"—supposedly petty—details of the suffrage (residential qualification, exclusion of women, etc.),[2] in the technique of the representative institutions, in the actual obstacles to the right of assembly (public build-

---

* Reprinted from V. I. Lenin, *The State and Revolution* in the *Selected Works of V. I. Lenin*, Moscow: Foreign Languages Publishing House, 1952, Vol. II, Part I, by permission of the Copyright Agency of the USSR.

[1] The Soviets have long proclaimed that they have already gone through the stage of the "Dictatorship of the Proletariat" and are now in the stage of the "Dictatorship of the Entire People." Violations of the rules of society are still taking place. But, they say, these are the acts of individuals and not the attempts of classes to take advantage of other classes. [Editor's note.]

[2] Such restrictions, prevalent during Lenin's day and during much of the history of Western democracy, have largely been lifted by now; voting restrictions based on race had an even longer history in the United States. [Editor's note.]

ings are not for "beggars"!), in the purely capitalist organization of the daily press, etc., etc.—we shall see restriction after restriction upon democracy. These restrictions, exceptions, exclusions, obstacles for the poor, seem slight, especially in the eyes of one who has never known want himself and has never been in close contact with the oppressed classes in their mass life (and nine-tenths, if not ninety-nine hundredths, of the bourgeois publicists and politicians are of this category); but in their sum total these restrictions exclude and squeeze out the poor from politics, from active participation in democracy.

Marx grasped this *essence* of capitalist democracy splendidly, when, in analyzing the experience of the Commune, he said that the oppressed are allowed once every few years to decide which particular representatives of the oppressing class shall represent and repress them in parliament!

But from this capitalist democracy—that is inevitably narrow, and stealthily pushes aside the poor, and is therefore hypocritical and false to the core—forward development does not proceed simply, directly and smoothly towards "greater and greater democracy," as the liberal professors and petty-bourgeois opportunists would have us believe. No, forward development, i.e., towards Communism, proceeds through the dictatorship of the proletariat, and cannot do otherwise, for the *resistance* of the capitalist exploiters cannot be *broken* by anyone else or in any other way.

And the dictatorship of the proletariat, i.e., the organization of the vanguard of the oppressed as the ruling class for the purpose of suppressing the oppressors, cannot result merely in an expansion of democracy. *Simultaneously* with an immense expansion of democracy, which *for the first time* becomes democracy for the poor, democracy for the people, and not democracy for the moneybags, the dictatorship of the proletariat imposes a series of restrictions on the freedom of the oppressors, the exploiters, the capitalists. . . .

Engels expressed this splendidly in his letter to Bebel when he said, as the reader will remember, that "the proletariat uses the state not in the interests of freedom but in order to hold down its adversaries, and as soon as it becomes possible to speak of freedom the state as such ceases to exist."

Democracy for the vast majority of the people, and suppression by force, i.e., exclusion from democracy, of the exploiters and oppressors of the people—this is the change democracy undergoes during the *transition* from capitalism to Communism.

Only in communist society, when the resistance of the capitalists has been completely crushed, when the capitalists have disappeared, when there are no classes (i.e., when there is no difference between the members of society as regards their relation to the social means of production), *only* then "the state . . . ceases to exist," and it *"becomes possible to speak of freedom."* Only then will there become possible and be realized a truly complete democracy, democracy without any exceptions whatever. And only then will . . . people gradually *become accustomed* to observing the elementary rules of social intercourse that have been known for centuries and repeated for thousands of years in all copybook maxims; they will become accustomed to observing them without force, without compulsion, without subordination, *without the special apparatus* for compulsion which is called the state.

The expression "the state *withers away*" is very well chosen, for it indicates both the gradual and the spontaneous nature of the process. Only habit can, and undoubtedly will, have such an effect; for we see around us on millions of occasions how readily people become accustomed to observing the necessary rules of social intercourse when there is no exploitation, when there is nothing that rouses indignation, nothing that evokes protest and revolt and creates the need for *suppression*.

Thus, in capitalist society we have a democracy that is curtailed, wretched, false; a democracy only for the rich, for the minority. The dictatorship of the proletariat, the period of transition to Communism, will for the first time create democracy for the people, for the majority, along with the necessary suppression of the minority—the exploiters. Communism alone is capable of giving really complete democracy. . . .

In other words: under capitalism we have the state in the proper sense of the word, that is, a special machine for the suppression of one class by another, and, what is more, of the majority by the minority. . . .

During the *transition* from capitalism to Communism suppression is *still* necessary; but it is now the suppression of the exploiting minority by the exploited majority.

Only Communism makes the state absolutely unnecessary, for there is *nobody* to be suppressed—"nobody" in the sense of a *class*, in the sense of a systematic struggle against a definite section of the population. We are not utopians, and do not in the least deny the possibility and inevitability of excesses on the part of *individual persons*, or the need to suppress *such* excesses. But, in the first place, no special machine, no special apparatus of suppression is needed for this; this will be done by the armed people itself, as simply and as readily as any crowd of civilized people, even in modern society, interferes to put a stop to a scuffle or to prevent a woman from being assaulted. And, secondly, we know that the fundamental social cause of excesses, which consist in the violation of the rules of social intercourse, is the exploitation of the masses, their want and their poverty. With the removal of this chief cause, excesses will inevitably begin to *"wither away."* We do not know how quickly and in what succession, but we know that they will wither away. With their withering away the state will also *wither away*.

8. WHAT IS FREEDOM?*

V. Denisov

Former Deputy-Editor-in-Chief, Novosti Press Agency

"The entire life of socialist society is based on the
principle of broad democracy. . . . Socialist democracy includes both political freedoms—freedom of
speech, of the press and of assembly, the right to elect
and to be elected, and also social rights—the right to
work, to rest and leisure, to free education and free
medical services, to material security in old age and
in case of illness or disability; equality of citizens of
all races and nationalities; equal rights for women and
men in all spheres of political, economic and cultural
activity. Socialist democracy, unlike bourgeois democracy, does not merely proclaim the rights of the
people, but guarantees that they are really implemented."

FROM THE PROGRAMME OF THE CPSU[1]

When people in Western countries read these lines in the Programme of
the Soviet Communist Party, they may object that all political parties talk
about freedom. The United States describes itself as the "free world"
and the "champion" of freedom. But communists reject what the capitalists call freedom. They declare that only socialism can provide real
freedom—freedom for all.

Which is right?

History has already given the answer.

Communists do not only promise freedom in their Programme.
They also explain what they mean by freedom. And—what is perhaps
the best argument—the Soviet Communists, who were the first in the
world to build socialism and have now set about building communism,
have shown in practice that the new social system liberates working people from all forms of oppression and exploitation, and provides the most
favourable social conditions for every man and woman to obtain real,
tangible and not merely formal opportunities for free and all-round development.

Man has today achieved such a level of maturity that people no
longer acquiesce in the absence or limitation of freedom. "Life without

---

* Excerpt reprinted from V. Denisov, *Communism Stands for Freedom*, Moscow: Novosti
  Press Agency Publishing House, 1962, by permission of the Novosti Press Agency and
  the Copyright Agency of the USSR.
[1] The Programme of the Communist Party of the Soviet Union was adopted by the 22nd
  Party Congress on October 31, 1961 and is, in essence, still in force today.

liberty is worthless,'' said Romain Rolland, the great French writer. Mankind possesses no prouder or more sacred word than "freedom". The history of mankind is the history of the struggle for liberation.

Many great sacrifices have been made for the cause of freedom. But its universal triumph has yet to be achieved. There are still nations fettered by the chains of colonialism.

Hunger and poverty still threaten the lives and health of certain sections of the population in many parts of the world, even in economically advanced countries. Scientists have invented many miraculous medicines—but epidemics still flare up, killing or crippling many people. Millions of families still live in slums.

Can large-scale unemployment, the lack of opportunities for young people to get an education or a trade, the banning of progressive political parties and the peace movement supporters, or the disfranchisement of large sections of the population for reasons of colour or property qualifications—all to be found in the capitalist world—be considered compatible with "freedom"?

In the light of such facts, how is one to understand freedom? What is it that freedom should give to the individual and to society as a whole? Where is the borderline between genuine and false liberty, between freedom for the few and freedom for all?

The rights and liberties of citizens may be solemnly proclaimed in a country's constitution, which describes those rights and liberties as "inalienable" and "natural". But is it sufficient to possess a right in order to enjoy it? The formal possession of a right is not enough; it must be confirmed materially. Otherwise, equality means merely formal equality in the eyes of the law, while man's actual status in society is determined solely by his wealth. As Anatole France pointed out, the millionaire and the pauper are equally free to sleep under the arches of a Seine bridge— but the former prefers to live in his mansion, while the latter does not have any choice. Society can give its members genuine freedom only if it can first and foremost guarantee their material welfare and economic independence. The degree to which any society is free is indicated by the material foundations of the freedom it extends to its citizens. . . .

Working people, who make up the vast majority of society, . . . need . . . first and foremost, freedom from want and oppression, freedom from fear for the morrow and for the future of their children. That is the principal freedom, the foundation of genuine economic and social freedom for the mass of the people. "Freedom of speech, of ideas and of conscience can acquire significance only given the freedom to live. . . . Therefore to judge whether or not freedom exists in a given society, it is first of all necessary to see whether there is unemployment there, how people are ensured the means of existence, how social security is given effect, and whether life is maladjusted. . . . If the basic freedoms are not provided in a society, it cannot, in essence, be considered free, no matter how many non-basic freedoms are provided," writes the Japanese philosopher Yanagida Kenzuro.

The most extensive and lavishly proclaimed freedom is worthless unless it has a material basis. Under such "freedom" man has only two alternatives—to fall into line, or starve.

The yardstick of genuine freedom is the existence of the economic basis necessary for the unhampered enjoyment of freedom by every member of society.

9. THE SOVIET "BILL OF RIGHTS"
NEW SOVIET CONSTITUTION, ARTICLES 39–69
compared with relevant sections of
THE UNITED NATIONS UNIVERSAL
DECLARATION OF HUMAN RIGHTS*

SOVIET CONSTITUTION

The Basic Rights, Freedoms, and Duties of Citizens of the USSR

UN UNIVERSAL DECLARATION OF HUMAN RIGHTS

Article 39

Citizens of the USSR enjoy in full the social, economic, political and personal rights and freedoms proclaimed and guaranteed by the Constitution of the USSR and by Soviet laws. The socialist system ensures enlargement of the rights and freedoms of citizens and continuous improvement of their living standards as social, economic, and →

Article 29

2. In the exercise of his rights and freedoms, everyone shall be subject only to such limitations as are determined by law solely for the purpose of securing due recognition and respect for the rights and

---

* Articles 39–69 of the Soviet Constitution are reprinted from *Constitution (Fundamental Law) of the Union of Soviet Socialist Republics,* Moscow: Novosti Press Agency Publishing House, Moscow, 1978, pp. 40–52, by permission of the publisher and the Copyright Agency of the USSR. The comparable parts of the UN declaration of Human Rights have been taken from the "Text of the Universal Declaration of Human Rights," *Yearbook of the United Nations,* 1948–49, New York: Columbia University Press, in cooperation with the United Nations, 1949, pp. 535–37. It should still be mentioned that articles 33–36 of the Soviet Constitution, not included here, deal with equality of rights of Soviet citizens, irrespective of "origin, social or property status, race or nationality, sex, education, language, attitude to religion, type and nature of occupation, domicile, or other status." Articles 37 and 38 deal with the rights of foreigners residing in or seeking asylum in the USSR and articles 158 and 160 with the rights of individuals charged with violating the laws. For the electoral system and the rights and duties of elected representatives (articles 95–107) see Selection 15 in this chapter.

cultural development programmes are fulfilled.

Enjoyment by citizens of their rights and freedoms must not be to the detriment of the interests of society or the state, or infringe on the rights of other citizens.

freedoms of others and of meeting the just requirements of morality, public order and the general welfare in a democratic society.

3. These rights and freedom may in no case be exercised contrary to the purposes and principles of the United Nations.

Article 40

Citizens of the USSR have the right to work (that is, to guaranteed employment and pay in accordance with the quantity and quality of their work, and not below the state-established minimum), including the right to choose their trade or profession, type of job and work in accordance with their inclinations, abilities, training and education, with due account of the needs of society.

This right is ensured by the socialist economic system, steady growth of the productive forces, free vocational and professional training, improvement of skills, training in new trades or professions, and development of the systems of vocational guidance and job placement.

Article 23

1. Everyone has the right to work, to free choice of employment, to just and favourable conditions of work and to protection against unemployment. . . .

3. Everyone who works has the right to just and favourable remuneration ensuring for himself and his family an existence worthy of human dignity, and supplemented, if necessary, by other means of social protection.

Article 41

Citizens of the USSR have the right to rest and leisure.

This right is ensured by the establishment of a working week not exceeding 41 hours, for workers and other employees, a shorter working day in a number of trades and industries, and shorter hours for night work; by the provision of paid annual holidays, weekly days of rest, extension of the network of cultural, educational and health-building institutions, and the development on a mass scale of sport, physical culture, and camping and tourism; by the provision of neighbourhood recreational facilities,

Article 24

Everyone has the right to rest and leisure, including reasonable limitation of working hours and periodic holidays with pay.

and of other opportunities for rational use of free time.

The length of collective farmers' working and leisure time is established by their collective farms.

Article 42

Citizens of the USSR have the right to health protection.

This right is ensured by free, qualified medical care provided by state health institutions; by extension of the network of therapeutic and health-building institutions; by the development and improvement of safety and hygiene in industry; by carrying out broad prophylactic measures; by measures to improve the environment; by special care for the health of the rising generation, including prohibition of child labour, excluding the work done by children as part of the school curriculum; and by developing research to prevent and reduce the incidence of disease and ensure citizens a long and active life.

Article 43

Citizens of the USSR have the right to maintenance in old age, in sickness, and in the event of complete or partial disability or loss of the breadwinner.

This right is guaranteed by social insurance of workers and other employees and collective farmers; by allowances for temporary disability; by the provision by the state or by collective farms of retirement pensions, disability pensions, and pensions for loss of the breadwinner; by providing employment for the partially disabled; by care for the elderly and the disabled; and by other forms of social security.

Article 44

Citizens of the USSR have the right to housing.

Article 25

1. Everyone has the right to a standard of living adequate for the health and well-being of himself and of his family, including food, clothing, housing and medical care and necessary social services, and the right to security in the event of unemployment, sickness, disability, widowhood, old age or other lack of livelihood in circumstances beyond his control.

Article 22

Everyone, as a member of society, has the right to social security and is entitled to realization, through national effort and international co-operation and in accordance with the organization and resources of each State, of the economic, social and cultural rights indispensable for his dignity and the free development of his personality.

This right is ensured by the development and upkeep of state and socially-owned housing; by assistance for co-operative and individual house building; by fair distribution, under public control, of the housing that becomes available through fulfilment of the programme of building well-appointed dwellings, and by low rents and low charges for utility services. Citizens of the USSR shall take good care of the housing allocated to them.

→ See Article 25 above

Article 45

Citizens of the USSR have the right to education.

This right is ensured by free provision of all forms of education, by the institution of universal, compulsory secondary education, and broad development of vocational, specialised secondary, and higher education, in which instruction is oriented toward practical activity and production; by the development of extramural, correspondence and evening courses; by the provision of state scholarships and grants and privileges for students; by the free issue of school textbooks; by the opportunity to attend a school where teaching is in the native language; and by the provision of facilities for self-education.

Article 26

1. Everyone has the right to education. Education shall be free, at least in the elementary and fundamental stages. Elementary education shall be compulsory. Technical and professional education shall be made generally available and higher education shall be equally accessible to all on the basis of merit.

→

Article 46

Citizens of the USSR have the right to enjoy cultural benefits.

This right is ensured by broad access to the cultural treasures of their own land and of the world that are preserved in state and other public collections; by the development and fair distribution of cultural and educational institutions throughout the country; by developing television and radio broadcasting and the publishing of books, newspapers and periodicals, and by extending the free library service; and by ex-

Article 27

1. Everyone has the right freely to participate in the cultural life of the com-

panding cultural exchanges with other countries.

Article 47

Citizens of the USSR, in accordance with the aims of building communism, are guaranteed freedom of scientific, technical, and artistic work. This freedom is ensured by broadening scientific research, encouraging invention and innovation, and developing literature and the arts. The state provides the necessary material conditions for this and support for voluntary societies and unions of workers in the arts, organises introduction of inventions and innovations in production and other spheres of activity.

The rights of authors, inventors and innovators are protected by the state.

munity, to enjoy the arts and to share in scientific advancement and its benefits.

2. Everyone has the right to the protection of the moral and material interests resulting from any scientific, literary or artistic production of which he is the author.

Article 48

Citizens of the USSR have the right to take part in the management and administration of state and public affairs and in the discussion and adoption of laws and measures of All-Union and local significance.

This right is ensured by the opportunity to vote and to be elected to Soviets of People's Deputies and other elective state bodies, to take part in nationwide discussions and referendums, in people's control, in the work of state bodies, public organisations, and local community groups, and in meetings at places of work of residence.

Article 49

Every citizen of the USSR has the right to submit proposals to state bodies and public organisations for improving their activity, and to criticise shortcomings in their work.

Officials are obliged, within established time-limits, to examine citizens' proposals and requests, to reply to them, and to take appropriate action.

Article 21

1. Everyone has the right to take part in the government of his country, directly or through freely chosen representatives.

2. Everyone has the right of equal access to public service in his country.

Persecution for criticism is prohibited. Persons guilty of such persecution shall be called to account.

Article 50

In accordance with the interests of the people and in order to strengthen and develop the socialist system, citizens of the USSR are guaranteed freedom of speech, of the press, and of assembly, meetings, street processions and demonstrations.

Exercise of these political freedoms is ensured by putting public buildings, streets and squares at the disposal of the working people and their organisations, by broad dissemination of information, and by the opportunity to use the press, television, and radio.

Article 51

In accordance with the aims of building communism, citizens of the USSR have the right to associate in public organisations that promote their political activity and initiative and satisfaction of their various interests.

Public organisations are guaranteed conditions for successfully performing the functions defined in their rules.

Article 52

Citizens of the USSR are guaranteed freedom of conscience, that is, the right to profess or not to profess any religion, and to conduct religious worship or atheistic propaganda. Incitement of hostility or hatred on religious grounds is prohibited.

In the USSR, the church is separated from the state, and the school from the church.

Article 19

Everyone has the right to freedom of opinion and expression; this right includes freedom to hold opinions without interference and to seek, receive and impart information and ideas through any media and regardless of frontiers.

Article 20

1. Everyone has the right to freedom of peaceful assembly and association.

2. No one may be compelled to belong to an association.

Article 18

Everyone has the right to freedom of thought, conscience and religion; this right includes freedom to change his religion or belief, and freedom, either alone or in community with others and in public or private, to manifest his religion or belief in teaching, practice, worship and observance.

Article 53

The family enjoys the protection of the state.

Marriage is based on the free consent of the woman and the man; the spouses are completely equal in their family relations.

The state helps the family by providing and developing a broad system of child-care institutions, by organising and improving communal services and public catering, by paying grants on the birth of a child, by providing children's allowances and benefits for large families, and other forms of family allowances and assistance.

Article 54

Citizens of the USSR are guaranteed inviolability of the person. No one may be arrested except by a court decision or on the warrant of a procurator.

Article 55

Citizens of the USSR are guaranteed inviolability of the home. No one may, without lawful grounds, enter a home against the will of those residing in it.

Article 56

The privacy of citizens, and of their correspondence, telephone conversations, and telegraphic communications is protected by law.

Article 57

Respect for the individual and protection of the rights and freedoms of citizens are the duty of all state bodies, public organisations, and officials.

Article 16

1. Men and women of full age, without any limitation due to race, nationality or religion, have the right to marry and to found a family. They are entitled to equal rights as to marriage, during marriage and at its dissolution.

2. Marriage shall be entered into only with the free and full consent of the intending spouses.

3. The family is the natural and fundamental group unit of society and is entitled to protection by society and the State.

Article 9

No one shall be subjected to arbitrary arrest, detention or exile.

Article 12

No one shall be subjected to arbitrary interference with his privacy, family, home or correspondence, nor to attacks upon his honour and reputation. Everyone has the right to the protection of the law against such interference or attacks.

Article 8

Everyone has the right to an effective remedy by the competent national tribunals for acts violating the

Citizens of the USSR have the right to protection by the courts against encroachments on their honour and reputation, life and health, and personal freedom and property.

$\longrightarrow$ fundamental rights granted him by the constitution or by law.

Article 58

Citizens of the USSR have the right to lodge a complaint against the actions of officials, state bodies and public bodies. Complaints shall be examined according to the procedure and within the time-limit established by law.

Actions by officials that contravene the law or exceed their powers, and infringe the rights of citizens, may be appealed against in a court in the manner prescribed by law.

Citizens of the USSR have the right to compensation for damage resulting from unlawful actions by state organisations and public organisations, or by officials in the performance of their duties.

Article 59

Citizens' exercise of their rights and freedoms is inseparable from the performance of their duties and obligations.

Citizens of the USSR are obliged to observe the Constitution of the USSR and Soviet laws, comply with the standards of socialist conduct, and uphold the honour and dignity of Soviet citizenship.

Article 29

1. Everyone has duties to the community in which alone the free and full development of his personality is possible.

Article 60

It is the duty of, and a matter of honour for, every able-bodied citizen of the USSR to work conscientiously in his chosen, socially useful occupation, and strictly to observe labour discipline. Evasion of socially useful work is incompatible with the principles of socialist society.

Article 61

Citizens of the USSR are obliged to preserve and protect socialist property. It is the
duty of a citizen of the USSR to combat
misappropriation and squandering of state
and socially-owned property and to make
thrifty use of the people's wealth.

Persons encroaching in any way on
socialist property shall be punished according to the law.

Article 62

Citizens of the USSR are obliged to safeguard the interests of the Soviet state, and
to enhance its power and prestige.

Defence of the Socialist Motherland
is the sacred duty of every citizen of the
USSR.

Betrayal of the Motherland is the
gravest of crimes against the people.

Article 63

Military service in the ranks of the Armed
Forces of the USSR is an honourable duty
of Soviet citizens.

Article 64

It is the duty of every citizen of the USSR
to respect the national dignity of other citizens, and to strengthen friendship of the
nations and nationalities of the multinational Soviet state.

Article 65

A citizen of the USSR is obliged to respect
the rights and lawful interests of other persons, to be uncompromising toward anti-social behaviour, and to help maintain public
order.

Article 66

Citizens of the USSR are obliged to concern
themselves with the upbringing of children,
to train them for socially useful work, and

to raise them as worthy members of socialist society. Children are obliged to care
for their parents and help them.

Article 67

Citizens of the USSR are obliged to protect
nature and conserve its riches.

Article 68

Concern for the preservation of historical
monuments and other cultural values is a
duty and obligation of citizens of the USSR.

Article 69

It is the internationalist duty of citizens of
the USSR to promote friendship and co-operation with peoples of other lands and help
maintain and strengthen world peace.

10. CONCERNING FREEDOMS, REAL AND IMAGINARY*
I. Alexandrov

It is common knowledge that the slogan with which the bourgeoisie moved
to power was freedom for the individual, which, as it later turned out,
meant primarily the freedom of private ownership of the means of production, that is, freedom to exploit the labor of others. When the working
class emerged on the political scene, it was with the idea of freedom for
the masses, for the working people themselves.

The proletariat also moved to power with the slogan of freedom—
freedom from exploitation, from social and national oppression. As for
individual freedom, the Socialist Revolution ensured it by winning freedom for the people, for the working masses. It opened the way to the
rounded personal development of everyone, not only of the narrow
"elite."

Needless to say, for every revolution, socialist or democratic, freedom is a very, very important slogan. But our program says that if freedom
runs counter to the emancipation of labor from the yoke of capital, it is
a deception. . . .

* Reprinted from I. Alexandrov, "Concerning Freedoms, Real and Imaginary," *Soviet Life*, July, 1976, pp. 20–21, by permission of the publisher and the Copyright Agency of the USSR.

MAIN ELEMENTS OF SOCIALIST DEMOCRACY

What are the main characteristics of socialist democracy?

They are: freedom from human exploitation; freedom from social and national oppression and racial discrimination; such basic human rights as the right to work, to education, to maintenance in old age, sickness or disability; the right to free medical care, rest and leisure; a high level of education to make it possible for the working people to run the government with greater competence, efficiency and responsibility; freedom of speech and freedom of the press, freedoms widely enjoyed by Soviet citizens; an efficient system of state agencies and public organizations, coordinated and guided by the generally accepted political vanguard, the Communist Party. This party of the working class expresses the fundamental interests of all classes and groups, of all the nations and nationalities of the country, and ensures that the power of the people will be used for creative and constructive ends for the general good.

It was socialism that, for the first time in human history, not only proclaimed but actually guaranteed that the working people would be free of the threat of poverty and unemployment and that their living standards would rise steadily. The Communist Party of the Soviet Union regards this as the primary goal of the country's economic progress. Economic security is an integral part of the Soviet way of life. Soviet citizens need never fear that they will not have a level of subsistence worthy of human beings.

FREE AND ALL-ROUND DEVELOPMENT OF THE INDIVIDUAL

But socialism provides people with more than a continuously rising standard of living and financial security. It creates increasingly favorable conditions for spiritual enrichment, for free and unhindered personality development.

The morality of the socialist system strikingly and undeniably manifests its truly free nature. Its ban on violence, brutality, racial superiority, propaganda for war and national prejudice, which has the force of law, is another manifestation of the sovereignty of the people and of the genuine humanism of socialist society. In the USSR, the education of young people, the literature and art, the entire social atmosphere are pervaded by respect for human beings, for their dignity, their right to build their life as they choose within the framework of the social system. For the first time in history this possibility is offered to all working people, to the entire people.

FALSE STEREOTYPES AND REALITY

The mass media of the Western countries have started a noisy propaganda campaign, obsessively repeating a number of false stereotypes. They include concoctions about the persecution of people for their opinions in the Soviet Union and other socialist countries; the ban by Soviet authorities on marriage between our citizens and foreigners; the barriers allegedly placed in the way of citizens of Jewish nationality who want to emigrate to Israel to reunite their families; the absence of freedom of religion in the USSR.

What is the real state of affairs? Of course there are individuals in the Soviet Union who express views that contradict communist ideology, as well as people who are frankly anti-Soviet, opponents of socialism. Ocassionally they are arrested, not for their views but an act that breaks the law.

It is unmitigated slander that in the Soviet Union "dissidents" are confined to "special psychiatric hospitals." As everywhere else in the world, it sometimes becomes necessary to hospitalize insane persons whose freedom of movement may be dangerous for society. Persons guilty of a crime can be committed to a psychiatric hospital only by a court, which makes its decision on the basis of the recommendation of a commission of medical experts. Insane criminals are treated medically exactly like other mentally ill people, and they are not kept in the hospital longer than is required by the state of their health.

Soviet medicine makes sure that only those suffering from mental disorders are subject to treatment. It is worth mentioning that a number of people who had been in psychiatric clinics in the USSR and who were made out to be "victims of the Soviet regime" by Western propaganda ended up in the same type of clinics when they went abroad.

FREEDOM OF RELIGION, MARRIAGE AND EMIGRATION

The West is particularly fond of capitalizing on the question of marriage between Soviet citizens and foreigners and of the Soviet citizens' freedom to go abroad. They describe at length and in detail the obstacles allegedly imposed by Soviet authorities. But that, too, is a malicious fabrication. The 5,500 Soviet citizens who married foreigners in the past few years and are now living in 110 countries are proof of this. As for leaving the Soviet Union, the West produces as illustration of "oppression" the three-fold decrease in 1975 (as compared with 1973) in the number of people leaving for Israel in order to be united with their families.

The decrease is the result of the fact that the number of those wishing to leave has dropped. The majority of the Jewish population in the USSR, like Soviet citizens of other nationalities, are dedicated to socialism and the Soviet system. The Soviet Union is their beloved and their only motherland, and they reject with indignation the very thought of leaving it.

Naturally, in considering applications to emigrate, government agencies take account of the need to protect the state. Those in possession of certain information, including military, military-industrial and other state secrets, are not permitted to emigrate for a certain period of time.

The number of such cases, however, is exceedingly small. Over the five years from 1970 to 1975 exit permits were granted to 98.4 per cent of those who applied for them, and only 1.6 per cent of the applications were turned down. These are the facts.

FURTHER PERFECTING SOCIALIST DEMOCRACY

The Communist Party of the Soviet Union displays constant concern for improving the political structure of Soviet society, of all the institutions of Soviet democracy. It believes this to be one of the most important directions of its activity. The specific ways of further perfecting socialist democracy, as Leonid Brezhnev indicated, are "still more active mass participation of the people in management; fuller implementation by the Soviets of their diverse functions in the administration of social life; a more consistent application of the principle of accountability of executive bodies to representative bodies; further strengthening of socialist legality; improvement in the activities of People's Control bodies."

The entire history of the Soviet Union is proof of the steady expansion and strengthening of democracy.

11. THE SOCIALIST CONCEPTION OF HUMAN RIGHTS, FREEDOM, AND DEMOCRACY*

Valentin Patyulin
D. Sc. (Law), USSR

The problem of individual rights and freedoms and of the relations between the individual, on the one hand, and society and the state, on the other, is among the oldest and most complex ones in human history both in terms of theory and practice. In the most general form it comprises the rights society gives to the individual and their guarantees and his duties to society.

We must note at once that in today's world there are widely contrasting views on the very idea of human rights and freedoms arising from the fundamentally opposite approaches to the problem adopted by the two different social systems.

The view in the Soviet Union and the other socialist countries is

* Reprinted from Valentin Patyulin, "The Socialist Conception of Human Rights," in *Human Rights in Socialist Society*, Moscow: Novosti Press Agency Publishing House, 1981, pp. 7–23, by permission of the publisher and the Copyright Agency of the USSR.

that equality proclaimed by capitalist society and its promises of equal protection of the rights of its members are merely formal. Can there be real equality between, say, Henry Ford and his workers? Do the press tycoon Henry Luce and the black unemployed in Harlem have the same rights in the exercise of freedom of speech and the press? Certainly not. In a society where there is no equality in ownership of the means of production the will of one person always encroaches on that of another and the freedom of one means the submission of others.

As Lenin said, ". . . the slogan of freedom and equality is merely the lies and humbug of bourgeois society, whose formal recognition of freedom and equality conceals actual economic servitude and inequality for the workers, for all who toil and are exploited by capital, i.e., for the overwhelming majority of the population in all capitalist countries."

Unlike capitalism, socialism is based on public ownership of the means of production. In other words, all factories and banks are owned by the nation as a whole and not by private citizens. This is the main, decisive condition for individual freedom.

With public ownership of the means of production labour is practically the only means of earning a living and the sole yardstick of human dignity. It is also a factor of genuine freedom and equality.

Last but not least, public property means public management of that property. The socialist state, managing the economy according to plan, acts in the interests of society as a whole, that is, of the entire people. In our view, the organisation and management of the national economy based on public property is the principal condition for ensuring democracy and the genuine rights and freedoms of every member of society.

The radical changes in property relations carried out in the socialist society give a qualitatively new meaning to the traditional democratic slogans of freedom and equality. This is also reflected in the fundamentally new approach to the position of the individual in society and in the creation of the necessary social, economic and political conditions for the fullest possible exercise of all the rights and freedoms.

Socialism linked the problem of the individual with the tasks of the revolutionary transformation of society. That signified an important step towards closing the traditional gap between formal and real democracy. Socialism has proved that genuine, not illusory, individual freedom can be achieved only if society and the state consistently carry out a series of wide-ranging measures. It is not enough to proclaim freedom. What is vital is to provide conditions in which all can exercise it.

The experience of the USSR and other socialist countries over the past several decades shows that democracy, individual freedom and civil rights and liberties are inseparable from the economic, political and cultural advancement of these countries.

Take the Soviet Union's experience, for instance. The first ever socialist revolution which took place in October (November), 1917, occurred in the world's largest multi-national country where there existed all forms of national oppression. It is not surprising, therefore, that one of the first documents issued by the Soviet government was the Declaration of the Rights of the Peoples of Russia. It proclaimed the right of the people of Russia to self-determination, and abolished all restrictions and privileges based on nationality or religion. These ideas were also reflected in the first Soviet Constitution adopted in 1918.

The new system created the conditions for freedom in the social sphere. The first, most important step in this direction was the abolition of relations of exploitation. Soviet socialist society also undertook to guarantee the right to a job for every citizen, which is the most important right of all. And what had been an idea in a political programme became a reality in 1930 when the dynamic growth of the socialist economy made it possible to put an end to unemployment once and for all.

Besides the right to a job, the right to free education also became law. The decree on education adopted in 1919 said that free tuition was necessary to enable everybody to play a meaningful role in the country's political life.

The right to work, to education, to maintenance in old age, to disability benefits and to free medical service made it possible for everyone really to exercise a whole number of social and political rights and liberties. As for the political freedoms—freedom of speech, of the press, of assembly, processions and demonstrations—the Soviet state not only made them into law, but also guaranteed them by nationalising the mass media such as publishing houses, radio stations, newspapers, magazines, recreation centres, etc. They came to belong to society as a whole and were used in its interests. . . .

Under socialism the putting of the interests of society before those of the individual is not an end in itself. What is more, the consistent implementation of this principle in the long run creates the best possible conditions for the development of the individual. This merging of public and individual interests, while ensuring the most effective functioning of the social system, guarantees the rights of every citizen and the steady and consistent extension of the rights and freedoms of all. . . .

Human rights and freedoms defined in the legislation of the socialist countries fall into three large categories: social and economic rights, political rights, and individual freedoms. This classification stems from the relations between the state and citizens under socialism in the socio-economic sphere, the political sphere, and in the sphere relating to the defence of their lives, freedom, honour and dignity. Soviet scholars believe that these three spheres most fully reflect the real position of the individual in society.

In this relationship each side has its own rights and duties which are defined in legislations. For example, the socio-economic and political rights set out in the constitutions of the socialist countries imply the obligation of the state to provide its citizens with real opportunities to exercise every aspect of those rights.

As for such rights and freedoms as the inviolability of the person and the home, privacy of correspondence and freedom of conscience, the state not only has the duty to guarantee them. The idea is that the state should not interfere in such aspects of private life which lie outside citizens' duties to the state. And when necessary the state is obliged to take action to protect citizens' individual rights and freedoms from unlawful encroachments by various institutions, officials or other persons. . . .

So how does the state carry out its duties? Take, for instance, the right to work, the most vital component of individual freedom. While in capitalist countries about 30 million people are now either unemployed or underemployed, in the Soviet Union economic growth has been accompanied by full employment for half a century.

Significantly, the present Soviet Constitution adopted on October 7, 1977, regards the right to work not merely as the possibility of getting a job and earning a living but as a guaranteed right of employment in the field corresponding to one's education, skill and interests, in other words, the right to choose a profession.

Furthermore, whereas the 1936 Constitution proclaimed the right to maintenance in the event of sickness or disability, the new Soviet Constitution guarantees the right to health protection. This guarantee is based on free medical service which was established more than half a century ago. Whereas the previous Constitution spoke of compulsory seven-year schooling, the new one provides for compulsory ten-year secondary education.

The new Constitution also proclaims the right to housing. The state ensures this right by the planned fulfilment of a large scale housing development programme, by promoting cooperative and individual housing construction and by the fair distribution of housing under public control.

It should be pointed out that most of the housing is made available to tenants without any key money, while rent and utility charges make up just three to four per cent of a working class family's income.

Besides socio-economic rights, citizens in the socialist countries also enjoy wide ranging political rights and freedoms such as the right to elect and be elected to government bodies and to take part in administering the state and associate in public organisations. This sphere also includes freedom of speech, of the press, and of assembly, and other liberties. All that is part of the socialist way of life. . . .

In the socialist countries citizens' participation in administering the affairs of state and society is far from being limited to sending elective representatives to government bodies. It is also very important that democratic principles in the field of production are being developed and strengthened.

In most cases workers take part in deciding key questions concerning the operation of their factories or offices through the trade unions. In the USSR about 127 million people or 98 per cent of all workers, office employees and students belong to trade unions. According to the current regulations, the unions monitor the observance of labour laws, safety rules and standards, and conclude collective agreements with the management on behalf of their members. Moreover, the unions manage the state social insurance funds; they are in charge of matters relating to pensions and other allowances. They also run rest-and-cure centres, preventoriums, holiday hotels, and sporting and tourist facilities.

The activities of people's control bodies are yet another important form of drawing the masses into administering state affairs. There is nothing of the kind in any of the capitalist countries. In the USSR over ten million people have been elected to people's control bodies. Their powers extend to practically all government institutions, from retail shops to the ministries. They have the right of access to any documents, including financial accounts. The purpose is to make the national economy even more efficient in the interests of the entire population.

Finally, besides the right to democratic representation, citizens in the socialist countries actively exercise their right to take part in what is known as direct democracy, in particular, the right to discuss and amend bills of national importance. A case in point was the nationwide discussion of the draft of the new USSR Constitution in 1977. The discussion lasted four months. It involved 140 million people or four-fifths of the country's adult population. Their proposals and comments resulted in the amending of 122 out of a total of 173 articles of the Constitution and in the introduction of one new article.

The constitutions of the socialist countries guarantee citizens equal rights in every sphere of economic, political, social and cultural activities. There are no privileges or restrictions here, direct or indirect, on grounds of social origin, party affiliation, sex, nationality, religion, property status or the length of residence. Citizens also have equal duties and obligations to the socialist state and society.

Citizens' equality under socialism means political equality irrespective of race or nationality, the equality of men and women in every sphere of economic, government, cultural and socio-political activities, and the gradual extension by the state and society of the principles of equality to the entire sphere of distribution of material benefits.

Thus the rights and freedoms in socialist society, seen as legal ties between the state and the citizens, can be characterised as follows: citizens' right to material well-being the conditions for which are to be provided by the state and society, and to having their social and cultural requirements met (socio-economic rights); the right to participate in managing the affairs of state and society (political rights); and the right to personal freedom, or freedom from state interference in the sphere of relations that lie outside citizens' duties to the state (individual freedom). These rights are guaranteed by Article 39 of the USSR Constitution. . . .

Courts play an important role in protecting citizens' rights in the USSR and the other socialist countries. Article 2 of the Fundamentals of Court Procedures of the USSR and the Union Republics points out that one of the vital tasks of socialist justice is to protect citizens' political, labour, housing and other individual and property rights and interests guaranteed by the Constitution. The socialist court not only protects the rights and legitimate interests of individuals and organisations and the honour and dignity of the individual, but also points out the conditions leading to encroachments on these rights and takes steps to combat and prevent law-breaking. . . .

The legal guarantees of the exercise and protection of citizens' basic rights and liberties are also written down in civil and labour legislations.

The USSR Supreme Soviet has adopted the Statute of the Rights of the Factory, Plant and Local Trade-Union Committees which provides one of the guarantees of citizens' right to employment. It says that no one can be dismissed from a factory, office or organisation at the management's initiative without the consent of the trade union committee. A similar purpose is served by giving citizens the legal right to appeal to court against dismissals.

According to Article 58 of the USSR Constitution, citizens have the right to lodge complaints against the actions of officials, state and public bodies with the respective administrative institutions. They can also appeal against such actions in court.

Citizens submit to state and public bodies proposals on political economic and cultural affairs as well as on amendments to legislation. In socialist society this activity is a widespread form of participation in administering the state, improving the work of the government machinery, enhancing people's control over its operation, and strengthening legality and law and order. . . .

The Fundamentals of Criminal Proceedings of the USSR and the Union Republics contain a number of provisions that protect the rights and legitimate interests of the defendants. For example, no one can be charged with an offense other than on the grounds of and according to the procedure established by law (Article 4); and no one can be convicted of a crime other than by a court of law (Article 7). The court, the public prosecutor and the investigating officer are duty-bound to ensure complete and unbiased examination of the circumstances of the case. They have no right to shift the burden of proof on to the defendant (Article 14). It is forbidden to base a conviction on surmises or conjectures (Article 43). A number of articles in the Fundamentals of Civil Legislation of the USSR and the Union Republics also provide for the protection of citizens' rights. And the same is true of the respective sections in the Civil Codes of the other socialist countries. . . .

The large-scale development of democracy which is characteristic of the socialist countries in recent years makes itself felt in the wider powers given to work collectives in managing directly the affairs of state and society. For instance, workers' collectives nominate candidates to government bodies at all levels and take an active part in election campaigns. They also exercise their right to control the activities of the deputies, including the right to recall those deputies who do not justify their confidence.

Thus the economic, political, legal and ideological guarantees of individual freedom in socialist society are closely, or to be more exact, inseparably interconnected. By supplementing one another they provide maximum opportunities for the exercise of human rights and liberties.

Furthermore, an inalienable feature of socialist democracy is that it not only respects individual interests but also combines them with those of society. Under socialism, freedom of the individual and his development do not at all mean unrestrained arbitrary actions on the part of the individual. The Marxist interpretation of these social categories has nothing in common with anarchistic views according to which the individual need not acknowledge the authority of any government. The logic of human relations calls for standards of behaviour that are binding for all and for a certain restriction of individual interests in the interests of society as a whole. That is why the socialist state and socialist society, while giving extensive rights and freedoms to citizens, also require that they perform certain duties and obligations.

The principle of combining citizens' rights and duties is not a discovery of socialism. It is commonly recognised in international law. For instance, the Universal Declaration of Human Rights adopted by the United Nations in 1948 underlines that "Everyone has duties to the community in which alone the free and full development of his personality is possible" (Article 29).

Citizens' rights and duties in socialist society express the objective correlation between the individual's freedom and his responsibility to the state and his people, his fellow citizens. Lenin said: "One cannot live in society and be free from society."

In full conformity with international law, the constitutions of the socialist countries impose on citizens such duties as the duty to safeguard the country's interests and enhance its power and prestige; the obligation to respect the rights and legitimate interests of other persons, to be uncompromising toward anti-social behaviour, and to help maintain public order; the duty to concern themselves with the upbringing of children, to train them for socially useful work and to raise them as worthy members of socialist society; the obligation to protect nature and conserve its riches; the duty to care for the preservation of historical monuments and other cultural values, and so on. It is the duty of every citizen of a socialist country to respect the national dignity of other citizens, to promote friendship and cooperation with other nations, and to help maintain and strengthen world peace. . . .

There is much talk outside the socialist world about the articles in the constitutions of a number of socialist countries which say that in exercising their rights and freedoms citizens should not damage the interests of the state or society or the rights of other persons. These articles are sometimes interpreted in the West as giving the government the right to persecute people on account of their convictions or "dissenting views".

Indeed, there are people in the Soviet Union and other socialist countries who express views that contradict communist ideology. There are also outright opponents of socialism. Some of them have to account for their *actions* before the law, but not for their *views*.

The very idea of extrajudicial punishment for a person's views is alien to socialist legality. This is clearly stated in Article 3 of the USSR Penal Code. "Criminal punishment," the Article says, "shall be meted out only to a person convicted of a crime, that is, who has committed, either deliberately or through negligence, an act regarded as socially dangerous by criminal law."

Similarly, criminal responsibility is also incurred for actions found by a court, in accordance with the law, to be either directed at undermining or weakening the existing socio-political system or at deliberately spreading false information to discredit the state and social structure. Again, these are actions envisaged by the Penal Code, and not views.

The criminal cases of those who are sometimes described as "prisoners of conscience" in the West show that these persons committed concrete acts of the above-mentioned type. These include fabrication of slanderous material about the internal and external policies of the socialist countries, its dissemination in printed form with the aid of foreign organisations and special services, speculation in foreign currency, and attempts to hijack airplanes, to mention just a few. . . .

And such legislation in the socialist countries does not contradict international law or the International Covenant on Civil and Political Rights. Articles 12 and 19 of the Covenant say that the exercise of the rights set forth therein is subject to restrictions necessary in any democratic society to protect national security, public order, the health of the population or public morality, as well as to ensure respect for the rights and freedoms of other persons. . . .

Democratic rights and freedoms constitute an important, distinctive feature of socialism. And they acquire a new, more profound meaning as its socio-economic and political foundations develop and grow stronger. The economic, political, ideological and legal guarantees of individual freedom are being steadily extended enabling citizens to exercise their rights and freedoms. This is a distinguishing feature of the social and state system under socialism.

12. SPEAKING ABOUT FREEDOM OF CONSCIENCE*
Editorial in the magazine *Kommunist*

The principal conditions ensuring real freedom of conscience are stipulated in the Constitution of the USSR.

– Citizens of the USSR are equal before the law, without distinction of origin, social or property status, race or nationality, sex, education, language, attitude to religion;

– All religions are equal in the eyes of the law, there can be no compulsion in matters of religion or atheism;

– Religion should not be used to the detriment of individual citizens or society as a whole;

– In the USSR the church is loyal to and separated from the state, and they do not interfere in each other's affairs.

Soviet law prohibits any infringement of the rights of believers, slighting them on religious grounds, insulting their religious feelings and preventing them from conducting religious worship. Similarly, the law protects atheists from hostile actions against them on the part of believers. Article 52 of the Constitution of the USSR guarantees citizens the right to profess or not to profess any religion, and to conduct religious worship or atheistic propaganda. Incitement of hostility or hatred on religious grounds is prohibited.

To refuse a job or a place in an educational establishment to a person, dismissal from work or deprivation of rights and privileges stipulated by the law or restriction in these rights on the grounds of a person's attitude to religion is a criminal offence punishable by law. . . .

Article 14 of the Constitution of Belgium states that freedom of conscience and religious worship are guaranteed the subjects of the Belgian crown, as long as the law is not broken during religious ceremonies. The Constitution of Switzerland (Articles 49 and 50) states that religious beliefs do not relieve any citizen of the Confederation of the performance of his civic duties, and the free conduct of religious worship is guaranteed inasmuch as the requirements of public order and good morals are not violated. Article 28 of the Constitution of Japan recognizes freedom of religion within the limits compatible with public law and order.

* Reprinted in *Sputnik*, November, 1980, pp. 45–48, by permission of the Copyright Agency of the USSR.

In general, there has never been a country which would remain indifferent to transgressions of the law on religious grounds.

The Soviet law does not allow religious meetings to be used for political campaigning against the state, for inciting non-participation in social life and advocating the shirking of civic responsibilities. The law prohibits cruel rites and rituals detrimental to health as well as deceitful actions that encourage superstitions.

The clergy in the USSR, to say nothing of the broad mass of believers, correctly understand these legal stipulations and adhere to them. However, there are religious extremists who venomously distort the essence of relations between the state and the church in the Soviet Union. It is they who circulate the rumours about religious persecution in the USSR.

Here is a case in point. The authorities in the Agdash district in the Republic of Azerbaijan, in the Transcaucasus, had to intervene to stop the activity of self-styled "saints", who told Moslem pilgrims to drink dirty water mixed with earth from the grave of "Haji baba piri". This was supposed to be a remedy for all diseases, including sterility. If the authorities had not acted promptly, an epidemic could have broken out.

There have been instances when leaders of the sectarian groups of Jehovah's Witnesses, Pentecostalists and Baptists forbade believers to join trade unions, watch television, apply for medical help. They sometimes tried to make people boycott the elections, destroy official documents, refuse to serve in the army.

These outrages of obscurantists, attacks against Soviet laws under the guise of religious sermons, infringements on the rights and duties of citizens are naturally counteracted on a perfectly normal legal basis. But this has nothing to do with freedom of conscience. . . .

The world has heard for many years, and even decades, legends about the forcible eradication of religion in the USSR and the administrative methods of struggle against the church, which have allegedly been elevated to the level of state policy. But bourgeois propaganda stubbornly remains silent about the fact that the Soviet state has adopted special legal acts protecting believers from any encroachment on their legitimate rights.

Soviet law forbids anyone or any organization to close down prayer houses and churches so long as at least a few worshippers gather there. . . . Those encroaching on freedom of conscience and worship must be strictly punished. . . .

At present there are more than 20,000 Orthodox churches, Roman Catholic churches, synagogues, Lutheran churches, Old Believer churches, mosques, Buddhist datsans, prayer houses of Evangelical Christian Baptists, Seventh Day Adventists etc.

In the past three years dozens of religious premises have been opened. Religious associations have the right to train their own personnel at secondary and higher theological educational institutions. They publish all the literature they require. The Russian Orthodox Church alone has more than 10 periodical publications. The Baptists, Adventists, Moslems and other believers also have their printed publications. It would be appropriate to mention that the finances at the disposal of the churches which come from parishioners' donations, are exempt from taxes.

The foreign "protectors of religion in the USSR" are trying to prove that Soviet citizens' children are forcibly torn away from religion, and that their parents are persecuted if they want to educate their offspring in their faith. In actual fact, the law does not prohibit religious education of children. It simply separates the school from the church. Religious education is quite possible and permissible on a private basis, the family. Children are completely free to attend church and take part in religious worship.

The legislation of the USSR and the Union Republics on public education emphasizes the equality of all citizens in receiving education, irrespective of race or nationality, sex, attitude to religion, property or social status. The Soviet state is responsible for the universal and equal scientific, technical and moral education of children and young people. But it has nothing to do with religious education, considering it the private affair of citizens.

Such is the real situation, and any unbiased person can easily see it. Many religious leaders who come to this country admit this truth. . . .

B
Elections à la USSR

"The masses must have the right to choose responsible
leaders for themselves. They must have the right to
replace them, the right to know and check each small-
est step of their activity."

VLADIMIR ILYICH LENIN

"The composition of the deputies to the organs of state
power reflects the social and class structure of developed socialist society. It affirms that workers and collective farmers, people directly engaged in production,
are widely represented in them."

NOVOSTI PRESS AGENCY

In Soviet national elections, there is only one single slate of candidates
presented to the electorate; the voters either deposit their ballot as is in
the ballot box or cross off the names of those candidates they oppose.
Moreover, there is only one official party in the Soviet Union, the CPSU,
and all elected representatives at all levels of government are either party
members or nonparty Bolsheviks (see page 154 above). To many Western
observers, this system of elections, as all the rest of the Soviet system
of government, is but a sham, a meaningless farce. Here is how one
strongly anti-Soviet Western analyst, G. Warren Nutter, formerly Assistant Secretary of Defense (1969–73) once phrased it:

> It was Lenin's genius to recognize the importance of embellishing
> the Soviet Systems with all the trappings of democracy. If the
> people want a constitution, give them one, and even include the
> Bill of Rights. If they want a parliament, give them that, too. And
> a system of courts. If they want a federal system, create that myth
> as well. Above all, let them have elections, for the act of voting
> is what the common man most clearly associates with democracy.
> Give them all these, but make sure that they have no effect on
> how things are run.[1]

To Marxist-Leninists, on the other hand, it is elections in capitalist
countries that are a sham. Marx and Engels wrote in the *Communist
Manifesto* that "political power, properly so called, is merely the organ-

[1] G. W. Nutter, *The Strange World of Ivan Ivanov*, New York, World Publishing Co., 1968,
p. 39.

ized power of one class for oppressing another."[2] And the founding fathers of "scientific socialism" explained that in capitalist society "the possessing class (the bourgeoisie) rules directly by means of universal suffrage,"[3] allowing the oppressed "once every few years to decide which particular representatives of the oppressing class should be in parliament to represent and oppress them."[4] In the United States, so Soviet leaders have always explained, the two major competing parties, the Democratic and the Republican Party, "both represent the interests of the exploiting classes. Therefore at election time there is bickering between various candidates representing the monopolists, the factory and plant owners— that is, the class whose domination the Soviet people ended back in 1917." The Soviets, on the other hand, are described as "agencies of true people's rule to which the people elect their finest sons and daughters, entrusting to them the sum total of power in the country."[5]

In the first contribution under "Western Views" (Selection 13), John N. Hazard describes Soviet elections as a process aimed at balancing "democratic aspirations . . . with the desire to retain strong leadership . . . a pattern designed to balance freedom of choice with control over what they (Communist party leaders) believe to be its irresponsible use." His assertion that there are no primaries can perhaps be challenged since representatives not only of the Communist party but also of such other social organizations as the local labor union, collective farm, unit of the armed forces, etc., participate in the selection process from which emerges the single nominee for any given post to run in the election.

In the second selection under "Western Views," Paul Hollander investigates the purposes of Soviet elections and concludes that they have no significance for the distribution of political power or for gauging public opinion, but that they might possibly help cement the loyalty of the Soviet people to their leadership.

The first selection under "Soviet Views" (Selection 15) consists of articles 95–107 of the 1977 Soviet Constitution, which describe the Soviet electoral system and the rights and duties of elected Soviet deputies. The next selection, taken from the Novosti Press Agency's Yearbook '80 USSR, further elaborates on the election process by which the deputies to the USSR Supreme Soviet are chosen.

Many Western analysts assert that no party other than the CPSU could legally run in Soviet elections (Hazard, for instance, talks about

---

[2] Karl Marx and Friedrich Engels, *The Communist Manifesto*, New York: Appleton-Century-Crofts, 1955, p. 32.

[3] Friedrich Engels, "The Origin of the Family, Private Property and the State," in E. Burns, comp., *Handbook of Marxism*, New York: Random House, 1935, p. 329.

[4] Lenin quoting Marx in V. I. Lenin, *State and Revolution*, New York: International Publishers, 1932, p. 73.

[5] These two quotes are from a campaign speech by Nikita S. Khrushchev (*Pravda*, March 17, 1962). Similar statements to that effect have been made by Soviet leaders and Soviet analysts of Western societies from the days of Lenin and Stalin to the present.

"the constitutional provision establishing the Communist party as the sole political party within the U.S.S.R."). While the CPSU certainly is the only political party in the Soviet Union today, the Soviets not only defend their one-party system as genuinely democratic but also maintain that there is nothing in principle in socialist society that would prevent a multi-party system. The existing one-party system in the USSR, they hold, is merely "a result of historic conditions." In this connection, it should be pointed out that there are indeed socialist countries in which more than one political party operates. In the German Democratic Republic, for instance, there are several political parties, including non-Marxist (although no anti-Marxist) parties. However, the slates of candidates are put together so that the SED (*Sozialistische Einheitspartei Deutschlands* or "Socialist Unity Party of Germany") remains in power.

WESTERN VIEWS

13. SOVIET ELECTIONS: CONTROLLED MASS PARTICIPATION*

John N. Hazard
Columbia University

A strengthened socialist democracy has been the theme since the fiftieth anniversary, but it presents problems to the Communist party leaders. Even with a tradition of firm leadership by the party of the political life of the country, Soviet citizens have become restless. Increasing numbers travel abroad to represent the state or to study or to tour. Ideas from abroad in a form sympathetic to Western democracies are still withheld from the masses by limitation of foreign newspapers except those published by foreign Communist parties, but foreign radio broadcasts can be heard. Soviet citizens know that modernized mankind now measures democracy in terms of opportunity to choose leaders and to influence policy formulation. The Communist party leaders cannot escape consideration of the reflection of these world-wide aspirations upon their own people. They are trying to meet the demand, but without sacrificing what they believe essential to progress at the U.S.S.R.'s current stage of economic and social development, namely strong leadership by the party.

* Excerpts reprinted from John N. Hazard, *The Soviet System of Government*, 5th Edition, Chicago: University of Chicago Press, 1980, pp. 56–60, by permission of the University of Chicago Press, © 1957, 1960, 1964, 1968, 1980 by the University of Chicago.

The Soviet state apparatus provides the means through which democratic aspirations are balanced with the desire to retain strong leadership. . . . Communists cannot bring themselves to open wide the gates to unrestricted selection of leaders and determination of policy. They insist on creation of a pattern of action designed to balance freedom of choice with control over what they believe to be its irresponsible use. The theme is to be controlled mass participation, differing from Stalin's concept in that emphasis is to be on participation rather than on control.

ELECTIONS AND THE ONE-PARTY SYSTEM

The key to mass participation in the eyes of the world is the electoral process, and since 1936 the Communist party has opened elections to all when deputies are to be chosen for the bodies comprising the representative agencies of the Soviet state apparatus. The restrictions existing until 1936 denying the vote to those who hired labor, served as priests or monks, or had been former members of the Imperial Police or the royal family were revoked at that time. Elections were simultaneously opened to every person of eighteen years of age and over, regardless of social origin, occupation, race, or creed.

Elections were also made direct for all levels of soviets. . . . Further, since 1936 all elections to the various soviets have been secret. Printed ballots are used, and curtained booths are provided for the voter to scrutinize and mark the ballot. Herewith, the U.S.S.R. is able to offer to its citizens and to the world a picture of general, direct, and secret elections, and to claim that it has established institutions that are the cornerstones of democracy.

To understand how little risk is really being taken by the Communist party in reforming the electoral procedure, the Westerner must note the counterweights that have been set up to prevent popular selection of state functionaries who might be unwilling to accept the guidance of the party. The most important of these counterweights is the constitutional provision establishing the Communist party as the sole political party within the U.S.S.R. No other political party may be organized in competition for votes.

While Western peoples do not consider one-party systems compatible with the processes of democracy, it must be admitted that there are parts of the world that are accepted as democratically governed and in which there is only one effective party because the competing party is traditionally too weak to make the slightest challenge to its rule. It is possible, therefore, for a system to merit attribution of the democratic label if there be only one effective party, but, in such cases, there must be a choice of candidates within that party. In many places this choice is provided through a party primary, in which the citizen can select the candidate he prefers. . . .

Opportunity for such choice of candidates is denied in the U.S.S.R. The Communist party holds no primaries, nor does it permit the placing of more than one name per office on a ballot. Nothing in the law prevents a multiple-candidate election. On the contrary, the new constitutional provisions applied in elections for the Supreme Soviet in 1937 provided for a ballot on which was printed the instruction to the voter to cross out all but one name. This same form of ballot is still in use. There is nothing in the regulations to show that there is no choice.

The nominating procedure provided by law appears to make possible the naming of more than one candidate for each office of deputy. Under this procedure, public organizations, such as sports clubs, trade unions, and co-operative associations, may propose candidates in addition to those named by the Communist party. However, none of these organizations may be a political party or conceal the mechanism of a political party under a mask, so it is clear that its basic program must conform to that of the party. It can be imagined that one organization would propose a candidate who would emphasize local school improvement, another might enter a candidate who favored building branch libraries or sports fields. All would have to favor basic party policies such as progression toward communism. None could seek to retrace steps from state-owned enterprise to private enterprise, but candidates could differ in emphasis and, easily, in ability.

In spite of the legal possibility of a choice of candidates in the elections of 1937, the first held under the new rules, there was no choice. On the day the ballots were printed, there appeared on each ballot only one name for each position. The individuals who had been nominated by different organizations within each district had been reduced to one, presumably after the executive committee of the party conference at the county or big-city level had made its selection from among the nominees. To this day, there has appeared on the ballot only one name for each place.

Soviet specialists argue that there is popular choice in selecting the single candidate. This is because names are sent to district electoral commissions by nominating groups in factories, universities, trade unions, sports organizations, and farms, and representatives of these groups extol their nominees before the commissions where final choice is made. Admittedly this is a method of choosing, but not by the general public, even though electoral commissions for the 1977 elections for local soviets comprised 9,223,355 citizens. These were thought representative in that 61.5% were workmen and collective farmers, 47.6% were women, 26.6% were under 30. Still, the party dominates the choice, for 35.7% of the commission members were party members and 17.1% were Komsomols. This permits selection of individual candidates to form part of a composite slate believed by party authorities to be desirable, since it includes nationally prominent figures as well as a balance between ages, sexes, professions, and party members.

Soviet defenders of the claim that the soviet system of government is democratic often point to the fact that citizens may cross out the name of the sole candidate appearing upon the ballot. The voter may even write in a name, so the defenders say. Soon after each election the electoral commission in each voting district publishes statistics on the number of scratches, and on each occasion a considerable number are reported. For example, in the 1975 elections for the Supreme Soviet, the scratches were said to have totaled 332,664 for deputies to one chamber of the Supreme Soviet and 245,750 for deputies of the other chamber. Reports on scratches show constant reduction, for in 1979 they dropped to 175,600 for one chamber and 185,422 for the other. In spite of these scratches all candidates were elected, for in no instance did the scratches exceed the number of affirmative ballots for a candidate.

In the local elections of 1977 there were reported 61 cases in which the single candidate for the position of deputy to a village, city, or county soviet failed of election because the total number of scratches constituted a majority of the votes cast. These failures were not many, however, for over two million deputies were successful in the elections at these local levels.[1] Clearly, the public opposition was to individuals and not to basic party positions.

The desire to express opposition to individuals led to proposals in the press in 1965 to give the voters a choice of candidates. No one needed to explain that the choice would not concern party programs, but only personalities and their concern for local issues. No change in electoral procedures has resulted, nor has there even been public discussion of the matter by high party officials. Still, the fact that they were published at all in a controlled press indicates some desire to extend the concept of socialist democracy to include a choice of candidates in an election, even when all have to adhere to the fundamental strategy of the party. . . .

14. SOVIET ELECTIONS: FOR WHAT PURPOSE?*

Paul Hollander
University of Massachussetts

The Soviet electoral system is at first sight a most puzzling institution, for the voter has no opportunity to select among alternatives. There is only one set of candidates and the only choice the voter has is to vote or not to vote for them. By "not voting" we do not mean abstention. The

---

[1] In the election of 1980, 2.3 million candidates ran for election to local soviets. Of these, 77 failed to poll a majority of votes cast and, hence, were not elected. (*USSR: Facts and Figures*, Moscow: Novosti Press Agency Publishing House, 1980, p. 14.) [Editor's Note.]
* Reprinted from Paul Hollander, *Soviet and American Society*, Chicago and London: University of Chicago Press, 1978, pp. 66–68 by permission of Oxford University Press.

Soviet voter has very limited opportunities to abstain from voting. All the organizations and agencies of the state swing into action at election times to make sure that all those eligible to vote do so. Entire army units are marched to polling stations, convalescing hospital patients are taken to vote, workers of the same place of employment cast their vote together. Sometimes residents of the same block join forces.[1] Not voting for the official list of candidates can only be accomplished by going to the polling station, entering the booth, and crossing out the candidates' names. In contrast, voting for the official candidates can be done simply by folding the ballot and putting it into the ballot box in full view of the local election committee. This procedure makes it obvious and public if the voter wishes to register his disapproval of the officially nominated candidates, and few Soviet citizens avail themselves of the opportunity to make their dissent so fully known. Soviet election figures testify to the startling unanimity of popular choices:

> The announcement, for example, of the 1962 elections to the USSR Supreme Soviet solemnly proclaimed that 99.95% of all eligible voters cast ballots in the elections and that 99.47% voted for "candidates of the Communist and non-Party Bloc" to the Council of the Union and that 99.60% provided the same endorsement to the Council of Nationalities. . . . These statistical triumphs were widely heralded in the Soviet press as a "majestic demonstration of the unity of the Soviet people."

From the official Soviet point of view none of this is surprising since the Soviet people are (supposedly) convinced that the Communist Party of the USSR and its candidates represent their interests most faithfully and effectively—hence they vote for them with predictable regularity.

Why, then, is it necessary to hold elections if the Communist Party and its candidates (to the local provincial, republic, and All-Union Soviet) can count on being elected by the entire Soviet voting population every year? What are the functions of elections under these conditions of apparent unanimity and social-political harmony? From the official descriptions, Soviet elections appear to be days of public rejoicing, gay occasions for the spontaneous affirmation of social solidarity and enthusiastic approval of the system. People sing and dance on the streets, contemplate with satisfaction the achievements of the past and indulge in delightful anticipation of yet greater future achievements. Against this official vision of the function and atmosphere of Soviet elections one may counterpose a more somber one. Probably there is a measure of popular satisfaction present since it is a public holiday. On the other hand, it is likely that most Soviet citizens view elections as a ritual which has little to do with

---

[1] The invalid is visited in his home by a representative of the local electoral commission, accompanied by a portable ballot box; the isolated weather observation team sends its votes from the northern frozen wastelands by radio. The network is so all-inclusive and so carefully articulated that it is virtually impossible to avoid voting.

their fate or with making political choices. There is very little, if any, expectation of choice to begin with—and this would temper disappointment or cynicism over the character of the electoral process.

What about the function of the elections for the rulers and the Soviet system? Elections are a part of the paraphernalia of popular democracy to which the Soviet regime has always paid lip service. It is a measure of the appeal of the slogans of democracy that few societies today, including the USSR, can abandon at least the pretense of being democratic. Obviously, the leadership does not view elections as having significance for the distribution of political power or for gauging public opinion. They are more likely to view them as rituals that may provide people with an illusion of participation, or as an occasion for pseudo-participation and the physical mobilization of the masses, trained to affirm unconditionally the candidates and the policies they symbolize. In keeping with Pavlovian behavioristic principles, Soviet leaders may believe that if people are made to "participate" in elections over a long period of time, they will learn to respond positively to these periodic exercises and perhaps will be persuaded that their action must have some political significance. If people have no choice but to vote for the party for decades, they may conclude that they favor it. This interpretation is especially plausible when the electorate has had very little experience of more meaningful elections. We do not know, of course, to what degree elections have helped to cement the loyalties of the Soviet people. It is clear, however, that they have an important ideological function for the leaders, who have persisted in staging them year after year.

SOVIET VIEWS

---

15. THE ELECTORAL SYSTEM AND THE RIGHTS AND DUTIES OF ELECTED DEPUTIES*

New Soviet Constitution, Articles 95–107

Article 95

Deputies to all Soviets shall be elected on the basis of universal, equal, and direct suffrage by secret ballot.

* Reprinted from *Constitution (Fundamental Law) of the Union of Soviet Socialist Republics*, Moscow: Novosti Press Agency Publishing House, 1978, pp. 72–77, by permission of the publisher and the Copyright Agency of the USSR.

Article 96

Elections shall be universal: all citizens of the USSR who have reached the age of 18 shall have the right to vote and to be elected, with the exception of persons who have been legally certified insane.

To be eligible for election to the Supreme Soviet of the USSR a citizen of the USSR must have reached the age of 21.

Article 97

Elections shall be equal: each citizen shall have one vote; all voters shall exercise the franchise on an equal footing.

Article 98

Elections shall be direct: deputies to all Soviets of People's Deputies shall be elected by citizens by direct vote.

Article 99

Voting at elections shall be secret: control over voters' exercise of the franchise is inadmissible.

Article 100

The following shall have the right to nominate candidates: branches and organisations of the Communist Party of the Soviet Union, trade unions, and the All-Union Leninist Young Communist League; co-operatives and other public organisations; work collectives, and meetings of servicemen in their military units.

Citizens of the USSR and public organisations are guaranteed the right to free and all-round discussion of the political and personal qualities and competence of candidates, and the right to campaign for them at meetings, in the press, and on television and radio.

The expenses involved in holding elections to Soviets of People's Deputies shall be met by the state.

Article 101

Deputies to Soviets of People's Deputies shall be elected by constituencies.

A citizen of the USSR may not, as a rule, be elected to more than two Soviets of People's Deputies.

Elections to the Soviets shall be conducted by electoral commissions consisting of representatives of public organisations and work collectives, and of meetings of servicemen in military units.

The procedure for holding elections to Soviets of People's Deputies shall be defined by the laws of the USSR, and of Union and Autonomous Republics.

Article 102

Electors give mandates to their Deputies.

The appropriate Soviets of People's Deputies shall examine electors' mandates, take them into account in drafting economic and social development plans and in drawing up the budget, organise implementation of the mandates, and inform citizens about it.

Article 103

Deputies are the plenipotentiary representatives of the people in the Soviets of People's Deputies.

In the Soviets, Deputies deal with matters relating to state, economic, and social and cultural development, organise implementation of the decisions of the Soviets, and exercise control over the work of state bodies, enterprises, institutions and organisations.

Deputies shall be guided in their activities by the interests of the state, and shall take the needs of their constituents into account and work to implement their electors' mandates.

Article 104

Deputies shall exercise their powers without discontinuing their regular employment or duties.

During sessions of the Soviet, and so as to exercise their deputy's powers in other cases stipulated by law, Deputies shall be released from their regular employment or duties, with retention of their average earnings at their permanent place of work.

Article 105

A Deputy has the right to address inquiries to the appropriate state bodies and officials, who are obliged to reply to them at a session of the Soviet.

Deputies have the right to approach any state or public body, enterprise, institution, or organisation on matters arising from their work as Deputies and to take part in considering the questions raised by them. The heads of the state or public bodies, enterprises, institutions or organisations concerned are obliged to receive Deputies without delay and to consider their proposals within the time-limit established by law.

Article 106

Deputies shall be ensured conditions for the unhampered and effective exercise of their rights and duties.

The immunity of Deputies, and other guarantees of their activity as Deputies, are defined in the Law on the Status of Deputies and other legislative acts of the USSR and of Union and Autonomous Republics.

Article 107

Deputies shall report on their work and on that of the Soviet to their constituents, and to the work collectives and public organisations that nominated them.

Deputies who have not justified the confidence of their constituents may be recalled at any time by decision of a majority of the electors in accordance with the procedure established by law.[1]

16. ELECTIONS TO THE USSR SUPREME SOVIET*
Novosti Press Agency

On March 4, 1979, elections to the USSR Supreme Soviet were held for the tenth time. These were the first elections to the highest body of state authority after the adoption of the new Constitution of the USSR in 1977, which gave fuller expression to the principle of each citizen's participation in state management.

The Law on Elections to the USSR Supreme Soviet adopted in 1978 incorporates many changes. First of all, the age qualification for candidates has been brought down from 23 to 21. Organisations with the right to nominate candidates now include work collectives, down to shops, sections, shifts and teams. Both Chambers of the USSR Supreme Soviet now have an equal number of deputies (750). The period allotted for the nomination of candidates and discussion of their qualities and competence has been increased. A candidate is now considered elected if he receives more than half of all the possible votes in his constituency and not only of those that have been cast in the elections, as was the case before. More attention is devoted to giving greater publicity to the work of electoral commissions, whose rights have been considerably expanded and whose membership has been increased. More favourable conditions have been created to encourage each and every citizen to take an active part in the election campaigns.

The new electoral legislation, like the preceding one, does not exclude the possibility of nominating and putting to the vote two or more candidates in one constituency. Traditionally several candidates are nominated but only one runs for election upon agreement between the nominators.

---

[1] Recalls, although not frequent, do occur. During the 1970s, out of more than two million deputies elected to Soviets at all levels, 4,000 were recalled. [Editor's note.]

* Reprinted from *Yearbook '80 USSR*, Moscow: Novosti Press Agency Publishing House, 1980, pp. 9 and 11–12, by permission of the publisher and the Copyright Agency of the USSR.

The nomination of candidates for deputies to the USSR Supreme Soviet in the constituencies is completed not less than a month before the elections. The right to nominate candidates is exercised by Party, trade-union, Young Communist League, co-operative and other public organisations, work collectives and meetings of servicemen in their units. Nominations take place at general meetings and anyone present can discuss any candidate, speak in his support or propose a motion for his rejection. The decision whether to nominate or reject a candidate is taken by a simple majority vote of those present.

The nominated candidates are then discussed at district pre-election conferences in which representatives of the electoral district's organisations, collectives and meetings take part. The candidate can be withdrawn by his nominators at any time during the pre-election campaign, or he can withdraw himself.

At the pre-election meetings the candidates receive mandates from the electors.

Candidates to the Soviets, as soon as they are registered by the district electoral commission, are invested with some of the guarantees inherent in the status of a deputy. Criminal proceedings cannot be instituted against a candidate without the consent of the Presidium of the USSR Supreme Soviet, and he cannot be arrested or subjected to administrative punishment by court decision. He enjoys the free use of all public transport in his constituency with the exception of taxis, and is released from his regular work or duties, while retaining his normal earnings, for purposes of meeting with his constituents and making pre-election addresses. All state agencies, public organisations and managers of enterprises and other establishments are obliged to render every assistance to the candidate.

The list of voters certifies the electors' right to vote on election day. It is drawn up by the executive committee of the local Soviets of People's Deputies for each electoral precinct. The alphabetical list, written in the language of the majority of the precinct's population, includes the name, age and place of residence of each voter who will be 18 by election day and who is a permanent or temporary resident of the precinct. . . .

If a voter leaves the precinct after the voters' lists have been drawn up and is unable to vote at his own polling station, the electoral commission provides him with a registration card enabling him to vote in any other constituency.

The pre-election campaign, in which any citizen can take part, is conducted unimpeded at meetings, in the press, on radio and television, and within the constituency—at election campaign centres and electors' clubs, which are provided with premises free of charge, and in the voters' homes which are visited by campaigners.

The pre-election campaign informs the voters of the candidates' work and public activities, their political, professional and personal qualities, explains to them the election law and reminds them of the time and place of the elections, encouraging them to cast their votes for the candidates of the bloc of Communists and non-Party people. Particular attention is devoted to young voters who are going to the polls for the first time. They are acquainted with the nominating and voting procedure.

The candidates themselves also take part in the pre-election campaign. They visit their constituencies and address their electors at meetings, conferences and rallies.

However, no campaigning is allowed in the polling premises on election day, to ensure the free expression of the voters' choice. . . .

Electoral commissions, from the Central Commission down to district and precinct commissions, are made up of representatives of public organisations, work collectives and military units. In the recent election campaign 1,661,406 public representatives worked in the country's 174,547 electoral commissions.

The commissions keep the electors informed of their meetings, decisions and measures. All their work is conducted in public and representatives of the press, radio and television are free to attend their meetings. . . .

Elections are held on the basis of universal, equal and direct suffrage by secret ballot. The law prohibits any restrictions whatsoever over voters' exercise of the franchise.

All citizens who have reached the age of 18 have the right to vote irrespective of their origins, social or property status, race or nationality, sex, education, language, attitude to religion, nature of occupation, and domicile, with the exception of persons who have been legally certified insane.

Each voter has one vote.

Deputies are elected by direct vote.

Every voter, regardless of where he may be on election day—on a train, or ship, at an Arctic station or on a research expedition—is guaranteed the right to vote. Electoral commissions take into consideration possible business trips, weekend trips and changes of permanent address. Those who happen to be out of town on election day can apply to any polling station where they receive their voting paper on submitting their registration card. . . .

Neither the candidates nor voters incur expenses related to the elections because all such expenses are met by the state.

Voting is held throughout the country, on a non-working day from 6:00 a.m. to 10:00 p.m. local time. At the polling stations sealed ballot boxes and polling booths ensure secrecy of the vote. . . .

If a voter cannot come to the polling station due to illness or disablement he is either provided with transportation or a member of the electoral commission brings the ballot box to his home. In remote areas where it is difficult to make a trip to the polling station voting papers are collected on the spot, provided at least three people reside there.

The voter crosses out the names of those candidates he votes against and leaves intact the names of those for whom he wishes to vote. Then he drops the voting paper into the ballot box.

The votes are counted by members of the electoral commission in the presence of representatives of the press, radio and television and the procedure thus receives wide publicity. The counting begins only after 10:00 p.m. even if all the voters in the constituency have been to the polls, for there may still be voters coming in with registration cards from other constituencies.

The total number of voters is determined by counting the number of ballots in the ballot boxes. Then the "for" and "against" ballots are counted.

Elections are considered invalid if less than one half of the electorate has voted, or if a district electoral commission has declared them invalid because of violations of electoral regulations at any polling station.

The results of the elections and the lists of the elected Deputies are published not later than one week after the elections. If none of the candidates has received the necessary majority of votes in his constituency or if the elections are declared invalid, new elections are held within a month.

C
The Dissidents

"For many years now I have been directly involved in the administration of justice, but I have never seen or read, and still do not know of the existence of a single Soviet law under which citizens could be prosecuted because of their political or religious views."

ALEXANDER SUKHAREV
USSR First Deputy Minister of Justice

It is by no means easy to define what constitutes dissent and who therefore is or is not a dissident. If an American citizen in 1981 disagrees with many of President Reagan's policies and says so to members of his family, is he a dissident? If he joins with others in an attempt to replace the Republican by a Democratic administration, is he a dissident? If he disagrees with the capitalist system altogether and wants to see it replaced by a socialist system, is he a dissident? If he joins with others and they take action, legal or violent, to replace the existing social system, are they dissidents? And the blacks who rioted in Harlem, Washington, Watts or Miami, were they dissidents? How about the Vietnam War defectors still living in Canada and Sweden today, or those who refuse to register for the draft now? And how about Father Berrigan, Stokely Carmichael, Malcolm X, Dr. Benjamin Spock, or Dr. Martin Luther King, Jr.? Were they dissidents?

Most Western analysts distinguish between opposition, which aims at replacing the existing rulers by others, and dissent, which has "no direct designs on power,"[1] but which, in the Soviet Union, "should still be viewed as a seed-bed of opposition."[2] There may be no specific law prohibiting a Soviet citizen from holding any political or religious views, as Sukharev said in the quote above; still, opposition and expressed dissent deemed harmful to society are both outlawed in the USSR. But the Criminal Code clearly distinguishes between them, although not by name. Articles 70 and 72 provide relatively severe punishment for "anti-Soviet agitation and propaganda" and for "anti-Soviet organization" aimed at

---

[1] Rudolf L. Tökés, "Dissent: The Politics for Change in the USSR," in Henry W. Morton and Rudolf L. Tökés, *Soviet Politics and Society in the 1970's*, New York: The Free Press, 1974, p. 10.
[2] Peter Reddaway, "The Development of Dissent and Opposition," in Archie Brown and Michael Kaser, *The Soviet Union Since the Fall of Khrushchev*, 2nd edition, London: The MacMillan Press Ltd., 1975, p. 123.

weakening or overthrowing the Soviet system (in other words, opposition). But articles 190 and 191 provide for relatively much milder penalties for individuals who, in writing or orally, spread "deliberate fabrications which discredit the Soviet political and social system" (in other words, dissidents). The legal maximum penalties for the latter offense are three years' imprisonment or five years' exile, and usually the penalties meted out are much lower. Probably the best-known Soviet dissident, scientist Andrei Sakharov, recipient of the 1975 Nobel Peace Prize, is at the time of this writing exiled in the city of Gorky; but by his own account, he is permitted to carry on there his scientific work, has an apartment, and his wife is allowed to bring him meat, butter and cheese from Moscow when they are not as readily available in Gorky.[3]

Most of the outspoken dissidents who publicly criticize the USSR (and that is what we shall henceforth mean by "dissidents") come from the ranks of those traditionally known as the intelligentsia.[4] Among the intelligentsia, with its important social role, high incomes, and many privileges, dissidents undoubtedly represent only a small minority. Many, if not most, of the members of the Soviet intelligentsia probably back the regime in principle, although not necessarily in all specific policies. Others are deterred by the possible, if not probable, loss of their high social position and by the threat of penalties. Still others, who are socialists themselves but disagree with the Soviet interpretation and implementation of Marxism-Leninism, refrain from taking a public stand because (as one dissident explained in an essay entitled "Why Are We Silent?") "the socialist intellectual who expresses himself freely before the Western public begins to feel, somehow, like a traitor . . . For socialist criticism is employed not only as a weapon against the socialist states but also against socialism, and against all those oppressed by poverty and racial prejudice in the Western world."[5]

Among those who are open dissenters, few offer concrete programs, and the ones who do are not in agreement among themselves. As just one example, the two best-known Soviet dissidents, Alexandr Solzhenitsyn and Andrei Sakharov, disagree strongly on the social system they would like to see emerging on Soviet soil. Sakharov, who favors SALT II as a "satisfactory embodiment" of the principle of genuine disarmament based on a strategic balance of power, advocates a pluralistic society with a mixed economy to be brought about "as a result of the peaceful convergence of the socialist and capitalist systems."[6] Solzhen-

---

[3] "Andrei Sakharov's Letter from Exile," *A Chronicle of Human Rights in the USSR*, October–December, 1980, p. 24.

[4] Jews who want to emigrate are not necessarily "dissidents" in this sense, since many of them quietly ask for exit visas to join their families. Leaders of religious dissent who publicly demand greater religious freedoms, such as schools to teach religion, also come to a great extent from the intelligentsia.

[5] Mihajlo Mihajlov, *Russian Themes*, New York, 1968, pp. 329–30.

[6] Sakharov, *op. cit.*, pp. 21 and 23.

itsyn, who opposed detente and seems to exhibit strongly nostalgic feelings for the social system of the pre-Soviet era, has little use for socialism. But Sakharov charges "that in reality, the nationalist and isolationist tendencies of Solzhenitsyn's thought, and his own patriarchal religious romanticism, lead him into very serious errors and render his proposals utopian and even potentially dangerous."[7] Yet, divergent as their views might be, all dissidents profess agreement on their demands for "human rights," by which they mean primarily the right to express their views freely, without restrictions or harassment by authorities.

Space limitations do not allow a detailed analysis of the dissident movement that has evolved in the Soviet Union since the 1960s. But in a general way the three Western non-Marxist contributions by David Kowalewski, Yuri Yarym-Agaev, and Elizabeth Scheets (which, in this case, include a Soviet émigré's views), briefly refer to some of the major dissident groups and focus their criticism on recent Soviet attempts to suppress them. Under "Western Marxist Views," Gus Hall, Secretary-General of the Communist Party of the United States, on the other hand, defends the position that a socialist society should not, "in the name of 'intellectual freedom,' make its press, TV and radio stations available to a handful of renegades so they can spread their vile slander against socialism, so they can spread their racism and imperialist propaganda." In Selection 21, the first selection under "Soviet Views," the Novosti Press Agency booklet *USSR, 100 Questions and Answers* also calls the dissidents "a pitiful handful of renegades," asserts that they are being incited by the CIA, that they advocate acts of violence which would be illegal under American law, and that the Soviet Union does not prosecute anyone whose views differ from those of the "majority of Soviet citizens" but has every legal right to deal firmly with individuals who violate Soviet laws.

As regards individual dissidents, the U.S., more often than not, sees them as courageous individuals, willing to risk their all in the defense of freedom and democracy, and honors them accordingly. The Soviets, on the other hand, usually treat them as liars, traitors, criminals, or mental incompetents. One such extreme example was Vladimir Bukovsky. With the U.S. as an intermediary, the thirty-three-year-old Bukovsky was exchanged on December 18, 1976 for Luis Corvalan, general secretary of the Communist Party of Chile. On March 1, 1977, he met with President Carter at the White House, urged U.S. commitment to human rights and subsequently was attacked by Soviet media for damaging U.S.-Soviet relations. According to Western sources, Bukovsky, the son of a writer, started his dissident activities by participating in literary protest meetings, involving himself in *samizdat* (underground self-publishing) and helping to plan demonstrations against the arrest of dissident writers. He was

---

[7] "The Solzhenitsyn/Sakharov Debate," *Kontinent*, New York: Doubleday, 1976, p. 13.

constantly in and out of Soviet prisons and claims to have spent "15 months of hell" in the Leningrad Psychiatric Prison Hospital.[8] But this is not the way the Soviets see it. In the second selection under "Soviet Views," B. Ruikovich presents the Soviet case against Vladimir Bukovsky.

Western analysts have often charged that Soviet authorities use mental institutions as disguised prisons where perfectly sane dissidents are placed for indefinite terms. In the final selection of this chapter, the Soviets first refute such charges in general and then give specific examples of Soviet mental patients who had been allowed to emigrate, describing what allegedly happened with them afterwards.

WESTERN VIEWS

---

17. HUMAN RIGHTS AND THE DISSIDENTS IN THE USSR*

David Kowalewski

Benedictine College

When the Universal Declaration of Human Rights was adopted by the United Nations in 1948, few observers would have thought that three decades later the document would become the most prized and discussed document in the Soviet Union. The Declaration has become the staple in the reading diet of many groups demanding civil, national, religious, and other rights in the USSR. Thus Lithuanian national dissident Simas Kudirka was catapulted into dissent by the document. The Universal Declaration of Human Rights was heady reading for . . . Simas. It seemed to have been written with his own case in mind. According to the Declaration, his human rights had been violated when the Soviet Union deprived him of his Lithuanian nationality, denied him the choice of a job, prevented him from leaving the country, blocked him from expressing his opinions. Numerous members of other groups constituting what is known as the human rights movement were similarly affected. Thus when the Soviet Union signed the Final Act of the Conference on Security and

---

[8] For greater detail, see for example the *1978* (Encyclopaedia) *Britannica Book of the Year*, p. 82.

* Excerpts reprinted from David Kowalewski, "Human Rights Protests in the USSR: Statistical Trends for 1965–78," *Universal Human Rights*, Vol. 2, No. 1, January–March, 1980, pp. 5–6 and 28–29, by permission of the author and the publisher.

Cooperation in Europe on August 1, 1975, promising to respect basic human rights, activists in Moscow, the Ukraine, Lithuania, Georgia, and Armenia shortly thereafter formed Helsinki Watch Groups to ensure that it did.

Although the Soviet regime pays respect to human rights in the abstract, the treatment of dissidents has been severe. The official media frequently brands human rights activists as anti-Soviet. Jews seeking emigration are labeled "renegades," while dissident Baptist presbyters are accused of parasitism, slander, and stealing money from believers. Newspapers described Georgian dissident Zviad Gamsakhurdia as an "extortioner" and criticized Russian Orthodox dissenters for their "hippie-style life." Equally revealing are official attitudes expressed informally. At the Office of Visas and Registration where he was seeking emigration, Pentecostal dissident Andrei Feder was told: "All the Helsinki Accords are only promises to us—for us they are not law." Likewise a police major in Voroshilovgrad told Pentecostals that the Helsinki Accords were "nonsense". . . .

Khrushchev's secret speech[1] had deep repercussions not only across the Communist world but at home as well. Dissatisfied groups increasingly questioned their conditions and began to manifest their dissent in numerous forms of verbal protest. The basis of new demands was no particular ideology but rather the principles of the Universal Declaration of Human Rights. . . . Protest demonstrations increased in frequency, to some extent in diversity of social base, and in geographical dispersion. Widespread emigration and arrests had little effect on their size and militancy. Concomitantly, dissidents became increasingly aware of other dissatisfied groups, and the extent of mutual cooperation rose dramatically.

In response, the Soviet regime acted with a high level of vacillation until 1972, when a wide-ranging and intensive attack on the human rights movement was launched. Dissidents rightly labeled this period a "crisis" in the movement. However, the depressant effect of intensified repression on the movement was short-lived. After a few years the frequency of protest demonstrations returned to high levels. The movement showed little sign of permanent damage. As dissident Valentin Moroz told his Ukrainian prosecutors, "You hurled a stone at every spark of life on the Ukrainian horizon, and every stone became a boomerang." Yet the regime shows little sign of giving in. . . .

However, the attitude of dissidents that basic freedoms are rights which are deserved by virtue of one's human existence and thus should be demanded as such is a sustaining impetus to the movement. Moreover, the belief that religious, economic, and other rights are primarily human

---

[1] Khrushchev's secret speech to the Twentieth Party Congress in 1956 at which he denounced Stalin for his "crimes." For the text of the speech, see *The Anatomy of Terror*, Public Affairs Press, 1956; for an abridged version, see Chapter II.

rights makes for a high level of tolerance and mutual support among dissenters—one of the movement's major strengths. Indeed, the growing conviction that human rights are indivisible, that "injustice in one part of the
earth threatens justice all over the world," has lent an international dimension to protest activities. On January 20, 1979, members of the Human
Rights Committee met with dissident representatives of the Polish Social
Self-Defense Committee—KSS"KOR"—in Moscow to establish principles of mutual cooperation.

Perhaps Andrei Sakharov summarized dissident thinking best.
When asked why he supported the Jewish right to emigrate to Israel, he
replied, "I am not supporting them as Jews, but simply as fellow human
beings." This notion—that without the exercise of one's rights one cannot
be fully human—makes political protest a fundamental requirement for
basic self-respect, and one not easily extinguished by the regime's labor
camps, prisons, or mental hospitals.

18. THE HUMAN RIGHTS SITUATION IN THE SOVIET UNION*

Yuri Yarym-Agaev†
Massachussetts Institute of Technology

The Soviet human rights movement was born in the 1960's and has continued to the present day. Historians consider this period of some 15 years
to be one generation. Some human rights activists are seventy years old,
while others are in their twenties.

Despite cruel repressions, the Soviet human rights movement continues. Anyone who decides to become a human rights activist knows
that he will most likely be arrested and imprisoned for many years. Nevertheless, people continue to join this movement.

Although the Soviet authorities are doing their best to stamp it out,
the Soviet human rights movement continues. Methods of suppressing
this movement have been the topic of Politbureau sessions. Millions of

---

* Reprinted from *A Chronicle of Human Rights in the USSR*, July–September, 1980, pp.
19–21, by permission of the publisher.
† Yuri Yarym-Agaev, a 31-year-old physicist and member of the Moscow Helsinki Watch
Group, emigrated from the Soviet Union on July 8 [1980] after several warnings from the
KGB that he would be arrested if he did not leave Moscow. A friend and classmate of
Anatoly Shcharansky, Yarym-Agaev signed appeals on behalf of Shcharansky, Yury Orlov
and Aleksandr Ginzburg while employed as a research associate at the Institute of Chemical Physics in Moscow. He was fired in January 1979 in connection with his dissident
activities.

Yarym-Agaev is currently a research associate at Massachusetts Institute of Technology. He read the following statement on September 16 [1980] before the Subcommittee
on International Organizations of the U.S. House of Representatives which was holding
hearings on the human rights situation in Eastern Europe.

roubles have been spent in this effort. And yet, this small group of people continues their activities. . . .

Why is it so difficult for the Soviet authorities to suppress the human rights movement?

This movement arose inside the Soviet Union. Soviet human rights activists were born in the USSR. They have studied and worked in that country. In fact, most Soviet human rights activists are well off by Soviet standards.

Perhaps the most vivid examples of the fact that Soviet human rights activists are successful members of their society can be seen in the following biographical facts: Academician Sakharov, is the youngest person ever to be elected a member of the Soviet Academy of Sciences: and leading physicist Yury Orlov, is a Corresponding Member of the Armenian Academy of Sciences.

I'd like to present a few less well-known examples: Vyacheslav Bakhmin, a founding member of the Working Commission on the Abuse of Psychiatry, which in its twenty-three Information Bulletins, has provided detailed proof of continuing Soviet abuse of psychiatry. The activity of this Commission helped gain the release of several Soviet citizens from psychiatric hospitals. In 1966, Bakhmin's enrollment in the prestigious Moscow Institute of Physics and Technology, was the start of a promising scientific career. For involvement in samizdat activities in 1969, Bakhmin was imprisoned for a year. Upon release, he managed to graduate from another scientific institute and became a computer specialist. Rearrested in February 1980, Bakhmin is now being held in Lefortovo Prison awaiting trial. On September 25 [1980], Bakhmin will have his thirty-third birthday.

Tatiana Osipova, a young woman of 31, is a trained philologist. She was arrested in May of this year [1980] for her participation in the Moscow Helsinki Group, which she joined in 1977.

Aleksandr Lavut, long active in the Soviet human rights movement, is a computer specialist. When Lavut was arrested in April, 1980, his scientific colleagues—none of whom had ever done anything like this before—sent a letter of protest to the Soviet officials. Such a move reveals the great respect people have for Lavut, both as a man and as a scientist.

I hope that these biographical sketches of a few Soviet human rights activists show that they are successful and respected members of Soviet society. This is the reason it is difficult for the Soviet authorities to suppress these people. . . .

The Soviet party bureaucracy cannot tolerate the existence of the Soviet human rights movement since they see in it a threat to the Party monopoly over all aspects of Soviet existence. This perceived threat is the main explanation for the sharp increase in repression in the USSR in the last year. . . .

In late November 1979, the Soviet authorities practically stopped Jewish emigration from Kiev, capital of the Ukraine. At present, there are 7,000 refuseniks in Kiev. In other Ukrainian cities, Jewish emigration was stopped even earlier. I would also like to point out that for members of other nationalities in the Soviet Union, it is almost impossible to emigrate from the USSR under any circumstances.

More information on the human rights situation in the USSR can be found in the documents of the Moscow Helsinki Group which have been translated and published by the Helsinki Commission. I would like to mention that the reports of the Moscow Helsinki Group on human rights in the USSR constitute a valuable source of independent information for the West. Despite all the attempts of the authorities to stifle our Group, we have managed to write about 100 documents since the Belgrade Conference.

The only aim of the Moscow Helsinki Group was to promote the implementation of the humanitarian provisions of the Helsinki Final Act in the Soviet Union. Nevertheless, on May 30, 1980, when I was called in by the All-Union KGB and told to leave the country, I was shown an official document in which the Moscow Helsinki Group was declared to be a hostile organization.

In light of these blatant human rights violations in the Soviet Union, the Moscow Helsinki Group feels that the West has two choices: either to discuss in detail these human rights violations—thereby supporting the Soviet human rights movement—or to ignore or gloss over this situation—thereby tacitly supporting the Soviet authorities in their suppression of the Soviet human rights movement.

19. HARD TIMES FOR DISSIDENTS
IN THE USSR*

Elizabeth C. Scheets
Radio Liberty Analyst

The wide-ranging repression of dissent currently taking place in the USSR is doubtless the most severe such crackdown since the Soviet dissident movement took shape in the late 1960s. Since the fall of 1979, well over fifty activists have either been arrested or brought to trial, and many more have been searched, interrogated, or harassed in other ways. Others have been forced to emigrate. Victims of this official campaign of harassment come from all corners of the broad Soviet dissident community, and their activities have varied considerably. They include persons attempting to monitor Soviet compliance with the Helsinki accords and those fighting for national and religious freedoms, for the right of workers to organize

* Reprinted from *Radio Liberty Research* (RL184/80), May 21, 1980, pp. 1–8, by permission of Radio Liberty.

themselves independently of state control, and for the possibility to publish without censorship. Whatever the focus of their struggle, they are persons committed to ideals not shared by the organs of power in the Soviet Union, and they have had to pay for their commitment.

A sensational move in the current clampdown on dissent in the USSR was, without a doubt, the action openly taken by the regime against Andrei Sakharov, a figure as prominent for his outspoken democratic views and years of service to humanitarian ideals (in 1975 he was awarded the Nobel Peace Prize) as for his scientific accomplishments. Sakharov, a leading figure in the Soviet human rights movement, was often regarded as untouchable because of his stature in the international scientific community; yet on January 22, 1980, following his outspoken stand on the Soviet invasion of Afghanistan, he was informed that he had been stripped of all govenment honors and state awards. Furthermore, Academician Sakharov was banished to Gorky (250 miles east of Moscow), where he and his wife live under close police surveillance.

The banishment of Sakharov from Moscow was a severe blow to human rights activists in the USSR since it virtually deprived them of a tireless and—of equal importance—internationally renowned champion of their cause. In spite of bitter protests in the West and repercussions in the area of East-West scientific exchange that it provoked, however, to date Soviet officials have stood firm in their determination to isolate the famed physicist. This incident would by itself be adequate evidence of the extent of hardening of the Soviet line, but the move against Sakharov is only one—albeit the most conspicuous—of many such pieces of evidence. For both before and after the action against Sakharov was taken, many of his cofighters in the struggle for human and civil liberties in the USSR fell victim to repression. A brief review of some of the targets of this repression will give some idea of the extensive nature of the official campaign.

THE SOVIET HELSINKI GROUPS

The signing of the Final Act of the Conference on Security and Cooperation in Europe on August 1, 1975, spawned a considerable amount of human rights activity in the USSR, and unofficial groups set up in various Soviet republics to monitor compliance with the provisions of the Helsinki accords have been in the forefront of much of this activity. They have also been a favorite target of official Soviet wrath, and since their establishment (the first was founded in Moscow on May 12, 1976) they have been an object of harassment by the authorities. The Moscow group, for instance, suffered a severe blow with the arrests and subsequent trials in 1978 of three leading members—Yurii Orlov, Anatolii Shcharansky, and Aleksandr Ginzburg. Repressions have not abated and have, in recent months, included the arrest or trial of other members. Thus, on December

12, 1979, Soviet poet Viktor Nekipelov was arrested; he has been charged
with anti-Soviet agitation and propaganda. Mal'va Landa was sentenced
in March of this year [1980] to five years of internal exile on charges of
anti-Soviet slander, and on April 10, 1980, Leonard Ternovsky, a member
since March, was arrested. . . .

Other Helsinki groups known to have suffered the recent arrest or
trial of members are those in the Ukraine and in Lithuania.

WORKING COMMISSION TO INVESTIGATE THE USE OF PSYCHIATRY FOR POLITICAL PURPOSES

The Soviet authorities have also turned their sights on persons associated
with the Working Commission to Investigate the Use of Psychiatry for
Political Purposes, which was formed in January, 1977. On February 12,
1980, Vyacheslav Bakhmin was arrested, while Feliks Serebrov was taken
into custody and sentenced to fifteen days for resisting the authorities.
Then, on April 10, the homes of Leonard Ternovsky, Feliks Serebrov,
and Irina Grivnina were searched, and the three were detained for questioning. Serebrov and Grivnina were later released; as noted above Ternovsky, who is also a member of the Moscow Helsinki group, was arrested. Aleksandr Lavut, who has had ties with both groups, was arrested
on April 29.

WORKER DISSIDENTS

The persecution of individuals involved with the unofficial Free Inter-
professional Union of Workers (SMOT), founded in October, 1978, continues. Last October, for example, Nikolai Nikitin was sentenced to one
and a half years in a labor camp on charges of anti-Soviet slander. In
March of this year, Mark Morozov, already serving a term of exile, was
charged with anti-Soviet agitation and propaganda, while Vladimir Borisov was forcibly placed in a psychiatric hospital. (At the beginning of
May, Borisov was released from detention in a psychiatric hospital; dissident sources have credited Western support for his case as the reason
for his release.) On April 1, SMOT member Mikhail Solovov was sentenced to three years in a labor camp on charges of malicious hooliganism.

RELIGIOUS DISSENT

Believers in the USSR whose activities extend beyond the narrow limits
set by the atheist state have also been victims of serious repression in
recent months. This repression has hit hard at several small but organized
groups and suggests that the authorities are intent on wiping out such
unauthorized initiatives.

The Christian Seminar. The Christian Seminar on Problems of Religious Revival was founded in 1974 as an informal study group that meets

in private to discuss Christianity in philosophical and theological terms. Since last fall, a series of arrests and trials on various charges has led to the imprisonment of several of its members. . . .

The Christian Committee. The Christian Committee for the Defense of the Rights of Believers in the USSR was founded in December, 1976. Soon after its establishment, members of the committee began to be subjected to various forms of intimidation, including attacks in the Soviet press and interrogations. Then, in November, 1979, Father Gleb Yakunin, one of the three founding members of the committee, was arrested. Since then, in March, 1980, another founding member, Viktor Kapitanchuk, has also been arrested.

The Catholic Committee. While no members of the Lithuanian-based Catholic Committee for the Defense of the Rights of Believers in the USSR (founded in November, 1978) are reported to have been arrested, the homes of two members, Alfonsas Svarinskas and Sigitas Tamkevičius, were searched in April of this year for seven hours.

In addition to the persecution of unofficially organized groups of believers, the Soviet authorities continue their repression of individual believers whose activities they consider untoward. A prime example of this was the arrest in January, 1980, of Father Dmitrii Dudko, a Russian Orthodox priest who first attracted notice in Moscow in the early 1970s for his sermons and frank question-and-answer sessions with his parishioners.

MOVES AGAINST *SAMIZDAT* PUBLICATIONS

Pressure has been stepped up against persons suspected of being involved in the preparation or circulation of *samizdat* journals. In recent months, searches have been carried out in the homes of Soviet citizens associated with the unofficial journal *Evrei v SSSR* (Jews in the USSR), and in March one of its editors, Igor Guberman, was sentenced to five years in a labor camp on charges of trading in stolen icons. In January, 1980, two editors of the Moscow *samizdat* journal *Poiski* (Search) were arrested. The moves against Yurii Grimm and Viktor Sokirko came only weeks after the arrest, in December of last year, of two other editors of *Poiski*, Valerii Abramkin and Viktor Sorokin.

The authorities have also harassed persons associated with *Khronika tekushchikh sobytii* (The Chronicle of Current Events). Searches have been carried out in the homes of some of these persons, and in November, 1979, Tatyana Velikanova was arrested. Velikanova, a leading Soviet human rights activist, was a founding member of the Action Group for the Defense of Human Rights in the USSR (formed in 1969) and was closely involved with the *Chronicle*. It is reported that she has been charged with anti-Soviet agitation and propaganda. Nor have *samizdat* publications in the republics been spared. In Lithuania, for example, since last fall the unofficial press has been subjected to an intensive crackdown by Soviet security organs.

This enumeration of targets of the current crackdown is by no means an exhaustive one. Besides the groups mentioned here, other Soviet citizens are also asserting rights, including persons in the non-Russian republics seeking national self-determination, Crimean Tatars wishing to return to their traditional homeland, Jews and Germans trying to emigrate, etc. These groups have also suffered at the hands of the authorities. Though incomplete, the list does provide some idea of the extensive nature of the current campaign to stifle dissent in the USSR. . . .

The scope and severity of the current repression of Soviet regime-critics suggests that Moscow is intent on delivering a staggering blow to the dissident movement in the USSR, by attacking important individuals and institutions in that movement. This internal hardening of line has been paralleled by one in foreign policy, as exemplified by the invasion of Afghanistan and the subsequent deterioration in East-West relations. Under the circumstances, it appears as if Moscow is no longer constrained by the reaction of Western public opinion to its actions and is willing to pursue its goals at home regardless of Western reaction. Still, it is difficult to predict the effect of foreign policy matters on the internal Soviet scene. Disregard for Western public opinion has often been evident in Soviet domestic actions, but it has been somewhat of an off-again, on-again affair. A Soviet "peace initiative" at this juncture could, if only for tactical reasons, be reflected in some kind of relaxation of the manner in which the authorities are currently applying their policy against dissent.

WESTERN MARXIST VIEWS

---

20. WHAT'S BEHIND THE HUE AND CRY FOR "INTELLECTUAL FREEDOM"?*

Gus Hall

Secretary-General, Communist Party, USA

The basic question is: "intellectual freedom" to what end, for what purposes? The basic thesis of Sakharov and Solzhenitsyn answers this question. Their purpose is obvious—to spread slanders and falsehoods about

---

* Reprinted from Gus Hall, *The Sakharov-Solzhenitsyn Fraud: What's Behind the Hue and Cry for "Intellectual Freedom?"* New York: New Outlook Publishers, 1973, pp. 28–32, by permission of New Outlook Publishers, 239 West 23rd St., New York, N.Y. 10011.

socialism, to spread apologies and to cover up and defend imperialism and every one of its crimes. Their cries for "intellectual freedom" are not to discuss birds, flowers or the weather or such problems as production, transportation, housing, health, science, energy or trade. Most important, their cries for "intellectual freedom" are not to discuss how to improve and how to speed up the building of socialism, but only to slander it in a fruitless attempt to destroy it.

So the obvious question to ask is: should a socialist society, in the name of "intellectual freedom," make its press, TV and radio stations available to a handful of renegades so they can spread their vile slanders against socialism, so they can spread their racism and imperialist propaganda? And another logical question to ask is: should a socialist country open the mass media to such elements to prove that socialism is "democratic?"

If, to prove its basic, democratic essence, socialism had to give a handful of vile slanderers free access to the media, then indeed there would be a serious crisis. And indeed it would prove nothing. The proof of socialist democracy is not dependent upon such gimmicks. Socialist democracy is not contingent upon the rights of a handful of renegades and traitors.

Socialist democracy is rooted in the basic principle of the defense of the socialist system. Socialist democracy develops and grows in the context of the realities of the struggle between the two world systems. Socialist democracy is not an abstraction, it is not a frill. It is an integral part of the building of socialism.

Socialist democracy is the elimination of racism and national chauvinism. Socialist democracy is the participation of the millions in the everyday decision-making process on all levels; it is the hundreds of thousands of people running the city councils, the courts, the Soviet Republics. Socialist democracy is the workers making all the basic decisions in the factories, the mines and the mills. Socialist democracy is in the election of government bodies on every level. Socialist democracy is in the millions of letters in the public press criticizing, proposing and observing their socialist society at work.

Socialist democracy is interdependent with the process and the level of socialist construction. It grows and develops in that process. As with all new phenomena there is an element of trial and error in this process, but the direction is clear. The direction is towards an ever broader participation of the masses in the decision-making process on every level and in all areas of life. Therefore, whether the mass media in the Soviet Union should be turned over to these betrayers must be seen in the above context.

Common sense says, absolutely not! From the point of reference of the defense of socialism, and the world-wide struggle against imperialism and racism, the answer is also clear—absolutely not!

Democracy and democratic rights are not concepts that can be dealt with in a vacuum. They cannot be separated from the struggles of real life because they are an inherent part of real life itself. For example, how can anyone seriously talk about "democratic rights" without taking into consideration the real-life experience of World War II against fascism and the more than 54 million people who were killed, the 90 million wounded, and the material losses which amounted to more than 4 trillion dollars? More than 20 million citizens of the Soviet Union were killed in that war. Should such developments be permitted again in the name of "democratic rights" and should we again permit the lynching and burning at the stake of Black Americans? Such developments cannot be separated from the *advocacy* of such policies.

A society cannot exist that does not put some limits on the rights of individuals making up that society. A most basic question is: restrictions to what end?

Under capitalism democratic rights are related to the 5% of the population having the "right" to continue exploiting the other 95% of the population. Because the ruling class is the 5% and the system is a system of exploitation, such a society is inherently undemocratic. The nature of capitalist democracy is determined by two factors. It is related to the level, to the challenge, of the opposition to monopoly capital. And it is related to the nature of the class struggle and the relationship of forces. The rise of the police-state structure that led to Watergate is related to both of these factors.

The *New York Times* is leading the pack in daily editorials and articles about the fact that Sakharov and Solzhenitsyn cannot get their books published in the Soviet Union. But in the United States the *New York Times* sings a different song. The *New York Times*, which makes such a fuss about the publishing of books in the Soviet Union, has a total ban on books written by Communists and absolutely refuses to mention, and especially to review, any books written by Americans who are Communists.

For every book not published in the Soviet Union there are one hundred not published in the United States. The publishing establishment has a stock answer: "there is no market" for such books. For over 100 years the United States publishing corporations, and this includes the federal government's press, have maintained a ban on publishing Marxist or Communist books. This, to the editors of the *New York Times*, is "intellectual freedom."

Many Communist leaders in the United States were convicted, and some of us served up to 8 years in United States prisons, for the "crime" and the charge of thinking dangerous thoughts. The *New York Times*, and for that matter most of the forces that are so excited about "freedoms" 3,000 miles away, were either silent or led the reactionary wolf pack.

How loud did these forces yell when the intellectual freedom, and the very life, of Angela Davis was at stake?

For more than 25 years Communists in the United States were denied passports and the right to travel outside the U.S.! Where was the hue and cry for "intellectual freedom" and the right to travel?

The issue of "democratic rights" has become an instrument in the struggle against socialism, and more specifically it is an instrument of anti-Sovietism. This is especially true in the United States, and U.S. imperialism has been trying to export its false concept of democracy and of socialism to all parts of the world in order to advance the interests of imperialism. If this is not so, how is it that these forces are silent about areas where there are real problems of democratic rights, areas where democratic rights do not exist, as in South Africa, Chile, etc.?

Socialist democracy is not and never will be like bourgeois democracy. In the socialist countries such as the USSR the people as a whole are the owners and the trustees of the economic establishment of the nation, and they operate it for the common good—this by itself is infinitely more democratic than anything in existence under capitalism. Because of this basic fact the essence of socialist democracy is more in the sense of self-regulation than in restrictions imposed by another class.

Under capitalism the people have no real voice about economic questions, except the power that comes from struggle. But prices, trade, wages, production schedules, profits, are prerogatives of monopoly corporations. The political structure, including the two-party system and the government, as well as the mass media, are also controlled by the monopoly corporations. Where the "democratic rights" of the masses are concerned is indeed a very narrow spectrum of life. The talk about "democratic rights" under capitalism is more rhetoric than real. In the context of being able to influence the course of events, the rights are more on paper than real. Even these rights are not gifts from monopoly capital; they are rights won by the working class and the people only through long, hard struggle.

The Sakharovs and Solzhenitsyns are howling at decaying windmills. The basics of human progress are that human society is in the midst of history's greatest transition—from capitalism to socialism.

On one side there are the varied forces of reaction, on the other the forces of the world revolutionary process. The struggle between them is determining at what speed civilization will advance and how soon it will reach new plateaus. The relationship of forces will determine what the sacrifices will be. The Sakharovs and Solzhenitsyns of the world can add to the confusion, they can add to the cost in human life and suffering in the struggle for this transition, but there is no way they can in any way influence the final outcome.

SOVIET VIEWS

21. THE TRUTH ABOUT THE DISSIDENTS*
Novosti Press Agency

WHO ARE THE DISSIDENTS? WHAT DO THEY WANT?

They are a pitiful handful of renegades. One of them, Andrei Sakharov, has said: "There are not more than thirty of us." They represent nobody but themselves in the USSR—thirty people out of 260 million.

But to say "nobody but themselves" is not quite accurate.

Former CIA agent Victor Marchetti and former State Department employee John Marks say they know not from hearsay but at first hand that the CIA secretly meddles in the domestic affairs of foreign countries. In their book *The CIA and the Cult of Intelligence*, they write on page 199 (London edition):

"The CIA has always been interested in reaching and encouraging dissidents in Eastern Europe and the Soviet Union. In the early days of the Cold War the agency sent its own agents and substantial amounts of money behind the Iron Curtain to keep things stirred up, mostly with disastrous results. In more recent times, operations against Eastern Europe and the USSR have become less frequent and less crude." But they have been conducted.

The juiciest and most important passages in their book, particularly in the chapter we have quoted from, were struck out by the American censor. One can only guess what figures, facts, operations and maybe names were given in the deleted passages.

But even what is left of the text makes it quite clear whose money supports the "dissidents" and whose bidding they do. Some of them have not denied this themselves when faced with material proof in court.

Press organs in major Western countries try to persuade their readers that the dissidents are not opposed to Soviet rule but only want to improve it, and that's all. This is unfortunately far from the case.

Listen to the appeals made by the more notorious dissidents and see where their sympathies lie.

". . . I am *against* Soviet rule," Anatoli Kuznetsov declared in the Paris emigre newspaper *Russkaya Mysl*. Sakharov calls on the West

* Reprinted from *USSR, 100 Questions and Answers*, Part Two, Moscow: Novosti Press Agency Publishing House, 1978, pp. 116–118, by permission of the publisher and the Copyright Agency of the USSR.

to exert "the strongest and most sensitive pressure on the Soviet authorities," and thinks all the public services and industry of the USSR should be put in private hands "except for heavy industry, freight and transport and postal service" (from a digest of his book in *Der Spiegel*).

In other words, back to capitalism!

Vladimir Bukovsky frankly told a press conference that from childhood he had dreamed "of an armed revolution against the Soviet government", "but nothing will come of it as long as the West follows the rule that it has no right to interfere in the internal affairs of the Soviet Union. That is why the Helsinki agreement is so dangerous."

And here is a no less frank admission. Asked what he really wanted, Alexander Solzhenitsyn declared in an interview to a neo-fascist Italian magazine: "A crusade against the Soviet Union."

We can understand the alarm of the London *Daily Mirror* which in indignation at Solzhenitsyn's pronouncements in Britain wondered if he really wanted a war to break out.

Do these people indeed realize what a "crusade" against the USSR would mean in present circumstances?

An interesting point is that dissidents qualify for punishment not only under Soviet law. Under American law too they could be brought to court.

Under the Logan Act "any citizen of the United States" entering directly or indirectly "without authority of the United States" into any contact whatsoever "with any foreign government or any officer or agent thereof with intent to influence the measures or conduct of any foreign government or of any officer or agent thereof, in relation to any disputes or controversies with the United States, . . . shall be fined not more than 5,000 dollars or imprisoned not more than three years, or both."

Would not the dissidents' appeals to the West "not to trade with the USSR", for instance, fall within the meaning of this Act? And their appeals to the West not to renounce the practice of trade discrimination against the USSR? Would not their appeals for interference in the internal affairs of the USSR qualify as crimes under the American Act?

WHAT LEGAL BASIS IS THERE FOR PROSECUTING DISSIDENTS?

First of all we must agree on the meaning of the terms we are using. If by "dissidents" you mean people who differ from the great majority of Soviet citizens only in their way of thinking, then no legal basis for prosecuting them exist. And nobody in our country is prosecuting such people. It is quite another matter if a "dissident" is a person commiting illegal acts, breaking the law. No one is allowed to do this. Such a person is tried in court only for specific acts stated to be illegal in the relevant documents.

22. DEPORTED, AND
GOOD RIDDANCE TOO*

B. Ruikovich
International Affairs Commentator

[Dissident Vladimir] Bukovsky was deported from the Soviet Union, and good riddance too.

Bukovsky's portrait has these days become a regular feature on Western television and in the press.[1] The propaganda machine is going full blast. A criminal, not long ago deported from the Soviet Union (and good riddance too) has been proclaimed a "hero," a man made to suffer for his divergent opinions, "a civil rights fighter" and, while at it, "a great writer" and "outstanding biologist." This propaganda hullabaloo has a sordid motive: to mislead the world public.

Now who is Bukovsky, what is his real, genuine portrait like? Bukovsky was thrice tried by a Soviet court, and thrice found guilty and convicted in full accordance with the RSFSR criminal code.

At least the following may be listed among Bukovsky's actual anti-Soviet actions: In the sixties he organized a bunch of anti-Sovieteers, the so-called "assault five." The five members went in for shooting practice in the woods, not at all training for duck hunting. The main aim of the anti-Soviet "united front" organization Bukovsky was trying to set up, was to fight against Soviet power, and terrorist acts against Soviet people were to become one of the main means in this fight.

While out of prison, Bukovsky never worked anywhere a single day, though he didn't subsist on his mother's pension, naturally. His Western friends paid him generously and regularly for his anti-Soviet efforts. And this criminal offender spared himself not in working those silver coins off. . . . On the instructions of an anti-Soviet [West German] organization, he arranged the illegal publication and distribution of diverse hostile leaflets and materials in the country. And to keep himself in the Western limelight he arranged public hooligan sallies in Moscow, not forgetting to invite Western correspondents to these sallies in advance.

While on the subject, a word about the correspondents. Abusing our country's hospitality, they transmitted to the West Bukovsky's slander regarding the Soviet Union. They were the ones who helped build up a myth in the West of Bukovsky, "the writer" and "the scholar" not even bothering to find out that this "scholar" had been expelled from

---

* This article was originally published in *Vechernayaya Moskva* on December 23, 1976. It was translated by Novosti Press Agency and published in English in *Press Bulletin* of the USSR Embassy in Canada, March, 1977 (1), p. 1. Reprinted here by permission of the publisher, the Novosti Press Agency and the Copyright Agency of the USSR.
[1] For a brief summary of the Western view on Bukovsky, see the editor's introduction.

Moscow University for poor academic progress in his very first, freshman year.

As a writer, Bukovsky's laurels are no less sorrowful; he never had anything of his published anywhere.

And, last but not least, what kind of a person is Bukovsky according to those who knew him closely and well?

"An avaricious, callous person. The kind of person who never extends a helping hand," "for cheap popularity and money he is ready to do anything"—that's how Bukovsky is characterized by people who knew him for many years.

Such are facts, not inventions. The facts about a person who is being lauded to the skies in the West.

According to reports in the bourgeois press, Bukovsky is now faced with a difficult problem—whether or not to accept the position of teacher at the Leiden University in Holland. Well, according to his Western friends, Bukovsky, who hardly managed to finish secondary school, may really be fit for the role of a university teacher. But we pity the students who will have to acquire their learning from this "great writer," "historian," and "outstanding biologist."

23. MAKING POLITICAL CAPITAL OUT OF MENTAL CASES*

Novosti Press Agency

SOVIET PSYCHIATRISTS ARE ACCUSED IN THE WEST OF USING MENTAL HOSPITALS FOR POLITICAL ENDS AGAINST DISSIDENTS. WHAT TRUTH IS THERE IN THESE ACCUSATIONS?

None whatsoever. Soviet psychiatrists make their diagnosis after thorough examination of the patient and at least three psychiatrists always have to take part in a consultation before a patient is sent for compulsory treatment. It should be noted that many "mentally sound dissidents" received psychiatric treatment in their childhood long before any manifestation of dissidence and they were already under observation at Soviet psychiatric clinics. But for some reason nobody at that time was campaigning for their release from the clinics.

We have always thought and we still consider public discussion of case histories in the mass circulation press to be a violation of medical

* The first five paragraphs have been taken from *USSR, 100 Questions and Answers*, Part Two, Moscow: Novosti Press Agency Publishing House, 1978, pp. 118–119; the rest, under the subheading "Specific Cases," from *Press Bulletin* of the USSR Embassy in Canada, June, 1977, p. 2. Reprinted by permission of *Press Bulletin*, the Novosti Press Agency and the Copyright Agency of the USSR.

ethics. That is why we have not sought to refute Western slanders by producing medical evidence, extracts from case histories and expert findings. But foreign psychiatrists, to whom the doors of Soviet mental hospitals have always been open, have been able to study this material on numerous occasions. Many of the "victims of psychiatric intimidation" who figured in sensational campaigns have again found themselves in mental hospitals on emigrating from the USSR, but this time in Western— not Soviet—hospitals. For what "dissidence" were they being put into hospitals now?

But where do the charges levelled against Soviet doctors originate? The "indisputable evidence of malpractices in Soviet psychiatry" turns out to be . . . assertions by people well-known for their hostile activities against the USSR and statements by patients themselves. You do not have to be a psychiatrist to know that most mental patients think themselves sane.

You don't need to be a doctor to realize that only a specialist is competent to diagnose an illness or refute a diagnosis. Nor does it call for great perspicacity to see that a campaign based on the opinions of people remote from medicine has nothing in common with a desire to establish the truth.

Specific Cases

Alexei Tummerman, formerly a groom at the Moscow race track, could talk himself hoarse trying to prove he was not a groom but Apix-Hannover, the famous racehorse that had been bought by the USA for 100,000 dollars, and his name would never have appeared in the papers. The groom owes his "fame" to the so-called dissidents who come to bet at the races. It was with their help he was proclaimed "a victimized dissident" in the West. He was offered a world tour during which he was to deliver a series of lectures against "psychiatric arbitrariness." However, he never set out on the tour because when he arrived in Israel he wound up in a clinic for mental cases.

The same thing happened to Lev Konstantinov, who was being treated in the Soviet Union for schizophrenia and who left for the West. While in a psychiatric hospital in Austria, Konstantinov wrote an expository letter to the Amnesty International Organization. Contrary to custom, he did not denounce the Soviet psychiatrists this time, but the Austrian. He castigated doctors Hutter, Rotter, Gerstenbrandt, Langer, Gross, and Pernhaupt for repeating the diagnosis of the Soviet physicians.

We could cite such cases as curious anecdotes if they did not concern people who are really suffering from a grave illness.

"It is a great misfortune that some of our patients are being used as tools in attaining dirty political aims which in themselves are flagrant violations of the principles of humanism," said Ruben Nadzharov, professor of psychiatry. "Finding themselves in the midst of political intrigues, the patients suffer from unfavourable psychic influences. That, however, does not trouble those who are striving to achieve political results at the cost of tragedy, which mental illness actually is. The "dissidents" who received treatment in our psychiatric clinics and later emigrated were put into mental institutions in the other countries as well. It is a pity, but that was to be expected since these people are really sick."

Yelena Stroyeva hanged herself in the toilet of a Paris flat on September 22, 1975. In despair she wrote the following lines: ". . . Bitter reality has smashed our concept of what Western democracy and freedom are. We have decided on a mad and irrevocable step. Everything here is cold and heartless, one feels that everything is based on business—from the shop-windows to the churches." Western propaganda had used Stroyeva for anti-Soviet campaigns though she was quite obviously a mental case.

In Paris last year, ex-"dissident" Yuri Titov, Stroyeva's husband and also a mental case, was forced to undergo psychiatric treatment. He had also been used regularly as an example of the persecution of dissidents in the Soviet Union.

It is still uncertain how the West is going to reward Leonid Plushch—give him Napoleon's cocked hat or put him in a strait-jacket. After his first eccentric outpouring, the *Ukrainian Voice* (published in Canada) wrote it was not known at present what political group Leonid Plushch would affiliate himself with if and when he recovered. If Plushch recovers and takes the right road, they say they will believe he has completely recovered his mental faculties. But what if Plushch does not recover his mental faculties and remains an inveterate Marxist, they ask. What is to be done with him then? In that case they feel they might have to isolate the dangerous and unwanted man from the rest of their healthy society. Another paper published a poem to the effect that Plushch should be packed away in a lunatic asylum and not let out as he had been by the Bolsheviks.

When on his arrival in the USA Plushch demanded at a meeting that Senator Jackson work for the release of Luis Corvalan Masser, the Uruguay Communist and his friends, the enraged audience cried: "You're crazy! Put him in a strait-jacket!" Since that day, that is, since March, 1976, Plushch's fate in the West depends completely on the political content of the views he spouts. At times he is proclaimed a great scholar and prophet, that is, when he slanders the Soviet Union, while at other times, when he turns his anger against Western democracy, he is declared a mental case.

Academician Snezhnevsky, a well-known Soviet psychiatrist, says: "It is a tragedy when the victims of the dirty anti-Soviet game are our patients, who are ill and suffering. It is immoral to use them for political intrigues."

VI

The Soviet Economy: Structure, Planning, Development

"Socialism has done away for ever with the supremacy of private ownership of the means of production, that source of the division of society into antagonistic classes. Socialist ownership of the means of production has become the solid economic foundation of society."

PROGRAMME OF THE COMMUNIST PARTY OF THE SOVIET UNION

"Socialism is inconceivable without planned state organization."

VLADIMIR ILYICH LENIN

"With every passing year, the Soviet Union becomes richer and more powerful. The advantages of a socialist over a capitalist economy become ever more evident. . . . The gap between us and the leading capitalist country, the United States of America, is steadily being narrowed."

N. V. PODGORNY
Former Chairman, Presidium of the Supreme Soviet

"Should the old planning methods be preserved, and given our present rate of growth, in 1980 practically the entire adult population of our country would have to be engaged in the administration and planning spheres. On the other hand, automation of accounting and administrative work, the introduction of electronic machines, will make it possible to solve the problem without undue inflation of the administrative apparatus."

V. S. NEMCHINOV (1894–1964)
Former Head, Laboratory for the Application of Mathematical Methods in Economics, Academy of Sciences, USSR

I N SOVIET SOCIETY, the means of production—the land, the factories, the retail establishments, the banks, the transportation system, etc.— are owned not by private individuals but by society at large, and are operated by the government, presumably in the interest of the people. In many ways, such a society can be thought of as a gigantic corporation that encompasses all the means of production—a corporation in which each citizen is an equal shareholder and in which the government acts as the board of directors, operating the corporation for the shareholders. The economic activities of this giant corporation, just like the activities of any other, must be planned in advance. The men in charge must plan what to produce, how many workers and how many machines to employ in different "departments," how much to offer in payment to workers of various degrees of skill and competence, what price to ask for each of the finished products, etc., etc. Production is supposed to be carried on according to plan by paid workers under the guidance and supervision of hired managers—in each of the divisions of large American corporations and in each of the enterprises in Soviet society.

The fundamental difference, then, between a planned economy and what is usually referred to as a free-enterprise system, is not that planning is required in one and not in the other, but rather that in the former, plans are made for the economy as a whole, while in the latter, individuals and business organizations plan only their own activities with the profit motive as a guide and with the forces of demand and supply as the coordinators of economic activity. Whether or not an additional 100,000 TV sets will be produced in a free-enterprise society depends upon whether or not the producers expect that they can sell them at a profit. In a planned economy, on the other hand, profitability is of secondary importance. Resources will presumably be allocated for the manufacture of the TV sets if, in the opinion of the planners, their production is in the best interests of society. If too many TV sets were produced in a competitive free-enterprise economy, sellers unable to sell them all at prevailing prices would put them "on sale." If the supply were insufficient, sellers noticing that prospective purchasers were willing to buy more TV sets than available would be induced to raise prices. In the Soviet Union, prices are changed only by orders from above, but the law of supply and demand still functions. If there were too many TV sets on the Soviet market and the government did not lower prices, they would gather dust on the shelves of the stores (since the economic meaning of "too many" is "more than can be sold at the prevailing prices"). If the supply were inadequate, queues would form in front of stores, with eager purchasers lining up to buy before the supply was exhausted.

This brief introduction should make the reader aware of some of the difficulties which beset those whose task it is to plan, supervise, and coordinate the economic activities of an entire nation, especially one of the size and complexity of the USSR.

Perhaps because of its economic system, perhaps in spite of it, but in any case under it, the Soviet Union has advanced in an historically short period of time from a relatively underdeveloped country, primarily of ignorant peasants, to a superpower second only to the United States in total output and military preparedness. It is this economic advance, this "closing of the gap" Soviet economists accentuate in their descriptions of the Soviet Union's economic progress and achievements. Westerners, on the other hand, tend to emphasize that the United States and also most other Western countries such as Canada, Australia, New Zealand, and virtually all the nations of Western Europe, are still ahead of the Soviet Union in per person incomes and living standards.

In spite of undeniable economic achievements, the Soviet system of planning and administration certainly also has its shortcomings, and even aspects of it which might have been helpful in the past in fostering economic growth might not prove equally helpful in coping with the ever-changing needs and requirements of an industrially advanced, mature socialist economy. Soviet analysts do not deny persistent inadequacies and deficiencies nor the need to correct them (and, indeed, Soviet leaders are constantly searching for, experimenting with, and instituting alterations aimed at improving economic performance). But they make it quite clear that they are not about to advocate the dismantling of the two fundamental aspects of their socialist economy—the social ownership of the means of production and the guidance of at least the major aspects of the economy by means of central planning. To them, these appear absolutely essential, not only for the building of a just and humane society with equal rights and opportunities for all, but also for the construction of an efficient economic system, capable of progressing without the inflation, unemployment, and economic insecurity that have always characterized Western free-enterprise economies. Many Westerners, on the other hand, focus their critical evaluations on what they perceive of as built in inefficiencies, and they talk, to cite one recent example of "failures and frustrations that stem from incurable flaws within its (the Soviet Union's) creaky system."[1] Another, recently published, very extensive Western analysis of the USSR reports that "per capita food consumption has . . . more than doubled since 1951, a feat unmatched by any other advanced nation," that industrial growth "has also been heady", and that the Soviet Union's gross national product "a mere 40% of the U.S.'s in 1955 is 60% today," (an average of some $6,000 for every Soviet man, woman, and child). Nevertheless, the same article also reaches the widely prevalent Western conclusion that "the Soviet economy has always been stultified by too much central planning, too little entrepreneurial incentives. Factories, farms and individual workers are caught up in a machine that spews

---

[1] Harrison E. Salisbury (renowned Western analyst of communist countries, formerly with the *New York Times*, but now retired), "The Real Threat to World Peace," *San Francisco Chronicle*, Feb. 3, 1981, p. F 1.

forth quotas and directives, sucks up output, inefficiently manufactures and distributes goods, and rarely awards incentives."[2]

This chapter focuses on the structure of the Soviet Union's system of economic planning and administration, and on the country's economic growth and development during the six-and-a-half decades of Soviet rule. While the various contributions to this chapter certainly shed light on the country's basic economic structure, space limitation precludes elaboration on all its various aspects, such as details on the operation of collective farms, the functions of labor unions, or the significance of the turnover tax. Such specifics must be relegated to a book on the Soviet economy. Living standards, economic welfare and the social security system, on the other hand, are covered in great length in Chapter VII.

In this chapter's first selection under "Western Views," Jahangir Amuzegar first presents a few basic data on "the world's biggest single enterprise" and then turns his attention primarily to Soviet planning— the types of plans, plan formulation, the planning apparatus, and, briefly, to alterations in the system of planning and administration under the post-1964 economic reforms. Next, Harry G. Shaffer reports in considerable detail on Soviet economic development, from the outset in 1917 to the beginning of the 1980s. In spite of obvious shortcomings, he finds the record impressive and admonishes the West "not to underestimate the past performance nor the economic potential of the USSR."

Holland Hunter, in the third selection, addresses himself to what he sees as some of the major economic problems facing the Soviet Union today, such as slow-downs in the rate of economic growth, inflationary pressures, disincentives to innovate, sectorially unequal economic development, and wholesale and retail services inadequate to cope with consumer demand. But the next selection, taken from a report by Henry Rowen, Chairman of the CIA's National Intelligence Council, to the Joint Economic Committee of the U.S. Congress, paints a much more favorable picture. While not minimizing persisting weaknesses, Rowen also points to great strengths in many areas of the Soviet economy. Senator William Proxmire, who released the previously classified report on January 8, 1983, commented that it showed that "the Soviet Union is perhaps the most self-reliant industrialized nation," and that "the ability of the Soviet economy to remain viable in the absence of imports is much greater than that of most, possibly all, other industrialized economies." He further remarked that "it is sobering to reflect on the possibility that Soviet economic trends might improve rather than grow worse."

European analysts have long been sceptical of highly negative American evaluations of, and dire American predictions for, Soviet economic performance. Summarizing the findings of a Joint Economic Committee study of European perceptions of Soviet economic trends, staff

[2] *Time Magazine*, (Special Issue on "Inside the U.S.S.R."), June 23, 1980, pp. 22, 23 and 49.

member Richard F. Kaufman reports that Western European experts do not question U.S. findings of current and prospective economic problems in the USSR, but disagree with the conclusions drawn therefrom, predicting instead that "Soviet economic growth will be sufficient to allow for continuing increases in defense spending and gradual improvement of the standard of living."

For as long as one can remember, Western free-enterprise societies have been plagued by virtually continuous and recurrently very severe unemployment problems. The Soviet Union, on the other hand, has been faced with the opposite problem for the past half a century: instead of mass unemployment, there has been a perennial labor shortage—and many Western analysts predict that it is going to get worse.[3] In Selection 6, Thomas Kent discusses Soviet successes with the elimination of mass unemployment and the country's struggle to cope with the problem of manpower shortages.

From the early days of comprehensive, detailed planning from the center, through the days of the economic reform movement of the late 1960s and the early 1970s, to the most recent modifications introduced in mid-1979 by a USSR Council of Ministers' resolution, the Soviet system of economic planning and administration has undergone changes and adjustments. In the next selection, Western Marxist David Laibman traces that system through its various stages. He in no way denies lingering shortcomings and flaws, which he attributes to a great extent to the fact that it is easy to change the rules but "much harder to change the people who operate them." These problems must and will be corrected, but, he concludes, "socialist planning is not the cause of Soviet problems, but rather a vital part of their solution."

Under "Soviet Views," the reader is first introduced to articles 10–18 of the new Soviet Constitution which make up the document's Chapter 2, entitled "The Economic System." These few paragraphs are elaborated on further in the next selection taken from *Fundamentals of Political Knowledge*, Moscow: Novosti, 1980, Chapter 4. It presents the official Soviet position on all basic aspects of the USSR's economic system, such as public ownership of the means of production, planning, money and prices, the role of profits, distribution, etc. While acknowledging that all problems have not been solved yet, this selection bestows high praise on the economic "triumphs of socialism." (Since the author uses many Marxist terms, and since some of the English phraseology differs from that usually found in American books on the subject, the editor has supplemented the piece with a series of explanatory footnotes.)

The next selection, 10, briefly compares the Soviet and U.S. econ-

---

[3] "A specter is haunting Soviet economic planners—the specter of labor shortages throughout the 1980's" is the way a recent CIA publication phrased it. (*USSR: Some Implications of Demographic Trends for Economic Policies*, Washington, D.C.: US Central Intelligence Agency, 1977, p. 2.)

omies, pointing to the Soviet Union's recent economic achievements that have substantially narrowed the gap between the two countries. The Soviet authors Boris Ponomarov and Valentin Kudrov readily acknowledge that the Soviet Union is still lagging behind the United States, not only in the production of many important lines such as automobiles, plastics, and electricity, but also in industrial efficiency, which they ascribe to the longer gestation period the United States had to develop her industrial system. They also express full awareness that new economic problems call for "recasting the system of planning and management . . . and improving performance." And Selection 11, from an editorial in the *Press Bulletin* of the Soviet Embassy in Canada, briefly summarizes what the Soviets see as the main economic advantages of socialism.

The final selection by Yuri Berezhnov gives the Soviet position on the manpower shortage problem, covered before by Thomas Kent under "Western Views." The problem is real enough, no doubt about it, but the Soviet author believes that accelerated automation and continued increases in labor productivity "give grounds for hoping that the Soviet economy will successfully cope with the shortage of manpower which so far exists in the USSR."

WESTERN VIEWS

---

1. ECONOMIC PLANNING IN THE USSR*

Jahangir Amuzegar†

Executive Director, International Monetary Fund

INTRODUCTION

The Soviet Union is the world's largest country in land area, the third most populated country on earth, and has a wealth of natural resources. . . .

Officially committed to implementing Karl Marx's communist philosophy, Soviet leaders have combined Russia's long tradition of government paternalism with largely borrowed Western technology to transform a relatively backward agricultural country with a population

---

* Reprinted from Jahangir Amuzegar, *Comparative Economics*, Cambridge, Mass.: Winthrop Publishers, 1981, pp. 267–71 and 273–77, by permission of Little, Brown and Company.
† Since the mid-1970s, Jahangir Amuzegar has also been Distinguished Adjunct Professor at the American University, and he is also Professorial Lecturer at the School of Advanced International Studies, Johns Hopkins University.

two-thirds illiterate in 1919 to an industrial superpower in a span of sixty years. The Soviet Union is now a world leader in many scientific and technical fields: space exploration, aviation, irrigation, medicine, atomic energy, and heavy machinery.

The Soviet public sector is by far the world's biggest "single" economic enterprise. Soviet planning authorities have to manage and co-ordinate some 350,000 economic activities (over 200,000 industrial enterprises, nearly 13,000 state farms, over 36,000 agricultural collectives, and hundreds of thousands of wholesale and retail outlets, schools, hospitals, resorts) everything from a repair shop to a research organization. Soviet planners also have to cope with some 5,000 product groups in an estimated 45,000 different business enterprises in fifteen federated republics. The enormous complex of this task is a testimony both to the Soviet Union's administrative skills and its well-publicized inefficiencies and shortcomings. . . .

Basic Economic Data

LAND AREA (sq. km.)	22,402,000*	
POPULATION (1980 estimate)	266	million
Net annual increase (1970–78 yearly average)	0.9	percent
Urban (percent of total, 1980)	65	percent
Working Age (15–64) (percent of total, 1978)	65	percent
LABOR FORCE (total civilian, 1979)	140	million
Agriculture, forestry, fishing (percent of total)	17	percent
Mining, manufacturing, construction (percent of total)	47	percent
Services, etc. (percent of total)	36	percent
GROSS DOMESTIC PRODUCT (market prices, 1979)	$1,500	billion
Per capita (1979)	$5,700**	
Average annual increase (1970–78)	5.3	percent
Public consumption (percent of GDP) ⎫ Private consumption (percent of GDP) ⎭	73	percent
Fixed capital formation (ratio to GDP)	26	percent
Savings (ratio to GDP)	27	percent
GROSS DOMESTIC PRODUCT (market prices, 1979)	$1,500	billion
Agriculture, forestry, fishing (share in GDP)	17	percent
Mining, manufacturing, construction (share in GDP)	62	percent
Services (share in GDP)	21	percent
FOREIGN TRADE		
Exports (percent of GDP)	5	percent
Imports (percent of GDP)	5	percent

* 8,649,420.8 square miles. [Editor's note.]
** The CIA's *Handbook of Economic Statistics* (1980, p. 11) gives the figure as $5,220. [Editor's note.]

THE COMMAND PROCESS

Historians of the Russian economy are quick to point out that neither the command mechanism nor the leading role of the state in national economic affairs has been a Communist party initiative in the Soviet Union. They point to Russia's long history of totalitarianism and the active participation of the state in domestic economic development, necessitated by Russia's relative economic underdevelopment. The concept of a centrally planned economy, however, was first embraced by the Soviet leadership in 1928 and introduced into the Eastern European countries (and the third world, as well as China) after World War II.

The Soviet leadership's uninterrupted grand strategy of rapid industrialization and high economic growth has been implemented mainly through a very high degree of central control. Under this process, basic national objectives have been determined by Communist party leaders and put to work with the help of an all-pervasive bureaucracy, using central planning, price manipulations, and material rewards—along with other noneconomic incentives, coercions and sanctions. The two most notable features of the Soviet economy are the almost total ownership and operation of the basic means of production by the state and the primacy of development planning. State ownership and control of resources is both an ideological imperative as well as a means of achieving broader sociopolitical goals. The Soviet Union is also a planned economy in the full sense of the term. . . .*

Soviet Planning

National planning determines and directs the economic life of the Soviet Union. Every industrial enterprise, every collective farm, every state agency, every geographical subdivision, every one of the fifteen republics, the autonomous regions, and the federal union has its plans. There is, in fact, an elaborate hierarchy of plans for a single factory, for a region, for a republic, for a ministry, and for the whole union.

Traditional Soviet economic planning—going back to the establishment of the State Planning Committee, or Gosplan, in 1921—has aimed at a centrally controlled mobilization and use of Russia's resources in the service of national goals. Soviet national planning is the oldest in the modern world.

Nature and Types of Plan. There are three time plans in the Soviet Union: a long-term twenty-year *general* plan, which sets forth certain

* The author focuses attention primarily on the industrial sector. The agricultural sector consists of state farms, owned and operated by the state similar to industrial enterprises; the collective farms, run and operated under considerable state influence by collective farmers; and the small subsidiary plots to which farmers (and also city workers if they want to) are entitled. On the latter, they grow crops or raise livestock for their own table or for sale on the collective farm markets at whatever prices their products will fetch—the only major free market in the Soviet Union. [Editor's note.]

long-range national goals for key sectors of the economy; a medium, five-to-seven year plan, or *perspective*, which is the core of Soviet medium-term objectives, particularly with regard to capital investments, and a guide for the preparation of short-term plans; and an annual, or *operational*, plan, similar to national budgets. Each plan specifies key output targets, manpower requirements, capital investments, and consumption objectives in physical and monetary terms. Perspective plans are nonoperational; they merely reflect the desired direction of economic activity. The only truly operational plan is the annual plan that prescribes actual production and distribution schedules for operating units. Annual operational plans are subdivided on the basis of operational periods (quarters and months) and operational levels (regional, district, or local).

The medium-term plans, usually for five years, consist of a series of input-output targets that foresee the course of development of national resources during the plan period, project certain growth rates to be attained in each sector and subsector of the economy at the end of the period, and prescribe, in detail, the institutional and organizational framework under which resources can be mobilized and put to use. Microeconomic targets for individual enterprises, sectors and subsectors (steel, cement, electric energy, or grains) are normally set up in physical volumes: tons, kilowatts, or bushels. Macrotargets such as the GNP, national income, public budget, savings, investment and foreign trade are presented in monetary terms (so many rubles). The overriding consideration in preparing the plans is not optimality and perfection, but practicality and chances of success. . . .

The annual plan is the concrete blueprint of detailed economic decision making. Each annual plan takes its cue from the main socioeconomic objectives of the five-year or seven-year plan, as the latter follows the broad perspective of the general long-term plan. The main task of each year's plan is to obtain three balances: a physical balance between inputs and outputs so as to ensure both full resource employment and efficiency, a monetary balance between total purchasing power of households and enterprises, and total value of goods and services so as to avoid shortages or unused inventories, and a foreign trade balance to make up domestic input requirements through imports and to pay for them by means of exports.

Plan Formulation. Officially and theoretically, national plans are the products of the "initiative and spontaneity of the working masses." In reality and in actual practice, the general tenor and direction of state economic plans are decided upon by the fourteen-member Communist party Presidium (the Politburo) and approved by the 287-member Central Committee of the Communist party, and by the party's Congress in its periodic conventions. In the Soviet economy, the "planner's preference" overtakes consumers' preference and sovereignty. The nexus of economic activity is the decisions made at the top of the hierarchical pyramid.

The formulation of the Soviet annual plan takes place in a hierarchical fashion in two directions: by individual enterprise proposals at the bottom up the bureaucratic ladder to the enterprise associations, regional economic councils, and the appropriate ministry all the way to the top party leaders in Moscow; and by master planners at the apex of Soviet hierarchy down the administrative chain of command to managers, workers, and peasants on production lines. The Gosplan in Moscow and its branches in the republics review ministerial requests for resource allocations and their planned outputs. After a good deal of "coordination and reconciliation" (bargaining) within the economic cabinet, the total available resources are allocated, on a "first-thing-first" basis, by the leadership. The "leading links," or top-priority items, present primary claims on resources, and they are served accordingly and in a fairly detailed fashion. Lower-priority targets receive their shares after the leading ones, and so it goes down the line until the resource supply is totally allotted to the competing claimants. Each ministry or agency proceeds to allocate its share of resources among its assigned tasks in the various republics. Ultimately, each industry, enterprise, collective farm, or distributing unit will receive its production quota and its materials ration. A similar procedure is followed in the allocation of consumer goods among wholesale and retail outlets, in the choice of investment projects, and in foreign trade (based on availability of foreign exchange).

The main directives or general guidelines of the plan are initially approved by the party Congress, with instruction to the government to work out the detailed document for subsequent ratification by the Politburo and the Central Committee. Upon their approval, the entire plan is submitted as a whole to the Supreme Soviet or the legislature. The exact role of Soviet legislators in amending planned provisions is not known to outsiders. The common guess is that deputies do not, as a rule, cause any major changes in the plan. The published version of the plan document contains only a limited number of important targets in a percentage form. Detailed targets, absolute figures, and supporting data are not normallly made public.

Planning Machinery and Supervision. Plan directives are communicated to the Council of Ministers or the cabinet by the party hierarchy. The ultimate responsibility for drawing up the plan document and supervising its execution rests with the State Planning Committee. At the operational levels, there are planning sections of government ministries, agencies, factories, and farms and service organizations. On the side, there is a large number of specialized and mainly advisory committees at the federal and republic levels, dealing with agriculture, construction, machine building, defense, and scientific research.

The plan's implementation, or "fulfillment supervision," is controlled and coordinated through several channels. First, the planning committees normally have their reporters in every major enterprise and can at all times discover sources of difficulties or negligence. Second, all transactions between state enterprises take place under formal contracts. These contracts specify the purchase of input factors from some factories and the sale of outputs to others. A failure to honor such commitments serves as an indication that the failing enterprise is not fulfilling its plans. Third, as every enterprise's deposits have to be kept in the state bank (Gosbank) and all transactions must be made by check, the failure to draw on these deposit accounts for the purchase of materials or to replenish these accounts through the sale of outputs may give warning signals. Fourth, both the government and the Communist party make official inspections of plant activities and report inefficiencies or wrong-doing. Finally, trade-union leaders in each enterprise are expected to serve as watchdogs of plan fulfillment, both as a duty and as a matter of self-interest in bonuses and premiums.

Soviet Financial Plans. The only other type of Soviet planning that matches the physical product or real output plan in magnitude and significance is the *financial* plan. Despite traditional socialist calls for eventually abolishing money and credit, the Soviet Union is a thoroughly monetized economy, where money, prices, savings, and bank credits are vital to the everyday functioning of the economic system. All incomes and all bonuses in the Soviet Union are paid and received in money. Transactions among individuals, enterprises, buyers, and sellers are conducted in monetary terms. Economic values, taxes, savings, and enterprise profits are expressed in monetary units.

The Soviet annual financial plans are prepared and administered by the Gosplan, the Finance Ministry, and the Gosbank. The principal aim of financial planning is to provide necessary and sufficient funds for the proper fulfillment of the physical plan. Funds are supplied in appropriate amounts by the state bank for consumer transactions, individual savings, and tax payments.

Performance of Soviet Plans. The Soviet government and the Russian press seldom publish detailed (particularly critical) accounts of Russia's economic performance beyond specific production data, but, on the whole, Soviet planning seems to have been successful in mobilizing domestic resources, and channeling them into high-priority investment outlets from the very beginning of the Soviet regime. Planners have also been able to force-feed the relatively backward Soviet economy of the pre-1917 era with modern (and mostly borrowed) technology to the point that the Soviet scientific and technological community has obtained a position of leadership in a number of major areas. Ambitious and knowingly unreachable targets determined from above have kept labor and management on their toes and under constant pressure to produce one of the world's highest rates of economic growth for a long time. Consolidation and "rationalization" of industry, transportation, and even agriculture under the plans have brought about considerable economics of scale.

On the negative side, Soviet planning, particularly in the early stages, has clearly been a process of trial-and-error, with each new plan trying to rectify the errors of the previous one. And the process is continuing. The results have obviously been less than optimal. The monumental task of bringing an intricate and sprawling economy under one centralized direction, coupled with an almost total lack of experience with planning on the part of early revolutionaries, must also have cost the Soviet Union and the Soviet nation an untold amount of waste and needless sacrifices.

State Enterprises

The whole of the Soviet economy, in effect, resembles a single mammoth business enterprise, made up of diversified units, directed by the Politburo of the Communist party and managed by state ministries and agencies on behalf of the silent shareowners, the Soviet people. . . .

As in a modern giant corporation, the underlying philosophy of Soviet planners is that "the whole is greater than the sum of its parts." Constituent units are directed and controlled by top management in such a way as to ensure the fulfillment of the conglomerates' objectives—not those of individual firms, subsidiaries, or factories. . . .

Every nonfarm enterprise—be it an electric power station, a newspaper publishing house, a sanatorium, or a department store—is a legal entity, chartered by the state for specific activities. Under the so-called *khozraschet* (full-accounting) principle, each enterprise is also operationally independent and fully responsible for its accounts; that is, it can buy, sell, and enter into contracts. The enterprise's initial assets, its working capital, and its operational policy are essentially provided by the state. It ordinarily buys its materials at stated prices, and in the amounts appropriated to it, from other enterprises, paying them by checks on its bank deposits; it gets paid for selling its goods or services to other enterprises or to households. . . .

The Soviet industrial enterprise is headed by a director, often an engineer, appointed by the appropriate ministry. The director is solely responsible for the enterprise's performance under the Soviet "one-man rule" system. The main responsibility of the director is to fulfill (or preferably, exceed) his plant's quota, to reach the "success indicators. . . .

Until 1965, the enterprise's workforce, wage bill, input-mix, output, inventories, prices to be paid for materials, and those received for product, the expected profits, and allocation for expansion and improvement were all centrally determined. The temptation was thus great to outsmart the planners by underestimating productive capability, overestimating costs, or using other tricks, thus ensuring planned targets and qualifying for bonuses.

In 1965, a new economic program was inaugurated with the avowed aim of loosening centralized direction and increasing the economic "levers" of profits, pay bonuses, and interest charges on capital as a means of raising productivity. Thus, factory operations were placed under the direction of factory managers within certain broad (mostly sales and profit) targets, instead of rigid physical production quotas by volumes. Success indicators became salability, not mere production. A greater share of profit was left to the discretion of enterprise managers to use for workers' bonuses or further reinvestment. . . .

Light industry goods have since been turned out with due attention to market conditions and with some price flexibility. Styles are allowed to be altered by managers to make them more attractive. Central planning directions are allowed to be bypassed in certain plants for the sake of higher quality and greater salability of consumer products. Under the new system, factories may receive orders directly from retail stores instead of the central planning agency. Nevertheless, managers still have to produce the types of things that the planners want. They must also fulfill some monetary quota—so many rubles' worth each year. They must make a certain minimum profit on their sale and turn a large portion of it over to the government. And they have to sell their products at predetermined, centrally imposed prices. . . .

As a still further step in the direction of profit-oriented reforms, the Twenty-fourth Communist Party Congress in 1971 approved a plan to reorganize Soviet industrial plants into larger "production associations," linking each plant with its own suppliers, sales outlets, marketing and research divisions, and designers. Under the new system—considered the most comprehensive since 1965—industrial plants in different provinces are to be placed under mid-level corporations, which can get their basic policies from the ministries, and direct individual plants accordingly. In this manner, the larger associations or public corporations are expected to be better able to attract skilled manpower, make a more rational use of resources, and take advantage of computerized technology. The role of industrial ministries is to be largely limited to overall planning, investment policy, and technological innovation.

2. SOVIET ECONOMIC PERFORMANCE UNDER THE PLAN*

Harry G. Shaffer

University of Kansas

To evaluate Soviet economic performance under the previous highly centralized, and the now somewhat modified planning apparatuses, one must

* A much more extensive, early version of this article was prepared for and delivered at the McMaster University Conference on Current Problems of Socialist Economies, held on October 23–24, 1970 at McMaster University, Hamilton, Ontario, Canada. The paper's original title was "Economic Performance under the Plan: The Soviet Union and East Europe." It was published in French under the title "Planification et croissance economique: l'Union Soviétique et l'Europe de l'Est, "9 Revue de l'Est, Vol. 2, No. 4, October 1971, pp. 75–122. The paper has been rewritten and updated by the author for inclusion in this book. Sections of the early version are used by permission of the publisher.

Table 1. Soviet Economic Growth 1950–80
(in percent)

	National Income or Product		Industrial Output		Agricultural Output	
	Official Soviet	Western Estimate	Official Soviet	Western Estimate	Official Soviet	Western Estimate
1951–55	70.4	42.4	84.8	62.4	23.7	26
1956–60	54.6	38.1	63.7	49.7	32.4	19
1961–65	37.1	29.9	51.0	37.5	12.4	14
1966–70	41.0	30.5	50.0	38.9	21.0	24.6
1971–75	34.0	20.7	45.0	34.1	13.0	−3.4
1976–80	24.0	17.9	33.0	20.7	9.0	6.9
1981–85 (plan)	18–20	—	26–28	—	12–14	—

look at the country's economic achievements and shortcomings in light of its own goals and not in light of what Western value judgment may consider desirable. In the case of the USSR, the leadership was motivated primarily by the aspiration of transforming the country into a military power capable of warding off any attackers and an economic power second to none. Hence, rapid industrialization became the paramount economic goal from the very outset. Priority was therefore given to the industrial rather than the agricultural sector, and to the producer goods rather than the consumer goods subsector. Only in recent years has greater allowance been made for the needs of agriculture and of the consumer.

During its sixty-five years of existence, the Soviet economy has had to operate under unusually severe handicaps. At the outset, it was an economy badly disrupted by World War I, with a population ill-equipped by background or education to meet the challenges of industrialization. Further disruption was caused by years of revolution, civil strife, and military intervention by several of the leading Western powers including the United States, followed by years of virtually total economic blockade by all the major industrial nations of the world that deprived the country of the benefits of substantial foreign investments and of extensive foreign trade, which had so greatly facilitated industrialization in the United States. World War II destroyed much of Soviet productive capacity, and later, the prolonged period of cold war, with its concomitant military expenditure, drained the country of resources that could have been devoted to the more rapid development of productive facilities. Then came the renewal and intensification of the armament race in the 1980s. Moreover, throughout the entire sixty-five-year period, the country was operating under an economic system untried in the history of industrialization. (On the plus side, one should point out, they did have the advantage of being able to utilize the technological know-how of already developed countries and to exact reparations, especially from East Germany, which offset a small part of the incredibly high costs of World War II.)

Table 2. Population and Output of Some Representative Commodities
(1913–1980, selected years)

A. Population

(in millions)

	1913	1929	1940	1949	1958	1969	1980	Population 1980 as multiple of 1913
	139.3	153.4	196.7	178.5	208.8	241.7	265.0	1.9

B. Some Representative Fuels, Producers' Goods, and Semidurable and Durable Consumer's Goods

	1913	1928	1940	1945	1958	1969	1980	Output 1980 as multiple of 1913
Electric power (1,000 mil. kwls.)	2.0	5.0	48.3	43.3	235.0	689.0	1,295.0	647.5
Steel (mln. tons)	4.3	4.3	18.3	12.3	54.9	110.0	148	34.4

Coal (mln. tons)	29.0	35.5	166.0	149.0	493.0	608.0	716	24.7
Oil (mln. tons)	10.0	11.6	31.1	19.4	113.0	328.0	603	60.3
Cement (mln. tons)	1.8	1.8	5.7	1.8	33.3	89.8	124	68.8
Mineral fertilizer (in conventional units, mln. tons)	—	0.14	3.2	1.1	12.4	46.0	104	—
Motor vehicles (thousands)	—	0.8	145.0	75.0	511.0	844.3	2,199	—
Footwear (mln. pairs)	68.0	58.0	211.0	63.0	356.0	635.0	744	10.9
All types of fabric (1,000 mln. linear meters)	2.7	3.0	4.5	1.8	7.5	10.3	13.1	4.9
Television sets (thousands)	—	—	0.3	—	979.0	6,600	7,500	—
Refrigerators (thousands)	± ±	—	3,500	300	1,675.0	3,700	5,900	—

Table 2 (continued)

C. Some Representative Agricultural Products
(five-year averages)

	1909–13	1924–28	1936–40	1946–50	1951–65	1966–69	1976–80	Output 1976–80 as multiple of 1909–13
Grain crops (mln. tons)	72.5	69.3	77.4	64.8	130.2	162.3	205.0	2.8
Raw cotton (mln. tons)	0.7	0.6	2.5	2.3	5.0	5.9	8.9	12.7
Meat, slaughter weight, (mln. tons)	4.8	4.2	4.0	3.5	9.3	11.4	14.8	3.1
Milk (mln. tons)	28.8	29.3	26.5	32.3	64.7	80.0	92.6	3.2
Eggs (1,000 mlns)	11.2	9.2	9.6	7.5	28.7	34.6	63.1	5.6
Wool (thousand tons)	192.0	157.0	129.0	147.0	361.0	393.0	460.0	2.4

In spite of all handicaps, the Soviet Union has advanced from a relatively backward and predominantly agricultural country to an economic power second only to that of the United States. When using official Soviet statistical releases in one's evaluation, one may question the methodology employed in computing official Soviet aggregate output data. One may challenge the accuracy of certain Soviet claims (for instance, indexes for long-run increases in real income), and one may take exception to the use of certain weights, for instance, 1926–27 prices which, in the opinion of Western economists, tend to overstate subsequent Soviet growth rates. But after all caution has been applied, figures computed by Western economists—though as a rule considerably lower than those released by the Soviets—still spell remarkable economic success in terms of overall, and even more in terms of industrial, development. It is probably fair to say that in spite of all shortcomings of the Soviet economic system one can point to, the annals of no other country show such rapid industrialization and such high growth rates sustained for so long a period of time.

FROM TSARIST RUSSIA TO THE FIRST FIVE-YEAR PLAN

During the quarter of a century preceding the outbreak of World War I, the fledgling manufacturing and mining sectors in Tsarist Russia grew at an average annual rate of about 5 percent—fairly high but far below average rates achieved by the Soviet Union during six-and-a-half decades of her existence. Overall national income, unfavorably affected by the relative inertia of the agricultural sector, grew much more slowly, perhaps at an average rate of 2.5 to 3 percent per year between 1860 and 1913. In 1894, Russia's per capita income was far below that not only of the United States but also of all major European powers, and there is strong evidence that it fell farther behind during the next two decades.

The first steps towards industrialization were taken in the pre-Soviet era, but in 1913, the high point of pre-World War I economic development, Tsarist Russia was far behind the leading industrial powers of the world. Agriculture accounted for more than 75 percent of those engaged in productive activities, and, together with industrial raw materials, for over 94 percent of her total exports. Only one-tenth of Russia's population was engaged in industrial pursuits and per capita industrial output was 13 times higher in Germany, 14 times higher in England, and more than 21 times higher in the United States than in Russia.

Russia's economic condition left much to be desired in 1913; and it deteriorated considerably during the subsequent eight years. As a consequence of World War I, the Revolution, the Civil War, and the concurrent and subsequent economic disorganization, the Soviet Union's industrial output had, by 1921, dropped to a small fraction of what Russia's had been before 1917, and amounted to between one-half and one percent of the industrial output of the world. When, after three or four years of war communism, and some seven years of a N.E.P. (see p. 31), the First Five-Year Plan was introduced in 1928, the Soviet economy had barely recovered its pre-World War I level.

1928–1940: THE FIRST THREE FIVE-YEAR PLANS

The introduction of the First Five-Year Plan in 1928 ushered in the era of detailed economic planning from the center. The years that followed were years of ruthless mobilization of resources, of extraordinarily high rates of forced savings and investment, and of primary concentration on heavy industry at the expense of the agricultural and consumer goods sectors. Much has been written about Stalin's inhumanity and about the great suffering of the Soviet people, and especially the peasants, during that era. Unfortunately, human suffering is not easily measurable, so that it would be difficult to determine whether or not it exceeded the suffering of British laborers, of slaves in the American South, or of immigrant workers in the New England textile mills during the first half of the nineteenth century, when England and the United States were in the throes of early industrialization. In any case, the industrially advanced Western countries all paid their price for industrialization in terms of hard labor and of consumer goods foregone so that efforts could be channeled into the erection of an industrial base. Yet most Western analysts consider the price exacted from the Soviet populace in the pre-World War II era unnecessarily excessive. But while one must reject the coldblooded ruthlessness of the Stalin era, one can hardly deny the economic achievements. While the West lingered under the harrowing experience of a prolonged and exceedingly severe depression, the Soviet economy continued to make rapid economic progress. The increase in heavy industrial production during the "first dozen years of forced industrialization," writes a well-known American Sovietologist,[1] "was unprecedented in international historical experience for a time period of this length. From a basically agricultural economy the USSR was catapulted into the first rank of industrial powers."

Official Soviet statistics claim an almost fourfold increase in national income for the period of the first two Five-Year Plans, from 1928 to 1937, and a more than fivefold increase from 1928 through 1940. The Third Five-Year Plan (1938–1942) had called for national income to be doubled. But under strained prewar conditions growth rates fell off and, moreover, appear to have been quite uneven. The output of capital goods, Soviet sources have it, rose by 53 percent from 1938 to 1940; but oil production increased by only 9 percent, iron and steel production by 3 percent, and the output of the electrical goods, automotive, tractor, trans-

---

[1] Stanley H. Cohn, *Economic Development in the Soviet Union*, 1970.

port, and the road-building and construction machinery industry was actually lower in 1940 than in 1937. Agricultural output increased but slightly during the three years preceding World War II. Western sources, using less favorable weights and prices than those used in official Soviet indexes, see aggregate Soviet output as having roughly doubled between 1928 and 1940—much less spectacular an accomplishment than that depicted by official Soviet figures, but still highly respectable.

In terms of the goals of the Soviet leadership at the time, overall growth was of much less import than the growth of the industrial sector. According to Soviet sources, industrial output increased almost sixfold between 1928 and 1940. Western estimates vary, but even the most conservative among the well-known ones grants a more than two-and-a-half-fold increase while some others come closer to Soviet figures than to those of their Western colleagues. Agriculture, languishing under the dual impact of enforced collectivization and priority for heavy industry, grew but slowly during the twelve-year period.

1941–1945: FOUR YEARS OF WAR

On June 22, 1941, Nazi Germany launched the largest land invasion and the most devastating war in history against the Soviet Union. By November, the German armies occupied territory roughly equal to the land area of the United States east of Chicago. On this occupied territory lived 10 out of every 25 Soviet citizens, and it accounted for 63 percent of all Soviet coal production, 68 percent of pig iron output, 58 percent of steel, 60 percent of aluminum, 38 percent of grain, 84 percent of sugar, and 41 percent of railroad lines. The four years of war cost the Soviet Union some twenty million dead, thirty million injured, and left many of her cities and towns and much of her agriculture, industry, and transportation system in shambles. Soviet statistics show staggering economic losses: some 1,700 cities and some 70,000 villages and other small inhabited communities were fully or partially wrecked and burned. Destroyed were some 4,700,000 houses, 127,000 schools, universities, and public libraries, 31,850 industrial enterprises, 15,800 locomotives, 428,000 railroad cars, and 65,000 miles of railroad track. Some 100,000 collective and state farms were wrecked and plundered, and the invaders slaughtered or shipped to Germany 7,000,000 horses, 17,000,000 cattle, 20,000,000 pigs, and over 100,000,000 chickens. Much of Soviet industry that miraculously survived the original German onslaught was systematically destroyed by the Russians in their "scorched earth" policy, by Soviet partisans during the Nazi occupation, or by the retreating Germans towards the end of the war, including the Donets basin, in which three-fourths of the Soviet mining potential prior to the war had been concentrated, and the Dnieper power works, pride of the First Five-Year Plan. In all, the country lost fully one-third of its entire capital stock. Soviet estimates to the effect that World War II delayed Soviet economic development by eight to ten years might well be too conservative.

National income dropped during the war years, and gross agricultural product dropped even more drastically. Gross industrial output suffered greatly, especially during the first months of warfare, but with all efforts devoted to the winning of the war, the armament industries sharply increased their output year after year.

According to Soviet sources, Soviet industry turned out in the course of the war 136,844 aircraft of all types, 102,500 tanks and self-propelled guns, and 489,900 artillery pieces, while receiving under lend-lease agreements 18,753 aircraft, 11,567 tanks and self-propelled guns, and 9,600 artillery pieces. In the closing years of the war, Soviet sources assert, lend-lease deliveries amounted to less than 3 percent of Soviet output. While Western sources do not deny that "the USSR produced the bulk of what was used" during the war, they point out that a large part of the increase in motor vehicles in the Soviet armed forces, from 272,000 to 665,000 during the war years, came from U.S. lend-lease, and that a significant number of locomotives and machine tools as well as significant tonnage of nonferrous metal and of cables and wire was provided for by lend-lease and by other imports.

1946–1950: THE RECONSTRUCTION ERA

The period of the Fourth Five-Year Plan, 1946–1950, witnessed exceedingly rapid restoration of the Soviet Union's war-torn economy. According to officially released Soviet statistics, the 1940 output of electricity was surpassed in 1946, of coal in 1947, of steel and cement in 1948, of pig iron and oil in 1949. In the war-devastated regions, the harvest of grain, sugar beets, flax, sunflowers, potatoes and other crops exceeded prewar levels in 1949, and by the end of that year, 90 percent of all houses in towns destroyed during the war were said to have been restored. Gross agricultural output, Soviet figures have it, reached the prewar level in 1950, and national income and gross industrial product in that year reportedly exceeded planned targets and were almost two-thirds and three-fourths respectively above their 1940 levels. Western estimates, though lower, also show considerable progress. Keeping in mind that overall production in 1945 was well below that of 1940, the first five postwar years were indeed years of highly creditable economic progress. American economist Norman Kaplan estimates Soviet GNP for 1950 as less than 18 percent above 1940, but according to his own computations, this represents a more than 50 percent growth for the five-year period 1945–1950.

1950–1980: THE LAST THREE DECADES

During the 1950s industrial output and national income continued to increase rapidly. Even agricultural production, after 1951, rose every year, jumping drastically to an all-time high in 1958. Consequently, towards the end of the decade, an exhilarated and overoptimistic Soviet leadership began to prepare a highly unrealistic Twenty-Year Plan. Adopted under Khrushchev's leadership by the Twenty-Second Party Congress in October, 1961, the plan predicted that by 1970 Soviet industrial output would surpass that of the United States and labor productivity would be twice as high in the USSR as in the U.S. According to that long-range plan, the Soviet Union would, by 1980, "occupy first place in the world in per capita production."

When sharply dropping growth rates reached a low in 1963, a year of bad crop failure, it became evident that the forecasts of the 1961 Twenty-Year Plan far exceeded the realm of possible achievement. But, on the other hand, those in the West who described the situation in terms of crisis or stagnation were obviously in error: the setback was but temporary. Although the Soviets could report only a 14 percent increase in agricultural output for the period of the Seven-Year Plan, 1959–65, they claimed increases of 53 percent in national income, of 60 percent in sales of goods through state and cooperative retail outlets, and of 84 percent in industrial output. Western estimates, somewhat lower as usual, still show considerable progress. (See Table 1.)

After 1963, industrial and overall growth rates recovered from their 1962–63 lows. Although not as impressive as during previous decades, they were again highly creditable. Agricultural output, so greatly dependent on weather conditions, had its ups and downs, rising somewhat faster during the second than during the first half of the 1960s, with growth rates oscillating (according to Soviet data) between a 10 percent increase in 1966 and a 3.2 percent drop in 1969.

IMPERFECTIONS AND ECONOMIC REFORMS

Soviet leaders have long pointed with pride to the economic achievements of the USSR. Yet after economic growth slowed down at the end of the 1950s, they began to encourage "constructive criticism," and during the early 1960s they themselves repeatedly expressed deep dissatisfaction with the efficacy of the planning apparatus and asked for alterations to improve economic performance. Apart from the general slowdown in growth rates, Soviet leaders showed concern, for instance, over the decrease in the rate of growth of labor productivity, and they called for steps to improve the situation.

According to official Soviet sources, labor productivity in industry increased 16.5 times between 1913 and 1968, and an unofficial Soviet computation by the Soviet Union's most famous statistician, the late S. Strumilin (who admitted that his calculations are necessarily "far from perfect"), arrives at a 22.8-fold increase in the productivity of Soviet labor during the first half a century of Soviet power, achieved with only a fivefold increase in the capital-labor ratio. But at the 23rd Party Congress in 1966, Kosygin reported that labor productivity had increased by an annual average of only 4.6 percent between 1961 and 1965 as compared with 6.5 percent during the preceding five-year period, and he demanded that "we must do everything we can to overcome the lag." Some non-Soviet sources show even lower increases in Soviet labor productivity in the early 1960s (although the rates are higher than those given for the United States), and there was apparently no improvement in 1968 and 1969.

Numerous other shortcomings became ever more apparent during the first half of the 1960s. The consumer goods sector continued to show a lack of variety and an inadequacy of quality often contrary to the intentions of the planners, insufficient supplies of certain inputs repeatedly caused production bottlenecks, and the hoarding of scarce capital goods by some enterprises interfered greatly with their optimum utilization. Convinced that economic performance could be substantially improved, the Soviets frankly recognized and openly discussed existing inadequacies. To correct them, they started to alter to some extent their system of economic planning and administration.

A system of detailed command planning from above and of highly centralized and strictly enforced administration of economic activities is particularly well suited for harnessing unused resources, for imposing forced savings, and for bringing about expansion primarily by net additions to plant, equipment, and to the industrial labor force. It is particularly well suited, in other words, to a relatively less developed economy embarked on a crash industrialization program.

But by the onset of the 1960s the situation had changed. The number of economic decisions to be made had increased gigantically, the single predominant priority goal (rapid industrialization) had been replaced by a great number of goals with equal or similar priority rankings, and the era of sellers' markets had drawn to a close in many sectors of the economy with the Soviet consumer, much choosier than before, no longer willing to accept whatever was available on the shelves. And probably most important, the epoch of "extensive" economic growth had virtually come to an end. Henceforth, growth would have to be attained increasingly not by adding inputs of land, labor, and machinery but by modernizing production facilities and techniques, by improving enterprise planning and organization, by economizing on inputs, by a more rational division of labor—in other words, by enhancing economic efficiency at the micro level.

The old system of planning and administration seemed ill-equipped to cope with economic conditions in an advanced socialist economy. It had become obsolete, a victim of its own successes. The Soviet leadership therefore found it necessary to introduce economic reforms aimed at extensive decentralization of economic decision-making at the micro level and at making increased use of market forces in resource allocation. This, however, did not mean that Brezhnev and Kosygin were about to preside over the dismantling of their socialist economy. There was nothing in the economic reforms that would imply the return of the means of production to private enterprise. The center has retained control, via the central plan, over the major economic proportions and, as a matter of fact, over virtually all macro-economic decisions. (In other words, central planning authorities continued to decide how much to invest in agriculture and how much in industry; but the director of a men's clothing factory could decide whether to produce more blue pants or more brown jackets).

Actually, the Soviet Union proceeded very cautiously with the revamping of her planning and administrative machinery, more cautiously than envisaged in the early 1960s, when growth rates were less satisfactory than in subsequent years. Soviet economic reforms have surely been much more limited in scope than those introduced in some of the Eastern European countries. In recent years, moreover, many industrial enterprises have been grouped together into enterprise associations, and some economic functions and varying degrees of power to make economic decisions, bestowed upon the enterprises in the late 1960s, have now been transferred to the management of these enterprise associations—an act widely interpreted in the West as a partial recentralization. And indeed, the "economic reforms" of the late 1960s and early 1970s are hardly ever mentioned anymore in official Soviet news media.

During the period of the Ninth and the Tenth Five-Year Plans (1971–1975 and 1976–1980 respectively), Soviet industrial growth rates continued their steady decline, and overall growth rates dropped even more (see Table 1 above). But it ill behooves us to be overcritical of Soviet economic progress. While most of the Western world has been suffering from both inflation and unemployment—and while the United States in addition has had to cope with high budget deficits, severe deficits in her international balance of trade, low rates of economic growth even in the industrial sector and, worse yet, occasional years of negative economic growth, declining or at best unchanged real spendable income of workers, and increases in the percentage of the population living beneath official levels of poverty—the Soviet Union has continued to make substantial economic progress, albeit in many areas more slowly than in the past. According to official Soviet sources, as compared with the preceding five-year period, national income increased by 34 percent during the Ninth and 24 percent during the Tenth Five-Year Plan period, industrial output by 45 and 33 percent respectively, and retail trade turnover by 40 and 29 percent. Labor productivity rose by almost 50 percent during the decade of the 1970s, average wages in 1980 were 1.4 times their 1970 level, and the income of collective farmers rose yet faster. Even the much-maligned agricultural sector, affected adversely by extremely bad weather conditions during two years of the Ninth and three of the Tenth Five-Year Plan period, has not been doing as badly as often assumed in the West. From 1976 to 1980, the all-important grain harvest averaged 205 million tons— just about three times what it was in the immediate pre-World War I era, and under the tzars Russia exported close to one third of its grain crops, while the Soviet leaders have been importing substantial quantities. (These continued grain imports from the West, it should be pointed out, are devoted primarily to livestock feed in an effort to further improve the citizens' diet—for it takes between 7 and 14 lbs of grain to produce one pound of meat.)

The U.S. Central Intelligence Agency's 1982 *Handbook of Economic Statistics* gives the per capita GNP of the USSR for 1981 as $5,930 (as compared with $3,590 for 1976, and $5,240 for 1980 figured in the respective year's U.S. dollar purchasing power equivalents). While this is still less than half that of the United States, it is, for instance, higher than that of Italy, almost three times that of Mexico, and more than eighteen times that of mainland China, and it places the Soviet Union squarely among the affluent nations of the world. Living standards, although rapidly rising during the 1970s, appear somewhat lower than would seem to be indicated by this figure of per capita GNP. This is so partly because in housing and in much of the durable consumer goods sector the Soviet Union can catch up only gradually with what the industrially advanced countries of the West have built up over decades and, in some respects, over centuries. And secondly, the USSR allocates substantial sums for military preparedness and devotes a much larger part of her GNP than most Western countries to the producer goods sector.

The 1981–85 Five-Year Plan, in progress as this book goes to press, is not a repetition of the overoptimistic plans of the Khrushchev era. Adopted under the Brezhnev-Tikhonov leadership by the Twenty-Sixth Congress of the CPSU in early 1981, it is conservative, realistic, and will in all probability be largely fulfilled. (For planned increases in national, and in industrial and agricultural, output, see Table 2, above.)

SOVIET ECONOMIC PERFORMANCE: AN ASSESSMENT

As has been shown, Soviet economic growth has been quite uneven. The Soviet Union's foremost economist and father of the First Five-Year Plan, Strumilin, now deceased, asserted a 238-fold increase in the output of the means of production during the first half a century of Soviet history, from 1917 to 1967, a slightly less than 38-fold increase in the output of consumer goods, and a tripling of agricultural production. Since then, in spite of greater emphasis on the consumer goods sector, the output of producer goods has continued to rise somewhat more rapidly, and overall industrial growth rates have, on the average, been several times higher than growth rates in the agricultural sector. But outstanding as the record has been in the producer goods sector on which most efforts have been concentrated, it has obviously not been unimpressive in the consumer goods sector either. Even in agriculture, where Soviet growth experience has left much to be desired, considerable progress has been made. *Per capita* growth in all sectors has necessarily been smaller than aggregate development. But since population has increased by only some 90 percent between 1917 and 1981, growth of per capita production has still been high throughout. Even per capita agricultural output has doubled over the past six-and-a-half decades and, because of substantial grain imports in recent years, consumption of agricultural products has risen even more. In this connection, it should perhaps still be mentioned that in the process of industrialization the structure of the labor force has so vastly changed that the agricultural output of the latter half of the 1970s (some three times, annually, that of 1913) was produced by much less than 25 percent (and by 1981, less than 20 percent) of the working population instead of the prerevolutionary 75 percent—a considerable improvement even since 1960, when still more than 46 percent of all gainfully employed were engaged in agricultural pursuits.

Computations of growth rates of economic aggregates such as national income, industrial output, real wages, etc., are strongly influenced by weights assigned to sectors and subsectors and by base years chosen. Especially when long time periods are involved, a certain degree of arbitrariness in the selection of weights and base years is inevitable. Western estimates often differ from official Soviet figures by a considerable margin. But, to be sure, Western estimates also vary greatly from one another, and at times there are substantial discrepancies when one and the same Western economist uses different weights.

On the other hand, there is relatively little disagreement on the growth of output of individual major commodities, expressed in physical units. At times, Western analysts will simply accept Soviet figures, especially in the case of principal industrial commodities; at times they will make adjustments of a few percent, especially when Soviet definitions change (such as the inclusion of milk sucked by calves in reported gross milk output, which started in the mid-1950s). These days, it is rare for a Western recalculation to be more than 10 percent below Soviet figures—even in the case of agricultural products. Under the circumstances, this author has felt at liberty to present, in Table 2, Soviet figures for the expansion of selected producer goods, consumer goods, and agricultural commodities from 1913 to the present. Aware that Western recalculations may be somewhat lower, he feels confident that the difference would not be substantial. (The CIA's *Handbook of Economics Statistics* gives, for instance, identical figures for 1980 for electric power, steel, and motor vehicles, and a slightly higher figure for cement production.)

In 1921, the USSR produced somewhere between one-half and one percent of the industrial output of the world; at the time of the outbreak of World War II almost 10 percent; and by 1980, with about 7 percent of the world's population, the Soviet Union laid claim to producing over one-fifth of the industrial output of the entire globe, by then, many times greater than sixty, or even thirty-five years ago. Western assessments of Soviet industrial growth rates are lower than official Soviet figures but seem to corroborate roughly the Soviets' claim to their relative position in the world as an industrial power. In any case, there is no doubt that the Soviet Union's industrial output is exceeded only by that of the United States and that she holds first place in the world in the output of many products essential for a great industrial power and for the achievements of high living standards. These include oil, coal, pig iron, steel, mineral fertilizer, cement, diesel and electric locomotives, sugar, butter, woolen fabrics, and leather shoes.[2] True, as shown above, Soviet economic progress was much slower during the 1960s and the 1970s than during the 1930s and the 1940s, and might well remain slow during the 1980s also. But slower growth does not mean economic decline. And recurring Western predictions of economic crisis and impending economic disaster which have proven patently wrong in the past are likely to prove patently wrong again, at least in the foreseeable future.

One should perhaps still point out that Soviet economic progress during the past two decades has been achieved in the face of several consciously self-imposed macro-economic decisions which, irrespective of any value judgment concerning their desirability, were bound to cause economic growth to slow down. First, both the average number of hours worked per week and the average number of days worked during the year have been reduced over the years and are considerably fewer at the beginning of the 1980s than they had been in the 1950s. Secondly, defense expenditures have continued to grow, perhaps on the average by almost as much as the growth in GNP. Thirdly, there was the conscious decision to respond to the Soviet people's rising expectations by placing relatively greater emphasis than in the past on the consumer goods sector, and fourth, closely connected thereto, the service sector (health, education, culture, trade) has been enormously expanded. Finally, to make possible increased rates of consumer goods and services output, the high rates of growth of fixed investment of the past have been allowed to drop sharply in recent years. Capital investments which had grown by more than 40

[2] So as not to unduly exaggerate Soviet claims, note should be taken that in the case of the last three items the United States makes much greater use of substitutes than does the USSR, namely margarine for butter, synthetic materials for wool, and plastic for leather shoes.

percent in the Eighth and Ninth Five-Year Plan periods (1966–70 and 1971–75 respectively), increased by only 29 percent during the Tenth, 1976–80 Plan period, and are scheduled to rise by only 12–15 percent during the current, 1981–85, Eleventh Plan period. Moreover, in recent years considerably higher percentages of total investment have been directed into agriculture, which has less of an impact on future growth rates than investment in industrial construction, machinery, and equipment.

There are many other achievements that could be added to those that have shown up in the figures presented above. In the supply of available medical and teaching personnel, for instance, the Soviets have exceeded the United States since the mid-1950s. Today, the USSR can boast of having fewer students per teacher and, per 10,000 population, more hospital beds and almost 50 percent more physicians than the U.S., claiming that her physician/population ratio (37.6 doctors per 10,000 population in 1981) is the highest in the world. As a result of improved nutritional and health standards, infant mortality rates have decreased spectacularly, from 273 per 1,000 live births in 1913 to 27.7 in the mid-1970s,[3] and life expectancy has increased over roughly the same period from 32 to more than 70 years. The Soviets have perhaps not gone far enough with their economic reforms, and seem to even have backtracked somewhat in recent years, but their planning and administrative mechanism is no longer inflexible. Having proven their willingness to tamper with it, they will undoubtedly make further adjustments as called for by ever-changing economic conditions.

In the meantime, Soviet per capita income and living standards are, to be sure, still far below those of the principal Western market economies and even behind those of some of the more advanced socialist countries such as the GDR and Czechoslovakia. The overoptimistic goal of surpassing the United States in per capita output has proven unachievable within the short time span allowed for it. However, even Western analysts, with estimates of Soviet economic performance lower than those of their Soviet colleagues, testify to the fact that the percentage difference has been narrowing rather consistently.

The record is available for all who wish to examine it. With this record before it, the West would be well advised not to underestimate the past performance nor the economic potential of the USSR. The United States is still ahead of the Soviet Union in total and per capita output, in consumption, and in living standards. But the Soviet Union has been

[3] For reasons yet to be determined, infant mortality rates seem to have increased during the latter half of the 1970s, and while no official statistics on the matter are available, Western estimates have them at well over 30 at the end of the 1970s—of course still only a small fraction of what they were in the pre-Soviet era, but obviously an issue greatly emphasized by Western analysts. [Interestingly, it appears that in the United States, overall death rates rose by 3 percent in 1980 (*Wall Street Journal*, March 3, 1981, p. 10), and that infant mortality rates in Washington, D.C. are above those of such countries as Jamaica, Cuba and Costa Rica. (*New York Times*, Jan. 13, 1981, p. 37.)]

steadily gaining on the United States. There may be disagreement as to exact percentage differences; but unless the trend of faster average growth rates in the USSR than in the U.S. is reversed, it is an arithmetically inevitable consequence that the economic gap will be closed sooner or later. The question is only when.

3. SOVIET ECONOMIC PROBLEMS*

Holland Hunter
Haverford College

After a long period of steady progress, the Soviet economy has entered an era of increasing difficulties. Policies and procedures that worked well in the 1950's and 1960's have yielded diminishing returns in the 1970's and now appear to face failure in the 1980's. . . .

I. MAJOR FEATURES OF RECENT SOVIET ECONOMIC EXPERIENCE

During the 1970's, output has been growing in the Western industrial world more slowly than during the 1950's and 1960's. Among the forces at work, higher energy costs have been significant. On a smaller scale, efforts to reduce environmental disruption have raised costs and slowed material output growth while raising its overall contribution to welfare. Higher labor costs, higher import costs, and diverse trade restrictions have hampered real gains.

Output has been growing more slowly in the USSR as well, but chiefly for other reasons. The costs of obtaining and using natural resources have been rising in real terms as high grade, well located resources have been depleted and less accessible supplies have been drawn on. Continued massive flows of annual investment in fixed capital formation have encountered diminishing returns, not significantly offset by technological progress. Soviet agricultural output growth has been set back by two very bad crop years (1972 and 1975), with some indication that climatic trends may have changed for the worse.

Though the rate of Soviet output growth has been slowing down, it is still positive. There have been no absolute declines in Soviet GNP since 1946. The recent growth rate, though lower than before, is still respectable. In a world economy where all major economies face growth constraints, recent Soviet overall growth performance appears impressive. It is its internal composition and qualitative characteristics that give concern to Soviet authorities and evoke criticism from outside observers.

* Reprinted from Holland Hunter, "Soviet Economic Problems and Alternative Policy Responses," *Soviet Economy in a Time of Change* (A Compendium of Papers Submitted to the Joint Economic Committee, Congress of the United States), Vol. 1, Washington D.C.: U.S. Government Printing Office, 1979, pp. 23–31.

The Soviet economy shares with the outside world a second common feature—inflationary pressures. Upward pressure on the price level in the USSR, however, does not reflect the usual wage-price spiral nor is it associated with large government budget deficits. Most wages and prices are controlled by the Soviet state, and official prices are only occasionally revised upward, in substantial general adjustments every eight years or so, with ostensible stability reigning in the intervening periods.

As for budget deficits, Soviet authorities have maintained balanced state budgets for several decades. Large hidden sales taxes and taxes on enterprise income siphon off enough current purchasing power to cover state outlays for national defense, education and public health, social security, and most fixed capital formation. The state budget does not, therefore, inject purchasing power into current income flows.

Chronic concealed inflation is nevertheless a serious problem in the Soviet economy. The pressures reveal themselves, not in sharply rising wages and prices,[1] but in chronic shortages, long consumer queues, pervasive economic inefficiency, and widespread corruption. Soviet authorities accept these malignancies as being less undesirable than market-clearing prices. For two decades the performance of the economy in delivering increasing output appeared to outweigh these operational defects, but in recent years reduced output growth has intensified inflationary pressures and focused more attention on these painful byproducts of the Soviet allocational mechanism.

The aggregate purchasing power of Soviet wages and salaries exceeds the ruble value of available consumer goods, priced at current official prices, so a growing mass of ruble savings in state savings banks and in currency outside banks hangs over the market. Soviet money wages are meant to provide material incentives for sustained effort and are further differentiated to attract labor, e.g., to jobs in the East and North. Thus Soviet authorities are both unwilling to curtail the public's purchasing power and unwilling to expand and reprice the flow of consumer goods; the resulting savings are thus not voluntary in the usual sense.

A major source of inflationary pressure is the regime's policy of providing job security to all Soviet men and women employed in state enterprises. Since unemployment is officially defined as a capitalist phenomenon, Soviet enterprises seldom fire workers. Padded employment rosters and swollen payrolls are the norm. It is therefore literally true that, apart from seasonal difficulties, unemployment scarcely exists in the Soviet economy. The economy suffers, however, from substantial underemployment of millions of workers in situations where layoffs would not reduce output. When Western firms squeeze out excess labor the consequences may be harsh unless alternative job opportunities are avail-

---

[1] Over the twenty-one year period from 1960 to 1981, consumer prices more than tripled in the United States but increased by a total of less than 36 percent in the USSR. (CIA *Handbook of Economic Statistics, 1982*, p. 58.) [Editor's Note.]

able; cost-minimizing efficiency in the firm can impose social costs on the society. Under the prevailing Soviet approach, by contrast, toleration of generous, not to say wasteful, staffing norms in Soviet enterprises facilitates social peace at the expense of substantial inefficiency. The real output per worker of the Soviet labor force is thus held down, and the potential output increments that might be obtained if the labor force were more efficiently allocated are not available to match the purchasing power embodied in current wages and salaries.

Another major source of inflationary pressure arises from the steadily growing demands of the Soviet public for the goods and services that make up an advanced standard of living. Soviet living standards have improved impressively over the last quarter century, but the regime's priorities have not enabled the system to keep pace with growing consumer demands.

While the Soviet economy has recently shared with other economies the problems of slower output growth and rising inflationary pressures, the USSR has also displayed its own unique problems. One that has been of increasing concern to Soviet authorities centers on the system's difficulties with innovation. . . . Decentralized market economies encourage and facilitate innovation, while the Soviet system in its present form thwarts the actual introduction of improved processes and products.

The incentives and disincentives that shape the behavior of Soviet economic decisionmakers serve to block the acceptance of innovations. Decisionmakers from top to bottom in Soviet industry seldom find it wise to replace old machinery and methods with new ones. Innovation is risky and its rewards are outweighed by its dangers. Official policy has called for industrial innovation but in practice the system protects the status quo. Where industrial assets are owned and operated by the state, officials show a natural tendency to protect and preserve these assets. If an innovation undermines the value of existing plant and equipment, ministerial and enterprise officials associated with the old assets will resist their displacement. Competition in a market economy forces old technology off the stage, penalizing with bankruptcy those who fail to adjust. No comparable pressure exists in the USSR.

On the contrary, long standing Soviet tradition preserves old capital plant and equipment to an extraordinary extent. Maintenance outlays are extensive, and equipment service lives run far beyond Western practice. This stubborn retention of aging and obsolete equipment means that the Soviet capital stock necessarily embodies antiquated technology. The difficulty is compounded by unusually long gestation periods for building and bringing fixed plant and equipment into operation.

Another unique feature of the Soviet economy is its lopsidedness. Because Soviet priorities over the last half century have focused on heavy industry and defense rather than civilian welfare, the economy displays large cumulative deficiencies in the stock of residential capital, urban social overhead capital, and the facilities required to supply public and private social services. In spite of a large nationwide program of urban residential construction over the last 20 years, there is still a serious housing shortage in the USSR especially where urban population is growing rapidly. . . .

Soviet growth policies over the last half century have also given inadequate attention to improvements in water supply, sanitary facilities, and paved roads. There is still a large national backlog of unmet demands for water mains, sewers, paved streets, and sidewalks. This kind of social overhead capital is provided in response to local demands expressed through local governmental units. Their voice has been weak in the USSR. Outside major cities, and once off major inter-regional highways, one immediately steps into a pre-twentieth century setting that is shockingly at odds with the USSR's position as a superpower.

Still another sectoral deficiency lies in the area of wholesale and retail trade. For sixty years the regime has been unwilling to make adequate provision for handling consumer goods and services; until recently, Soviet citizens could be appeased by comparisons between their genuine improvement and the extremely straitened circumstances of the 1930s and 1940s. Under current conditions, however, with more vivid awareness of contrasts between Western living standards and continued Soviet shabbiness, claims from this quarter can no longer be slighted. By comparison with Western Europe, North America, and Japan, the USSR is still stunted in respect to the developed needs of a mature economy. Effective economic performance in the 1980s may require deliberate attention to these needs as a key instrument in maintaining morale, raising productivity, and eliciting sustained effort.

II. ELEMENTS OF A MULTIFACETED SOVIET DILEMMA

Mounting evidence over the last several years has made it increasingly clear, both to Soviet leaders and to the outside world, that these strains in the Soviet economy require new answers. The input increases that formerly underlay Soviet output growth are no longer in sight. The pressure on Soviet labor supplies means that improvements in per-worker productivity, formerly merely desirable, are now crucial. Similarly the contribution of added capital plant and equipment, for several decades a central feature of Soviet growth, must somehow be raised to a new level of effectiveness. In both respects the economy is under pressure to shift from extensive to intensive methods, laying stress no longer on sheer quantitative increments but placing new emphasis on qualitative improvement. . . .

In casting about for specific ways to upgrade its economic activities, the USSR has become interested in a variety of Western high-technology areas. Giant projects like the Tolyatti passenger automobile plant and the Kama River truck plant symbolize the willingness to import advanced industrial technology in hopes of stimulating Soviet technological progress. Sophisticated equipment is being imported to improve resource extraction. Automated feed lots mark a comparable effort in agriculture.

In seeking to improve the effectiveness of economic planning and management, the USSR has been working out organizational blueprints for a very extensive system of information collection and processing designed to link all levels of production and administration into a national network of centralized economic management. . . .

It is already evident from Soviet experience to date that the transfer and application of contemporary Western technology in these fields requires a degree of flexibility that is simply not compatible with the present Soviet economic system. Large projects in heavy industry require a systems approach going far beyond specific aggregates of machinery. An isolated product or process cannnot be effective if put down in a surrounding economy that is incapable of supplying inputs of adequate quality and reliability. The typical high-technology product today achieves maximum effectiveness only as part of a complex network of suppliers, servicing facilities, distributors, and customers. Backward and forward linkages extend in many directions.

Effective technological transfer now requires a systems approach to the innovation, covering managerial aspects of production organization along with the narrow physical aspects. The present Soviet system, however, has great difficulty accommodating these relationships. In computer use, for example, it is standard Western practice for the computer manufacturer to make available very extensive servicing arrangements so that the hardware can be maintained and the user can be assisted in making effective use of the facility. These vendor services are utterly foreign to Soviet practice. But without prompt informed support of both hardware and software by a vendor organization, no computer user can learn how to make the computer deliver its full potential. The unsupported user is likely instead to have an expensive and largely idle piece of equipment on his hands. . . .

In the sphere of agriculture, a somewhat similar dilemma confronts the regime. Western observers have long been critical of the costly and ineffective performance of giant Soviet state farms at one end of the organizational spectrum, and tiny peasant private plots at the other. Intermediate size farms, operated under on-the-spot guidance, diversified and decentralized for alertness to local conditions and responsiveness to local opportunities, are missing from the Soviet scene. Yet it is in this direction that the greatest promise lies for lowering costs and improving capital and labor productivity in agriculture.

The dilemma appears to be that the organizational changes required to meet the new conditions confronting the Soviet economy do not fit within the present economic and political institutions of the USSR. Powerful vested interests in the Party and the state bureaucracy find changes along these lines to be unacceptable. Decentralized agriculture would give free rein to the "petty-bourgeois soul of the peasant proprietor." A systems approach to technological innovation would concede major initiative to plant management both as salesman for the plant's products and as free ranging purchaser of inputs. It is evidently feared that enterprise-level initiative would permit "localist tendencies" to divert resources from the Party's priorities into profitable consumer-oriented activities.

4. THE SOVIET ECONOMY: STRENGTHS AND WEAKNESSES*

Henry Rowen

Chairman, National Intelligence Council, U.S. Central Intelligence Agency

I. INTRODUCTION

    A. How is the Soviet economy doing?
       1. Confusion regarding the Soviet economy abounds.
       2. We believe, however, that this confusion results not so much from disagreement over Soviet economic performance as from uncertainty as to how to interpret that performance.
       3. Western observers have tended to describe Soviet economic performance as "poor" or "deteriorating" at a time when Soviet defense spending continues to rise, overall Soviet gross national product in real terms continues to increase, and Soviet GNP is second in size only to that of the U.S.
    B. These characterizations are not wrong.
       1. Given past rates of economic growth, the gap between Soviet performance and plans and expectations, and the marked departure from standards of economic efficiency, the record compiled by the Soviet economy in recent years has indeed been poor.
       2. Results that are unsatisfactory when measured by this yardstick, however, do not mean that the Soviet economy is losing its viability as well as its dynamism.
    C. In fact, we do not consider an economic "collapse"—a sudden and sustained decline in GNP—even a remote possibility.
       1. Our projections indicate that growth in GNP will remain slow but positive.

---

* Reprinted from *Central Intelligence Agency Briefing on the Soviet Economy,* Statement of the Honorable Henry Rowen, Chairman, National Intelligence Council, Central Intelligence Agency, Before the Joint Economic Committee, (U.S. Congress), Subcommittee on International Trade, Finance and Security, Dec. 1, 1982.

2. Growth is being retarded by a combination of factors. Some are beyond Soviet control, and some reflect the weaknesses of the Soviet economic system that even the new Andropov regime is not likely to change. Other factors holding down economic growth represent policy choices—for example, the allocation of resources to defense—that could be modified but are unlikely to change much in the near term.

3. Nevertheless, we expect annual growth to average one to two percent for the foreseeable future. Per capita consumption could level off or even fall slightly. . . .

II. SOVIET ECONOMIC OBJECTIVES AND PRIORITIES

A. Turning first to Soviet economic objectives and priorities, we believe that Soviet economic activity has always focused on building military power.

1. But the Soviet leadership has also always placed great stress on rapid economic growth.

2. The good life for the Soviet populace, in the form of a rising standard of living, has been of importance to Moscow too for almost 30 years. But improvements in the welfare of Soviet consumers have generally been subordinated to the demands of the military and to the high rate of capital investment necessary to insure fast GNP growth. It appears, though, that consumer interests are now being treated somewhat less cavalierly. Breaking precedent, the 11th Five-Year Plan calls for capital investment to grow more slowly than consumption.[1]

3. In pursuit of these national objectives, successive regimes have given heavy industry priority status because it is the source of military hardware and investment goods.

4. Meanwhile, despite some experimentation with decentralized forms of economic administration, the Soviet leadership has remained firmly committed to strict central planning and management of most economic activity. The justification has been that rigorous centralization is required for fulfillment of national objectives.

B. Soviet economic performance in terms of the objectives and priorities established by the leadership has been mixed.

1. The Soviet Union has built an exceedingly powerful military

---

[1] The draft directives for the 1971–1975 Five-Year Plan also set industrial targets for consumer goods higher than for producer goods. But actual growth rates achieved over the five-year period were slightly higher for the latter than for the former. [Editor's note.]

force. Under Khrushchev the emphasis was on strategic nuclear programs, but Brezhnev presided over an across-the-board expansion and modernization of all Soviet forces. . . .

2. While developing its military power, the USSR has until recently been able to maintain a rapid rate of economic growth.

   a. Soviet GNP, as measured by CIA, grew at an average annual rate of 4.6 percent from 1950 through 1981. During the same period US GNP increased by 3.4 percent per year.

   b. Soviet growth, however, has steadily slowed during this period—especially after 1978. The average annual rate of increase in GNP was about 6 percent during the 1950s, 5 percent during the 1960s, and nearly 4 percent between 1970 and 1978. In 1979–81, yearly growth averaged less than 2 percent. This year [1982] we expect GNP growth to be about 1.5 percent.

   c. To a remarkable degree, the slowdown in Soviet economic growth has a parallel in OECD[2] countries. During the first three years of the seventies, OECD GNP increased at the rate of 5 percent per year. The crisis induced by OPEC[3] oil prices brought OECD growth to a halt in 1974–75. Then in 1976–79, GNP resumed a respectable rate of growth of 4 percent per year. In 1980–81, however, GNP growth in the OECD collapsed to 1.2 percent per year.

   d. The slowdown in the USSR in part reflects four consecutive poor or mediocre harvests. But most sectors of the economy have been sluggish, especially industry.

      (1) In large measure, industrial performance has been held back by the emergence of serious bottlenecks unconnected with agriculture. Growth in industrial output, which averaged almost 6 percent a year in 1971–75, fell abruptly in 1976 and in 1976–81 averaged just slightly over 3 percent annually.

      (2) The decline in growth has been steady. Industrial production grew by only 2 percent in 1981 and is expected to rise by 1½ to 2 percent this year.

3. The higher priority accorded to military strength is suggested by the continued rise in defense spending at the average annual rate of 4 percent that has prevailed since the mid-1960s. . . .

---

[2] OECD = Organization for Economic Cooperation and Development. An international organization of primarily Western countries, created in 1960 for the purpose of stimulating economic progress and world trade. Member countries include most West European nations as well as the United States and Canada. The only socialist country in OECD is Yugoslavia. [Editor's note.]

[3] OPEC = Organization of Petroleum Exporting Countries. [Editor's note.]

4. At the same time, leadership concern about consumer welfare seems to have somewhat diluted the commitment to growth.

   a. The share of Soviet GNP allocated to fixed capital investment—the driving force behind Soviet economic growth—has more or less stabilized in the last few years at about 26 percent (factor cost), compared with about 20 percent in 1960.

   b. Slowing investment growth is explained partly by bottlenecks in sectors providing building materials and machinery. But it probably also stems from a political decision to protect Soviet consumers in a time of tightening economic constraints.

   c. Nonetheless, consumption still accounts for only 55 percent of Soviet GNP, far below the share in most non-Communist industrialized countries. . . .

III. BASIC STRENGTHS OF THE ECONOMY

A. We turn now to our discussion of the strengths and weaknesses of the Soviet economy. We will look first at the USSR's economic strong points, starting with those attributes that shore up the economy as a whole, and then move on to identify specific sectors that are performing in a particularly effective fashion.

B. The sheer size of the economy, reflecting the substantial growth since World War II, is one of its strengths. Soviet GNP in 1982 equals about $1.6 trillion, roughly 55 percent of US GNP this year. Per capita GNP is almost $6,000.

C. The population is also large, currently numbering about 270 million. The labor force totals about 147 million and, by world standards, is well-trained and well-educated.

   1. Literacy is by now almost universal in the USSR. The educational level of the population has been rising rapidly. Twenty-three percent of those over 16 in 1979 have completed at least a secondary education (10th grade in the Soviet Union) compared with only 14 percent in 1970. In 1979 an additional 7½ percent also had completed higher education, compared with 5 percent in 1970.

   2. A particular effort is being made to expand the education of the indigenous nationality groups in the Central Asian republics. The USSR wants to upgrade the skills of the relatively large pool of labor available there and possibly encourage outmigration by assigning these better educated young people to labor-short areas. Graduates of higher, specialized secondary, and vocational-technical schools receive compulsory work as-

signments at specific enterprises where, it is hoped, they will continue to work.[4]

3. The emphasis on mathematics, engineering, and science in Soviet schools is also a plus for the technologically oriented Soviet society. About one-third of total instruction time in secondary schools is devoted to mathematics and science. There are serious flaws, however, in Soviet education, including too much rote learning and, at the university level, narrow specialization early on.

D. Another of the strengths of the Soviet economy is the tremendous accumulation of capital assets that has occurred since World War II.

1. The value of gross fixed capital assets—buildings, machinery, equipment, and the like—amounted to over 1.74 trillion rubles in 1980 according to Soviet published data. The value of Soviet capital assets expressed in constant prices increased almost 11-fold between 1950 and 1980 and about 4.4-fold from 1960 through 1980—long after the USSR had recovered from wartime devastation.

2. This phenomenal expansion reflects the allocation of a large and, until recently, rising share of Soviet resources to capital investment. The rapid growth of capital assets has resulted in a more than threefold increase in the amount of capital per worker. The rise was almost 3½-fold in industry and over fivefold on state and collective farms.

3. Two-thirds of the stock of capital assets is concentrated in industry, agriculture, transportation and communications, and construction. Only about 15 percent of total gross fixed capital consists of housing or is used to provide services to the population such as health care and education.

4. Although the rapid accumulation of capital assets is one of the Soviet Union's strengths, the capital stock includes a disproportionately large share of worn out and technologically obsolete equipment. Soviet policies have kept retirement rates of existing assets artificially low and have prolonged their service lives through repeated capital repairs.

E. The USSR is exceptionally well endowed with natural resources.

[4] All Soviet education is free and the great majority of students also receive substantial stipends, generally adequate to cover their living expenses. In exchange, students are expected upon graduation to work for two or three years in their chosen field at a place they are needed. Because of a labor shortage, there are usually lists of places to choose from, and the better students get first pick of locations. But while the law for such postgraduate assignments is on the books, there are no provisions for penalties. In other words, a student who were to refuse such assignment may be looked down upon, his "anti-Socialist" behavior might be recorded in his work book that he must show when applying for jobs, but he cannot be jailed or fined for it. [Editor's note.]

1. Beginning with energy, the Soviet Union has about 40 percent of the world's proved reserves of natural gas—the 30 trillion cubic meters under Soviet control exceed the reserves of all [other] industrialized nations combined.

   a. Soviet reserves of coal account for 30 percent of the world's total recoverable reserves and are sufficient to insure over 200 years of output at current rates of production.

   b. The Soviets do not publish figures for oil reserves, as they do for gas and coal. Our estimate is that oil reserves, at least in West Siberia, are substantial, though increasingly difficult to exploit.

2. The USSR is abundantly stocked with other important raw materials.

   a. According to Soviet studies, iron ore reserves amount to about 60 billion tons—some 40 percent of the world's total.

   b. With as much as one-fifth of the world's forest resources, the USSR has a virtually inexhaustible source for producing wood and wood products.

   c. In addition, the Soviets claim—and may well have—the world's largest reserves of manganese, nickel, lead, molybdenum, mercury, and antimony. They also say that reserves of chromite, gold, platinum-group metals, zinc, and copper are among the largest in the world and sufficient to support Soviet mine production for many decades.

   d. The Soviets also have substantial reserves of potash and phosphate rock—raw materials for the production of chemical fertilizers—although a large portion of the newer phosphate deposits consist of poor quality ore.

F. With its wealth in human, capital, and material resources, the USSR is highly self-sufficient—another of the economy's major strengths.

1. The high degree of Soviet self-sufficiency in vital raw materials is shown by its position as a net exporter of a large number of these materials. Net exports of energy—mostly of oil and natural gas—now total about 4 million barrels a day equivalent or about 15 percent of total energy production.

2. The Soviets are major exporters of precious metals, ferrous and non-ferrous ores and metal products, chemicals, and timber. Because of expected gains in output the Soviets will be able to expand sales of key minerals such as platinum group metals, nickel, cobalt, manganese, chromite, and gold during the 1980s. We also anticipate major increases in Soviet exports of ammonia, nitrogen, and potash fertilizer and methanol.

3. Though highly self-sufficient, the USSR is not autarkic. Indeed, for at least the last decade, trade with the West has been

an important element in the USSR's efforts to modernize the Soviet economy and render it more efficient.

  a. The Soviets now must rely on Western imports of capital and technology to increase or maintain production of some of the raw materials in which they are abundantly endowed and self-sufficient.

  b. Imports from the West have become critical to Soviet efforts to improve, or simply maintain, the quality of the Soviet diet. In 1981, imports of grain and other agricultural products reached almost $12 billion, or about 40 percent of the USSR's total hard currency purchases.

  c. But despite the large-scale expansion in agricultural imports, the Soviet Union remains basically self-sufficient with respect to food.

   (1) These imports are intended mainly to prevent a decline in meat consumption and are not essential to maintaining an adequate quantity of food consumption.

   (2) At 3,300 calories, average daily food intake is equivalent to that in developed Western countries. Grain production is more than sufficient to meet consumer demand for bread and other cereal products.

4. To summarize, when we say the USSR is self-sufficient, we do not mean that the Soviets neither need nor benefit from trade.

  a. Imports, particularly from the West, can play an important role in relieving critical shortages, spurring technological progress, and generally improving Soviet economic performance.

  b. What we do mean is that the ability of the Soviet economy to remain viable in the absence of imports is much greater than that of most, possibly all, other industrialized economies. Consequently, the susceptibility of the Soviet Union to economic leverage tends to be limited.

G. In considering fundamental strengths, the highly centralized, rigid system of administering the economy—while perhaps the Soviet Union's major economic millstone—has had its advantages in enabling the leadership to mobilize resources in crash programs to achieve priority objectives.

  1. The prime example of this capability has been Moscow's success in building up its military might. This has been achieved through centrally-directed mobilization and allocation of the USSR's highest quality human and material resources and a rigorous system of quality control in military production that prevents the shoddiness so characteristic of Soviet civilian output.

2. Centrally directed concentration of resources does not of course work everywhere. Agriculture, which we will discuss in more detail later, is an example. . . .

H. We turn now to specific areas where Soviet economic performance has been especially strong.

   1. As we mentioned, natural gas has been a major Soviet success story. It will play a pivotal role in meeting the energy needs of the economy in the 1980s, particularly as a substitute for crude oil in industry and in home use but also as a potential hard currency earner.

   2. The nuclear power industry, although it has not met the full expectations of the leadership, has also done quite well. We estimate that the annual increase in nuclear-generated electricity will increase by about 17 percent a year during 1981–85 and supply about 11 percent of the country's electricity by the end of the period.

   3. Development and production of some Soviet natural resources are proceeding at respectable rates despite the obstacles of remote location and conditions that make extraction exceedingly difficult.

      a. The USSR is second only to South Africa in the production of gold. Production in 1981 was about 325 tons. Its stock of gold is about 1900 tons, worth over $25 billion at current prices.

      b. Soviet production of platinum-group metals, nickel, and cobalt will jump sharply during the 1980s. Output of these resources will be adequate to meet domestic needs and also to provide increasing quantities for export.

      c. Prospects for production of those resources located in more easily accessible regions look even better. Rich new deposits in Kazakhstan and Georgia should generate sizable increases in production of both chromite and manganese.

IV. BASIC WEAKNESSES OF THE ECONOMY

A. We will now look at the weaknesses or vulnerabilities represented on the Soviet economic ledger. We will focus first on problems stemming from circumstances beyond Soviet control and then turn to the shortcomings and vulnerabilities of the economy that are inherent in the USSR's system of economic planning and administration. Then we will consider specific weaknesses.

B. Soviet economic performance has been hurt in recent years by declining increments to the labor force and by the increasing difficulty of extracting and transporting vital energy and other raw material inputs.

1. Because of lower birth rates in the 1960s, an increase in the number of workers reaching retirement age and a rising mortality rate among males in the 25 to 44 age range, increments to the working-age population have been declining since the mid-1970s. The falloff became particularly sharp starting in 1980, and increments will remain very low throughout this decade.

   a. From 1971 to 1981, the working-age population grew by about 23 million. In 1981–91, it will increase by only about 4 million people. The decline in growth of the labor force— that is, of people actually employed—will be less, largely because of a rise in the share of the population in the 20 to 39 age group, where labor force participation rates are highest. But the decline in growth will still be substantial. The increment to the labor force in 1981–91 is expected to be only 9 million, compared with 19 million in 1971–81. With participation rates in the labor force already very high, there are few unemployed people to draw on to offset adverse demographic conditions.

   b. Other factors will aggravate the labor shortage. Large-scale migration from the countryside to urban areas, formerly a rich source of labor supply to the rest of the economy, has slowed considerably in the past decade. The agricultural sector itself faces shortages of qualified manpower in most areas. This problem is compounded by the fact that rural residents in the Central Asian republics, where increments to the working age population will be highest and where there still is substantial redundant labor, are reluctant to migrate.

2. As we noted earlier, the Soviet Union is blessed with enormous quantities of a large array of raw materials. But in many instances these materials are increasingly inaccessible, and thus the cost of exploiting them has been rising sharply. This has been strikingly true of Soviet energy resources.

   a. With the decline in production in the Volga-Urals oil fields in the mid-1970s, growth in Soviet oil production has come from West Siberia, much of it from the giant Samotlor field. However, production in this field probably has peaked, compelling the Soviets to seek oil in even more remote and forbidding regions. In 1981–85, just to achieve the slowest growth rate planned in oil output since World War II will require greatly expanded drilling and pumping operations.

    b. Decades of mining have depleted the underground coal mines of the European USSR. The Soviets must tunnel deeper shafts and mine thinner seams just to maintain coal output at current levels. During 1976–80, for example, more than 80 percent of new mine output was needed to offset depletion at older underground operations.

    c. Even the extraction and distribution of natural gas has grown considerably more expensive.

      (1) Natural gas deposits in the old producing areas— North Caucasus, Transcaucasus, Ukraine, Volga-Urals, and western Turkmenistan—are severely depleted. More and more gas must be piped from central Asia and especially Tyumen oblast to replace exhausted local supplies.

      (2) Such long-distance transmission of natural gas requires construction of lengthy pipelines and a great many compressor stations, a very expensive operation.

    d. Easily accessible supplies of many non-energy raw materials have also been exhausted.

      (1) The Soviets have largely depleted reserves of copper, nickel, and bauxite in the Ural Mountains and are beginning to tap deposits in northern Siberia or, in the case of bauxite, are exploiting non-bauxite ores and boosting imports. Similarly, the richest deposits of phosphate rock in the Kola peninsula have been depleted, forcing the Soviets to move to lower-quality deposits in Siberia.

      (2) In the case of iron ore, the Soviets have depleted their richest deposits in the Western USSR. To compensate for declining ore grades, increasing amounts of investment must be devoted to ore-enriching facilities, raising both production costs and manpower requirements.

      (3) The Soviets are also faced with the depletion of forests in the traditional logging areas of the northwestern USSR. Government planners have chosen to overcut these forest tracts beyond the point of natural regeneration so that, at least temporarily, the scale of operations in Siberia could be held down. But when loggers are forced to expand operations in Siberia—and the Far East—recovery costs will be high because of the distances involved, the harsh climate, and the lack of infrastructure.

3. The increase in fixed capital investment has also slowed markedly in recent years. This deceleration can be seen as both

forced upon the leadership by shortages of key inputs and—
as I noted earlier—as a conscious policy choice.

   a. Growth was 7 percent a year in 1971–75, slowed to about
       5 percent a year in 1976–78, and fell sharply to an average
       annual rate of only about 1.5 percent in 1979–80.
   b. Growth picked up in 1981—fixed investment rising by 3
       percent—but the 11th Five-Year Plan calls for investment
       in 1981–85 to rise by less than 2 percent a year. This is by
       far the lowest planned rate of increase in the post World
       War II period.

C. Because of tightening demographic, investment, and resource
    constraints, the traditional Soviet economic growth formula of
    relying on lavish use of labor, capital, and material inputs is no
    longer applicable.

   1. The Soviets themselves have long recognized the need for a
       new approach. For at least a decade they have been stressing
       the necessity of switching from an extensive to an intensive
       pattern of growth. This means essentially that growth must
       largely spring from productivity gains—from more efficient
       use of resources for any given level of technology and from
       faster technological progress.
   2. But the productivity of capital has actually been falling for
       several years, and labor productivity has been rising at stead-
       ily declining rates. For this, shortcomings in the Soviet system
       seem largely to blame, a matter to which I will now turn.

D. The Soviet economic system is peculiarly ill suited to promote
    efficiency and technological progress. Four features of the system
    help to explain why.

   1. First, economic planning and management are highly cen-
       tralized, with resources allocated mainly by administrative
       fiat. Reforms aimed at increasing the degree of enterprise au-
       tonomy have generally come to naught.

      a. Indeed, central control over economic activity has been
          on the increase for the last several years, as indicated by
          an increase in the number of commodities that are allocated
          in physical terms according to central planning decisions.
      b. The arbitrary nature of central decisions on allocating in-
          puts and assigning outputs, which is aggravated by the ab-
          sence of prices that accurately reflect relative scarcities,
          precludes efficient planning.

   2. Along with overcentralization, the goals the central authorities
       impose on the economy have generally been unrealistic. Faced
       with a gap between what they want to do and what is possible,
       Soviet leaders have tended to call for productivity gains and
       material savings that are beyond the system's capacity.

    a. The economy thus chronically operates under conditions of strain and shortage. And the number and severity of supply bottlenecks have been increasing in recent years.

    b. With inputs regularly hard to come by, enterprises have a strong incentive to hoard. This intensifies bottlenecks and leads to more hoarding, in a depressing circle of waste.

3. Overcentralization coupled with unrealistic planning has meant that the behavior of factory directors is largely dictated by the urgency of meeting the plan imposed by higher authorities.

    a. Fulfillment, however, is generally measured by multiple and often inconsistent "success indicators" of varying degrees of priority, such as physical volume of output, gross value of output, value added, material savings, and productivity.

    b. The principal drawback of this system is that managers often strive to meet the targets even at the expense of what is economically rational from the standpoint of the central authorities and society as a whole.

    c. For example, if gross value of output is a prime goal, waste is encouraged, as managers seek to make their production as material-intensive as possible.

    d. The Soviet Union is currently elevating value added in production to the position of the prime success indicator. Though probably less perverse a target than gross value of output, it, too, is subject to abuse. For example, it could induce managers to increase employment at a time of labor stringency.

4. Finally, Soviet economic performance has long been impaired by the separation of research, development, and production into different organizations. Each organization operates according to different planning targets.

    a. Scientific Research Institutes do basic research and are paid for successful completion of research projects whatever their practical benefit to the economy.

    b. Design Bureaus develop the blueprints for new equipment and are largely rewarded for the successful testing of the prototype. Rewards are only loosely linked to successful incorporation of the new product into serial production.

    c. Production plants, meanwhile, are rewarded for increasing both physical output and the value of output.

      (1) The introduction of new products at a plant initially disrupts serial output, jeopardizing plan fulfillment and resulting rewards.

      (2) The Soviets have no competitive marketplace to force

both developer and producer to introduce better products and technologies. Indeed, hostility to technological change at the producer level is characteristic of the Soviet economy—as Yuri Andropov told the Central Committee of the Party.

d. Because of this division of labor and the system's rewards, Soviet products remain in production for an inordinately long time, new products frequently embody only minimal change, and the fruits of truly advanced research impact on serial production only with great delay. Over the last decade and a half, the Soviets have reorganized development and production establishments to deal with this problem. But the problem persists.

E. Moving from generalizations to particulars, we will look now at the areas in which the USSR seems particularly weak or vulnerable.

F. Historically, agriculture has been the economy's leading problem sector. Its performance over the past four years has strengthened its claim to that dubious distinction.

1. After peaking in 1978, farm output fell steadily through 1981, when it stood over 10 percent below the 1978 level. This year [1982] production is expected to rise but by only about two percent.

2. The grain crop, which reached a record high of 237 million tons in 1978, has not reached 190 million tons in any subsequent year. Last year the grain harvest was so low that Moscow never announced a figure, although unofficial statements put the crop at 158 million tons.

3. Production of meat—a key commodity in the regime's drive to better the Soviet standard of living—has also fared poorly. It reached 15.5 million tons in 1978 but has been below that level since, ranging from 15 to 15.3 million tons over the last four years.

4. Bad weather has been a major factor in the decline in agricultural production since 1978, but harsh weather and unfavorable geographical conditions constitute a permanent threat and obstacle to agriculture and only partly explain why Soviet efforts over the years to boost farm output have not yielded more dividends.

a. Mishandling of the sector by the Soviet authorities has also had much to do with its disappointing performance.

b. Management and planning processes are much too centralized. Farm efficiency is seriously handicapped by constant intervention of unqualified officials regarding what to plant, when to plant, when to harvest, and the like.

    c. Prices of both farm inputs and outputs set by the central authorities are encouraging an assortment of output that is inconsistent with the national plan. At a time when Moscow is striving to expand output of meat, milk, and eggs, relative prices are such that farmers find it more profitable to concentrate on growing crops.

    d. Though investment in agriculture has been heavy—over a quarter of total investment outlays has gone to the farm sector for many years—much of it has been misdirected.

       (1) There has been too much emphasis on construction, not enough on equipment.

       (2) Furthermore, the quality of farm machinery is low, with the incidence of breakdowns high.

    e. Deliveries to the agricultural sector of needed material inputs, such as fertilizers, have been insufficient while the proportion of aged and unskilled workers in the farm labor force—which accounts for about 20 percent of the total labor force—is high.

    f. The regime has also failed to take maximum advantage of the potential of the private sector[5] in agriculture, even in periods, such as the present, when it is encouraging expanded output there.

5. In recognition of the rising popular demand for quality food, Brezhnev told the Central Committee in late 1981 that food was the most important "political and economic problem" of the 11th Five-Year Plan.

    a. The increase in demand reflects rising consumer expectations and incomes. The inability to satisfy that demand is a function of both stagnant output of most livestock products and the regime's unwillingness—reinforced by Poland's experience—to raise prices in state stores.

    b. The leadership has attempted to ease the imbalance between supply and demand by allowing various local rationing schemes under which customers may purchase only limited amounts of certain foods in state stores. But long lines for meat, milk, and milk products remain widespread. To soften the impact of shortages on the work force, the regime has redirected substantial amounts of quality foods from public state retail outlets to special dis-

---

[5] The author refers here to the private plots, the small pieces of land that all farmers (and even city workers who want to farm on weekends) can have for their own use. On these subsidiary plots they have their house and barn and they can raise crops or livestock for their own table, for sale to the state, or for sale on the collective farm market, the only major free market in the Soviet Union where prices are basically set by demand and supply. [Editor's note.]

tribution outlets in factories and other economic enterprises.

6. Against this background, Brezhnev last May unveiled his Food Program—in preparation for a year-and-a-half. The objective of the program was to boost Soviet food production and reduce dependence on imports—quickly. The Food program attacks agriculture's problems from three directions:

   a. First, it reorganizes the agricultural administration by creating commissions at all levels of government to coordinate agricultural operations and all related activities, ranging from sectors providing supplies to agriculture to the processing, distribution, and marketing of farm output.

   b. Second, without significantly raising previous targets for total expenditures, the program seeks to redirect investment to weak links in the food production chain. Investment in sectors producing machinery for agriculture is to rise sharply. To reduce waste, investment in on-farm food processing and storage facilities has been given top priority. More investment in rural housing and roads is scheduled to improve farm-to-market transportation and stem the flow of younger workers to the cities. Upgrading the plant and equipment in food processing is another major target.

   c. Third, financial incentives are to be raised. Prices paid by the state to farms for a large variety of agricultural products will increase on January 1 [1983]. At the same time, prices paid by the farms for equipment, fuel and fertilizer will be lowered.

7. For the most part, however, the Food Program represents relatively minor variations of old policies.

   a. One exception is the reorganization of agricultural administration, which—by increasing friction and confusion within the bureauracy—is likely to cause more problems than it solves.

   b. The basic defect of the Program lies in its omissions. It does nothing to reduce day-to-day bureaucratic interference in agriculture, and it does not do enough to restructure prices or to change the incentive system so that rewards are directly keyed to performance.

G. As the recent meetings of the Communist Party Central Committee and the Supreme Soviet made clear, there are very serious problems in other sectors as well.

   1. The Soviet steel industry, for example, has become a major bottleneck.

      a. Shortages of steel, especially high-quality products, are holding back the growth of civilian machine building and other priority sectors of the civilian economy.

b. The appetite of the Soviet economy for steel is probably unparalleled—and a reflection of its relative technological backwardness. Last year the USSR with little more than half the GNP of the United States used 103 million metric tons of rolled steel products compared with US consumption of 94 million tons.

c. The shortages of steel won't be remedied quickly.[6] Investment requirements to cope with the declining quality of ore are escalating rapidly, and new capacity requires long gestation periods before it can be brought on stream. In addition, supplies of coking coal and iron ore are likely to continue to be tight in the next several years.

2. Transportation is another sector responsible for recent poor economic performance. Snarls on the railroads—the backbone of the system—have disrupted economic activity across the board, but most particularly in the delivery of raw materials such as coal, iron ore, timber, scrap-metal, and chemical fertilizer.

a. The Soviet economy requires a large volume of transport services not only because of its size and complexity but also because the country's resources and people are spread widely over a very large land mass.

b. Compared with North America and Europe, the USSR is poorly served by year-round water transport, and government policy has held back the development of an adequate highway system. The brunt of the transport burden, therefore, has fallen to the railroads.

c. The railroads, however, appear to have reached their capacity ceiling with present technology and facilities. Consequently, the transport sector will find it difficult to support economic growth through the next several years at least.

3. In the energy field the leadership faces rather different problems in the coal and oil industries.

a. Coal production, which dropped during 1979–81, has been hampered by deteriorating underground mining conditions at larger, established mines, by shortages of labor and declining labor productivity, and by insufficient capital investment.

---

[6] It should be kept in mind, though, that the Soviet Union is by far the world's largest steel producing country, with a 1981 steel output of 149 million tons as compared with 109 million tons for the United States. (CIA *Handbook of Economic Statistics, 1982*, Washington D.C.: Directorate of Intelligence, Central Intelligence Agency, 1982, pp. 26–27. [Editor's note.]

   b. Oil production continues to increase, though slowly.[7] Even
      the very small growth of the last few years has required
      an enormous effort.
 4. Finally, shortages of raw materials and depletion of fuel and
    power supplies have caused a marked slowdown in the pro-
    duction of construction materials.
   a. Current output, for example, increased by less than 2 per-
      cent annually during 1976–80 compared with nearly 5½
      percent annually in the preceding five year period.
   b. Shortfalls in the production of cement, roofing materials,
      construction resources, and wall materials have restricted
      construction activity throughout the economy.
H. As we emphasized earlier, the Soviet economy does not depend
   on trade for survival. Total imports equal about 12 or 13 percent
   of GNP, those from the West—only about 5 percent. But, because
   of the difficulties just enumerated, the elimination or easing of
   critical bottlenecks and the achievement of key elements in Soviet
   development plans are closely tied to imports from the West.
 1. The USSR will have to import a broad range of Western oil
    and gas equipment if it is to minimize the fall in production
    in fields where depletion is at an advanced stage, increase
    output elsewhere, and help locate and develop reserves.
   a. Pipelaying equipment capable of handling large-diameter
      pipe is produced only in the West, and we estimate that
      the Soviets will need to import 15–20 million tons of steel
      pipe during the remainder of the 1980s to build the pipelines
      they have scheduled.
   b. They will also continue to need sophisticated exploration
      equipment, high capacity submersible pumps for the oil
      fields, and probably high-powered turbines for gas com-
      pressor stations.
 2. Soviet requirements for quality steel should result in annual
    imports of steel other than pipe of about $2 billion (current
    prices) at least until the mid-1980s.
 3. Imports of chemical equipment and technology probably will
    continue to be large, reflecting the still antiquated character
    of some parts of the chemical industry and the importance of
    the industry for agricultural production.

[7] This represents a change from some earlier CIA estimates that predicted that Soviet oil
production would start falling off rapidly by the early 1980's and that soon thereafter the
USSR would need to import oil. (See, for instance, CIA, *Prospects for Soviet Oil Production, April, 1977.* See also the summer 1979 prediction by former CIA director Admiral
Stansfield Turner in *Hearings before the Subcommittee on Economy in Government of
the Joint Economic Committee, Congress of the United States, Ninety-Sixth Congress,
First Session,* Part 5, June 26, 1979, Washington D.C.: US Government Printing Office,
1980, p. 16. He predicted that by 1985, oil production would fall to 10 million barrels per
day and might even drop as low as 2 million barrels a day. [Editor's note.]

4. Imports of grain and other agricultural commodities have soared in recent years and almost certainly will remain high. Grain purchases in 1979–82 averaged more than 30 million tons a year.

I. The USSR's ability to earn the hard currency it needs to pay for its Western imports is, however, already under pressure and may well diminish in the future.

1. The main reason is the leveling off and possible decline in Soviet oil production.

   a. Because domestic consumption will continue to rise and because of ongoing demands from Eastern Europe, we expect oil exports to the West—which account for about half of Soviet hard currency merchandise export earnings—to fall.

   b. According to our projections the rise in hard currency earnings from stepped up exports of natural gas will only partially offset the anticipated decrease in receipts from oil.

2. Other factors also have restricted Soviet hard currency earning capacity.

   a. Primarily because of the softening of energy prices, Soviet terms of trade vis-a-vis the West will be less favorable in the 1980s than they were in the 1970s, when upward spiraling oil and gold prices brought the USSR windfall gains.

   b. In addition, demand for Soviet raw materials will be weak if Western economic activity fails to pick up.

   c. Soviet manufactured goods, which are generally not competitive in Western markets, are unlikely to take up the slack.

   d. Finally, less developed countries, including OPEC countries, probably will be less able to pay cash for Soviet arms.

3. The Soviet capacity to buy from the West is of course backstopped by the USSR's huge stock of gold. But the USSR is reluctant to undertake massive sales of gold in an uncertain market because of the downward pressure that Soviet sales exert on prices.

4. On balance, the unpromising export outlook suggests that the USSR may have to make do with little if any increase in real imports in the 1980s.

J. The USSR's relations with Eastern Europe add another dimension of strain. Because it wishes to maintain political and social stability in Eastern Europe, the Soviet Union has given favorable economic treatment to five of the six Warsaw Pact countries—Czechoslovakia, East Germany, Bulgaria, Poland, and Hungary. The exception has been Romania.

1. This special treatment, or "assistance", has taken two basic forms: Subsidization and credits.

   a. Subsidies have not been given directly. They have instead been extended through preferential terms of trade. That is, Eastern Europe's terms of trade vis-a-vis the Soviet Union are more advantageous than those that would prevail if Eastern Europe conducted that same trade with the non-Communist world.

   b. In essence, the USSR sells energy, mainly oil, and other raw materials to Eastern Europe for less than world market prices and pays more than world prices for the manufactured goods it buys from Eastern Europe.

   c. Estimates of the cost to the Soviet Union of giving preferential terms of trade to Eastern Europe are rough—and controversial. According to the highest Western estimate we know of, these subsidies totaled almost $70 billion in 1960–80, with about 90 percent of this amount accumulating after 1974. The huge jump implicit in subsidies reflects the explosion in world oil prices in 1973–1980 and the large rise in opportunity costs to the USSR of its oil exports to Eastern Europe.

   d. The credits come mainly from the trade surpluses the USSR has consistently run vis-a-vis Eastern Europe since the mid-1970s, although the Soviet Union has also given some direct hard currency assistance to Poland.

2. Eastern Europe, battling severe economic problems of its own, continues to depend on Soviet assistance. But economic stringencies in the USSR have increased greatly the cost to the Soviets of aiding Eastern Europe.

3. The USSR apparently has decided to give reduced priority to Eastern Europe's economic needs in the future. Soviet oil exports to Eastern Europe were cut this year, and the USSR's trade surplus with the area apparently declined. Soviet subsidies will probably fall too. But a drastic cut in exports of raw materials and in trade credits and subsidies is unlikely.

V. UNCERTAINTIES ATTACHED TO THE GROWTH FORECAST

A. Andropov's advent to power has not altered our assessment of Soviet economic prospects.

   1. The exogenous factors impeding economic growth are not affected by the change in leadership.

   2. Moreover, Andropov's comments to the Central Committee point to no significant changes in economic policy.

    a. He indicated that he will take a cautious approach to economic reform.

    b. He further made clear that defense and heavy industry will retain their priority.

  3. The smattering of economic targets for 1983 announced at the Supreme Soviet meeting a week ago [November, 1982] are overambitious, suggesting that relief of economic strains and bottlenecks from more realistic planning is not to be expected.

B. Andropov is, however, in an extremely early point in his reign. Thus major policy changes *could* lie ahead. For this reason—and for reasons unrelated to leadership changes—our forecast of average annual growth in real GNP of 1 to 2 percent could be off the mark.

  1. Growth could be *more* rapid, for example:

    a. If the USSR enjoyed a run of good luck with the weather, leading to a succession of good harvests.

    b. If the new leadership were willing to undertake a substantial reallocation of resources from defense to investment.

    c. If the new regime were able somehow, perhaps by diverting resources from defense to consumption, to improve morale and labor productivity.

    d. Above all, if efficiency could be boosted by mitigating some of the most damaging features of the existing system. Productivity might be raised, for example, without a drastic overhaul of the system through

      (1) more balanced allocation of investment to end the neglect of such vital sectors as transport, and by

      (2) stopping the proliferation of success indicators and of overlapping lines of authority that has characterized the so-called "reforms" of past years.[8]

    e. If Andropov—his rule securely established—undertook basic changes that significantly reduced centralization and gave substantially greater play to market forces, the prospects would be even better. Such a reform, however, would be constrained by the imperatives of maintaining political control in a large multinational society. Furthermore, attempts to implement reform would encounter stubborn noncompliance by party and economic bureaucrats.

  2. Growth could be *less* rapid, for example:

    a. If the bad weather of the last few years continued, causing a permanent depression in agricultural output. In any case, there is a theory, substantiated by evidence, that the generally favorable weather that prevailed between the early

---

[8] The economic reforms of the 1960s actually called for the discontinuation of most success indicators and their replacement primarily by one: profits. [Editor's note.]

1960s and mid-1970s was an aberration. Although the weather for crops in the past several years was surely worse than any long-run average, a return to the pre-1975 conditions is unlikely.

    b. If the new leadership decided to accelerate the growth in defense spending at the expense of investment.

    c. If the ripple effect of current bottlenecks intensified.

    d. If public cynicism and apathy deepened markedly or active unrest developed.

3. Of these possibilities, serious widespread unrest—as the Polish experience suggests—is the one most likely to hit aggregate output the hardest. However, we consider such an eventuality unlikely. . . .

5. WESTERN EUROPEAN PERCEPTIONS OF SOVIET ECONOMIC TRENDS*

Richard F. Kaufman

Staff Member, Joint Economic Committee, U.S. Congress

1. INTRODUCTION

The way Soviet economic trends appear to us influences many U.S. policies and programs. This applies particularly to allocations of resources for defense. Unfortunately, Soviet secrecy and incomplete statistics make it difficult if not impossible to know all the facts. U.S. policymakers have come to rely heavily on the intelligence community for information about the Soviet economy.

This staff study sets forth the result of a study that was made to understand how West Europeans view the Soviet economy and whether, or in what way their views differ from those of the U.S. intelligence community.

The study was based on a series of in-depth interviews of government officials and private experts in August, 1977, in four countries—France, the United Kingdom, West Germany, Sweden and NATO and SHAPE headquarters in Belgium. A number of documents prepared in various foreign ministries and in NATO were examined. Interviews were conducted at economic, foreign and defense ministries in the countries visited, NATO headquarters in Brussels, SHAPE headquarters in Le Mans, and a number of public and private research institutes and universities.

* Reprinted from *Western Perceptions of Soviet Economic Trends*, (A Staff Study Prepared for the Use of the Subcommittee on Priorities and Economy in Government of the Joint Economic Committee, Congress of the United States), Washington, D.C.: U.S. Government Printing Office, 1978, pp. 1–8.

2. U.S. INTELLIGENCE PERCEPTIONS

During the past 2 years the U.S. intelligence community has significantly altered its estimates of Soviet economic trends.

In a broad [1978] assessment, *Soviet Economic Problems and Prospects*, the CIA concludes that Soviet GNP growth is likely to decline by the early and mid-1980's to between 3 and 3.5 percent annually, and could drop as low as 2 percent in that period. This outlook, substantially more pessimistic than earlier ones, is based on predictions of worsening problems in the energy sector, a slowdown of labor force growth, a slowdown in the growth of capital and labor productivity, an inefficient and undependable agriculture sector, a probable return to less-favorable weather for crops, and a possible shortage of steel. The Defense Intelligence Agency (DIA), disagrees with the prediction of a decline in Soviet oil production,[1] but agrees that the Soviet economic growth rate is slowing and could go as low as 2 percent in the 1980's.

3. WEST EUROPEAN PERCEPTIONS

European officials and private experts in the countries visited are, in general, skeptical about the U.S. intelligence community's bleak forecast of the Soviet economy. Europeans agree that the Soviets face serious economic problems but the prevailing attitude is that they are no more intractable than are the West's problems and are balanced by many positive aspects. . . . Criticism of the CIA and DIA overall forecast for the Soviet economy is widespread. None of the persons interviewed believe a crisis is pending or that growth rates will decline to the levels forecast by the U.S. intelligence community. Europeans tend to discount the more dire forecasts as a renewal of the predictions frequently made in the past of "imminent collapse" of the Soviet economy. A number of experts, when asked to comment on the U.S. estimates, recalled earlier Western judgments that proved erroneous, such as the Soviet economic system resting on "feet of clay."

At the risk of oversimplifying a complicated subject, Europeans who have made assessments of Soviet economic prospects can be said to fall into two groups. One group contends that the growth slowdown stems from the Soviet system of central planning and that problems will get worse unless fundamental reforms are adopted. The second view is that with all its limitations central planning has served the U.S.S.R. well and that most of its economic problems can be handled through improvements in the system. They believe the command economy can be made more efficient. To characterize the two approaches in another way, one type of observer focuses on the recent unsuccessful efforts of the Soviet

---

[1] This refers to earlier, pre-December, 1982 predictions. For revised CIA estimates on Soviet oil production, present and prospective, see the preceding selection. [Editor's note.]

Union to "catch up" with the West; the other notes the distance traveled since the Revolution and the continuing incremental gains. . . .

But even those who indict the Soviet system predict steady although slower growth. Most hedge their projections with the possibility that foreign trade, productivity improvements and other factors could improve growth prospects. Others maintain that what matters is not the shortfalls between plan and performance but the state of the economy from one year to the next. They argue that national income has been growing and should continue to grow. Some add that many Westerners do not understand that Soviet planning is a decision-making process, that plans are made to be adjusted and that the planners know the results will differ depending upon circumstances.

All of the persons interviewed recognize that the high growth rates of the past will not be matched in the future. Soviet leaders seem to acknowledge this when they speak publicly of the problems of a "mature" economy. Most European observers of the Soviet economy understand that it faces serious shortcomings. They do not question the descriptions of the shortcomings in U.S. intelligence reports. What they do challenge are the conclusions American intelligence experts have drawn about what the current difficulties imply for the future. It is significant that, in NATO's view, Soviet economic growth will be sufficient to allow for continuing increases in defense spending and gradual improvement of the standard of living. . . .

European analysts do not regard the 3 percent range growth forecasts for the Soviet Union as alarming. Although that rate represents a slowdown for the U.S.S.R., growth of from 3 to 4 percent is considered quite satisfactory in most Western countries. A growth rate of 2 percent for the Soviet Union would be viewed with greater concern. However, most analysts are highly skeptical that the slowdown will go that far.

A principal reason for skepticism is rejection of the idea of an impending Soviet energy crisis. As mentioned earlier, European analysts are much less critical of the Soviets than is the CIA for alleged mismanagement of their oil fields. If the Soviets solve their fuel problems GNP could grow from 3 to 3.5 percent annually in the 1981–85 period, according to the CIA's own analysis.

Many experts are also optimistic, with reservations, about Soviet agriculture. It is difficult to identify the factors that will provide the basis for future growth of production. The farm labor force is declining, a decrease in the rate of capital formation seems likely, and there will be no significant increase in the land under cultivation. Further, there is always the chance of crop disasters due to bad weather.

But it is also true that in the past 25 years there have been remarkable gains on agricultural production (3.4 percent annually since 1951) and per capita food consumption (100 percent since 1951), and those who have observed these achievements are unwilling to predict a reversal of the long-term trend.

The key question about Soviet agricultural prospects concerns productivity. Significant improvements in productivity could enable the Soviets to overcome the admittedly serious obstacles they now face and even release part of the labor force to other sectors. Europeans argue that no one knows enough about the Soviet Union, perhaps not the Soviet leaders themselves, to confidently predict whether or not, or by how much, productivity will increase.

A further reason for skepticism about U.S. intelligence forecasts is that Europeans have reason to doubt the accuracy of economic forecasting. The level of confidence in forecasts is especially low with respect to efforts to predict what will occur in the Soviet Union, some Europeans say. . . .

6. SOVIETS HAVE THEIR OWN MANPOWER PROBLEMS*

Thomas Kent
Associated Press correspondent

On March 13, 1930, an unemployed Moscow plumber, Mikhail Shkunov, finally got a job. He was the last person registered with the Soviet capital's central unemployment office, and after he went to work, the office closed for good.

Shkunov, who is now retired, is officially recognized here as the last unemployed man in Moscow and in the Russian Soviet Federated Socialist Republic.

The official media often refer to him when they make the claim that there is no unemployment in the Soviet Union.

Soviet officialdom considers the abolition of joblessness as one of the greatest accomplishments of Soviet communism.

But the elimination of mass unemployment has not solved all the nation's manpower difficulties. Some analysts, in fact, say the threat of limited joblessness persists in part of the country. And authorities freely acknowledge other problems with the labor force that are cutting into Soviet economic efficiency.

In such major cities as Moscow, the labor market seems at first glance to be in robust shape. No one worries about being jobless, and factories and offices are busy.

"I don't even bother to tell my grandchildren about how I was the last unemployed person," said Shkunov, now 75 years old.

"Young people these days aren't interested in hearing about it,"

* From an AP report from Moscow by correspondent Thomas Kent, published in affiliated newspapers throughout the US on June 2, 1981. Reprinted here by permission of the Associated Press.

he added in an interview with The Associated Press in his two-room Moscow apartment. "They don't even believe that unemployment really existed."

The Soviet Union got rid of unemployment by massive manpower-training programs, huge construction projects and state control of all major industries. Inefficiencies and planning problems have left many workers worse off materially than their Western counterparts, but mass unemployment is gone.

Moscow and other major cities, in fact, now face unemployment in reverse: up to 100,000 jobs are said by officials to be vacant on any day in the Soviet capital, jobs that could add to national productivity if filled. Nationally, two million jobs are said to be vacant.

Many of the jobs are low-level jobs that school and university students don't want.

"The job of a store clerk is an interesting and honorable one," says a poster designed to attract students to a Moscow retail-trade vocational school.

At the same time that some parts of the economy beg for workers, others are overstaffed. The Soviet press complains that factory managers, worried about fulfilling high output quotas, keep surplus workers on as "insurance."

But many Soviet citizens seem convinced that it is better to give people a job, even if their work is unnecessary, than to make them feel useless by keeping them at home on unemployment compensation.

"The way the Soviet Union is set up, paying unemployment compensation is impossible," said one young Moscow worker.

"Unemployment is the worst thing," said Shkunov. "I remember how I used to sell my own clothing for money. I remember the lines at the unemployment office."

There are some signs that low-level unemployment is appearing again in the Soviet Union.

Soviet press reports speak of "surplus labor" areas in the southern Caucasus Mountains region and Soviet Central Asia, where the birth rate is high. Although these reports avoid the word "unemployment," they acknowledge that more labor-intensive industries are needed to soak up workers.

Citizens from these areas are encouraged by high salaries and fringe benefits to emigrate to other parts of the nation, including Siberia, where many natural resources are located and a labor shortage is holding back economic development.

But many people in the nation's sun belt are apparently reluctant to travel to the north. And even if they are temporarily unemployed, they are entitled to free medical services, subsidized housing and other benefits available to Soviet citizens in general.

Some "intellectually" trained citizens in cities—university humanities graduates, translators and others—also complain of a form of unemployment when jobs directly in their specialities are unavailable. Many take jobs in allied fields, hoping for more suitable posts later.

Most official effort in the employment field now seems devoted to finding enough people for jobs that are vacant. Complicating the picture are a declining birth rate in recent years, and huge construction projects— such as the Baikal-Amur railway in the Soviet Far East—that need large amounts of labor.

Taking births and deaths into account, the overall Soviet population is growing at about 0.8 percent a year—while the government wants economic output to grow 18 percent to 20 percent in the 1981–85 period.

School pupils in some areas already help with agricultural work, soldiers are being used on the Baikal-Amur project and authorities are paying retirees to work part time.

They include Shkunov's 73-year-old wife, Yevdokia, who still works at a factory.

"They asked me to come help them part time," she said. "They've got a labor shortage there now."

WESTERN MARXIST VIEWS

---

7. STAGES OF SOVIET ECONOMIC PLANNING: SUCCESSES AND SHORTCOMINGS*

David Laibman†

Editor, *New World Review* and *Science and Society*, Associate Professor of Economics, Brooklyn College, and CUNY

The Five-Year Plans are now a firm tradition in socialist practice and thought throughout the world. They are applied in the development strategies of socialist countries, and of developing countries embarking on a socialist-oriented path; they symbolize the goal of rapid, sustained, comprehensive growth and the lifting of formerly underdeveloped and over-exploited economies and peoples to the threshold of modern technology and living standards. An appraisal of the progress of planning and socialist economic development in the USSR always has meaning, therefore, beyond the borders of that country alone; and this is true despite the fact

* Reprinted from David Laibman, "Incentives, Planning and Socialist Construction," *New World Review*, May–June, 1981, pp. 34–40, by permission of the publisher.
† The author extends his thanks to Dr. Vadim N. Kirichenko, Director of the Economic Research Institute of the State Planning Board (Gosplan), who spoke at length with the author while this article was in preparation.

that there is no Soviet "model" that can be installed ready-made elsewhere, and that there have been serious problems and obstacles as well as basic success in the Soviet experience.

We may well begin, then, with a summary table that shows both the progress and the gaps between promise and performance that characterize the Soviet economy. With a summary of earlier stages of socialist construction and the concepts appropriate to those stages as background, we will be able to consider the changes in planning and management now contemplated or under way, and offer some thoughts about the future.

Several things emerge from this table. First, and of foremost importance, is the fact that the Soviet economy has grown steadily and significantly, and at rates which for the most part outstrip the performance of the capitalist economies. Industrial output, for example, has grown by almost 80 per cent in the decade covered by the 9th and 10th FYPs, compared to (about) 40 per cent in the United States. If we were to examine the annual or quarterly figures, we would also see that USSR growth is steady and proportional, while that of the US is zig-zag, with spurts alternating with declines. Nothing in the Soviet data leads to any conclusion other than a reaffirmation of the balanced and rapid character of socialist economic growth, combining the advantages of comprehensive planning, full employment, and high rates of investment.

The second conclusion, however, points to a clear recent tendency for the plans to be *incompletely* fulfilled, with actual results below the targetted levels, and a tendency for the plan targets themselves to be lowered in each successive plan. This of course is the source of the literature on the slowing-down of the Soviet economy. While the data do not support the lurid accounts of a "crisis," they still should be of concern to serious observers.

Five-Year Increases in Various Indicators of the Soviet Economy,
Over Three Five-Year Plans
(Per Cent)

	9th FYP 1971–75		10th FYP 1976–80		11th FYP 1981–85 Planned (Guidelines)
	Planned	Actual*	Planned	Actual*	
National Income	39	28	26	20	18–20
Industrial Output	47	43	36	24	26–28
Labor Productivity (Industry)	39	34	31	17	23–25
Agricultural Output (annual average)	20–22	2	16	8	12–14
Real Per Capita Income	31	24	21	18	16–18

* Note that "actual" figures used here are generally lower than those supplied by the Soviets, but higher than Western non-Marxist estimates. [Editor's note.]

Stages of Planning and Management

In the prewar period, beginning with the GOELRO electrification plan and control figures of the 1920s and the First FYP, 1928/29 to 1932/33, planning was essentially *project planning*. Resources were earmarked for major industrial construction projects and drawn from the rest of the economy, which limped along as best it could, making do with whatever was left over. While this early form of planning was essential in laying the foundations of industry and establishing irreversibly a culture of industrialization and urbanization among the country's fledgling working class, it clearly did not yet amount to a system of *overall* planning, in which all of the sectors of the economy are prefigured into a consistent whole.

During the first post-war decades, such a system emerged. It is useful to characterize this system as one of *comprehensive* planning, which includes but is not limited to *central* planning. Nevertheless, in this, second, stage, the bulk of the actual planning was done at the center, by the State Planning Board (Gosplan). In this system of "detail planning from above," the producing enterprises were given detailed lists of plan indicators, or targets, specifying for the enterprises a complete assortment of planned outputs, techniques to be used, material inputs and machinery to be used, size of the wage fund, etc. For their part, the planners at the center, relying on whatever data they could gather, would construct "material balances—tables specifying the sources and uses of each product. By juggling the material balances, the planners worked to achieve rough consistency among all the inter-industry flows—a consistent plan—which would then be the basis for physical allocations of capital goods to enterprises, and final outputs to the retail trade network. Enterprise plans were specified in terms of physical units of output, either by weight or by number of items; increasingly, toward the end of this period, in terms of the ruble value of output.

This system was a major breakthrough in planning. For the first time—one hopes it will not seem hyperbolic to say, *in history*—there existed an *intentional economy*: one in which the system of economic activities is appropriated to human consciousness, foreseen, subjected to human control. . . .

The system of centralized planning—the lower phase, as it were, of the stage of comprehensive planning—permitted rapid and *balanced* growth (as compared with the earlier project-planning stage). It shared with that earlier stage, however, the feature that growth relied almost entirely on extensive sources.

The limitations of the system are well known (some critics of socialist planning know *nothing* else!) To summarize briefly: In the absence of accurate, up-to-date information, the planners formulate enterprise plans on the basis of previously achieved levels. If an enterprise produced

x units of output last year, this year it will be given a plan to produce, say, $1.08x$. Enterprises are thus given an incentive to conceal reserves, to hold back on possible innovations, and to distort the information given to the center. Results are measured in tons of output or number of units produced; if the first, the enterprise will concentrate only on heavy items, if the second only on light ones. In either case, there is no incentive to produce spare parts; hence no spare parts. If the plan is set in terms of the value of output, the enterprise is encouraged to use expensive materials rather than cheaper ones, since the material cost is included in the price of output. Even more fundamentally, a detailed plan handed to the enterprise from above is bound to be inconsistent, since it is based on poor information. The target for output may, for example, be unreachable if the enterprise stays within the plan for materials cost or wage fund, or vice versa. In this case, the enterprise management is free to violate the plan as it chooses, and the effectiveness of planning itself is weakened.

The solution to the inherent weakness of the early top-down approach was to complete the system of comprehensive planning by the addition of planning at the enterprise level. Thus *comprehensive* planning combines central planning with planning at the lower levels. It is crucial to understand that central and decentral planning complement and require each other. To strengthen one level is to strengthen the other; the problem of "centralization *versus* decentralization" is a pseudo-problem. Decentral *planning* is entirely different from atomistic decentralization, in which the local units act in isolation from one another and in ignorance of the aggregate outcome of their activity.

The question which emerges at this stage is: How are central and decentral planning made to fit together? The answer: by a system of *iteration*, repeated flows of information from the center to the localities and back again. Gosplan formulates overall targets for industries and the Ministries break them down to the enterprise level. The enterprise thus gets from the top not a detailed plan, but the outlines of a plan: general output (*not* the detailed assortment of output), an upper limit to employment, a target for productivity increase, and a few others. The enterprise then works out *its own* plan in detail, and when it does so it conveys that information (including a detailed shopping list!) back up to the center. The center, then, must revise its overall plan in the light of the new information, reformulate the material balances to a fit, and send the control figures back down. The enterprise then adjusts its plan accordingly, and sends its figures back up. Down, up, down, up. With each iteration, the plan, alternately disaggregated and reaggregated, gradually approaches consistency; this occurs, one hopes after not too many iterations, when the plans as revised by the enterprises are consistent with the figures received by them in the last round. If the divergence get smaller each round, the plan is said to *converge*. Once convergence is achieved, the plan is locked into place.

To complete this picture, it should be added, first, that, in a major development of the 1970s, there is now in most industries a middle level of planning between the Ministries and the enterprises—the industrial associations. These bodies combine the resources of several enterprises in the areas of research and development, marketing, consumer research, etc.; they are constituted on a representative basis out of the enterprises themselves. Finally, the large and increasing role of the trade unions in organizing worker participation at all levels should be mentioned. Union involvement is guaranteed in the collective agreement, and covers everything from the initial planning phase to the administration of large parts of the enterprise funds.

How can it be insured that the enterprises, given the discretion to formulate their own plans within the overall guidelines handed to them, will act in the general social interest by assuming ambitious plans? How can the distortions, mentioned above, caused by physical output targets or value-of-output targets, be avoided? Here is where the economic reforms, begun in the mid-1960s, come into the picture. Enterprises are rewarded for superior performance by the share of their profits which they get to keep. This share is paid into three funds—material stimulation (bonuses, etc.), housing and cultural, and investment. Now the critical feature of the new formulas for assigning profits to these funds is that the reward is greater if an enterprise plans ambitiously—in the language of the planner, if the enterprise assumes a *taut* plan. If, for example, the current performance of the enterprise is assigned an index of 100, and the enterprise thinks it can achieve a level of 110 next year, it will do better by assuming a plan of 110 and just meeting it, than it would by assuming a plan of 105 and overfulfilling the plan by 5.

In principle, the problem of distortion is met in the following way. In place of the various output, productivity, cost reduction and capital-saving indicators of performance, use just one: the *realized net rate of profit*. (We will see later why this cannot quite be done in practice, at least not yet.) This means that goods will not count toward plan fulfillment unless they are *sold*; that the single indicator will reflect all improvements in productivity, cost reduction, efficient use of capital. (It is important to remember that prices are set by central or local planning bodies, and the enterprise cannot raise its profit by means of price increases.)

Now, the economic reform was begun, with pilot experiments as all things in the USSR begin, in 1965; the major transition to the new system was completed in 1968. Yet it is precisely in the decade of the 1970s that growth rates fall. Evidently, the "crisis" of the extensive system continues to make itself felt; there is an even more serious labor shortage looming over the horizon for the 1980s. If the sources of extensive growth have largely dried up, as evidenced by a fall in the share of investment in national income from 30 to 25 percent in recent years, why has the economic reform not been effective in switching the Soviet economy over to a path of intensive development?

While the answer to this question must be speculative, it is not hard to speculate. You can change the rules; it is much harder to change the people who operate them. Enterprise managers and their staffs are now asked to plan; to innovate; to seek out their own customers and their own sources of supply; to decide on their own investment program, and even to finance it if necessary by borrowing from the state bank. . . .

Speaking frankly: An entire generation of Soviet managers had the attributes of caution; ability to take orders from the top without questioning; ability to skillfully reconcile discrepancies in those orders. With that generation in the prime of life, it has been difficult to remove it, to "kick it upstairs." Moreover, it would be wrong to do so! The "old-style" economic leadership is, in addition to being "old-style," a group including many heroes—heroes of the war, and of the economic reconstruction after the war. . . .

And this brings us to the present.

On July 12, 1979, the USSR Council of Ministers approved a resolution, entitled: "On Improving the Planning and Enhancing the Effect of Economic Management on Raising the Efficiency of Production and the Quality of Work." While many of the changes enacted are not yet firm—they were in fact a major consideration in the discussions preceding the 26th CPSU Congress—some idea can be given of the direction of change in the works.

The time horizon of planning is being extended: there are now 20-year Comprehensive Programs and 10-year Perspective Plans, developed on the scale of the country as a whole and for individual republics and localities. These long-term documents are not obligatory plans, containing targets which the producing units are required to meet; but neither are they mere forecasts. They embody fundamental planning choices, concerning the development of cities, the location of industry, the forms of scientific and technical progress and their association with the production process, the changing role of the educational system, etc. They are based on careful studies and projections, and seek to make explicit the most basic goals of advanced socialist construction. The long-term plans will be interlinked and continuously reformulated: the 10-year plan for 1981–1990, for example, will eventually give way to a 10-year plan, at the same level of generality, for 1986–1995.

The five-year plans are to be given greater importance, and to become, for the first time, the *operative* plans. This means, in particular, that FYPs will be installed for the individual enterprises; up to now the FYPs have been developed only at higher levels, and only the annual plans broken down to the producing units. Further, under the new rules the norms for deduction into the enterprise funds—called "appraisal indicators"—will be stable for the entire five-year period. The enterprises will therefore get the full benefit from achieving productivity goals and successfully introducing technical change, without having to worry about whether the norms will be revised before their efforts take effect.

An enterprise now has, in addition to the plan and the collective agreement signed with the trade union, an Enterprise Passport. This contains a complete specification of the enterprise's capacities and inventories of equipment, and the basic norms of their operation, developed not from achieved levels but from "substantiated" engineering parameters. The Passports are designed to help both in the formulation of plans and in the appraisal of results. For example in establishing a target for productivity increase, and in measuring the extent to which that target is met, the "base" level of productivity will not be some average of the level of current practice, but rather will be derived from *norms* which identify what is possible given the existing technology. . . .

The changeover to self-financing of enterprises is to be completed, and the attitude "don't worry; the state will make good any losses" uprooted once and for all. In this connection, the enterprise funds will be greatly increased in importance. Enterprises will have both the rights and the rubles to develop their own large-scale reconstruction plans. They will also have more control of their wages funds; following a successful experiment in which 1,200 enterprises participated, enterprises will be entitled to keep any part of the wages fund saved by reducing the workforce. (This is a dissemination of the Shchekino experiment of the early 1970s; it is of course carefully monitored by the trade unions as well as the management bodies so that the saving is carried out by means of innovation, not speedup or overloading, and that the workers displaced are retrained and relocated to their own satisfaction.). . . .

A final innovation, which really deserves an article by itself, will be the extension of the brigade form of organization within the enterprise. There have always been teams, or brigades, of workers in the enterprises—face-to-face groups of workers small enough so that each member of the brigade can know every other. These are the basic production collectives. What is new is that the brigades will increasingly be going over to self-financing and responsibility for developing and fulfilling their own plans. This, of course, takes place within the enterprise plan, which in turn falls within the plan of the industrial association and the overall industry-wide and economy-wide plans; brigade planning represents a new step in the iterative chain, which only becomes possible when the technology of information flows and the economic and political level of the workforce have developed to a sufficient degree. Together with a rise in the responsibility and importance of the brigade, there is a certain shift toward collective piece rates—wages paid in proportion to output achieved, but not by each individual, rather by the collective as a whole. This is a form of *material* incentive which promotes *collective* consciousness, and which can only be developed when skill and consciousness levels, and differentials, make it possible. . . .

It should be apparent from even this cursory survey that Soviet socialist planning is in a very exciting stage of its development. Planning technology, including the use of optimal programming, modeling, mathematical techniques, computerized information processing and transmission, is developing by leaps and bounds (in this regard we may note that the computer industry, as a priority industry and a special project of the 10th FYP, continues to grow at more than twice the rate of industry as a whole). More people than ever before are involved in the planning process. Both central planning (as seen in the almost 75 per cent increase in the number of commodities planned centrally) and decentral planning (the emergence of enterprise FYPs, self-financing, and planning at the brigade level) are expanding. The plan indicators are becoming more sophisticated and powerful. . . .

Soviet planners at all levels make use of a variety of indicators, both as plan targets, or goals, and as measures of performance. Above, the ideal of a single indicator—realized net rate of return—was mentioned. Why, then, do planners still rely on a list of indicators—per cent fulfillment of contracts, net productivity increase, per cent reduction in cost, share of high-quality products? Isn't there still a possibility that some of these goals may conflict with others? It would appear that the level of information (quantity; quality) available at present does not permit the formation of a single, reliable indicator; to unify the indicators ahead of the real possibilities would result in loss of information and planning distortion. The Soviet position on the tradeoff between multiple and unified indicators must be determined by the concrete development of planning in that country.

All in all, and mindful of the disappointing trend in growth rates, there is good reason to suggest that the USSR is entering a *third stage* in its planning system; one which brings the comprehensive planning mechanism of the second stage to fruition by perfecting the indicators, bringing the decentral planning process off of paper and into existence, and streamlining central planning so that it can concentrate on fundamentals. . . .

Compare Soviet economic performance with that of the capitalist countries, and there is ample reason to reaffirm the view that socialist planning is not the cause of Soviet problems; rather it is a vital part of their solution. The problems indeed only appear as problems against the background of the monumental achievements of the Soviet economy: stable growth; full employment; financially sound cities, transportation, medical and educational systems; elimination of poverty and social disorganization; a degree of income and wealth equality unknown elsewhere; rapid social and cultural development. . . .

SOVIET VIEWS

8. THE SOVIET ECONOMIC SYSTEM*
Constitution of the USSR, Articles 10–18

Article 10

The foundation of the economic system of the USSR is socialist ownership of the means of production in the form of state property (belonging to all the people), and collective farm-and-co-operative property.

Socialist ownership also embraces the property of trade unions and other public organisations which they require to carry out their purposes under their rules.

The state protects socialist property and provides conditions for its growth.

No one has the right to use socialist property for personal gain or other selfish ends.

Article 11

State property, i.e. the common property of the Soviet people, is the principal form of socialist property.

The land, its minerals, waters, and forests are the exclusive property of the state. The state owns the basic means of production in industry, construction, and agriculture; means of transport and communication; the banks; the property of state-run trade organisations and public utilities, and other state-run undertakings; most urban housing; and other property necessary for state purposes.

Article 12

The property of collective farms and other co-operative organisations, and of their joint undertakings, comprises the means of production and other assets which they require for the purposes laid down in their rules.

The land held by collective farms is secured to them for their free use in perpetuity.

The state promotes development of collective farm-and-co-operative property and its approximation to state property.

Collective farms, like other land users, are obliged to make effective and thrifty use of the land and to increase its fertility.

---

* Reprinted from *Constitution (Fundamental Law) of the Union of Soviet Socialist Republics*, Moscow: Novosti Press Agency Publishing House, 1978, pp. 23–28, by permission of the publisher and of the Copyright Agency of the USSR.

Article 13

Earned income forms the basis of the personal property of Soviet citizens. The personal property of citizens of the USSR may include articles of everyday use, personal consumption and convenience, the implements and other objects of a small-holding, a house, and earned savings. The personal property of citizens and the right to inherit it are protected by the state.

Citizens may be granted the use of plots of land, in the manner prescribed by law, for a subsidiary small-holding (including the keeping of livestock and poultry), for fruit and vegetable growing or for building an individual dwelling. Citizens are required to make rational use of the land allotted to them. The state, and collective farms provide assistance to citizens in working their small-holdings.

Property owned or used by citizens shall not serve as a means of deriving unearned income or be employed to the detriment of the interests of society.

Article 14

The source of the growth of social wealth and of the well-being of the people, and of each individual, is the labour, free from exploitation, of Soviet people.

The state exercises control over the measure of labour and of consumption in accordance with the principle of socialism: "From each according to his ability, to each according to his work." It fixes the rate of taxation on taxable income.

Socially useful work and its results determine a person's status in society. By combining material and moral incentives and encouraging innovation and a creative attitude to work, the state helps transform labour into the prime vital need of every Soviet citizen.

Article 15

The supreme goal of social production under socialism is the fullest possible satisfaction of the people's growing material, and cultural and intellectual requirements.

Relying on the creative initiative of the working people, socialist emulation, and scientific and technological progress, and by improving the forms and methods of economic management, the state ensures growth of the productivity of labour, raising of the efficiency of production and of the quality of work, and dynamic, planned, proportionate development of the economy.

Article 16

The economy of the USSR is an integral economic complex comprising all the elements of social production, distribution, and exchange on its territory.

The economy is managed on the basis of state plans for economic and social development, with due account of the sectoral and territorial principles, and by combining centralised direction with the managerial independence and initiative of individual and amalgamated enterprises and other organisations, for which active use is made of management accounting, profit, cost, and other economic levers and incentives.

Article 17

In the USSR, the law permits individual labour in handicrafts, farming, the provision of services for the public, and other forms of activity based exclusively on the personal work of individual citizens and members of their families. The state makes regulations for such work to ensure that it serves the interest of society.

Article 18

In the interests of the present and future generations, the necessary steps are taken in the USSR to protect and make scientific, rational use of the land and its mineral and water resources, and the plant and animal kingdoms, to preserve the purity of air and water, ensure reproduction of natural wealth, and improve the human environment.

9. THE ECONOMIC SYSTEM OF THE USSR*
Novosti Press Agency

A real socialist society has been created in this age by the effort and through the struggle of the working class and the masses led by Communists. The word *socialism* is associated in the minds of millions of men and women in different corners of the globe with the living example of the Soviet Union and the community of socialist countries.

In different socialist countries the new social system is in different stages of maturity. In the USSR, an advanced socialist society has been built. A knowledge of its economic basis and political superstructure, of the principles on which the life of the state and society is organized, and of the ideology, law and morals prevailing in it, help one to form a well-rounded picture of socialism as the first phase of communism.

PUBLIC OWNERSHIP AND THE PURPOSE OF PRODUCTION

Economic Foundation of Socialism

In the Soviet Union the means of production belong to society. This determines the nature of the relations of production, of the socialist eco-

---

* Reprinted from *Fundamentals of Political Knowledge*, (no author given), Moscow: Novosti Press Agency Publishing House, 1980, pp. 78–105, by permission of the publisher and the Copyright Agency of the USSR.

nomic system. In the land of Soviets there is neither a class deprived of the means of production nor a class of private owners. Nobody there is privileged or, conversely, unfavourably placed with respect to ownership of the means of production. As a result, it has become impossible to turn the means of production into capital, and to turn labour power into a commodity[1]. *Public ownership rules out the exploitation of man by man.*

Where there is no exploitation, and people may not appropriate the products of the labour of others, one's own work is the only lawful source of livelihood.[2] Public ownership rejects parasitism, living on others, and imposes on all an equal duty to work.

As the products of labour are placed at the disposal of society and are then distributed among people, remuneration of labour depends entirely on national wealth: the richer the society, the better off are its members. They all have an interest in the growth of socialist production. Common economic interest brings people together. *The socialist relations of production are relations of co-operation and mutual assistance between workers who are free from exploitation.*

Development of the socialist national economy is determined by the united will of the whole of society which is the owner of the means of production, not by any disunited and conflicting actions of separate groups or individuals. Public ownership rules out anarchy in production,[3] economic crises and unemployment, and makes it possible (and also necessary) to plan the development of production consciously and purposefully. In other words, the predominance of public ownership means that production is no longer ruled by the blind, spontaneous laws of capitalism, but is subject to the *economic laws of socialism* which are studied and utilized by society. . . .

In the Soviet Union, the bulk of the means of production and other material values is in the possession of the socialist state, i.e. it is *state (or public) property*. The state, on behalf of the people, enjoys all the rights of the property owner, including alienation of property (e.g., it may sell machinery and other goods to foreign countries).

State property is for the use of all Soviet people. Workers in the factory use machines and machine tools; scientists use the research equip-

---

[1] In Marxist terminology, a "commodity" is a produced good that is sold on the market. Under Soviet conditions, consumer goods are considered commodities; producer goods are not because they are not for sale proper, but are allocated to the productive units, even though the latter may be charged a price for them on the enterprise's and the state's record books. Under capitalist conditions, labor power, according to Marx, is also a commodity that is bought and sold on the market like any other commodity. [Editor's note.]

[2] Although not specifically spelled out here (as it usually is in official documents), it is understood that this applies only to able-bodied citizens and that a Socialist society takes care of its children, its disabled, its old. [Editor's note.]

[3] Marxists assert that under capitalism there is "anarchy of production." In other words, production is not centrally planned, and so the system proceeds by trial and error. For example: in a town a hamburger stand makes a lot of profit, so competitors start opening up others, until there are too many, and some of them have to go out of business. Under socialism, the necessary number of such hamburger stands as well as their location would be centrally planned. [Editor's note.]

ment at scientific centres and laboratories; students have the use of school buildings, tools at workshops and instruments at laboratories.

It is not, however, individuals, but state organizations and enterprises—part of the great political whole—that dispose of state property.

Managers of enterprises and organizations are given powers by the state to dispose of material values, while working people are granted the right to control the executives' actions.

Two Forms of Socialist Property

In the Soviet Union, the state owns the bulk of the means of production. Simultaneously, some of the means of production and other material values belong to working peasants' associations, such as collective farms and other co-operatives. State property and collective farm-and-co-operative property are of a similar nature, being two forms of public, socialist property, on which the socialist relations of production are based.

Besides these principal forms of socialist property, there is also the property of trade unions and other public organizations, which they require to carry out their purposes under their rules.

The main distinction between the different forms of socialist property is the extent to which the means of production are socialized. State property consists of the means of production socialized on a national scale; they, therefore, are the property of the people as a whole. Collective farm property consists of the means of production socialized on a scale of an individual agricultural enterprise; they, therefore, are the property of a group of people.

State ownership plays the leading role in the system of socialist ownership. This is so not only because it extends to all the basic means of production. Thanks to state ownership, all parts of the national economy are linked together so that the economy can be developed according to a single plan. State ownership prompts citizens to have national interests at heart and to think in terms of the well-being of the country as a whole.

This does not mean that those whose work is connected with collective farm property are in a worse position than others. As a part of the people, they are co-owners of state property. Collective farm property is a form of property which corresponds to today's level of development of the productive forces in the countryside, and creates conditions for increasing production.

As there are two forms of socialist property, so there are some distinctions in remuneration of labour. Those employed at state-run factories and organizations receive money wages and salaries. Collective farmers receive payment in cash and kind in proportion to their contribution to the common economy and depending on the farm's income. They also have subsidiary small holdings from which they may derive additional income.

Under a 1969 party and government decision, collective farmers now draw guaranteed monthly payment for their work at the farm. This reduces the difference between remuneration of labour in agriculture and industry.

One part of a collective farm's income goes to form *the consumption fund* from which the collective farmers are paid for their work. The other part goes to *the indivisible fund*.

The indivisible fund consists of the means of production, farm machines, implements, collective-farm power plants, transportation facilities, buildings intended for production and cultural purposes, work and commercial livestock, and materials and money intended for expanding collective-farm production. This fund may not be used to make payment to members or drawn upon to make payment due those leaving the collective farm.[4]

The indivisible funds have been created by the efforts of collective farmers, with the help of of the entire Soviet people. Thirty years ago collective farm property consisted of the socialized means of production of the peasant economies, i.e. horses, ploughs, harrows, and other implements. Today it consists chiefly of tractors, combines, lorries and other machines produced at the country's socialist industrial enterprises.

The two types of socialist enterprises also differ in the forms of management.

The manager of a state-run enterprise is appointed by the state and is accountable to it for the performance of the enterprise. The supreme body of a collective farm, on the other hand, is a general meeting of its members which elects the board and chairman. Collective farmers deal with questions of organization and management of the farm on the basis of the country's laws and Collective Farm Rules; they adopt plans, proceeding from the interests of both their farm and the state, approve reports, decide on the distribution of income, and so on.

The socialist state maintains close economic contact with collective farms. It supplies them with farm machines, fertilizers, and selected seeds; organizes the training of farm managers and agricultural specialists; maintains a veterinary inspection service; promotes the dissemination and introduction of advanced know-how; grants credit to collective farms; and buys produce from them.

Personal Property

Besides public property, there is also personal property under socialism. It may include articles of everyday use, of personal consumption and convenience, the implements and other objects of a small holding, a house, and earned savings.

---

[4] In other words, the machinery, tools, and equipment that constitute the "indivisible fund" are not the personal property of any one collective farmer, but belong to the collective farm as such, for use by its members. [Editor's note.]

Under the Constitution, citizens may also be granted the use of plots of land for a subsidiary small holding (including the keeping of livestock and poultry), for fruit and vegetable growing or for building an individual dwelling. Citizens are required to make rational use of the land allotted to them, and the state and collective farms provide assistance to citizens in working their small holdings.

Personal property under socialism has nothing in common with capitalist private property.[5] Its basis is earned income, and it may not be used to the detriment of the interests of society or as a means of deriving unearned income.

As national wealth increases, more and more products become available for the satisfaction of citizens' private needs. Accordingly, personal property tends to increase. This process is regulated through a system of payment according to the quantity and quality of work done, through a price policy for consumer goods, and through the development of social consumption funds, which we shall discuss further on.

The personal property of citizens and the right to inherit it are protected by the state.

The Goal of Socialist Production

In a society where the means of production belong to the working people, production is carried on in the interests of society as a whole, and the goal of production is not profit but the well-being of citizens.

Socialist production serves the purpose of raising the people's living standards; this is not only evidence of the humane nature of the socialist system, but also *an economic necessity*. Satisfaction of the people's material, and cultural and intellectual requirements is essential to the development of the main productive force of society, i.e. people.

In conditions of the scientific and technical revolution, production not only satisfies the traditional requirements (food, clothing and shelter), but also gives rise to new wants. Before anybody wanted a TV set or a refrigerator, they had to be designed and produced, and their cost had to be at a level at which the mass of consumers could afford to buy them. And for this, products must be turned out on an ever larger scale, and their quality must be continually improved. This applies not only to the consumer goods industries, but also to heavy industry, which turns out machines, equipment, and other means of production for all branches of the national economy.

To raise the people's living standards it is necessary to meet both their material and their cultural and intellectual requirements, to satisy their thirst for knowledge and for mastering the treasures of national and

---

[5] More specifically, by Marxist terminology, *personal* property refers to consumer goods, which under socialism or communism, as well as under capitalism, belong to their individual owners. Capitalist *private* property, on the other hand, refers to the private ownership of the means of production in capitalist societies. [Editor's note.]

world culture. In socialist society, the need for "intellectual nourishment" grows rapidly, and to satisfy this need, more and more money is invested in public education, the film industry, the press, radio and television, and in the building of new theatres, libraries, palaces of culture, and so on.

All this can be created—and it is being created—by the collective effort of the people, on the basis of public ownership and the utilization of the achievements of science and technology. The development of science and engineering is what makes it possible to expand and perfect production in line with the aims of socialism, and to ensure a steady growth of labour productivity, national wealth, and people's well-being.

Thus, the main economic law of socialism consists in uninterrupted development of production on the basis of collective work and advanced technology, for the sake of the fullest possible satisfaction of the constantly growing material, and cultural and intellectual requirements of all members of society.

Under capitalism too, material and cultural goods are produced, and their consumption, on the whole, increases. Nevertheless, if we compare the goals of capitalist and socialist production, we see that there is a fundamental difference between them. The goal of capitalist production is to secure profit, and the production of use values is merely a means towards that end. The goal of socialist production is to attain higher material and cultural standards for the people.

PLANNING

What Planning Is About

Every enterprise in a socialist country is a part of a single economic organism united by public ownership of the means of production. The latter belong to one master—the people. And where there is one master, there is one common goal and one programme of action—the plan.

The plan is a state document which distributes available resources among the industries and sets the targets with respect to the growth of production and living standards, development of culture, the volume of home and foreign trade, and so on.

Planned economic development is one of socialism's major advantages over capitalism. For the first time in its long history, society exercises control over the conditions of production and carries it on purposefully and systematically, saving much social labour in this way. Society rids itself of the destructive effects of competition and anarchy in production and is free from economic crises.[6]

Conscious economic regulation does not mean, however, that plans are drawn up without due consideration of a great many interrelated fac-

---

[6] In Marxist terminology, as well as in nineteenth-century economic terminology in general, the word "crisis" refers to what today we would call recession or depression. [Editor's note.]

tors. Obviously, we cannot plan the construction of new factories unless we know that there will be enough raw material for them. We cannot raise the target for shoe production in the coming year ten times because it is impossible to get the necessary additional raw material all at once.

This leads us to an important conclusion, namely, that planning reflects the operation of one of the objective economic laws of socialism—*the law of balanced, proportionate development of the national economy*. This law, which makes economic planning possible, requires that the different branches of the economy should be in a definite proportion to each other or be adjusted in size relative to each other.

Utilizing the law of balanced, proportionate economic development, the state establishes and maintains the desirable proportions of the different economic sectors. But that does not exclude the possibility that partial disproportions may arise as a result of errors or natural disasters. Such disproportions are temporary and cannot lead to the destruction of productive forces, to unemployment or economic crises.

One way of dealing with these partial disproportions is provided by government reserves. Socialist society creates reserve stocks of raw materials, fuel, consumer goods and money so as to allow production to proceed under all circumstances and, most important of all, to ensure that people do not suffer from shortages, should there be a natural disaster.

Birth of the Plan

Plans must reflect the objective law of balanced, proportionate development of the economy. State bodies must master this law and learn to apply it and draw up plans in line with it.

Plans may be *short-term* or *long-term* (i.e. drawn up for some years ahead).

Long-term planning is the more important. It shows most clearly the capacity of a socialist state to foresee the course of economic development and, moreover, its capacity to carry out a system of effective measures determining the overall trends of economic development.

What kind of indicators are included in long-term plans? Long-term plans set the rate of development of production and the proportions of different sectors in this development, and determine the amount of investment to be made in each industry, republic, and economic area; they provide for the construction of new industrial centres, major enterprises and roads and highways and the technical reconstruction of different industries and enterprises. In the Soviet Union long-term plans are usually drawn up for a period of five years. . . .

Long-term plans are carried out on the basis of short-term (yearly) plans. Short-term plans make it possible to control the step-by-step fulfilment of the long-term plan and to adjust the targets set by the latter so as to make them more exact and concrete.

An important part in determining what targets should be set by the plan belongs to the drawing up of *balances*. The idea of a balance in this case directly corresponds to the meaning of the word, i.e. a state in which no one part overweighs another.

Every balance consists of two parts, namely, receipts and expenditures. The first part keeps account of all available resources, and the second, of all expenditures to be made during the period covered by the plan.

When all the balances have been drawn up and co-ordinated, the final draft of the plan is submitted for approval to the highest state legislative bodies. After it has been approved, the plan becomes law and is binding on all. Should the plan fail to be observed or fulfilled in any one industry, it will harm the entire national economy, for the other branches of production, transport, trade, finances, and so on, will be affected.

The plan-regulated development of the Soviet economy ensures its high growth rates and makes it possible to increase national wealth and raise the people's living and cultural standards. . . .

Prices

In the capitalist economy, prices are formed spontaneously at the market. In conditions of socialism prices are established by the state in accordance with the state plan (except for collective-farm market prices),[7] with account taken of various economic and political circumstances, but primarily on the basis of the value of the goods produced.

The price of a commodity is usually set so that it is as close as possible to its value, i.e. the amount of labour expended on its production. The more exactly the price reflects the value of a commodity, the easier it is to see how profitable this or that kind of equipment, raw material or production process is.

Utilization of the law of value[8] makes it possible to provide material incentives to the introduction of new technology and improve the organization of production. This helps to ensure the growth of labour productivity and reduce the cost per production unit.

In some instances, however, the state deliberately allows prices to deviate from value. This is done in the interest of increasing social production and promoting the well-being of citizens. It is done, for example, when it becomes necessary to use part of the income produced in some sectors to accelerate development of other sectors that are of vital importance for the national economy, or to regulate consumer demand and thus also the pattern of consumption. For example, prices of chil-

---

[7] Prices on the collective-farm market are not established: they vary, depending on supply and demand. At the same time, these prices are influenced by the state, as the bulk of the produce of collective farms is sold at fixed prices at state-run shops.

[8] By value, or exchange value, as Marx uses the term, is meant the average labor time necessary in that particular stage of economic development, with the given stage of technology and the means of production available ("socially necessary" labor time, Marx called it). [Editor's note.]

dren's goods are often lower than their value while some goods (cigarettes, vodka, etc.) are sold at prices higher than their value. Hence, in a socialist economy deviation of prices from value is permitted when it serves the interests of society as a whole.

Money under Socialism

Money performs its usual functions also under socialism. All commodities are compared in value to money commodity, so that it serves as an instrument for measuring their value. Gold is the money commodity under socialism too.

Money is indispensable to trade. It is *the means of circulation*, without which nothing can be bought or sold.

When wages and salaries are paid to factory and office workers; when socialist enterprises get loans from the State Bank and when they pay them off; when tax and insurance payments are made; when money income is distributed among collective farmers; in short, whenever money changes hands without anything being bought or sold, money performs its function as *a means of payment*.

Money is also *a means of accumulation*. Plants, factories, and state and collective farms keep their earnings and spare money at a State Bank. The state uses these accumulations and savings to expand production, create reserves, and provide loans to various enterprises and organizations.

There is a vast difference in the role money plays in capitalist and socialist society. Under capitalism money turns into capital, becoming a means of exploitation and appropriation of the labour of others. Under socialism, money cannot turn into capital; it cannot buy a factory, a plant, labour, land, a power station or anything of that kind. In capitalist conditions money is the instrument of the spontaneous market laws. In a socialist state, money is used as the universal means of keeping account of, and controlling, the production and distribution of goods, as a means of controlling the amount of labour and the amount of consumption.

Under socialism money is a necessary means of distribution according to work done. Paying money for consumer goods, citizens receive a share of the social product in proportion to the quantity and quality of the work done by them.[9]

The state judges the efficiency of an enterprise with the help of money. The money expenditures of an enterprise show the amount of labour required to produce a particular kind of goods, and the amount of raw material and fuel expended in the process; the wear of equipment; they show the cost of management, and the cost of transporting goods and of delivering goods to the consumer. Money control over the per-

[9] See footnote 2 above. [Editor's note.]

formance of socialist enterprises is an effective method of economic management.

An important role in the settling of accounts between socialist countries is played by the transferable rouble—a collective socialist currency. It forms the basis of the currency system of the Council for Mutual Economic Assistance[10] and helps perfect financial relations among its member countries.

MANAGEMENT OF THE ECONOMY

The socialist economy, owing to its planned character, opens up good opportunities for stable and rapid economic growth. Such opportunities are not, however, realized spontaneously, but through a system of economic management.

This system implies the use of diverse techniques and methods. In order to master it, one must have a good theoretical grounding and sufficient practical experience. To begin with, let us see what the basic elements of this system are.

Each socialist enterprise (a plant, factory, mine, power station, state or collective farm, etc.) is a socio-economic unit, a group of people working in a certain branch of the economy. The purposes, rights and duties of state enterprises are set out in the Socialist State Industrial Enterprise Regulations, and those of collective farms, in Collective Farm Model Rules.

An enterprise has the necessary means of production, such as machines, equipment, materials, raw material, fuel, transportation facilities, and so on. All this forms its *production assets* which fall into two large groups, namely, fixed assets and assets in turnover.[11] Fixed assets include industrial buildings and installations, equipment, transmission facilities (electricity grids, pipelines, etc.), transportaiton facilities, and instruments and tools. Assets in turnover consist mainly of raw material and basic and auxiliary materials, purchased semi-finished products, fuel, spare parts, and the money with which to buy all this.

The overall indicator showing how efficiently fixed assets are utilized is *the output-capital ratio*[12] or output per invested rouble. By increasing the output-capital ratio, an enterprise can raise output with the fixed assets it has, without additional investment. The output-capital ratio can be increased by different methods, and is a reliable yardstick of production efficiency.

[10] The Council for Mutual Economic Assistance, often abbreviated as COMECON, CEMA, or CMEA, is roughly East Europe's equivalent of West Europe's Common Market. [Editor's note.]

[11] In English-language Marxist terminology, usually referred to as fixed and circulating capital. [Editor's note.]

[12] In professional literature, usually called capital-output ratio. [Editor's note.]

Socialist society sees its interest in utilizing available resources as effectively as possible. The more economical is the use of raw material, fuel, electric power and other means of production, the greater the output at the same cost.

Economy can be achieved not only by a thrifty use of raw material and basic and auxiliary materials, but also by increasing labour productivity. A steady rise in labour productivity, improvement of technology, systematic lowering of the expenditure of human labour, thrifty use of raw material and basic and auxiliary materials, fuel and electric power, and reduction of waste and spoilage in production are all indispensable to economy. In short, economy is the method of socialist management which consists in producing more quality goods at minimum expenditure of the means of production and labour. The principal means towards this end is the operation of enterprises on *a profit-and-loss basis*.

This means that an enterprise must pay its own way, always earning more than it spends. Only an enterprise that makes more than it spends is profitable and can contribute money to the State Budget and help meet social needs, as well as expand its own production and provide additional material incentives to its labour force.

Socialist enterprises have a sort of gauge which accurately registers their efficiency. It is *product cost* which shows how much an enterprise spends in order to produce a certain kind of good.

In calculating the cost of the product, account is taken of the expenditures on raw material and auxiliary materials (lubricants, paints, etc.), fuel and electric power, depreciation (i.e. compensation for the wear of the instruments of labour—buildings, machines, and equipment), and wages and salaries; deductions for social insurance; and administrative expenses. When the expenditures are added up, the total is divided by the quantity of output and the cost of a production unit is determined. Thus, *cost is what an enterprise spends in terms of money on the manufacture and sale of its products*.

Profit and Profitability

By looking at the cost indicator we can see how an enterprise is getting along. But it does not tell much about its performance from the standpoint of the interest of the country's economy as a whole. For that we need to turn to other indicators, namely, *profit and profitability*.

Profit is the difference between wholesale price and output cost; in other words, it is that part of the surplus product made by the labour force of an enterprise which remains at the disposal of the enterprise after its products have been sold (or realized).

Under socialism, the profit of an enterprise cannot become unearned income. It has nothing in common with capitalist profit, as it is used for the satisfaction of the needs of society as a whole and of its members.

Compared with the cost indicator the profit indicator gives a more complete picture of the performance of an enterprise.

The effort to bring down cost often conflicts with the effort to improve ouput quality. Additional outlays made by an enterprise to raise quality of its products may result in substantial savings in the utilization of the products. For example, aircraft engines of improved design enable the country to save thousands of millions of roubles. But such additional outlays increase cost. If we judge the performance of this enterprise by cost only, we may get the impression that it has become less efficient, as the cost of output has increased. But, if we judge its performance by the amount of profit it earns, we shall conclude, quite correctly, that its performance has improved: its profit increased since high-quality goods fetch a higher price. Thus profit, when it is due to improved quality of output, is to the advantage of both producer and consumer.

Needless to say, setting a target for profit does not make cost reduction less important.

But the total sum of profit does not yet tell everything about the performance of an enterprise. To appraise that, one should also use the indicator of profitability, which expresses the relationship between the amount of profit earned and the cost of the fixed assets and assets in turnover.

LABOUR AND DISTRIBUTION

One of the most important changes in the conditions of work under socialism consists in full employment. In 1930, the last labour exchange in the USSR closed its doors, and since then the younger generation of Soviet citizens know what unemployment is only from books and from newspaper reports from capitalist countries.

Soviet people have an opportunity to choose their trade or profession, type of job and work in accordance with their inclinations and abilities, with due account of the needs of society. Every citizen is guaranteed free vocational and professional training and education. Everything is done to enable young people to find jobs without difficulty or delay. Every enterprise has a definite number of jobs reserved specially for secondary school leavers.

Soviet law safeguards factory, professional and office workers from unlawful dismissal. The management may fire an employee only in cases specially provided for by the law, and that only with the consent of the trade union committee. A dismissed worker has the right to take the matter to court, and should the latter find that his dismissal was unlawful, it will not only have him reinstated in his job, but will make the management pay him for the time of his enforced absence from work.

As the productive forces advance, *working hours are reduced*. Workers have more and more time left for leisure, education and private life.

By far most of the factory, professional and office workers in the Soviet Union have a five-day workweek, with two days off. At enterprises where the character of production and the conditions of work make it inexpedient to have a five-day week, employees work six days, with one day off, but their working day may not be longer than seven hours. According to the Soviet Constitution, the number of hours in a workweek may not exceed 41. Doctors, those engaged in arduous jobs, and those under 18 years of age have a shorter workweek. Adolescents under eighteen, although they work shorter hours, are paid the same wages as adults working full time on the same job.

Overtime work is strictly limited in the Soviet Union. The management may ask personnel to work overtime only as an exception, and that with the permission of the trade union.

Those engaged in arduous jobs, besides working shorter hours, have longer holidays.

Every worker is expected to know safety rules well, and some workers have to take a special examination in industrial safety rules.

Labour discipline is strengthened under socialism through efficient organization of production and a well thought-out system of moral and material encouragement of both individual workers and whole work collectives.

The present level of the productive forces is not yet high enough to allow the introduction of the communist principle of distribution, the gratuitous satisfaction of everybody's needs irrespective of their individual contributions to the public coffer. On what principle, then, are material goods distributed under socialism?

Distribution under socialism must promote the steady growth of national wealth and simultaneously provide for a continuous rise in the living standards of every working man and woman. These requirements are fully met by the socialist principle, "From each according to his ability, to each according to his work," i.e. remuneration of labour depending on its quantity and quality.

Payment according to work performed makes it possible to implement another economic principle of socialism, i.e. the principle of *making every worker economically interested in the results of his work*. The better a person works, the more he gives to society, the higher his pay. This prompts people to work to the best of their ability and improve their qualifications.

Besides wages, which are the chief source of citizens' incomes, a large proportion of their material, and cultural and intellectual requirements are satisfied at the expense of what is known as *social consumption funds*.[13]

---

[13] For greater detail on consumption and social welfare, see Ch. VII below. [Editor's note.]

Even at the dawn of Soviet government, when the first boarding schools, crèches and similar institutions appeared, Lenin called them "the shoots of communism", and he bade us to cherish them and build them up. Today there is a whole system of such institutions in the Soviet Union. Free public education and health protection, old-age and disability pensions, government grants for students, family allowances, and many other kinds of social insurance are all financed from public funds.[13]

The main purpose of the socialist emulation movement is to achieve the best results in work. Socialist emulation also means helping those who lag behind advanced workers, it is an effort to achieve an overall upsurge of production. While in a capitalist economy every technological improvement is kept secret from competitors, under socialism emulation facilitates rapid and broad introduction of all innovations.

One important aspect of socialist emulation is its character-building influence. Taking part in socialist emulation, one develops qualities essential to every working person, such as resourcefulness, industry and purpose. Upholding, together with his comrades, the honour and prestige of his factory, collective farm or organization gives a worker a sense of identity with his collective, makes him feel responsible for its success and fires him with a desire to become better and better at his trade.

Reproduction

Reproduction, or a constant uninterrupted renewal of the process of production, is a necessary condition of society's existence.

When social production does not grow, and is of the same size year after year, we have simple reproduction, in which case the expended material values are merely replaced. But when the volume of production increases, we have expanded reproduction, in which case society does not merely replace the expended material values, but produces additional means of production and articles of consumption.

Let us see to what laws socialist reproduction is subject, and how the new material values produced are distributed.

The total amount of material goods produced in a society over a definite period (e.g., a year) form *the aggregate (or gross) social product.*

In its physical form, the aggregate social product is divided into the means of production and the means (or articles) of consumption. Accordingly, there are two big subdivisions of social production: *Subdivision I—Production of the means of production, and Subdivision II—Production of consumer goods.* With reference to industry, these subdivisions are called respectively Group A and Group B.[14]

What conditions must be present so that all enterprises would be

---

[14] Perhaps somewhat more precisely, Group A and Group B refer to the respective goods produced by Subdivision I and Subdivision II. [Editor's note.]

able to satisfy their needs for raw material, fuel and plant, and all citizens would be able to buy at the shops the articles of consumption they need, and, consequently, production would be able to continue?

First of all, there must be enough output in Subdivision I to replace the means of production consumed, i.e. to make up for the wear of machines and buildings and replace the expended raw materials, fuel, and so on; and then, to provide for the further expansion of social production as a whole.

Simultaneously, as many articles of consumption must be produced in Subdivision II as are necessary for the fullest possible satisfaction of the needs of all citizens. The rate of expansion of production and the rate of technological progress of the industries in Subdivision II depend above all on the amount and quality of the means of production provided by Subdivision I. Hence the absolute need for *priority growth of the production of the means of production*.

The law of priority growth of production of the means of production means that, with the help of correct planning, those industries are developed faster which accelerate technological progress and assure higher productivity of labour in all other industries.

Production of the means of production is not, however, an end in itself. Means of production are needed, after all, in order to produce more articles of consumption and improve the people's living standards. For this reason, the development of heavy industry is accompanied by a continuous growth in the production of the means of consumption.

If we look at the aggregate social product in terms of its value, it will amount to the sum total of values produced in all spheres of material production.[15] It falls into two parts. One part goes toward replacing the means of production that have been expended. Actually, this is *"old" value*, which, with the depreciation of the means of production, is transferred to the manufactured products. The other part is designed for personal consumption as well as for the expansion of production, maintenance of the workers engaged in non-productive spheres, and accumulation of reserves. All new value produced makes up the *national income*. In material terms, national income consists of the means of production and of consumer goods, i.e. raw materials, basic and auxiliary materials, machines, machine tools, bread, sugar, clothing, footwear, books, and so on. Apart from that, national income is calculated in terms of money.

Total national income is divided into *an accumulation fund* and *a consumption fund*.

---

[15] In Soviet national income accounting, only *material goods* are counted. In other words, direct services not rendered in the process of producing material goods (such as the services of a doctor, lawyer, or even a planner) are not counted as part of total output. [Editor's note.]

The consumption fund is used for the satisfaction of personal and social needs. It is divided into a wages fund from which are paid the wages and salaries of those engaged in material production, and a social consumption fund which is expended on the remuneration of labour of those engaged in science, public education, the cultural field and the health service; on social security; and on the maintenance of state machinery and the armed forces. The consumption fund comes to about three-quarters of the total national income.

The accumulation fund falls into three parts. One is used for the expansion of production; another, for the capital construction of social facilities, such as schools, hospitals, kindergartens, crèches, houses, and so on; and a third forms a reserve and insurance fund. The accumulation fund is of great importance, for no expanded reproduction is possible without it.

All funds, with the exception of that part which is placed directly at the disposal of socialist enterprises, are centralized. This is achieved with the help of *the state budget.*

The income and expenditure plan of the budget is the basic financial plan of the socialist state. It shows where the means come from and for what purposes they are to be spent.

Means are channelled to the state budget from the socialist enterprises as a part of their net income, and from the collective farms in the form of income tax. Personal income taxes make up only a small part of the state budget.

Society of Working People

With the building of socialism, the class pattern of society undergoes a radical change. As private property and the exploitation of man by man disappear, so do the exploiting classes, while the labouring classes and sections of society become quite different from what they were before, and the entire system of social relations acquires a new aspect.

The workers are the most numerous class in Soviet socialist society. They account for almost 62 percent of the country's population.

Owing to the central role it plays in production, its rich political experience, the high level of its political and social awareness and its good organization, the working class plays the leading role in society. The working-class party—the Communist Party, which is the political vanguard of the Soviet people—organizes and guides the development of society.

The other principal class of Soviet socialist society is the peasantry, which accounts for 15.7 percent of the population. The peasants began to develop along the socialist path in the 1930s.

Along with material incentive to work, there are under socialism also moral incentives. The latter emerged immediately after the victorious

October revolution. The emancipation of labour from exploitation aroused tremendous enthusiasm among the masses and inspired them with a desire to build a new society and make life happier for everyone as quickly as possible. That was a great moral incentive to work.

How material and moral incentives are combined is seen best of all in the socialist emulation movement.

The farmers come ever closer to the working class in conditions of work and cultural standards. Collective farmers work in large socialist economies based on joint work and use of machinery.

The development of industry, urban growth and increasing mechanization of agricultural labour reduce the proportion of farmers in the country's population.

The intelligentsia is a rapidly growing section of Soviet society. They are, for the most part, trained experts engaged in material production, science, technology, the cultural sphere, the health service and public education, and in state and social administration.

Under socialism, the ranks of the intelligentsia increase as more and more people from the other classes and social groups join them; they are closely linked with the people and serve their interests.

Belonging to one social section or another carries with it no political privileges. All citizens in the USSR enjoy equal rights in administering the state and have the same duties to the state. There are no clear-cut border lines between classes in Soviet society. If they wish, workers may become farmers, and vice versa; young men and women from working-class or peasant families may pursue intellectual professions after appropriate academic preparation. Such mobile boundaries between classes are evidence of their drawing together.

Clearly linked with this is another feature of social relations in the Soviet Union, that is, the social, political, and ideological unity of society in which the working class is the leading force. This unity arises from the fact that, socially, all working people in socialist society enjoy equal rights and have the same basic interests; politically, they are united by the building of communism under the guidance of the Communist Party; and ideologically by Marxism-Leninism. . . .

The triumph of socialism has brought about some other major changes in social relations. Socialism has done away with the antithesis of mental work and physical labour, and of town and country—that ugly feature of the exploitative formations. It has abolished the social conditions under which intellectual work was a special domain reserved for the propertied classes, and the villages could be exploited by the towns.

At the same time, it would be wrong to think that under socialism all problems have been solved. In the course of building a classless communist society, essential distinctions between mental and physical labour and between town and country will have to be abolished, and conditions provided for a gradual disappearance of distinctions between classes.

10. THE SOVIET AND THE U.S. ECONOMIES: CLOSING THE GAP*

Boris Ponomarov and Valentin Kudrov

One in every five manufactured products in the world today is made by Soviet workers. This, let us note for the sake of comparison, is more than the whole world produced in 1950. The Soviet Union has the world's second largest economic potential, with only the United States, the richest Western nation, ahead. Moreover, the gap is steadily narrowing.

Soviet industrial production, which, for example, in 1950, was less than one-third of American was upwards of 80 percent of the US industrial output in 1979. Further change can be expected, perhaps, by the end of this year (1980); for the first six months of 1980, Soviet industries showed a 4.2 per cent rise, while American industries showed a five percent decline.[1]

Over the period 1970–1979, national income in the USSR grew 57 per cent, whereas in the USA it grew only 33 per cent; industrial output in the USSR grew 72 per cent, whereas in the USA, only 41 per cent. As a result, the gap between the levels of economic development of the two countries has narrowed considerably. The national income of the USSR is now almost two-thirds of that of the USA.

Four-fifths of the national income in the USSR is used directly for consumption, housing and cultural construction. Real wages grew on an average by more than 15 per cent during the period 1975–80, while the income of collective farmers grew by 26 per cent. On the whole, real per capita income grew 17 per cent over the past five years, and doubled over the past 15 years.

Over the next five years it is planned to ensure a further 16 to 18 per cent increase in the real per capita income of the population.

The Soviet Union leads the world in oil production (its output was a mere 14 per cent of American production in 1950), steel production (the 1950 output was 30 per cent of the American), mineral fertilizer (as against 31 per cent of the American output in 1950) as well as in the production of pig-iron, coke and cement, and the output of trunkline diesel locomotives and grain harvesters. Western commentators usually argue that

---

* This selection has been put together from two sources. The third, fourth, and fifth paragraphs are from a TASS summary of an article by Boris Ponomarov, scheduled for publication in the *World Marxist Review*, as published in English in *New World Review*, March–April, 1981, p. 3. The rest is from Valentin Kudrov (Guest Editorial, courtesy Novosti Press Agency), "Soviet Economy: Closing the Gap," *New World Review*, November–December, 1980, pp. 3–4. Reprinted here by permission of the publisher, the Novosti Press Agency and the Copyright Agency of the USSR.

[1] According to the CIA's 1981 *Handbook of Economic Statistics*, pp. 38–39, Soviet industrial output in 1980 rose by 3.6 percent, and U.S. industrial output dropped by 3.5 percent. [Editor's note.]

this has been achieved at the consumer's expense. However, the USSR has moved to the fore in production of many consumer goods as well. For example, the Soviet Union now produces nearly as much butter as the next three leading producers, West Germany, the USA and France, put together. The USSR is making 1.5 times as much sugar out of its own sugar beet crop as the United States, nearly twice as much leather footwear and cotton fabrics, and four times as much woollen fabrics. These items provide a considerable proportion of the national revenues both of the USSR and the United States.

The Soviet Union is the only major industrialized country to have virtual self-sufficiency in home-produced energy resources. However, the shifting of major production centers into the little developed eastern areas (these now contain almost 90 per cent of the surveyed Soviet reserves of oil, coal, natural and casing-head gas and hydropower resources) makes for a rising rate of capital consumption by the fuel and energy producing industries. These absorb about one-third of the entire Soviet industrial investment even at this juncture. Considering also manpower shortage in the country's eastern regions, the complexity of the energy supply situation is quite obvious.

However, the system of economic planning provides for solutions to this problem. Work is nearing completion on an integrated national power grid. New enterprises in non-ferrous and ferrous metallurgy, chemical, pulp-and-paper industries will be built predominantly in the country's eastern areas, close to the sources of low-cost fuel. Energy-producing capacities totalling 5.3 million kw were installed at nuclear power plants in 1976 through 1979.

In 1980 the Soviet plan is to produce over 600 million tons of oil and gas condensate, more than 700 million tons of coal and 435,000 million cubic meters of natural gas.[2] That means that the USSR will keep its lead in the world's oil and coal-mining industries, while sharply increasing the production of gas (its output has more than quadrupled in the last 15 years). This will enable it not only to supply the growing national industrial demand, but to continue exporting coal, oil, gas and other energy-bearing minerals (the Soviet Union exported 2,400 million tons of fuel in the 1970s).

The USSR is lagging behind the USA for the time being in some important lines of production, as plastics, synthetic fiber, motor vehicles, electronic equipment, paper and cardboard. It is still considerably outdistanced in the production of electricity even though the Soviet Union (with its overall output of 1,239,000 million kwh in 1979) is ahead of Japan, West Germany and Canada, put together (which rank third, fourth and fifth in the world respectively).

[2] Actual output figures for 1980, according to Soviet sources, were 603 million tons of oil and gas condensate, 716 million tons of coal, and 435 billion cubic meters of natural gas. (*Pravda* and *Izvestia*, Jan. 24, 1981, p. 1) [Editor's note.]

The United States, which has a longer industrialization record, does have greater industrial efficiency. However, the integrated system of management and planning provides advantages to the Soviet economy, allowing it to concentrate efforts and resources in major areas. For example, there has been particularly rapid progress over the past decade in the industries crucial to technological progress—power, machine-building, chemical and petrochemical industries. Their growth rates today are twice as high as they were in 1970.

In the last ten years the USSR has doubled its output of manufactured goods. The United States has taken 16 years to double its industrial production, West Germany 17, France 18 and Great Britain 26 years. Moreover, in contrast with the USSR, the pattern of growth rates in most of the industrialized Western countries and, above all, the United States, looks very much like that of the temperature of a fevered patient with its ups and downs.

However, although the dynamics of production in the USSR does look quite good against the background of the Western countries, the tone of the comments by Soviet leaders and the press is very critical. The possibilities and advantages of planned economy are not always turned to account in full.

There has been a process of recasting the system of planning and management and one of improving the performance of all the sectors of the economic machinery in the USSR in the past few years. The need for this has arisen, above all, from determination to maintain high and stable growth rates under changed economic circumstances.

The Soviet economy had been developing for years through the enlistment of fresh resources. At present, with a giant economic potential available, there has to be a different approach to economic growth. The new strategy, which will determine the development of the Soviet national economy in the next few decades, lays emphasis on intensive growth factors and fuller and more rational utilization of the material, manpower, financial and natural resources involved in production.

11. ECONOMIC ADVANTAGES OF SOCIALISM*

Editorial
Press Bulletin

It is true that, on occasion, a few capitalist countries reach rates of industrial development and growth of national income close to or even

---

* Reprinted from "The Advantages of Socialism," *Press Bulletin* (USSR Embassy of Canada), May 1977, p. 8, by permission of the publisher and the Copyright Agency of the USSR.

higher than the USSR's. And some people may ask as a result, what then are the advantages of socialism.

The first point to note is that these high rates are achieved only by a few capitalist countries and only for limited periods.

The occasional economic "booms," from Western Germany to Japan, mean only that capitalism has found, and will certainly go on looking for, economic reserves.

In the recent past crises spread throughout the whole capitalist world. . . .

In our country we have stable progressive development without crises or recessions—and that is possible because it rests on public ownership [of the means of production].

Of course, economic growth is not the only indicator of the advantages of a particular system.

The most important is the way the national wealth is distributed.

It is plain to see that in the richest capitalist countries there is a tremendous gap between the luxury of some and the poverty of others.

Historically speaking, socialism is young. It is only 65 years since the first steps were taken to create it—and those steps were, it must be stressed, taken by a country which was far from socially and economically advanced.

It is therefore natural that though we have made great leaps forward, we still lag behind certain countries in production and consumption of certain goods.

This is a situation the Soviet mass media make no attempt to conceal.

Moreover, we admit that we have something to learn from other countries in technology, organization of production, and trade.

Incidentally, the West also learns many things from us.

State planning, originated by socialism, wins more and more supporters in the West.

And many of the developing countries get inspiration from us in building their economies.

There is one important thing that should never be overlooked.

Under socialism production and consumption are not ends in themselves.

Nobody in a socialist country works for somebody else.

That explains why the Soviet worker is usually eager to help develop new technology.

He is in a completely different position from the Western worker, who is afraid that automation and the introduction of new machinery and new processes will threaten him with unemployment.

Confidence in tomorrow, the feeling of freedom and the feeling of involvement in all the affairs of one's factory, collective farm and the country as a whole—these are, in my view, the main advantages of our socialist system, our Socialist way of life.

12. PROBLEMS OF MANPOWER SHORTAGE*
Yuri Berezhnov
Correspondent, TASS News Agency

The recent period, which in the capitalist world has been marked by an unprecedented growth of unemployment, is distinguished in the USSR by a further growth of the diametrically opposite difficulty—a shortage of manpower. And in the period from 1981 to 1990 the absolute growth of the able-bodied population in the Soviet Union will decline to less than a third of what it was in the previous decade.

BIRTH RATE

The causes of this phenomenon are common knowledge. One of them is the decline in the birth rate as a result of remote consequences of the Second World War. Another factor which must be taken into account is that young people are increasingly involved in education now that universal secondary education has been introduced in the USSR. The reserves have been drawn in to the limit: more than 94 per cent of the able-bodied population have already been brought into the socialized economy.

Is there a way out of this situation, bearing in mind that nearly two million jobs are vacant in the USSR's national economy, and the demands of the economy are growing?

The new mills and factories of Siberia, the Far East and other regions will alone require in the near future from 800,000 to a million workers annually.

The way out is obvious—it is necessary to continue increasing labour productivity all over the country. In 1970–79, despite a certain slowing down in its growth rates due to a number of reasons and in the first place to irregularities in raw material supplies, labour productivity rose by 42 per cent, whereas in the USA the corresponding increase was only 17 per cent.

AUTOMATION

Secondly, investments are distributed in such a way as to finance, above all, the reconstruction of existing mills and factories. The mechanisation

* Reprinted from Yuri Berezhnov, "Economic Growth with a Shortage of Manpower," *Soviet News*, Feb. 17, 1981, p. 1, by permission of the publisher and the Copyright Agency of the USSR.

and automation of manual operations, especially loading and unloading, as well as other jobs, from which millions of workers can be released, will be actively stimulated.

Owing to these and other measures, it is planned to increase the productivity of socialised labour in 1981–85 in conformity with the draft Guidelines for the Social and Economic Development of the USSR by 17 to 20 per cent and to ensure through this at least 85–90 per cent of the increase in the national income. In industry this index will show an even more considerable growth—23 to 25 per cent—and in the socialised sector of agriculture: 22 to 24 per cent.

PRODUCTIVITY

In many branches of the economy—agriculture, oil refining, the coal and fishing industries, non-ferrous metallurgy and others—it is planned to ensure that the increase in output takes place almost entirely through more productive work.

It must also be stressed that in the early 90s the situation in the field of labour resources will improve. These resources will increase through the generations of the 70s—a period when the birth rate again increased.

The acceleration of scientific and technical progress and the rational use of labour resources are two problems which must be solved. The approach to be used in the 11th and subsequent five-year-plan periods gives grounds for hoping that the Soviet economy will successfully cope with the shortage of manpower which so far exists in the USSR.

VII
Living Standards and Social Welfare

"The Party and the government are consistently taking measures to raise the living and cultural standards of Soviet people. The slogan 'everything for the sake of people, for the benefit of people' is law in our country and we shall unswervingly follow it."

>   LEONID I. BREZHNEV,
>   Late Secretary-General, CC CPSU and Chairman,
>   Presidium of the Supreme Soviet

"To achieve steady advances in the economy and the improvement of the people's well-being—this is both our responsibility to the Soviet people and our international duty."

>   YURI V. ANDROPOV
>   Secretary-General, CC CPSU

"The CPSU sets the historical task of achieving in the Soviet Union a living standard higher than that of any of the capitalist countries."

>   Programme of the Communist Party of the
>   Soviet Union

INTERNATIONAL COMPARISONS of living standards are by no means easy. While Western observers and Soviet analysts acknowledge that living standards are higher in the United States and in most of Western Europe, even an approximation of how much better off the U.S. citizen is than his Soviet counterpart is not only difficult but also open to subjective interpretation. There are fifty percent more doctors per thousand population in the Soviet Union than in the United States and their services are offered free of charge, but medicines and hospital supplies are much more readily obtainable here than there. The Soviet worker spends some 3 or 4 percent of his income on rent as compared with some 20 percent for the American worker, but in the major cities especially, apartments are often hard to come by, are on the average much smaller, and often have fewer amenities than those in American cities. Theaters, concerts, movies, and sport events are either free or very low-priced in the USSR, but there are many more color television sets and telephones per hundred families in this country. Income taxes, which so greatly reduce the take-home pay of American workers, are very low in the Soviet Union and there are no wage deductions for social security at all. But a good part of the Soviet citizen's expenditures on consumer goods may go for the payment of the "turnover tax"—that difference between the cost of producing and marketing a consumer good on the one hand, and the price charged to the consumer on the other. This difference varies from negligible or even negative amounts in the case of commodities the Soviet leadership wants to encourage (such as children's shoes or books) to high percentages in the case of low-priority consumer goods (reportedly well over 100 percent on vodka, for instance). Warm underwear, fur coats, and fur-lined boots are essential consumer goods for the citizens of Novisibirsk and Vladivostok; air conditioning is a high priority item for the inhabitants of Los Angeles and San Diego. The services of real-estate agents, stock brokers, investment counselors, tax consultants, or corporation lawyers do not constitute a part of the expenditures of Soviet citizens, but time-consuming trips to the collective farm markets on the edge of town to get good cuts of meat or high-grade fruits or vegetables are not necessary for the American shopper, who can purchase his groceries readily at the neighborhood supermarket.

Apart from such discrepancies as the ones mentioned above, international comparisons of living standards, especially between countries with such diverse economic systems as the US and the USSR, are difficult to make for other reasons also. Per capita income, for instance, can become a meaningless concept, unless income distribution is taken into consideration. An "average family income" of $100,000 per year does little good to ninety-nine families in a hundred-family community in which one family earns $10,000,000 per year and the other ninety-nine nothing. While this example may be too drastic an illustration, the fact remains that extremes of wealth and poverty are incomparably greater in the United States than in the USSR; in the former, the median family income is thousands of dollars per year less than the average income,[1] while in the case of the latter, the average is not thrown off by multi-million ruble incomes on the top. Counting for comparison's sake only the income of workers (or only incomes directly generated by work), as some Soviet social scientists have proposed, would make more sense from the point of view of an ideology which rejects rent, interest, and profits as sources of individual incomes.

[1] The "median" is a "middle" number, with no more than 50 percent of the items above and no more than fifty percent below that number. By "average" is usually meant the "arithmetic mean," a number obtained by adding all the items and dividing by the number of items.

The frequent comparisons in Western popular magazines of how many minutes or hours it takes for John (an average American worker) as compared with Ivan (an average Soviet worker) to buy a pair of shoes, a television set, or a small automobile are often scientifically invalid. This is not only because of the kinds of goods usually selected for such comparisons—which rarely include those cheaper in the Soviet Union, and almost never services provided at virtually no cost[2]—but also because purchasing power per hour of wage-income has little significance to the worker who is unemployed, or involuntarily works only part time, for much of the year—and there is widespread unemployment in the United States as compared with a labor shortage in the Soviet Union.

The income of Soviet workers, under the present system "on the road to communism," is supposedly distributed according to the quantity and quality of their work. But in international comparisons of living standards, Soviet writers always emphasize also the public consumption fund, which distributes goods and services free of charge (such as education), not according to work performed but according to citizens' needs—consumption, in other words, the cost of which is born by society at large rather than by the individual consumer. And beyond that part of income per se, the knowledge that it is available, and the security that it will be forthcoming when needed is presumed to also have a substantial impact on the quality of life of Soviet citizens. Here is how the late party leader Brezhnev put it in his address to the Twenty-Fifth Party Congress in 1976:

> One of the great achievements of socialism is that all Soviet citizens are assured of their future. Their work, their abilities, and their energy will always find fitting use. Their children will be given a free education. Society will never abandon them in case of misfortune. They will be given given free medical treatment, a pension in the event of permanent disability, and security in old age.

Although there may be some dispute as to the *precise* per capita value of such consumption from the public consumption fund in the USSR, there is no doubt that it plays an important role in the economic well-being of the Soviet citizen and leaves the Soviet workers a large percentage of their income for such expenditures as food or clothing.

No matter how one measures it, there is no denying that the living standard of the Soviet citizen today is considerably higher than it was at the time of Stalin's death. It is also considerably higher than the living standard of most any country in Asia, Africa or Latin America with such possible exceptions as Israel, Japan, and perhaps Taiwan, and probably higher also than the living standard in many Western countries such as Portugal, Turkey, Greece, or Puerto Rico, especially if one accepts the Soviet proposal to compare income of workers only, i.e., if one excludes

---

[2] More scientific studies, published in professional journals, are more likely to take such goods and services into account.

from any comparison those classes in society which derive the major share of their income from the ownership of wealth, rather than from their labor. On the other hand, Soviet economists acknowledge that overall consumption of material goods in the USSR still lags behind the United States and most of Western Europe, although they emphasize that the gap, such as it is, has been narrowing. The selections in this chapter are intended to be illustrative not merely of consumption and social welfare as it has developed in the Soviet Union over the years, but also of the somewhat divergent views as to what constitutes the "good life."

In the first selection under "Western Views," Gertrude E. Schroeder and Barbara S. Severin trace the development of Soviet consumption and income over a quarter of a century, from 1950 to 1975. The editor has added a column for 1978 to the first two tables in the selection to bring them more up to date, and has supplemented the selection with a brief section by M. Elizabeth Denton on the outlook for the 1980s. Schroeder and Severin find that the Soviet citizen's living standard in 1975 was two-and-a-half times what it had been in 1950 but conclude that it is nevertheless still far below that of his Western counterpart. They would probably not agree with Robert Knight, chief of the *U.S. News & World Report* Bureau for Moscow who, after spending three years in the Soviet Union in the late 1970s, wrote that he had the impression that over the last two decades "sufficient progress has been made to keep most people happy and content."[3] But other Western observers of the Soviet scene would seem to agree with Robert Knight. American correspondent Marc Greenfield, for instance, wrote recently:

> This is the first generation of Russians since their revolution that has not known war or starvation, and their living standards, though low by our criteria, are higher than most Russians can remember.
> As for freedom, they seem to find enough of it in Russia's vast open spaces and in freedom from economic insecurity. With jobs guaranteed by the state, people can spend their last ruble without worrying about the next paycheck.[4]

In December, 1982, the Joint Economic Committee of the United States Congress released a long and rather technical report on Soviet economic growth and development from 1950 to 1980, prepared by the U.S. Central Intelligence Agency, that shows very considerable achievements and great improvements in living standards. The second selection under "Western Views" consists of a brief summary of the CIA's findings as reported in a press release by the Joint Economic Committee of the United States Congress.

---

[3] *U.S. News & World Report*, July 16, 1979, p. 26.
[4] Marc Greenfield, "An American's View of Life in Moscow," *San Francisco Chronicle*, Jan. 26, 1983, p. F 6.

Fitzroy MacLean, next, also acknowledges "enormous advances" over the past quarter of a century. However, like other Western (and Soviet) observers, he finds supplies still often inadequate to meet rising demands, and quality and variety still well below what is available in the West. But he focuses his article less on that than on what he sees as the rise of consumerism and the development of different lifestyles and of a new class structure in the Soviet Union that has taken the place of "the standardization of Stalin's days and the control which went with it."

The fourth selection, taken from the 1981 *Europa Yearbook*, provides a brief introduction to the USSR's social welfare system.

Sara Harris, originally from New York but married to a Soviet journalist and permanently residing in Moscow with her two children, where, in 1978, she pursued her studies for a Ph.D. degree in economics, gives a Western Marxist's insight into life in Moscow on a relatively low family income of 300 rubles per month. While money needs to be watched somewhat with so low an income, she still has nothing but praise for what she describes as a highly satisfactory life style, concluding that "our family is able to live a full, healthy life, without skimping on that most important element—the children, their health, their security, their education and their future."

In the first two selections under "Soviet Views," Moscow Univerity Professor Margarita Bunkina and Novosti Press Agency commentator Gennadi Pisarevsky draw comparisons between living standards in the USSR and in the West. They readily concede that "to this day the standard of living in the USSR is still below the average standard of living in such developed capitalist countries as the United States, West Germany and others"; but they try to make a case against "biased bourgeois press reports" which depict living conditions in the Soviet Union as much less favorable than they actually are and neglect areas of relative advantage for the Soviet citizen, be they low prices of such necessities as food staples and transportation, stable rents, unchanged for over half a century, or free education and medical care. In the final selection under "Soviet Views," put together from two separate articles by Borris Rakitsky and Pyotr Margiev and a Novosti Press Agency booklet, the authors focus their attention first on the Soviet Union's "social consumption funds" per se, and then specifically on three areas for social welfare measures in the USSR, namely housing, health and old age. As regards old-age pensions, it should be pointed out that Soviet citizens automatically "retire" when they reach a certain age—men at age sixty after twenty-five years of work, women at age fifty-five after twenty years, and both earlier in numerous professions and jobs deemed "strenuous or hazardous to health." But "retiring" merely means going on pension and does not mean that the worker has to stop working. The last section of this selection addresses itself to the topic of the pensioner who continues to work.

WESTERN VIEWS

1. SOVIET CONSUMPTION AND INCOME
1950–1975*

With some supplemental data for the latter half of the 1970s and predictions for the 1980s

Gertrude E. Schroeder

University of Virginia

Barbara Severin and M. Elizabeth Denton

Economic Analysts, U.S. Central Intelligence Agency

Meeting in the Kremlin in early 1976 for the 25th Party Congress, the leadership of the Soviet Communist Party could look back with both pride and frustration on the fruits of its policies affecting the welfare of the population over the preceding quarter century. The period (1950–1975) was one of relative peace and quiet, witnessing none of the upheavals of the preceding 25 years—the advent of central planning, the collectivization of agriculture, the political purges, World War II with its catastrophic loss of life, property and production in the economy. Even with restored output by 1950, the population had benefited little from the advent of socialism. Per capita consumption was not much above the level of 1928 or 1913, and the goods and services provided were primitive and inferior in mix and quality, even for a semi-developed country. The subsequent quarter century has brought great progress, particularly in quantitative terms. By 1975, the level of living of the Soviet people was more than double that of 1950 and had gained significantly relative to industrialized countries of the West. Qualitative gains were much less spectacular. . . .

* Except for the last two sections, reprinted from Gertrude E. Schroeder and Barbara S. Severin, "Soviet Consumption and Income Policies in Perspective," *Soviet Economy in a New Perspective* (A Compendium of Papers Submitted to the Joint Economic Committee, Congress of the United States, October 14, 1976), Washington D.C.; U.S. Government Printing Office, 1976, pp. 620–739. The section before the last on "Outlook for Consumption in the 1980's," is reprinted from M. Elizabeth Denton, "Soviet Consumer Policy: Trends and Prospects," *Soviet Economy in a Time of Change* (A Compendium of Papers Submitted to the Joint Economic Committee, Congress of the United States, October 10, 1979) Vol. I, Washington, D.C., U.S. Government Printing Office, 1979, p. 776. The last section on "Prospects for a Market Alternative," is reprinted from Gertrude E. Schroeder, "The Soviet Economy on a Treadmill of 'Reforms'," *op. cit.* p. 340.

I. CONSUMPTION—THE RECORD

A. Overall

During the period 1951–75—the Fifth through the Ninth Five-Year Plans—per capita consumption of all goods and services increased about 2.6 times, an average annual rate of 4 percent. Progress was uninterrupted but quite uneven, with the greatest gains being made during the 1950's. After relatively low rates of growth during the early 1960's, per capita consumption accelerated in the late 1960's, only to be followed by another slowdown during the early 1970's. Poor agricultural performance was the main cause for the slowdown in consumption in both 1961–65 and 1971–75. The slowdown affected all categories of consumption except household services. In contrast to the pre-war years, consumption of goods and household services rose more rapidly than communal consumption (state-provided education and health). Despite such rapid progress, per capita consumption in the U.S.S.R. is still only about one-third of that in the U.S. and well behind that of Western Europe. The disparities are even greater when allowance is made for the inferior quality and limited assortment of Soviet goods and services.

B. Food

Although it is the slowest-growing category, per capita food consumption has more than doubled in real terms during the past quarter century. Year-to-year gains have varied widely, depending on the size of the harvest. In addition to quantitative gains, the quality of the diet has improved markedly in a direction typical of developing countries—more meat, milk and vegetables and less bread and potatoes. The average person ate over twice as much meat in 1975 as he did in 1950. Per capita consumption of fish and vegetable oil also doubled, while that of eggs, sugar and fruit more than tripled. In contrast, per capita consumption of potatoes was half what it was in 1950, and consumption of grain products has declined. Even so, the average Soviet citizen still gets about half his daily calories from bread and potatoes and eats less than half as much meat as do his counterparts in the U.S. and Western Europe. Moreover, in 1975, consumption of bread and potatoes still exceeded the "rational consumption norms" established by Soviet statisticians for long-range planning purposes by over one-fifth, and consumption of meat, milk and eggs was below these norms by over one-quarter. Only for sugar and vegetable oil were the norms exceeded.

C. Soft Goods

Per capita consumption of soft goods expanded about four-fold during the past 25 years. Gains were nearly twice as great during the 1950's as during subsequent years. This group includes clothing, shoes, haberdashery, fabrics and a wide variety of other soft goods, ranging from soap to publications. Factory-made clothing has been rapidly displacing home-sewn garments, resulting in a slowing growth in consumption of fabrics and rapid growth in outlays on ready-made garments. The average person now buys three pairs of shoes per year, compared with only one pair in 1950, and the U.S.S.R. has now met the "rational norm" established for consumption of this item. The quality, style and variety of soft goods have also improved markedly, even though they still appear shoddy and drab by Western standards. Imports of these goods in recent years have added quality to the wardrobe of consumers affluent enough to pay the high prices fixed for them or having the credentials to purchase them at low prices in special stores not accessible to the general populace.

D. Durables and Miscellaneous Goods

In 1950, a consumer durable goods industry was almost non-existent in the U.S.S.R., and sales of durables and miscellaneous common household items represented only about 5 percent of total retail sales of non-food goods. A quarter century later the U.S.S.R. had developed sizeable capacities to produce ordinary durables such as sewing machines, washing machines, refrigerators, furniture, radios and TV's, and had established belatedly a moderate-sized passenger car industry. Sales of such durables in 1975 comprised about one-fifth of total sales of non-food goods. Overall, per capita consumption of durables and miscellaneous goods increased twelvefold during 1951–75, an average annual growth of 10.4 percent. Although most Soviet consumer durables are of poor quality and obsolete design by modern standards, ordinary durables, nonetheless, are becoming a feature of most Soviet households. Indeed, some families now own two or more of some durables. Automobiles are a striking exception, since only about 4 of every 100 families owned one in 1974—the consequence of the government's long delay in deciding to produce cars for sale to the population in large quantities.

By far the largest gains in consumption of durables took place during the 1950's, when explosive growth occurred in production of washing machines, refrigerators, vacuum cleaners and television sets from very low levels. Subsequently, growth in sales of such conventional durables slowed greatly, but after 1970 the number of automobiles sold at retail rose over eight-fold—from 123,000 to 924,000:[1] their sales probably approached 4 billion rubles in 1975.

E. Housing and Personal Services

Per capita consumption of services tripled during 1951–75, and in contrast to all other major categories grew more rapidly in the 1960's and 1970's than in the 1950's. This group consists of housing, utilities, personal transportation and communication, repair and personal care, and a variety of recreational and cultural services paid for by the population. Personal transport

---

[1] According to official data, total vehicle production for 1980 was 2,199,000 of which 1,327,000 were passenger cars. (*Pravda* and *Izvestia*, Jan. 24, 1981, p. 1.) Western sources predict passenger car output in the USSR in 1985 at 1,500,000. (Toli Welihozkiy, "Automobiles and the Soviet Consumer," *Soviet Economy in a Time of Change, op. cit.,* p. 815.) [Editor's note.]

and communication services grew most rapidly over the period, expanding over fivefold. In contrast, the total housing stock rose by only 75 percent, reflecting an increase in per capita living space in urban areas from 4.7 square meters in 1950 to 8.1 square meters in 1975 and somewhat larger gains in rural areas. The majority of urban families now have their own apartments, a great gain over earlier years, when most urban families shared kitchen and bath facilities with several neighbors. All housing now has electricity, and the use of gas is growing rapidly. Despite these visible gains, Soviet housing remains crowded, drab and monotonous and represents an area of great consumer frustration and relative neglect.

F. Communal Services

Government outlays on education and health services more than tripled over the past quarter-century, representing a growth in real per capita expenditures of 3.4 percent annually. Such expenditures now account for about 7 percent of gross national product, a large share for a country at the Soviet level of development. The two sectors have expanded at similar rates, and both have experienced reduced growth rates since 1965, a result consistent with slowing population growth. In education, this substantial effort has resulted in an increase in the median number of years of schooling of persons aged 16 years and older from 5.0 years in 1950 to an estimated 7.7 years in 1975. The goal of a universal ten-year (high school) education is close to being realized.[2] The large-scale investment in higher education is evidenced by the fact that 84 out of every 1,000 persons working in 1975 had completed college, and an additional 667 had some college or secondary specialized education; in 1959, the corresponding figures were 33 and 400.

In health, the Soviet effort is reflected in reductions in general and infant mortality rates to levels that compare favorably with those of Western industrialized countries. According to Soviet statistics, the number of doctors per 10,000 population rose from 14.6 in 1950 to 32.6 in 1975, and the number of hospital beds per 10,000 population rose from 56 to 118 during the same period. By all accounts, the quality of health care varies greatly among regions and is far better in cities than in rural areas and for elite groups than for the general population. Although the quality of both personnel and facilities may be poor by Western standards, the U.S.S.R. has developed a generally adequate public health system available to everyone without direct charge. The costs of such an extensive system have been kept low mainly by fixing low wages for health service personnel.

II. PERSONAL INCOMES

Along with rapid growth in quantities of goods and services consumed, the past quarter century has brought remarkable changes in the growth

---

[2] Virtually completely realized by the end of the 1970s. [Editor's note.]

and structure of personal incomes. First of all, money incomes have increased steadily and rapidly. The Table below presents the available data on disposable money incomes. In considering these data, it should be noted that they understate total current money incomes by several percent, because of the absence of data on such incomes as prisoners' wages, various kinds of money payments not included in the regular wage fund, receipts from sale of property and from private nonagricultural activities, and others. Per capita reported money incomes quadrupled during 1950–1975, rising somewhat more rapidly than per capita retail trade and household services (3.7 times). Incomes grew more rapidly during the 1960's (6.5 percent annually) than during the 1950's (5.2 percent annually). A cutback in growth to 1.9 percent annually was registered in 1971–75.

Table **4.** Growth of Money Incomes and Outlays Per Capita, 1950–75
[in rubles]

	Disposable money incomes	Money outlays on goods and services
1950	220.5	226.2
1955	282.8	287.5
1960	366.1	406.3
1965	492.9	499.1
1970	685.1	696.3
1975	871.6	842.1
Average annual rates of growth:		
1951–55	5.1	4.9
1956–60	5.3	7.1
1961–65	6.1	4.2
1966–70	6.8	7.0
1971–75	4.9	3.9

The rise in money incomes has been spread quite unevenly among major groups of the population. Nonagricultural workers experienced a growth in average annual money earnings of 3.1 percent annually. Average wages increased nearly twice as fast during the 1960's as during the 1950's. In the latter period the growth in earnings reflected mainly rising productivity and a higher level of skill and education of the labor force. Also, in this period the workweek was reduced by one-sixth, a major wage reform was carried out in the industrial sector, and the minimum wage was raised substantially. In the 1960's, the minimum wage was again raised—from 20–30 rubles per month to 40 rubles and then to 60 rubles per month. The wage reform along with large increases in wage levels was extended to the long-neglected service sectors. During the latter half of the decade, average wages were raised significantly as a result of increased bonuses paid from profit-based incentive funds established by the general economic reform launched by Kosygin in late 1965. The acceleration in the growth of money earnings, along with an even greater increase in the level of savings deposits, led to a policy of severely restricting the expenditure of incentive funds in 1971–75. Another round of wage reforms was launched and reportedly completed in the so-called "productive" sectors: it involved an increase in the minimum wage to 70 rubles per month, establishment of new wage scales and tightening of work norms, and increases in regional and other such pay differentials. Substantial wage increases were also made for major groups of workers in education and health.

Throughout the entire period, money wages of agricultural workers increased over three times as fast as wages of nonagricultural workers. In part, this spectacular growth reflects the monetization of the collective farm sector. In 1953, only about 40 percent of total wages paid to collective farmers by the farms was paid in cash; the rest was paid in kind. By 1973, nearly all wages were paid in money. As a result of this change, the large rise in agricultural procurement prices,[3] and a deliberate policy of gradually raising collective farm wage rates to the level of state farms, money wages of collective farmers increased at an average annual rate of 13.6 percent during 1951–75. At the same time, wages in state agriculture were raised more rapidly (4.9 percent annually) than wages of all other state employees (3.1 percent annually). . . .

With respect to consumption-in-kind, the evidence points unmistakeably to a steady decline in its share in total farm household incomes. One Soviet source reports that in-kind incomes (including in-kind payment from collective farms) comprised 15 percent of the total personal consumption fund in 1950, 12 percent in 1960, and about 8 percent in 1973. From this information, coupled with available data on farm and non-farm money incomes, it can be estimated that average farm incomes were 41 percent of non-farm incomes in 1950, 64 percent in 1960, and 86 percent in 1973. . . . Whatever the "true" figures may be, the term "revolution" is certainly appropriate to describe the large rise in farm incomes over the past 25 years, both absolutely and relative to non-farm incomes.

Another major development affecting the level of personal incomes is the rapid rise in transfer payments, which increased over 6 times during the past 25 years. These payments consist mainly of state pensions, var-

---

[3] Prices paid by the state for farm products sold to the state. Each collective farm is obligated to sell certain minimum quantities to the state at prices set by the state. Additional output over and above the required minimum can be sold either to the state also, at substantially higher prices, or on the collective farm markets where prices are determined by market forces of demand and supply. Alternately, the collective farmers may keep such additional output for their own use. [Editor's note.]

ious kinds of welfare benefits and stipends for students. In 1950, pension and welfare payments amounted to a mere 19 rubles per capita; in 1975 they amounted to 123 rubles. Their growth has been far more rapid than the growth in wages, reflecting not only gradual aging of the population and increasing wages (to which pensions are tied), but also large increases in minimum pensions and liberalization of other welfare programs. In the mid-1950's, a major reform raised pensions and disability benefits, liberalized eligibility requirements, and set minimum pensions of 20–30 rubles per month. During the 1960's, a formal system of pensions for collective farmers was established, patterned after the system for state employees and partially financed by the state budget. During 1971–75, pensions and benefits for various categories of workers were further increased, eligibility rules for collective farmer pensions were liberalized, and (in 1974) a system of family allowances for low income families was introduced. In 1972, stipends for students were increased by 25 percent.

Up to now, the discussion has concerned money incomes alone. Consideration of real incomes requires a price index that measures changes in the cost of living with reasonable accuracy. The index used in previous JEC studies to express per capita disposable money income in real terms is a combination of the official Soviet index of state retail prices and an index of prices on collective farm markets derived from official data. . . .

To provide an alternative to the official index and to give some idea of what actual price changes might have been, an "alternative" index was calculated; it is the price index that is implicit in a comparison of indexes of goods sold in the retail trade network in constant and in current prices.

Real per capita disposable money incomes grow quite a bit more slowly, when the "alternative" consumer price index is used as a deflator than they do when the official retail price index is used. During the entire period 1951–1975, the former shows a less than fourfold growth, compared with a more than fivefold growth shown by the latter index. The former increases more slowly than the latter in all periods, with the differences being greater in more recent years. . . .

III. SOME CONSEQUENCES OF SOVIET CONSUMPTION AND INCOME POLICIES

Since the early 1950's, Soviet policies in the area of consumption and personal incomes have reflected a large-scale effort to redress in part the gross imbalance in the economy which was Stalin's legacy. At the same time, the leadership strove to do so with a bare minimum of change in Stalinist arrangements for production and distribution of goods and services. Rapid growth in quantities of basic goods and services, along with essentially unchanged institutional arrangements over the past quarter century, has produced a number of serious problems in the consumer sector. The problems may be grouped in two categories: (1) those relating to provision of the mix and quality of goods and services that people want, when and where they are wanted, and (2) those relating to the presence of a large overhang of liquid assets in the hands of the population. The two groups of problems are related, as are the constraints on their solution imposed by current dogma and institutions.

A. Problems of Quality and Mix

By about 1960, the needs of the population for basic goods had essentially been met. People had enough to eat, and the quality of the diet had steadily improved; they also had minimum stocks of clothing and shoes and a few common durables. With basic physical needs satisfied and with rising incomes, the general seller's market long characteristic of the Soviet consumer sector came to an abrupt end. People began to buy selectively; they rejected goods of obsolete design and shoddy quality. . . . The current situation, does not involve an overall buildup of inventories relative to sales, but rather a selective build-up in stocks of particular goods.

In recent years, the Soviets have attempted to cope with inventory pileups of slow-moving goods by conducting nationwide sales at greatly reduced prices and covering the resulting losses for retail stores with budget subsidies. There is much lament in the press over the high cost of these sales. . . .

At the root of this persistent problem is the chronic inability of enterprises producing consumer goods to turn out products with the quality, design and mix that consumers wish to purchase. . . .

Another problem related to product mix concerns imbalances in the availability of complementary goods. Recent examples cited in the press include: a plethora of cameras and acute shortages of film; tape-recorders but no tape; lenses but no eyeglass frames; flashlights, transistor radios, electric shavers but no batteries. . . . An acute shortage of some random household items, such as meat grinders or bread boxes, frequently creates a hue and cry in the press, which ultimately results in large surpluses. Shortages of a product in particular geographic areas and surpluses in another are common, even though supply and demand may be balanced overall.

Press reporting on these indicators of pervasive imbalances in consumer goods markets in 1975 did not differ essentially from what it was 10–15 years earlier. The reasons for the chronic problems are the same. First, there is the "second class" status and secondary priority of the industrial sectors making consumer goods and of the distribution and service network catering to consumers. This situation prevails, notwithstanding [the late] Party Secretary Brezhnev's excoriation of those who treat consumer goods as a "second-class" sector. The true status of the sector is reflected in practice in the relatively inferior quality of materials and manpower allocated to the sector and the relatively low wages and generally inferior social status of trade and service jobs.

Second, incentives throughout the supplier-producer-transport-distribution chain are geared mainly to fulfilling plans for output or other activity measured in rubles or physical units or both. The change in labels introduced by recent economic reforms (from gross value of output to sales) and the addition of success indicators, such as profits and labor productivity, have not altered the fact that in actual practice the real priority attaches to fulfilling plans for output, with emphasis on physical measures. Moreover, when value indicators (cost, output, profits) are indeed used to measure and reward performance, they continue to be based on arbitrary prices set by administrative bodies in ever greater detail. As a consequence, some goods are "profitable" to produce and others "unprofitable", regardless of demand (e.g., spoons, but not knives and forks; sofas and armchairs, but not kitchen chairs). Some products are "profitable" for retail stores to sell (e.g., alcoholic beverages) and others bring losses because of low trade markups (e.g., fish, vegetables, canned fruit, eggs, jam, laundry soap and windowglass). Continuous tinkering with prices and success indicators during 1965–1975 has left the basic problems largely untouched. Although one or another abberration may have been removed, others have been created.

Third, although management of food processing and soft goods production is concentrated in the Ministries of Food and Light Industries, production of durables and miscellaneous household items is scattered among dozens of ministries. This sector has simply been allowed to grow like Topsy, much of it as side-line operations in enterprises in heavy industry. In 1975, 50 ministries and organizations were in charge of the production of such goods, whose share in output of heavy industry rose from 10 percent in 1970 to 12.4 percent in 1975. . . . In 1971, for example, 9 ministries produced 35 models of washing machines in 35 plants, only 11 of which were specialized.

Fourth, connections among the several links in the chain from materials supplier to producer to distributor to seller of consumer goods are administrative or bureaucratic rather than economic in nature. The U.S.S.R. has not found a method for ensuring that each link in the chain is rewarded or punished economically, depending on whether retail customers buy or do not buy a given product. A chemical plant making dyes, for example, cares only to fulfill its own plan as measured by the relevant rubles or tons; it is not affected economically by the fact that the printed cloth in which its dyes are used fades, or the colors run after the first washing by a Moscow housewife. For the most part, the worst that will happen is for the plant to be roundly scolded in *Pravda*. Although ultimately some feedback may occur, the mechanism is slow and cumbersome. The system of economic contracts, "direct ties," fines and penalties for contract violation has proved ineffective, and the multiple tinkerings with these arrangements over the past decade have improved matters only marginally.

B. Money Incomes, Goods Availability and Accumulation of Liquid Assets

Much attention and argument among Western analysts has centered on the question of the interpretation of these facts: (1) per capita savings deposits have been rising over the past two decades at an average rate of about 15 percent annually, more than twice as fast as both per capita disposable money incomes and per capita outlays on goods and services; (2) by 1975, per capita savings deposits had reached 357 rubles; (3) total savings deposits amounted to 91 billion rubles in 1975, equal to 43 percent of total retail trade turnover in that year and amounting to over 5 months' earnings for the average state wage and salary worker. These and similar data and calculations have been used, in particular, to suggest the presence of a sizable and perhaps growing amount of repressed inflation in the U.S.S.R. In other words, the rapid buildup in liquid asset holdings in the form of savings deposits is taken to mean that people are being "forced" to save, because the government has failed to provide the goods and services that people wish to purchase at their income level.

These facts and interpretations of them involve several issues. First of all, the true rise in consumer prices cannot be measured. While there are published data on price changes in official markets (state retail trade network and collective farm markets), these data have long been suspect. As indicated in II above, the implicit price index calculated by juxtaposing independent measures of real consumption and Soviet retail sales in current prices shows an average annual price increase of 1.3 percent over the past 20 years. The official Soviet indexes show almost no increase. Comparison of the two indexes suggests that a slow rate of price increases in official markets has been hidden by a faulty price index.

Second, by all accounts extensive "unofficial" or "parallel" markets coexist with official markets. There is no way to measure either the size of these markets or price changes in them. . . .

Third, there is the question of whether the state has been able to achieve reasonable balance between aggregate money incomes and aggregate money expenditures, allowing for a planned growth of savings at "normal" rates that one would expect. . . .

Fourth, questions arise about how to interpret the notable buildup of savings deposits. Why do people save in the Soviet Union? Is the savings rate abnormally high compared with other countries? . . .

Although comparisons are tricky, because there are no data on currency holdings in the U.S.S.R., the savings rate does not appear to be abnormally high in the U.S.S.R. . . .

IV. OUTLOOK FOR CONSUMPTION IN THE 1980's

The Soviet consumer has made admirable strides during the Brezhnev years even though progress has been uneven and the pace of improvement has slowed in recent years. As the 1980's approach, the leadership will find that substantial gains in consumer welfare will be even harder to achieve.

A change in basic weather patterns could frustrate Soviet plans for a large rise in farm output, particularly in the livestock sector, and increase dependence on grain imports.

The easy gains—large quantitative gains from a low base—have been made, and future achievements will depend largely on qualitative improvements. The Soviets traditionally are weak in this area because the present incentive system is not geared to rewarding innovation and improved quality.

Stringent projections for the economy as a whole in the early 1980's will increase competition among resource claimants for investment, labor, and foreign exchange. If the past is repeated, the consumer will lose this battle.

At the same time, changes in demand will maintain pressures for increased consumption. Although population growth will remain low, those in the 25–34 year age group will increase proportionately more, and these are prime consumption years. One mitigating factor is the fact that population growth will be greatest in those republics with the lowest relative per capita consumption. Growth in money incomes, even restrained, will put the greatest pressure on those consumer items with the poorest near-term prospects for growth—meat, high-quality durables, and personal services. Moreover, the traditional emphasis on mass satisfaction of basic consumer wants will make it difficult and costly to satisfy the more sophisticated and individualistic demands of the future.

V. PROSPECTS FOR A MARKET ALTERNATIVE

In the long run, radical economic reforms involving the introduction of market arrangements in some form might alleviate the chronic malaise in the consumer sector and boost productivity. To be effective, such NEP-like reforms would have to include abolition of directive plans for producing units, replacing central allocation of producer goods with market exchanges, freeing of most prices and introduction of incentives based on profits. Transition to such a system of "market Socialism" would surely result in serious economic difficulties in the short run, including inflation and unemployment, and rupture existing fabrics of political and economic power. The idea would be fiercely resisted by the state bureaucracy, where jobs, careers and political influence would be at stake, as well as by the Party bureaucracy, whose jobs and control over resource allocation would be threatened, along with, perhaps, its very raison d'etre.

Faced with uncertain long-term benefits, certain high short-run costs and strong opposition, a Soviet leadership of any presently foreseeable stripe likely would not opt to take such risks, even more since long-held ideological positions are also at stake. The Party probably would seriously consider NEP-type reforms only if it faced a severe economic crisis, such as evident economic paralysis, declining production and widespread popular unrest. As long as present working arrangements continue to yield modest, even if declining, increments in annual output, the leaders as well as the led, will probably prefer to put up with the familiar deficiencies of the system, rather than to embark on untried and ideologically distasteful paths with unknown payoffs and certain disruptive consequences. After 60 years of experiences with a Socialist economy run by government agencies nearly everyone seems to have devised ingenious ways to turn its shortcomings to his individual advantage.

2. RISING LIVING STANDARDS AND STEADY ECONOMIC GROWTH IN THE USSR: A BRIEF SUMMARY OF A NEW CIA STUDY*

Joint Economic Committee, Congress of the United States

The Soviet Union has experienced steady economic development and improving standards of living over the past 30 years, despite continuing problems, especially in housing, according to a study conducted by the Central Intelligence Agency[1] and released by Chairman Henry S. Reuss (D-Wis.) of the Joint Economic Committee.

The study (prepared for the Joint Economic Committee) reports that:

○ The standard of living of the Soviet people has improved rapidly during the past 30 years. Real consumption per capita nearly tripled, rising at an average annual rate of 3.5 percent. Still, So-

---

* Reprinted from Joint Economic Committee, Congress of the United States, *Press Release*, December 25, 1982.
[1] Central Intelligence Agency, Directorate of Intelligence, *USSR: Measures of Economic Growth and Development, 1950–80*, Washington D.C., (U.S. Government Printing Office) December 8, 1982. The study is a somewhat technical, detailed report on the Soviet economy and economic performance, consisting of four parts, i.e., "Gross National Product of the USSR, 1950–80" (by John Pitzer); "An Index of Industrial Production in the USSR" (by Ray Converse); "An Index of Agricultural Production in the USSR" (by Barbara Severin and Margaret Hughes); and "An Index of Consumption in the USSR" (by Gertrude E. Schroeder and M. Elizabeth Denton). [Editor's note.]

viet living standards remain well below those in the United States, Japan, and most of Europe, both East and West.

○ Availability of housing has increased very slowly, with per capita living space in urban areas in 1980 still remaining below the minimum norm for health and decency set by the government in 1928.

○ The quality of diet in the USSR has improved greatly, shifting toward a pattern of less reliance on bread and potatoes and more reliance on meat and dairy products—a shift typical of other countries as per capita income levels rise.

○ National economic accounts constructed for the Soviet Union along conventional Western lines confirm the Soviet economy has experienced rapid growth since 1950. The output of the Soviet Union in 1980 was about four times the level in 1950, the result of an annual average growth rate of 4.7 percent.

○ Measured in 1970 prices, expenditures on investment have climbed from 14 percent of GNP in 1950 to 33 percent in 1980. The growth of investment reflects partially the traditional Soviet emphasis on growth through rapid increases in capital stock. (In comparison, U.S. investment, including housing and inventory, has gone from 17.5 percent of GNP in 1950 to 13.8 percent in 1980). However, the growth rate for investment in the Soviet Union has slowed sharply from 11.5 percent per year for the 1950s to an average of 5.8 percent per year since 1960. (Comparable figures for the United States are 1.1 percent per year for the 1950s and 3.5 percent per year since 1960).

○ It is believed that total defense expenditures in the Soviet Union amounted to 11–13 percent of GNP in 1970 and have increased at an average rate just above the growth in GNP. Therefore, the share of GNP allocated to defense has increase slightly. (In comparison, defense spending in the United States was 7.4 percent of GNP in 1970 and 5.2 percent of GNP in 1981).

○ Total agricultural output (crops and livestock) increased at a rate of 4.3 percent in the 1950s, at a rate of 2.1 percent in the 1960s, and at a rate of 3.7 percent in the 1970s. (In comparison, total agricultural output in the United States grew 2.1 percent in the 1950s, 1.0 percent in the 1960s, and 2.3 percent in the 1970s).

3. THE RISE OF CONSUMERISM IN THE USSR*

Fitzroy MacLean

Correspondent, London *Telegraph Sunday Magazine*

The Soviet Union is developing in directions that are not always in accordance with the hopes and aspirations of its Founding Fathers or, for that matter, of the present Government. In the past decade a consumer revolution has dramatically raised living standards. At the same time a class structure has emerged. Together, these forces are changing the face of Soviet society.

Soviet citizens, unlike those of thirty or forty years ago, have come to expect a sustained improvement in living conditions. Though still infinitely patient and long-suffering by Western standards, they have become much harder to please. For most of them, prices are a secondary consideration to availability. Though there have been enormous advances over the past twenty-five years, the quality and range of goods in the big stores still do not compare with that in the West.

Even so, Russian shoppers can now choose among several makes of cameras, radios, tape recorders, and television sets—some made in the Soviet Union and some imported, probably from East Germany. There also is a larger range than formerly of clothing, shoes, groceries, furnishings, and sporting goods. And there is never any lack of customers buying them.

One immediate effect of the consumer revolution is a flourishing black or gray market to supply needs neglected by the State. In the Ukraine, for example, sailors—foreign as well as Russian—from the port of Odessa head for the nearest peasants' market and sell at several times their original cost whatever foreign cameras, radios, watches, tape recorders, perfumes, and nylons they have been able to smuggle in. The authorities wink at this.

Small-scale private enterprise is flourishing: dressmaking, plumbing, painting, electrical work, carpentry, bricklaying, and other trades. In theory all of these should be officially sanctioned and licensed by the State. In practice, however, the best way to get a job done is either to do it yourself or to employ a moonlighter working either in his spare time or on his employer's time—and using materials which, to judge by newspaper reports, often started life as State property.

A class of middlemen has sprung up in these gray areas of the economy which makes a good thing on the quiet out of wedding supply to demand by cornering desirable goods and releasing them at the most

---

* Reprinted from Fitzroy MacLean, "Pressure from the People," *Telegraph Sunday Magazine*, March 9, 1980, by permission of the publisher.

opportune and profitable time. Exactly how much they make by their illicit but nonetheless useful activities is a closely guarded secret. But one can be quite sure that they take into account that in general goods and services are in greater demand than money.

One important development is the privately owned automobile. Four or five million Russians now own cars. This scarcely compares with the West, but the number is increasing. Suddenly a growing number of Soviet citizens has become more mobile, more independent, and more status-conscious.

The internal combustion engine has brought trouble in its wake— road accidents, pollution, congestion, and crime. The photographs of "wanted" men outside Soviet police stations and the accompanying descriptions of their crimes attest to the high rate of auto theft.

In the Soviet Union cars are not marketed by slick, fast-talking salesmen. Demand still so greatly exceeds supply that there is no need for advertising. Nor are the cars displayed in glossy showrooms. With only two or three makes to choose from, a potential customer has little difficulty making up his mind. He places his order at the appropriate office and waits up to five years to be notified that it is ready to be picked up at a depot. He pays cash, and drives it away triumphantly. Spare parts are in short supply, but Russians are immensely ingenious, and here again a "fixer" with friends among drivers of official cars can be useful.

Nothing is more confusing than to try to form an accurate idea of the standard of living of various categories of Soviet citizens. Prices and earnings do not tell the whole story; there are other factors to be taken into account.

The average industrial wage is around $275 a month; agricultural workers earn less. Most wives work. (In theory there is equal pay for women, though, as elsewhere, women seem to be employed mainly in the lower paid jobs.) A couple with two children, earning about $600 a month, will spend $300 a month on food.

But this is only a beginning. In the Soviet Union the State is the producer, importer, and retailer of practically all goods and services as well as the universal landlord and universal employer. It is therefore in a position to fix all prices, rents, and wages and to regulate the availability of all goods to meet the requirements of Government policy. Thus, for social reasons, rents and rail fares are deliberately kept low (around $15 a month for a two- or three-room apartment, and $50 for a 1,200-mile rail journey), while the price of vodka is deliberately kept high at $10 a quart.

The State also controls the trade unions, whose function is to increase productivity, not wage rates. Workers are constantly reminded that it is their duty to the Soviet Fatherland to produce more.

The prices of State-manufactured goods in State shops are, not unnaturally, State-controlled nationwide. In principle a bath towel costs the same in Soviet Central Asia as it does in Moscow. There is therefore no such thing as bargain hunting. What there is—under a system where both production and distribution are likely to be capricious—is the enormous satisfaction, after a long chase, of finding something you really want to buy.

In rural areas, choice is often limited to one or more rough-and-ready village shops. In the cities, shops form part of most big housing developments. Shoppers make expeditions to the big department stores only on special occasions. In Moscow the most spectacular of these is GUM, across the Red Square from the Kremlin. Built about 100 years ago in the form of a multiple shopping arcade on three floors under a lofty glass roof, it is like nothing else in the world.

It is visited by several hundred thousand potential customers a day. Here they can buy food, clothing, linens, grand pianos, fur hats, and television sets. They line up three times: once to make purchases, once to pay for them, and once to pick them up.

In this extremely status-conscious society, advantages vary according to rank. Nominally, those possessing privileges cannot share them with outsiders, but human nature being what it is the aides, personal assistants, and relatives of the great reap the privileges of hangers-on the world over.

Achieving rank is a question of seniority, ability, favoritism, and luck. At all levels of the hierarchy, special perquisites go with special jobs: official rations, official houses, official cars, and the services of official personnel. All are far more desirable than mere money. Instead of waiting in line for admission to some restaurant where the food is likely to be inferior, it is far more agreeable to be a member of a select club, such as the House of Writers, where one can lunch or dine in congenial company and where service and food are excellent.

Special perquisites are not the only advantage high-level workers enjoy. They also are paid wages far higher than the average. . . .

Taxes do not make the same dent in the Soviet Union as in capitalist countries. Funds for the national treasury can be raised in any number of ways in a country where the State controls the means of production, distribution, and exchange.

Most people, by our standards, pay practically no tax. Even the highest rates of income and inheritance taxes are only in the region of 12 per cent, though in theory private earnings, if declared, are subject to a higher rate. . . .

Absenteeism is a problem. So is alcoholism. In the Soviet Union, as elsewhere, some people work longer and harder than others. Moreover, a great many people in all walks of life take time off to supplement their income on the side. The fixer, the wrangler, the moonlighter, and the pilferer all exist under Communism as they do under capitalism. And, despite talk of "overtaking" the U.S. economically, the Soviet industrial worker still produces only half as much as his American counterpart does.

Working schedules in Soviet factories are usually erratic. In theory there is a forty-hour week, but if, toward the end of the month, The Plan is not running to schedule, double shifts go into effect. Once the crisis has passed, there is an easing.

Side by side with changes in the economic spectrum have come even more significant and deeprooted social changes. Of these, the most important politically is the increasing stratification of Soviet society. Six decades after the Bolshevik Revolution, what amounts to a hereditary ruling class—one might almost say an aristocracy—is emerging.

For more than a quarter of a century, those in positions of power and responsibility in politics, the armed forces, industry, finance and trade, diplomacy, the arts, and the academic world have not only been consolidating their own positions, but have been insuring that their children and grandchildren will have a good start in life. It is easier to get a good job if your father had a good job; in the Soviet Union, as elsewhere, a good start makes all the difference—as does the inherited wealth that usually accompanies it.

No less important politically is the appearance, for the first time in Russian history, of a firmly established middle class, bringing with it the social stability and bourgeois virtues lacking under the Czars. It also bridges the dangerous gap that long existed between the highest and lowest levels of Russian society—between the rulers and those "dark masses" who, barely a century ago, were still being bought and sold as serfs. Not as elegant, self-assured, or sophisticated as the upper class, these new bourgeois nonetheless know what they want and are beginning to get it.

Throughout the Soviet Union they can be seen shopping at the big stores, putting their money on a horse, spending their evenings at the theater or ballet, driving their medium-size family cars into the country on their days off, and enjoying their holidays at the better resorts. The comparatively modest privileges they enjoy clearly act as an incentive to the working class to work a little harder—and so, with time, luck, and shrewdness, in their turn to climb a little higher up the social ladder.

The Soviet scene today presents infinitely more variety than it did ten years ago. There is no longer a dreary uniformity. Not only are there now several different social classes; there are different lifestyles to go with them.

All kinds of cracks appear in the old monolith. Some people look shabby; some are chic; some are trendy; others favor conservative styles. Some, with long hair and eccentric clothes, are deliberately bohemian or intellectual in appearance. Others, in track suits and gym shoes, in crash helmets or ski pants, proclaim their enthusiasm for some sport.

The standardization of Stalin's day, and the control which went with it, are becoming things of the past. . . .

4. SOCIAL WELFARE IN THE USSR: AN INTRODUCTION*

Europa Yearbook 1981

In the 1981 budget the State allocated 45,800 million roubles for social insurance and security, or almost 12 per cent of total budget expenditure. Apart from a complete range of social security benefits (disability pensions, loss of wage earner, student grants, maternity benefits), pensions are paid to retired men at 60 and women at 55 and average 60–70 per cent of their salary prior to retirement. Employees in enterprises where the work conditions are arduous may receive pensions five or ten years earlier than is the norm. In 1980 there were 48.6 million people receiving retirement, disablement or army pensions in the U.S.S.R. A new social security scheme for old and disabled collective farm workers has been introduced. The centralized fund of the scheme is made up of deductions from the farmers' wages made by the collective farm, and of allocations from the state budget.

There is a streamlined system of public health services providing medical aid for the entire population. The public health services are supervised by the Ministry of Public Health and the Ministries of Public Health of the Union and Autonomous Republics, through regional (territorial), district, and city Boards of Health, under the corresponding Soviets of Working People's Deputies. All medical services and treatment are given free of charge, as are drugs and medicines in hospitals. In 1978 state allocations for free medical aid totalled over 8,000 million roubles. The U.S.S.R. has a total of 35,000 outpatients' clinics of various kinds. Public health institutions (hospitals, special clinics, maternity health centres, etc.) administer free services. In December 1977 there were 24,000 hospitals, and 121 hospital beds per 10,000 of the population. The number of doctors totalled 893,400 (34.4 per 10,000 of the population). In addition to these hospitals there is a large network of sanatoria and holiday homes. Accommodation for children, and in tuberculosis sanatoria, is free of charge. Working people are generally charged a nominal fee—usually about 30 per cent of the cost. Infant health centres and children's polyclinics have been set up as part of the public health system in order to watch over the health and proper physical development of all children. At the age of 16 years the child is transferred to an adult polyclinic. There are more than 500,000 hospital beds for children. Workers temporarily unable to work due to sickness receive a sick leave benefit on the basis

---

* Reprinted from *Europa Yearbook 1981*, London: Europa Publications Limited, 1981, p. 1219, by permission of the publisher.

of a certificate issued by the adult polyclinic. Disabled workers are either transferred to lighter work or given a disability pension.

Rents are controlled and on average amount to 3 per cent of family expenditure.

WESTERN MARXIST VIEWS

---

5. MAKING IT ON $400 A MONTH— SOVIET STYLE*

Sara Harris†

Ph.D. Candidate in Economics, Moscow University

How would you like to live on $400 a month—before taxes—with two children? We're doing it. Well, not exactly. We're living on 300 rubles, which is the equivalent of $400 at the exchange rate. ($1.00 = 75 kopeks or 0.75 ruble.)[1] But this is a low figure for a family of four even in Soviet terms. My husband, as an editor, gets 200 rubles a month but I am still a graduate student and receive only a stipend. So how do we do it?

Once I asked each member of the family, in jest, what we should buy if we happened to win 1000 rubles in the state lottery. I never expected the answers I got, except from Dimka, aged five, who responded with "a truck-load of ice cream and watermelons." My husband, Alek, suggested we buy the summer house we saw selling for that price in the country last year. What? There must be more important things we could spend it on! Ten-year-old Andre had the quickest response: "What do we need all that money for?" That's ridiculous, I thought. As an "efficient American," I'll find the most effective way to spend that money without simply blowing it on ice cream and watermelons.

---

* Reprinted from *New World Review*, July-August, 1978, pp. 20–22, by permission of the publisher.

† Sara Harris, born and raised in the New York City area, is married to Soviet journalist Alexander Kamenshikov and lives in Moscow with her husband and their two children. At the time she wrote this article in 1978, she was working on a Candidate of Science degree (roughly equivalent of the American Ph.D. degree) in economics at Moscow University. She is listed here under "Western Marxist Views," although she could possibly also be listed under "Soviet Views."

[1] In 1981, 300 rubles were approximately $480 at the official exchange rate, and of course only a fraction (perhaps one-fourth or one-fifth) of it on the black market. Between 1978 and 1981, prices of the "constant" items have remained unchanged, some of the more expensive items under "variable expenses" may have increased somewhat in price—not the staple food items—and wages have gone up by perhaps 10 percent. [Editor's note.]

1. First of all, we could put it toward the children's higher education. But how? It's already free. In fact, the longer you study in the Soviet Union, the more you get paid for studying, no matter which technical school, institute or university you're in. As an undergraduate, I was given first 35, then 45, and later 50 rubles a month. (The Government increased stipends during the last five-year plan; also seniors and "A" students get an additional bonus.) Being a graduate student, I contribute 100 rubles a month to the family budget. Sports facilities, special interest clubs, music lessons, for me and the kids are also free of charge. The only area of education that isn't totally free is nursery school where the government subsidizes only 4/5 of the total cost.

ITEM	AMT. (IN RUBLES):	% of TOTAL (ROUNDED TO 0.1%)
CONSTANT* EXPENSES		
Rent (incl. heat, water, gas)	14.71	4.9
Taxes (the only tax we pay is income tax)	20.00	6.7
Union Dues	2.00	0.7
Electricity	4.00	1.3
Transportation	10.00	3.3
Nursery School	12.50	4.2
Education (grade school and all higher education)	0	0
Health Care	0	0
Subtotal:	63.21r.	21.1%
VARIABLE EXPENSES		
Food and Household Supplies	150.00	50.0
Clothing	35.00	11.7
Culture (incl. books, movies, theatre, school supplies, etc.)	12.00	4.0
Other (gifts, household furnishings, trips, etc.)	39.79	13.2
Savings	0	0
Subtotal:	236.79r.	78.9%
Grand Total:	300.00r.	100.0%

* The word "constant" is used in a relative sense, Utilities and transportation do vary, + or − a few rubles. Nursery school can be less, if Dimka was absent, but never more.

2. Then, I'll put the money toward medical bills. Even if we're lucky enough to avoid a hospital stay, what growing family can avoid an occasional flu, innoculations, the dentist, oculist, or at best, the maternity ward?

Our family has been far less fortunate. In twelve years of family life we've managed, in part, two tonsillectomies, an appendectomy and a broken arm, a total of six months of specialized sanatoriums for the children, oculists, cardiologists, surgeons, neurologists, some top specialists in their field, a complete set of dentures (pardon my frankness), two years of orthodontia, and at least 75 house calls by the doctor. (Not bad, considering that I'm still going to school!) The total cost for twelve years—55 rubles ($63). That was the price of the fancy metal put into my husband's month last year by the dentist. All the rest was and will be free, with no insurance costs. We do, however, have to pay for medicines. Although the price of all medicines was lowered last year by 10 percent, a good antibiotic can run as much as 3–8 kopeks a tablet.

3. Well, how about beating the rent hike and paying the rent way in advance? That's a good idea! Our utilities went up last spring—82 cents—for the first time since we moved in five years ago. So now rent plus all utilities except electricity, which we pay for according to usage and averages four rubles ($5.33) a month, cost us 14 rubles and 71 kopeks ($19.60, a month for four rooms and two balconies. That means that with 1000 rubles we can pay the "landlord" for more than five and one-half years to come! I'm afraid that won't work. I've heard of people here not paying rent to the government for months at a time, but I've never heard of paying five years in advance!

4. We could always put the money toward a new car? Let's just say car, since we don't have an old one. If I had a car, I would drive to the country once in a while, or to distant friends. I doubt that I would drive to the university or to work. The subway is a twelve minute walk from our house with not one major street to cross. Then it takes five kopeks plus twenty minutes to be in the center of town. The bus, also five kopeks, is a block from our house. I'm not sure I would want to fight the traffic in a car, or miss my morning walk for that matter. Andre goes by himself by public transportation to swimming lessons, to clubs at the Pioneer Palace, to Grandma's house on the other side of Moscow. I can just see myself becoming his personal chauffeur if we had a car. It would ease the shopping, it is true. I would do less package carrying. But, come to think of it, there are no through streets the four blocks between our house and the shopping center, just apartment houses and parks.

5. In that case, why don't we just put the money in the bank for a "rainy day"? My husband and I have five rubles in the bank. The last transaction in our bankbook was over two years ago. Some people do save, but what we earn we spend. With no fear of unemployment and no need to save for old age or disability, we don't think in terms of putting

money away. If we have money left over at the end of the month, which happens but not often, we'll buy something for the house or the kids or just blow it on a restaurant or fruit.

When cherries or grapes are in season, my family can eat five lbs. at one sitting. The same is true of apples, peaches, oranges, bananas. . . . I've given up trying to satisfy my family's appetite for fruit. I just buy as much as I have money in my pocket for when I happen upon a shipment of something.

By spring I usually start saving a little toward vacation. Each year we get out of the city for a month or more. Three summers the family traveled more than 800 miles to the Black Sea, several times we rented a cabin on a lake not far from Moscow. This year the whole family went to a resort on the Volga river 125 miles north of the city, where we swam, went boating, gathered wild berries in the forest and fried fresh mushrooms over an open fire. All told, transportation included, the 24 days cost the family 300 rubles—a month's income. I got a big discount as a student but Alek and the boys had to pay the full price so it was a good deal more expensive than most resorts where the union pays up to 70 percent of the cost. But if you consider that I received my stipend and Alek his full salary for that month, we didn't really have to put away much in advance for our holiday. Andre's month away at camp cost 23 rubles which is about average and probably less than I would have spent on him if he had stayed home those four weeks.

Two years ago my husband and I took a trip to the US. (Our relatives helped. That is still beyond our pocketbook.) We had saved up 250 rubles. Thirty rubles we put aside for our return; after all we have two dependents. The rest, 220 rubles, we spent on gifts for our American friends and relatives.

6. What's left, except to spend the money on a trip abroad? Tours to Cuba were advertised this summer on the bulletin board at the University. A few years ago my girlfriend took a tourist fling to London while her husband babysat. Alek said they are selling ten-day package tours to Italy at his job for 450 rubles, including tips. Now we're getting somewhere! My husband and I could go together and have some money left over for souvenirs!

Wait a minute! We haven't won that lottery. Besides, it would be foolish to assume that we could find nothing else to spend money on but a trip abroad. It is enough to look at our monthly budget to discover the weak spots (see Table, p. 431):

The "constant" column, a little over 20 per cent, covers the monthly essentials after which we are free to spend on consumer goods. Any increase in income would go into the variable column, where the more we earn the more we will spend. (With the possible exception of "culture." Twelve rubles is enough to provide each member of the family with a movie a week, a major theatrical performance once a month, plus

a few new books for the family. Alek disagrees with me here. He insists
that a few new books a month is not enough.)

The 50 per cent for food reflects, in part, my philosophy of not
skimping on our health and we don't. Most families I know spend more
like 30–40 per cent on food. But then again, their incomes are larger.
Although we eat meat frequently, we still don't buy all the smoked fish
and snacky extras that we would if we let our tastes rather than our
pocketbook, or waistlines for that matter, dictate the shopping.

Clothing is the major sore spot. We buy clothes when we need
them and not when we simply want them. Alek could use a new winter
coat. The house could afford papering, and I am watching for my chance
to have some cabinets built.

Obviously, we are not delighted by the fact that our income is small.
At the same time, we do not have to dream of winning a lottery. Despite
pinching here and there on a coat or a piece of furniture, our family is
able to live a full, healthy life, without skimping on that most important
element—the children, their health, their security, their education and
their future.

SOVIET VIEWS

6. THE SOVIET CITIZEN AS A CONSUMER*

Margarita Bunkina†

Moscow University

Production and consumption of goods has existed since human society
emerged. In different historical and social conditions the inter-relationship
of production and consumption assumes different forms, but it invariably
remains very important.

In the last analysis the aim of production is to satisfy human
needs. . . .

In so far as the means of production are not privately owned by
individuals but belong to society as a whole, social production is carried

* Reprinted from Margarita Bunkina, *Socialist Economics Today*, Moscow: Novosti Press
  Agency Publishing House, 1981, pp. 34–43, by permission of the publisher and of the
  Copyright Agency of the USSR.
† Margarita Bunkina is professor of economics at Moscow University, has published nu-
  merous books and articles, and has travelled widely in the West, lecturing to university
  students and faculty on the Soviet economy.

out in the interests of all citizens. This is laid down in Article 15 of the USSR Constitution, which says in part that "the supreme goal of social production under socialism is the fullest possible satisfaction of the people's growing material, and cultural and intellectual requirements.

With this aim in view the state concerns itself with rising productivity and the efficiency of production and improving the quality of work, and sees to it that the national economy develops dynamically, systematically and proportionately.

Sometimes sceptics who know about the life of Soviet people only from biased bourgeois press reports express doubt about the feasibility of the aim of socialist production. They point to the fact that to this day the standard of living in the USSR is still below the average standard of living in such developed capitalist countries as the United States, West Germany and others.

Others lay special stress on the fact that for a long time the rates of development of Soviet heavy and extractive industry (i.e. producer goods industries) were quite high, whereas the production of articles of personal consumption grew more slowly. Let us take a look at consumption under socialism from a specific practical point of view.

People purchase particular goods to the extent that they are able to do so. In the Soviet Union the main source of income is wages, which Soviet people receive in accordance with the quality and quantity of their work in social production. It will be noted that wages and salaries are systematically increasing while the prices of basic foodstuffs and manufactured consumer goods are remaining stable.

But family's real income is not confined to the earnings of its working members. The size of the real income is influenced substantially by the fact that no payment has to be made for education at any level, for training to improve qualifications or for any kind of medical service. The state-financed social consumption funds pay for free and reduced-cost vouchers for accommodation at sanatoriums and holiday homes. The state pays pensions to the aged and disabled and monthly allowances to the students of higher and specialized secondary schools, covers 80 per cent of the cost of maintaining children in creches and kindergartens and a large part of the expenditure in maintaining housing, so that rents claim not more than 3–4 per cent of the family budget. Economists have estimated that real per capita incomes in the USSR are doubling roughly every fifteen years. This means that within the lifetime of a single generation consumption rises several times to a qualitatively new level.

A comparison of average indices of per capita consumption under capitalism and socialism, to which bourgeois researchers often refer can obscure the real state of affairs. The relatively high average consumption of material goods in the United States and other "rich" capitalist countries conceals, on the one hand, the inordinate luxury of millionaires' families, and on the other, the misery of the lower strata, such as a large part of the non-white population in America. The socialist system ensures a systematic rise in the living standards of the broad masses of the working people in town and country, that is, of the population as a whole.

It is true that the Soviet Union is still lagging behind the developed capitalist countries in per capita consumption of particular foodstuffs (vegetables, fruit, vegetable oil, meat), in the quality of clothing and footwear or the number of cars, transistor radios or tape recorders per head of population. But these problems are not being ignored by the Communist Party and the Soviet Government. Large capital investments are being made to improve and further develop the consumer goods industries. . . .

In productivity, too, the Soviet Union has yet to draw even with a number of capitalist states. In 1979, for instance, the productivity of social labour in the USSR was roughly 40 per cent, and production per employee in industry and agriculture 55 per cent and 20–25 per cent, respectively of the US level.

What is the explanation for the fact that American workers and farmers outperform their Soviet opposite numbers by a factor of 2 to 4? The main reason is the higher technological level of US industry and agriculture. Judging by the rates of development of production, however, the time is not far off when this lag of the Soviet Union will be eliminated. . . .

Already there are spheres of production and consumption where the advantages of socialism, its social achievements, are obvious. These include the volume and level of consumption of values in the cultural field. Every Soviet family subscribes, on average, to at least four newspapers and magazines. In 1978, theatres and concerts were attended by 120 and 160 million people, respectively. (According to UNESCO statistics, such attendance in the United States and the West European countries taken together was one-fifth of the Soviet figure).

An analysis of the consumption of material and cultural values and services by the population would be incomplete if we did not touch upon the structure of retail prices.

Under socialism the prices of goods and services are determined and changed by the state in a planned way. The prices of goods must reflect their cost, that is to say, the socially necessary expenditure on their production. So the price of, say, a deluxe pair of shoes is higher than that of mass-produced ones, and hand-made furniture in precious wood costs more than furniture made from plastics. But the prices of goods cannot be an exact mirror reflection of their cost. Under capitalism, for instance, they fluctuate under the impact of supply and demand, the arbitrary actions of the monopolies, and other factors. Under socialism prices also take supply and demand into account. A high demand for fashionable goods not yet in mass production can account for their higher price. But the main factor in pricing policy under socialism is its aim to satisfy the basic requirements of people and shape these requirements.

There are many goods and services whose prices are much lower than their cost.

This is true, first, of bread, sugar, meat, milk and dairy products, vegetables and other staple foods.

Secondly, it is also true of the prices of books and especially textbooks, magazines and tickets to exhibitions, concerts, cinemas and theatres.

Thirdly, the prices of children's goods and of medicines are much lower than their cost.

Furthermore, thanks to state budget subsidies the population spends comparatively little on transport and services (public transport fares, the prices charged by repair shops, at hairdressers and so on).

Last but not least, rents are low, having remained unchanged since 1928. Every year the state allocates vast sums for the upkeep and repair of housing. The rents paid by the population cover not more than one-third of this expenditure.

On the other hand, there are goods whose prices are much higher than their cost. These goods are either goods which are not prime necessities (cut glass, silver and gold articles and so on) or products whose consumption it is desired to reduce (such as liquor).

The state periodically adjusts prices to bring them closer into line with the necessary cost of production. The prices of some prime necessities (clothing from man-made fibre, TV sets and other cultural and household appliances) are reduced because production and supply are increasing. While the prices of the main categories of commodities sold through the retail network remain stable, the prices of several goods (natural fur and articles made from it, of rugs and carpets and of imported wine) have been raised. Such price increases have not to any appreciable extent affected the bulk of consumers, but have enabled the state to mobilize additional resources for maintaining the constantly growing fund of housing and for assisting agriculture (through raising the state purchasing prices of meat and milk).

Such price adjustment measures are criticized by certain bourgeois sociologists who claim they widen the gap between the prices of basic foodstuffs and so-called luxury items to be found in many homes today.

It is true that in our day no one any longer regards rugs, cut glass and other such things as luxury items. But they are not prime necessities, either. We believe that the structure of prices existing in the socialist countries and the measures taken to readjust them are quite justified by the socialist way of life because they meet the needs and interests of the working people.

We referred earlier to sceptical comments about consumer goods production relatively lagging behind the manufacture of producer goods in the USSR. Let us return to this question. Part of the national income is not consumed by the population directly but is used in the form of what economists call accumulation for expanding production. Accumulation, i.e., additional capital investment for the development of production and activities in the non-productive sphere,[1] is necessary for *extended reproduction* or, in other words, for the constant renewal of production on an ever greater scale. Without this, further growth of consumption is impossible; if, for instance, the fleet of tractors is not increased and improved while productivity remains unchanged, more crops can hardly be grown. Or if we do not take care to increase the manufacture of weaving looms in good time, we shall hardly be able to turn out more textiles. . . .

In the 1930s and the early postwar years, expenditure on productive needs (especially on the renovation and extension of producer goods production for the manufacture of means of production themselves) grew at quite a rapid rate—not because of any disregard for the working people's needs, of course. It was generally understood that consumption could not be increased without first building an adequate material and technical basis and equipping war-ravaged agriculture and manufacturing industry with modern machinery. In addition, being surrounded by capitalist countries in those years, the Soviet Union was in constant danger of military invasion and had to see to its defense—and the higher military spending is, the more difficult it is to improve the standard of living of the population. Moreover, such expenditure is even more injurious to the socialist than to the capitalist economy, for the former has no relatively excessive capital, no chronic underutilization of production capacities or unemployment. For many years Soviet people had to allocate resources for defence at the cost of slowing down the growth of consumer goods production.

In our time also, military spending weighs heavily on the working people of the world. The freeing of mankind from the arms race would release vast resources, helping to solve on an international basis such problems as environmental protection and the tapping of new energy sources and the riches of the ocean, to combat disease and to improve the life of many millions of people now suffering hunger and misery. The ending of arms manufacture would free mothers from fear for the future of their children. That is why the socialist countries come out steadfastly for curbing the arms race, reducing armaments and easing international tension, for world peace.[2]

---

[1] See footnote 15 on p. 398. [Editor's note.]

[2] Economists, East and West, have pointed out that military expenditures pose a greater burden on a full-employment than on a less-than-full-employment economy. Since the former makes full use of its productive capacities (to the best of its ability), increased military expenditures will necessitate decreased expenditures in other sectors. When a country operates below its "production possibilities," it could increase both "guns and butter" simultaneously. [Editor's note.]

7. THE "AVERAGE CITIZEN" IN THE U.S. AND THE USSR*

Gennadi Pisarevsky
Commentator, Novosti Press Agency

The statistical "average Soviet citizen" is less well-to-do than the "average American." Everybody knows that there are more material comforts available in the United States than in the Soviet Union, things like housing, goods and services. But while these are important, there are many other things essential for a person's well-being that cannot be measured in dollars or rubles.

In the USSR, for example, there is work for everybody who wants it. As a matter of fact, jobs look for people in our country, not the other way around. From the economists' point of view, this has its negative aspects: Having gotten work easily, a person sometimes also as easily leaves it. The Soviet Government has even been forced to increase the time (from two to four weeks) that a person has to stay on the job after handing in a resignation notice.

All education in the Soviet Union is free. The cost of a university diploma, for example—the 42-month wage of an "average" parent—is fully covered by the state. The state also pays for all medical services, which are rendered according to the individual's need, not according to his or her ability to pay.

The overwhelming majority of Soviet families, more than 80 per cent, receive housing that is built with funds from the state budget. Rent in the USSR is the world's lowest. Utility charges are also very low. The cost of electricity, gas, telephone, water, including hot water, and central heating has not changed since 1948. Take the telephone bill, for example. A family pays 2.50 rubles per month regardless of the number and duration of conversations. The gas bill comes to 16 kopecks a month per individual regardless of the amount of gas used. True, gasoline prices went up in 1978: A liter of gas now costs from 15 to 20 kopecks.

For more than 30 years the fare on city public transportation facilities (excluding taxis) has not changed and, irrespective of distance, comes to 5 kopecks for the bus or the subway, 4 kopecks for the trolley bus and 3 kopecks for the streetcar.

By American standards, wages in the USSR are not high. Industrial workers average 180 to 200 rubles (288 to 320 dollars) a month. But in the Soviet Union taxes, housing, transportation, medical care, education,

---

* Reprinted from Gennadi Pisarevsky "Economy: Dynamics and Difficulties," *Soviet Life*, August, 1980, p. 25, by permission of the Novosti Press Agency Publishing House and the Copyright Agency of the USSR.

electricity, heating, and so on, add up to less than 20 per cent of the family budget. That means a family can use as much as 80 per cent of its income for goods, services, entertainment and savings.

In the USA, it is just the opposite. Up to 80 per cent of family income goes for taxes, housing, transportation, education, medical treatment, insurance payments and other such things.

In order to avoid being reproached for bias, I shall once again note: The standard of living in the USA is higher than in the USSR, just as, incidentally, it is higher than in many other countries. But the standard of living in the USSR is nowhere near as low as it is professed to be in the West. . . .

8. SOME SOCIAL WELFARE MEASURES: HOUSING, HEALTH, OLD AGE*
Borris Rakitsky, Pyotr Margiev, et al.
Novosti Press Agency

In the Soviet Union distribution according to the work performed determines personal income. Yet, progressive as it is, this method of distribution cannot abolish the unequal levels of social consumption which may be due to unequal capacity for work, the size of family, the number of dependents, and so on.

Therefore, if payment according to work were the one and only principle of distribution, the actual prosperity of working people, even assuming equal earnings, would depend mainly on how many wage earners and dependents there were in a family. This would inevitably result in unequal opportunities in terms of medical care, education, skills, training, and satisfaction of other cultural and intellectual needs.

By making services available free of charge—which is the mainspring in the mechanism of the distribution of the social funds—socialist society purposely separates the satisfaction of some personal needs from individual incomes, giving everybody access to education and medical care, good homes, and other social benefits, regardless of personal income.

Distribution of a portion of the national income through the social

---

* The introductory paragraphs and the first two sections on housing and health care have been taken from *USSR, Today and Tomorrow: People's Wellbeing* (no author given), Moscow: Novosti Press Agency Publishing House, 1978, pp. 18–28, except for the introductory part to the section on health, entitled "A Grim Legacy," which comes from *The Soviet Union Today and Tommorrow: Health Care* (no author given), Moscow: Novosti Press Agency Publishing House, 1979, pp. 6–7. The third and fourth sections have been taken respectively from Borris Rakitsky, "The Right to a Secure Old Age," and Pyotr Margiev, "The Pensioner Who Goes on Working," both from *Soviet Weekly*, Feb. 10, 1979, pp. 8 and 16. Reprinted here by permission of the publishers and the Copyright Agency of the USSR.

consumption funds increases social equality. Of course, not every family draws on this source to the same extent. This is one manifestation of the social justice of socialist society.

The Soviet state continuously increases its material assistance to low-income and large families, granting more and more benefits to working mothers. For example, in 1973 the number of days with full pay a mother can miss to tend her sick child was brought up to ten, and in 1974, allowances for children of low-income families were introduced.

Child-care facilities are financed out of the social consumption funds. It costs more than 450 roubles a year to keep a child at a kindergarten, and about 500, at a creche. The state foots almost 80 per cent of the bill. Collective-farm kindergartens and creches are maintained 100 per cent by the farms.

People receive their share of the social consumption funds not as workers but as citizens. Thus, pensions, allowances, scholarships are usually granted to members of society who do not work either permanently or temporarily.

One of the most important purposes served by the social consumption funds is to ensure an equal start in life to all young people, regardless of parental income and social standing.

How is it done? Parents do not need to worry about how they are going to pay their children's tuition at school or college. Education is free. Moreover, undergraduates are paid monthly scholarships.

The system of advanced training at all levels, which is highly developed in the Soviet Union, is also free. Society foots the bill in this case too.

If we sum up the income of a typical Soviet family of four in terms of cash allowances (benefits, scholarships, pensions, paid leaves) and in terms of free education, medicare and subsidised housing, the total will be a considerable sum amounting to roughly a third of the aggregate volume of material goods and services consumption. . . .

Some critics of the Soviet system ask, "Does it make any difference if you pay tuition and the doctor's fees out of your own pocket or if you get less and pay for the same things indirectly, through the State Budget?" The situation in the Soviet Union allows all citizens, regardless of income, to enjoy major social benefits equally. With the help of the social consumption funds, the socialist state assures, not in word only but in deed, every person a right to these benefits, enabling all members of society to enjoy them on equal and fair terms.

THE ARITHMETIC OF RENT

When they asked a member of the Executive Committee of the Moscow City Council what they did about people who lacked the money to pay rent and whether they evicted such people, he was flabbergasted.

"Dear me," he said, "I'm afraid I cannot cite any instances of this kind. Some people do accumulate arrears. It happens when someone goes away on a long business trip or something like that. But not because the rent is more than they can afford. Still, even if we imagine a hypothetical case like that, the authorities have no right to evict a family. I have never heard, let alone experienced, anything of that kind."

In no other country are houses constructed on the same scale as in the Soviet Union.

The new Soviet Constitution proclaims—for the first time ever—citizens' right to a dwelling. It is worth noting that this vital right is being ensured in a country where during World War II fascist invaders ruined 1,700 towns and levelled to the ground 70,000 villages, leaving 25,000,000 persons homeless.

In the Soviet Union no one who moves into a new, comfortable flat is subjected to a means test. The idea would never occur to anyone since his credit as a tenant is guaranteed by the state, not by his bank account. The majority of flats are granted by the state free of charge. This is the guarantee of the right to a dwelling, augmented by low rent, which is also written down in the Soviet Constitution.

Incidentally, rent has not changed since 1928. With electricity, gas, central heating and hot water, it does not exceed, as a rule, 3 per cent of the income of an industrial worker's family. Rent is not raised despite the fact that it covers less than a third of the state's expenditure on housing maintenance. The state annually allocates about 5,000 million roubles from the social consumption funds for the maintenance of houses and municipal services.

Monthly rent ranges from half a kopek to 13.2 kopeks per square metre of floor space. Rent is based on the rooms only, not on the kitchen, hall, corridor, bathroom and toilet (these are rent free).

A family pay nothing for the plumbing, radiators, gas range and other facilities.

The cost of public utilities in the Soviet Union is as follows. Electricity costs 4 kopeks per kilowatt-hour; gas costs 16 kopeks a month per person, regardless of the amount consumed; heating costs about 5 kopeks per square metre of living space; a telephone costs 2 roubles 50 kopeks a month, regardless of how often or how long it is used (trunk calls[1] are charged separately).

Since flats are received free of charge and rent is very low, every Soviet family, regardless of social status or income, can have a good home. The Soviet state considers providing flats to be a social service, not a commercial proposition. It is worth noting, that according to UN figures covering the last five years, rent increased by 44 per cent in France, 58 per cent in Spain, and 77 per cent in Austria. In West Germany,

---

[1] Long distance calls. [Editor's note.]

many people are compelled to move to houses with practically no conveniences on the outskirts of cities and towns.

The continuous construction of houses demands enormous investments of money, labour and machinery. Practically a fifth of total capital investment in the economy or much more than is invested in several key industries put together, is allocated for housing.

Only ten years ago, mostly small flats were provided. They consisted of small, often adjoining, rooms, small kitchens and halls. The objective at that time was to enable people to move from shared into separate flats. Industrial-type construction provided the only correct answer in those circumstances.

Now it is no longer a minimum of conveniences that is required but real comfort. In the last fifteen years, the standard flat changed four times. The rooms and kitchens were made larger, the layout was improved, new architectural ideas were applied. Modern designs of dwellings take account of climatic conditions. In houses being built in the North flats have special rooms for drying clothes, while in those to be built in the South, protection from the sun and artificial cooling are provided.

Naturally enough, this increases the cost of construction. In 1971–1975 a square metre of floor space cost the state an average of 150 roubles. In 1976–1980, despite rapid progress in construction technology, the cost is 170 roubles. Nevertheless, Soviet citizens pay the same 13.2 kopeks per square metre of floor space.

Such is the arithmetic of rent in the Soviet Union.

The watchword of the home production program in the Soviet Union is: A comfortable flat for every family—one room for each member of the family plus a living room.

Soviet people are often asked why they refuse to consider the housing problem as solved. After all, in the past sixty years available housing has increased almost 20 times, while the population has hardly doubled. Why are more than two million flats a year being built instead of curtailing construction as might be expected? There is nothing to wonder at. So far we still have not enough flats to go around. That's the first reason, and there's another reason too. Soviet society is growing richer all the time, and people are becoming harder to please. A flat that seemed to be perfect twenty or thirty years ago is now often regarded as a relic of the past. Old houses have to be renovated; obsolescent houses are also replaced with modern ones.

Flats provided by the state free of charge are the main but not the only source of housing. Those who have the money and do not want to wait can join a building co-operative. Currently there are about 25,000 of them in the Soviet Union. A three-room flat costs approximately 10,000 roubles, and the state grants a loan for up to 60 per cent of the cost of the flat, payable over 15 years.

Many private houses are built mostly in the suburbs and the countryside. Loans are granted in this case too. At present, one family in ten builds a home at its own expense.

Every year more than 2,300,000 flats are provided in the Soviet Union. One could say that every year a city like Moscow or Greater Paris is being built. And although the housing problem on the whole has not yet been solved, notable successes have been achieved in this field. Today average floor space per person is 12 square metres whereas in 1945 it was 5.5 square metres.

HEALTH

A Grim Legacy

The good health of the people is a nation's great asset. The way a country conserves and builds upon that asset gives fair indication of the nature of the social structure of that country, its qualities and its achievements.

In prerevolutionary Russia there was no unified health service. Much depended on charitable organisations. There was one doctor for 5,700 people and only about one in a thousand could receive hospital treatment. Moreover, the majority of the doctors had their practices in the big towns of the European part of the country. More than a third of towns in Russia and the vast outlying areas had no hospitals at all.

Incomplete records reveal that every year in Russia more than a million people died of infectious diseases. Each year seven million people fell ill with malaria alone. Two hundred and sixty-nine new-borns in every thousand died during their first year. Forty-three per cent of children died before they were five. The average life expectancy was 32.

"We inherited an indifferent, hypocritical medical bureaucracy, an inadequate rural and urban medical service, a helpless industrial medicine and the awareness that step by step the country was sliding towards degeneration," wrote Zinovy Solovyov, one of the distinguished organisers of the Soviet health service.

IF YOU ARE UNWELL

It would be no exaggeration to say that among the good things of life health ranks first.

In the Soviet Union, if you fall ill, you do not need to worry about doctors' bills. When you go to see a doctor or call one or go to the hospital you do not need to count your money or ask yourself if you can afford the expense or how it will affect the family budget. The Soviet Constitution ensures all citizens the right to free medical treatment. This right is also enjoyed by all foreigners who come to the Soviet Union, tourists, journalists, specialists and workers.

In the socialist world, medicine is not a lucrative business; it is not commercialised. It is a social service. And this refers to the production of medicines as well. The price of medicine is the lowest in the world. Medicines are sold with no profit in mind, and in cases of serious illness (e.g., tuberculosis, dysentery, epilepsy), are issued free of charge.

In 1976, the Soviet Union had 862,000 practicing doctors of all specialities or nearly a third of the world total. This means, first of all, that medical assistance is easily accessible. Soviet citizens are used to having a doctor everywhere, not only at the village or district polyclinic but also at the floating fish-factory, at the sports stadium, in the kindergarten and the Young Pioneer summer camp. There is a growing number of factory and shop doctors.

This army of doctors receives annually about 2,500 million patients. This means that everyone visits a doctor 9–10 times annually on the average. Ambulance teams annually answer 70 million calls. Every minute 200 ambulances rush to patients urgently in need of help.

"Often enough, the calls are prompted by caution," the Soviet Health Minister, Academician Boris Petrovsky, once told foreign journalists "But we do not mind. On the contrary, we encourage patients to see a doctor before the disease has done irreparable damage." In the Soviet Union each year more than 160 million people are subjected to prophylactic medical examinations. All infants during the first year of life are periodically visited (without being called) by a pediatrician. They are examined by a psychoneurologist, an orthopedist, an eye-specialist, and an ear, throat and nose specialist. A child in its second year is examined by a dentist and a specialist in the treatment of speech defects.

These examinations cost the state a lot of money. Is it well spent? According to medical statistics, large-scale prophylactic examinations have revealed that one person in eight showed symptoms of ischemia after age 45. The patients did not suspect that they had this disease, and so, would not have consulted a doctor on their own.

In the Soviet Union, everyone who falls ill is paid a temporary disability allowance. The allowance is sufficiently large. Most working people receive compensation equal to their full wages. The time during which one may draw the allowance has no fixed limits. Temporary disability allowance is paid from the first day of illness until complete recovery.

In the Soviet Union women's health is protected by special laws. Expectant and nursing mothers may not be fired or have their wages lowered. They may not be refused employment. Should this be recommended by a doctor, the management is obliged to transfer a pregnant woman to a lighter job with the same average wages as before.

Besides her regular paid leave, an expectant mother is given 112 additional days of paid maternity leave (56 before and 56 after childbirth). If there be an abnormal delivery or if two or more babies are produced in one birth, postnatal leave is prolonged to 70 days. And all this time the mother receives her full wages or salary.

Health depends on many factors. To give real protection, the state must not only ensure a competent public health service for treatment and prevention of diseases, but must also take measures to improve factory and home conditions and provide sufficient facilities for wholesome recreation.

The Soviet state introduced regular annual holidays with full pay. The holiday may be 15 to 48 weekdays long, depending on length of service, conditions of work, and type of work. People usually spend their leave at a sanatorium, a holiday home, hiking or on a tour.

Workers engaged in key industries are granted additional leave if they have worked at the same factory for a certain number of years. A steel worker, for example, who has worked at his mill 2 to 6 years, is entitled to 3 to 10 days' leave in addition to his 24-weekday holiday. Those working in the Far North are granted another 18 days off. In this way, a steel worker in the Far North may enjoy 51 weekdays of paid leave. Wages paid for the duration of the holiday are computed on the basis of average earnings during the previous 11 months. If you fall ill during your holiday, the holiday is prolonged accordingly.

The Soviet Union has 14,000 holiday centres of all kinds, tourist camps, and sanatoriums. They can accommodate almost 2 million people simultaneously. In 1976, organised leisure and treatment facilities were used by 48 million wage and salary workers and their families. Anyone can afford it. Accommodation at a sanatorium, for example, costs 121 roubles on the average.[2] However, only 20 per cent of the passes are sold at full price, the same proportion is distributed free of charge, and the rest are sold at cut rates—for 30 per cent of their real cost, i.e., 24-day rest including rooms, meals, and treatment costs 36 roubles.

In 1977, such passes to sanatoriums and holiday homes were made available to 8,600,000 persons.

Foreign tourists often marvel at the way rest and leisure is organised in the Soviet Union. It is a great surprise for them, but for a Soviet citizen, it is just part of the usual Soviet life-style. . . .

About 11 million schoolchildren annually spend their summer vacations at the hundreds of thousands of Young Pioneer camps in the countryside. Their parents pay only a third of the cost, i.e., 8 or 10 roubles for 26 days. Large families and unmarried mothers do not pay anything at all. All the expenses are defrayed by trade unions. For children who do not go to the country in summer there are recreation grounds run by schools, clubs and Young Pioneer centres for out-of-school sports and health-building activities.

Until recently, almost all holiday homes and holiday hotels were primarily for adults. Lately, however, it has become popular to spend holidays with the family. Passes to family holiday homes are given free

[2] For 24 days. [Editor's note.]

or sold at 30 per cent of the cost whether or not the rest of the family works at the establishment which issued the pass. To cite an example, a family of four pays 40 or 50 roubles for a 12-day stay at a holiday home. That is one rouble daily per person.

THE RIGHT TO A SECURE OLD AGE

A secure old age is one of life's basic human rights, a yardstick with which the humanity of a society can be judged.

The Soviet Constitution guarantees "the right to maintenance in old age, in sickness and in the event of complete or partial disability or loss of a bread-winner."

And this is not just a legal formality, but is carried out in practice in everything that concerns the life of the elderly.

The Soviet Union has 46 million pensioners—30 million of them old-age pensioners.

Their proportion in the population has been steadily increasing— in recent years at the rate of about 800,000 a year.

This is not surprising, of course.

Apart from the aging of the population caused by the drop in the birthrate resulting from the severe losses in the second world war, life has been considerably prolonged by the vastly improved social conditions and the advances of medical science. The Soviet Union now has an average life expectancy of 70 years—twice as long as in 1917.

With the country's increasing prosperity, it was possible in 1964 to extend retirement pensions to collective farmers who, in a sense, are self-employed—co-operative owners of their farms.

Today there are 12 million collective farmers receiving retirement pensions.

Pensions are non-contributory. Not a penny comes from the worker's pay-packet.

They are financed entirely out of social funds; state budget allocations and deductions from the incomes of factories, offices, organisations and co-operatives.

A special state co-operative fund is responsible for paying collective farmers' pensions.

All pensions are tax free.

The right to a full retirement pension is granted at 60 to men with a 25-year work record, and at 55 to women with 20 years' service.

If they work 10 years beyond retirement age or they have 15 years' unbroken service at one place of work an extra 10 per cent is added to the pension.

A person with one disabled dependent gets 10 per cent added to the pension, and with more than one dependent, 15 per cent.

Certain occupations and working conditions bring earlier pensions.

Men and women who have worked in the Far North, for instance, for 12½ and 10 years respectively, may retire five years earlier, and the retirement age is 50 for men working underground, in hot shops or in other arduous conditions.

Among other privileged groups are women who have brought up five or more children and working war invalids.

The work record includes army service, leave for attending university or technical courses and time spent on any other civic or work commitment.

Pensions range from half to the whole of average earnings, with the percentage higher for the lower income groups.

There is a ceiling to the amount that can be received as a pension, so the pensions of the people in the top income brackets, no matter how high their earnings may have been, cannot exceed it.

Pensions are granted to widows unable to work, irrespective of age.

The able-bodied get a widow's pension if they are 55 within five years of the husband's death.

In the event of the loss of a breadwinner, pensions are paid for underage children, elderly parents or disabled dependents.

Pensions are delivered by post, paid directly into a savings bank or, if the pensioner is working, together with wages at the place of work.

All the paperwork connected with issuing a pension has to be done in advance.

The law sets a time-limit of within ten days of the date a person reaches retirement age, but in practice it is usually completed in two or three days.

Everything possible is done to encourage pensioners to remain active. Many of them play a useful part in local government, welfare departments and party and other organisations.

They retain close contact with their former places of work and continue to join in the social life of the enterprise, enjoy the holiday and other facilities provided, and pursue their hobbies at its clubs and sports centres.

Care for the health of the pensioner is, of course, of prime concern.

They have at their command the whole range of free medical services, from routine health check-ups to the assistance of the country's leading specialists.

Pensioners who are unable to care for themselves may go to state-financed homes for the elderly.

At these they have their own rooms, furniture and belongings, and are cared for by experienced domestic and medical staff.

They can still pursue their own interests and enjoy the recreational and social activities provided.

In common with working people throughout the country pensioners have benefited by the rising standard of living.

Minimum pensions for factory and office workers increased by 50 per cent, and for collective farmers by 70 per cent in the 1971–75 period.

And under the 1976–80 five-year plan pensions have been raised again for miners and iron and steel workers.

It should be noted that shop prices, rents and the cost of services have remained absolutely stable, so these increases are genuine ones.[3]

Further increases are in the pipeline for all sections of the population.

Plans are afoot to raise the minimum pensions for workers and collective farmers and to widen the range of benefits for invalids, large families and pensioners who wish to continue working.

The Pensioner Who Goes on Working

Should a healthy person on reaching retirement age give up work?

It has to be recognised, of course, that by the time people are due for retirement they are no longer in their prime. But have they outgrown their capacity for socially useful work?

In the Soviet Union increasing attention has been paid to this in recent years—not only for the benefit of the expanding national economy but also to provide a fuller and more satisfying life for the elderly.

In 1964, only about one person in ten of retirement age went on working. By 1976 just about a quarter did.

With no unemployment, and even a shortage of manpower in some branches of the economy, choosing a job is no problem.

Working pensioners, of course, are subject to the same labour legislation as others as regards wages, holidays, social security, sick leave, etc.

They receive holiday vouchers, housing and other benefits on a par with other workers.

They cannot be refused employment or sacked on the grounds of being pensioners. And a person who stays on in his job but finds it a strain can be transferred to a lighter job or to part-time work.

A Labour Research Institute survey in several Soviet republics showed that in Latvia four in five pensioners were working four hours a day.

---

[3] Since this was written, there have been some consumer price increases in the Soviet Union, for instance, for furniture, gasoline, and vodka. But prices of what they consider absolute necessities (such as rents, in-city transportation, milk, bread, etc.) have remained unchanged. Overall, the CIA's 1977 *Handbook of Economic Statistics*, p. 43, shows no increase at all in the Soviet Union's consumer price index from 1960–1975 (as compared, for instance, with 83% for the US or 202% for Japan) and a 1% increase for 1976. But the CIA later revised that index and the *Handbook's* 1980 edition, p. 43, showed increases of 13.6% for the 1960's and 18% for the 1970's. [Editor's note.]

In the Russian Federation 41 per cent were doing four hours a day and 38 per cent six hours.

In the Ukraine, 29 per cent did four hours and 40 per cent six hours.

And in Georgia, 31 per cent four hours and 42 per cent six hours.

Pensioners employed in branches of the economy where there is a shortage of labour, in medical establishments, rural teaching and in the distributive trades and other service jobs receive their full pension tax-free in addition to their wages.

ABOUT THE EDITOR

Harry G. Shaffer is Professor of Economics and Soviet and East European Studies at the University of Kansas. He has visited and carried out extensive interviews in the Soviet Union and all the socialist countries of East Europe except Albania.

Dr. Shaffer has published widely in the field of Soviet and East European Studies. He has to his credit ten books, more than forty articles, and numerous book reviews published or reprinted in seven languages in such journals as *The American Economic Review, The Slavic Review, Problems of Communism, Soviet and East European Foreign Trade*, and *Christian Science Monitor*, among others. He has given papers and invitational lectures at numerous conferences and universities in the United States, Canada, and Germany.